Leah loved dri

She had a sudden clear memory of being snuggled up against Jeff in this very seat, and for one second, the past fourteen months of their separation were swept away. Instead of being on a stupid search to dig up the past, they were headed off for a weekend of fun and love.

"Pretty country," Jeff said, breaking into her thoughts. "All farmland and meadows."

Leah sighed. Back to reality. "Ever wish you were a farmer instead of a lawyer?" As if she cared.

"Sure, but never when five o'clock rolls around and I can choose to stay in bed if I want to."

"With who?" The question was out before she could stop herself. When he didn't answer, Leah looked up to find Jeff smiling.

"That concerns you, does it?"

"I have to know who to name when I file the divorce papers, don't I." *That* took the smile off his face. Too bad it made her feel so immeasurably sad.

ABOUT THE AUTHOR

"Why did I write a book about a heroine who tries to find her birth mother?" says Muriel Jensen. "Well, I'm adopted myself, and my three children are all adopted, so I guess it's pretty obvious why the whole subject fascinates me." Muriel and her family make their home in Astoria, Oregon, just where the Columbia River empties into the Pacific.

Books by Muriel Jensen

HARLEQUIN SUPERROMANCE
422–TRUST A HERO

HARLEQUIN AMERICAN ROMANCE
283–SIDE BY SIDE
321–A CAROL CHRISTMAS
339–EVERYTHING
358–A WILD IRIS
392–THE MIRACLE

Don't miss any of our special offers. Write to us at the following address for information on our newest releases.

Harlequin Reader Service
P.O. Box 1397, Buffalo, NY 14240
Canadian address: P.O. Box 603,
Fort Erie, Ont. L2A 5X3

Bridge to Yesterday

MURIEL JENSEN

Harlequin Books

TORONTO • NEW YORK • LONDON
AMSTERDAM • PARIS • SYDNEY • HAMBURG
STOCKHOLM • ATHENS • TOKYO • MILAN

Published September 1991

ISBN 0-373-70468-2

BRIDGE TO YESTERDAY

CHAPTER ONE

JEFF ALDEN LEANED back in his chair and propped a pair of dusty wing tips on the corner of his littered desk. With lazy brown eyes he watched his estranged wife pace across the office to the place where his law degree hung on the oak-paneled wall. She studied the parchment with sudden concentration, then—just as suddenly—lost interest in it. She turned around to face him, the black-and-white wool of her skirt flaring around her trim legs.

He braced himself against the impact of her wide pale green eyes. Though he and Leah had been separated for over a year, the feelings she aroused in him hadn't diminished. She still made his pulse race, his temper rise, his blood run hot and his heart ache. He maintained his relaxed pose as she perched on the corner of his desk. He noted the vulnerability in the line of her bent head and slumping shoulders, but resisted the impulse to offer comfort. She'd refuse it and he'd get angry.

"So what do you think?" she asked. Her manner was a little aggressive despite the defeated look she wore. He couldn't remember once in the two years they'd been married when she'd asked him what he thought about anything. Leah always did what *she* thought was right, confident that it was. She'd gather data scrupulously, weigh it all carefully and make a swift, clean decision. She'd have made a fine attorney, but had been a very difficult wife.

Jeff watched her rub the pleat between her eyebrows and lowered his feet, reaching into his side drawer for a bottle of aspirin.

He went to the bar across the room and poured a glass of water. Coming back to the desk, he offered the glass to Leah, shook two aspirin into her hand and sat down again. "I think it's a bad idea, too," he said finally. "But I don't see how you can stop her."

"But *you* can stop her," Leah insisted urgently, the tailored black wool of her jacket a perfect foil for the drama of green eyes and porcelain skin framed by short dark hair. Her small stature and doll-like features robed in the high-fashion styles she preferred always made him think of a little girl playing dress-up. But that was only one of the incongruities that made up Leah Alden. "She's coming to you for help, Jeff, and I want you to discourage her. Tell her it's foolish and dangerous and that she'll only get hurt. Tell her she's silly to look for her birth parents when she was loved and pampered for eighteen years by the finest adoptive parents two kids ever had."

"Silly?" Jeff challenged quietly. "That's not fair, Leah." As her brow pleated further, he added, "Take the aspirin, will you?"

She obeyed, popping both into her mouth and tossing her head back to swallow. The delicate line of her throat brought Jeff a sharp memory of how she tasted there.

"Not fair?" she repeated hotly, setting the glass aside, her eyes warming with emotion and a trace of temper. Jeff suppressed a smile. Now this was the woman he knew. "What do you mean, not fair?"

"I don't think foolish and silly are fair words to describe what she wants to do. Ill-advised, maybe, but not silly." He folded his arms across his chest and studied Leah closely. "I can understand her curiosity. Aren't you ever curious about your natural parents?"

Leah had always stoutly maintained that it didn't matter where a person came from. Who that person became was all that was important. Though there were times when he thought he saw a question in the depths of her eyes, he had yet to hear her admit any need to know about her biological parents.

"No," she replied coolly. "If they didn't want me, I don't want them."

"You don't know the circumstances," Jeff pointed out mildly. "Maybe they had little choice."

Leah looked at him squarely. "If I had a child, it would be taken from my dead body and no other way."

"I know, Lee, but you're strong and equipped to deal with life. Everyone isn't so blessed. What may seem like just forty miles of bad road to you could be an impassable obstacle to someone else."

"But how could a woman give up the fruit of her own body?" Her question was just a little desperate, and Jeff answered in a calm, controlled tone of voice.

"To see that it's fed and sheltered perhaps if she isn't able to do it. To provide for it a life she knows she'll never have."

Unconvinced, Leah waved her hand dismissively. "Well, it doesn't matter. We're talking about my sister Susan, not me. Jeff, you know how she is—all feelings and volatility and big dreams. What happens if her mother's dead or in a mental institution or a prison? What if she was involved in things that have never touched Susan's life? She's going to get hurt no matter what we find."

"I gather you've tried to explain that to her?"

Leah looked heavenward in exasperation. "Until I was blue in the face and she threatened to gag me. She won't listen to a word. Since we found that photograph, she's been absolutely insufferable about this."

"Did you bring the photo with you?"

Leah slipped off the desk and crossed to the leather sofa where she had dropped her purse. She produced the photograph, walked around the desk and handed it to Jeff as she took the client's chair facing him. They leaned over the photo, dark heads almost touching.

"We found it in an envelope of family papers when we were cleaning out the house. It was wrapped in Mom's lingerie in a bottom drawer."

"What makes Susan so sure it's her?" Jeff asked, studying the out-of-focus image of the giggling infant in the arms of a woman of indeterminate age. He turned the photo over. On the back was inscribed "Baby and Gerda Szabo."

"Mom and Dad have—" Leah stopped herself, swallowing a swell of emotion. "They called her 'Baby' since the day the caseworker brought her to us at about that very age. It even slipped out once in a while as she grew older. You remember."

Jeff smiled, still studying the photograph. "Yes, I do. But the photo's fuzzy. Neither the baby's nor the woman's features are clear. Why does she think it's her mother?"

"Because she wants it to be. And I suppose there's an even chance."

Jeff handed the picture back to Leah and turned in his chair to face her. "Can you judge an approximate year from the clothes?"

Leah shrugged. "It's difficult to tell from the baby's things, and the woman's wool coat and kerchief are pretty timeless. Maybe Eastern European. What do you think?" She handed the photo back to Jeff, and he turned with it to the window.

"Could be. Big-city skyline in the background."

"Sue and I have stared at it for hours. We couldn't find anything in the fuzzy detail to tell what big city. Could be Boston or Chicago or New York."

Jeff handed back the photo. "Could even be as near to us as Portland."

Leah put the photo back in her purse and returned to her chair, falling into it with a ragged sigh. "Jeff, I don't want to do this. I don't want Susan to do this. I have a bad feeling about it. What if her mother turns out to be a prostitute or something?"

Jeff shook his heady wryly. "The truth remains the truth whether we know it or not."

"Then why does she have to know?"

"The best reason in the world. Because she wants to know. When does she plan to see me about this?"

"She's going to call to invite you to dinner on Saturday."

Jeff arched an exaggeratedly surprised eyebrow. "And you agreed to having me as a guest?"

"When she moved in with me after Daddy died, I swore that no sacrifice was too big for me to make Susan feel secure and happy." She gave him a dry grin as she shouldered her purse. "I can handle having you over for dinner."

He laughed. "You sweet talker. What's on the menu?"

"I'm not sure. Sue's cooking. She's not too experienced, so you and I are both taking our chances."

Jeff stood to walk her out of the office. "You didn't tell me this was going to be a dangerous case," he teased, holding the door open as she paused before walking through. She smiled back at him, and for a fleeting instant all the dark days before their separation dissolved and some of the old magic was back. They had loved laughing together almost as much as they enjoyed making love.

"So how have you been?" he asked softly, leaning against the door. "Still holding Minding Your Business together?"

She nodded. "We're doing well. No matter how sophisticated office equipment becomes, the efficient secretary will always be the heart of smooth operation. And my temporary office aides are among the best." She smiled with proud conviction. "We might even show a profit this year."

He'd never resented her dedication to her work, though all that energy directed at business rather than life had been hard for him to understand. "Good for you. Is Susan still on staff?"

"Part-time. She was supposed to start college this fall, but now that this whole thing about her natural parents has come up, she's flatly refused to go. We argue about it all the time. She wants to be free to do whatever she has to do to find them." Leah shook her head. "I'm seriously considering running away."

Jeff couldn't hold back the skeptical laugh. "You? Old 'remain calm and never back down till the enemy is beaten' Alden? Somehow I can't picture that." Then he noted a trace of real weariness in Leah's eyes and his tone sobered. "I imagine it's been difficult having to face something like this with Susan so soon after your father's death."

Jeff had gone through her mother's death with Leah two years previously, and he remembered how fiercely Leah loved and how deeply she grieved. When her father died six weeks ago, he'd been unable to take her into his arms at night, to make love to her and force her to think of life rather than death. They'd already been separated almost a year, and all he'd been able to do was offer some small comfort at her father's graveside.

"Of course, if you'd like to escape," he added, slanting her a grin, "you know where you can come for sanctuary."

"Jeff, don't be charming," she scolded, walking through the empty outer office to the elevators. "You were as relieved to separate as I was. Don't pretend you want me back."

"I wanted us to separate because, at the time, it was the only way out of the anger we were both feeling." He reached past her to press the down button. "I didn't expect it to last this long."

"It's better this way."

"For whom?" he asked.

"Both of us." She smiled teasingly at him. "You should be grateful that I no longer have a right to tell you that your shoes need a shine and your office curtains should be replaced."

"I am," he agreed with heartfelt sincerity. The smallest pinch of disappointment showed on Leah's face. The elevator doors parted, and Jeff held them open for her as she stepped into the empty cubicle.

"I'll ride down with you," he said, following her inside and pressing the ground level button. The doors closed, and they retreated to opposite corners as the car began to move. "There are things I miss about you," he said quietly. "I had hoped we could come to a point where you could shine your shoes and replace your curtains and let me handle mine my way."

She looked at him as though he were dense. "You can't compartmentalize things like that in a marriage. Everything you do affects me."

"Only because you can't learn to mind your own business." He knew he shouldn't smile as he said that, but it was so true that he couldn't help it.

Leah closed her eyes. He could almost hear her counting to ten—by twos, probably, because it was more efficient. "We're incompatible on all levels," she said finally. "Just accept it."

The car bounced slightly to a halt, and the doors parted on the ground level of the office building. They stepped out onto a tobacco-colored carpet in an old, ornate lobby.

"We made love well," Jeff disputed, pushing the heavy double glass doors open for her. They walked into the cool breeziness of a September evening.

"Yes," she conceded, running lightly down the steps and turning to the parking lot. "But if you recall, by the time we separated, we couldn't do *that* without fighting. Our marriage was a mistake, Jeff." They had reached her elegantly waxed Chrysler LeBaron. She rummaged in her purse for her keys.

"So when are you going to file for divorce?" he asked mildly, leaning against her front fender.

Her hands stilled for a fraction of a second. Then she produced the keys and tucked her bag under her arm.

She looked at him, her eyes carefully unrevealing. "You're the attorney," she said. "You know all about that stuff. Why don't you file?"

He shrugged as though the reason was obvious. "Because I don't want to file."

Leah, too, shrugged. "Well, I have too much on my mind right now to think about it."

"What's held you back for the past year?" He was goading her, and he knew it, but he hated it when she let the cool control take her over.

"The fact that you have Smythe," she returned, fitting her key into the door lock, avoiding his eyes. "And I don't want to be divorced from him."

Jeff leaned on the open door as Leah slipped into the car. "If you're going to demand equal custody of a springer spaniel," he warned, "you're definitely going to have to be the one to file."

"He was yours when we got married. I don't even have the right to claim him." Leah turned the key in the ignition and put her hand on the gearshift.

Jeff reached into the car to pull the seat belt away from its slide and hand her the buckle.

"Thank you, my lord." She snatched it from him and snapped it into place. "I have only ten blocks to go."

"Most accidents happen within a half mile of home. For someone who's so meticulous about everything else, you should take a little care with your personal safety."

Leah closed her eyes to summon patience. "That's one thing I don't miss about you, Jeff."

"What?"

"The lectures."

He smiled. "You mean there are some things you do miss about me?"

"It was nice when there was someone else around to get up in the cold dark to turn off the alarm and put on the coffee." Leah shifted and moved slowly away. "See you Saturday."

"Right." Jeff waved as she pulled away.

LEAH ROLLED her window down and drew in a deep gulp of air as she turned onto the highway. Jeff always made her feel as if she were choking, as though she might become hysterical despite a lifetime dedicated to maintaining control. Her calm had always annoyed him because he was passionate about everything. She wondered what he would think if he could see how she shook inside sometimes when she was maintaining a cool demeanor.

She'd thought she'd braced herself for this meeting, but she hadn't been as ready as she'd hoped. Of course, Jeff's ability to shift from thoughtful friend to judicious partner in the bat of an eye had always been a quality that unsettled her. She liked things in their place. One's personal life should never enter into business; it disturbed and distracted. And she hadn't wanted to talk about them; she'd wanted to discuss Susan.

She found it alarming to realize that a whole year hadn't diminished his impact on her senses one bit. The water glass, warm from his hand, his dark gaze across the elevator, his tall, solid presence beside her made her mind recall in vivid detail long nights spent under the erotic blanket of his body and sleepy mornings when he'd cradled her with a tenderness so selfless that it had been hard to remember the sensual devil of the night before.

And she had the most curious feeling that those lazy brown eyes saw right through her. Several times today he'd watched her with an expression she remembered from the days they'd lived together. It was as though he were looking for something in her that he thought she was hiding from him. She hadn't understood that look then, and she found it confusing now.

All in all, Leah wasn't sure that her meeting with Jeff today had been profitable. He sounded as though he was on Susan's side, and she'd hoped to get him on hers. Leah knew Jeff's opinion carried weight with her younger sister. He would have been a valuable ally in convincing her that this search on which she was about to embark was a mistake.

Now she wished she'd never gone to him for help. Not only was he going to be a problem about Susan, he was going to be a problem for her, Leah, as well.

Leah had spent the past year building a life without Jeff by employing the careful orderliness that was a basic part of her nature. Without Jeff's casually sloppy presence underfoot, the home they'd shared in Seaside, and in which she now lived with Susan, was tidy, free of clutter and quiet. There was no one steaming the bathroom mirror while she tried to put on her makeup, no one getting pancake batter all over her kitchen floor. No one pushed her to one small corner of the bed at night, and no one pulled the covers off her. For a brief period she'd been free to cook what she chose, go where she wanted to without consulting anyone. She was free, and life was orderly.

Inviting her sister to move in with her after their father's death had restricted Leah's freedom some-

what, but except for the matter of the search, Susan
was undemanding. She was happy to help around the
house and at the office, and if Leah disregarded her
sister's tendency to dramatize, Susan was fun to have
around. Life had begun to settle into a subdued but
fairly comfortable pattern after the funeral. Then she
and Susan had gone to prepare the home where they
had grown up for listing with a Realtor.

Leah had found Susan's birth certificate concealed
in the folds of a piece of their mother's lingerie, undis-
turbed since her death. It was in a large envelope with
a marriage license and other family papers.

"I haven't seen this in ages!" Leah said to Susan,
who was taking clothes out of the closet and folding
them into a box. "Trust you to decide to make your
entrance into the world at 2:17 a.m.!" She sat on the
edge of the bed to study the document, then, as Susan
came to sit beside her, discovered the photo clipped to
the back of it.

"Who's that?" Susan asked, leaning an elbow on
Leah's shoulder. Her long blond hair was tied back
with a blue bandanna found in a drawer, her cheeks
flushed from working in the bottom of the closet.

"Got me," Leah said, glancing over the woman
holding the laughing child. She turned the photo over.
"Baby and Gerda Szabo." She read aloud from the
inked inscription, stumbling a little over the unfami-
iar last name.

"Oh, it must be me," Susan said lightly, snatching
the photo from Leah's hand. "It's such a cute baby,
even though the picture's fuzzy."

Leah looked over her shoulder as she studied the
faces closely. Despite the age and poor quality of the
print, it was apparent both subjects were smiling.

Susan studied the back again, her lips moving as she silently reread the words. "Baby," she said thoughtfully. "Mom and Dad always called me Baby." After a moment Susan's head came up slowly. "Lee," she said breathlessly, "do you . . . do you think it's me?"

Leah put down the marriage certificate she'd been studying and looked at the photo again. "Could be," she said. "The baby is blond and looks a little giddy."

Her attempt at humor was lost on Susan who continued to stare at the image of the woman and child.

"If that's me," Susan said, her voice distracted, "I wonder if that's . . . her?"

"Who?"

Susan swallowed and looked at Leah again. "My mother," she said.

Leah felt her first shiver of trepidation. "I guess we'll never know." Getting to her feet, she carefully folded the negligee in which the envelope of family papers had been wrapped. She wanted to end the discussion; she could see the direction in which Susan's mind was moving and didn't like it.

"I'd *like* to know," Susan said with sudden stubbornness.

"I don't think even Mom and Dad knew who your real parents were." Leah put the negligee in a box and wove the flaps to close it. "As far as I remember, a caseworker brought you here when I was twelve. You were about six months old."

"About the age of the baby in the picture." Susan looked over her birth certificate and sighed. "I wonder why they change the names on these things to make it look like you were born to the people who adopted you?"

"For the protection of the child and the adoptive parents, I suppose," Leah said, shoving the box aside. She closed the box Susan had been filling and stacked it beside the other. "I think the idea is to tie up the new family unit—to protect us from whatever happened before we were adopted—and probably to protect the people who put us up for adoption."

"Protect them from what?"

"Their own mistakes maybe." Leah shrugged philosophically.

"What if I don't want to be protected?"

"The law does it, anyway. Come on, let's take a coffee break. I brought some éclairs from the Boardwalk Bakery."

Susan sat at the round table in the kitchen while Leah brewed coffee for herself and pulled a soft drink out of the refrigerator for her sister. Keeping the refrigerator stocked had eased the painful and difficult chore of clearing away a thirty-year accumulation of possessions.

"Are you going to see Doug this weekend?" Leah asked, putting the two sinfully large desserts on the table.

"We're no longer an item," Susan reported grimly. Then she slanted her sister a grin. "I'll take the biggest one of these. I know how scrupulously you watch your figure."

"What happened between you two?"

"I turned him down one too many times, I guess."

Leah frowned. "Turned him down?"

Susan gave her sister a look that told her she was definitely the more naive of the two despite the disparity in their ages. "Sex, Leah."

"Oh."

"There aren't too many virgins my age."

"Shocking." Leah spoke calmly, licking cream from her fingers. "It's an old story, Suzie. Kids who use their heads instead of their glands are often in the minority. Be proud of yourself."

Susan gave her another worldly wise look. "Everything's changed since you were a kid."

Leah nodded dryly. "All those years ago. I know it has, but a young person can grow up just so fast and still have enough time to do it right."

For a long moment Susan stared into her cola. Then she sighed and, pushing the drink aside, leaned across the table toward her sister. "Don't you ever wonder who you are, Lee?"

"Nope," Leah replied without hesitation. "I'm Leah Blake Alden, owner of Minding Your Business. I never doubt that."

"You never wonder what happened before you were brought here to live?"

"Never."

Susan took a sip of her drink, then put the glass down, running her index finger thoughtfully around the rim. "Well, I do. I thought about it a lot after Mom died, but I was afraid Daddy wouldn't understand if I asked him, so I haven't done anything about it."

Leah tried to look forbidding. "I'm the one who wouldn't understand, Susan."

Susan straightened in her chair, obviously surprised by Leah's reaction. Her soft mouth hardened into an aggressive line. "Why not? You're the same as I am— a woman without a past."

Leah tried heroically not to laugh at that theatrical remark.

"There's an old axiom about never looking back. That's good advice, Suzie. If your parents had wanted to keep you, or been able to, they would have. Since they didn't, perhaps it's best not to examine the reasons."

Susan leaned toward her sister urgently. "Don't you want to know if you look like your mother or your father? If that shiny black hair and those killer wide eyes were given to you, by him or her? Don't you want to know how they thought and what they felt? How can you not care?"

Leah was beginning to feel just a little panicky and fought to remain calm. "I care that Ed and Selena Blake loved us with all their hearts, gave us everything they were capable of and were there for us every time we turned to them. I don't need to know anything else."

"It has nothing to do with them!" Susan said, her cheeks flushing with the first traces of anger. "I loved them very much, too, and will always love them. I just want to know who brought me into this world!"

"Who bore you is the least important fact about you, Susan," Leah responded a little too loudly. "You are beautiful and intelligent and strong. Why does it matter what components made you that way? You *are*. Don't risk hurting yourself by trying to uncover information that was probably withheld with good reason."

Susan stood, scraping her chair aside. "You go ahead and be content with the way things are, Miss Perfect. I want to know, and I'm not afraid of being hurt."

Susan had stormed away, and they'd driven to Leah's house in silence. When two days had passed without the subject being raised again, Leah thought she'd heard the last of it. Then she'd returned home from work one evening to find Susan slumped in a chair in a room filled with long, early-evening shadows.

"What's the matter?" she asked in alarm.

"I called the courthouse. Then I called the health office. Then I called the vital records office in Portland," Susan said tonelessly. "They said my files are sealed. No one can tell me anything about my natural parents."

Leah put down her briefcase and walked over to sit on the arm of Susan's chair. She switched on the light on the table beside them. "I told you the laws are made to protect everyone involved."

"If I want to go any farther with this," Susan said, "I have to get a court order. Then they can open the records."

Leah felt her second shudder of fear.

Susan sat up, then got to her feet. "So with my inheritance from Daddy I'm going to hire Jeff and get him to do it for me." She looked down at Leah with an expression that was half challenge, half plea. "Will you help me?"

"I don't think it's a good idea," Leah said, her voice not as firm as she'd intended it to be.

Susan nodded. "I know. You didn't think it was a good idea when I wanted a punk streak of purple in my hair, but you helped me do it. Will you help me with this?"

"Suzie, you're laying yourself open to all kinds of—"

"Will you?" Susan insisted.

Leah sighed deeply. She had always helped Susan. She had taught her little sister to ride a bike, to roller-skate, how to apply makeup, and she had convinced her that she would live when her first boyfriend went to the prom with her best friend. "Of course," she said.

"Good!" Susan started toward the kitchen. "I'm going to call Jeff and invite him for dinner on Saturday so we can talk to him about it. Want a sandwich?"

CHAPTER TWO

LEAH WAS NERVOUS. Susan was preparing what looked like a passable sweet-and-sour chicken dish, fresh fruit on a bed of lettuce waited in the refrigerator and a bottle of Riesling was chilling. The table was set, coffee was perking and Susan was humming as she put the rice on to steam. Everything was ready but Leah.

She poured a cup of coffee and leaned against the kitchen counter, watching Susan move capably around the kitchen. The girl had such potential in so many areas, Leah thought. Susan had a flair for the artistic, she did very well in school and she was considering a career in commercial art. She was neither defeated by housework nor a slave to it; she simply handled her share. She was going to be a perfect wife for some man—a well-rounded woman who could have her career and her family and deal well with both. And for a teenager who'd had her share of grief early, she was well adjusted and optimistic. Leah hated the thought of anything throwing Susan off course.

The apprehension Leah had first felt when she and Susan found the photo had grown since she'd talked to Jeff. She had the most uncanny feeling that this search for Susan's parents was going to change things, was going to cause disorder in the life she, Leah, was finally getting under control.

"Why are you so jumpy?" Susan asked as she gave the aromatic chicken concoction a stir. "You've seen Jeff lots of times since you've been separated. He treats you like a sister or a good friend. This shouldn't change anything."

It shouldn't, but she had a feeling it was going to. Usually too sensible and methodical to credit hunches, Leah thought this one just too strong to ignore.

Susan brought a spoonful of the sweet-and-sour chicken across the room to Leah, her hand cupped under it against drips. "I promise to monopolize Jeff all evening, so you don't even have to talk to him if you don't want to. What's the verdict?"

Leah tasted cautiously, then nodded with sincere approval. "Yum. You can do *all* the cooking from now on."

"Hopefully we'll be too busy during the next few weeks to cook at home. Oops! There's Jeff. I'll let him in."

Susan dropped the spoon into the sink and raced across the kitchen, tearing her apron off as the sound of the door chime sang through the house.

With a sigh of resignation Leah took a match from the wall holder and went into the dining room to light the candles.

The three of them were sitting over coffee an hour later, Jeff studying the photo Susan had produced, while she explained how she and Leah had found it, what Susan thought it meant and what she would like do to about it.

"What makes you think it's you?" Jeff asked, failing to display the enthusiasm it was obvious Susan had been hoping for.

"The baby's blond," Susan said. "And we found the photo with my birth certificate."

Jeff studied it, then looked long and hard at his sister-in-law. "That's reaching a little, Suzie. This photograph is out of focus. This could be almost any baby with fair hair."

"Read the back."

"I have. 'Baby and Gerda Szabo,'" he read dutifully. "Do you have any idea how many parents call their baby 'Baby'? Also, it's hard to be sure, but the woman in this photo looks close to fifty. She's more likely an aunt or even a grandmother, not the mother."

While not refusing to help, Jeff was calmly putting every possible roadblock in Susan's path. True to Leah's request, he behaved as though he had never seen the photo before and had never been approached by her for help.

"And how does Leah feel about this?" he asked Susan.

"She's against it, of course," Susan said, a trace of frustrated temper in her voice. "Miss Perfect has no questions about anything. It doesn't matter who you came from, you know, but who you become." Susan had quoted her sister's philosophy sarcastically, and Jeff turned to her, a scolding eyebrow lifted.

"Don't resent Leah because she's able to have faith in herself without knowing her past. She's a smart businesswoman and she's made a home for you."

"I'm sorry," Susan said hesitantly. She glanced up at Leah, red-faced. "I'm sorry," she said again. "It's just that it's frustrating that I can't make either of you see how I feel."

Susan was close to tears, and Leah pushed a water glass toward her, her own throat tightening in sympathy. "Let's move to the living room," she said, pushing her chair back. "Would you build a fire, Jeff? I'll get more coffee."

When Leah returned with the tray, Jeff was standing before a dancing fire, brushing the knees of his gray wool slacks. The ribbed hem of his blue sweater rested lightly on muscular hips as he moved to sit beside Susan on the sofa. Leah, trying not to notice, concentrated on getting the tray to the coffee table without spilling. She handed a mug of coffee to Jeff, a glass of cola to Susan, then sat by the fireplace in a chair that was angled to face the sofa.

"Lee is wonderful." Susan picked up the thread of their conversation. "I'd be the first to admit that. She can stand alone, sure of who she is. But I'm not like that." She frowned, groping for words. "I'd like to know where I came from. I was happy with Mom and Dad—it has nothing to do with them. I just want to know who made me what I am, and if we can find out—" she swallowed and looked pleadingly at Jeff "—I'd like to know why they let me go."

Jeff looked at the girl levelly. "What if your mother was a prostitute and had to give you up to . . . continue working?"

Susan nodded. "I've considered that," she said in a small voice.

"What if your parents are still alive?" Jeff went on relentlessly, as though he had her on the witness stand. "What if they didn't care about you when you were born and never will? What if we find them and you confront them and they simply don't care?"

Susan drew a shaky breath. "Then I'll know. Whatever the reason was, whoever they are—I think I can live with knowing. It's not knowing that hurts."

Jeff put his coffee mug aside and faced Susan, his elbows resting on his knees. Leah saw his total involvement, his caring and, for one brief instant, wondered painfully where her relationship with him had gone wrong.

"Suzie, I'm sure that's how you feel now, but you have to think about this carefully before you decide to go ahead." He took hold of her hand to assure himself of her attention. Susan watched him, wide-eyed. "Whatever we find out, whether they're dead or alive, whether they wanted you or not, your life will be changed because of it. You've been nurtured and loved. You have everything going for you. You could be risking your future with this search. If you can handle what you learn, it'll become part of you and make you different from what you are now. If you can't handle it, it'll still be part of you and will haunt you till the day you die. Think hard, Suzie. Is it worth that?"

There was a moment's heavy silence, then Susan asked quietly, "Isn't there a saying about how the truth will make you free?"

"Sometimes freedom isn't all it's cracked up to be," Jeff said. "It has a way of putting you out there all by yourself."

"I have you and Leah," Susan pointed out with a smile. "There's no way this would change that, is there?"

Finally, at a loss, Jeff looked at Leah.

"Of course there isn't," Leah replied firmly. "You and I are sisters even though we don't share the same blood. Nothing will ever change that."

"Then," Susan said gravely, "I'd like to go ahead. Where do we start? How do we get a court order?"

Jeff shook his head. "We don't. You'd have to have a life-or-death medical reason, and even then it isn't always granted."

"But that isn't fair!"

"Maybe. But that's the law."

"So what do we do?"

"We work around it. We start with the information on your birth certificate—"

"But it's wrong!" Susan interrupted him, her eyes brimming, her chin quivering dangerously.

Leah moved from the chair to sit beside Susan, expecting Jeff to become impatient with her.

To her surprise Jeff put an arm around Susan and hugged her to him. "It isn't wrong. It's altered," he corrected quietly. "And it has the state and county in which you were born."

Susan took the handkerchief Jeff offered her and looked up at him doubtfully. "Yamhill County, Oregon. That's only a hundred miles away, but it isn't much to go on."

He looked at her evenly now, the kindness tempered with honesty. "That's the plain truth, Susan. We don't have much to go on. It's going to be hard, tedious work. There will probably be lots of blind alleys, leads that prove nothing and people who won't want to be bothered with what's so important to you. If you've lost hope already..."

"No, I haven't." Susan sniffed and gave him a shaky smile. "I guess I'm kind of...you know." She made a spiral motion with her index finger.

Jeff smiled teasingly. "Crazy?" he guessed.

"Wound up," she corrected, scolding him with a teasing elbow in the ribs.

Jeff nodded in understanding. "Okay. But you'll have to pace your emotions. It's going to be a long, hard process—I guarantee it."

"I will. I promise." Susan sat a little straighter. "So where do we start in Yamhill County?"

"In McMinnville," Jeff said, sipping his coffee. "We'll go down and stay as long as it takes us to find anything. You were born at McMinnville Hospital. It's more than likely your mother lived in that area."

A thought occurred to Leah that had escaped her attention until that very moment. "This will cost a lot of money," she said, frowning at Jeff.

"There's my inheritance," Susan began.

"Sue, that's a very small amount when you consider taking trips, spending nights in motels, eating out..."

Jeff shrugged and put his cup down on the coffee table. "I'll take care of it, and we'll square up later."

"That isn't fair," Leah insisted. "This isn't your search." She knew he had a lucrative practice, a healthy savings account and a plump IRA but, after all, she and Susan were no longer really his family. She couldn't allow him to absorb the cost of this venture. "Susan isn't your responsibility. She's mine."

Jeff gave her a challenging look. "And whose responsibility are you?"

"My own."

He rolled his eyes heavenward. "I keep forgetting. If you're suddenly demoting me to nonfamily status, then maybe you can allow me to be a friend and to help accordingly."

"I wasn't—"

"Shut up, Lee. I have responsibilities that I feel seriously, whether or not you admit they're mine."

"Are you guys going to fight, or are we going to decide—" Susan interrupted, but before she could finish the telephone rang.

"I'll get it." Leah ran for the kitchen, grateful for the excuse to terminate the conversation. She remembered suddenly where her relationship with Jeff had gone wrong. They had gotten married.

"Hello!" Her tone of voice reflected her mood, and there was a startled silence on the other end of the line.

Then a young male voice said hesitantly, "I'm trying to reach Jeff Alden. This is his office calling."

"Hold on a moment, please." Leah placed the receiver on the counter and shouted to Jeff from the kitchen doorway. "Telephone."

He looked up from the photo he was studying with Susan.

"It's your office," Leah explained.

Jeff excused himself to Susan and brought his empty coffee cup with him into the kitchen. He held it out to Leah as he picked up the receiver.

"Hello," he said. Then, after a brief pause, he added, "Hi, Charlie. What's up?" His coffee cup filled, Jeff lifted it in a salute to Leah, who made a face at him and turned away. "So what did you find out?" he asked, pausing again to sip the hot brew. "Well. Good work, buddy. Would you mind bringing the stuff to me on your way home? Then I can look it over at home tonight." He rattled off the address. "No, it's my wife's."

Leah paused in the act of fitting a cup on a spindle in the dishwasher. "Your ex-wife," she whispered at him.

He put a hand over the mouthpiece. "You're not my ex until we're divorced."

She rolled her eyes. "You're splitting hairs."

He grinned. "I'm a lawyer. That's my job. No," he said to the person on the other end of the line. "Just a friendly dinner. She's sort of a client. Will you get over here with that stuff, or do you want to go back to filleting fish to support your law school habit?" As Jeff cradled the receiver, Leah closed the door on the dishwasher. "Charlie Barrett, my clerk, going to bring a brief by for me to look at this weekend. You don't mind, do you? We'll just be a minute."

"Of course not. Why should I mind?" Leah asked, her eyes widely innocent. She turned the kitchen light off as she passed into the other room and left Jeff standing in the dark. It was curious, she thought, that he was the emotional one, yet he could seem so unaffected by her presence when she was bothered by his. *Bothered* was a broad term, but it seemed to suit the way he made her feel—annoyed, upset, sometimes amused, often touched, never controlled. She had to be controlled.

She had reached the sofa before he wandered out of the kitchen. He looked at her assessingly over the rim of his cup as he approached the chair she'd occupied earlier. She was jumpy beneath that cool exterior. When she was truly calm, she could look him in the eye and stare through him. When she was acting calm, she looked everywhere else but into his eyes. He knew she'd thought she'd gotten away with that little deceit for two years, but she hadn't. He watched her turn her attention to the photo Susan continued to examine and felt a certain satisfaction.

Within fifteen minutes the doorbell rang, and Susan went to answer it. Leah stood. "I'll get him a cup of coffee. Do you need a refill?"

"No thanks." He caught her hand as she tried to move past him. "And Charlie doesn't drink anything but cola or beer. Sit down and relax."

She looked down at his hand, then into his eyes with a haughty disdain he remembered well from the last month they were together. When she didn't know what to say, she could be brutal with a glance.

A year ago he would have walked away. Today he'd been without her long enough to realize that if he wanted her back he had to take a stand. With a deft yank he pulled her into his lap. She was instantly flustered and beside herself with indignation. He loved it.

"That look didn't scare me when we were together," he said quietly, "and it doesn't scare me now, so quit posturing. You're in no danger from me. I'm here for Susan, not for you." While he spoke with detached amusement, he was fiercely aware of the softness of her in his lap, the scent of her perfume that always clung to her and had clung to him for months after he'd moved out of their house, the touch of her satin blouse against his skin. Nearly overpowered by her femininity, he realized abruptly how masculine his life had been the past year. How lonely. But he schooled his features carefully, knowing he'd be lost if she sensed his vulnerability.

Leah felt hard muscle under her derriere, broad shoulder under the arm she held against the back of the chair. His eyes were so close, so dark, and filled with that intimate, knowing look that made her feel exposed. She'd seen the satisfaction there when she'd struggled against him for a moment, so she forced herself to sit calmly, to speak softly. "Then you won't mind letting me up," she said.

He laid an arm lightly across her knees as she tried to stand. "But I do. I remember long, rainy evenings the first few months we were married when we sat like this for hours. Do you remember?"

She did. Her mind was suddenly filled with them. She forced herself to remember also that, on the night of their second anniversary, he'd been dancing with Mrs. Dunwiddie. "That was a lifetime ago, Jeff," she said with a sigh.

Susan walked into the room, trailed by a tall young man with a briefcase tucked under his arm. "Charlie," she said breathlessly, "this is my sister—" Then she paused and looked at Leah with what seemed like unfamiliarity. "My sister... ah..."

"Leah," Leah provided helpfully.

"Yes. Leah. Of course." Susan looked less than convinced. "And this is my brother-in-law..." Again she paused, obviously at a loss.

"Jeff," Jeff said. "But he knows me, Suzie. We work together."

Charlie approached the chair where Jeff still sat with Leah in his lap. He studied the intimacy of their seating arrangement a little uncomfortably. "Pleased to meet you, Mrs. Alden." Then he frowned at Jeff. "Or is she still? Mrs. Alden, I mean."

"Not for long," Leah replied, wiggling out of Jeff's grip. "Sit down, Charlie. Would you like a soft drink?"

But Charlie was looking at Susan, and Leah was sure he hadn't heard the question.

Susan pushed the young man to the sofa. "Sit down. I'll get you a cola." She ran off to the kitchen, her eyes bright and her color high.

Leah took over Jeff's chair when he joined his clerk to look over the documents. The chair was warm from Jeff's body, and Leah felt her own body absorb the heat. A faint scent of him lingered, and she wondered with a little frisson of panic what was happening to her.

Susan put a cola in front of Charlie, then took Jeff's cup to refill it. Afraid that her sister, in her current state of distraction, might burn herself, Leah followed her into the kitchen.

"Cute, isn't he?" Leah teased softly, leaning against the counter as Susan poured the coffee.

Susan closed her eyes dramatically. "Isn't he just the most gorgeous thing you've ever seen?"

Actually, Jeff was the most gorgeous thing Leah had ever seen, but she was trying not to think about that now. "He is cute. And a law clerk. Appears to be bright and ambitious, too."

Susan gave her a small frown. "That's important to you, isn't it?"

"What?"

"Ambition."

Leah thought about that for a moment. "No intelligent woman wants a couch potato for a husband. Ambition is important. It means a man is looking to the future, that his career, his life are organized."

"Like yours."

Leah was becoming annoyed. "What do you mean?"

Susan added the few drops of cream that were all Jeff put in his coffee. "When you were in Portland last Saturday and Milly took over the office for you, she told me you were thinking about expanding your business services."

Leah shrugged. "That's just a dream at the moment. We're doing well. It's time to look forward."

"Daddy used to say that was the problem between you and Jeff," Susan said, studying her sister with genuine concern.

Leah straightened away from the counter, her spine stiffening. "What?"

"That Jeff was always looking around, enjoying things, and you were always looking ahead, planning to enjoy things."

As Susan walked away to deliver Jeff's coffee, Leah stood still in the middle of the kitchen, contemplating that remark. Then she drifted across the room to push open the sliding glass door. The night was dark and chilly and full of all the wonderful smells of autumn.

The busy beach town of Seaside stretched out below her, hundreds of lights marking the lively main thoroughfare. Laughter drifted up to her along with the sound of the surf and traffic noise from the state highway that connected Seaside to Astoria.

Leah loved this house and this small town. She loved the unabashed commercial fun of the turnaround, humming with tourists in the summer, quietly romantic and nostalgic in the winter. She loved her business. She loved her employees, who had all become friends. She admired and respected the businesses who called on her for help. And nothing matched the satisfaction of knowing she had someone well qualified to fill a key clerical or secretarial position. She loved knowing that, in a pinch, she could fill almost any job herself.

She hated being without Jeff. They couldn't live their lives together—she'd accepted that when they separated—but he had added something to her life that was missing now. She'd spent the past year trying to analyze just what that was as she rebuilt her life in its new pattern of order and solitude.

Whatever was missing had nothing to do with her dependence on him; they had never had that kind of a relationship. She had always been as strong as he, as capable, as smart. But some hidden quality, some little spark that had given everything a different dimension was missing.

Free of Jeff and his sloppy habits, his erratic hours and his preference for the impromptu, Leah had finally achieved the orderliness she so needed. But happiness hadn't followed.

"Are you reading the stars?" Jeff's deep voice just behind her ear startled her out of her thoughts.

"No." She rubbed her arms against a sudden gust of wind. "I just love this view. Pretty soon it'll be too cold to do this. Where are Susan and Charlie?"

"Would you believe playing backgammon in the den?" Jeff asked with a smile in his voice.

Leah turned to look at him in surprise. "Backgammon?" Then she nodded knowingly. "I see. Love is in the air."

He laughed. "I think it's a stage-ten alert. But don't worry. Charlie's a great kid. He goes to law school one semester a year and works the other semester to put himself through."

Leah turned back to stare into the darkness, rubbing her arms once more. "Maybe a romantic diversion is good for Susan. It'll take her mind off this thing for a little while."

Suddenly Leah felt Jeff's arms wrap around her, and the chill of the evening dissipated as he joined his hands in front of her, their weight resting comfortably under her breasts. She stiffened as her body jumped in alarm.

"Relax," he said quietly. "I'm offering body heat, not seduction." He tightened his grip ever so slightly and asked gently, "You're really afraid for Susan, aren't you?"

"I am," she agreed, unable to relax. Her body was rioting. "She's just not as strong as she thinks she is. Who could be at eighteen?"

"I know. But she's going to do this with or without us. At least we'll be **there** to pick up the pieces or cheer her on, however it turns out."

Leah tilted her head back and to the side to look at Jeff. "Speaking of launching this project—if we can't get a court order like Susan thought, there's no real reason for you to be involved in this. We won't need an attorney."

"I've been invited to be involved," he reminded her. "By Susan."

"Because she thought she needed an attorney."

"And because she loves and trusts me as a brother-in-law."

"It'll take a lot of time."

"That's why I have a partner. So I can get free when I have to. I'm part of this, Leah. You'll have to adjust to the idea."

There was silence for a moment, then Leah asked softly, "Jeff, do you remember why we separated?"

"Yep." He replied easily. "Because we couldn't live together."

"I mean specifically."

He shifted to lean against the doorframe, moving her body with his. "To the best of my recollection I forgot to tell you I was having a late session with a client, and when it got complicated and I walked in the door just before midnight feeling amorous, you threw me out."

"You reeked of perfume," Leah reminded him archly.

"Mrs. Dunwiddie was rather effusive," he laughed. "She loved to hug me. Actually, that night she cried on me. And I think she was wild for my body. I'm in real demand out there, you know."

"It was our anniversary."

He dropped his arms. "I apologized and explained. You threw me out, anyway."

Leah tried to remember his explanation and couldn't. It had involved Mrs. Dunwiddie. That was all she could recall.

"Lee, why are we talking about this all of a sudden?" Jeff asked. "Come on inside. I'm getting cold." He pulled Leah back into the warm kitchen and slid the glass door closed. The room smelled of coffee and pineapple.

"Because Susan told me earlier that ambition was important to me," Leah said, sinking into a kitchen chair. "She said it as though it made me a terrible person."

"You're not terrible," Jeff said, leaning a hip on the counter. "A little overorganized maybe, but not terrible." He smiled tauntingly, and she frowned at him.

"Order is important in life."

Jeff nodded. "Sure it is. But for some of us too much order makes us claustrophobic, and we can't live that way. But if you're happier on an established course without room for deviation, then that's how you should live, and you aren't required to explain yourself to anyone—even Susan." Jeff kissed her forehead affectionately. "I'd better round Charlie up before he invites himself to breakfast. Thanks for dinner, babe. And try not to worry about Susan. Promise?"

Leah swallowed a pointed rise of emotion. She missed being called "babe." "I promise."

"Good. Good night."

Jeff disappeared in search of his clerk, and Leah turned the kitchen light off and went back to the sliding glass door, opening it just enough to lean her body through. She inhaled deeply of the pungent night, feeling her lungs draw in the air and deposit it in the large empty area in the region of her heart.

CHAPTER THREE

LEAH DROVE HOME from Portland in the darkness of early evening, three new word processor/typewriters in the trunk of her car. Business was picking up, and she needed more equipment and two more good typists. Usually she enjoyed the trips to the big city to replenish supplies or add a piece of office furniture, but today she'd been distracted by the fact that, in two days, she and Jeff and Susan would travel to McMinnville to begin the search. She was now committed to Susan's quest, but the approaching reality of it made her nervous.

"I have a case in court on Monday," Jeff had explained to an impatient Susan over lunch at the Mikado, a Japanese restaurant upstairs in Seaside Town Center. The aroma of hamburgers, pizza and Greek gyros from other concessions teased their nostrils as they sat at a table in the gallery's communal dining area. "And Leah has to go to Portland Monday. We'll marshal our resources and start out Wednesday morning."

"Why not Tuesday?" Susan asked.

"Because I have paperwork and Lee has to get statements out to clear the decks for a few days."

"You'll be so busy covering the office for me Monday and Tuesday," Leah said cheerfully, nibbling on the morsel of *gyozo* speared on the tip of her fork, "that time will just fly."

Susan put her hamburger down and reached into Leah's plate for a bite of the meat-and-vegetable mixture wrapped in wonton skin. She dipped it carefully in the little paper cup of dark sauce. "Great con job, sis. I suppose you'll expect me to file, catch up on the typing on that manuscript you're working on for Diane Hankins and change that winking fluorescent tube over your desk." She examined the exotic morsel on the tip of her fork. "You're sure this is good?"

"Delicious. Anything you'd care to do would be appreciated, but don't worry about the light. Wally said he'll change it for me when he has a minute."

Susan chewed thoughtfully on the *gyozo*, then turned to her brother-in-law. "Did you know that the illustrious owner of Waltham's Sporting Goods next door to Minding Your Business is after your wife?"

Jeff shrugged, looking at Leah with a teasingly accepting air. "Half of Seaside is after my wife. That's the price a man pays for being married to a gorgeous woman."

"Separated from a gorgeous woman," Leah corrected, pulling her plate away as Susan reached for another piece of her lunch.

"It's interesting that you keep feeling the need to make that distinction," Jeff noted, leaning back in his chair with a glass of Japanese beer in his hand. "Yet you never do anything to make the separation permanent."

"Just keeping the record straight," she said, backing off from the subject. What he said was true, and because she didn't understand it, she didn't care to consider it. "I thought attorneys liked things in order."

Jeff studied the soft turmoil in her eyes and smiled knowingly. "Sometimes confusion is more revealing than order."

"What time Wednesday?" Susan had asked, apparently trying to draw them away from the pointed banter that always seemed to develop when they were together. Jeff had turned to her and they had begun to finalize plans.

Now, as Leah passed the Seaside city limits sign, she breathed a heavy sigh. Her thoughts had been chaotic all day, and she'd found nothing revealing in them—only that nagging sense of irritation disorder always brought. She was worried about Susan getting her hopes up. She was worried about spending all of Wednesday, or maybe longer, in Jeff's company. And she was worried about her business. While she accompanied Jeff and Susan in this search, her availability for work would be unpredictable. Though she knew she could depend on Milly, her office assistant, to keep things running smoothly, she liked to be on hand herself.

Leah pulled into her driveway, thinking that she should call a staff meeting in the morning to explain the impending disruption of their established routine.

When she entered her house, she was surprised and a little alarmed to find it empty. Checking her watch, she discovered that it was just shortly after eight. She went to the refrigerator where she and Susan left notes for each other fastened to the door with a cat-faced magnet. There was nothing but the grocery list she'd started that morning.

Leah began making a mental list of all the places where Susan could be: with Charlie, with Jeff, with her friend Shelly. Then the telephone rang. She went toward it with a mild sense of foreboding.

"Hello?"

"Hi, Lee. It's Jeff."

"Jeff." Leah felt relieved by the very sound of his voice. "Hi. I just got in from Portland. Have you seen Susan? She isn't home and I—"

"I'm with her right now," Jeff interrupted. There was an instant's pause and Leah braced herself, knowing something was wrong.

"What's the matter. Where are you?"

"We're at the hospital, but we're ready to leave right now. Just sit tight. Charlie and I are bringing her home."

Leah closed her eyes. "What happened?"

"She broke her leg," Jeff said, then hastened to add, "but it's a simple fracture and everything else is okay. She's in pain, but they've given her something. Get her bed ready—we'll be home in fifteen minutes."

"I KNOW YOU SAID Wally would fix the light," Susan murmured, wincing as she shifted against the bank of pillows Leah was stuffing behind her. "But it was almost closing time and Milly had to leave early to pick up a prescription. I was restless and . . . well, I thought I'd try it." She shook her head, her usually expertly made-up face now pale and drawn from the afternoon's ordeal. "Bad move. I didn't realize how hard those ten-foot fluorescent tubes are to handle. I sailed right off the ladder." She gave Leah a grimace. "I killed your philodendron on the way down. Good thing the phone fell with me. It was a lot easier being able to call Jeff from right there on the floor. God, I feel awful."

Charlie, who had carried Susan in with great care and deep concern, now looked across the bed at Leah in obvious distress. "What can we do for her?"

Jeff began to draw him gently away. "The medication should take effect pretty soon. Why don't we get out of here and let Leah make her comfortable?"

"Jeff!" Susan called urgently, trying to sit up and gasping as pain made it impossible.

"Will you quit moving around," Jeff scolded gently, going back to the bed to lean over her. He took the hand she held out to him. "What, Suzie?"

Large tears pooled in Susan's eyes as she pulled him down to sit beside her. "Thanks for coming when I called. I know you and Charlie were busy..."

"We were just on our way to the Shilo for a drink." He shrugged away her thanks, then grinned. "We considered letting you lie there till we were finished, but..."

"Jeff?" Susan ignored his teasing, her mind obviously occupied with something else.

"Yeah?"

"About McMinnville on Wednesday..."

"We'll just postpone everything until you can get around," Jeff assured her, patting the hand he held. "No problem."

"No!" Susan said forcefully. "I want you to start without me."

Surprised by her request, Jeff looked at Leah as she sat on the other side of her sister. "Sweetie," Leah said, "we don't want—"

"Please," Susan insisted. She turned back to Jeff and squeezed his hand. "Please, Jeff. If I have to wait three or four weeks, I'll go crazy. Start without me and just let me know what's going on.''

"Suzie, I can't leave you home alone with a broken leg," Leah said with big-sister authority. "It's out of the question.''

"I'll bet Delia would come and stay with me," Susan suggested. "And Charlie would check on us, wouldn't you, Charlie?''

Susan turned her woeful, tear-filled blue eyes on the young man standing at the foot of the bed, and he became speechless. Finally pulling himself together, he cleared his throat. "Of course I would. Who's Delia?''

"She was a friend of our mother's," Leah explained.

"Please?" Susan's overtly wheedling expression was suspended by a sudden yawn. "Call her now and see if she's free. I'll sleep better if I know everything's going to go as we planned. Please?''

Running out of arguments, Leah turned to Jeff for reinforcement. "Jeff, will you *do* something."

"Right." Jeff got decisively to his feet and started out the bedroom door.

"Where are you going?" Leah demanded.

He stopped and turned to her, inclining his head in reluctant acceptance of the situation. "To call Delia.''

"Je-eff!" Leah gave his name two frustrated syllables as she followed him along the corridor and through the living room. "I won't leave her. She'll need me.''

Jeff went into the kitchen and stopped at the wall telephone. "What she needs is to know that you care about her concerns as much as she does and that you'll do this for her." Jeff picked up the telephone book from its pocket on the pegboard organizer behind the phone. "Delia Crockett, right?" he asked, beginning to flip through pages.

Recognizing that the battle was lost, Leah took the book from him, replaced it and pushed him away from the phone. "*I'll* call her," she said with ill grace.

As Jeff watched her stab out Delia's number, he couldn't dispel the feeling that Leah needed this experience, that it would do her good to delve into the corners of life and be forced to deal with the untidiness that often lived there. True, she would be delving into the lives of Susan's parents rather than her own life, but ultimately they were all entwined. She was bound to be affected, to have her orderliness mussed a little by the endeavor. He had to help her toward that end before the warm woman inside her was lost forever to routine and organization.

"She'll do it," Leah reported grimly, replacing the receiver with a little more force than necessary. "I'll tell Susan."

Jeff leaned against the counter and watched Leah walk across the living room, the sway of her neat hips in burgundy wool slacks forcing a longing sigh from his lips. He was getting tired of this separation, he thought with sudden resolution. If he was going to make a move to win her back, he couldn't have asked for a more golden opportunity. There had to be a way that her systematic approach to life could coexist with his more serendipitous ways. He was determined to find it.

BETWEEN SEASIDE on the Oregon coast and McMinnville in the Willamette Valley were over one hundred winding miles of beautiful countryside. The gleaming evergreens that lined both sides of the road were interspersed with the red and gold of vine maple and the small shiny leaves and the red-orange fruit of the huckleberry. Rich green hills appeared and disappeared as the highway meandered, and a lonely farmhouse occasionally provided a break in the heavy forest off the road.

It was a clear, crisp day, and Leah was feeling cautiously optimistic. When she left the house that morning, Susan had been resting comfortably with Delia firmly in charge. The fact that Jeff and Leah had finally agreed to begin the search had settled Susan's nerves considerably, and Leah realized resignedly that, at this point in time, that was what was important. Charlie had called from Jeff's office to assure her he would stop in and spend time with Susan after work.

Relieved that her sister was well cared for, Leah was able to relax and absorb the atmosphere around her. The times she had ridden in the car beside Jeff were among her happiest memories of their two years together. Every other weekend they'd been off on a picnic or a jaunt to Seattle or Portland to shop or off for a couple of days at the beach. Sometimes they'd talked incessantly, the beautiful Northwest scenery barely noticed. Other times they'd been comfortably silent, each ensnared by the beauty surrounding them. She felt herself slipping into that feeling of contentment now.

Leah had a sudden, clear memory of being snuggled up to Jeff in this very seat, her hand resting on his knee, his arm holding her close to his side. For one swift moment the past fourteen months were wiped away and they were in the car, headed for a weekend of fun and love.

"Feeling okay?" Jeff asked.

Leah looked up in alarm to find his quick, sharp glance on her before he turned back to the road. She was sitting primly on her end of the bench seat, her seat belt buckled.

"Fine," she said, trying to push aside the nostalgic past and deal with the present.

"Everything's going to be all right," he promised.

"I know." She tried to sound convinced. "I don't think I've been to McMinnville since high school football games."

"I get there a couple of times a year on business. It's such a pretty place. The farmland and the meadows are so different from our fir-covered hills."

Leah noted the wistfulness in his voice and was a little surprised by it. "Ever wish you were a farmer instead of a lawyer?"

He smiled at the road. "Every time I buy a steak. But never when 5:00 a.m. rolls around and I can choose to stay in bed if I want to."

"With whom?" The question was out before she could stop herself. When it met with silence, Leah looked up to find Jeff studying the road, his smile deepening.

"With Smythe usually," he replied.

"And unusually?"

He turned to look at her over the arm that guided the steering wheel. "Does it matter to you?"

"Of course it does." She leaned back against the headrest and closed her eyes. She didn't want him to misunderstand what he might see there. "I have to know who to name when I file, don't I?"

There was another long silence. Jeff continued to stare ahead, but with a skeptical smile on his face now.

"I'm not seeing anyone. Although celibacy is wearing a little thin. What about you?"

She shrugged without opening her eyes. "Too busy."

She heard him make a small sound of amusement. "Story of your life. Do you ever wonder why you're running so fast?"

She sat up in her seat, her eyes opening wide, the mellow mood dissipating. "I have things to do. Unlike you, to whom life is a lark."

"It's not a lark," he denied quietly, "but neither is it a sentence at hard labor."

"If your father hadn't worked hard, you wouldn't be a Harvard graduate with a stock portfolio."

He glanced at her quickly, anger suddenly alive in his eyes. "If my father hadn't worked so hard, I might have gotten to know him. My mother might have liked to stay home once in a while. And the stock portfolio is mine."

Leah regretted having brought the subject up. She knew Jeff's childhood had been difficult and lonely. His mother had died young, and his father, the owner of a major New York publishing house had missed most of the major events in Jeff's life because of business. He'd chartered a private plane to fly to Seaside for Jeff and Leah's wedding, then left immediately after, unable to stay for the reception. Jeff had been furious. Leah remembered looking into a face very much like Jeff's, seeing a sad emptiness under the facade of smiling hyperactivity, and felt empathy.

"I'm sorry," she said. "But there's something to be said for hard work and an organized life-style. You shouldn't discount it completely because your father is obsessive."

He glanced in the rearview mirror, then at the speedometer, slowing down to comply with the reduced speed limit as they drove into McMinnville. "It was frightening to me," he said with another glance at her, "that you were showing signs of living the same way he did."

She shook her head and folded her arms. "You think anyone who tries to plan and works past five o'clock should be compared to your father. And if you do feel that way about me, I'll file for divorce as soon as this business with Susan is over."

"I suppose," he said to the windshield, "that it would be easier than admitting that you had anything to do with our marriage going wrong, easier than trying to fix it."

She sat up in a huff, instantly offended. "And I suppose you didn't?"

"I did. I admit it."

"Big of you. Do you want to admit to Sylvia Dunwiddie while you're at it?"

He looked at her as though she were a child who had just made a transparent excuse for a transgression. "There's nothing to that, and you know it."

Leah folded her arms and stared at the windshield. "Then why *did* you come home smelling of Obsession?"

"I explained about—"

"The client who loved to hug you," she interrupted coolly. "I know. And on our anniversary. If you think I'll believe that, you don't know me very well after two years of marriage and one year of separation."

"Who does know you very well, Leah?" Jeff asked. "You don't even know yourself. How can I be expected to ever understand you when you keep running away from me?''

She was beginning to get angry, but she tamped down the hot words, replying instead with dignity, "You had your chance, Jeff."

His laugh was quick and humorless. "Two years with a mannequin in a mask isn't a chance."

In the heated argument that had ensued the night they'd separated, Jeff had maintained that it was neither his working late nor his basic lack of organization that had opened a chasm between them, but Leah's own inability to be open and giving.

"You're always so prim and formal!" he'd said accusingly. "Makeup always on, never a hair out of place. You're not real, Leah!" Then, to prove his point, he'd grabbed the neck of her ivory silk negligee and yanked it angrily. The gown had torn, falling into a soft pile of rag at her feet. She had simply looked back at him haughtily, small breasts swelling as she'd drawn a steadying breath. She hadn't moved or flinched.

She would never forget the way he'd looked at her then. In his smoldering brown eyes had been that searching look she'd become familiar with, but it was quickly replaced by acute disappointment and finally followed by defeat.

"Even when you're naked you aren't vulnerable," he'd said. "You're still wearing armor and a mask. There's no getting through to you, Leah."

She'd told him to get out, expecting him to argue, possibly explain a second time why he'd been out with a client on their anniversary and come home at midnight. But he'd simply gathered up a change of clothes and his sad-eyed dog and left.

His reference to her as a mannequin with a mask made the hurt of that night fresh, and she shuddered a little with pain.

She expelled a long, shaky breath. "Maybe we'd better stick to discussing why we're here and leave everything else for our attorneys."

Jeff forced himself to relax, calmly turning his attention back to the road. He was convinced that Leah referred so often to divorce because she didn't really want one. But getting her to see that was going to be a project of grand proportions. He would need every ounce of strength and energy he possessed. There was no point in wasting either when she was intent on behaving like an ice cube.

It was midmorning in McMinnville, and the humming little town was alive with activity. Patrons were coming and going from fast-food restaurants, supermarkets, garden shops and all the other stores and offices along the main highway.

Jeff pulled into a parking spot in front of a two-story ivy-covered building. On this fall day the library's parklike setting, complete with maple trees in their flaming colors, was breathtaking.

"You have the photograph?" Jeff asked as he turned the engine off.

Leah sighed impatiently, "Yes, of course I have the photograph. But do you really think the woman in it is recognizable?"

"Possibly to someone who knew her," Jeff replied.

Leah looked doubtful. "Okay. I'm to show it around and see if anyone recognizes the woman while you check the phone book and the genealogy files for the name Szabo. Do you have paper and pen?" she asked, looking pointedly at his empty hands.

"No," he replied, opening his door. "But I'm sure you do. Ready?"

After a short half hour in the library, they emerged, the mood between them no more congenial than when they'd gone in.

"That was a complete waste of time," Leah said as he opened the car door. "How'd you do?"

"No Szabos in the phone book or in the genealogy files." Jeff walked around and got in behind the wheel. "But I was playing with the card file while waiting for you and found a biography of a Hungarian freedom fighter named Szabo."

Leah blinked. "Are you suggesting Susan's descended from a freedom fighter?"

"No," he replied patiently. "Only that she could be of Hungarian descent. I wasn't sure what nationality the name Szabo was. Now I know."

That seemed like precious little to her, but she had enough respect for detail to know that it could mean the difference between success and failure in anything. "So what's our next stop?"

"The *News Register* office. It's just a couple of blocks away. Keep your eyes open," he directed as he pulled out into the main street traffic. "I'm not sure if it's right or left off this street, but it's on one of these downtown blocks."

Within a few minutes they were parked in front of the newspaper office.

"I understand we're going to look for birth announcements that were posted on the day Susan was born," Leah said as Jeff opened the door for her. "But if all records are sealed when a child is adopted, wouldn't that sort of information be prevented from appearing in the paper?"

"When an infant is adopted, yes," Jeff agreed. "But you said Susan was a couple of months old when she came to your home. So the adoption wasn't planned before or even when she was born. It was a later result of whatever happened to her parents. So the announcement probably made the paper."

Leah squared her shoulders. It sounded like a long shot to her, but then the whole project was an exercise in sheer bullheadedness.

After they'd explained their project to the receptionist, Jeff and Leah were seated at a table in a back room of the noisy office. Jeff checked the microfilm while Leah double-checked him by looking through the yellowed 1972 editions. They were held together in a large black binder. Propped on her elbows, one of her knees on a chair, she bent over the unwieldy books. Carefully she made a list of every girl born on October 17, 1972, and the names and cities of origin of the parents.

"Found any Szabos?" Jeff asked, staring into the microfilm reader.

"Nope." Leah shook her head. "I've found Chan, Harrison, Clayborne, Dulude, Nagy, Kelly, Villasenor and Gray. What about you?"

"Matches my list." Jeff turned off the viewer and went to look over Leah's shoulder. "Let's go through the clipping files and see if we can find anything on any of these people. An accident or a death could be a reason for giving up a baby and give us the correlation we're looking for." He smiled and pointed to the top four names on her list. "You take those and I'll do the rest. I think we can safely put Chan and even Villasenor at the bottom of the list."

Leah nodded with a grin. Susan's fair features bore no apparent trace of Chinese or Hispanic ancestry.

An hour later Leah sat across from Jeff, poring over the clippings they had picked out of the newspaper's files.

"Patricia Dulude was named Ladies League Woman of the Year in 1978," she read to Jeff. "She had three children at the time, one of them a six-year-old girl. We can scratch the Duludes." Leah did so with a bold swipe of her pen.

"George Clayborne died in 1987," Jeff reported, running the tip of his pen along the clipping. "He left a wife and two daughters, Karen Stevenson of Seattle and Lisa Clayborne, fifteen. We can disregard the Claybornes."

"The Kellys were both in a serious automobile accident in January 1973." Leah looked up at Jeff, a small ripple of excitement running along her spine. She was becoming involved in this project, despite her objections. "If things got bad for them . . . or if one of them died after this story ran . . ."

Jeff understood what she left unsaid. "Right. And Janos Nagy was reported missing in action in Vietnam in 1972. That could be a possibility, too. So how does our list look now?"

Leah checked her notes. "Well, if we're doing this right, we're down to four names. We found nothing on the Harrisons or the Grays, so there's no reason to cross them off, and the Nagys and the Kellys are maybes. I suppose we should save Chan and Villasenor on the chance that none of the others work out."

"Okay. I'll make copies of these clippings. Be right back."

As Jeff disappeared into the outer office, Leah replaced the other clippings in their envelopes and put them back in the files. Sad, she thought, that the grief she learned about in these clippings brought them closer to finding Susan's parents.

"Will these be safe in that bottomless purse of yours?" Jeff handed her the copies of the clippings, neatly folded into an envelope. His brown eyes were lazy and teasing, his manner suddenly lighthearted and flirtatious. Leah felt her heartbeat quicken, her somber mood evaporate.

She lifted her cavernous leather satchel onto the table and took the papers from him. "It's big, but I know where everything is in it. Just remember how many times it carried your camera," she reminded him dryly, "and your sunglasses and your winter gloves."

Jeff hefted the purse and grimaced. It amused him to be reminded of this one facet of her life she'd never seemed to be able to sort through and organize. "Good Lord, Lee! I'm just concerned about your getting a hernia."

Leah slung the purse over her shoulder with deliberate ease. "Nothing to it. I'm built to take it."

"Mmm." He gave her a look that was half thoughtful, half critical. "Leah of the steel spine. Sometimes I forget. Let's have some lunch."

"Now it's back to the library?" Leah asked as she pushed aside a plate that still held half of a club sandwich. "Do you want this?"

Jeff pulled it toward him, and in one bite half of the remaining piece of sandwich was gone. He nodded, swallowing. "We'll see if we can find any of the names on our list in the phone book."

"And if we can't?"

"I've asked for help from a detective friend. He says if we can just get some names, he can find almost anyone through the Department of Motor Vehicles. He's working on finding Gerda Szabo right now." The rest of the sandwich disappeared and he took a sip of coffee. "If we find anything in the phone book, we'll have a little time to check out addresses before it's dark."

Leah's heart jolted anxiously at the prospect of actually approaching a strange woman and asking her if she could be Susan's mother. Looking at it from the woman's point of view, it seemed like such an invasion of privacy. Didn't everyone have a dark little corner in their life that they kept scrupulously secret? But remembering how much Susan wanted to find her natural parents, Leah resolved with a sigh that she would have to do it.

Noting her pensive and distant expression, Jeff reached across the table to cover her hand with his own. It felt small and cold. "Nervous?" he asked gently.

Leah looked up at him with a grim smile. "Terrified. It hasn't occurred to me until this minute what a hurtful thing I'll be doing by asking questions."

"The questions could be hurtful only to Susan's parents," he said earnestly, squeezing her hand. "And, depending on the circumstances under which they let her go, maybe they'll be happy to find her. But—" he ran his thumb along her knuckles and smiled doubtfully "—I really don't think we'll find them this early in the process. It could happen, but I doubt it."

He released her hand and, picking up the check, led her toward the cashier. As they walked out onto the parking lot, he put a companionable arm around her shoulders. "So relax. And remember that I'll be along to prevent anyone from slugging you."

Leah looked up into his teasing grin and couldn't prevent herself from laughing at the picture his words brought to mind. Then, as she suddenly became aware of the warmth of his arm around her and the way her arm had snaked around his waist with the old, familiar ease, the laughter stopped and the moment was suspended.

The valley had a different fragrance than the coast, she noted absently as her surprised green eyes locked with his watchful brown gaze. It was more floral—less primitive—as it swirled around her on a soft midafternoon breeze that stirred the hair at the crown of her head and lifted it away from her cheeks. The sky was bright blue behind Jeff's dark head, but she couldn't focus on it. She couldn't pull away from the tempting darkness of his eyes.

"I'm always right behind you," he said softly. "Whether or not you know I'm there."

Her lips parted. She wanted to tell him that she was aware of that. She wanted to thank him for how quickly he'd come to her side when her father died and how persistently he'd remained to shield her from wellmeaning friends and neighbors. She wanted to thank him for caring this much about Susan.

She opened her mouth to speak, but Jeff leaned down and covered it with his own. He'd read the gratitude in her eyes and didn't want to hear it, so he silenced it in the only way that was bound to leave her speechless.

She tasted the same—warm, soft, sweet. He took advantage of her surprise and moved his lips over hers, wondering how she would react. He felt her instinctive response, the inclination of her body, the crumpling of his shirtsleeve in her hand. Then she pushed away from him, her eyes as angry with herself as they were with him. He noted with satisfaction that she had a little trouble catching her breath and her hands were shaking.

She adjusted her purse strap on her shoulder and tugged at the hem of her sweater. "We're here on Susan's business," she said, lifting her chin in the old, controlled pose. "Don't forget that."

He put her into the car, closed the door and leaned into the open top over her. "We have some unfinished business of our own. Don't you forget it."

CHAPTER FOUR

"Box 291. Here it is." Leah checked the note in her hand against the number on the large country mailbox as Jeff pulled to a stop. The box had been enameled Williamsburg blue, and someone had painted a stately goose on it complete with a big red bow and a trail of little goslings.

Leah turned to Jeff, her eyes reflecting nervousness. "Someone here is obviously an artist. Susan's very artistic."

"They could have bought the box, Lee," he said calmly, studying her sudden pallor. "Want to find a motel and come back in the morning when you're fresh?"

She looked at him, trying to determine whether he was motivated by concern for her welfare or lecherous plans of his own. His eyes were so honest, his expression so open that she felt guilty for having entertained the doubt and lowered her eyes.

"I would like to get you in bed," he admitted, a thread of amusement in his voice as he read her mind. "But not in one you put quarters in. You're sure you're up to this?"

Leah spared him an impatient side-glance to acknowledge the joke, then turned forward determinedly as they cleared a narrow lane and turned into a circular drive. "No. But I promised Susan."

A barking golden Labrador strained at the end of a chain tied to the front porch of a yellow two-story farmhouse. It was a cheerful place, Leah thought. An apple tree to the right of the house was heavy with fruit, and white, yellow and purple mums grew around the house, following the angle of the stairs. On the porch green plants hung from the rafters, and white lace curtains hung at the windows. One was moved aside as she watched, then a tall blond woman stepped onto the porch, shading her eyes against the low angle of the sun.

Leah's heart lurched as she opened her door.

"Want me to come?" Jeff asked quietly.

She turned back to him. "Thanks, but if it is Susan's mother, she might find it easier to talk if I'm alone."

"All right." Jeff settled into the corner of his seat to wait. "Go easy," he cautioned.

Yes, she thought, stepping out of the car and smiling at the woman who watched her. *Easy.* It occurred to her that she had no idea what to say. *Pardon me, but are you my sister's mother?* Or, *I know it's bold of me to ask, but did you abandon your baby daughter eighteen years ago?* Maybe she could try, *I'm sorry, but I understand your family was involved in a serious accident, and I wonder if that forced you to . . . ?*

There was no delicate way to pry into a stranger's past, and she clung to the open car door for a moment, ready to chuck the plan before she even started. If Susan was so determined to find her parents, she could do it herself when she was well. But the thought of her sister lying in bed and waiting to hear what Leah was able to discover stirred her sense of responsibility. She squared her shoulders and pushed the door closed.

"Hello, Mrs. Kelly," she said, walking toward the porch. "I'm Leah Alden." She stopped several feet from the Lab, which barked threateningly and pulled against its chain. "I'm visiting from the coast."

The woman nodded, obviously waiting for more information before she offered to quiet the dog or move down the steps. She wore jeans and boots, Leah noted, and a gray sweatshirt covered with berry-colored stains that could have been paint. She was slender and leggy like Susan. Leah tried hard to think clearly.

She joined her fingers and smiled nervously. "I'm on a kind of a . . . strange mission."

The woman nodded again and waited.

"I'm trying to help my sister look for her mother," she blurted, hoping it would sound more sensible said aloud than it had in her mind. It didn't. The woman frowned and nodded again. The dog barked.

"She's adopted," Leah went on before she lost courage. "We both were. Susan was going to come with me, but she broke her leg changing a fluorescent—" She stopped, feeling foolish, and put a hand to her head. "I'm sorry, Mrs. Kelly, I'm not doing this very well."

Lucinda Kelly walked down the six porch steps and quietly said, "Sunbeam, hush." Then she walked to within inches of Leah and ordered in the same voice with which she had calmed the dog, "Start again."

A corner of Leah's mind still reacting normally considered the fact that this woman was too calm and reasonable to be Susan's mother. But genes were tricky, she knew, and she had made a promise.

"I'm here," she began, "to find my sister Susan's mother. All I have is Susan's birth certificate, saying that she was born in McMinnville on October 17, 1972.

I checked at the *News Register* for all the birth announcements for that date."

The woman smiled. It wasn't a smile of happiness or even cheer, but one of simple understanding. "I gave birth to a daughter on that day."

Leah swallowed. "I know. Is she..." Leah glanced away nervously. "Do you..."

"Do I still have her?" The woman looked less insulted by the question than interested. "Yes, I do. But why do you think I might not?"

Leah looked her in the eye, deciding she was a woman who deserved honesty. "This will sound heartless to you, Mrs. Kelly, but after we found the names, we looked through the newspaper's clippings file for any further mention of the names on our list, hoping it might tell us something. I read that you and your husband were involved in a serious accident two months after your daughter was born." She swallowed again. "I thought if either of you had... died, the other might have put your new baby up for adoption."

Lucinda Kelly shook her head. "We don't give our babies away where I come from."

Leah put a hand to her eyes and shook her head. "I can see that. But apparently they do it where my sister and I come from. I had to ask. I'm sorry."

Suddenly the front door of the farmhouse burst open and a young woman Susan's age erupted onto the porch. She wore a red sweater and jeans, and a mass of dark hair swung around her shoulders. The dog ran up the steps to jump on her, tail wagging, body bent double in its excitement.

"Hi," she said to Leah as she bent down to kiss the dog's snout. "I didn't mean to intrude. I heard the car while I was getting dressed and thought it might be Michael."

Lucinda Kelly smiled at Leah. "Michael's her boyfriend." Then she extended a hand to the girl. "Come here, sweetie. This is Joy," she said, putting an arm around her daughter's shoulders. "Joy, this is Leah Alden. She's on a quest to find her adopted sister's mother."

Joy had her mother's handsome looks and an ebullience that reminded Leah sharply of Susan. But Leah had to admit to herself a little sadly that the girls had simply youth in common and not parentage.

Joy put an arm around her mother's waist and laughed teasingly. "Well, this is *my* mother and you can't have her."

All heads turned at a whirring electrical sound, and Leah saw a wheelchair speed along a concrete sidewalk between the house and an outbuilding behind it. The man in the chair was broad-shouldered and handsome with a thick thatch of graying black hair. In his lap, enjoying the ride, was a fat yellow-eyed tabby cat.

The man held up a mobile phone. "Joy, it's Michael."

"Oh!" With a delighted squeal the girl ran to him. They exchanged a laughing remark that Leah couldn't quite hear, and Joy ran up the porch steps with the phone.

"That's what the accident did to us," Lucinda said softly. "But Joy's been a comfort rather than a burden."

As her husband approached, Lucinda reached out to catch his hand and introduce Leah.

"It's been a pleasure meeting all of you," Leah said, her throat tightening, a swell of emotion she couldn't quite interpret filling her chest.

Lucinda gave her a hug, holding her for a moment. "I'm sorry you have to keep searching, but we're a family, whole and entire. Always have been."

Leah drew away and looked into her eyes. "I hope there's someone like you at the end of my search," she said. "Bye." She hurried back to the car as the Kellys waved at her. She watched through the windshield as they went around the side of the house, still hand in hand. At a wooden ramp Lucinda got behind the wheelchair and pushed.

"So that was the result of the accident," Jeff observed grimly.

Leah nodded, concentrating on swallowing the lump in her throat. "The daughter's name is Joy," she said, her voice strained and high. "And that's what she is to them."

Jeff hooked his hand around her knees and pulled her beside him. "Are you all right?"

"No." She leaned her forehead wearily against his upper arm. "I feel like sobbing."

"Go ahead," he suggested gently.

She sighed and straightened up, shaking her head. "No. We have to pace ourselves. Isn't that what you told Susan? It's probably going to be a long and difficult search." She looked back at the modest farmhouse, where the front window was catching the setting sun, and shook her head wistfully. "But it would be nice if Susan's family were something like the Kellys."

Jeff eased around the curved driveway to the lane that led to the highway. "The address I have for the Harrisons," he said, opening a map of McMinnville

and putting it in her lap, "is on a little back street behind the library. You ready?"

"Yes." Leah buckled her seat belt, made some notes
on a pad in her purse, then spotted the circle he'd made
on the map. It was almost evening, and she had to
strain to read the names.

James Harrison's house was a two-story, turn-of-the-
century house like most of the homes in the older section of McMinnville. It was in disrepair, and two wide
flower boxes at each front window were filled with naked stems. A battered pickup, the hood tied down with
a stout rope to the bumper, was parked at the curb. As
Jeff parked behind it, Leah looked at the house with
trepidation.

"I'm coming with you," Jeff said, reaching across
her to open her door. Strains of heavy metal blared
from an open window. A woman standing on the porch
of a prim little house next door glared at them, clutching the sides of her sweater around her.

A tall, muscular young man in a T-shirt answered the
door, a beer in his hand. His eyes lighted on Leah with
interest. Then he noticed Jeff and frowned suspiciously. "Yeah?"

"Hello, we're looking for James Harrison," Leah
said politely.

"Never heard of him," the man replied, taking a
swig from his beer.

"The phone book lists him at this address," Leah
persisted.

"Phone book's wrong. I live here."

"How long have you been here?"

"God, feels like forever."

"Specifically, how long?" Jeff asked.

The man thought. "Specifically," he returned the word with mild scorn. "Three months, anyway."

"You bought this place?"

"Renting."

"Where do you send your checks?"

"Look." The man straightened to his full height, several inches taller than Jeff, and looked belligerent. "I been clean since that little business at the Rooster. I got rights, you know."

Jeff nodded. "I know all about your rights. I'm a lawyer. This has nothing to do with you. We just want to know how to find Harrison."

"Well, I don't know nothin' about him. I send my rent check to a real estate office here in town. If you want to know about him, ask the old lady next door." He peered around his front door and made a face at the old lady, who was obviously trying to overhear their conversation. She put her nose in the air and turned away. "The old biddy knows everything about everybody." Then he slammed the door in their faces.

It was now dusk, and Jeff took Leah's elbow as they made their way over the sidewalk broken by the roots of a huge maple tree to the little house next door. The woman met them halfway down the stairs.

"He's a cretin," she said with an inclination of her white head toward her neighbor. "What do you want to know?"

Leah explained.

The woman nodded, obviously pleased to impart what she knew. "Mr. Harrison moved his family to Arizona about four months ago. Wife needed a better climate. Has arthritis. Bad." She cramped her own perfect white fingers to illustrate the problem. "Boy was upset. He was on the football team."

"Did they have a daughter?" Leah asked.

The woman nodded. "Amy. About twelve. Nice little girl. Loved my oatmeal cookies."

Leah felt herself stiffen. "Wasn't there an older girl? About eighteen?"

"Wendy. But she didn't go with them. She got married a year ago." The woman leaned closer to Leah and whispered, "Had to."

Leah released her breath, half relieved, half disappointed. "Thank you. We appreciate your help."

The woman shrugged bony shoulders under the stretched sweater. "Somebody's got to watch the neighborhood."

In the car again Leah and Jeff looked at each other. She looked tired and disappointed, and that worried him. He was discovering that it was one thing to want her to experience a little of life's grimness for her own good and another to see that confused, lost look in her eyes. He cared too much to remain unaffected by it.

"The list is dwindling," he said bracingly. "That's a good thing."

She looked at him wearily. "I know. I just wish I had something more positive to tell Susan when we get home."

He smiled gently. "She didn't expect you to find her parents the first day out."

Leah gave him a wry side-glance. "You know Suzie better than that. Of course she did. She wants things to happen now."

"Don't we all really? Deep down?"

It was a gentle question, an offer to share a basic human frailty at a time when she was vulnerable. But Leah was determined not to be vulnerable in this. She was doing this for Susan, and though she couldn't love

Susan more if they shared the same blood, this was in reality Susan's search and not hers. It had nothing to do with Leah's life. And if meeting the Kellys had left her a little shaken, it was because she admired courage, not because a little corner of her being had opened up and realized that orderliness would never have kept the Kellys together. Something else had.

Leah buckled her seat belt. "It takes time to get an education, time to organize your life, time to plan. Susan's got to see that, or she'll never be happy."

Jeff turned the key in the ignition with a small groan. "What does that leave time for when you're finished?"

She looked at him in surprise. "You're never finished. It's an ongoing task."

"So when does the fun begin?"

Leah sighed. "Life isn't about fun. It's about accomplishment, responsibility...."

Jeff shook his head and pulled away from the curb. "We don't have to look for *your* roots. You're probably a great-great-granddaughter of some warrior queen."

The beautiful Sunset Highway became treacherous after dark, and Jeff concentrated on guiding the car along its elaborate twists and turns. Halfway home, he stopped for dinner at Camp 18, a restaurant and gift shop constructed of whole logs and surrounded by a museum of old logging equipment.

Leah seemed tired and preoccupied, so he let her pick at her salad. He ate his own sandwich with a quiet efficiency he thought would do credit to her philosophy of not sparing time to enjoy things, then drove home.

She fell asleep the moment they were back in the car.

LEAH AWOKE to a curious change in cadence from the rumble and roll of the car that had put her to sleep. Her head wasn't leaning against the cold window, but against a faintly scratchy wool through which she could feel heat and the unmistakable thrum of life. She lifted her head suddenly and collided with Jeff's chin.

"Careful," he cautioned, his voice filled with amusement. He shifted her in his arms and shouted, "Down, Smittie! You're going to kill us all."

Leah found herself clutching his neck for balance as she tried to focus on the dimly lit stairway. "Where are we?" she asked groggily.

"My place," he replied. "It's twenty minutes closer than yours, and I thought it was a little late to wake up a household with an invalid in it."

Sleepily she leaned back against his shoulder. In her semiconscious state, spending the night at Jeff's seemed more a cause for philosophical amusement than concern. "And this keeps me handy so you can plan my seduction."

"Planning's your department," he reminded quietly, topping the stairs and taking a right turn down a dark corridor. "I just let things happen. But don't let that stop you from planning *my* seduction."

Leah held on as Jeff kicked a door open, carried her into a cool, dark room and placed her on a silky bedspread. It was cold where it touched her cheek and her stockinged legs, and she immediately missed the warmth of Jeff's touch as he pulled away from her and straightened. Something leaped up beside her and began to lick her face.

"Smythe!" she cried, delighted to embrace the pet they'd shared for two short years. He was unflinchingly loyal to his master, but he'd loved her, too, and she had spoiled him shamefully.

Jeff turned a bedside light on, revealing a spacious room with oak furniture and soft green walls. Beside her, the spotted brown-and-white springer danced excitedly, licking her and whining his delight. Leah forced herself into a sitting position and hooked an arm around the dog as she examined her surroundings. She'd never been in Jeff's home before and she was surprised by the lack of alarm she felt at being brought here in the middle of the night.

"Your room?" she asked.

It was a moment before he could answer. A memory had come to him of Leah in the middle of the bed, her hair fanned over the pillow, Smythe trying vainly to wake her. For all her organization she hated getting up in the morning. More than once in the two years they'd been together, he'd gotten her out of bed by climbing back in with her and waking her up in a way that had left both of them charged for hours.

"Guest room," he replied after a moment, ignoring the ache in his body the memory had created. He pointed to a corner. "Bathroom's in there. It's well stocked with soap, shampoo and toothpaste, but no girl stuff, I'm afraid."

He reached into a dresser drawer to pull out a T-shirt. "This do for pajamas?"

Suddenly Smythe raced out of the room, and his claws could be heard clicking down the steps to the living room. Leah lay back on the bed, holding the T-shirt up and letting the neatly folded square fall open. "So I'm to plan your seduction with no girl stuff and wearing a T-shirt?"

She wished she hadn't said that the moment the words were out of her mouth. She'd never been a tease, but she felt strangely perverse after this unusual day, and a little disturbed by his calm, even assessment of her in the middle of the bed.

He regarded her for one long moment, his dark eyes darkening further before he smiled. "That's the trouble with planning. It always seems to require particular ingredients. When you just let things happen, you need nothing at all but nature and desire." He went to the door and turned for one last look at her. "Shall I wake you for breakfast?"

She had to pull her eyes from the smoldering quality in his. "I'll be up, I'm sure. Thanks. Good night."

Smythe raced back into the room, a soggy six-inch rawhide bone between his teeth. He dropped it onto her stomach as though offering a gift, then sat back on his haunches, waiting to be thanked.

"Want me to put him out?" Jeff asked.

Leah scratched the dog's head and sighed. "No thanks. I'll enjoy the company."

Jeff closed the door, trying to ignore the wistful quality in her voice. It didn't necessarily mean she would have preferred his company to that of the dog.

LEAH SLEPT FITFULLY, unable to relax. The bed was cozy and warm, the house quiet, the dog a comfortable weight against her side. But Jeff was somewhere down the hall. She wasn't concerned that he might visit her in the night to claim some leftover right from their marriage—what worried her was more complicated than that. She felt tense with awareness of his nearness as though *she* might be the one to make a move toward him and disturb the comfortable fortress of organization and control she'd built around her life. The fact that the thought even crossed her mind caused her serious concern. She tossed and turned, finally discarding the wrinkled T-shirt sometime during the night.

She awoke before the sun was up, the blankets down to her waist, her upper body chilled by the coolness of the room. Grabbing yesterday's clothes, she took a peek out the window and saw a gloomy, cloudy sky stretched over a choppy ocean and an empty stretch of sand. She showered, put on fresh makeup and brushed her hair until her scalp tingled and every residue of the restless young woman of last night had been replaced by her controlled self.

It occurred to her as she reached for the partially open bedroom door that Jeff had closed it when he left her the night before. Then she remembered it was his habit to take Smythe for a walk every morning, rain or shine. He'd probably come for the dog earlier and left the door open rather than risk waking her.

She'd flipped the light off and was halfway down the hall before she remembered how she'd awakened this morning—T-shirt tossed aside, blankets down to her waist. Was that the view Jeff had seen when he opened the door? She went warm all over, leaning weakly against the wall for a moment as a little groan escaped her.

Then she pulled herself together and ran briskly down the stairs, chiding herself for her little adolescent fantasies. The man was gorgeous and she missed his body, but their marriage hadn't worked and they were in each other's company now only because of a strange circumstance. She had to remember how far she'd come in the past year. Life was organized, her business was growing, and she knew where everything in her life, physical or personal, stood. She liked that. It hadn't yielded quite the sense of accomplishment and fulfillment she'd expected, but she was comfortable with it. She wouldn't risk that now for anything.

The kitchen was small but well equipped, with a wide window with a view of the beach. As she looked out to assess the possibility of rain, she saw Jeff and Smythe running along the waterline. Jeff wore red shorts and a gray sweatshirt that ballooned behind him in the wind. Smythe ran ahead, then stopped, barking at his master to catch up. When he did, the dog ran on again, ecstatic over his morning workout.

When they reached a level with the house, Smythe angled across the sand toward it, Jeff following. As he drew closer, Leah noticed the beads of moisture on his hair, curling it, making it look blue-black. A V of perspiration plastered the sweatshirt to his broad chest and his straight, muscular legs pumped with grace and efficiency. He stopped several feet from the window, still unaware that she watched, to rest his hands on his knees and breathe.

Leah drew quickly back, her heart fluttering erratically. She pulled the coffeepot from the back of the counter and found a canister beside it. She dropped its lid noisily as she opened it. The image in her mind of his strong, supple body running toward the house was superimposed over a mental picture of herself, blanket down to her waist, breasts exposed and chilled. Her thoughts drew one image against another, and her movements with the coffeepot were arrested as she seemed to feel his warm, brawny arms wrap around her, dispelling the chill. The kitchen door opened, and she dropped the coffeepot's basket onto the floor.

"Good morning." Jeff stood just inside the door, still breathing deeply. After jumping happily on Leah, Smythe went to his water dish and drank noisily.

"Hi." Leah snatched the basket off the floor, ran it under the hot water and dried it off. She kept her back to Jeff while she filled the coffeepot. "I'll fix breakfast while you shower."

"Sleep well?" he asked. She felt him move up behind her, but she didn't turn.

"Yes, very well," she replied lightly. "You?"

"No," he replied. His voice was right behind her ear, and she stopped in the act of fitting the filled basket into the pot. The male scent of him mingled with the aroma of the ground coffee. Her hands became unsteady, and something fluttered in the region of her stomach. "I was distracted by the knowledge that you were just a door away from me. You still toss around a lot in your sleep."

She shrugged off the net of his seductive voice and plugged in the pot. "Had a lot on my subconscious, I guess."

"Mmm," he replied softly. "Must have made even the T-shirt feel heavy."

Leah closed her eyes against the sure knowledge that he'd seen her without the shirt and turned to him, the expression in her green eyes wry. "A gentleman would have let that pass."

He appeared unrepentant, a slow grin spreading across his face, which was dark with early-morning beard. "We both know I was never a gentleman. And how many times have I seen you completely naked? Why should that embarrass you?"

She raised an eyebrow and tried to look forbidding. "Because you no longer have the right."

He studied her for a moment, a brief flare of anger in his eyes replaced by amusement and a glow of confidence that completely unnerved her. He took her chin between his thumb and forefinger and leaned down to look into her eyes. "As long as you blush so prettily at the knowledge that I've looked at your body, I retain the right to do so." He kissed her quickly, then left the room, calling over his shoulder, "Bacon, eggs over easy, wheat toast."

CHAPTER FIVE

LEAH SERVED GRAPEFRUIT, cold cereal and toast. When Jeff took his place across the table from her, looking vaguely disappointed, she said airily, "This is better for you. So what's our next step?"

He was showered and shaved, wearing a white shirt and subtle tie that coordinated nicely with the slacks of a gray suit. He looked impeccable, professional, and Leah watched him with trepidation, thinking this was just what disturbed her about him. One moment he could be a bearded devil in shorts and a sweatshirt. The next, he could be transformed into the consummate businessman, appearing to have little interest whatsoever in her as a woman. She wasn't sure which bothered her most—his change of persona or the loss of his flirtatious manner.

Jeff speared a wedge of grapefruit, deliberately concentrating on his breakfast. She looked uncertain and pouty, and he liked that. The sight of her small but perfect breasts this morning had destroyed the tenuous hold he'd maintained on his sanity during the night as he listened to her tossing and turning, moaning softly and sighing. He'd had to run an extra two miles just to keep his body under control. It pleased him that she was suffering a little.

"I'll turn the remaining names on our list over to Herbie," he said. "There's nothing for us to do but wait until he finds something."

"Herbie?"

"The detective."

"How long do you think it'll take?"

He shrugged. "He expected an answer from Salem in a couple of days. Of course, there's always the possibility her name won't be found."

Leah nodded glumly. "She might have passed away. Or maybe she's too old to drive."

"But we still have the other names on the list. We'll find something."

Leah shook cereal into a bowl, a line between her eyebrows. "I hate to think the trail's cold already."

"Why?" Jeff asked, taking a sip of coffee. "Do you believe in Susan's quest, after all? Are you enjoying it?"

She frowned at him and replaced the box with a firm thunk. The suggestion that she might be finding pleasure in the search and in his company was irritating. "Of course not. I just don't want Susan to be disappointed."

He glanced at her and smiled as he spread jam on a triangle of toast. "You're not concerned for yourself?"

Leah poured milk on the cereal. "Why should I be? It's Susan's life, not mine."

"But Susan's life is tied to yours. What if we find her parents in . . . in New Jersey or Florida, and she moves away to be with them? What if they're ill or just old, and she wants them near her and needs you to accept that? This is bound to mess up your orderly life a little."

Leah put her spoon in the bowl with a clatter and sat back to glare at him. "That's what you want, isn't it? You want to see me floundering. Well, I hate to disappoint you, Jeffrey, but you're not going to see that. I have a grip on things, and I'm not going to lose it just because Susan's trying to find her parents and I'm being forced to spend time with you. Whatever Susan finds, I can handle it. I can even help her handle it. And as for you..."

She was lying through her teeth, but she squared her shoulders and looked down into her cereal so that she wouldn't have to face him. She hoped the gesture looked casually unconcerned rather than cowardly. "I can deal with you messing up my life. You do it so thoroughly that it may appear to have an effect on me, but it won't be lasting, I assure you."

He was silent for so long that Leah had to look up to assess his reaction. She fixed a haughty, distant expression on her face. She had to fight to retain it when she met Jeff's dark, direct gaze. He wore that knowing look that always shook her to the core, that undermined her every attempt to keep herself to herself.

"Really?" was all he said, with an indulgent "let her think that if it makes her happy" quality in his voice. It was enough to make her wish she had airfare to Borneo.

LEAH MET CHARLIE coming out of her house as she ran up the porch steps. Jeff had dropped her off at home before going on to his office. "How's Susan?" she asked.

"Grumpy," Charlie replied, stopping as she cleared the top step. "I suppose she's in pain. Delia just gave her another pill. But she won't eat anything. Any news?"

"A few leads maybe." Leah patted his arm. "Thanks for checking on her. I really appreciate it. Jeff can give you more detail. I've got to see Susan and get to the office."

"Anytime." Charlie ran down the steps to a red rattletrap of a truck and leaped into it. He roared away with a belch of smoke and a nasty noise that Leah was sure spoke of many mechanical difficulties.

"If you won't eat," Delia was saying firmly to Susan as Leah walked into the bedroom, "then you should at least drink the juice. Your body won't heal if it doesn't get proper nourishment."

Susan sat poutily against her bank of pillows, her eyes clearing as she spotted Leah in the doorway. "Lee! What did you find out? Tell me!"

Leah took the untouched glass of juice from the tray and handed it to Susan. "Drink that and I'll tell you." She handed the tray to Delia, who rolled her eyes toward the ceiling to indicate what the past twenty-four hours had been like. Leah smiled at her sympathetically. "Have a cup of coffee and I'll be right down."

Delia left with the tray, and Leah sat on the edge of Susan's bed, pointing at the full glass in her hand. "I'm not kidding. Drink that, or I won't tell you what we've found."

Susan blew a disgruntled breath, then spent the next ninety seconds downing the glass of juice in three swallows. Putting the glass aside, she focused on Leah. "All right. Tell me."

"Well, so far," Leah said calmly, trying to imply that what they'd learned was important, though it truly seemed like very little, "all we know is who you *don't* belong to."

Susan's shoulders sagged visibly.

Ignoring Susan's disappointment, Leah went into chatty detail about searching the *News Register*'s files, then tracing down the families on the list they were able to find. She handed Susan the list, hoping having something tangible to look at would buoy her spirits.

Susan looked over the list, her pale face fixed in a frown. "What are the red check marks?"

"Those are families we eliminated because they have daughters your age."

"What about the ones that aren't checked?"

"They're possibilities, but we couldn't find any evidence of them still in McMinnville."

Susan put the list aside, shaking her head. "I knew it was hopeless."

"Suzie," Leah said reasonably, "it isn't hopeless, it'll just take time. This was our first day out, after all. Jeff told you it wouldn't be easy."

Susan sighed, her head moving restlessly against the pillows. "I know. I'm sorry. Go ahead to work. I'm going to sleep for a while."

"All right." Leah stood to lean over her and draw the blankets up. "Promise me you'll eat some lunch?"

"I'm just not hungry," Susan grumbled into the pillow. "The pain pills make me sick."

"Because your stomach's empty. You'll feel better if you eat something. Give Delia a break, okay?"

Susan opened one eye to glare at her, then settled into the pillow. "Bye," she said.

Delia, a plump dark-haired woman who'd been having morning coffee with Selena Blake for as long as Leah could remember, shook her head smilingly over

Susan's attitude. "What she really needs is someone to break her other leg," she said. "Then she'd realize how good she's got it now. Don't worry, Leah, I'll stay with her while you're at work, and I'll move back in when you have to leave again. I didn't raise four boys to let one little girl get the best of me."

Relieved that Susan's nurse wouldn't be quitting under pressure, Leah showered and changed into a pinstriped gray suit. The long, closely cut jacket covered a silky white shirt with a man's collar held together by a filigreed Victorian pin Jeff had given her one Valentine's Day.

She called goodbye to Susan, then to Delia, hurrying out of the house, eager to get to the office. She always knew what she was doing there. It was one place where she felt that, whatever happened, she would be on top of it. After meeting the Kellys, sparring with Jeff and arguing with Susan, she desperately needed to feel she had something under control.

"I'm SORRY. She isn't in at the moment. Ah...may I take a message?" Milly Griffin asked as she waved at Leah from the desk across the front office of Minding Your Business. Milly was sopping up a milky brown puddle in the middle of her desk with tissues and looked thoroughly harassed.

Leah waved back and walked through to her small office beyond, hoping there was no important correspondence under the puddle. But before Leah had time to sit behind her desk, Milly appeared in her office doorway. She was tall and spare with a wry sense of humor that belied her prison-matron appearance. And she typed ninety-two words a minute. Leah couldn't have managed without her.

"Don't get comfortable," Milly said. "Sandy called in. She apologized up and down, but she and Jack are splitting up, and she needs the day to move out. She promised to be in tomorrow."

Leah nodded. Inconvenient but not impossible to deal with it. "You can cover for her at Daniels Insurance?"

"Sure. But we have another job. One-day coverage with lots of typing and a lunch date."

Leah raised an eyebrow. "A lunch date?"

"They need notes taken at a lunch meeting with one of their clients."

Smiling, Leah pushed her chair back under the desk. "Is this a dream job, or what? Just to show you what a great boss I am, you can have the lunch date and I'll take Daniels Insurance."

With a reluctant grimace that made Leah immediately suspicious, Milly shook her head. "I'm not qualified. They need a legal secretary."

Leah folded her arms. "Who are they?"

Milly paid close attention to straightening Leah's desk blotter. "Alden and Foster, Attorneys."

"Milly..."

"Well, Mr. Foster called," Milly explained hurriedly. "I didn't know what to do. Even when we're swamped, you don't like me to turn anything down without talking to you and, I mean, you and Jeff have a civilized separation and you just went to McMinnville with him. It can't be that much worse to work at his office for a day. How did all that go, by the way?"

Leah sank onto the edge of her desk, feeling any sense of control over anything escape her entirely. She'd come to the office hoping to put Jeff and the search behind her for a couple of days, but even that brief respite seemed doomed.

"Nothing encouraging," she replied. She explained their exploration of the newspaper's files. "We eliminated half the names almost immediately. Now we're waiting to hear from a friend of Jeff's who's checking Department of Motor Vehicle's files."

Milly grinned. "So you've got nothing better to do today than look pretty in your husband's office."

Leah glowered at her and walked past her to the coffeepot in the outer office. "How'd you like to work for another agency? This is Jeff's little manipulation. We parted this morning in the middle of an argument. This is his way of having the last word. He knows I'm too much of a professional not to show up."

"You parted...this morning?" Milly asked significantly, following her.

Leah scolded her with a look as she poured a cup of coffee. "Spare me your insinuations. We got back very late last night, and his house was closer than mine. I slept in his guest room."

"You're always asking my opinion on business," Milly said, going to her desk for her cup. She paused long enough to toss the soggy tissue into her wastebasket. "You should listen to me in matters of the heart."

"Milly, you're single."

"That doesn't mean I don't recognize the ideal man when I see him."

Leah smiled beatifically and stepped aside from the pot while Milly poured a cup. "If you think Jeff is ideal, you can have him. I give him to you."

"He wants you," Milly said, her expression suddenly grave. "Is that what makes you run away from him?"

Leah blew into her cup to cool the coffee, then brought her head up sharply at Milly's question. "What?" she asked ominously.

"The fact that he needs you so much. That you're afraid he'll get to the real you?"

Leah rolled her eyes impatiently. "Are you telling me you think this woman—" she pointed her index finger at her chest "—is artificial?"

Milly appeared to consider her answer. "Not deliberately, no."

Stunned by the implication in her friend's reply, Leah put her cup down and went back to her office for her purse. The day was deteriorating quickly. She may as well put in an appearance at Alden and Foster and let it crumble completely.

She turned from her desk, slinging her purse over her shoulder, to find Milly blocking her doorway. "I meant," Milly said evenly, "that one day you have to accept that efficiency and organization may make a business hum but not a man. He needs warmth to draw him, affection and laughter to hold him." Before Leah could question her advice she added, "I never married, but that doesn't mean I never had the chance. Or that I don't regret failing to take it. See you tomorrow."

Leah walked the two blocks to the offices of Alden and Foster, Attorneys. It was pouring, but she had her umbrella and walked slowly, breathing in the freshness of the rain, the salty ocean smell and the tempting, sweet aroma of caramel corn coming from the open door of a vender. The street was dearly familiar to her, but everything else in her life at the moment seemed alien. What had happened to the uncomplicated life she'd been building as a single woman only weeks ago? It was now crowded with a miserably un-happy younger sister, a friend who, after a close asso-ciation of five years, told her she wasn't real, and a husband she'd thought she'd found a comfortable spot for on the back burner of her life, who now had ev-erything boiling over. She was losing it. She couldn't get a grip.

"LEE, BABY!" Alan Foster wrapped Leah in a bear hug in the middle of a reception area filled with wait-ing clients. She was embarrassed but didn't struggle. It would have been like trying to break free of a sweetly exuberant King Kong.

Glancing surreptitiously around as Alan led her through the reception area to a desk outside his pri-vate office, she saw no evidence of Jeff.

"My secretary's ill today," Alan explained, pulling her chair out for her and snatching the plastic cover off a state-of-the-art electronic typewriter. "And I have two contracts and a lease that have to be ready by noon. Thank God you were available. Jeff tried to tell me you were off yesterday and had too much to catch up on at the office. I'm glad I didn't listen to him."

Leah smiled thinly at the man who'd been Jeff's best friend since law school. "What does he know?"

"You're a champ, Leah. There's a great lunch at the Tolovana in this for you."

Certain it would have been rude to admit that she'd rather be brown-bagging it in her office, Leah tried to look appreciative. "Great. Well, bring on the con-tracts."

At least she didn't have to deal with Jeff. She al-most felt guilty for thinking he'd arranged for her presence here—almost but not quite. She was sure if he'd thought of it, he'd have done it.

WHEN LEAH PULLED the last sheet of the lease out of the typewriter, she glanced àt her watch. It was 1:15. The office was quiet, only a skeletal crew remaining through the lunch hour. She carried the lease and the two contracts into Alan's office—and stared in surprise at his vacant, high-backed leather chair. She'd been so engrossed in her typing that she hadn't noticed he'd left.

So much for lunch at the Tolovana, she thought, dropping the work onto his desk. Something more important must have come up.

"Ready?"

Leah spun around at the sound of Jeff's voice. He stood in the office doorway, shrugging into his suit coat.

Jeff straightened his lapels, watching her squelch the surprise in her eyes, but not before he saw it. He'd caught just a glimpse of pleasure in her quick glance before she'd lowered her eyes.

"Ready for what?" she asked, folding her arms. She'd shed her suit jacket, and her arms outlined the full curve of her breasts under her silky blouse. Memories of a time when he'd been free to touch her almost swamped him. But he pulled himself together. When he put his mind to it, he could be as tough as she was. He just had to work harder at it.

"Lunch at the Tolovana Inn," he replied. "I'm meeting a client and you're taking notes for me. Didn't Alan tell you?"

"He implied I was lunching with him."

"You misunderstood."

Jeff met her level gaze across the small area of tweed carpet that separated them. He didn't flinch, and neither did she. "So you are responsible," she said.

"For what?" he asked innocently.

"For Alan's secretary being 'sick.'"

He laughed. "That's one you can't blame on me. She's got strep throat. Caught it from her son."

"Why isn't *your* secretary taking notes at this lunch?"

"She's on vacation," he replied with believable calm. "You remember. Sally always goes to New Hampshire to be with her folks when the leaves are turning." Leah knew that to be true, but it didn't allay her suspicions.

"And you're working without a replacement?"

"Alan's secretary was filling in when she had time." He grinned. "Maybe you'd like to stay on until Sally comes back."

Leah breezed past him to get her jacket. "In your dreams, Jeffrey."

The client was already waiting for them when the Tolovana's maître d' led them to their table. She was a generously built woman of medium height with furs and diamonds and hair in fashionably curly disarray. Leah guessed her age at fifty.

"Jeffrey, it's about time!" the woman said in an affectionately scolding tone as she rose to welcome Jeff with a hug. "I've turned away two mashers while waiting for you, and a waiter with his heart set on an afternoon of sin or a big tip, I'm not sure which. How are you, darling?"

"Great, Syl." As Jeff emerged from the woman's embrace and reached back to pull Leah closer, the fulsome scent of Obsession wafted around her, and something she couldn't quite focus on niggled at her mind. "You've never met my wife, Leah. Lee, this is Sylvia Dunwiddie, one of Alden and Foster's favorite clients."

Leah couldn't have been more surprised had Jeff poured a glass of water over her. Anger would have followed closely if she'd been sure what to be angry about—that Jeff had brought her to this meeting without warning or that this obviously indulged middle-aged woman had been the cause of many sleepless nights for Leah and, ultimately, the dissolution of her marriage.

Though Leah had lost control of everything else that day, she stoutly maintained control of herself. Knowing Jeff watched her closely for a reaction, she extended her hand politely. "I'm pleased to meet you, Mrs. Dunwiddie." She spared Jeff a lethal side-glance. "My husband's spent so much time with you in the past that I feel as though you're part of the family."

To her complete surprise Sylvia wrapped her in a fragrant hug, apparently missing her subtle sarcasm. "Thank you, Leah. You're such a pretty thing that I guess it just follows you'd be understanding, too. Here, sit by me..." She pulled out the chair beside her and shooed Jeff to the other side of the table. "I've taken the liberty of ordering white zinfandel. You do like that, don't you?"

Without warning, the woman's cheerful manner cracked, and Leah found herself easing Sylvia into her chair as her chin quivered and she delved into a snakeskin purse for a hanky.

"I'm getting a divorce, Jeff," Sylvia said, dropping her purse onto the floor without regard for what Leah guessed was a several-hundred-dollar price tag, and put the hanky to her nose. "And you're not going to talk me out of it this time. Jordan Dunwiddie may be a fine man, but he doesn't need a wife. He needs a valet. Someone to see that his clothes are ready, his appointments kept and his bets on the bowl game taken to his bookie."

"Sylvia!" Jeff cautioned under his breath, barely holding back a grin as he looked around to see if anyone had overheard her.

"Don't try to shush me, Jeff," Sylvia warned, straightening in her chair. The fur of her silver fox jacket rippled as she waved her hanky. "I've had it. I've left him and I'm not going back. I'll make do on my own."

Jeff sighed. "Where are you staying?"

"In the bridal suite at the Shilo," she replied in the same pathetic tone one might use to admit renting a room at the Y. "The whirlpool in the hot tub is being repaired," she added, her tone growing more injured.

As Sylvia concentrated on refolding her hanky, Jeff caught Leah's eye, his own bright with laughter. The corner of his bottom lip was caught between his teeth. In spite of all she'd been through this morning and Jeff's shameless manipulation of this luncheon, she felt amusement bubble up in her. To cover it she reached into her purse for her notepad. Jeff gave her the barest shake of his head, and she straightened again. Right. It might be best if all of this woman's remarks weren't committed to paper.

Mercifully the waiter came with the wine. Sylvia ordered crab all around, a high-handed gesture to which no one felt inclined to object.

"He hasn't taken me to bed in over a month," Sylvia announced quietly, but with such sudden frankness that Leah's head came up. Jeff, more used to his client's candor, simply met Leah's startled look with a wink and turned back to Sylvia.

"He's almost sixty, Syl," Jeff said reasonably, his voice lowered to confine it to their table. "And he's just closed a multimillion dollar deal for that land on the highway. That kind of thing doesn't just happen. He's worked day and night for it. Give him a break."

Gracefully Sylvia dipped a crab leg in drawn butter. She looked at Jeff with royal disdain. "I don't care about his deals. We could live in luxury for the rest of our lives without ever making another dollar. I want some attention paid to me. I want to have fun. I'm tired of being overlooked in Jordan's almighty quest for deals. He made a 'deal' with me thirty-two years ago, and if he doesn't want to keep it, I'll find someone to subcontract."

"Sylvia," Jeff scolded.

She raised an eyebrow at him. "And don't take that tone with me. Jordan's almost sixty, as you pointed out, but he has stamina that would amaze even a young stud like yourself when he puts his mind to it." She sighed and dusted her hands over her plate. "Unfortunately he isn't even putting that to it lately. No, I'm tired of waiting for him to notice me. I want out. And I want you to get me out. Gracefully." Sylvia turned to Leah and asked intimately, "You understand, don't you, dear? A woman needs more in life than business and 'things.' She needs to know she's loved, she needs to know her man wants to stay home with her once in a while, she needs to know..." Sylvia sighed and closed her eyes. "She needs to know that she can put on a black lace negligee in the middle of the afternoon. That she can call her husband at the office, tell him what she's wearing..." She laughed throatily, wickedly. "What she's thinking...and that he'll come home and make all her fantasies reality."

Inexplicably caught in the woman's private thoughts, Leah came to with a rush of color to her face and no breath in her lungs. There had been a time just like that in the first few months of her marriage, when she'd stayed home to catch up on paperwork without the disturbance of the office phone and been seduced by thoughts of her new, virile husband. He'd been home in fifteen minutes, and memories of that afternoon still haunted her dreams. She had to clear her throat before she could speak.

"I...your husband probably..." Stammering, she glanced up at Jeff, saw the same memory in his eyes and struggled to maintain her equanimity. She cleared her throat. "As a businesswoman myself, Sylvia, I can see your husband's side. It takes so much time and energy to keep a business in the black, much less prospering."

Sylvia poured more wine. "Isn't he required to expend some energy keeping his marriage prospering?"

"Maybe right now," Leah suggested, "he needs you to take care of that while the business is consuming all his time. It'll benefit both of you eventually."

Sylvia folded her arms on the table and stared gloomily into the pale wine. "That would work if tomorrow didn't bring just another deal. If I remain the stalwart, supportive wife, he'll never remember I'm here, and I'll rot away like a moldy fig."

Leah touched a finger to the fur jacket Sylvia had shrugged off onto the back of the chair. "You don't seem to be entirely forgotten."

For the first time since they'd all come together, Sylvia looked deeply into Leah's eyes. For a woman who appeared so frivolous, Leah thought, she had eyes like Rasputin. "I'd rather have his arms around me than this fur," she said. "And if you don't understand that, then I fear for my friend Jeffrey here. So, darling." She turned her attention to the man about whom she'd expressed concern. "When can we file? Now that I've decided I'd rather not dawdle."

Leah sat back in her chair, letting the conversation drift around her as she tried to recover from being pinned by Sylvia Dunwiddie, then dismissed. The woman was hardly your typical matron. Still, Leah found it difficult to dislike her. But she couldn't dismiss the feeling of having been shaken and placed in a corner.

"What do you mean, three weeks?" Sylvia was saying when Leah roused herself.

Jeff flipped studiously through a leather-bound appointment book. "I have a full schedule, Syl, and some important personal matters that have to come first. Alan can handle it for you if you want it done immediately."

Sylvia pouted. "I don't want Alan."

"Then I'll start proceedings for you in three weeks."

Sylvia sat back, eyeing Jeff suspiciously. "I don't care how long you make me wait. I won't change my mind."

Jeff tucked the book into his breast pocket and shrugged. "You're a big girl, Sylvia. Whether or not you get a divorce is your business. I'm just telling you I can't get the paperwork going for three weeks."

She sighed, accepting defeat. "Then three weeks it is." She turned to Leah with a dry smile. "Now there's a man who knows how to live. Personal business takes precedence over a client with big bucks. If *you're* the personal business, darling, you're a lucky woman." She patted Leah's hand and signaled for the waiter. "Let's have dessert. Lunch is on Alden and Foster, isn't it?"

CHAPTER SIX

"ARE YOU REALLY tied up for the next three weeks?"
Leah asked. The Cadillac was stopped while Jeff
waited to make a left turn out of the restaurant's parking lot. A red Porsche pulled up beside them, the driver
honked, waved and sped off in the other direction like
a competitor at Le Mans. It was Sylvia.

Jeff shook his head, cautioning "Hold on" as he
took advantage of a gap between cars and turned with
skillful speed into the traffic. Rain pelted against the
windshield and drummed on the roof. Leah felt a little
as though she and Jeff were confined in a diving bell.

"I could fit it in," he said, glancing at the rearview
mirror, then setting the speed control. "But I know if
she has time to think about it, she'll change her mind."

"Why is that important to you?" Leah asked.
"Maybe her marriage is over."

Jeff gave her a scolding glance. "Because I like her.
Because Jordan's a great guy and too many marriages
die of impulsive decisions. I see it all the time."

It was on the tip of Leah's tongue to defend their
separation, certain that had been a significant statement intended for her. Then she remembered that,
though they'd argued for months before the breakup,
the decision to separate had been the hot, spur-of-the-
moment result of a quarrel.

"Anyway," Jeff went on, "I know Jordan loves Sylvia. He's sort of an absentminded genius type. He just gets all wound up in the fascinating intricacies of his business and forgets to tell her how important she is to him. But I saved their marriage once. I'd like to do it again."

Leah gave him a look of censure. "You destroyed ours in the process."

"I explained to you," he said evenly, "that I was supposed to meet with Sylvia and Jordan at the Shilo. Sylvia arrived, but Jordan didn't. He'd had a worker hurt, but we didn't know that. Anyway, Sylvia finally left, very upset that Jordan hadn't shown. I went back to the office to pick up a gift I'd bought you and pull some files out for the following day."

He glanced at her to see if he still had her attention. When he saw that her green eyes were watching him grimly, he went on. "Sylvia had gotten about ten blocks and had a fender bender. She was so upset that the police didn't want to send her home alone, and they couldn't reach Jordan, so they called me—her attorney. I tried to call you from Sylvia's to warn you I'd be even later, but the line was busy."

She'd called his office, Leah remembered, to find out what was keeping him. When there had been no answer, she'd assumed the worst. "I don't remember you telling me all this," she said defensively.

He slanted her a grin. "I'm not surprised. You didn't listen. You called me some not very nice names, and things deteriorated from there."

Leah sighed, torn between guilt at having misjudged the situation and annoyance at the way he'd manipulated her this afternoon. "It was rotten of you to surprise me like that. You could have warned me who the client was."

"I knew if I told you," he reasoned without removing his eyes from the road, "that you'd refuse to come. And I wanted you to see for yourself what she's like. That I have no designs on her, and that, despite her hugging and kissing, she has none on me."

Leah shook her head at his presumption. "You were taking a chance. I could have made a scene and walked out on both of you."

He glanced at her then, his eyes gentle. "One up side to your controlled nature is that your manners are always impeccable. In a social situation I've never seen you surprised or annoyed into making a bad move."

Leah accepted the compliment in silence, warmed by it, but disoriented, as well. "I can't believe," she said after a moment, "that you remember something good about me."

It sounded like a bald bid for reassurance that his memories weren't completely negative. She tried to look as though it didn't matter.

"I remember a lot of good things," he said with flattering swiftness. Then he slanted her a wicked grin. "Want to have dinner at my place and remind me of a few I might have forgotten?"

His flirting pleased her, reassured her, but it didn't seem wise to let him know. She leaned against the headrest and scolded halfheartedly, "I thought we were talking seriously."

"I'm serious about missing you physically," Jeff said. He glanced at her, saw that she'd distanced herself from the argument and decided to indulge a slightly Machiavellian side of his nature. "I know that means nothing to you," he said with a careless sigh. "You made time for sex, you even seemed to enjoy it, but I don't think you ever lost yourself to it. Control doesn't allow you to do that.''

Her head came off the headrest immediately, her little bubble of self-satisfaction punctured. ''What do you mean?'' she demanded.

''I mean,'' he explained quietly, passing a small pickup loaded with firewood, ''that you kiss dispassionately and you make love without giving in to it.'' He eased back into the right lane. ''That's all. Don't take offense.''

''Don't take offense?'' She rose beautifully to the bait. ''You make me sound like an inflatable doll, and you don't want me to take offense? Why do you claim to miss me physically if I was so unsatisfactory?''

''I didn't say you were unsatisfactory,'' he corrected with a quick, innocent glance at her. ''In fact, the talents you did apply to lovemaking were artful, if not...passionate.'' He felt her bristle. Leah prided herself on applying everything she had to everything she did. He knew she'd be unable to ignore the suggestion that there had been something she hadn't done perfectly. ''I just can't help but wonder,'' he pressed quietly, ''what it might have been like with feeling behind it.''

She made a small sound of anger. ''Pull over,'' she ordered.

''Lee, we're on the high—''

''Pull over!''

Jeff complied, turning off onto a soft shoulder that led into the woods. The moment he turned off the engine, Leah was out of her seat belt. With one hand on the upholstery and the other on the dash, she faced him, green eyes dark with challenge.

"If our lovemaking ever lacked...passion," she said, her voice stiff, "it wasn't *my* fault."

Jeff pretended unconcern. She was a hairbreadth from the edge. "Look, all I meant was that a warm woman brings things to a relationship that a...a...cool woman—"

He got no farther. Her eyes ignited, and she pinned him to his seat with her body, her hands gripping his shoulders, her mouth opening on his with the delicious artistry that had haunted his dreams for a year. Her tongue swept his lips and the rim of his teeth, stroked his tongue, then withdrew. He felt a moment's desperate disappointment until he realized she was just getting more comfortable.

HE EASED HER onto his lap, cupping her hip in his hand to protect her from the steering wheel. She opened his jacket, pressing her silk-covered breasts against his chest. The thin broadcloth of his shirt did little to disguise the warm curve of her. She covered his face with kisses, dipped her tongue in his ear and went back to his mouth with an earnestness that made everything inside him shudder with sensation.

He threaded his fingers into her hair and held her still while he plundered her mouth, giving and taking until he felt her gasp for breath. Her soft cheek rubbed against his temple, and she groaned as he nipped at her earlobe, her jaw, the small V of flesh at her throat.

He felt her tremble, heard her little whimpers that sounded like distress but that he knew meant satisfaction, and he felt as though life had been restored to him after a long, dark year.

Leah was aware of his hand inching up her thigh. She still dreamed about his touch—and not always at night.

Sometimes, in the middle of a transcription, she'd remember what it had been like to lie under him, the object of his tender attention, and feel with sharp clarity the sweep of his long, warm fingers, their wicked ability to taunt and tease her, as though he had no other intention but that. Then he would find the pulsating heart of her and bring her to delicious pleasure in a matter of seconds.

As Jeff's hand slipped under her skirt, passion inched up around her, threatening to close over her head. She wanted Jeff to give in to it, to let him take her wherever it would lead and hang the consequences. It required one small step over the edge, one drifting movement of her body into his.

But long conditioning, fortified by the year she'd spent alone tidying her life, organizing her future, reminded her that they were in a car on the side of a state highway—and that they were legally separated.

For an instant those facts registered, but didn't really matter. She wanted Jeff, anyway; she wanted to be his again. But when she concentrated hard on stepping over the brink, something held her back. Some vague fear, some elusive detail, some half-formed but powerful insecurity pulled her back. She pushed against Jeff's chest until he freed her hair and only his hand on her thigh held her in place.

She gasped for air, her eyes turbulent, her cheeks pink as she struggled back from the edge of surrender. Then she looked into Jeff's eyes and saw a mild "I told you so" in their dark depths. He'd been right, she realized in as much alarm as surprise. She'd come on like a woman with a purpose, but she'd gotten just so far and then backed away.

Jeff watched confusion cross her eyes, then distress. Despite his personal disappointment, he felt sympathy for her. She'd always held back from him; he'd sensed it on their wedding night. But he didn't think she did it deliberately or even consciously. It just happened. That reluctance to give everything was just a part of her, somehow entangled with the compulsion to be organized and controlled. He didn't understand it and knew she didn't, either.

They'd have to sort it out before they could be truly happy together, or even, he suspected, before she could be happy with herself. Maybe he wanted too much from her; he didn't know. Since the first time he'd seen her as a temp in his office, he'd wanted to hold her, protect her, possess her.

She looked at him now, self-deprecation deep in her eyes. She hadn't wanted to draw back.

He felt guilty now that what he'd considered a well-deserved little joke had hurt her. He pulled her down until her head rested on his shoulder. Smoothing her skirt, he just held her while traffic zoomed by only yards away and rain drummed on the roof and windows.

"SHE ATE AN ICE-CREAM BAR that Charlie brought this afternoon," Delia reported, taking her coat from the hall closet as Leah dropped her purse and briefcase onto a chair and kicked off her shoes. "Other than that I don't think Susan's eaten a thing all day."

Leah gave the small woman a hug. "Thanks, Delia. I appreciate your being so patient."

Delia secured the silver-dollar-size button on her gray coat and smiled cheerfully. "It's all right. Before my husband died your mother sat with him for four hours every afternoon so I could get some rest. And after he died your father was always running over to handle a plumbing crisis, mow my lawn, talk to my son when I had no words left to tell him he was heading for trouble." Her smile took on an edge of sadness. "I owe them a lot. Now I owe you."

Leah hugged her again, words caught behind a lump in her throat. She remembered those times. Her mother and Delia had shared a friendship that defined the word. It touched her to know that it endured even now.

"There's a pot roast in the oven," Delia said, letting herself out. "Try to relax."

Leah stood for a moment in the foyer, caught in the snare of Delia's memories. She could see her parents' faces in her mind's eye, her plump mother's bright blue eyes and ready smile, her tall, quiet father's watchful look over wire-rimmed glasses. She could hear their voices, remember their touch, feel their love envelop her even now when she felt the loss of them like a physical pain.

"Leah?" Susan called from her bedroom. "Did I hear you come in?"

Leah hesitated before answering, holding her memories for an extra moment. They made Susan's search seem even more distasteful and unnecessary to her.

"Lee?" Susan called again.

"Coming," she replied, turning toward the bedroom with a private smile. Their parents had loved and indulged Susan. They'd probably understand what she was doing better than Leah did.

Susan sat in the middle of the big bed, the television's remote control in one hand and a can of cola in the other. Her hair was combed and styled, her makeup perfect.

"Feeling better?" Leah asked, leaning over to give her a hug before perching on the edge of the bed. "You look wonderful."

Susan returned her hug but seemed no more animated than she had been in the morning. She turned off the television and shrugged one shoulder. "I knew Charlie was coming by this afternoon. I didn't want him to see me looking like death."

Leah nodded. "What did you do today?"

"Slept. Watched *All My Children.* Talked to Charlie." A spark of interest crossed Susan's face. "He brought me a couple of videotapes, so I asked him to move the VCR up here. You don't mind, do you?"

"Of course not. What did he bring?"

"*Suspect, Anatomy of a Murder* and *The Jagged Edge.*"

Leah laughed. "Think he's studying to be an attorney?"

Susan giggled, her mood lightening. "Sounds like it, doesn't it? What's for dinner?"

"Delia put a pot roast in the oven. Are you hungry?"

Susan nodded. "All I've eaten is—"

"An ice-cream bar Charlie brought you," Leah finished for her. "I know."

Susan folded her arms and frowned. "Your spies are everywhere. So what did you do today?"

Leah told her about filling in at Alden and Foster and accompanying Jeff on a business lunch. "And the client turned out to be—" she leaned sideways, propping a hand on the mattress and pausing a few seconds for drama "—Sylvia Dunwiddie."

Susan's eyes widened and she leaned toward Leah, one hand covering a small squeal. "You're kidding! Did you scratch her eyes out?"

Leah pretended to be affronted by the suggestion. "Of course not. I was the picture of grace and dignity." She straightened and added wryly, "Besides, she's about fifty, dripping with fur and jewels and an outrageous manner—and I liked her."

"Leah, she flirted with your husband. She broke up your marriage."

Leah plucked at the bedspread, remembering the way Sylvia had hugged Jeff. She'd been feminine, effusive, a little dramatic, but not seriously sexual. It was obvious that she liked Jeff, and she probably treated all men she liked with excessive attention. "I don't think so," Leah said. "I think she's just . . . spoiled and sensitive and needs a little more attention than most women. I think I was wrong about that."

Susan leaned a little closer. "Then it was all a mistake? You and Jeff are getting back together?"

Alarmed by that suggestion, Leah got to her feet, her manner suddenly brisk. "There was more wrong with our marriage than Sylvia Dunwiddie."

"You still love each other," Susan said. "Everybody knows it. You're just—" She stopped, glanced at Leah guiltily, then leaned back against her pillows. "Never mind."

Leah knew she would hate herself for asking. "You may as well tell me. You won't be able to stand it and neither will I. I'm just what?"

Susan considered her for a moment, then sighed reluctantly. "You're afraid of him."

Leah stared at her, dumbstruck. "I'd have cheerfully killed him several times, but I have never been afraid of him."

Susan gave her a look that caught her full attention. It was dark and grave and startlingly mature. "I didn't mean you were afraid he'd hurt you physically. I meant . . . he messes you up."

Leah nodded, thinking she understood Susan's statement. "His untidiness drove me crazy, but I . . ."

Susan closed her eyes and shook her head, then pinned her again with that look. "I mean he messes *you* up, and it's like you have this image of yourself—like you just said—of grace and dignity. Jeff gets through all that to find what's underneath, and you don't like it."

Leah stared at her for a moment, half surprised that Susan had analyzed her so profoundly and half insulted by her conclusion. "I think the ice-cream bar has gone to your head," Leah said, turning toward the door. "Try to rest and I'll bring dinner up in a little while."

Leah ran down the stairs to the kitchen, anger flushing her cheeks. She remembered a quiet few moments in Jeff's car earlier this afternoon when he read the cowardice in her eyes. She'd expected him to point it out to her, to make her acknowledge it. Instead, he'd sensed her own disappointment in herself and taken her into his arms. Susan was right. He messed her up royally.

JEFF LAY ON the leather sofa in Alan's office, his elbow propped against the back, his long fingers dangling a chain of paper clips several inches from his face.

Behind his desk Alan observed him with a pitying frown.

"I don't know what to tell you," he said. "Half the time I don't understand Emily. The other half I *do* understand her, and the fact that a grown woman thinks like she does makes me fear for life as we know it. They're not like us, Jeff. They need stuff we don't understand. Sometimes even stuff we don't have. Accept it."

"If I accept that," Jeff said moodily, making the paper clips sway, "then I have to let her go. I can't do that."

"Well, what have you got now?" Alan asked. "You've been miserable for a year, and now that you have to see her regularly over this thing about Susan, you're even more miserable."

"There are moments when I get close to her," Jeff said. "Even a moment or two when she seems to be trying to move closer to me."

Alan was quiet. The subtle noises of an office closed for the day filled the silence. A clock ticked, Alan's adding machine hummed and laughter from the janitorial crew working in the reception area filtered back. "Is that enough for you?" he asked finally.

Jeff let the chain fall onto his chest and dropped his hand to his forehead. "I don't know. For now, it's better than the past year, I guess." With a groan he swung his legs over the side of the sofa and sat up. He fixed Alan with a feeble grin. "Paula enjoy her day off with pay?"

Alan grinned back. "She did. Paula hates typing contracts, anyway. And when I explained why, she was happy to stay home. Her wages today, however, come out of your share of the profits."

Jeff got to his feet. "Gladly."

"How'd Leah take meeting Sylvia?"

Jeff flexed a stiff arm. "With her customary aplomb. I think by the time lunch was over she even liked her."

"Sylvia after a divorce again?"

"Yeah. I told her I didn't have time to handle it right away. Hopefully she'll change her mind."

Alan shook his head. "Poor Jordan. Trying to make sense of Emily is bad enough. Imagine trying to make sense of Sylvia." Alan shuddered. "So if Leah saw that Sylvia wasn't the siren she thought she was, that blows her reason for asking you to leave, doesn't it?"

Jeff buttoned his top shirt button and straightened his tie. "Not really. That's what caused the blowup, but there were other underlying reasons." He shook his head and sighed. "Everything's in layers with Leah. Nothing is simple."

Alan came around the desk and walked Jeff to his office door. "You know buddy," he said, clapping him on the shoulder, "there are easier ways to live."

Jeff smiled at him grimly. "Not with her. Thanks for listening. See you in the morning."

Alan frowned after him. "Right. Hey!"

Jeff stopped just beyond the door. "Yeah?"

"Did you get the message that your dad called?"

Jeff nodded, his expression unrevealing. "Yeah. Didn't say what he wanted."

Alan shrugged. "Maybe he just wanted to keep in touch."

Jeff raised a doubtful eyebrow. "I haven't heard from him since the wedding."

"The man came three thousand miles to see you, and you chewed him out."

"He gave me an hour of his time on my wedding day. Wow."

"We all do what we can, you know?" Alan said reasonably.

Jeff sighed, thinking too much of his friend and partner to tell him he had no idea what he was talking about. He sketched a wave. "Good night, Alan."

In his own office Jeff packed up his briefcase, wondering what Leah was doing tonight. Coddling Susan probably. For a moment he let himself remember how it had felt to hold her, to feel her trusting and quiet in his arms. Then he closed his briefcase with a decisive snap, deciding there was little to be gained by self-indulgence. He'd go home and settle back with a pizza and a Bloody Mary and plan his strategy. As for his father, he'd done fine without him for years, and he was sure the reverse was true. Why meddle with a good thing?

TURNING THE DIAL on his answering machine to playback, Jeff dropped his jacket on the back of a chair and reached into the refrigerator for the tomato juice.

"Mr. Alden, this is Paula. Thanks for the day off! Hope it worked. If I can't have you, I'd like Mrs. A. to get you back. Bye." The beep signaled the end of the first message.

"Jeff, darling," Sylvia's voice said cheerfully, "forgot to thank you for lunch. Your wife is beautiful, though a little serious, but time tends to fix that. Except in Jordan's case. Also forgot to mention that I want custody of the Scotties. Will that be a problem? I know you don't have time for this for a couple of weeks, but call me when you can. Don't forget I'm at the Shilo. If I don't answer, have me paged at the bar. Ta-ta."

Jeff was shaking his head as he tested his Bloody Mary. "Hey, ugly, if I wanted to leave a message, I'd have called Western Union." Jeff put his glass down at the sound of the gravelly voice and walked toward the answering machine in the desk alcove at the far end of the bar. "I know, I know," the voice went on, "you're doing your Perry Mason thing somewhere and someone's life or fortune hangs in the balance. Well, I'm just a paper pusher, but I've got the skinny on the Gerda Szabo frau. Call me."

Jeff began dialing before the beep sounded the end of the call.

CHAPTER SEVEN

"YOU FOUND HER?" In a blue velour bathrobe and bare feet Leah brushed the hair out of her eyes, then gripped the telephone receiver with both hands. "Already?"

"Herbie was more efficient than I expected," Jeff said, sounding alert despite the early hour. She'd always resented that about him. "She's eighty-three and living in a home for senior citizens in L.A."

"And she's still driving?"

"No," Jeff replied, "But she has a state identification card, so Herbie was still able to find her through the DMV. We have a ten o'clock flight."

"Who?" she asked, concentrating on the little tick of foreboding in her midsection instead of the issue at hand.

There was silence for a moment. "You haven't had your coffee yet, have you?" Jeff asked.

"No," she admitted. "I was just making it."

"Okay, listen carefully." His voice was gently indulgent with a smile in it. "I'm picking you up in an hour. We're driving to the airport to catch a flight to Los Angeles. You with me so far?"

"Jeff—"

"Good. When you hang up, plug in the coffee. Then call Delia, have her come by early and tell her you'll be gone for a couple of days. Then you'd better call Milly."

She couldn't leave for the airport in an hour. She had an office to run, Susan's breakfast to fix, a . . .

"And wear something comfortable, will you?" Jeff went on. "It's a two-hour drive to the airport and two and a half hours to L.A. with an hour's stop in San Francisco. You don't have to look like Nancy Reagan to travel. See you at seven."

The proper telephone calls made and her suitcase half-packed, Leah hurried into Susan's room and groped blindly in the bottom of her closet for the makeup case her sister had borrowed several weeks before.

"What are you doing?" Susan asked sleepily.

Leah explained.

"It's under the bed." Susan sat up, rubbing her eyes. "Where are you going?" Then, as realization struck her, she asked excitedly, "Did Jeff find something? Tell me! Have you found her?"

Susan closed the closet door, knelt to grope under the bed and found the square case. She pulled it out and blew a formidable collection of dust off it. Calmly, struggling to sound enthused, she explained about Jeff's call.

"Oh, Lee!" Susan exclaimed. "You've found her. I knew it would happen." She fell back against the pillows and covered her face with both hands, completely unaware that she was reversing her conclusion of yesterday. "I knew it, I knew it, I knew it!"

"Now don't get carried away," Leah cautioned. "We don't know anything for sure yet. We've found a woman with the right name, but so far that's all we know."

Susan lowered her hands and clapped them together. "Oh, Lee. How many women can there be named Gerda Szabo?"

Leah opened the case to make sure everything she needed was there. "In Hungary probably lots. Where's my toothbrush holder?"

"I dropped it in a john at Mount Hood," Susan said impatiently, reaching out to catch the sleeve of Leah's robe and yanking on it. "Lee, why aren't you excited?"

Leah pulled away from her, impatience and fear bubbling to the surface. "You know why I'm not excited. I told you I thought this was a mistake. You should just be grateful for the family you have, go to college and forget all this."

"Before I start living *my* life," Susan snapped angrily, "I want to know who I am. College isn't going to tell me that, is it?"

Leah closed the case and made a conscious effort to lower her voice. She couldn't remember yelling at Susan since they'd been children. "College will prepare *you* for life—the you who exists regardless of who your biological parents are."

"You keep harping on college," Susan shouted, "because you want me to be a clone of you—cool, organized, in control! Well, I don't want to be a zombie. I want to be flesh and blood. I want to live and do things instead of just learning about them and spending all my time making money so that maybe someday I might try to do them if I'm not dead yet!"

Her diatribe delivered, Susan fell back against her pillows and folded her arms, turning her face to the wall.

Leah stared at her for a moment, her feelings crushed. She'd have been the last one to point it out, but she'd done a lot for Susan. Hearing how her sister viewed her life-style and her goals was a brutal blow to her ego and the sense of family she'd struggled so hard to preserve since the death of their father.

"Well," she said quietly, walking to the door. "I'll miss you, too, sweetie." She closed the door behind her, changed into jeans and a green-and-white Portland State sweatshirt, packed the makeup case and greeted Delia with a hug and a cup of coffee. Then she went out with her bags into the early-morning dampness and sat on the top step to wait for Jeff.

He pulled up promptly at seven, stowed her bags in the trunk, then put her into the passenger seat. Slipping in behind the wheel, he took a white paper bag from the console and put it in her lap. His eyes went over her dark expression, and he asked quietly, "Row with Susan?"

The bag contained something warm, and she held it to her for a moment, ignoring his question while she enjoyed the sensation. She felt cold to the core of her being. She knew it was foolish to be hurt by Susan's words yet, oddly, she knew Jeff would understand. "She called me a zombie."

He put a hand to her hair and combed his fingers through the side. "She's probably grumpy and in pain, and you were handy. I'm sure she didn't mean it."

"I'm not." She sighed and opened the bag. "What's this?"

"Coffee and a cinnamon roll," he said, straightening in his seat and turning on the engine. "Sit back, relax and have breakfast. I thought it might make up for rushing you."

The gesture was thoughtful, typical of the startlingly sweet things he was capable of when he wasn't infuriating her. In light of her argument with Susan it was doubly welcome. She put a hand on his forearm and squeezed. "Thank you."

Jeff forced himself to take her touch lightly. She didn't have to know he felt it everywhere. "Sure," he said. "Buckle up."

LEAH FOLLOWED JEFF through the throngs of people at Los Angeles International Airport, feeling as though the Boeing 727 had deposited them on another planet—one whose spin in the universe was twice the speed of Earth's. People hurried by them with baggage carts, rushed past them on the moving sidewalk and ran up and down escalators. She watched in fascination, wondering if a Seasider's pulse could ever acclimatize itself to this pace.

Jeff stopped at one of the many banks of doors leading outside, waiting for her to catch up. She laughed up at him, distracted from her concerns about the trip. "I feel like a hick in the big city."

He grinned. "I think that describes both of us."

Leah watched people pour through the doors to disperse into the long string of taxicabs and the acres of parking lot beyond. "How do we get to wherever it is we're going?"

Jeff, carrying his bag and hers, pushed the door open with his shoulder. "There's a limousine and driver waiting for us."

Leah stopped halfway through the opening and stared at him. "You're kidding!"

He shook his head. "This is all on my expense account. We might as well do it in style."

Leah shook her head. "Jeff," she explained, "you don't pad your expense account when you're the one who'll ultimately foot the bill." She blinked, then asked suspiciously. "Or is it me, as your client, who'll be paying for this?"

His dark gaze went slowly over her face, feature by feature, then rested on her eyes with wicked suggestion. "Maybe we can cut a deal."

In the bright Southern California sun she found it hard to be annoyed by his teasing. She stepped through to the sidewalk, saying over her shoulder, "You sound like a big-city wheeler-dealer already. I'm not sure a hick like me should make deals with you."

Jeff let the door swing closed and followed her, stopping beside her to put the bags down. "Then your answer to me should be, 'Have your people call my people,'" he said, feigning a Hollywood air. "And we'll let the underlings handle it."

She made a face. "That's a little antiseptic for my taste."

He looked pleased. "I'm glad to hear it. There's our limo." He pointed beyond the string of taxis to a stretched black Cadillac. The liveried driver, an older man with a considerable paunch, stood on the sidewalk holding a sign over his head that read Alden. Jeff waved at him and picked up their bags. The man hurried toward them with a broad smile and a gait that was regal despite his girth.

"I'll take those for you, sir. Ma'am." He tipped his hat at Leah and relieved Jeff of both bags, hurrying to stow them in the trunk of the limousine. Then he opened the passenger door and ushered them into the lush interior.

Once behind the wheel, he turned to smile at them over the back of his seat. "Where to, sir?"

"The Beverly Hills Hotel, please," Jeff replied.

The driver nodded without surprise, but Leah turned to gape at Jeff as the limousine moved into the jumble of traffic. "Jeff," she whispered reasonably, "you can't afford the Beverly Hills Hotel. And I can't afford it, either. I've seen it on *Lifestyles of the Rich and Famous.*"

He put a shushing finger to his lips and an arm around her shoulders. "You're going to make the driver think we can't afford to tip him. He's liable to drop us downtown somewhere and we'll never be heard from again."

Leah emitted a small groan and relaxed against his shoulder, thinking that they really had been dropped into a different dimension. Palm trees, limousines, and eighty-degree weather in October were as foreign to her as the red sky of Mars.

"PINCH ME," Leah said an hour later as she sat in the middle of a large bed topped with a canopy and hung with elegant draperies.

Jeff, walking past her to hang his jacket in the closet, raised an eyebrow. "Anywhere I want?"

Too impressed with her surroundings to even acknowledge his teasing, she spread her arms hedonistically. Opulence was eroding her customary reserve. "Do you believe this place? I don't even mind that you could afford only one bungalow."

Jeff hung up the jacket, then walked back to the suitcase. "Because you trust me to be a gentleman, or because you're dying to ravage my body?"

She acknowledged that with a roll of her eyes. "Jeff you're such a mouth. Because the sofa looks comfortable and I know you'll sleep well in the living room while I lie here like the Queen of Sheba in the lap of decadent luxury."

He smiled at her indulgently as she rubbed a stockinged foot on the silky bedspread. "You mean you could adapt to the good life?"

"Oh, probably not." She fell back against the mattress, her arms outstretched, and giggled at the canopy. "But for a day or two it's wonderful and such a relief from my life at the moment."

Jeff put a knee on the bed and leaned over her, a hand on either side of her waist. His expression apologetic, he said, "Then I'm a cad to remind you that we should call the convalescent home."

Leah plummeted to earth. She looked up into his face, her eyes dark and resigned. "I guess we should get it over with."

"It's going to be all right," he assured her firmly.

She sighed and nodded. "Yeah." Her tone was unconvincing.

He leaned down to plant a light kiss on her lips. "Try not to worry until we know there's something to worry about."

She forced a smile. "Will you make the call? You always sound so important on the phone."

He looked disappointed. "Only on the phone?"

"Yes," she replied. "In person you're sincere, and that diminishes your clout. But on the phone people are inclined to do what you want because you sound so in charge."

"In charge, huh?" Slipping a hand under her waist, he pulled her to his chest and brought them both to their feet. "Maybe that's an attitude I should take with you."

Nose to nose with him, she smiled sweetly. "Only if you want to make your next court appearance in a body cast."

He released her suddenly, and she fell back against the mattress with a little squeal. "Such a romantic," he said with a shake of his head. "I'll make the call."

Leah occupied herself with a quick shower. She slipped into fresh underthings she'd brought into the bathroom, reapplied her makeup, then slipped into a yellow cotton skirt and top she'd retrieved from her summer things. She peered around the bathroom door to find Jeff hanging up the phone. She wandered into the bedroom, brushing her hair.

He came toward her, smiling. "Reprieve. It seems Gerda Szabo and four other residents of the home have been taken on an outing that will keep them away until later this evening. I made an appointment to see her tomorrow after lunch."

Leah felt both disappointed and relieved. It would have been good to put the task behind her, but she didn't look forward to prying into an old woman's past.

"So what do you want to do this afternoon?" Jeff asked.

Leah looked at him pleadingly, certain he would refuse. "Want to go window-shopping on Rodeo Drive?"

"Oh, Leah..." he began to protest.

She fixed wide green eyes on him. "Please?" she asked, remembering a time when she'd been able to get almost anything she wanted from him with the right approach. He never fell for whining, but he'd been a pushover for a melting glance.

"Lee, there's Universal Studios, the Music Center, Disneyland, and you came a thousand miles to go shopping?"

Heady with the afternoon's reprieve and the luxury that surrounded her, Leah threw caution to the wind. She put her hands on Jeff's hips and drew him closer, her eyes still fixed on his. "Please?"

She saw his eyes react, felt a subtle tension in the muscles under her hands. He cupped her elbows, his touch light and loose. "Coax me," he prompted softly.

Without wondering why, Leah accepted that that was just the encouragement she'd hoped for. Slowly she raised her arms to loop them around his neck, rose on tiptoe, inclining her body against his for balance, then raised her mouth to his. Jeff seemed willing to let her take the initiative, remaining quiet and pliant as she moved her lips over his, wound her fingers in his hair to hold him closer as she kissed his ear, nibbling and sighing as she traced its shape with the tip of her tongue.

Jeff's assumption of control was swift and thorough. His hands swept up her back, crushing her to him. He took a fistful of her hair and tugged until she dropped her head back. He stilled her marauding mouth with his own, his bold tongue reminding her of past intimacies, hinting at the potential for more still ripe between them. His hands stroked over her with the skill of a man who knew his work.

Again Leah found herself on loose ground at the edge of a precipice. As she tottered, torn between jumping out into space or jumping back, Jeff made the decision for her. He raised his head, held her to him for a moment while he drew in a breath, then pushed her gently away.

"I'm convinced," he said with a wry smile. "Shopping it is. Give me ten minutes to shower and change."

HOWARD DROVE THEM to a busy corner of Rodeo Drive, then pulled over to let them out.

Jeff checked his watch. "We'll need at least...three hours?" he said, glancing at Leah for confirmation. She nodded. "Three hours. Would you pick us up back here, please?"

Howard nodded, giving Jeff a sympathetic shake of his head. "Shopping, sir?"

Jeff looked at the driver with new interest. "I don't suppose I could pay you to go in my place?"

Howard smiled respectfully. "I'd prefer to die in my own bed, sir."

Jeff nodded and squared his shoulders dramatically. "I understand. See you at five."

Leah frowned at the driver. "Don't encourage him, Howard." She hooked her arm in Jeff's and started down the street. "Come on. The exercise will do you good."

In truth Jeff felt as though he could spend days this way, Leah's arm in his, walking lazily along under a smiling sun. She was happy and carefree this afternoon, her smile constant, her laughter quick.

She would try to tug him toward a shop she considered interesting, and the least resistance on his part would earn him that big-eyed look and the pressure of both her arms wrapped around his upper arm in an enticing manner he doubted any man could resist. He pretended reluctance with shameless frequency.

She bought a silk scarf for Susan and chocolates for Delia and Milly. She looked longingly in the windows of an exclusive boutique, then, finally, still staring wistfully over her shoulder, began to lead him away. He resisted.

"Don't you want to go in?" he asked.

She shook her head halfheartedly. "No. I'll just see things I want and can't have."

"Who says you can't have it?"

"It's designer stuff, Jeff," she explained, as though he were slow. "It's out of my price range."

Jeff started toward the door. "Come on. I think you should have something to remind you of Beverly Hills."

Leah stood her ground, holding him back. "No! You can't afford these prices, either, believe me."

"Let's find out for sure." He pulled, dislodging her, and she had no choice but to follow him into the store. An elegant blond saleswoman attached herself to them immediately. Before they left half an hour later Jeff had bought Leah a sand-colored handkerchief jacket and box pleat trousers.

Leah was afraid to speak. She loved beautiful clothes, but she'd never expected to own a Donna Karan design, much less expected to receive it as a gift. Jeff carried the large white-and-gold box under his arm, apparently unmindful of the fact that the money he'd just spent would be enough to buy the assets of her entire company.

"This was crazy," she grumbled as they walked toward their appointed meeting place with Howard.

"It looked beautiful on you," he said. "And I don't want to hear any more about it."

"When we leave here, I won't have any place to wear it."

He continued walking. "I'm taking you to Ixtapa for our fourth anniversary. You can wear it then."

"Jeff," she said gravely, "this didn't buy you a reconciliation."

He stopped suddenly, his eyes darkening dangerously as he looked down at her, his indulgent mood eclipsed by anger. "Do you really want to be paddled in the middle of Rodeo Drive?" he asked ominously.

She'd seen this mood before and she knew enough to be a little uncertain of her position. "I just wanted you to understand," she said reasonably.

"Well, I'd like you to understand," he said, a furious edge to his words, "that it was a gift and not a bribe or a suggestion of payment of any kind. You were enjoying Beverly Hills and so was I. I wanted you to have something to remind you of that when you're back to the grind of daily life in the real world."

"You said . . ." she began.

"I mentioned our fourth anniversary," he said, his manner still stiff and angry. "I know. Not because I thought I'd bought you, but because I intend to get you back. We belong together, and I won't rest until I get under that stiff starch you cover yourself with and find the real Leah. You love me. I know you do. You're just afraid to admit it because it means you'd have to loosen up and give something, and that's just not in the plan for a lady who's into getting." He walked around her and down the street to where Howard waited with the car.

She followed him, ashamed and depressed.

IN THE POLO LOUNGE at the Beverly Hills Hotel Leah watched one celebrity after another walk past their table. Many of the names on daytime television kibitzed with faces everyone knew from the movie screen. Susan would be green with envy when she told her. Leah was simply pale with misery.

Though Jeff had been flawlessly polite for the past three hours, he'd resisted her every effort to engage him in conversation. Across the table from her he looked dark and elegant in a somber suit. He expended a lot of effort avoiding her eyes, but when he had to look at her, he did it quickly and without masking a very neutral disinterest. The situation reminded her grimly of the last months of their marriage.

Then she'd felt free of any responsibility for his mood. Tonight she remembered all he'd done to help her with Susan's search, the luxuries he'd lavished upon her—and how she'd thanked him by suggesting that it had all been a bribe. She was miserable.

The waiter arrived to take their order. When Leah indicated she wasn't ready, Jeff went ahead with his. When the waiter turned to her again, she closed the menu and handed it back to him. "Crow, please," she said with a smile. "No dressing, no trimmings, just straight up, talons curled."

The waiter stared at her without changing expression.

"Leah..." Jeff warned quietly.

"Hemlock to drink," she added to the waiter. "A wedge of lime, no ice."

Twice, the waiter tried to speak, then turned to Jeff with a weak, "Sir?"

"Oh, and humble pie," Leah said, putting her hand on the waiter's elbow to reclaim his attention. "You do have that? I might as well have it à la mode." She glanced at the murderous look in Jeff's eye, then back at the waiter with an accepting sigh. "It's probably going to be my last meal."

Jeff reopened his menu and scanned it quickly. "Bring the lady the prawns," he said to the waiter, then glanced up at her, his eyes dangerous. "Soup or salad?"

She smiled at him sweetly. "I'm already in the soup."

He sighed. "Salad, please," he said, "and a spritzer with lime." He handed the menu to the waiter, who accepted it and stepped away without turning around, as though afraid to put his back to them.

Jeff regarded her evenly across the candlelight. He knew what she was trying to say, but he was in no mood to make it easy for her. "You'll have to put it more clearly than that."

Leah met his gaze. "Do I finally have your attention?"

"Another scene like that," he said, "and you might have more of it than you want."

Leah ignored the threat. "I'm sorry about this afternoon," she said sincerely. "What I said was stupid and uncalled for. But I can't make up for it if you're going to continue to pretend I'm not here."

In the designer jacket and pants she wore she was difficult to ignore. Jeff drew a deep sigh and concentrated on shedding his anger. He considered it a good sign that his silence bothered her.

Leah saw the line of his jaw and shoulders soften and pressed her advantage. "You can even have the bed tonight, and I'll sleep on the sofa."

Jeff gave her a fractional smile. "You're just afraid I'll leave you to meet Gerda Szabo alone."

Leah reached across the table to capture his hand as he reached for his water glass. "No," she said penitently. "I was getting used to our being friends and confidants again, and I miss it. I apologize."

"All right." He turned his hand to lace his fingers in hers, his eyes warming as they looked over her face. "Forget it. You look beautiful."

The waiter returned with their drinks, gave a puzzled look at their hands linked on the table and left with a frown between his eyes.

Jeff leaned across the table. "He thinks you're weird."

Leah laughed. "I don't think he's sure about you, either. He's probably talking about us in the kitchen right now." Leah sobered suddenly, feeling bold now that the tension had eased between them. "Jeff?" she asked, drawing her hand back to toy with the straw in her bubbly drink. She concentrated on it for a moment, then looked at him and saw that he was watching her, waiting. "Why do you care so much?"

He gave her question just a moment's thought, as though to be sure there wasn't a trick in it. Then, apparently, deciding there wasn't, he replied frankly, "Because I love you. I thought I'd made that clear."

"But you love me even when I say cruel things to you."

He shook his head, dismissing the point. "That's not the real you."

Leah abandoned her drink and leaned back in her chair with a small sound of distress. "Why does everyone keep saying that?" she demanded in a whisper. "Susan and Milly said the same thing, that I'm somehow not real, that I'm hiding someone else inside. But this is me!"

He studied her for a moment, his expression both critical and understanding. "Mostly. Until someone tries to analyze you or understand you. Then you pull in like a turtle and someone else comes out—someone who puts us off with facts and figures and everything in order so that you don't have to field the questions anymore."

Frustrated, Leah asked, "But why would I do that?"

Jeff smiled gently. "If I knew that, we'd still be married. Want to dance?"

Mellow music wafted out from a small band in the corner. Leah put her napkin on the table and asked dryly, "How do you know which turtle you'll be dancing with?"

He laughed and put an arm around her to lead her to the dance floor. "I'll just think of it as a very sophisticated shell game."

CHAPTER EIGHT

LEAH SURFACED from sleep without opening her eyes. She detected light beyond her eyelids and smiled to herself. They'd made it. It was morning. After dinner and more dancing last night, they'd come back to their bungalow and gone to their separate beds like two very organized adults. She felt good about that. A year ago she probably wouldn't have been able to trust Jeff to cooperate. Maybe he was growing up, absorbing a little of her practicality.

With a little sigh of contentment she rolled over— and collided with something hard—Jeff's elbow. He was sitting beside her in bed, reading the morning paper.

She was on her knees in an instant, her hair in her eyes. "You!" she cried heatedly.

"Relax," Jeff said calmly, reaching a hand out to clear the hair from her face. "I'll do a lot for you, but I won't be found sleeping on the sofa when room service comes to deliver breakfast."

She crossed her hand over her breasts, just covered by blue silk held up by thread-thin straps. "They're coming?"

"They've been," he corrected, indicating the tray on the bedside table. "Eggs Benedict or spinach omelet?"

Leah couldn't decide why finding Jeff in bed with her should upset her so. It was because she'd thought he was doing things her way, she concluded, only to find that, as usual, he operated only in his unique fashion. Had she, just a moment ago, thought she was changing him?

And they were going to the convalescent home this morning to meet the woman from Susan's photograph. Depression tried to nudge aside her annoyance with Jeff. Then she decided she wouldn't be defeated by either of them.

"Neither, thank you," she said coolly, getting out of bed and pulling on the robe draped over the foot. "I have things to do."

Jeff recognized her mood. He'd unsettled her, and she hated that. She would become doubly efficient this morning to show him she wasn't affected by waking up and finding him in bed with her.

She called home and spoke to Delia, interrogating her about how Susan was and whether or not she was eating. Then she spoke to Susan, explaining that they hadn't been able to visit Gerda Szabo yesterday but would do so today. She maintained a friendly but businesslike tone, as though she were certain nothing would come of the encounter.

Then she called her office and asked Milly to review the day's assignments with her. Apparently satisfied, she left a few instructions, then hung up the telephone.

"Why don't you call the President," Jeff suggested, looking up from the financial page. "Maybe you could organize Central America or Eastern Europe."

She stuck her tongue out at him and went into the bathroom. He longed for the good old days when a man could swat a bratty wife and not go to jail for it. Another day with her and he might risk it, anyway.

JEFF AND LEAH FOLLOWED an aide down a pristine hallway that smelled of antiseptic and aging humanity. The smells weren't unpleasant, Leah thought, but very basic, like the truth of growing old.

At the end of the hall they turned right and stopped in front of a closed door.

"Gerty's sharp," the aide said, "but forgetful. Her eyesight's not bad for her age, but she's vain about wearing her glasses. Her hearing's remarkable. I warned her that she'd be having guests who wanted to talk to her about the past. She was delighted." The woman opened the door and ushered Leah and Jeff inside.

"Gerty, these are the people I told you about," the aide said.

A small, fragile white-haired woman in a straight-backed chair near the window turned as they approached. Her face was almost as white as her hair and was crisscrossed with wrinkles, but her blue eyes sparkled and she fixed them with a warm, toothless smile.

"This is Mr. and Mrs. Alden," the aide said. "Gerty Szabo." The aide disappeared, and Leah found herself looking down at the little woman, at a loss for words.

"Please sit down," Gerda said with a gracious sweep of a small wrinkled hand toward the single bed. Jeff and Leah sat side by side.

When Leah still said nothing, Jeff pointed to the book in the woman's lap. "I hope we haven't disturbed you."

Gerda closed the book and tucked it into the corner of her chair. "Not at all. It is a book of poems I brought with me from Hungary. Poems are important, but sometimes other things are more important."

"That's...what we'd like to talk to you about," Leah said hesitantly. "About when you first came here."

The woman smiled inquiringly. "I will be happy to tell you, of course, but why? You are writing a book perhaps?"

"No." Leah put her purse aside and leaned forward, her elbows on her knees. "I...we..." There was something less terrifying about including Jeff in her questions. "We think you might know someone we know. Someone we're trying to find."

"Who is that?" Gerda asked.

Simply Leah explained about Susan's search.

"But I came here as a servant girl," Gerda explained. "I did not meet very many people."

"When our father died," Leah said, "my sister and I were clearing out his things and our mother's, as well, and we found this photograph. It has your name on the back."

Leah handed the photo over, wondering if there might have been a mistake, if they were wrong about everything. It was difficult to find any similarity between the small, faded woman in the chair and the robust one in the photograph.

Gerda looked at the photo blankly, then raised her head and frowned. She reached for her glasses, put them on with great concentration, then looked at the photo. Despite its poor quality her reaction was immediate. She put a hand to her heart and her lips began to quiver. Leah felt her pulse jolt, and reached out to comfort Gerda.

"It is," the woman said, "my Iliana's baby."

The breath seemed to leave Leah's lungs, but she struggled to think clearly, to resist jumping to conclusions. She drew a photo of Susan out of her purse. "Mrs. Szabo, this is my sister." She handed her the photo. "Do you have any idea if she's the baby in the photograph?"

Gerda dutifully studied the photo while time ticked away in the small room. "I can't say," she replied after a long time. "It was so long ago. She could be, but I don't know."

"Can you tell us what happened when that photograph of you and the baby was taken?" Jeff asked.

Gerda nodded, putting both photos on her lap and removing her glasses. Her eyes were filled with tears and seemed to have lost their sharp focus, as though her mind had already slipped back in time. "She was leaving Los Angeles to look for Janos." She smiled sadly, distantly. "She wanted a photograph to remember me."

"Was Iliana your daughter?" Leah asked.

Gerda shook her head. "I worked for her family. In Hungary the Arpads were wealthy and important, and I was Iliana's nurse."

"Who was Janos?" Jeff asked.

"The Arpads came to the United States," Gerda explained, "and we stayed for a while with a family who had also come from Hungary the year before. It is difficult, you see, to learn the language well enough to find a job that will pay enough to support rent and all the other bills of living."

Jeff nodded. "What was the family's name?"

"Nagy," Gerda replied.

Leah felt another jolt. Nagy was one of the names on their list. She looked at Jeff and felt his hand move up her back in a gesture of comfort and support.

"My Iliana," Gerda went on, "fell in love with Janos Nagy, the host family's son. Iliana became pregnant." She sighed sadly, looking from Leah to Jeff. "That was an unhappy situation in those days. In the old country it was a very dark sin." They nodded understanding, and she drew a deep breath and continued. "Both families were outraged. Janos was made to leave his home, and we never heard from him again. The Arpads moved into their own apartment and put Iliana into a maternity home. We escaped the revolution, but the family was destroyed all the same."

"Gerda." Jeff leaned forward to draw her out of her thoughts.

She focused on him. "Yes?"

"You're saying that the Arpad family came to the United States at the time of the revolution in Hungary?"

"Yes," Gerda confirmed.

Jeff turned to Leah. "That was in the fifties. Susan was born in 1972."

"Then she cannot be Leah," Gerda said.

Leah felt Jeff turn to her instantly, but it was a moment before the impact of the woman's quiet remark struck her. *Then she cannot be Leah.* Leah. The sound of her own name was like a blow to the stomach, and a trembling began deep inside her that she seemed unable to control. She stood and crossed the small space that separated her from Gerda's chair and got down on her knees in front of her. "Leah?" she whispered.

"Yes. Iliana named her little girl..." Gerda stopped, looking down into Leah's face. She put a hand to her chin and lifted her face to the light. She made a small sound of astonishment. She framed Leah's face in her hands and stared down at her. Her mouth began to work unsteadily again, and a solitary tear coursed down her cheek. She looked up at Jeff and pointed to a table on the other side of the bed. "There is a photograph over the table."

Jeff walked around the bed and found a dusty frame on the wall, hidden from view across the room by the large shade of the table lamp. He stared at the image in it, then took it down with a hand grown suddenly unsteady. He went back to hand it to Gerda and sat on the bed again, beginning to understand the mystery of the baby in Susan's photograph.

Leah saw the grief in Gerda's eyes as she looked at the framed photo. Tears were now running freely down her face as she turned the frame so that Leah could see it.

It was a portrait of a girl in Hungarian costume, a coronet of flowers in her hair, ribbons streaming through the dark mass that fell to her shoulders. She was on the brink of womanhood, the contours of her face still a little plump, her light eyes smiling but shadowed. She looked like a child with fears. Leah stared at the face that might have been a portrait of herself fifteen years ago. Her tears beaded on the dusty glass covering the photograph as she realized that Iliana had been her mother and not Susan's.

Gerda leaned over to wrap her in her arms. "Leah," she wept. "Leah."

Leah clung to the small woman, her mind awash with confusion and a grief she felt without understanding it. She cried for what she'd discovered, and for all the things she would never know.

When Gerda leaned into her chair as though exhausted, Jeff drew Leah back beside him on the bed. "Where is Iliana now?" he asked Gerda gently.

"I haven't heard from her in almost thirty years," she replied. "When the photograph was taken, she was going to Portland in Oregon to look for Janos. He had told her he was going there when his father threw him out and that he would send for her."

"Did he never write?" Leah asked.

"If he did, Iliana's parents intercepted the letters. They were very bitter because of her shame, and they disowned her." She shook her head sadly, her voice faltering. "Iliana spoke so little English and was not well equipped to make her own way. She had always been a willful child, but she was frightened of things, too. Her mother was very strong and always scolded her because she was sensitive and a little delicate. Because of that I don't think Iliana believed in herself as a girl has to, to live on her own. She wrote to tell me she hadn't been able to find Janos, that she was destitute and had to give up her baby. I never heard from her again. I continued to stay with the Arpads, and we moved from the address she had. When I wrote to her, my letter was returned as unforwardable."

Leah sat on the edge of the bed without moving, trying to take in what she'd been told. She couldn't begin to absorb it, to relate it to who and what she was and find a place for it in her life. All she could grasp was that they were at a dead end. The only clue they still held was nearly thirty years old.

Gerda reached out to pat her arm with the philosophical acceptance of a woman who had survived hardships and knew her own ability to go on. "You must take her photograph and her letters." She directed Jeff to the bottom of her closet and an ancient trunk. "They are tied with ribbon, under my wedding dress."

Jeff got them and handed them to Gerda.

"I want you to keep the photograph," Leah said, her throat constricted with emotion. "It's all you have left of her."

"We will trade photographs," Gerda said with a smile. "I will give you the one of your mother, and you will give me the one of me and you. I will feel less lonely now, knowing you are...somewhere, being happy." She smiled from Jeff to Leah. "This handsome man makes you happy, is that not true?"

Jeff and Leah exchanged a rueful look, and Gerda laughed softly. "Ah, yes, he makes you angry, too, but that is men. That is love. Here." She handed Leah the letters. "They are in Hungarian, but perhaps you can have them translated. It will help you know your mother just a little. Perhaps it will even help you find her. If you do, tell her Gerda still loves her."

"I will." Leah knelt before the old woman's chair and took her into her arms. "Thank you for everything. I know this wasn't easy for you."

"Life is hard," Gerda said, firmly patting her back. "Only love makes it livable. Don't forget to write me and tell me what happens."

"If I find her," Leah said, drawing back to look into her eyes, "I'll bring her to see you."

Gerda nodded, her eyes grave. "But if you don't," she cautioned, as though to warn or prepare her, "you will send me a photograph of *your* baby." Then she smiled.

Leah didn't even consider the complexities involved; she simply promised.

JEFF WANDERED around the bungalow's elegant living room, a gin and tonic in his hand. In the other room Leah sat in the middle of the bed, Iliana's letters spread around her. She couldn't read them, of course, but perhaps she hoped to absorb something from them, something that would point them in her mother's direction.

He couldn't analyze how she felt about what they'd discovered. She was keeping him at a careful distance. That was always her reaction to things she didn't understand, to situations where she was presented with the possibility of failure. Confronted with circumstances she couldn't organize, she operated in private so that her confusion wouldn't be witnessed.

He was used to being left out emotionally. His mother had always treated him with vague affection and had never stayed around long enough to listen to his tales from school, his plans, his dreams. She'd always had somewhere to go, someone waiting for her.

He'd seen even less of his father. Adam Alden had commuted from Manhattan to their Connecticut home on weekends and spent much of that time closed in his upstairs office. Jeff remembered constant quarrels between his parents. His mother's death in an automobile accident when he'd been eleven had resulted in his being sent to boarding school.

It was then, he remembered, that he'd written his father off. If he couldn't see how much he loved him and wanted to know him and be with him, Jeff had thought, then managing without him would be no problem. He'd had lots of practice.

Jeff ran a hand over his face, downed the contents of his glass and wondered why he was thinking about that now. He supposed he was feeling Leah's pain, not recalling his own. He wondered also what his father had called about—but not enough to return the call.

He didn't have to glance at his watch to realize the lateness of the hour. His shoulders ached from the tension of feeling Leah's shock and confusion. He went to the door of the bedroom to ask her if there was anything she needed before he went to bed. She wore that blue silky thing, the matching robe that covered it slipped off one shoulder. Her hair was tumbled, her face pale as she looked up from the letter in her hand.

"It's after midnight, babe," he said quietly.

She nodded. "You go on to bed. I'm going to sit up a while longer." She looked fragile, on the brink of snapping.

"There's a little more coffee in the pot from room service."

"I'm fine. Good night." She returned her attention to the letter, and Jeff went into the living room to make up the couch. It unfolded into a double bed, but he didn't bother opening it. A single bed wasn't quite as lonely as a double bed with no one on the other side.

HE WOKE UP the moment she touched him. The living room was in darkness, her hand on his bare shoulder cold and trembling. "What?" he asked anxiously, sitting up.

"I found something," she said. Her voice was trembling, too.

He reached up to turn on the lamp on the table beside the couch. They squinted at each other in the sudden glare. Leah put a letter two inches from his nose. "Marilyn White. See that? Marilyn White."

He closed a hand over her wrist and pushed it back until he could focus on the small, clean script.

"See it?" she demanded.

He had to read three lines of indecipherable words before he found the name.

"It's in so many of the letters," Leah said excitedly. "She mentions her over and over. She must have been someone important to her. Call your friend who found Gerda and ask him to find Marilyn White. Now, Jeff. Please!"

"Lee, it's the middle of the night," he reminded her, concerned by her desperate expression.

"But it's an emergency!"

He put a hand to her face, trying to get beyond the tension in her. "Leah, Herbie can't do anything until the DMV office opens in the morning." He glanced at his watch. "It's just a couple of hours."

She glared at him a moment, then pulled away from him. "All right," she said stiffly and walked back into the bedroom.

He followed her, feeling helpless and ill equipped to help her through this. She stood near the foot of the bed, her stiff, almost naked back to him. He took her arm and turned her to face him, prepared to coax her into going back to bed with the promise that he'd call Herbie at eight o'clock.

But her face crumpled and she flew into his arms. At least he knew what to do about that, he thought, sighing with relief as he closed his arms around her. "It'll be all right," he whispered, rocking her from side to side. "It'll be okay."

"What if she's dead?" she sobbed, her fingernails digging into his shoulder.

"Then she's still your mother."

She pulled back from him, still holding him, her color hectic, her eyes fevered. "I want to find her!" she cried, weeping. "I want to look into her face."

"I know," he soothed.

"I mean, I thought I didn't care! I always said if my parents didn't want me, I didn't want them. But..." She shook her head as a sob overtook her. Aching for her, Jeff held her and waited. "But she was a sad-eyed little girl who couldn't even speak the language, and her parents threw her out!"

"I know."

"Oh, Jeff." She fell against him again, her sobs deep and racking. "I've just dismissed her all this time."

"You didn't know."

She continued to sob, then finally quieted, still leaning against him, as though she needed his support to stand. "I feel I don't know anything, even now," she said, her voice neutral and weary. "Everything is inside out and upside down. I'm not who I thought I was."

He kissed her temple, stroking a hand gently up and down her back. "Your past is different, but you're the same. Nothing changes that."

"It does," she said. "Because I built myself. I didn't know where I came from, so I constructed a woman I thought should be perfect, so that none of the bad things that might be inside me would show. You called it a mask and armor." She drew back and leaned her forehead against his chin. "You were right. That was why I told you to leave. Because you found me out. You knew. Under all that organization was a little girl who was afraid of everything." Her face crumpled again, and she bit her lip to stop fresh tears from falling. "I knew the minute I looked into that portrait.

Even before I recognized that all the other features were mine, too, I looked into Iliana's eyes and saw myself—the girl who didn't know who she was.''

"Well, now that you know who's inside," he said softly, leaning down to look into her face, "you don't have to worry about hiding her anymore. There's nothing bad in you. You're composed of a couple of kids who loved each other too much to be patient or cautious. Love's a good thing to be made of."

There was a trace of irony, even jealousy in his tone, but Leah was too mired in her own shock and confusion to hear it. Still, she clung to him, feeling the warm, naked solidity of his back under her hands like a life preserver that would keep her afloat until life stopped tossing her around.

Jeff felt her tremble against him and turned her in his arm to lead her to the side of the bed. "Come on," he said, leaning down to throw the blankets back. "Get into bed and try to get some sleep. I promise I'll call Herbie the minute the office is open."

She resisted his efforts to put her into bed, leaning farther into him when he tried to pull her away. "Leah," he said patiently, "you've got to—"

"Make love to me, Jeff," she said, her arms clinging to him as though she would never let him go. "Please? Now?"

Jeff dropped his cheek against the top of her head and expelled a sigh that hurt. How many times in the past year had he dreamed she would whisper those very words? How many times had he mentally plotted his reaction? He would sweep her up in his arms, he'd thought, without giving her time to think, knowing that was always dangerous with her. She might indulge an instinct for a moment, but then she'd stop to analyze, remember the dangers, consider the consequences, and they'd both lose their chance to be together again. No, he'd pin her to the pillows before she could reconsider and fill her until there was nothing on her mind but him, nothing in her heart but his love spilling over into her.

And now he couldn't do it. Though he was a believer in trusting instinct over second thought, he knew she was too emotionally adrift to trust hers at this moment. Someone had to give her dangerous proposal a second thought. Grimly he realized it had to be him.

"No, babe." Firmly he pulled her head from his chest and looked into her eyes. They brimmed with confusion, disappointment and fear. "Not tonight."

She sniffed, still holding him. "But... why?"

How in God's name did he explain, he wondered, that he wouldn't make love to her because he loved her too much?

"Because," he said quietly, cautiously, "it'll just compound your confusion. It's what you want tonight because I'm the only thing in your life that hasn't changed. Tomorrow, when you've had a little time to adjust to what you've learned, you might feel differently."

She rose on tiptoe to rub her hot, damp cheek against his. He closed his eyes as her beaded nipples beneath the thin gown rubbed against his bare chest.

"What if I told you," she said, "that I knew I was wrong to let you go the moment you left? That I've been missing you and dreaming of you for a year? That I've wanted you back since I went to your office to tell you about Susan?"

He fought down his body's response to her with a self-control he'd never have guessed he possessed.

"Then I'd ask you to hold those thoughts until tomorrow. If I still fit into your life, ask me again. Because when I make love to you, we're committed forever, Leah. I won't let you out of my life again."

She slid down to the soles of her feet with a sigh and leaned her forehead against his pectoral muscle. "Then will you stay with me and hold me tonight?" She raised tearful, pleading eyes to his. "I need you, Jeff."

He couldn't refuse her, though the prospect of a slow and ugly death held less horror for him than lying all night with her in his arms and keeping his promise to himself.

"All right," he said, "get in."

She scrambled into the middle of the bed and turned to wait for him. He reached over to the bedside lamp switch and, in the instant before the light went out, saw her raise her arms to him. She cuddled into him with a familiarity that seemed to erase the year they'd lived apart. She found the same spot on his shoulder where she'd always pillowed her head, rested her arm across his waist and flung a leg over his, her bare, frigid foot running up and down his shin in search of warmth. Seeing no point in fighting his fate, Jeff laid his arm along her, closing his hand over her bare shoulder and holding her close.

"My foot cold?" she asked, moving her hand distractingly along his side.

He tightened his elbow against it to still its movement. "You're still made of ice from the knees down. Go to sleep."

"I'm sorry," she said, pulling her foot back.

Despite his torturous situation Jeff smiled into the darkness. She'd always done that. Then the moment he'd drift off to sleep, she'd replace her frozen foot and send him three feet off the mattress. Something about that small, intimate detail relaxed him.

He put his foot out in search of hers. "Oh, come on. You'll only put it back on me when you think I'm asleep." He connected with her frosty foot almost immediately, and she hooked hers over his, laughing softly as she cuddled even closer.

"You were always going to buy me those socks with batteries in them," she reminded, her voice sounding thick and sleepy. "But you never did. How come?"

"Because," he said, reaching a hand up to brush her hair back and caress her cheek, "I never really minded your cold feet."

But she was already asleep, her breath flowing in rhythmic little puffs across his chest. He stared at the ceiling, not even trying to close his eyes. Somehow this night had ceased to be about sleeping.

CHAPTER NINE

THE SHRILL RING of the telephone awoke Leah. Groggily she reached a hand out and dragged the phone to the pillow. "Minding Your Business," she sighed. "Good morning."

"Lee?" Susan's voice woke Leah more effectively than a brass band would have.

Leah sat up in bed, remembering suddenly where she was and what had happened. Susan. Poor Susan. She would be so disappointed. "Hi." She forced a cheerful tone. "I'm sorry. I guess I overslept. How do you feel?"

"I'm fine," Susan replied. "Did you get to see Gerda Szabo. Is she...?"

"No," Leah replied quickly. Then she added with more enthusiasm, "No, she's not your mother, but...I learned some important details from her."

There was a disappointed silence, then Susan asked predictably, "What?"

What? Leah asked herself. *That the baby in the photo is me and not you? That we're on the trail of my mother, not yours?* "I know it's hard for you to wait, Suzie," she said gently. "But I'd like to tell you in person. We'll be home tomorrow afternoon."

"Why not today?"

"Because..." She looked around helplessly, wondering where Jeff was, judging by the silence of the bungalow that he was gone. Then she spotted the note on his pillow.

"Gone to try to get the letters translated," it read. "Be back by lunch."

"Leah?" Susan prodded.

"Because…Gerda gave us another name," she said, hating herself for hedging, "and Jeff's going to call his detective friend and ask him to try to find her. Then he wants to check out a few other details."

Susan sighed. "Then we're not really that close to finding her?"

Leah closed her eyes. "It's hard to tell, Sue. We might just round a corner and find all the answers."

"Okay." Susan's crestfallen tone tore at Leah. Knowing she had nothing to offer her but more disappointment hurt even more. "See you tomorrow."

"Cheer up," Leah said. "I bought you something in Beverly Hills."

"That's great." Susan's voice didn't echo the sentiment.

Unable to bear another moment, Leah said cheerfully, "You're going to love it. See you tomorrow."

Leah showered and dressed in the jeans and sweatshirt she'd worn on the plane. Her life seemed suddenly to lack structure, and the casual clothes suited her sense of alienation. She called room service, then ignored the fruit and croissant on the tray, pouring cup after cup of coffee and pacing the rooms, torn between concern for the fragile threads of her past and the blow she would have to deal Susan when she got home.

When Jeff let himself into the bungalow, the packet of letters and a file folder tucked under his arm, Leah stared at him from the window where she'd been watching for his return. Now she couldn't seem to move, both drawn and repelled by what he held.

He came toward her, dropping the packet and folder on the coffee table before putting his hands on her shoulders. "I found a professor of Slavic studies at UCLA. The English translations are in the folder."

She sank against him. The courage she'd gained last night by lying in his arms drained away as she faced learning the truth. "I'm afraid," she admitted.

"That's all right," he said, hugging her to him. "Everyone's afraid of something. You've always thought fear or failure were crimes, but they're not. They make you real, Leah."

She sighed and drew away from him, giving him a small smile. "Would you call room service and order more coffee? I drank everything in the pot."

"Sure."

Leah sat on the sofa and, after a moment's hesitation, pulled the folder into her lap. She opened it as though it contained something of great danger. Then she sighed, swallowed, picked up the top sheet and began to read.

She read for hours. There were only nine letters, each translated into less than two double-spaced pages, but she read the nuance in each word, read the meaning between the lines, then read them again as the image began to form in her mind of the desperate young woman who was her mother.

The first letter sounded hopeful.

Dear Gerda:

I have rented one room in a hotel in Portland. Tomorrow I am going to see about work. Leah has been very good and plays always with the little

rabbit you made for her. Janos will be so proud of
her. I will find him. I know I will find him.

The second letter was also hopeful. She'd found
work cleaning houses for a janitorial company that
didn't mind that she spoke no English as long as she did
her work well. The sister of one of the girls she worked
with had agreed to watch Leah for a reasonable
monthly fee. "Still no word of Janos," she wrote.
"But I will find him."

Then the tone of her letters began to change. "I have
moved into a small apartment," she wrote early in
November, "because the hotel was no longer safe. My
room was broken into a third time, and only the intervention of my neighbor, a man in his seventies who has
a gun, prevented the two men from taking my purse. I
cannot afford to have a telephone or even heat, but
Oregon is not as cold as Hungary. Still no word of
Janos. I am not sure where to turn next."

Leah drank coffee and continued to read, not even
noticing Jeff when he brought the pot, then disappeared.

"Leah cries from hunger and the cold at night," Iliana related to Gerda. "I have done so poorly for her
that I could die. My friend at work said that I should
call the welfare office, that they will help with a little
extra money until I can find Janos. I have an appointment to see a woman named Marilyn White tomorrow, but I will have to miss an afternoon's work. My
boss was very unhappy."

Though circumstances seemed to improve a little
with the help of the caseworker and the small welfare
stipend she'd arranged for, Iliana grew more despondent over the absence of any news of Janos.

Tears slid down Leah's cheeks as she read one of the later letters. "I cannot tell you the loneliness I feel or how difficult it is to go from day to day with this burden of despair. Mrs. White has tried to help me locate Janos, but she has found nothing. I think Leah senses my desolation because she seems always so unhappy. I begin to think I must do something for her, though there seems to be little I can do for myself."

Iliana's last letter to Gerda held the answer to the question that was Leah's life, though she'd never been able to admit to herself until last night that it had been important.

"I have decided to give Leah up for adoption," Iliana wrote. "I work long and hard, and I have help from Mrs. White, but still I am not able to give her the things a child should have, the proper care of a doctor, the attention of a mother who is filled with love and hope. I feel as though I sever my own arm, but I must think of her. I have now accepted that I must live my life without Janos, but I know he would want me to give our daughter the opportunity to be happy that we could not have. I pray that God and Leah will forgive me."

Jeff paced the bedroom and listened to the silence. Then the sound of Leah's sobs drew him to the doorway of the living room and he hesitated, wondering if he had a right to assume a share in her pain, or if she would resent his intrusion.

Her face puffy and pink, she looked around, as though searching for him. He took a step into the room, and she held a hand out to him. He went to her, and she drew him down beside her, putting the translations into his hand. "Oh, Jeff," she said, tears spilling over. "Read these."

She leaned against his forearm while he read, the original letters clutched to her chest. When he finished, he put both arms around her while she wept. "Well," he said softly, "you don't ever have to wonder again if you were loved or not. You were all she had left, and she gave you up to give you a better chance."

"Jeff," she whispered, "I don't know what I'll do if we can't find her."

"If we find Marilyn White," he said, holding her with one arm while he leaned forward to top up her coffee cup, "she'll probably have access to Iliana's records. If they got to be friends, they might even still be in touch."

"Maybe she couldn't learn to live without Janos," Leah speculated, staring into the dark brew in her cup. "Maybe she . . . died."

"It's been a long time," Jeff said. "Many things could have happened. But I don't think it's wise to try to guess until you know more. Why don't you take a bath, soak out all the tension of the past few days, and I'll take you out to dinner?"

Leah agreed halfheartedly, getting up to do as he suggested because she had no idea what else to do. Time and reality were in a kind of warp, and she didn't know which way to move.

In a tubful of bubbles from a bottle she'd found on the counter, Leah relaxed, leaned back and tried to think. It was habit. However confused she might become, she had to try to find a way through it, to organize at least the little things so that the big picture wasn't so forbidding.

She felt different. This disorderliness in her mind was new to her, but it wasn't that. It was the strange vacancy in the center of her being, a hollowness less related to grief or loss than to simple change. The woman she'd thought she was, was no longer there. The woman she might become wasn't formed yet.

There was a freedom about this she had never experienced before. Though there was still so much to be discovered, so much still uncertain, there was no more need to hide her fears under a facade of control; she came by them naturally. Her mother had been afraid. And no wonder, she thought, closing her eyes and trying to focus on her mental image of the portrait that looked so much like her. She thought of the lonely young woman, little more than a child, shunned and abandoned by her family, lost to her lover, having to give up her child—and pain rolled over her in waves. Was it because the woman had been her mother and some primal echo in her blood responded to her plight that she felt her sadness so completely? Or was it because she was now stripped of the armor and the mask Jeff so despised that she was more open to emotion?

Jeff. She remembered inviting him into her bed the night before and smiled over his reply. For all his lack of structure and order his integrity was polished and in place. Now love flowed over her as she thought about all he'd done for her on this trip. He'd surrounded her with luxury to make the meeting she'd so dreaded less frightening. When her whole world had cartwheeled, he'd been the one to try to right it for her, getting all the information he could, having the letters translated. Then he'd left her alone to find her mother in them and, ultimately, herself.

Curiously Leah knew who she was now. She might never find Iliana, but she was born of Iliana's love for Janos, and that gave her a sense of rightness she'd never known before, despite the love of her adoptive parents.

And the tragedy of their love unlived gave her a new perspective on her own relationship. It had never been Jeff's disorderliness that had so infuriated her, but his ability to see through her mask to the vulnerable woman underneath, his ability to put his finger on her fear and make it ache because she couldn't discard it. He'd been trying to make her recognize it, to admit to it—she could see that now. Fear and failure make you real, he'd said this morning. Well, she thought wryly, as she rose out of the suds and toweled off, she must now be real enough for anyone.

JEFF LAY ON HIS BACK on the bed, slipping in and out of a doze as early-evening shadows darkened the room and an occasional splash came from the bathroom. A few minutes rest and he'd be refreshed.

He stirred, opening his eyes, focusing in confusion on the canopy overhead before he remembered where he was. He prepared to sit up—and discovered he was being held down by an elbow and a chin propped on his chest. Leah's green eyes were watching him with a concentration that suddenly alerted every nerve ending in his body.

"Hi," she said lazily.

"Hi." His reply was just a little wary. "How long have I been asleep?"

"About an hour."

"Have you been staring at me that long?"

"Yes," she said, not moving. "Making up for lost time."

"Ready for dinner?"

"Not hungry."

"You need a change of scene."

She smiled a little. "You could make love to me on the sofa. Or in the back of the limo. Of course, in that case, we'd have to send Howard somewhere."

He tried to prop himself on an elbow, but she lowered her lips to the jut of his ribs and he lost muscle control. He fell back against the mattress with a groan. His pulse was beginning to thrum.

"The practical thing," he said slowly, as though determined to do it, "would be to give this a little time. Wait until we get home, until this whole thing..."

She pulled herself up and sat primly beside him in a blue towel, her dark hair falling over one eye. She tossed it back. "I want you now," she said with what sounded like complete conviction. "And not because I'm lost or confused. It would stabilize my world if we made love. I can't deny that's true. But this time I'd like to make love to you for what I can give you, not what I can get. When we lived together and we made love, I felt validated. I was so insecure deep down and you—" she dipped her head, looking uncharacteristically shy "—seemed to take such pleasure in me."

He slipped a hand up into her hair, tilting her face so that he could look into her eyes. "I did," he said, his voice and his heart heavy. "You make love as expertly as you do everything else."

"The other day in the car," she reminded him, "you said you'd like to know what it would be like to make love to me when I could put real feeling behind it."

"Yes."

"I can do that now." She leaned across him again, smiling into his face. "The woman in me needs you, and I was always afraid of that because I wasn't sure what was inside me to give back. You're always so in-

NO RISK, NO OBLIGATION TO BUY... NOW OR EVER!

CASINO JUBILEE
"Match'n Scratch" Game

Here's how to play:

1. Peel off label from front cover. Place it in space provided at right. With a coin, carefully scratch off the silver box. This makes you eligible to receive one or more free books, and possibly other gifts, depending upon what is revealed beneath the scratch-off area.

2. You'll receive brand-new Harlequin Superromance® novels. When you return this card, we'll rush you the books and gifts you qualify for ABSOLUTELY FREE!

3. If we don't hear from you, every month we'll send you 4 additional novels to read and enjoy. You can return them and owe nothing but if you decide to keep them, you'll pay only $2.92* per book, a saving of 33¢ each off the cover price. There is *no* extra charge for postage and handling. There are *no* hidden extras.

4. When you join the Harlequin Reader Service®, you'll get our subscribers-only newsletter, as well as additional free gifts from time to time just for being a subscriber!

5. You must be completely satisfied. You may cancel at any time simply by sending us a note or a shipping statement marked "cancel" or returning any shipment to us at our cost.

YOURS FREE!

This lovely Victorian pewter-finish miniature is perfect for displaying a treasured photograph and it's yours absolutely free — when you accept our no-risk offer!

*Terms and prices subject to change without notice. Sales tax applicable in NY.

CASINO JUBILEE
"Match'n Scratch" Game

CHECK CLAIM CHART BELOW FOR YOUR FREE GIFTS!

YES! I have placed my label from the front cover in the space provided above and scratched off the silver box. Please send me all the gifts for which I qualify. I understand I am under no obligation to purchase any books, as explained on the opposite page.

(U-H-SR-09/91) 134 CIH ADE2

Name

Address   Apt.

City   State   Zip

CASINO JUBILEE CLAIM CHART

🍒🍒🍒	WORTH 4 FREE BOOKS, FREE VICTORIAN PICTURE FRAME PLUS MYSTERY BONUS GIFT
🍒🍒🍒	WORTH 3 FREE BOOKS PLUS MYSTERY GIFT
🔔🔔🍒	WORTH 2 FREE BOOKS

CLAIM N° 1528

▼ DETACH AND MAIL CARD TODAY! ▼

HARLEQUIN "NO RISK" GUARANTEE

▼ DETACH AND MAIL CARD TODAY! ▼

tense and so thorough that I was afraid of losing my identity in you." She shook her head. "Now I understand that losing that identity doesn't matter. The woman I'd invented was getting lost in you because she wasn't real. But I'm real now, Jeff. Still afraid, still uncertain, but able to give because that's what love is, isn't it? Giving, anyway?"

Jeff wrapped both arms around her and turned so that he lay over her, her cool body beginning to tremble in the warm room. Then he saw in her eyes that she trembled for him, and every caution he'd entertained evaporated. Loving was dangerous; nothing could safeguard lovers from its consequences. Iliana and Janos had certainly learned that. Whether she was truly ready to commit to him again or not, he was going to make love to her because he knew no other way to tell her how deep his love for her went or how eternal it was.

He tossed her towel away, doffed his briefs and T-shirt and lay with her in the middle of the bed, the blankets pulled up. "You could have caught pneumonia," he scolded, "lying like that for an hour."

"I wanted you to look into my eyes when you woke up," she whispered. "And I knew when you did that you'd chase the chill away."

He did that now because he was surprised to find himself nervous. So he concentrated on rubbing warmth into her back, her hips, her thighs. She shook the focus of his attention by kissing him slowly, lingeringly, by teasing his mouth open with the tip of her tongue and invading. Hooking an arm around his neck, she brought herself tightly against him, relaxing her body into the planes and hollows of his as she reveled in the pleasure of being flesh to flesh with him once more. "Oh, Jeffrey" was all she could say. There were no words to describe how good, how right, it felt.

Jeff felt her gesture of surrender and let the sweetness of it lap around him. It wasn't submission, but an entrusting of herself to his love. "Leah," he whispered, humbled by the gift he'd once thought she might never be able to give.

Leah gave herself over to his loving ministrations. The firm strokes that had been intended to rub warmth back into her body had changed to caresses of an entirely different kind. She felt the control he exerted in the long, careful sweeps down her back and over her hips. They were tender enough that warmth rose in her, but firm and possessive enough that heat billowed deep inside her, in a part of herself she'd almost forgotten in the year they'd been separated.

Gently he drew her leg over his hip and reached into her with a tender authority that drew a ragged sigh from her. She began to feel as though the core of her was melting, as though she could become molten and change. This was the part of loving him that used to frighten her. In a moment she would be mindless and clinging, a frightening experience for a woman who prided herself on remaining cool in all circumstances.

But she couldn't seem to focus on that now. It had ceased to be important. The past had exploded in her face, life had fallen around her in shapes and pieces she didn't recognize and couldn't yet reassemble, yet she felt so free. She had been conceived in love, raised with love, married to love. She could give it back. She wondered in a corner of her mind not occupied with Jeff's hands why that had once seemed so difficult.

He found the pulsing heart of her and stroked with devastating artistry. The tension and the cry built simultaneously inside her. She barely had time to register the exquisite torment on the brink of fulfillment before warm, delicious eddies of pleasure broke over her. The cry escaped her on a note of surprise. She'd experienced this before but never with this intensity, this depth of feeling that went beyond the physical to a new awareness of herself and Jeff, a new concept of their unity.

In the darkness of the bedroom her eyes were bright with discovery. "Jeff, I . . . love you. God. I do!"

He understood her surprise. There was even more love alive between them than he'd hoped. In fact, it felt as though nothing had died, that all they'd ever had together had simply lain in wait for this moment, to blossom again with its newness, crowding them with love.

He crushed her against him. "I love you, too. I have always loved you. I will always love you."

Leah heard the fierceness in his declaration and marveled that it could match the intensity of her feelings. The need to show him what was beyond her power to explain became of paramount importance.

She knelt astride him, cupped his face in her hands and planted a kiss in the hollow of his throat. She nibbled along his jaw, down the corded muscles in his neck, then dipped the tip of her tongue into the indentation of his clavicle.

He ran his hands up her thighs, but she stopped him, putting them back on the mattress. "Don't distract me," she scolded with a laugh. "You know how I like to do things my way. Carefully. Methodically. With my full attention to detail."

With a little groan he took two handfuls of bed sheet. "I'm a man on the edge of madness, Lee," he warned.

She blew a line gently down the middle of his chest and felt the stomach muscle quiver under her. "Then let me push you over," she said, her voice growing husky with desire. "You're the one who taught me that surrender is what it's all about."

"Clever me," he complained, gasping as she traced the jut of his ribs with her fingernails, then dipped into the cavity at his waist. She wriggled backward to continue her torture, and he gasped again.

She wanted desperately to touch him, but her power over him was intoxicating and she knew that his desperation would only bring him more pleasure. She reached behind her to draw her fingernails from his knees to his hipbones, then back again and up until she was sure he was as mindless as he had made her. Then she closed her hands over him.

But she enjoyed her supremacy no more than a moment before he lifted her hips up and entered her. She uttered a little cry of surprise that became, almost instantly, a gasp of rapidly mounting pleasure. Jeff moved under her in a slow circle, linking fingers with her as she leaned backward in response to the tension building in her. Still moving, he drew her forward, then let her lean back, drew her forward again and let her recline. She said his name the same moment he groaned hers, sanity shattering, love bursting, bodies bound in a single pulse in a moment beyond imagining.

Leah fell against him, her body sprawled over his, limp with physical fulfillment and a happiness so deep that she clung to Jeff, waiting to understand it. The feeling was so exquisite that she felt as though there must be a corona of light around her.

"It's because you loved me," Jeff explained, holding her so close that she wasn't surprised he'd read her mind.

"But I loved you before."

"This time you made love to me with nothing hidden or held back. You gave me everything you had and took everything I offered. I guess that's love in its most perfect form." He pulled her down beside him and settled her against his side. "We belong to each other again. And this time it's forever."

Leah reached up to kiss his chin. "Yes," she said. "Forever."

CHAPTER TEN

IT WAS RAINING in Seaside. Leah stood in the cold downpour, wondering if Beverly Hills and all that had happened there had been a dream. As she looked at her small lawn and comfortable but very ordinary two-story house, it was difficult to realize that she'd just spent three days in one of the Beverly Hills Hotel's famous bungalows and that she'd walked down the streets of one of the glitziest cities in the country. She couldn't even begin to consider what had happened to her personally.

Jeff slammed the trunk of her car and carried her two bags to the foot of the porch steps where she stood. He studied her expression of vague disorientation and laughed softly. "Culture shock?"

She smiled in response. Rain was dampening his hair, dotting the shoulders of his leather jacket. She felt the hair at her temples begin to frizz. "It was eighty-two degrees at LAX this morning."

The color of his eyes deepened as he leaned down to kiss her. "I'm still registering over one hundred and eighty. Hear the rain sizzle when it hits me?"

Laughing, she hugged him, then leaned back to look into his eyes. "Still? Being home hasn't diminished your ardor?"

He tried not to worry that she'd even asked. She'd been through a lot. He could expect her to be uncertain about a lot of things. "No," he replied. "Because it's ardor motivated by love. It takes more than a change of climate to shake that."

Leah liked his answer. She saw the suggestion of concern in his eyes and felt humbled by the knowledge that he needed as much reassurance as she did. She pointed to the bags he carried. "Then where's *your* bag? Aren't you coming home?"

Jeff liked her questions. He felt himself relax. "I only have two hands."

Leah nuzzled his cheek and giggled wickedly. "Really? I could have sworn I felt six or eight last night."

"Style and enthusiasm," he explained, nipping at her earlobe. "You were pretty versatile yourself."

"I was inspired." She sighed and faced the house. "I suppose we should go inside."

"Yes," he agreed. "Unless three days in Southern California have made you amphibious."

"Lee! Jeff!" The front door flew open, and Susan appeared in the opening, wearing a sweatshirt and a pair of jeans with one leg slit to accommodate her cast. She leaned on two crutches, which she shifted awkwardly to let them in. "I thought you'd *never* get back." As she leaned on one crutch to move the other, the scatter rug on which it landed slid and she fell sideways with a little scream. Leah reached for her, but Charlie appeared from behind the door and caught her before she fell.

"Didn't I ask you to wait until I could help you with the door?" he asked, an edge of impatience to his voice. "You're not good on these things yet."

"You didn't come fast enough," Susan retorted.

Charlie gave Jeff a look of pure male frustration. Leah saw it and guessed that the past few days of helping Delia with Susan hadn't been easy.

"My goodness, you're soaked," Delia exclaimed, coming around them to push the door closed. "Run upstairs and dry off. Dinner's just coming out of the oven."

"But I—" Susan began.

"There'll be plenty of time for questions when they're dry," Delia said firmly.

"I'll come up with you, Lee," Susan said, beginning to hobble toward the stairs.

"No, you won't." Charlie closed a hand over her arm, stopping her progress. "You'll break your other leg. We'll wait here."

Susan turned to Leah with a long-suffering look. "He has done nothing but boss me around since you left."

"And if he hadn't been here," Delia said, folding her arms with an air of constructive tattling, "she'd have lived on corn chips. She would have died of multiple fractures when she tried to wash her hair in the shower with her leg sticking out and fell. I had to call Charlie at Jeff's office to help me pick her up. And I'd have gone to jail because of the fuss she caused when I slit the leg of her jeans so she could wear something other than a nightgown. You'd have thought I was torturing her." Delia gave Susan an injured look. "I was only trying to help."

"They were my best jeans," Susan explained, fully expecting everyone to understand.

"Had Charlie not come by to help," Delia said, "and if he hadn't stepped between us once or twice, I'd probably have killed her. So don't let her bad-mouth him. I'd marry him tomorrow if he'd have me."

Charlie put an arm around the much shorter, much rounder woman's shoulders. "Would you be willing to support me so I can finish law school, and make that scrumptious beef barley soup for me whenever I want it?"

Delia smiled up at him. "In a minute."

Charlie smiled back. "Then tomorrow's good for me."

Susan, close to tears, turned to Leah for sympathy. "They've been like that since you left! The minute you were out the door they ganged up on me."

"It took both of us," Delia said judiciously, "to keep her from disaster. Go dry off. Dinner's getting cold."

Upstairs, Leah toweled her hair, now certain telling Susan what she'd discovered was going to be worse than she'd imagined. Her sister was obviously strained to the limits of her still-minimal maturity and upset enough about Charlie's defection to Delia's camp to make disappointment fatal.

She tossed the towel aside, and her hair tumbled in her face. She saw Jeff waiting for her, a shoulder propped against the bathroom doorjamb. "Now," he said with a grin, "that's an interesting look."

Leah turned to the mirror and peered through the fine network of wet hair. She put a hand on her hip and turned back to Jeff. "This look made Tina Turner a bundle."

Jeff shook his head. "It was her legs."

Leah lifted the hem of her wool skirt to midthigh. "I've got those, too."

With a gleam in his eyes Jeff stepped into the bathroom and closed the door behind him.

"Dinner's getting cold, remember?" Leah said, laughingly backing away from him, her concern about Susan temporarily forgotten.

"Then behave yourself." With three steps he had her backed into the corner between the shower and the towel rack. "And don't tempt me with appetizers if there isn't time for them."

He had a hand on the wall on either side of her head, and though he didn't touch her, she felt his nearness like a stroke. Warmth emanated from his body, and a flattering, exciting desire from his eyes. She put her hands on his chest. "Well, maybe one."

He leaned down to capture her mouth, vanquishing every thought in her head that didn't involve him. When she wrapped both arms around his neck, he straightened, lifting her off the floor. He held her to him with one arm, the other hand slipping up her skirt, coping with her slip, then reaching inside her panty hose to take a bold handful of her bottom. She groaned against his mouth, lost in him and his possessive touch.

"Whatever's going through your mind right now," he said into her ear, his voice breathless, "hold the thought until later tonight."

Still suspended from his neck, she fought to focus her attention on a reply. "I wish you were wearing a kilt," she whispered, "so I could pay you back."

"You can pay me back later," he said, lowering her to the floor, "and I'll wear any damn thing you want." He withdrew his hand, slapped lightly where he had just caressed, then smoothed her slip and skirt down. He went to the door and grinned back at her over his shoulder. "Move it, will you? Dinner's getting cold."

With a hand that trembled Leah combed her hair into order, pushing the thought she'd been instructed to hold to the back of her mind. If she wasn't going to alienate Susan completely, she had to plan her strategy.

WHEN DELIA TRIED to leave after putting dinner on the table, Leah insisted she stay. "I've brought you something from Beverly Hills," she coaxed, "but I think it's in Jeff's bag and that's still in the car. I'll get it after dinner."

Jeff helped Susan drop into a chair, then pushed it to the table. She raised an eyebrow at him. "Sharing a suitcase? You two getting chummy?"

"Yes," he replied, startling her into staring. "We're back to sharing everything. Comfortable?"

She nodded vaguely. "Thank you."

"All *right*." Charlie and Delia exchanged a high five before he seated her.

"We knew it was just a matter of time," Delia explained to Leah, who looked surprised by their reaction. "I'm glad you were smart enough not to waste any. Now be careful of this sauce. I like it spicy, but you might want to try it first."

Dinner was more relaxed and congenial than Leah had dared hope. Jeff and Charlie talked a little business, Delia caught Leah up on the local gossip, and Susan, possibly warned by her companions of the past three days to save her questions for later, concentrated determinedly on her food, though she ate very little.

After dinner Jeff brought in his bag and Leah distributed gifts. Delia left, clutching her box of chocolates. Jeff and Charlie disappeared into the living room, talking shop.

Leah and Susan resumed their places at the kitchen table. Leah made a pot of tea while Susan waited patiently. Leah took down the delicate china cups her mother used on special occasions or when Delia came to tea and poured.

"Mom's good cups," Susan noted, turning awkwardly in her chair to face Susan as she sat in the chair next to hers. "I can't decide if that means bad news or good news."

"It means," Leah said carefully, pushing the sugar bowl toward Susan, "that whether you find your mother or not, there's no *bad* news in your life. You were loved by the parents who raised you. You're loved now by Delia and Jeff and me. And it sounds as though Charlie wouldn't even be here right now if he didn't care a lot already."

Susan ignored Leah's careful cushioning and read between the lines. "We're not going to be able to find her," she said flatly.

Leah drew a breath. "Not exactly."

Susan sighed. "What, exactly?"

"The baby in the photograph," Leah said, "was born in 1959."

Susan considered the fact for a moment, then Leah watched as the entire structure of her sister's hopes and dreams to find her natural parents dissolved in her eyes. Susan had thought the trail might have become more elusive or that the hope of finding them at all had grown slim. But she had never considered that the search had begun on an error and that her dreams had no foundation at all.

She stared at Leah, her blue eyes wide and stricken. "It isn't...me?"

Leah felt Susan's pain, yet beside it, traitorously, her own frail excitement. Sadly, guiltily, she shook her head. "It's me."

Susan's stunned look remained. It was a moment before she demanded, "What?"

Slowly, with as much detail as she could remember, Leah explained. She told Susan about the meeting with Gerda, about the photograph of her mother and the letters Jeff had had translated. She told her what they contained. "I put them on your bedside table so that you could read them."

She longed for a glimmer of understanding in Susan, one small glimpse of a smile to tell her she was happy for her. She knew Susan was very young to be expected to deal with such a major disappointment with grace and compassion, but it had become very important to Leah. Susan was all she had left of her childhood, of the family in which she'd learned her values and grown to maturity, of the family that now was lost to her except for the girl staring at her in resentment.

"I'm happy for you," Susan said.

They were the words Leah wanted to hear, but the dead tone with which they were spoken was almost more painful than an angry retort would have been.

"You win again," Susan went on. "You get to continue to be perfect."

"Sue..." Leah protested quietly.

"Miss Perfect," Susan interrupted, her voice rising. "You didn't even want to know about your parents, yet things work out so perfectly for you that you found yours while looking for mine. And your mother even turns out to be someone who loved you."

Cut deeply, Leah asked, "Would you prefer that she hadn't?"

"I'd prefer that she was mine!" Susan shouted at her. "I'd prefer that once, just once, you'd fall flat on your face, and *I'd* be the one to look good."

Leah sipped her tea and tried to appear calm. "Living in the shadow of a big sister has been hard on—"

"It's more than living in your shadow!" Susan screamed. "It's being smothered by it! You're the one who did everything for me. Helped me when school was hard, gave me a job at your office, gave me a place to live when Daddy died."

"How can you blame me for that?" Leah demanded.

"Because you're pushy and demanding. Because everyone thinks how good you are, and no one thinks about me, having to live up to all that! You're the big success, the cool professional. I'm just the flighty little kid hanging on your coattails."

Susan pushed herself up from her chair, the bulkiness of her cast knocking it backward, sending the crutches leaning against it clattering to the floor.

"Susan!" Leah shouted, reaching out to steady her. Susan yanked away.

"Whoa," Jeff said quietly, appearing with Charlie at the kitchen door. He moved slowly between them, frowning from one to the other. "What's going on?"

Leah sank back into her chair, propped an elbow on the table and put a hand to her throbbing forehead. "I didn't explain things very well," she said wearily, "and Susan's understandably disappointed."

Charlie righted Susan's chair and Jeff eased her back into it. "I told you in the beginning," he said, "that this would be difficult. That it would take time."

Susan cast one dark, vaguely remorseful look at her sister, then raised large tear-filled eyes to Jeff. "You didn't tell me you'd find her mother instead of mine."

Jeff studied her in confusion for a moment, then turned to Leah. "What did you tell her?"

Leah dropped her hand, puzzled by the question. "The truth. That I was the baby in the picture. That Iliana is *my* mother."

"Leah," Jeff said, pulling up a chair to place it between them, his tone implying that she'd obviously missed some very important point. "We first found the Nagy name by using the information on *Susan's* birth certificate."

Leah stared at him for several seconds, waiting for the significance of that detail to register. She looked at Susan, who was also staring. Her anger was dissolving, a very tentative hope rising in her eyes.

Leah put a hand to her head, rubbing between her eyebrows. "You'll have to explain to me what it means, Jeff."

He spread his hand. "I don't know what it means. Except that it makes it obvious Susan is involved in this somehow."

"God." Leah drew a deep sigh. "How did I miss that?"

Jeff smiled gently. "Other things claimed your attention at the time. I'm sorry I didn't say anything about it. I assumed it had occurred to you."

"Well." She looked at Susan, her eyes carefully neutral. Hurt feelings and acute disappointment at Susan's attitude made her want to burst into tears. "I'm sorry, Sue. I didn't deliberately mislead you, I just... didn't quite grasp the whole picture."

Tears were running down Susan's face. An apology was beginning to form, but Leah didn't think she was ready to cope with it yet. She stood and carried the two teacups to the counter. "I have lots to catch up on at the office tomorrow," she said. "I think I'll go to bed early."

Jeff put an arm around her shoulders. "I'll walk you up."

At the top of the stairs he turned her in his arms and pulled her close. "I heard what Susan told you," he said softly. "It was rotten, but you know she didn't mean it."

The only thing that prevented Leah from bursting into tears was that she felt she'd done nothing in the past few days but cry on his shoulder. She was certain he must be getting tired of it. She nodded against him. "I know."

"But it hurts, anyway, doesn't it?"

"Yes."

Jeff held her close for a minute, then let her go. "I'll be up in a little while," he said, walking her to the door of her room—their room once again. "Just clear your mind and try to rest."

She turned to open the door, then looked back, catching his arm as he began to walk away. He raised an inquiring eyebrow. "I'm glad you're home," she whispered.

He smiled and reached out to pinch her chin. "Me, too. See you in a few minutes."

Jeff ran down the stairs, then walked across the darkened living room. Hearing the authoritative sound of Charlie's voice, he slowed his pace, listening as he went toward the kitchen.

"You were big enough to take this on," he was saying, apparently to Susan, "when you thought it would get you what you wanted. When you thought it hadn't, you turned on Leah, who put her life on hold to run all over creation for you."

"But she told me—" Susan tried to protest.

"I know. So it turns out maybe the woman they learned about has something to do with you, too. But whether she does or doesn't, Leah treats everyone with kindness. She didn't deserve the things you said to her. You acted like a brat." There was a pause, then the sound of a chair scraping back. "I guess," Charlie said, a note of sophisticated weariness in his voice that made Jeff smile despite the circumstances, "I just keep forgetting how young you are. When Jeff comes down, tell him I went to get Smythe."

"You don't have to do that." Jeff stepped into the kitchen, and Charlie stopped just short of colliding with him.

"Oh. Hi. I don't mind." He glanced at Susan, who was crying into her folded arms. "After Suzie worked her over, Leah probably needs you. Anything else you want from the house?"

Jeff clapped his shoulder. "If there is, I'll get it tomorrow. Thanks, Charlie. Why don't you just continue to stay at my place for a few days? We'll probably be off again if Herbie finds anything."

Charlie nodded. "Thanks. Regular office hours tomorrow?"

Jeff walked him to the door. "Yeah, but you can have the morning off. You'll need time to get married."

Charlie looked at him blankly.

"You proposed to Delia," Jeff reminded. "You have three witnesses."

"Oh, yeah." Charlie laughed, then shook his head. He sobered suddenly, jutting his chin in the direction of Susan's sobs. "I thought you'd read my mind for a minute. I know it's early, and all, but I was giving some thought to maybe...Susan and I one day. But after what she said to Leah tonight..."

Jeff nodded, following him onto the porch. Rain still fell torrentially, forming a sheet of water beyond the porch roof. "She's beautiful and smart, but she's still very young. It's a fact of life that all of us—" he grinned down at Charlie "—even those of us who are seasoned and mature, will at some point in time behave like fools. We need the people who love us to understand and forgive us."

Charlie jammed his hands into the pockets of his down vest. "So you think I was wrong to tell her what I thought."

"No." Jeff folded his arms and leaned a shoulder against the porch post. "Just don't assume that her behavior tonight means she wouldn't be a good bet as a wife one day. She's emotional and quick-tempered, but she's warm and enthusiastic and basically good and kind. She's just caught in a turmoil that's bound to bring out the worst in anybody."

Charlie ran a hand over his face and stared at the rain. "Maybe I'll be a monk."

Jeff laughed. "I wouldn't give you ten minutes in a monastery."

"Just a bachelor, then."

"Nah, that's a waste of manpower."

"Marriage hasn't been easy for you," Charlie argued.

Jeff nodded, wryly acknowledging the truth in that statement. "But easy isn't what it's all about, or we wouldn't be back together again."

Charlie shook his head. "I don't understand."

Jeff shrugged. "I don't, either. Life's full of mysteries, and love's one of them."

"Well." Charlie shook Jeff's hand. "What do you want me to do with Smythe?"

"Just let him in the door," Jeff said. "He'll find his way upstairs. See you tomorrow. And thanks for all you did while we were gone."

"Sure."

Jeff waved Charlie off, then closed the door. He turned into the shadowy living room and saw a bent-over figure on crutches waiting for him. Though there were no lights on, the fire he'd laid earlier in the evening picked out Susan's disheveled blond hair and the tears on her face. Compassion swelled in him, but so did a healthy anger. He struggled to indulge neither.

"I'm going up to Lee," he said. "You want to stay down here and watch television, or do you want me to take you upstairs?"

"I'll stay down here," she said in a small voice. "There's a pillow and a blanket on the sofa from this afternoon."

"All right. Good night." He started toward the stairs, but she said his name, the pathetic quality in her tone making him stop and turn to her.

"Thank you," she said, swallowing with obvious difficulty, "for explaining me to Charlie. For... explaining me to me."

Jeff put his hands in his pockets and went toward her. "You were pretty awful, Sue," he said frankly. "I can think of a lot of times when Leah helped you out of trouble or made things easier for you in one way or another. And money's the least important thing she's given you, but just because she makes it look easy, don't think it's a piece of cake for her to support the two of you and keep a business running successfully."

"I know that," Susan said thickly. "I guess I hate that she's done so much for me, but she's so efficient that there's nothing I can do for her."

"Kindness," he said significantly, "is appreciated by everyone."

"I know," she whispered. "I'm sorry."

"I hope so. But Leah's the one who should hear it."

She looked hesitantly toward the stairs. "She's probably asleep by now."

He doubted that she would be, but he thought Susan's having to deal with a guilty conscience all night might be a good thing. "There's always first thing in the morning."

She nodded. "Right. You go on up."

"Charlie's going to be letting Smythe in."

"I heard."

"I just didn't want you to be frightened when he unlocks the door."

With a grim smile she raised a crutch. "I'm better able to handle attackers than I was before."

He smiled back, leaning down to kiss her cheek. "Then I leave you in charge."

JEFF WALKED STEALTHILY into the cool, dark bedroom. He sat carefully on the edge of the bed and pulled off his shoes, tossing his clothes beyond the night table where he hoped there was still a chair. He heard his belt fall to the floor with a thunk.

"I moved the chair after you left," Leah said from the expanse of bed behind him. "I thought it was too convenient a place to drop stuff. Seems I'm going to have to put it back." Her hand gliding gently over his back took any sting out of the gentle criticism.

"Couldn't sleep?" he asked, easing under the blankets. He pulled her close.

"No," she said, snuggling into him.

He brushed her hair back and kissed her forehead. "Did you clear your mind of everything like I told you?"

"Mostly."

"Susan's very sorry," he assured her. "And not just because Charlie chewed her out."

"He did?"

"And very well, too. I think she regretted what she'd said before you even came upstairs, but she was still too upset to know what to do about it."

Leah sighed against him. "I know. I've had a little time to think about it, and I understand how she feels, I guess. I have pushed her about college. I shouldn't do that. And the bad news I dumped on her was unnecessary and all my fault, anyway."

"That was just honest confusion."

"I know. But I feel badly about it, anyway. I'll talk to her in the morning."

"Well, if you've come to this serene understanding of her and yourself," he said, "what's on your mind that's keeping you awake?"

"A couple of hours ago," she said quietly, kissing his throat, "in a corner of the bathroom, a lustful image of wild debauchery was introduced to my mind by a gentleman of considerable skill and dubious intentions who suggested that I retain the thought until later." She wriggled her lower body closer. "You know how obedient I've always been."

"No," he said.

She slapped his chest. "Well, give me credit for a late start, anyway."

He coughed theatrically. "Since you asked so nicely—"

She put a hand over his mouth. "Do you want to hear what's on my mind or not?"

He nodded emphatically. She lowered her hand and placed it so that she had to explain no further.

Later they lay side by side, staring languorously into each other's eyes in the evening darkness. Then something struck the bedroom door open, shattering the silence. Smythe leaped into the middle of the bed, effectively separating them. He licked first Jeff's face, then Leah's, then Jeff's again, whining his delight at Jeff's return and the added bonus of finding Leah with him.

He took her affectionate strokes and scratches as his due, rolling onto his back between them to allow them easy access to his sensitive chest. He stretched his back legs and curled his front paws in ecstasy. He turned his face to Leah, his long tongue curling out to kiss her chin.

"Oh, I've missed you Smitty," Leah said, nuzzling him and patting his solid chest.

He whined in response, saying, "I've missed you, too," as clearly as any spoken words.

Jeff shook his head. "Great. There goes a year of discipline down the tubes."

"Oh, sure," Leah said dryly. "From the man who cooked a turkey when Smythe wouldn't eat after surgery."

"Well..." Jeff said lamely. "The smell of turkey cooking always brought him into the kitchen."

"I rest my case."

"Who's the lawyer here?"

"The same guy who's a patsy where this dog is concerned."

Jeff snapped his fingers and pointed to the foot of the bed. "Where you belong, Smythe," he said firmly.

Smythe went without complaint, happy to curl up on their feet and renew his old habits.

Jeff and Leah wound their arms around each other and settled into the pillows with a mutual sigh. It was all so dearly familiar that Leah closed her eyes, wrapped in a rosy glow.

OVER THE RUSHING SOUND of the shower Jeff sang a rhythm and blues tune in a key Leah was sure had never been heard before. Feeling rested and refreshed, she smiled at the sound and hurried downstairs. Her mind was already occupied with the myriad details she would have to deal with today.

Two things brought her to a stop at the bottom of the stairs. One was the smell of breakfast drifting out from the kitchen. The other was the sight of Delia, who'd been preparing breakfast since she'd come to care for Susan, seated on the sofa watching *Good Morning, America.*

"Good morning," Leah called.

Delia turned away from the screen to smile, raising a glass of orange juice in greeting. "Good morning." When Joan Lunden's voice announced the next segment with famous chef Wolfgang Puck, Delia returned her attention to the screen.

Leah followed the aromas into the kitchen and stopped in the doorway at the sight of Susan puttering over the stove. Actually, her actions were more frantic than puttering. With a towel tucked into the waistband of her jeans, she hobbled from a frying pan in which potatoes browned to a griddle where bacon sizzled, then to a bowl on the counter in which she whisked an egg mixture.

The table was set and fragrant coffee dripped in the coffee maker. Leah guessed that this was in the nature of an apology.

Susan turned away from the stove as Leah approached. Her cheeks were flushed, her eyes bright, her countenance sheepish but free of last night's anger and resentment. "Good morning," she said. "I apologize for what I said last night." Nervously she twirled the spatula in her hand. "I was being a jerk. I'm sorry."

"I've forgotten it," Leah said. That wasn't entirely true. She'd chosen to put it all aside, to attribute Susan's resentments to the frayed state of her nerves. But she understood that even if Susan had managed to keep those things to herself, she still felt them—and felt them strongly by the way they'd burst from her, like something long held under pressure. Leah looked into the pan of potatoes, sniffing appreciatively. "Jeff's going to think he died and went to heaven."

"Lee." Susan caught her arm, reclaiming her attention. Her eyes were wide and grave. "I know what you're thinking. That I'm sorry I let those things out, but that I still feel them."

"It's okay," Leah said. "You're entitled to how you feel. I . . . am pushy and demanding."

"Yes, you are," Susan agreed, "but you're also kind and supportive and unselfish and a lot of other things

I take for granted. And I know when you do push me, it's because you care. I care, too. I guess I just resent that you can feel so sure of yourself when I have all these fears and insecurities inside."

Sure of herself. Leah knew Susan wouldn't understand if she laughed. "I'm not sure of myself, Suzie," she admitted, giving her a quick hug. "Particularly now. I feel as though my whole world is upside down. I don't want to lose you, too, in the process."

Susan held her fast. "I think that was part of the reason I got so upset. When I thought you'd find your mother and that it had nothing to do with me, I thought you'd go your way and I'd be left alone."

Leah pulled away from her, her expression clouded. "Susan, you couldn't be more important to me if we were related by blood. I'd never abandon you."

Susan nodded penitently. "I know. I'm sorry."

They held each other for another moment, then pulled apart as the doorbell chimed. Susan pointed her spatula toward the door. "You want to get that? I've got to turn the potatoes."

Leah hurried into the living room and found Delia already opening the door to Sylvia Dunwiddie. She was dressed in silk and fur this morning, but her mood was grim.

Spotting Leah, she walked around Delia with a charming smile and a "Thank you, dear," then wrapped her arms around Leah with alarming force. "Leah, I *must* talk to you. Please tell me you have time."

"You're sure you don't want Jeff?" Leah asked, drawing her toward the kitchen. "Have you eaten? My sister Susan's just fixing breakfast." Susan spun away from the stove, a plate piled with omelet, bacon, potatoes and toast in her hands.

"Suzie, this is Sylvia Dunwiddie," Leah said, her eyes pleading with Susan to keep her speculations about Sylvia's claims on Jeff to herself. "She's a client of Jeff's. Can you fix her something?"

Susan blinked, then recovered instantly. "Of course." She put the plate in the warm oven and smiled across the table at Sylvia. "I'm fixing western omelets." Her eyes flickered over Sylvia's elegant appearance. "Would you like me to hold the red and green pepper?"

"Oh, no," Sylvia said, pulling out a chair and sitting down. "I'll have both, please. Thank you." She frowned at Leah, who took the chair beside her. She shrugged her fur onto the back of the chair and pulled off her fawn gloves. "I'm so glad you're back," she said quietly. "I'm absolutely at wit's end. Jordan hasn't called me once."

"You left him, Sylvia," Leah reminded her gently.

Sylvia waved the gloves dismissively. "Well, yes, but I've done this before, and he's always called me and tried to get me back. It's been almost a week and not a word." She sighed and her bottom lip began to quiver.

It occurred to Leah that Jeff knew her very well. He'd predicted this would happen, given time. But she guessed that even he didn't suspect it would happen so quickly.

"I thought you were anxious to get a divorce?"

Sylvia put both hands over her eyes. A solid gold charm bracelet tinkled musically. "I guess I don't know what I want. I get so furious with him for not noticing me that I leave him. Then I miss him so much that life without him rapidly loses its appeal." She lowered her hands and, with a heavy sigh, leaned back in the chair. She turned to Leah, her big eyes despondent. "I want you to tell me how you got Jeff back. He looks at you like he can't get enough of you. How do I get Jordan to do that?"

Susan put a steaming plate in front of her. Sylvia inhaled the aroma and groaned, giving Susan a beatific smile. "Thank you, sweetie. I haven't eaten since yesterday morning. This looks wonderful."

Jeff walked into the room, buttoning the cuff of a white shirt with a narrow blue stripe. He looked devastatingly handsome. Leah's heart almost stopped when she looked up into his eyes and saw the look Sylvia had just envied.

"Good morning," he said to Leah, his tone so intimate there might have been no one else in the room.

"Oh, Jeffrey!" Sylvia flew out of her chair and into Jeff's arms. Still looking at Leah, he held his hands away from Sylvia with palms up to indicate his helplessness. Leah grinned, nodding to indicate she understood his innocence.

He brought Sylvia to the table, looking down in wonder at the morning's fare. "Wow," he said.

As he took his chair, Susan hobbled over and put a bowl of cereal at his place. With a wink at Leah she turned away. Jeff caught her arm. "What's this?"

Her expression innocent, she replied, "Cheerios."

He looked significantly from Leah's plate to his own. "That's all?" he demanded.

Susan smiled. "Want a banana?"

Jeff smiled back. "Do you? Permanently affixed to your nose?"

Susan giggled. "Just wanted you to know I'm me again."

He considered her for a moment. "Is that supposed to comfort me?"

"Yes." She leaned down to kiss his cheek, then picked up the bowl of dry cereal. "Be right back with your real breakfast."

Charlie arrived several moments later, smiled a little self-consciously at the group around the table, then cornered Susan at the other end of the kitchen. An earnest conversation ensued, followed by a hug. Then Susan went back to her task and Charlie took a place at the table. "Man-to-woman ratio looks a little lopsided," he explained. "I'll help out."

"Good morning," Jeff said. "Noble of you. You been by the office yet?"

"Yeah." He rolled his eyes. "You've got a big day. Steed and Folsom are coming in to talk about bankruptcy proceedings. I dug the files out for you. Alan sent me by to make sure you were coming in today to handle it."

"Sure. What's new with...?"

As Jeff and Charlie talked shop, Susan and Sylvia discussed clothes. Delia wandered in for more coffee, topped up everyone's cups, then went back to the living room, apparently pleased to be relieved of her duties for a morning.

Leah thought how strange it was to have everyone talking about torts and patterned panty hose when her life, and possibly Susan's, hung suspended like a baby's mobile, various parts moving, spinning, tilting. Their lives could change in an instant—or never—depending on whether or not Herbie could find Marilyn White.

Jeff noted her grimly pensive distraction and hooked an arm around her neck to pull her toward him and kiss her gently. "You're to have only positive thoughts," he said firmly, "until we know differently. All right?"

She smiled up at him. "All right." She went back to her breakfast, having little trouble considering herself lucky despite the emotional confusion. She had Jeff back.

CHAPTER ELEVEN

"SYLVIA, this is Milly Griffin, friend, co-worker and confessor." Leah drew Sylvia toward Milly's desk. "Milly, this is Sylvia Dunwiddie, a client of Jeff's."

Milly gave Sylvia's extravagant appearance a mildly critical but tolerant survey, then offered her hand. "Welcome to Minding Your Business."

"Sylvia and I were talking over breakfast," Leah explained, "and didn't have a chance to finish our conversation. Would you hold my calls, please?"

"Sure. Shall I bring coffee?"

"When you have time. Come on, Sylvia." Leah ushered Sylvia into her office, took her fur and hung it on the coat tree. It looked ridiculous there, and somehow discarded, but Sylvia didn't seem to mind. She was already baring her soul.

"I feel like an absolute fool," she said earnestly as Leah took her chair behind the desk. "And I know I look like a fool, but damn it! I love him. Why can't I be married to him on my terms?"

Leah considered how she'd thought of Jeff as fatally disorganized and uncommitted to his career—only to discover that when she needed him, his go-with-the-flow nature had allowed him to put everything else in his life aside for her. She hated to think what she'd have done in Los Angeles without him. When she first met

Sylvia, she'd been on Jordan's side. Now, suddenly, it was easy to sympathize with her.

"I know how important he is to this community," Sylvia went on. "But I also know that when he never remembers me, I feel bitter and angry and my willingness to make allowances for his busy schedule evaporates."

"Have you explained that to him?"

"Before I left him I'd seen him all of six hours in an entire week. It's hard to get down to gut feelings when he's in the shower, on the lawn mower or asleep."

Leah had to smile. "Have you tried jumping on the lawn mower?"

Sylvia looked rueful. "I'd jump on him if he'd stay home long enough." The expression turned quickly to one of desolation. "I can't believe he hasn't called even once. I told him where I was going."

"Maybe he feels abandoned," Leah suggested. "You've got to talk to him. Maybe he has no idea how desperate you are to have more time with him. You said yourself you never have time to talk to him about it."

Sylvia crossed one leg over the other and swung her expensive Italian shoe forward and back. She thought for a minute. "I told him once that I refused to have to make an appointment to see my husband. But that's what it would take."

"Then maybe you should do that."

The telephone rang once. Instinctively Leah reached for it, then remembered she'd asked Milly to hold her calls.

"How did you get Jeff back?" Sylvia asked. "Did you go to him, or did he come to you?"

Leah shrugged. "He was always around to see if I needed anything. I guess when the time came that I did, and he was there, I realized that the things about him that annoyed me weren't a fraction as important as how much I needed him and how eager he always was to be there for me."

There was a rap on the door. Then Milly elbowed her way in with two mugs of coffee. She set them on the desk. "I know you asked not to be disturbed," she said, "but I just need a quick answer from you. We have a client on the line who sounds desperate for a secretary right now. We haven't anyone to send but you. Do you have anything going today?"

Leah took a sip of coffee. "Who's the client?"

"Dunwiddie Developers," Milly replied, then suddenly making the connection to the woman to whom she'd just been introduced, she laughed. "Well, isn't that a coincidence?"

A 150-watt, three-way light bulb went on over Leah's head. She smiled at Sylvia. "Tell him we'll send someone over within the hour."

When Milly closed the door behind her, Sylvia returned Leah's speculative look, clearly confused by it. Then light dawned, and she lowered her swinging foot to the floor. "Oh, no," she said decisively. Then, true to her nature, she quickly vacillated, smiled and asked hesitantly, "Do you think?"

JEFF BROKE HIS BREAD STICK in half and dipped the end into a pat of butter. "If you're looking for representation in your divorce, Jordan," he said, pushing the bread sticks toward his companion, "I have to warn you that Sylvia's already asked me to represent her."

Jordan Dunwiddie nodded, his preoccupied frown making Jeff wonder if he'd really heard him. Dunwiddie was short, round and bald and gave the appearance of being someone's dotty uncle. He had one of the finest minds in business Jeff had ever met, but communicating with him always made Jeff feel as though Dunwiddie assimilated information in ways other than the usual. His eyes always wandered around the room when he spoke instead of making eye contact with the person he addressed, and his answers didn't always seem to relate to the question. It was as though he dispensed with the part of the conversation he considered unnecessary and just moved ahead.

Jordan surprised Jeff by replying appropriately. "I knew she would. No, I don't want legal advice, I need...personal help."

Jeff tried not to look shocked. "Oh?"

Jordan leaned his arms on the table, looked around the room as though slowly cataloging all its occupants, then looked Jeff in the eye. "Is she...seeing you?"

Jeff looked at him blankly and repeated, "Seeing me?"

Jordan's eyes never flinched, but he swallowed perceptibly. "Sleeping with you," he clarified.

Jeff lost the battle to appear unshaken. He dropped his bread stick into his cup of coffee and almost overturned his water glass as he tried to retrieve it. Steadying the glass, he frowned at Jordan. "No," he said, "and if you think I'm picking up the tab for this lunch after that, you're mistaken."

Jordan held Jeff's gaze. He didn't look convinced.

Jeff leaned back in his chair, his expression firming. "Who told you to stay out of the Clipsan Condos venture even though it would have meant a bundle for Alden and Foster? Who saved your bacon when that kid fell off your scaffolding and sued you, blaming the rig? Who—?"

"You're talking about courtroom skill and business integrity," Jordan said. "I'm talking about . . . sex."

Jeff was almost too surprised to be angry. "In my line of work," he said patiently, "we don't usually bust our butts for our clients, then go to bed with their wives."

Jordan considered for a moment, then said, apparently still unconvinced, "Sylvia's a beautiful, seductive woman."

Jeff sighed. "She is, but I have my own, thank you."

Jordan looked surprised. "I thought you were divorced."

"We were separated. We're back together."

Jordan studied him for a moment, then smiled grimly. "I apologize. I've accused her of carrying on with you several times, and she'd never really denied it."

Jeff rolled his eyes. "You know Sylvia! Her conversation is a series of one-act plays. She's always in the role of the indulged but neglected woman. She might even like being neglected a little, or she'd have really left you long ago."

Anger flashed in Jordan's eyes, and Jeff saw the look that had made the man a millionaire. All his energy and power came into sharp focus. Fortunately, Jeff thought grimly, he'd gone head-to-head with Leah. Nothing scared him anymore.

"You know it's true, Jordan," he went on, braced to duck if necessary. "Sylvia is the only thing in the world you're afraid of. After thirty years and two kids, you still don't have her figured out, and because you can't tie her up in a neat package like some clever stock deal, you find it easier to stay away."

Jordan's face was red to the fringe of hair above his ears. "Look, Alden..." he began in a choked voice.

"If that wasn't true," Jeff persisted, "you'd have done something about her long ago. You'd have made time for her, because you know she loves you, or you'd have let her go. Instead, you put up with her running off. Then you beg her to come back, and when she does, you don't change anything."

Jordan's color receded and he became subdued and pale. He picked up a glass that had contained bourbon and water and stared at it. "I don't understand her," he admitted quietly. "I don't know what to do with things I don't understand. I just let her do what she wants. Then when she runs away, I beg her to come back. But when she does, I still don't know what to do with her."

Jeff wished he didn't have clients coming in this afternoon. He could have used a drink himself. "Do you think any man," he asked, "truly understands any woman?"

Jordan shrugged. "You got your wife back."

"Because I love her, not because I understand her. And because, under all the junk that got in our way, she loves me, too." He shifted in his chair, then leaned earnestly toward his companion. "And you can get Sylvia back on the same principle. She loves you, but she needs things from you—not perfect understanding—just your time, your tolerance, your affection, your shoulder. You've got to give, Jordan, or you'll lose her."

The man who'd bought a multimillion-dollar beachfront hotel project on the verge of bankruptcy and turned it into the hottest resort in the state looked as though Jeff had set him an impossible task. "She does scare me," he said with a shake of his head. "When the kids were home, it wasn't so bad. We sort of dealt with each other through them. But since it's been just us again, she looks at me with this kind of desperation, as though she needs something from me that's so important, so complex that I'm sure I don't have it."

"All she wants is love, Jordan."

"I'm not a very complex man, you know. Business is very straightforward."

"So is love," Jeff said. "You give it or you don't. I think you should call her. Make a date with her to talk it over."

Unaccountably Jordan's confusion turned into a spare but definite grin. "I don't have to do that."

"Why?" Jeff asked warily.

"Because she's at my office right now."

That surprised Jeff for an instant. Then he decided it was silly to be surprised by anything Sylvia did. But Jordan's behavior was cause for concern. "You mean, she's waiting for you at your office and you're here with me?"

Jordan shook his head. "She's not at my office as Mrs. Jordan Dunwiddie. She's there as Sylvia Dunwiddie, temporary office help sent by Minding Your Business."

Jeff laughed before he could stop himself, then quickly sobered. "You're kidding. How did that happen?"

Jordan shook his head. "I was hoping you could tell me."

Jeff uttered a gasp of helpless amusement. "I told you I love Leah, but I don't always understand her." He sobered suddenly. "Then why did you call me to meet you for lunch?"

Jordan's grin widened. "I left Sylvia filing invoices and answering the telephone. I figured I'd find out if you were seeing her. If you were, then I'd know it was over. If you weren't, I hoped you could tell me what to do when I got back from lunch."

"Jordan," Jeff pleaded, "I'm not a marriage therapist."

Jordan accepted that with a nod. "But I don't even speak the language. What should I do?"

Jeff sighed. "Take the afternoon off, take her home, make love to her until she whimpers, then promise her you'll schedule two or three afternoons a week just for her."

Jordan put a hand to his heart, amusement coming to life in his eyes. "Two or three? I'll be sixty-one in January."

Jeff shrugged that detail away, grinning. "Sylvia told us you have stamina that would amaze even a young stud like myself. That's a quote."

Jordan blinked, then barked a laugh. "When was that?"

"About a week ago when Sylvia invited me to lunch to ask me to represent her in the divorce. I told her I didn't have time to get to it for a couple of weeks."

"You're that busy?"

Jeff shook his head. "I'm that smart. I knew she didn't really want it. I suspected that you didn't, either, but why haven't you contacted her since she left?"

Jordan shrugged. "Pride, I guess."

Jeff nodded understanding. "My advice is chuck it. Then take her home and make sure she never wants to leave you again."

"Right. Thanks, Alden." Jordan stood decisively, straightened his tie and coat and started away from the table. Then he turned back, picking up the tab and grinning at Jeff. "Sure you won't reconsider paying for lunch?"

Jeff shook his head. "No way. I lost my wife for a year because she thought the same thing you did."

Jordan shook his head. "Devilish little woman, your wife."

Jeff laughed. "Tell me about it."

BEFORE JEFF HAD his jacket off, his secretary, just back from her vacation, walked into his office and put a note on a stack of folders on his desk blotter. "There's a gentleman on the phone who wants to speak to 'Ugly,'" she said.

He put his jacket on the brass coat tree and walked to his desk. "Isn't Alan in his office?"

She grinned. "He was specific about asking for 'Ugly Alden.'"

"Ah." With a grin he waved her out the door and propped his feet on the corner of his desk. "Herbie," he said into the receiver, "how the hell are you?" He picked up the note Sally had left and saw that his father had called again.

LEAH TURNED to a fresh page of copy, completely engrossed in the new Diane Hankins fantasy novel.

The Gypsy's engines labored beneath Meris's blood-slickened hands. Her breath came in quick, fear-filled gasps. Smoke rose thickly in the near-darkness of the engine room. Blindly she ran a hand across the floor, searching for the access panel to the escape pods. Behind her came a slither of sound. She spun around to see a Company soldier materialize out of the whorls of smoke, a stunner aimed at her head.

Turning another page, Leah picked up the story without pause, not even noticing the cross-outs and editor's marks. "She felt a breath behind her, the barest inhalation of a—"

A breath sighed against Leah's neck as teeth closed over the long, slender muscle there. She screamed murderously, ripping her earphones off and leaping out of her chair. Still screaming, she turned to confront Jeff, who stood innocently behind her chair in a long khaki raincoat, the collar turned up.

"I love to make you scream," he said suggestively, his eyes filled with amusement as he reached out to pinch her chin.

She slapped his hand away, half horrified, half entrapped by his laughter. "You beast!" she said, still slapping at him as he drew her into his arms. "I was typing a scary scene, and you took ten years off my life!"

He kissed her soundly. "Tonight I'll give you ten years back."

She let herself be held, pretending it was against her will. "What are you doing here, anyway?"

He held her close for one moment, then pulled her away, his expression sobering as he looked down into her eyes. "Got a phone call from Herbie."

Leah felt air leave her lungs in a rush. "And?"

"Marilyn White has retired to Portland. I have her address."

She swallowed. Already? She'd been so sure it would take longer, that she'd have more time. Dread and excitement warred within her. "He's sure it's the right one? That's probably a fairly common name."

"It's her. She was a caseworker for Children's Service from 1953 to 1981."

Leah closed her eyes. "I'm scared, Jeff."

He pulled her back into his arms. "I know, Lee. It's a step closer, but it might lead nowhere. This could go either way. Do you want to stop now? It's an option, you know. You don't have to do this."

Leah sighed against him and pulled back, her eyes quiet. "That was what I thought just a week ago. Now it's the key to me. I have to know. And I'm sure Susan does, too."

Jeff nodded. "All right. Let's go tell her."

SUSAN TOOK THE NEWS without the enthusiasm Leah expected. She looked mildly pleased, closing the magazine she'd been reading and smiling up at Leah and Jeff. "That's great. You guys want some coffee? Delia should be back from the market any minute. I'm sure she'll have cookies or something to go with it."

Leah pushed lightly on Susan's shoulder as she tried to stand, then sat in the chair next to hers. "I thought you'd be excited." Confused by Susan's reaction, she felt her way cautiously.

"Oh, I am." Susan replied in a tone that failed to support the words. "When are you leaving?"

Leah shot a worried glance at Jeff as he took the chair on the other side of Susan. "In the morning," he replied. "Don't you want to come?"

Susan smiled and shook her head, concentrating on her fingers joined together on the table. "I'm still kind of clumsy. I'll just be in the way. And somebody has to stay with Smythe."

"Susan." Leah took her hands and turned her toward her. "This all started because of you. Checking the births recorded on the day you were born turned up the Nagy name—the people Gerda worked for. We don't understand how, but you're involved."

Susan shrugged a shoulder. "Maybe. But you're the baby in the picture. Iliana Arpad is *your* mother." She straightened her shoulders and forced a shaky smile. "I read the letters."

Leah nodded, tightening her jaw. Just the thought of the letters was still enough to make her lose her composure.

"She loved you so much," Susan went on. "When you find her, I don't want to mess it up for you. I don't want you to worry about whether or not I'm jealous or hurt or anything. I just want you—" her smile slipped, and she drew in a breath that sounded like a sob "—to be happy."

Susan dissolved into tears, and Leah pulled her into her arms, strengthened by her concern. "Suzie," she said quietly, "you're my sister. Nothing will ever change that for me. And now that I know what it feels like to have to know—" She pulled her away and looked into her eyes. "Suzie, after we find my mother, we'll start all over again until we find yours. I promise."

"I'm so sorry about yesterday," Susan said, weeping. "That was small and stupid."

"Forget that," Leah said firmly. "I understand how you felt. I want you to come."

Susan sniffed and tucked her hair behind her ears. "I'd like to come."

The sound of a bark came from the living room, followed immediately by a streak of brown and white racing into the kitchen, trailing a leash. Smythe ran to Leah and Susan, allowed himself to be stroked and fussed over, then went to Jeff, putting his forelegs on his master's knees and kissing his face.

"Oh, sure," Jeff scolded while ruffling the dog's ears. "Now I'm second fiddle, and you still expect me to act like your best buddy."

Smythe barked and kissed him again, confirming his accusation.

Delia, her unbuttoned coat falling off one shoulder, a loaf of French bread tottering dangerously out of a grocery bag, slouched into the kitchen. Jeff went to take the bag from her. Leah helped her into a chair.

"What happened?" Susan asked.

"I . . . thought . . . it would be nice," Delia gasped as she collapsed against the back of the chair, "to take Smythe for a walk."

"It wasn't nice?" Leah guessed.

Delia shook her head. "It wasn't a walk. It was more like . . . I had grown jets. We started out at a fast walk that turned into a run, and by the time we reached the supermarket, we were airborne." She sighed, her eyes unfocused. "There are grapefruit all over aisles one and two, and you know the dinnerware they're offering with a purchase of ten dollars or more? This week it was going to be dessert plates." She shook her head again. "Not anymore."

Jeff turned away from the counter, unable to decide whether to laugh or call Alan and tell him to prepare for a hefty suit. "Is that all?"

Delia sat up, appearing to recover. "Except for the pork chops and the chicken. I don't think they'd have caught us if Smythe hadn't sat with the chicken in his mouth, as though he'd retrieved it out of the brush."

Leah looked at Jeff, her mouth unsteady. Susan had succumbed to hysterics.

"What?" Jeff asked defensively. "So he's a retriever. And he likes to do his own shopping." He winced. "Did they present you with a bill?"

"I told them you'd be in touch." Delia struggled to her feet. "May I have the evening off?"

"Of course," Leah said. "In fact, you can have tomorrow off, too. We're all going to Portland."

Delia smiled. "News?"

Leah shrugged. "Maybe. We'll let you know."

Delia went to the counter and opened one of the tall cupboards. "I'll put the groceries away before I go."

Jeff caught her hand. "You go home. I'll do that."

"But it'll be easy for me," she told him with a bland smile. "My right arm is eight inches longer now."

"DINNER OUT WAS a good idea," Leah said, pulling Jeff to a stop at the window of a clothing shop. The store was closed, as all the shops along Broadway were at that time of the evening, but Leah pretended interest in the window, taking the opportunity to look beyond Jeff to the bench a block away where Charlie sat with Susan, his arm around her shoulders. "Susan seems more relaxed, don't you think?"

He glanced toward the bench, then back at the window. "Yes." He looked down at her indulgently. "You're like butter on a skillet, though. 'Come on, Jeff,'" he said, mimicking the suggestion she'd made a few moments earlier. "'Let's take a walk. You and

Charlie stay here, Susan. I'm sure you need to rest your leg.'" He laughed softly, resuming his own quiet baritone. "As though they really want to be sitting there in forty-five-degree weather that seems to be sprouting gale winds."

To support his comment a gust of wind swept up the street, leaves and paper dancing and swirling ahead of it. She frowned up at him. "I thought she might want some time alone to talk with Charlie. Someone her own age would understand how she feels."

Jeff pulled his hand out of his pocket and put his arm around Leah. She leaned into him, wrapping her arm around his waist as they wandered farther up the street. "What about you?" he asked. "Do you need someone to talk to?"

She sighed. "I think I'm okay. But then, I always do—until I come face-to-face with something that startles me, like my mother's picture or her letters. Then I realize how different the beginning of my life was from what I'd thought. Then I'm not okay. I come apart."

"Living is about change, isn't it?" he asked gently. "Maybe you come apart to pull yourself together into someone a little bit different, someone affected by what she's learned. There's nothing weak or wrong with that."

Leah stopped walking and looked up at him, her other arm also coming to rest at his waist. In the light of an antique streetlamp she smiled at him, her eyes soft with love. "Have you always been so sane? How could I have never seen that in you?"

He wrapped his arms loosely around her. "Maybe it's a new development," he said, absorbing the look in her eyes, feeling it warm his blood. "I used to want you to be the way I wanted you—freer, more relaxed, more willing to let me into every little corner of your mind and your soul." He inclined his head, his expression wry. "After I lost you, I got to thinking maybe that was my hang-up as much as yours. I got so little from my parents that I was determined you weren't going to keep any part of yourself from me. Now I have a lot less pride. I'll take you however I can get you. You can have the private places in your mind and your soul as long as you're near me, smiling at me, loving me."

"Oh, Jeff." Leah leaned against him for a moment, drawing his warmth and his strength into her, trying to absorb his tolerance and his tenderness, as well. God, she had a lot to learn. She stood on tiptoe to offer him her mouth. He took it gently, but she dipped her tongue into his, trying to tell him something for which there simply were no words.

"Mmm," he said throatily, holding her closer. "Time to go home. Come on."

They were halfway down the block, walking quickly arm in arm, when a restaurant door burst open across the street and Sylvia marched out. She turned in the middle of the sidewalk to shout at someone lost to view in the doorway. "Forget it! Just forget it! Go to Dallas. Make your deal. I'll go to Monte Carlo without you. Maybe the prince would like some female company!" She walked into the street and around her car, her high heels clicking angrily on the pavement.

As she fumbled with her keys, a door slammed and a short, bald man stormed onto the sidewalk.

"Jordan?" Leah whispered to Jeff.

"Yeah," he replied, not taking his eyes off the man. He watched Jordan stare at Sylvia as she dropped her keys, swore, leaned down to pick them up, then fumbled with the lock again. He seemed to struggle with a moment of indecision before shouting authoritatively, "Sylvia! You come back here!"

"All right," Jeff said under his breath.

Sylvia looked at her husband over the top of the car, apparently surprised for a moment that he had followed her out of the restaurant. Then she tossed her head. "Goodbye, Jordan," she called. She fitted the key into the lock and opened the door.

Jordan continued to stand in the middle of the sidewalk. Sylvia tossed her purse into the car, slipped behind the steering wheel and pulled on her seat belt.

"Sylvia Dunwiddie!" Jordan roared suddenly, striding around the car to pull the door out of her reach as she grabbed for the handle. "You are coming home with me!"

"You're going to Dallas, remember?" her voice reminded from inside the car.

"You're coming with me."

"I have no wish whatsoever to go to Texas."

"I will make time for you," he said reasonably, his voice still edged with anger, "but you have to make time for me."

"I'm going to Monte Carlo."

"In January. First you're going to Dallas. Move over."

"I will not." Her denial was followed by a little scream of alarm when Jordan reached into the car.

Afraid he meant Sylvia bodily harm, Leah tried to push Jeff in their direction, saying, "Jeff! He's—"

Jeff resisted, covering her hand with his and shushing her. Jordan straightened, holding the end of the shoulder harness. "Move...over," he said again, enunciating carefully.

There was muted grumbling, a moment of scrambling, then Jordan slid into the empty driver's seat and pulled the door closed. The car roared to life immediately and sped away, doing a quick circuit of the turnaround before racing up Broadway to the highway.

Leah looked up at Jeff, saw him smiling at the Dunwiddie's exhaust and slapped his shoulder. "Don't stand there grinning like a chauvinist. What if he hurts her when they get home?"

Jeff took her hand and pulled her along as he headed for Charlie and Susan. "Jordan Dunwiddie isn't capable of hurting anyone, least of all Sylvia. He was just desperate to be heard. I don't blame him."

"He frightened her," Leah accused.

Jeff didn't seem to find that cause for concern. "You think her running away didn't frighten him? Why do you think the man's shouting when he can negotiate a deal for days on end and never raise his voice? *He's* scared."

Leah looked doubtful. "You're guessing."

"No," he said quietly. "I'm experienced."

Leah stopped in her tracks, pulling Jeff to a stop. He pointed to the bench in exasperation. "Babe, they're probably frozen to Popsicles by now."

She ignored that, her eyes dark. "Do you mean that you were frightened when we broke up?"

"Yes."

"No kidding?"

"No kidding."

"Why?"

"I did the same thing Jordan just did because I was desperate, too." He sighed and added quietly, "Only it blew up in my face. You were supposed to be shaken into finally listening to me. Instead, you told me to go.''

''I didn't mean it,'' she whispered.

He pinched her chin and gave her a thin smile. ''Then you shouldn't have been so convincing. Come on. You're shivering.''

As they approached Charlie and Susan, Leah chuckled. Their noses were red, their breath billowing around them, but they seemed unaware of any discomfort. They had eyes only for each other.

''And you were worrying about them freezing.''

It was another half block to the car and the four proceeded toward it. Jeff and Charlie fell back as Leah helped Susan hobble ahead, answering her questions about Sylvia Dunwiddie and the fuss on the street.

''Do you have plans for tomorrow?'' Jeff asked Charlie.

Charlie shook his head. ''You need me to feed Smythe if you don't get home from Portland tomorrow night, right?''

''No,'' Jeff corrected. ''I'd like you to come with us.''

He looked surprised. ''Sure. I'd like to. But how come?''

Jeff shrugged. ''It might help Susan.'' Then he grinned. ''And it'll sure help me. One woman in an emotional turmoil requires all one's wits and energy. Two might be more than I can handle alone.''

''Hey,'' Charlie cautioned. ''You're dealing with a novice here, remember? What makes you think I'd know what to do.''

''When you're in love, it's instinctive,'' Jeff said.

Charlie nodded, apparently deciding to trust that truism. "Can I bring my Grateful Dead tapes?"

"No."

CHAPTER TWELVE

"TURN THAT WAY on Comstock," Susan directed from the back seat, frowning over a map spread across her and Charlie's knees.

"You're sitting behind me, Susan," Jeff said patiently, trying to watch the traffic all around him on the busy, rainy Portland suburb streets. "Which way is 'that way'?"

"Left."

"No, it's right," Charlie corrected quickly. "Turn right, Jeff."

"Charlie," Susan argued, "he'll end up on the golf course!"

"The golf course is east! He wants to go west! Trust me, Jeff. Turn right."

"Only if you've brought your clubs, Jeff," Susan warned sweetly.

"Susan, give it to me," Charlie said. There was a furious rustle of paper in the back seat. Jeff glanced at Leah with a roll of his eyes and turned right.

"Up is north, down is south!" Susan insisted. "Nothing changes that, Charlie."

"But we're coming from the top of the map and heading south!" Charlie sounded at the end of his rope. There was more rustling. "He has to turn right to go west."

There was a long silence. "Oh," Susan said.

Charlie went on more patiently to explain their position.

Jeff glanced at Leah again, half frustrated, half amused. "Why did we give her the map?" he asked softly.

Leah smiled. "To give her something to do because she was driving us crazy with her license plates game."

"All right, so I'm no navigator," Susan said defensively.

There was a loud silence while no one corrected her. "Okay, okay!" she went on. "I won't say another word this whole trip."

Jeff glanced at the rearview mirror. "Would you write that down, Suzie? Charlie, did you bring my notary seal?"

While everyone laughed, Susan struck him on the back of the head with a bag of potato chips.

THE WHITE, gray-trimmed ranch-style house that matched the address Herbie had given them for Marilyn White sat on a large lot at the top of a hill. Long-needled pines grew close to the back of it. Colorful flower beds were breathing their last gasps of red, yellow and purple. An old maple at the front of the lot was aflame with November honey, crimson and brown. The broad lawn was half buried under their color. Jeff pulled up under the tree and turned off the engine. In the dreary midafternoon light the house looked dark, and the driveway was empty.

Leah felt her heart sink. The woman wasn't home. Susan leaned over the back of the front seat. "Maybe we should have told her we were coming, after all," she said, her tone heavy with disappointment.

"We didn't want to give her a chance to refuse to see us," Leah reminded her.

"Why don't we just wait?" Charlie suggested. "Maybe she'll come back."

Even as they were all settling comfortably in the leather upholstery to wait, the creak of a gate at the side of the house turned their heads in that direction. Through the gate came a plump figure in brown woolen pants, with thick white socks in blue tennis shoes showing under them. A blue corduroy jacket tied high at the neck fell over the woman's ample bosom. Wisps of gray hair escaped from a blue-and-white crocheted hat with a pom-pom.

The woman held a rake in one hand and, with the other, was pulling a deep green plastic trash can on wheels. Two tabby kittens scampered around her feet as she made her way agilely across the lawn. Her laughter and her baby talk to the kittens could be heard in the car.

Leah swallowed, gathering courage.

"If we all get out," Jeff said, "we'll probably scare her to death."

The woman had noticed the car now and watched it with caution, if not mistrust. A gust of wind blew the leaves, and the kittens pounced on one, then another, then abandoned them and rolled each other over and over on the grass.

"Want to come, Suzie?" Leah asked, opening her door.

"I guess." Susan sounded as reluctant as Leah felt, but she got out of the car and walked with Leah toward the woman.

"Mrs. White?" Leah asked, stopping several feet from her.

"Yes," the woman replied politely, leaning the rake against the trash can. "How can I help you?"

Leah smiled, thinking that only someone who'd been a devoted public servant most of her life would ask that. Not a suspicious "What do you want?" but a concerned "How can I help you?"

Leah offered her hand. "My name is Leah Alden, and this is my sister, Susan Blake." Susan remained shyly behind Leah's shoulder, and Marilyn White smiled at her wistfully.

"I've always wanted to look like that," she said, pulling off her gloves. "Blond and willowy. In-stead..." She held her hands away from her plump body and gave Leah and Susan a rueful grin. "And it wasn't any better when I was younger, just a little higher maybe, a little firmer." She sighed, then re-turned to business. "What is it? United Way? Moth-er's March of—"

Leah shook her head. "Nothing like that. We found your name in some letters Iliana Arpad wrote to a friend of her family's many years ago." Leah hesi-tated, expecting it all to fall apart at that moment—that she wouldn't be the right Marilyn White at all, despite all Herbie's assurances. But she saw instant recogni-tion in the woman's eyes. More than that, she saw emotion swell in the soft brown gaze as it narrowed against the cold afternoon wind.

"Iliana," the woman said, her voice no stronger than the wind. She shook her head, a gesture Leah couldn't quite interpret. Refusal? Regret? "That was a long time ago."

"Thirty-one years ago," Leah said.

Marilyn nodded, her expression pensive. "That long? Like so many things that affect our lives, it could have been a lifetime ago or yesterday. But what—?" She stopped, a sudden tension in her stance. She focused on Leah's face, her dark gaze going over it feature by feature. Then her eyes widened and she said again, in a whisper of disbelief, "Leah? Iliana's Leah?"

Leah's throat closed. She had to nod because she couldn't speak.

Marilyn's eyes filled, and a broad smile formed as she put her hands on Leah's arms. "You're so much like her. It does my heart good to look on your pretty face. Can you come inside?"

"We'd love to, but..." She pointed to the car where Jeff and Charlie waited.

"Husband?" Marilyn guessed.

"Yes," Leah replied. "And a friend. We've come from Seaside."

"Then you must be ready for tea and muffins. Bring the men inside. I have lots. Gardening and baking are all I do these days."

Marilyn White's home was a cozy haven in an afternoon grown increasingly windy and dark. Mismatched overstuffed furniture was placed in a U shape facing a brick fireplace. On a thick, rough mantel a dozen framed photographs caught the light as she turned on several small lamps around the room.

"If one of you gentlemen will stoke the fire, I'll put the kettle on." Marilyn pulled off her hat, smoothed the fine strands of silver that had escaped a plump bun at the back of her head and walked purposefully into the kitchen.

Jeff folded to his knees to add a log to the quiet fire, then distributed the embers with the poker. Leah stood behind him, the upper part of her body leaning forward over him to study the photographs. Marilyn didn't appear to be in any of them, nor could Leah find a face that resembled Marilyn's among the many adults and children smiling at her. She concluded that these weren't photos of family. Then, with a little gasp of surprise, she found a photo of her mother.

"Jeff, look!" She tugged on his shirtsleeve until he got to his feet, dusting his hands off and looking down at the photo she held. It was Iliana in a plain camel coat and simple shoes. She stood alone on the small lawn of a little house. Leah saw the difference in her face immediately. It was no longer the youthful face of the young Iliana in ethnic dress. It was a more mature, knowing face. Still, none of the sadness Leah had read in her letters was visible in her eyes. She looked as though she might be in her early twenties. She was smiling at the camera, or whoever was behind the camera, and Leah knew with sudden certainty, with that echo in her blood that seemed to cause her as much pain as joy, that Iliana had done it. "She found Janos," Leah whispered. "Look at her face."

"Yes, she did." Marilyn bustled into the room, a tray laden with plates, forks, a platter of fat muffins and a teapot, its spout steaming with some aromatic brew. Jeff took the tray from her and placed it, as she directed, on the old trunk used as a coffee table. Marilyn poured as her guests sat down, Leah and Susan on the love seat. Next to it, nearer the fire, was a chair with a pair of glasses folded on a Sidney Sheldon novel on its arm. Jeff and Charlie sat at opposite ends of a sofa on the other side of the trunk. Marilyn distributed plates, forks and napkins, then passed the muffins. "I hope Earl Gray tea's all right," she said, pointing out a particularly plump muffin to Charlie. "I never could drink coffee." She sniffed the air appreciatively. "Doesn't that bergamot give off a wonderful aroma?"

Leah didn't think she could swallow anything more than the fragrant tea, but, afraid to hurt the woman's feelings, she selected a domed blueberry muffin. Susan sat quietly beside her, smiling when she turned to her, the gesture intended to be supportive and reassuring. Leah patted her knee in gratitude.

Marilyn took the chair, turning her body away from the fire so that she could look at Leah. "Now," she said, as though deliberately putting aside the social niceties and getting to the point, "what do you need from me?"

Briefly Leah told her about the photo Susan had found and the search it had begun, about her visit with Gerda Szabo and the discovery that Leah was the baby in the photo and that Iliana, the daughter of the family Gerda had worked for, was her mother. She told her about the letters and how often and affectionately Iliana had mentioned the caseworker who'd helped her in so many ways.

"In the last letter she wrote to Gerda," Leah said, "she told her that she'd given me up because she couldn't make enough money to see that I had what I needed and she couldn't find my father. She said you'd found a family to adopt me."

Marilyn nodded sadly, her dark eyes remembering. "Your mother was so young and so alone. She tried hard to be brave, but it was almost impossible for her, with her meager knowledge of English, to earn enough to pay child care and still provide everything you needed. When it seemed that Janos had disappeared off the face of the earth, Iliana decided the best thing she could do for you was give you up." Marilyn sipped her tea and swallowed with difficulty. "Please never think it was a decision she made lightly. She loved you so much. She was very ill afterward. For weeks I thought she would just give up and die. But she went on. There was simply nothing else to do."

She drained her tea, then held her cup out toward Charlie, giving him a charming smile. "Would you bring me more, young man. Thank you. Once I'm settled, these old bones can't be disturbed without painful complaint. Help yourself to another muffin. You're a growing boy. Now, where was I?"

"She went on because there was nothing else to do," Susan prompted.

"Yes." Marilyn sipped. "Iliana managed for another year, though she was never very well. I kept a close eye on her." She sighed. "I never married, you see. My clients took all my time and energy. And Iliana was special. I looked into those great, sad eyes and knew she'd simply lost too much, too young, been too hurt to make it on her own. I determined to try again to find Janos. On a hunch I checked the armed services through the Red Cross. We found him."

Leah stroked a finger over the glass on the photo she still held in her lap. Pain, joy, relief rolled inside her, one emotion uppermost, then the other. "You can tell by her smile in this photo," Leah said to herself. She didn't realize she'd said it aloud until Marilyn responded.

"Yes, you can. Janos took that picture when they were stationed in San Diego."

"They got married, after all?" Susan asked.

"Yes." Marilyn smiled, then grew serious. "Janos, thinking Iliana no longer cared because she hadn't answered his letters, joined a fishing crew in Alaska as a cook. He'd been sent away when Iliana's pregnancy was discovered. He hadn't known she'd been sent to a home for unwed mothers and disowned by her parents. Because her mother intercepted his letters, Iliana, of course, had no idea he'd written over and over and twice sent her money to join him in Portland. By the time she had you, Leah, she borrowed money from Gerda and made her way to Portland, figuring it was where he'd gone. But, of course, he was in Alaska. He spent a year there, then joined the navy."

"How could any parents be so cruel?" Susan demanded in quiet indignation.

"Oh, Susan." Marilyn shook her head. "Abominable things are done in the name of judiciousness and morality. Sometimes people prop up their own fragile identities by making a bold display of stamping out someone else's frailties. Iliana's parents had been important people reduced to the status of immigrants in a place that treats everyone the same. Perhaps they took out their disappointments on her."

Susan put an arm around Leah, as though to comfort her for what her mother had been through. "So were they happy when they finally found each other?"

Marilyn's smile returned. "Very. It broke their hearts to leave Leah with the Blakes, but the adoption was final by then. They felt they'd already done her enough harm and didn't want her to suffer anymore." Marilyn gave Leah a gentle look. "I was in touch with the Blakes, and they couldn't thank me enough for having found you for them. Iliana knew how much they loved you, and she and Janos decided it wouldn't be fair to take you from what you knew as your family. They comforted themselves with the thought that they could have more children.''

Marilyn took a last sip of tea and placed the cup on the right arm of the chair. Then she turned back to Leah with an expression both gentle and sad. Leah felt a pain begin to grow in her middle. No, she thought, trying to ward off what she knew was coming. Please, no.

''Janos stayed in the navy, and they continued to try to have a baby. But as cruel fate would have it, when Iliana finally became pregnant, Janos was assigned to Vietnam. He moved her in with friends in Mc-Minnville before he left.''

McMinnville. Four bodies straightened in their chairs.

Leah turned to Susan, who stared at her for a moment, apparently afraid to reach the obvious conclusion.

Marilyn said quietly, ''You were the baby born in McMinnville, Susan.''

Leah watched the shock flare in Susan's eyes, felt her own body tremble deep inside with the truth she'd never suspected. Susan put both hands to her mouth, covering a sound that was impossible to identify as pleasure or grief. Tears fell onto her hands, and Leah wrapped an arm around her.

''But how did we come to be together?'' Leah asked Marilyn, confused.

Jeff, already suspecting the substance if not the details of the answer, came across the room to stand behind Leah. He put his hands on her shoulders and suddenly she, too, knew. Tears began to fall freely. Marilyn was crying, too.

"Late in the summer of that year Janos was reported missing in action." Leah clutched one of Jeff's hands, holding tightly to Susan with the other. Everything inside her seemed to settle into a cold puddle of grief. But she listened to Marilyn, needing to know every small detail.

"A week after Susan was born, Iliana developed an infection, and I think at that point..." She shook her head, obviously fighting for composure.

Charlie carried the teapot across the room, refilled her cup and handed it to her. She took a long, slow sip, then a deep breath. "She was just too weak and tired and beaten to fight anymore. When she was dying, she begged me to see that Susan was placed with Leah. The Blakes agreed, but as you, Leah, were now twelve years old, it seemed best to leave your relationship and the past a secret."

As Susan sobbed on her shoulder, Leah sat perfectly still, feeling the doomed spirits of the parents she'd never known. It was indeed a cruel fate that could take something that began as love in flower and turn it into one tragedy after another until one lover died an unspeakable death in a foreign jungle and another in a hospital bed, broken and alone. For a moment her grief was almost more than she could stand.

Then Jeff asked quietly, "So Janos is dead also?"

"I'm not sure," Marilyn replied. Susan's head came up, and Leah turned toward Marilyn. "That is, he came home from Vietnam when the prisoners were freed in 1973. When he learned Iliana was dead, he got in touch with me to find out about the baby." Her voice broke, and she went on softly, "He wept when I told him she'd been placed with her sister."

"He's alive," Susan whispered, clutching Leah's arm.

"He didn't seem at all well to me," Marilyn cautioned. "He'd been living for two years under conditions we can't even imagine—and wouldn't want to. He was a man over six feet tall, weighing only about 140 pounds. His complexion was ashen, and he was hollow-eyed. And it's been sixteen or seventeen years since I've spoken to him."

"Do you have any idea where he went?" Jeff asked.

Marilyn closed her eyes to think, a frown marring her forehead. "I've such a poor memory these days." She rubbed a forefinger on the frown lines. "He said something about going to... Washington. He and a friend he'd been in the prison camp with were going to..." She shook her head angrily. "Oh, I can't remember!"

"Did he go back to fishing?" Jeff prompted.

Marilyn snapped her fingers and sat forward in her chair, her eyes bright. "He joked that he never wanted to see another boat as long as he lived. But his friend's family owned a restaurant. That was it! In Spokane, I think. Or was it Seattle? He said he would keep his feet on solid earth from now on." Her enthusiasm dimmed, and she looked candidly at Leah and then Susan. "I want you to find him, girls. I really do. But I want you to be able to bear the disappointment if you don't. He was ill when he came here. And learning that Iliana was dead took what little light there was out of him. You have to consider," she said softly, thickly, "that he might not have made it."

Susan sobbed, and Leah let Charlie take her sister's weight as he sat on the arm of the love seat. Leah nodded grimly. "Yes, I know." Her father and mother seemed to have been doomed to tragedy the moment they fell in love. Would the darkness that pervaded his life allow him to still be out there somewhere, waiting to be found by the daughters he'd never once laid eyes on? Leah's shoulders sagged. She couldn't muster the spirit to believe it.

Susan reached out to touch her arm. "Maybe," she wept, "he...just went on because there was nothing else to do. Like our mother did."

"That's right." Jeff stroked Leah's hair, then gave it a playful tug. "If you get your determination from him, he's probably governor of Washington by now. Marilyn, may I use your phone?"

"Here." She offered her hand. "Pull me out of this chair and I'll show you where it is."

Jeff obliged her and they disappeared into the kitchen together. Charlie, still holding Susan, leaned across her to squeeze Leah's arm. "If he's out there, Jeff will find him," he said confidently.

Leah nodded blankly, unable to absorb the words through an almost overwhelming sense of loss. Iliana was dead. Janos wouldn't have wanted to live.

"You don't believe he's alive, do you?" Susan asked, her voice tight with emotion.

Leah wanted to reassure her that she did, but the words just wouldn't form. Still, years of big-sistering made her try to point out the positive. "This has never been that important to me, except that now I see it from a different perspective." She squeezed Susan's hand. "We're sisters by blood. It isn't the fact that we have genes in common, but that we come from the same two people who loved each other and—" her voice faltered and she drew a breath to go on "—tried so hard to be together. That's very important to me now."

Susan fell against her, sobbing, all efforts to be strong and think positive defeated by the facts. "He's dead, isn't he?" she cried. "I know he is. And he never saw us—either one of us. That's so sad."

Cold, hard truth found a place inside Leah and settled in. Her tears dried up. Emotion swelled for one awful, painful moment, then fell in on itself, deflated. It was over.

Jeff walked back into the room, his expression quiet. Over Susan's head Leah looked at him inquiringly.

"I just checked Information for Spokane and Seattle on the chance that Janos Nagy might be listed." When she raised an eyebrow, appearing only politely interested, he studied her for a moment before he answered the unspoken question. "Nothing. But he could have an unlisted number."

She dismissed that possibility with a shake of her head and a stiffening of her shoulders that caused a small niggle of alarm to begin at the base of Jeff's spine. "The operator would have told you that."

Leah stood up, brisk and businesslike, as though they'd all come to discuss insurance or aluminum siding. She gave Marilyn a quick hug. "Thank you, Marilyn, for your time. I know this wasn't easy for you, but I appreciate your sharing what you know with us."

Jeff saw Marilyn's blink of surprise, Susan and Charlie's glance up at Leah. "Well, of course, dear," Marilyn said politely. "Now that you know how to reach me, call or come by if there's anything else I can do."

It was dark and cold as they trooped out to the car, Marilyn following behind to stand under the tree and wave them off. They decided against staying the night in Portland—that is, Leah did.

"I have to be at the office in the morning," she said in a tone that was calm and reasonable and contributed greatly to Jeff's rising unease. "And you do, too, don't you?"

"Not necessarily," he replied.

"If you run a business," she said flatly, "you should be there."

They also decided against stopping for dinner—that is, Jeff did. Susan was sobbing in Charlie's arms in the back seat. For some reason he didn't understand, Leah had retreated into her old persona that was all edges and no soft places. And his stomach was rapidly filling with panic.

Come on, he told himself bracingly. *It isn't like you to jump to conclusions. This doesn't mean the old Leah is back, just that the new one is upset and confused. She needs time. And you're good at waiting around.*

But he felt the wind blowing through the breach between them. Just this morning he would have sworn that nothing could separate them again. Now he wasn't so sure.

With Charlie dropped off at his place, Jeff pulled into the driveway behind Leah's car and turned off the engine. The sudden silence filled him with a strange sense of finality.

Leah went ahead to open the door and turn the lights on, and Jeff helped Susan out of the car and up the porch steps. "Do you think he's alive?" Susan whispered. Leah could be heard in the kitchen, checking her answering machine.

"I think there's a chance," he replied frankly. "Possibly slim, but a chance."

Jeff smiled at her and lifted her off her feet. "I'm going to keep looking," he promised. "If he's alive, I'll find him. Meanwhile, you need to settle down, get some sleep and try to pick life up where you left off. If he's alive, it could still take a while to find him. If he isn't, then you have to think about the rest of your life. Okay?"

"Okay." With a sigh Susan leaned her head against his shoulder. When he deposited her at her bedroom door, she gave him an extra hug before letting him go. "Thanks, Jeff. I love you."

He kissed her cheek. "I love you, too, sis. Good night."

Leah was already in the shower when he reached their bedroom. Wearily he pulled off his clothes and tossed them onto the chair she had put back in its place. In T-shirt and briefs, waiting for his turn in the shower, he put his briefcase on the bed and opened it, pulling out his calendar to check the next day's schedule.

He was relieved to see nothing of earth-shattering importance on it. He'd be preoccupied tomorrow; he could already tell. Leah would probably come out of the bathroom in a few minutes, in the tailored blue pajamas he used to hate, give him a look of vague surprise as though she wondered what he was doing cluttering up her life, then peck him on the cheek. She would pull the blankets back neatly, methodically fluff her pillow and say good-night. Then she would lie precisely in the middle of her side of the bed and go to sleep. Tomorrow he'd be wondering how to save his marriage.

When the bathroom door opened, he tossed the calendar back into his briefcase, snapped it closed and put it aside. Then he turned, bracing himself for that look so that when she gave it to him he wouldn't throttle her. But he was probably the one wearing a look, he thought an instant later—an adolescent, dumbstruck look.

She wasn't wearing the tailored pajamas. She wasn't wearing anything. Her lush, ivory breasts and softly rounded hips turned his will to mush as she came into his arms, fragrant, warm and faintly moist from the shower. He was aware of one moment of strong confusion before even that sensation muddied, and he could focus on nothing but the woman he held in his arms.

Leah's fingers went into his hair. "Are you tired after that long drive?" she whispered in concern.

"No," he replied softly against her ear. He could feel her pulse beating hard against his cheek, and it spurred his own body's tempo. "You?"

Her answer was to let her body fall backward, pulling on his neck as her knees went slack. He sank with her into the cool, silky spread, then farther into the deep, dark magic of night-long lovemaking.

CHAPTER THIRTEEN

JEFF HAD NO IDEA what the hell was going on. He'd been right about one thing. He was preoccupied and virtually useless at the offices of Alden and Foster the following day.

He wasn't sure if his marriage was in trouble. But another night like last night and his mind would be in trouble. And his body. He and Leah had driven each other from one side of the bed to the other, from the head to the foot and back again, changing positions, techniques and probably the orbit of the earth. Then she'd left the house this morning in a white blouse and a navy blue suit, briefcase in hand, with a perfunctory kiss for him while he shaved, and a blasé "See you tonight."

God.

He didn't understand what she was feeling, except that, logically, it must involve grief and pain. Just why that had turned her into a demon in bed, he wasn't sure.

Decisively he dialed Herbie. He had to find Janos Nagy or know for certain that he hadn't survived the countless tragedies of his life. He had no idea why, after this painful search, Leah had suddenly chosen to consider it over without conclusive evidence. But, hopefully, when they knew Janos's fate, one way or the other, they could make some sense of their lives together.

FOR THREE DAYS Leah worked day and night, too busy for lunch or breaks. She covered for Sandy because she was moving back in with Jack—and had sprained her right hand in the process. Diane Hankins's novel was within ten days of deadline with two hundred pages still to be put on the word processor. Leah clung to the work as salvation.

Pressure was building inside her until she felt like a boiler with a faulty release valve. Her natural parents were dead, and she'd accepted it. She and Susan were natural sisters, and that was a bonus for which she was very grateful. She and Jeff had resolved their differences and picked up the threads of their marriage. She should be able to resume a normal life again. But that didn't seem to be happening.

Outwardly she was the cool, efficient woman she'd been before the search had begun. It had always been her style to do a dozen things at once, and she appeared to have retained the skill. With a staff still one woman short she managed to see that all jobs were covered, and when that meant she had to go on a call, she did all the in-office jobs like the Hankins manuscript and mailers by herself after hours. Minding Your Business hummed like a well-oiled machine, but there was a squeak in its owner that was rapidly building into a scream. Hysteria lay just inside her cool facade, a breath away from manifesting itself.

She kept it under control by releasing the pressure with her nightly lovemaking with Jeff. Wrapped in his arms, she divested herself of all her tensions, and he willingly absorbed them, driving her as she drove him until for several blissful moments she forgot that scream held under its fragile lid. Then he would cushion her head on his shoulder and settle down to sleep, and it would all start coming back—the tension, the panic, the fear she didn't understand.

Leah blinked at the green letters on the dark screen of her computer monitor as they blurred into an indistinguishable smear. She closed burning eyes and opened them again, hoping the letters would come into focus, but they didn't. She let her head fall back, then forward with a little groan as every cramped muscle from her neck to her waist protested the movement.

"You coming home sometime tonight? It's almost midnight."

Jeff's voice behind her made her turn in her chair, then wince when her neck stiffened. He came into sharp focus, long and lean and vaguely dangerous to her carefully capped nerves. He wore jeans and a short leather jacket open over a black turtleneck. He paused in the doorway to her office, his eyes dark with an expression that mingled impatience with concern and just a trace of that look that told her he understood things about her she didn't know herself.

She smiled wearily at him across the office. "Hi. I forgot to look at the clock. I'm sorry." She turned back to the computer, entered the command to save, then shut it down. She stood to reach for the plastic cover and gave another little groan when her shoulders cramped.

Strong fingers settled on them and began to knead. Leah let herself go limp, the cover hanging from her hand, forgotten, as Jeff massaged her. Dexterously he rubbed across her shoulders to her neck, back to the subtly rounded joints, then in again. With his fingers gripping her collarbone, his thumbs worked circles over her shoulder blades.

"Ah!" Leah cried out when he touched a particularly stiff knot.

"Sorry." He pushed her toward the small tweed sofa that had come from their first apartment, eased her facedown onto it and sat on the edge at her hip.

He pulled the prim blouse out of the waistband of her skirt and pushed it up to her bra line. Then he bracketed her waist with his hands and began to work his thumbs along her spine. She alternately groaned and sighed, shifting as his touch brought pain one moment and relief the next.

Her eyes closed, her awareness beginning to drift, Leah raised her head when Jeff said, "Sylvia Dunwiddie called."

This time her groan had nothing to do with Jeff's ministrations. "She's leaving him again."

He laughed softly. "No. She's staying. They want us to come for dinner tomorrow night."

Leah opened her eyes at that and raised herself on her elbows to look at him over her shoulder. "Really? Why?"

His right hand continued to rub, even though she had turned. "They seem to think they owe their reconciliation to us."

Concealing a grin, Leah laid her head back down on her arm. "Really?"

Jeff gave her bottom a light swat. "Don't play the innocent. I know all about your creative deployment of troops when he called you for an office temp."

With a mellow laugh she rolled onto her back. "I thought it was very resourceful of me."

The small, covered buttons on her blouse slipped free of their buttonholes with her turn, and the silk separated over a lacy white bra that seemed not quite filled until she sat up. Then smooth ivory flesh swelled out, and he lost his train of thought for a moment.

Her actions had been deliberate, he was sure. She'd been working him over in just this way all week— sweetly but ruthlessly engorging his senses with her charms. Every time he thought he was on the brink of understanding her behavior, she stroked him or moved against him, and the answer eluded him again.

Leah met his eyes and saw the knowledge there that he was onto her. Not completely, but close. Guilt tried to rise in her, but she forced it down, choosing instead to look him in the eye and let him see that her desire for him was insatiable. Did a wife have to explain a lust for her husband?

As Leah leaned forward to capture his mouth while pushing his jacket off, Jeff realized they weren't even going to make it home tonight before he was lost to her yet again. His wits began to scatter as she pulled his face to her breasts and fell backward, bringing him with her. As delicious as her sudden insatiability was, he thought, he had to find the reason for it. He was beginning to feel like a man who should be paid when the evening was over.

LEAH LOOKED UP at the knock on her office door. Milly peered around and smiled. "Diane Hankins wants to know how you're coming with her manuscript and if there's any way she can have it by Friday." When Leah looked back at her blankly for a moment, Milly said helpfully, "Today's Wednesday."

Leah sighed. "I only have fifty pages left, but I have a full day tomorrow and a mailing to do tomorrow night."

Milly shrugged. "Then I'll tell her no. I'm sure she'll understand. This is three days earlier than what you'd agreed upon, anyway."

"No." Leah stopped her before she closed the door. "Tell her she can have it. I'll just do it tonight."

"You're going out tonight."

"Not anymore. When you're finished with her, get me Jeff, please."

Milly sighed, frowned and closed the door.

Several moments later Milly buzzed with her call.

"Jeff, I can't come tonight, after all," Leah said, her tone exaggerating a disappointment that was completely false. "I have to get that fantasy manuscript out by Friday, and I've already told you what tomorrow is going to be like. Will you make my apologies to the Dunwiddies?"

"No." The answer was swift and unmistakably nonnegotiable. "I'm picking you up in an hour."

Bristling, but remembering just in time that combative behavior only made him more stubborn, Leah said reasonably, "Jeff, this isn't a gift shop. I can't just close the door and go home at five o'clock. I have respon—"

"Susan can do it tomorrow," he interrupted.

"Susan has a broken leg."

"Susan doesn't type with her leg."

Leah gripped the phone with both hands and drew a breath. But before she could offer a retort Jeff continued quietly. "You've used her as an excuse for working eighteen hours a day for the past week. She's asked you twice to give her something to do at the office.

Maybe she can't go out on a job, but she can certainly sit at the word processor and finish the manuscript."

Forgetting her own psychology, she asked loudly, "When did you give up the law for office services? If I want to work eighteen hours a day, I don't need an excuse, nor your approval!"

"Jordan Dunwiddie works longer hours than that, but he chose to make some time in his life for you—to thank you for helping Sylvia. I'm sure you can find time to accept his gratitude." Leah recognized his courtroom voice and, for a moment forgot her stiff anger in her fascination with its deep-timbered intimidation. Knowing the warm and open, if sometimes deplorably stubborn man behind the voice, she found it amazing that he could pull off the other persona so successfully. "I'll be by to pick you up at five-thirty. Be ready or be prepared to explain to downtown Seaside why you're being carried out of your office like a load of salmon. See you."

Leah slammed the receiver down with a growl. But anger changed instantly to panic. She couldn't go to the Dunwiddies and while away a lazy evening with talk of love and marital adjustments. The scream would erupt. The terrible tension would snap and...and then what? That was the worst part. She didn't know. She would probably be sent to a mental hospital because she'd never be able to explain to anyone what was happening in her head. Or in her heart. She couldn't remember ever being so frightened.

True to his word, Jeff was at the office at 5:30. Unwilling to give him the satisfaction of thinking he'd managed her, she pretended there had been no problem to begin with.

"I spoke to Susan," Jeff said, standing aside as she locked her files, "and she'll be happy to come in early tomorrow and stay until the manuscript is finished."

Without looking at him she crossed the office, dropped her keys into the open purse on her desk, then slung the black leather pouch over her shoulder. "That was kind of you," she said evenly.

"You need a break," he said to her back as she went to the small table where she'd placed a bouquet of cut flowers she'd bought for their hosts.

She gave him a quick guileless glance as she crossed to the door. "It appears I'm going to get one. Are you coming? Or would you like to be seen leaving the office like a load of salmon?"

Jeff walked lazily toward her, willing in his testy mood, to meet the challenge she'd thrown out. "Think you could do it?"

She gave him a bland smile over her shoulder as she headed for the outer door. "I'd happily die trying."

THE DUNWIDDIES' HOME was precisely what Leah had expected. It was draped, upholstered, carpeted and appointed with only the elegant and expensive. There was no pretension about it, simply the unembarrassed extravagance of people enjoying their wealth. She was surprised to find herself comfortable sipping Bollinger and dipping crackers into a colorful vegetable pâté.

Despite the supposed purpose of the evening, Jordan and Jeff spent a large part of it discussing business while Leah sat on a stool in the kitchen, watching Sylvia baste four fragrant game hens. The woman worked with a skill and ease Leah would never have guessed she possessed in domestic matters.

"Did I ever tell you I was a lowly secretary when he married me?" Sylvia reminded when Leah shared the thought aloud. Sylvia looked suddenly stricken. "No offense intended, of course. By lowly I meant..."

Leah waved away any suggestion of hurt feelings. "So what happened when you walked into his office last week?"

Sylvia gave the hens a nod of satisfaction and closed the oven door. She wiped her hands on her blue-and-white striped apron, then pulled it off. Underneath was a black wool sweater with a V-neck adorned with feathers and jewels. It was worn over black silk pants. She looked sophisticated and ready to giggle—a paradox, Leah realized. But, then, that was Sylvia.

"He has this manner in the office, you know..." Sylvia lowered her eyebrows and lifted her chin, affecting an imperious expression. Leah thought of Jeff's courtroom voice and nodded understanding. "And he said, 'Hello, Syl. Have you come to your senses?'"

Sylvia snatched her champagne glass off the island where she'd been working and took a sip. Then she placed it on the other side of the bar from where Leah sat. She folded her arms on the Dutch tile and looked blasé. "Well, I have a look, too," she said, raising a superior eyebrow. "Only I use it mostly when my backhand beans the people in the next court." She swung an imaginary racket. "Or the saleslady refuses to take back the jeans that were roomy enough when I tried them on, but shrunk somewhere between the Junior League Luncheon and the Merchants' Association Banquet." She fixed Leah with the look. "I said, 'No, Jordan. I've come to my assignment. I'm now employed by Minding Your Business.'"

She broke into girlish laughter. "I thought he was going to need CPR. Anyway, the crash course you gave me in new office machines before sending me over helped a lot. I was a model of efficiency. Well, actually..." She looked vaguely guilty for a moment. "There's a quarterly report that I think I accidentally sent with a folder of stuff to New Zealand. But he hasn't noticed it yet, so I'd rather not mention it for a while."

Leah choked on her champagne. "Until the IRS comes to shut him down for not filing? I think you'd better tell him right away." Then, as an afterthought, she asked, "New Zealand?"

Sylvia nodded. "I was ordering a fur. Anyway, we got along politely, and he went out to lunch with your husband. When he came back to the office, he told me he was tired of our silly bickering and that we needed to talk." Sylvia shrugged an elegant shoulder. "That was what I'd wanted all along, so I agreed." She paused, her color rose and she shook her head, her eyes unfocused. "What an indescribable afternoon. Whew!" She came back to Leah with a toss of her head. "Well, after that we did talk. I told him what I wanted, and what I was willing to concede, and he promised he'd be home every weekend and several nights a week. Then he took me out to dinner and we bumped into a friend of his, Bill Webster, who built the Riverside Mall in Astoria. He mentioned a deal they'd made to build one upriver." Sylvia rolled her eyes. "Well, I've been *there* before. When he's onto something new, I don't see him for weeks. So I ran out of the restaurant."

Leah nodded. "Jeff, Charlie, Susan and I were out for dinner that night. We were walking up Broadway when you came out to your car. We saw Jordan get in."

Sylvia twirled the stem of her champagne glass, a self-deprecating smile on her lips. "He took me home and told me I had two choices. If I wanted no part of his life, I could pack my bags and leave and I'd never hear from him again, or I could come to work for him and learn what his life was all about. He said that he had too many projects under way to simply abandon them, but that he'd do his best to ease out of the running of the business if I would just be patient. That's when he explained that one of his men would be supervising the deal with Webster."

Leah reached across the bar to pat her arm. "I'm glad you chose to stay. Jeff has a lot of respect for Jordan."

Sylvia nodded, smiling broadly. "The reverse is true, too. The day Jordan invited Jeff to lunch he was trying to find out just what my status was. He asked Jeff if we were sleeping together."

Leah's eyes widened. Sylvia laughed. "Jeff made him pay for lunch." Then she sobered. "I think he also gave my husband a few things to think about, because he hasn't been this attentive in years." She wagged an eyebrow. "He also hasn't been this forceful. It's been fun."

"I'm happy for you."

Sylvia studied Leah consideringly, then selected a cracker from the platter she'd brought into the kitchen to refill. She covered it with the last of the pâté from the plate and handed it to Leah. She asked candidly, "Did you two have a fight before you came?"

Leah gave her a mildly offended look, surprised she would voice such an observation. Then she decided it was silly to be offended about anything with Sylvia. She explained she'd tried to back out of the evening because of the manuscript and Jeff's reaction.

Sylvia came around the bar to sit on a stool beside her. "You're getting ready to run from him again, aren't you?"

"No, I'm not," Leah denied. For one strange moment she sincerely thought she was being honest. Then she wondered if Sylvia was reading the tension and panic just under the surface of everything she did.

"I've done it enough times myself, Leah," Sylvia said quietly. "I recognize the signs. You've bumped into something you can't handle, and you're back to the stiff little number I met at the Tolovana."

Leah regarded the last sip of champagne in her glass, then drank it down. "Maybe that's who I really am."

"I've seen otherwise," Sylvia said. "Is it the search thing... about your parents?"

"No." Leah helped herself to another cracker and ate it dry, averting her eyes. "We found they were both gone. I'd understood that could happen. I've accepted it."

Sylvia sighed, her expression grave. "I'm sorry. But that doesn't mean you're dead, too, you know."

Again Leah looked at her in surprise. How did Sylvia know that was precisely how she felt? Before she had a moment to reflect on it, Jordan came into the kitchen, the platter that had held vegetable sticks also empty. "You're falling down on the job, Syl," he joked, going to the refrigerator. "At the office this would go on your work evaluation. Didn't I see another pâté in here?"

As Sylvia, grumbling affectionately, went to help him, Leah took the opportunity to escape into the living room. She regretted the action when Jeff, enjoying the moonlit view of the ocean from the French doors that opened onto a patio, turned to her with a smile. That feeling of dangerous contents under pressure that she'd held at bay all evening began to seep through her calm facade. With a forced smile she went into the arms Jeff held out to her and pretended to enjoy the view. She felt as though someone had just lit the end of a long fuse attached to that volatile something inside her.

JEFF FELT THE TENSION emanating from her. They sat in a corner of the plush sofa, his arm around her, her fingers laced in his at her shoulder. She was talking and laughing with Sylvia about a spring cruise to Alaska, but her body felt as though there was no spark of life in it. He remembered the long hours she'd been working and began to feel guilty. Though the pace she'd set this week had been of her own choosing, it was after midnight and she must be exhausted.

"Much as I hate to break this up," he said with a quick glance at his watch, "I have court in the morning and Leah always starts early."

While Sylvia went for their coats, Jordan shook Jeff's hand and gave Leah a hug. It was hard to find the wily businessman or the angry husband of the other night in this congenial and generous host.

"I'm glad you were able to come. We wanted you to know how much we appreciate what you've both done for us." He grinned down at Leah. "You're a clever woman." He glanced up at Jeff with a rueful quirk of his brow. "Watch yourself. That's the most dangerous kind." As Sylvia walked back into the room, handing Jeff his jacket and helping Leah into hers, Jordan inclined his head her way. "I know whereof I speak," he said quietly to Jeff.

She raised an eyebrow at her husband. "Whereof? What are you talking about?"

"Us," Leah said, her smile stiff, but not, Jeff knew, from Jordan's teasing. "He was making a chauvinist joke."

"He called you clever," Jeff pointed out.

"As though it were a dirty word."

"When men are clever," Sylvia said, "it's a sign of wit and genius. When we're clever, we're being tricky."

"That's because you always apply the cleverness to matters that would best be handled in a straightforward way," Jordan said. "That's why you confuse us."

Sylvia sighed at Leah. "They get confused and blame us."

Leah shook her head over the injustice. "Now *that's* clever."

On the way home Leah suddenly started chattering about how unromantic a spring cruise to Alaska would be—not that anyone Jeff knew of had ever dreamed of doing such a thing. Tolerantly he listened to her verbal pictures of guests wrapped in leggings, parkas and woolen hats, reclining on lounge chairs or doing aerobics. "They probably ice-skate on the swimming pool." She gave a dramatic shudder. "In my mind it would never replace a cruise to sunny Mexico." She snapped both fingers over her head, shouting, *"¡Olé!"*

Jeff glanced away from the road to smile at her, knowing that was what she expected. But his mind was busy comparing her amusing "ice cruise" with her behavior since they'd come home from Portland. She'd been more than cozy in bed, but out of it she'd kept him at a careful distance. He'd been trying hard to figure out why, but he was sure the answer, like the woman who was the question, was complex. Still, he was suddenly very tired of the mystery and the position in which it placed him. He wanted an answer. Tonight.

CHAPTER FOURTEEN

LEAH HUMMED LOUDLY while she filled the kettle and pulled cups down from the cupboard. The tune was from a Linda Ronstadt album she kept in the office for the nights she worked late, something about one lover pleading for another to respond if he was "still within the sound of my voice...." But nobody was. Her mother and father were beyond all sound, beyond all efforts to find them, no matter how determined they were.

The picture of her mother on Marilyn's mantel kept flashing in her mind's eye, and she kept forcing it back. She was dead, Leah told herself calmly. The man behind the camera, whose face Leah had never seen, was dead, too. The search was over. She'd thought she'd accepted that. She could put it out of her mind if she concentrated, but nothing would erase Marilyn's voice, saying gently, "You have to consider that he might not have made it." She had to keep humming louder and louder to erase the sound.

The urge to scream her anger was almost over-whelming. She was sure if she'd been a woman who'd spent a lifetime indulging her emotions, they'd have control of her right now. But she knew how to deal with this. She knew how to go on. And she still had Jeff.

A little dart of fear stabbed deep inside her at that thought. Several times tonight she'd turned and found his watchful eyes on her, seeing inside her, reading things, spotting, she was sure, all the inadequacies there.

"You're getting ready to run," Sylvia had said. "I recognize the signs."

Leah put two tea bags in the pot and filled it with boiling water. Sylvia didn't know what she was talking about. She needed Jeff. The only peace she could find these days was in his arms.

She put the tea things on a tray and carried it into the living room, a smile on her face, though her heartbeat suffocated her.

JEFF WAS ON HIS KNEES in front of the fire she'd asked him to build when she entered the room. He didn't look up, trying to keep his thoughts focused, his resolve in place.

He braced himself as her scent floated toward him. The next moment she was on the carpet beside him, her arms wrapped around his neck, her breast pressed against his arm. "Want me to spread a blanket?" she asked softly.

"No." He rose to his feet, pulling her with him, then placing her carefully away. "Tonight we're going to talk instead of making love."

He saw the flash of fear in her eyes. She tried to hide it with a wrinkle of her nose and a sinuous movement of her arms toward his neck. It was almost his undoing. "Can't we do both?"

"No!" he said loudly. She jumped back, her eyes startled. "At least you don't seem to be able to," he added more quietly. "Now sit down."

She turned away from him with a careless shrug and went to the sofa. He took the moment to fill his lungs with air. She was better at this kind of confrontation than he was because she remained calm, and he didn't. But he had to find a way to stay cool. He had to win this one.

She kicked her shoes off and sat on her knees in the middle of the sofa, so that at whichever end he chose to sit, he'd be easily within reach. Her face composed, her eyes blank, she folded an elbow on the sofa back. "Okay, what is it?" she asked casually.

What a gift that detached, vaguely disdainful look was, he thought. It might have fooled someone else, but he saw behind it to the dark turmoil that had been there since they'd come home from Portland. He sat on the arm of the sofa and looked down at her. "That's the question," he said quietly. "What is it, Leah?"

She shrugged delicately. "What is what?"

"What's frightening you so much that you don't really want to know if your father's dead or alive?" he asked. "Why can't you come home early enough that Susan will still be up to talk. And why can't you talk to me? Why are you using me like some treadmill to expel your sweat and energy on, then walking away? What's wrong?"

She'd looked away when he asked the first question, and then she stared at her knees, smoothing her skirt over them. "Nothing's wrong," she answered lightly.

Without raising his voice he demanded, "Then why can't you look at me?"

She sighed and raised her eyes to his. They were vacant of all expression. She pasted on a smile. "Nothing's wrong," she repeated.

He folded his arms. "Now take off the mask and look at me."

She rolled her eyes as though he bored her, then slapped her hand impatiently against the sofa back. "Jeff, you think anyone who isn't sobbing or laughing isn't being honest. You think anyone who's calm is a fake."

"You're not calm," he said, looking deep into the carefully bland eyes and seeing that he was right. "You're a step away from screaming hysteria."

He saw her fight the instinct to get up and walk away. Instead, she sat correctly on the edge of the sofa and began to pour tea. "If that were true," she said, her voice and manner deliberately cool, "it would be my business."

Jeff considered her stiff back and shoulders. "I'm your husband. That makes it my business, too."

"Well, that's always been the problem with us," she said. Her face and her tone held a definite pout as she turned to offer him a cup. He considered those good signs. She was losing the pose. "You have to see inside my head. You have to understand every thought, or you feel left out. That's stifling."

The accusation was calculated to make him angry; it always had in the past. But he understood now that she was right, and he remained calm. He leaned forward to take the cup, then placed it on the coffee table. "That's true. It used to make me crazy that you wouldn't share your thoughts and feelings with me. But now I'm only worried about the feelings you can't share, the ones that seem to hurt you so much. I don't like to see you in pain."

She gave him the first honest look he'd seen in her eyes since that afternoon in Portland. It hurt him to his soul that what he saw was wariness in her face rather than trust. "Sometimes pain has to be a private thing," she said.

"If someone loves you," he said earnestly, "you never have to hurt alone. Tell me what you're feeling."

She growled and slapped the cushion beside her. "I'm just upset, that's all. You know what's happened. In the space of two weeks I've discovered who my natural parents were and that they're both dead. Isn't it natural that it upsets me?"

"You don't know that your father's dead," he reminded her. "And you're not just upset, you've shut down . . . except for sex, and even that hasn't relieved the pressure building inside you. You're about to blow, Lee."

Leah sprang to her feet and marched to the fire. She folded her arms and stared moodily into it, her pretense at control slipping away. "You'd like that, wouldn't you?" She demanded, turning to glare at him. "Ever since you've known me, you've been waiting for me to fall apart. You won't feel like you have your life together until I'm a helpless bundle in your arms and you can take over for me. Well, that's not going to happen!"

That wasn't true, and had never been true, but Leah felt as though she were losing her grip on everything—even the truth. In her mind she heard the loud sizzle of her own fuse.

He looked at her for a moment, his gaze level and calm. Then he stood to join her near the fire. "Is that the reason you're giving yourself for trying to drive me away?"

Something about that question jarred her. "Drive you away?" she asked in disbelief. She spun around to look into his face. He was only inches away, and she felt the warmth emanating from him, almost stronger than the warmth of the fire. Need became a pain inside her. "For a week now I've been trying to show you how... how important you are to me," she whispered.

Jeff raised a doubtful eyebrow. "As a toy? A piece of exercise equipment? A sedative?" He gave her a long, quiet look of censure. "Did you really think I wouldn't notice?"

Ashamed and embarrassed, and angry at him for seeing inside her, she gave him a sarcastic little laugh. "Sorry I frightened you. You can use my nymphomania as cause when you file for divorce. I'm going upstairs—"

He caught her arm as she tried to walk past him. "You're not leaving. And you're not driving me away."

She yanked on her hand, suddenly furious. When he tightened his grip, she swung her other hand at his face. He dodged it easily, turning her. She lunged her body forward, toward the stairs, hoping to break his grip around her waist, but he only tightened it, propping her against his hip and lifting her feet clear of the carpet. Enraged, she screamed, kicking and flailing as he carried her back to the sofa and dropped her onto it.

She was free, but she was still screaming. She heard herself with some surprise, but didn't seem able to stop. Frightened because the sound of her own voice seemed so alien, she made one last attempt to run. Jeff, now seated on the coffee table facing her, yanked her down easily and sat her so that her knees were trapped between his.

Leah let her head fall against the back of the sofa and drew in deep gulps of air, trying to fight back the sobs building in her chest. She wasn't going to lose it now. She wasn't.

Then his hands closed over her knees in a comforting gesture. It was the last thing she'd expected from the hands she'd been unable to escape just a moment ago, and while she was distracted by his kindness, the sobs broke through her defenses. Jeff moved to the sofa and took her in his arms.

"I want my mother!" She wept into his shoulder. "I want to see her, Jeff. Just once."

With no solution to offer her, no balm for her pain, Jeff simply held her tighter.

"I wanted to find her. I wanted to tell her I understood."

"She knows that, Leah."

"I didn't want her to be dead."

"Of course you didn't."

"But for so long I didn't care. I just thought..."

Jeff rubbed gently between her shoulder blades. "Don't torture yourself with that. You had no way of knowing what happened."

Leah sighed and drew a ragged breath. "For two weeks I thought..." She shook her head as words failed her, then struggled on. "We were so close to finding her."

"I know," Jeff said.

"It's just so hard," she went on after a moment. "To know that I'll never...ever...see her."

Jeff bided his time for a moment, understanding that her primal cry expressed only part of the problem. He waited until she relaxed against him. Then he asked, "Why don't you try to find your father?"

She stiffened away from him instantly, but he wouldn't free her. "Because he's dead." She dragged both hands across her eyes and made a desperate effort to compose herself. "I know it. I can feel it."

She looked into his eyes with an expression he understood immediately. *Don't press this,* it said. It was a warning that everything they'd rebuilt in the past two weeks could be gone in a minute.

He didn't think twice about it. Her future was on the line here, and he wasn't going to let her compromise it. He drew his arms away so that he could say what he had to say without being distracted by her, without being tempted to chuck it all and let her remain closed up if it meant she'd stay with him.

"That's just a cover-up, Leah," he said quietly. "The only death we know about for sure is the death of the new you. Didn't last long, did she?"

She drew back and looked at him as though he'd slapped her. Her eyes widened in horror. Her bottom lip trembled. He had to work at remaining unmoved.

"You told me yourself," he went on mercilessly, "that you built your old self out of pieces you thought would be perfect, but that she didn't count because she was manufactured. After you read your mother's letters, there was a new you—open and ready to feel. You'd thought there'd be only good things to feel. You'd find your mother after all these years, and you could expunge your guilt for all the years you didn't care by being a loving daughter now. You'd have all that love."

Leah backed away farther, but he caught her wrist before she could escape completely. "And then you discovered she was dead. That you wouldn't have what you wanted and you'd still have the guilt." Leah stared at her lap, and he shook her wrist to reclaim her attention. She looked up at him with eyes filled with angry tears. "So you shut down the new Leah and brought back the old cardboard one."

She pulled against him, but he held firm. "Then why are you still here?" she asked, her voice deadly quiet. "No one's holding you. You ran away from me once before."

"You pushed me away," he corrected, "just like you're trying to do now."

"Oh, that's right." She laughed without amusement. "Too much sex. That usually draws men closer. You'd think someone who's not wild about putting in a full day's work would have more energy."

"I have the energy," he replied calmly, "but not the stomach for sex that means nothing. I can get that anywhere."

She indicated the door. "Like I said..."

"You'd like me to just walk out of here," he said, resisting another of her attempts to break free, "because then there'd be nothing to remind you of what you can be when you don't run scared. No one to make you think of a family in McMinnville that's still together because love binds them to each other, not plans or schedules or orderliness. No one to remind you of a few days in Beverly Hills that showed you what life is really all about, and I don't just mean our making love. You found the mother who really, truly loved you and the man with whom she'd made you. No one to make you think of a couple of white-haired old ladies who loved others more than themselves."

With a fierceness that surprised him she tore away from him, but he followed her, trapping her between the fire and the stairs.

"For once in your life you opened up," he said, sidestepping toward the kitchen when she tried to get around him, "but you discovered that it costs you to be accessible, that it's scary and it hurts. And you're not going to take that chance again, are you? To find your father you'd have to open up again, maybe let yourself be slapped down with the absolute confirmation that he's dead—and for all your efficiency and organization, you don't have the guts for it. So you just make yourself too busy to bother."

Leah stopped trying to evade him and simply stood still. He watched her freeze over, even her anger hardening into something he couldn't reach. "Perhaps," she said, her eyes, her voice without expression, "you've transferred the importance of a father from yourself to me. You can't deal with your father, so you insist that I find mine."

He sighed, stung. "My father has nothing to do with this."

"Your father has nothing to do with anything," she replied. "You won't let him. Talk about shutting down. Did you ever take a good look at yourself, Jeff? How long are you going to blame your dad for the fact that your mother didn't care? Maybe he worked such long hours because it was preferable to being home."

Jeff shrugged, letting the pain slip over him and slide away. That didn't matter now. "It was his choice. Whatever his reason, he lost me in the process. But your father is Susan's father, too. She wants to find him. Doesn't that matter to you?"

Leah folded her arms. "She doesn't. We talked about it. She thinks it's better to just leave things as they are."

"You talked her into that, you mean," he accused.

"No, I didn't. Look, if you can choose to live without your father, why can't we?"

This argument was growing ugly tentacles, so he got down to the issue at the bottom of it all. He faced her, hands loosely on his hips.

"I won't live with you like this, Leah," he said. He waited for some reaction from her, some small sign that it mattered. He saw tears brim in her eyes. Then she turned away from him to stare into the fire. The line of her shoulders was stiff.

"I thought you said I couldn't drive you away." She said it like a joke, as though she were poking fun at the bold statement on which he already seemed to be reneging.

"You haven't," he said, his voice sounding heavy to his own ear. His heart was leaden; he wasn't entirely sure he could do this. "At least not completely. I'll always love you, and I'll always be there if you need me, but I won't live with you if you're going to close yourself off to me everywhere but in bed."

"I know," she said, quoting him to himself. "You can get that anywhere."

"So can you, Lee." He grabbed his jacket off the back of the chair and went to the door. He hesitated, every breath in his lungs a burden. "Goodbye."

Only years of careful control kept Leah from running after him and pleading with him to stay. Still, she had to turn away from the fire for one last look at his face. It was pale, tight, grim. The scream she'd expelled just minutes ago was there again at her throat. She swallowed it because it was counterproductive, and she had to start all over again—on her own. "Goodbye, Jeff."

He looked at her hard, one long, last moment. Then he walked into the darkness and closed the door behind him. Leah put both hands over her mouth to stifle the sound she'd thought she'd swallowed, then sank to her knees on the carpet. The old control was gone, some terrifying, unmanageable vulnerability left in its place. Doubled over with pain, her head touching the carpet, she sobbed.

"Leah!"

Leah looked up to find Charlie running toward her, Susan hobbling after him as fast as she could. But Smythe reached her first, whining and licking her face as his tail swished, apparently not certain if her position on the floor was cause for alarm or a game.

"What happened?" Charlie asked worriedly, taking hold of her arms and pulling her to her feet. "Are you ill? Did someone hurt you?" He put her on the sofa, and Susan sank down beside her, putting a hand to the teapot. Apparently finding it still hot enough, she poured tea into the empty cup.

Leah watched the steam in mild surprise. Could her life have really fallen apart in less time than it took a pot of tea to grow cold?

"Drink a little," Susan ordered, shooing Charlie toward the kitchen. "There's brandy in that cupboard over the dishwasher. Leah, what happened? Just tell me if you're okay."

Leah nodded, swallowing a mouthful of tea. It spread warmth down her throat and into her stomach, and she felt the barest trace of normalcy return. "I'm okay. I'm sorry I frightened you. It's just..." She drew a deep breath, took another sip of tea and pulled herself together to explain. "Jeff and I had a fight, that's all. He's gone."

"Oh, Lee..."

Leah shrugged a shoulder, feeling emotion swell inside her despite all her efforts to pull the cloak of control around her. It simply wasn't there. "He wants me...us to find our father." She looked into Susan's eyes, saw concern and pain there and took her hand. "You understand, don't you, Suzie?"

Susan closed her other hand over Leah's. "Yes, I do."

"You're not just saying that because I want to let it lie?"

Susan shook her head firmly. "No. I want it to be over. We'll just go on like we were. I've got all the forms to enroll at Portland State for winter term."

Leah hugged her, pleased but saddened. In a few short months Susan would be leaving her, too. In the space of two weeks she'd gone from regaining her husband and almost finding her family to having no one.

Taking charge, Susan sent Charlie home and helped a now-composed Leah up to bed. "I'm going into the office with you in the morning," she called through the bathroom door, turning the bed down while Leah changed into her nightclothes. "I'll finish Diane Hankins's manuscript and help you get caught up. I can work full-time in the office until school."

Leah came out of the bathroom in a pair of tailored blue pajamas. She felt empty and exhausted. "Thanks, Suzie. But I don't want you to wear yourself out. If you can just get Diane's manuscript ready to go, just a few hours a day after that would help me a lot, and you'll still have time for Charlie and having fun before you go to school."

Susan hugged her. "Jeff will come back, Lee," she said bracingly. "I know he loves you."

Leah fell onto the edge of the bed and kicked off her slippers. "No, he won't. He loves me, but he can't live with me because he thinks I'm shriveled up and a coward."

Susan frowned. "Shriveled up? You mean . . . old?"

That would have been easy to agree to at the moment, Leah thought with grim humor. "No, I mean...closed up. Like the old me." She smiled thinly up at her sister. "Did you know there was an old me and a new me?"

"Yes," Susan said. "The difference when you came home from Los Angeles was blinding. Even when I could have killed you for having what I thought I had no part in, I could see the light in you." Her eyes ran over Leah now and grew sad. "It's out, Lee."

Leah looked back at her in momentary dismay. It was one thing to feel dark and dead, but another to know it was obvious to someone else.

Susan encouraged her to lie down and pulled the blankets over her, then sat beside her as Leah had done for her hundreds of times. "Don't worry about it," she said, smiling. "There's a new me, too. I know now that I should have listened to you in the first place. I should never have started all this."

"Sue . . ." Leah propped herself on an elbow.

"All it's brought us is grief. We thought we'd found our mother, then . . ." Her voice broke and she shook her head and drew a steadying breath.

Leah put a hand on her arm. "Susan, I—"

"It's best that the past remain in the past." Susan patted Leah's hand and stood. "It'll be better this way. We'll just put it all behind us. I'm going to stop being such a cheerleader and try to get a better grip on things. Sleep well." She leaned down to kiss Leah's cheek.

"Take your time in the morning. I'll get breakfast. I told Delia she doesn't have to come anymore."

Susan reached for the lamp, and the room went dark. The door closed behind her, and Leah lay alone in the bed, thinking with a feeling of panic that the little cheerleader had just walked out forever. The search had killed something in Susan, too, and Leah felt almost worse about that than she did her own problems.

JEFF JOGGED along the hard-packed sand, Smythe looking back over his shoulder, waiting for the command to cut to the right toward the house. Instead, Jeff pointed ahead. Smythe hesitated, as though he might complain, then caught up and ran on, resigned to the morning's longer workout.

Jeff needed it this morning. It had only been four days, but already he missed Leah so much that it was all he could do not to pack his things and move back in, whichever woman was there—the old one or the new one. But he knew that would assuage his loneliness only temporarily, then her stiffness would infuriate him again and he'd regret going back. No. He had to wait it out. Maybe she'd come around. Maybe she was missing him, too. Trouble was, she could miss him and never let herself believe it. He tried not to think about that; it made him realize how truly hopeless his position was.

Charlie was waiting at the back door when Jeff dragged up the steps fifteen minutes later.

"Longer run than usual this morning?" Charlie asked, handing him a towel.

"Thanks. Yeah." Jeff dried the perspiration from his hair, then looped the towel around his neck. "Had breakfast?"

"No. And I've already invited myself."

Jeff walked into the kitchen to find the table set for two. Orange juice had been poured and a box of doughnuts sat in the middle of the table. Jeff looked at Charlie suspiciously. "You lost the Miller versus Miller report?"

Charlie looked affronted. "Of course not."

"You forgot to pay my parking ticket, and I now owe the city twenty-five dollars?"

Charlie rolled his eyes. "Paid that two days ago."

"Then what?"

"Alden versus Alden," he said, pulling up a chair across from Jeff. "It's affecting the Blake/Barrett partnership."

Jeff frowned at him over a large maple nut roll. "Why?"

Charlie selected an apple fritter from the box, then studied it halfheartedly before looking up at Jeff. "All Susan does these days is work. She's at the office all the time, she won't break for lunch, she stays overtime with Leah, and she's…" Charlie frowned worriedly. "She's different, Jeff. I don't understand it, but I think it has something to do with their dad. She says she doesn't want to find him, but I don't believe her."

"Why not?"

Jeff pushed the fritter away, his blue eyes wide and anxious. "Because she always looks like she's about to cry. She puts on this front of being so busy and so cool, but you can see in her eyes that she's miserable. I don't know what to do."

Jeff gave him a wry look over the rim of his juice glass. "Ain't love grand?"

"Can't you do something?"

"I'm out of Leah's life, Charlie. And I don't want to get between Leah and Susan. They need each other." Even if Leah was turning Susan into a clone of herself, it wasn't his place to interfere.

"So what do I do?"

Jeff shrugged. "Wait. For a large part of my life I've been waiting around for Leah to realize she needs me. But if you feel the need to take more positive action, you have my blessings."

"If I knew what to do, I'd do it. But I don't. So I guess I'll wait with you." Charlie looked glumly at the juice in this glass. "You got any vodka for this stuff?"

CHAPTER FIFTEEN

"COME ON, let's go home." Leah covered the box of letters she was folding into the envelopes Susan was printing out with the computer. "We'll finish this tomorrow."

Susan held up the last floppy disk to be printed out. "We only have one more file. Then we'll be finished. It'll just take an hour."

"It won't gain us anything but exhaustion," Leah said, gathering up Susan's envelopes and tapping them into order in a box. "Tomorrow we can print them out while we're stuffing the rest of these and we won't lose any time."

"But—"

"No." Leah took the disk Susan still held and placed it back in the file. Then she gave her chair a spin away from the computer. "You've been here since seven this morning. I'm so far ahead now that I'll have to give Sandy and Peg two days off next week in order to let the work load catch up. We're going home."

"All right, all right." Susan put on the slip-on canvas shoe she'd kicked off and tugged up the sock that still covered the bare toes of her mending leg. "God, I'll be glad when I get this thing off. It slows me down until I could just scream."

Leah, packing up her briefcase, glanced at her sister in growing concern. The cheerleader had indeed vanished. In her place was a one-legged fiend who did the work of three people and was always looking for something more to do. She'd turned down Charlie's invitations to lunch and the movies and never seemed to entertain a thought that wasn't related to Minding Your Business or her sudden, overwhelming enthusiasm to go to college.

She never giggled anymore. She seldom even smiled. Leah took several steps toward her, looking into the tense and tired contours of her face as she shrugged into a long fleece jacket, and for the first time in their lives saw a similarity in their features. Despite Susan's willowy height and her fair hair and complexion, Susan somehow reminded Leah of herself. She realized what the likeness was, and it struck her like a kick to the ribs. Susan looked tight and closed up, and miserably unhappy. Leah had been looking in the mirror at that same face for days now.

All other concerns put aside in light of her discovery, Leah took Susan's wrist and pulled her toward the sofa.

"What—?" Susan protested, though following docilely. "I thought we were going home."

"In a minute." Leah pushed her down and sat beside her. "What is it, Suzie?"

Susan blinked at her. "What is what?"

Leah heard shades of another such conversation, but put it out of her mind, concentrating on the importance of this one. "What's bothering you?"

Susan looked back at her for a moment, her eyes filled with guilt. Then she dropped her gaze and put a hand to her head. "I'm sorry," she said wearily. "I know how you feel."

Leah frowned at the top of Susan's blond head, an unpalatable suspicion rising in her. "About what?" she asked.

Susan sighed and looked into Leah's face, her eyes apologetic. "About our natural parents."

"Well, my question," Leah said gently, "was what are *you* feeling? Were you fibbing when you agreed that the past should stay in the past?"

"No," Susan replied with all evidence of honesty. Then, with a sigh, she leaned against the back of the sofa and stared at the ceiling. "At least I wasn't lying then. At that point I didn't want to find him." She rubbed absently at her ribs. "But there's like an ache here. I tried to just put him out of my mind, but I can't. The knowledge that our father could be out there is like a shadow I can't outrun." She closed her eyes and a solitary tear slid down her cheeks. "It might be almost easier knowing for sure that he was dead."

Leah began to see through the confusion of her sister's words. "Susan...honey, sit up." Leah pulled on Susan's arms until she sat forward, sniffing and tossing her hair back. "Jeff will put his friend on it if we ask. We can still look for him."

"No," Susan said quickly, shaking her head. "No. I'll get over this. Let's just go on as we are, you and me..."

Seeing herself reflected in Susan's eyes, Leah let herself accept the truth. "You and me working ourselves to death, trying to shake the shadow, trying to get so tired that there isn't time to think about what we could have if we only had the courage?"

Susan's eyes grew wider and more desperate. "No. No, I don't think I could take finding him and..." She closed her eyes against the thought, whatever it was, and shook her head again.

"And what?" Leah persisted, confused now by her sister's reaction.

"Don't you get it?" Susan asked, her voice a loud whisper of pain. "He'll hate me."

Leah gasped in surprise, frowning at her. "What for?"

Susan got to her feet, turning on Leah as she followed. "Because I killed her!" she screamed. "Because they found each other after that awful time of being lost and having to give you up. Then he went to Vietnam and endured God knows what for two whole years. Probably the thought of her was the only thing that kept him going, and then he came home to find that—" Susan's face crumpled and she began to sob, pointing a finger at her own chest "—I killed her. After all that."

"Oh, Susan." Leah wrapped her arms around her and held her, silently making a decision as she let her sister cry. "That's nonsense," she said firmly. "Marilyn said she hadn't been well for sometime. If we're going to go into that kind of blaming, then it was my fault, too. I'm the one who started it all for them. If it hadn't been for me, they'd have both gone on to do whatever they'd planned in the first place."

Susan pulled away and dropped her hands. "You had no control over being conceived," she pointed out reasonably.

Leah raised an eyebrow. "Did you?"

Susan considered that for a moment, then lifted both hands to her face. "No," she said wearily. "But somehow I feel so responsible. And I don't want to see that in his face."

Leah handed Susan her purse and grabbed up her own. "We're going home to get a good night's sleep. Then we'll talk about this tomorrow. I think we're both too tired tonight to make sense."

Susan sighed and dropped her hands. She watched Leah turn out the lights, then followed her to the door. "You always make sense. I've been trying hard to be like you, but I don't think I'll ever have the gift."

Leah gave her a grim smile. "Maybe you're lucky," she said, pulling the door closed behind them, then testing the knob to be sure it was locked. She was just beginning to realize that making sense of a senseless situation was no virtue at all.

JEFF WALKED into his office a full hour early to prepare for court. It wasn't that he'd turned over a new leaf, but his body seemed to have given up sleep, and he'd grown tired of fighting it. With his briefcase in one hand and a paper cup of coffee in the other, he tried to shoulder his office door open. It didn't budge. Right. He'd even beaten the secretaries in this morning.

He put his briefcase down at his feet, delving into his pocket for keys. The door opened, startling him so that he sloshed hot coffee onto his hand. Swearing, he found himself face-to-face with Leah. At least he thought it was Leah. The surprise of finding her in his locked office an hour before Alden and Foster opened for business was less shocking than the sight of her in old jeans, her Portland State sweatshirt, her face without makeup and with her hair scraped back into a ponytail no bigger than his thumb.

She pulled the door open wider. "Come in," she said. "Don't worry about the coffee. I made some. I didn't think you'd mind me using my old key."

Jeff strode to his desk, determined to be as calm as she was, despite her appearance. In reality he was torn between wanting to kiss her senseless and shaking her until she saw things his way. He knew neither approach would work with her, but he couldn't deny himself the satisfaction of entertaining them for a moment.

He watched her walk across his office to the coffeepot. The sway of her round bottom in her jeans caused him to hang his jacket on empty air rather than the brass coat tree at which it was aimed. By the time she'd turned around, carrying two full cups of coffee, he'd retrieved the jacket from the floor, hung it up and taken his place behind his desk.

She handed him a cup, then sat on the edge of his desk, giving him a smile that was barely there. "Good morning."

He leaned back in his chair, his arm stretched out so that two fingers caught the handle of his mug. "Good morning," he replied. "Don't tell me. Your clothes have been stolen, and you need a lawyer."

She sipped her coffee, giving him a reluctantly amused glance. "My clothes haven't been stolen."

"Too bad." Jeff looked disappointed. "Some skinny male midget with designs on a Madison Avenue career is missing a good bet."

Leah sighed. She looked tired, he thought. Maybe she wasn't sleeping, either. "I know you've never liked my clothes. But they're practical and they look professional."

He shrugged and waved aside further discussion of her wardrobe. "What do you want, Lee?"

In his heart she replied, *I want you back, Jeff.* Or, *Jeff, I want to come back to you.*

But she stiffened her spine, frowned into her cup, then looked at him with soft green eyes and broke his heart—again. "I need you to do something for me."

Hurt, he shook his head and shrugged. "Too late. Alan started the paperwork on our divorce yesterday. You'll have to find someone else for your odd jobs."

Her look of horrified surprise was worth the lie—for about four seconds. Then he watched her cave in on herself and felt his own pain doubled by the added burden of hers. She went pale, and her mouth opened to speak, then closed as though she'd thought better of it. She took another sip of coffee.

"Are you divorcing Susan, too?" she asked.

He made an impatient sound, letting her believe the question had trapped him into listening to her request, when he was actually pleased to have an excuse. "So tell me," he said ungraciously.

"She lied about not wanting to find our father," Leah said simply. "The only reason she didn't want to keep looking for him is that she's afraid he'll hate her for causing our mother's death."

Jeff's careful pose of unconcern slipped. "What?"

Leah nodded. "I know. It's silly. But she's a bundle of nerves over this, and frankly..." She sighed and put her cup down, giving him a look he couldn't quite decipher. There was pain in it and longing and emotions too layered for him to identify one by one. "So am I," she finally said. "She was upset, and she thought the way to handle this was to be like me. But it was making her crazy. I could see it."

Leah slipped off the desk and tugged her sweatshirt down, holding on to the hem of it with both hands. "Please," she said politely. "You don't owe me anything. In fact, the scale's overbalanced on the other side. But would you call Herbie and see if he can find out if our father is dead or alive?''

Jeff studied her for a moment, from her short hair pulling out of the minuscule ponytail to her faded jeans, then asked quietly, ''Are you going to be able to deal with this? I mean, you look a little... strung out already.''

''I'm not strung out,'' she said, appearing mildly offended by the suggestion. ''I'm just... loose.'' With the tip of her index finger she wiggled the pen in his desk set back forth. Her voice grew tight and a little high. It sounded anything but loose. ''If he's dead, I want to be able to deal with it. If he's alive, I want to be able to help Susan finish what she started.''

He nodded, wanting more than anything in the world to pull her into his lap and let her cry. But despite her claims at looseness she was tighter than a drum, and he could do nothing but stand by and watch. Well, almost nothing. ''What's this going to do for you?'' he asked softly, knowing she was opening herself to risks she'd rather not face so that Susan would be forced to deal with hers. She'd never been short on nobility.

She shrugged a shoulder, still playing with the pen, and gave a nervous little laugh. ''Kill or cure, I guess. So, will you?''

Jeff reached across his desk, plucked a slip of paper from a crush of notes in a spiral rack and held it out to her. Frowning, she took it from him and read it. He knew the address by heart. ''Janos Nagy,'' it read. ''1511 Pacific Lane, Heron Harbor, Washington.''

She looked at him in astonishment.

''I called Herbie when we got back from Portland,'' he explained, leaning back in his chair. ''I'd never have done anything about it if you hadn't changed your mind. But I hoped you would."

She fell into the client's chair facing his desk and put a hand to her mouth. It was shaking. He watched her eyes go over and over the address before she finally folded the slip of paper and put it in the pocket of her jeans.

"He's alive," she said, her voice reflecting wonder.

"Yeah," he said.

She shook her head. "He must be . . . something."

Jeff had been thinking about that in the three days since Herbie had called with the address. Janos Nagy must be some tough-hided, single-minded hard-nose. No wonder Leah was such a paradox. She was half misplaced aristocrat and half tenacious hero.

She leaned toward him and asked quietly, hopefully, "Will you come with us?"

It never occurred to him to refuse. It would have been easier certainly, but for all his casual, easy ways he never left anything unfinished. He'd started out with her on this quest, and he'd see it through with her.

"Sure," he said. "Tomorrow?"

"Let me talk to Susan, and I'll let you know for sure." She stood up, her shoulders squared under the baggy sweatshirt, her jaw firm. "She might need a little time to adjust to the idea. Do you have any idea where Heron Harbor is?"

"On the coast," he replied. "Almost to the Canadian border. It's a well-to-do community of boaters and sport fishermen."

She nodded, absorbing that without apparent reaction. She gave him a fractional smile. "Thanks, Jeff. I'll call you after I talk to Susan."

He nodded. "Okay."

She shouldered the large satchel that went everywhere with her and went to the door. She pulled it open and started through. Sounds were beginning to filter in from the outer office. Paula and Sally were talking and laughing, file drawers closed, the smell of coffee brewing was everywhere. She turned to look at Jeff, and he saw her make the smallest movement toward him, then abort it, as though she wanted to run into his arms but couldn't quite let herself do it. Against every instinct he remained still. He couldn't take love from her; she had to want to give it. "Bye," she said.

He waved and raised his cup. "Thanks for putting the coffee on."

She gave him a smile that broke his heart a second time. Then she was gone. He fell against the back of his chair, as though he'd just experienced hand-to-hand combat. He put a hand to his chest. Heart-to-heart combat had to be worse. But things were looking up. She'd decided to find her father, after all, to open herself up to all that would mean. And she wanted him along. He let a little bubble of hope rise in him. He wasn't dead yet.

"No, I DON'T need any laundry done for the trip," Susan said, snatching the filmy underwear Leah had taken from the foot of her bed and placed in the laundry basket. She held it protectively against her chest, her expression mutinous. "Because I'm not going. Somebody's got to run the office. We should both be there today, but you're running around here like a chicken with—"

"Her head cut off?" Leah finished, wrestling Susan for the underwear and winning. "You're right. I am. I'm nervous and excited and frightened, and I'm not afraid to admit it. There's something very comforting about losing your head. It makes you think with your heart, and there are some situations where that's the only thing you can do."

She hurried down the hall, then down the stairs with the laundry basket, Susan thumping noisily behind. "What's gotten into you?" she demanded. "If you insist on doing this, the logical thing would be to call him first and see if he wants to see us. He might not, you know. He might have another family."

Leah went through the kitchen to the laundry room, putting the basket on the dryer and opening the lid of the washer. "We'll watch the house first," Leah said, scooping clothes into the machine. "If that seems to be the case, we can call from the nearest pay phone."

Susan folded her arms. "You can't make me go if I don't want to."

Leah added liquid detergent, closed the lid and set the dials. She looked up at Susan, an elbow on the machine, the other hand on her hip. "Who controls your food, shelter and paycheck?"

Susan gasped in indignation. "That's mean!"

Leah nodded without remorse. "You have to do this, Susan, or you'll wonder your entire life what he was like. And you'll kick yourself for not having the guts to find out." She sighed, putting a hand on the empty place just under her breasts. "I have to do it because I've always been afraid to know who I really was. I used to think my parents were selfish and rotten, and I didn't want to be like that, so I created Leah Blake, woman in control. Now that I know what they were like and what they went through for the tiny bit of happiness they had together, the woman I created looks like such a fraud. So I'm afraid, too. I know how you feel. But we have to do this."

Susan's mouth was pursed to prevent its trembling. "What if he does have another family and doesn't want anything to do with us?"

Leah put an arm around her shoulders. "We have another family, too, remember? They're not here, but we'll always have them. And whatever happens we have each other." She smiled into Susan's flushed face. "Come on. Ed and Selena Blake didn't raise a couple of cowards, did they? Let's do this for us. And let's do it for them."

Susan hugged her fiercely, then pulled away and asked conditionally, "Is Jeff coming with us?"

Leah nodded.

"And Charlie?"

"When I call Jeff back, I'll ask him to invite Charlie along."

Susan looked at her for another moment, then nodded. "Okay. But if he doesn't like us, I'm going to tell him this was all your idea."

"And if he does like us?"

"Then I started the whole thing and you didn't want any part of it." She smiled and patted Leah's shoulder. "Excuse me. I have to pack."

THE FIVE-HOUR DRIVE seemed to take an eternity. Refused her post as navigator, Susan drove her companions to distraction with a geographic locations game. "You say the name of a city or a state or a country," she instructed, "and the next person has to say a name that starts with the last letter of the name you said. Ready? Ohio." She poked Charlie to indicate that it was his turn.

"Ohio," he repeated, thoughtfully, taking up the challenge. "Okay, I've got it. Oz!"

"That's not a real place," Susan protested.

"You didn't say the place had to be real."

Susan gave him an affectionate shove. "Okay, Lee, your turn. Something that starts with a *Z*."

Only half-attentive, her mind occupied with controlling an almost debilitating nervousness, she had somehow absorbed the rules of the game. She tried to think. *Z*. There had to be something, but she couldn't call it to mind. Traffic slowed at a congested exit, and Jeff closed his fingers around the nape of her neck. He pulled her toward him, leaning sideways to whisper in her ear, "Zimbabwe."

After the long days without him, the touch of his gentle fingers and his breath in her ear made her look at him without comprehension, her eyes unfocused.

He leaned over again and repeated the word.

"Zimbabwe," she said absently, straightening. The traffic moved, and he turned his attention to it.

"Are hints allowed?" Charlie asked. "I don't think hints should be allowed. Is there a prize for the winner? Did we decide that?"

"Hints are allowed," Susan said cheerfully, "'cause Leah's a little slower than the rest of us." She smiled at her sister, who was alert enough to glower at her over her shoulder.

"Your turn, Jeff," Charlie said. "*E*."

"Eeepanema!" Susan shouted.

Charlie elbowed her with a groan.

"What?" She feigned hurt feelings. "I just said hints were okay."

"Eeepanema?" Charlie laughed.

"It's a beach in Portugal or Brazil or somewhere. There was a song."

Jeff grinned at her in the rearview mirror. "Ipanema starts with an *I,* sweetie. Thanks for the help."

"Geez," Charlie said feelingly. "I hope your father hasn't become an English teacher."

THE TOWN OF HERON HARBOR was strewn along the folds of a piny hillside that dropped to a windy beach. The afternoon had grown cold, and the rain waited overhead in dark, glowering clouds. Leah watched large drops of it plop against the windshield as a gas station attendant popped the hood and checked the oil. Jeff had gone into the service station to ask directions to Pacific Lane. In the back seat, Susan nervously brushed her hair while Charlie patiently held her mirror. No one in the car had said a word since they'd passed the Heron Harbor city limits sign.

Then Jeff was back, the attendant closed the hood, patted it and said, "You're fine." Jeff handed Leah the directions and pulled out of the station onto the little town's quiet main street.

She gave him a look filled with nerves and uncertainty.

He glanced at her with a quick smile, as though he'd felt it even though he hadn't seen it. "You're almost home free," he said. "It's going to be all right."

With Susan and Charlie now involved in a serious discussion over whether she should or shouldn't tie her hair back with a ribbon, Leah asked quietly, "And if it isn't all right?"

Jeff looked back at the road. "Then you have to remember everything you had before this ever came up."

Leah considered that. Ed and Selena Blake would always be Mom and Dad to her. They were the parents of her childhood if not of her blood, and they'd been as good and kind as any child had a right to expect. She'd lost their physical presence, but not their love. That would be with her always.

Before this came up she'd been separated from Jeff for a year, and she'd been lonely and rigid and searching desperately for what was missing in her life. Now that she'd had him back for several weeks, she couldn't adjust to life without him again. Life had no color, no music, no light. He'd been flawlessly polite since the night he'd left. He'd agreed to help her when she'd asked him, but he'd given no indication that he missed her or that he wanted her back. The prospect of the rest of her life without him was too grim to contemplate.

She looked up at the street signs as they neared an intersection, then down at the note in her hand. "Right on Burnham Hill Road," she directed.

He complied, and the car wove down a steep incline to a narrow residential street. Pacific Lane. Leah looked at several blocks of elegant homes, each set back from the street on double lots. There were expensive cars in the driveways.

"Leah?" Susan said in a small voice.

"Yes?"

"I'm scared."

Leah smiled at her over her shoulder. "You're doing better than I am. I'm terrified."

Jeff pulled up in front of a large white plantation-style home complete with columns and veranda. Leah double-checked the address. Susan drew in a noisy breath. "Is this it?"

"Yes," Leah breathed. Her voice had abandoned her, but her heart was beating like a trip-hammer in her breast. For a moment she could do nothing but stare at the house.

"No car in the driveway," Jeff noted.

Charlie pointed through the window. "Could be in the garage. But there are no lights on."

"If he's not home, I'll die," Susan said with all sincerity. "If he is home, I'm going to be sick."

"You're not going to do either," Leah said, forcing herself out the door and to her feet. "Come on. Let's do it."

Susan followed her onto the sidewalk, and Leah looped her arm in hers, not wanting her to run off at the last moment. They went quickly up the walk, up the few steps that led to a colonnaded veranda. Leah rapped firmly on the door with her free hand.

Except for the sound of the surf a quarter of a mile away, the silence was loud. Leah waited for the vibration, for the subtle sound beyond the door that indicated someone was coming. Nothing. She rapped again. Nothing. Susan groaned. Leah felt disappointment rise in her like a shriek.

"We'll have dinner and try again," Jeff said when they returned to the car.

"I don't think I can eat anything," Susan said.

"You skipped lunch," Jeff said. "You can't miss dinner, too. I saw a seafood place just beyond the gas station."

Charlie made a sound of approval. "I'm starved."

At the restaurant Susan played with a cup of chowder and ate french fries from Charlie's plate. Leah nibbled at a shrimp cocktail and finally pushed it away half-eaten.

"What time is it?" she asked Jeff.

He looked at his watch for the fourth time in ten minutes. "Seven-fifteen. We've only been gone from the house twenty-seven minutes. Let's give it a little longer."

She nodded, giving him a grim smile that acknowledged she was being difficult. Silently he put an arm around her and pulled her close to him in the booth.

Jeff drove back to Janos Nagy's address at eight o'clock. There was still no car in the driveway and no light on in the house.

"What do you bet," Susan asked despondently, "that he left yesterday for a month in Europe?"

"Susan," Jeff scolded gently.

"Maybe he's working late or had a meeting," Charlie suggested.

Jeff turned off the engine and settled back in the seat. "We'll wait for a while. If he isn't back in a couple of hours, we'll get a motel and try again in the morning."

Leah thought she might be dead from the tension by morning, or Susan would drive her to murder. Either way, if Janos Nagy did come home, he'd be minus one daughter.

Without waiting to be invited Leah leaned against Jeff, knowing he'd put his arms around her and let her settle in his strong embrace. At this point in their relationship he was only offering comfort and support, but she wasn't proud. She needed it.

Jeff asked Charlie to hand him the jacket Leah had tossed into a corner of the back seat. He covered her with it, tucking the collar in at her neck. She snuggled comfortably and prayed, *Please come home, Janos Nagy. Please come home.*

For an hour every car that passed brought her straight up in her seat. But each went on into the night until there was no movement at all on the street. The quiet neighborhood was asleep. Leah leaned back against Jeff and went to sleep herself.

She was awake in an instant when Jeff stirred. "Is he here?" she demanded, straining to see the dark driveway.

"No. It's almost eleven," he said. "We should find a place to spend the night."

Leah looked longingly at the dark house, wanting desperately to see a light go on and a figure move beyond the window. But there was nothing. She looked over her shoulder at Susan, who also stared at the house.

"Couldn't we wait just a little longer?" Susan pleaded.

Leah turned to Jeff.

He turned in his seat to shake his head apologetically at Susan, then at Leah. "You wouldn't want to give him that kind of shocking news at midnight, would you? It'll probably be hard enough on him as it is."

Leah felt guilty. She'd thought so hard about what finding their father would do for her and Susan and so little about what it would do to Janos Nagy to come face-to-face with the pain of his past.

They found a small motel in a huddle of pine trees back from the beach. Leah and Susan were relegated to one room and Jeff and Charlie to the other. With Susan breathing evenly in the twin bed on the other side of a pale wood telephone table, Leah stared at the ceiling.

She longed for Jeff's arms, for their double bed at home. If she closed her eyes, she could imagine Jeff's sturdy shoulder under her head, his arm across her waist, holding her to him. She could feel her legs entangled with his and Smythe's weight on them. But in the face of this mission, imagination was short-lived and reality returned to remind her that she was alone in a single bed. And the sleeping arrangements had nothing to do with the impropriety of letting Susan and Charlie share a room. She had been alone in her bed at home for a week now, and she would be alone when this was over, because she'd found it so difficult to be the open, sharing woman Jeff wanted.

But she was changing. Necessity was changing her. She'd finally seen in Susan that running from reality gained you no ground. But was the change too late to save her marriage? A cold finger of dread ran down her spine when she remembered that Jeff had filed for divorce. Proceedings could be easily stopped if he wanted to stop them, but would he? What guarantee would he have that she could finally be a warm half of this relationship, that she could let him be what he was and soften her own inflexibility so that she could enjoy it in him and love him for it? None.

Leah rolled onto her stomach and buried her face in her folded arms. Organization and compulsive attention to detail might run a business, but they guaranteed nothing, she realized, in a man/woman relationship—except that one would see it in organized detail when it all fell apart.

IN THE NEXT ROOM Jeff, still dressed, sat in a chair near the small window and looked out at the neon sign that flashed Vacancy. Charlie lay on his stomach on one of the single beds, dead to the world.

Jeff wondered if Leah was asleep. Probably not. She was trying hard to be calm so that Susan would remain calm, but he could see that she was ready to scream with the frustration of being so close to finding her father and having him just out of reach.

He wished he could hold her in his arms tonight, but he knew that even without Charlie and Susan along they might not have shared a bed. He wouldn't have assumed, and he was reasonably sure she wouldn't have asked. She had other things on her mind right now. A solution to their difficult marriage was probably on a back burner somewhere, waiting for time and quiet to work it out.

Anyway, much as he wanted to, he wouldn't make a move toward her until she made one toward him. She'd sent him away twice. She would have to be sure what she wanted before he came back. She had to need him.

There was suddenly a commotion from Charlie's bed as he turned over, punched his pillow into order, then fell back against it with a disgusted groan.

"Can't sleep?" Jeff asked, drawing the curtain closed.

Charlie sighed. "Injustice keeps me awake."

"Injustice?"

Charlie raised himself on an elbow and regarded Jeff with a frown. "Yeah. I finally get to a motel with two beautiful women and end up sharing a room with *you.*" He fell back with another groan. "I wonder if Vincent Bugliosi needs an office clerk?"

Jeff reached a leg out to kick the foot of Charlie's bed. "Shut up and go to sleep."

"Where do you think he is?" Charlie asked soberly.

"Vincent Bugliosi?"

Charlie made an impatient sound. "Janos Nagy."

Jeff stood up and stretched. "Got me. But pray that he's home in the morning."

"We should be there early in case he did come home last night but leaves for work really early."

"Yeah. I set my watch alarm for 5:30."

"Am I getting overtime for this?"

Jeff smiled in the dark. "You're not even getting straight time. I've been buying all your meals and putting you up. What more do you want?"

As Jeff walked around to his bed, he heard an indignant sputter from the other one. "Susan never thinks she can eat, so she doesn't order anything. Then she picks off my plate. This mattress is lumpy, that Vacancy sign will probably flash in my brain for the next three weeks, and I'm going to wake up at 5:30 in the morning, looking at your face. Talk about perks of the job."

In T-shirt and briefs Jeff climbed into his bed. Charlie was right. The mattress was lumpy. "I paid your tuition for next year," he said.

There was loud silence for a moment, then Charlie's voice demanded, "What?"

"I paid your tuition for next year," Jeff repeated, settling into the pillow, which was also lumpy. "So you can study straight through without having to take a semester off to work to pay your way through the next one. If you save your money this year, you'll be able to afford a few luxuries—like a truck that runs."

"It runs," Charlie said, mildly defensive. "Well, not in reverse, but it runs. Jeff, I . . ."

Jeff closed his eyes and tried to clear his mind of images of Leah alone in her bed. "I just thought it would be a good investment. You're going to make a good lawyer, and you're probably going to end up as my brother-in-law. It's in my best interest to get you educated.''

"Jeff..."

"Good night."

"Thanks."

"Shut up."

CHAPTER SIXTEEN

JANOS NAGY WAS HOME. At least there was a late-model Volvo in the driveway.

"Oh, God, oh, God, oh . . ." Susan muttered in the back seat of Jeff's car.

Leah closed her eyes, forcefully mustered courage out of the depths of a tenacious cowardice, then opened her eyes and turned to Jeff. "Tell me again," she said in a small voice, "that it's going to be okay."

Unable to resist the impulse, he cupped the back of her silky head in his hand and planted a quick, firm kiss on her lips. "It's going to be okay. And if it isn't—" he paused for a moment, looking deep into her eyes "—well . . . it will."

Leah wanted time to read every subtle complexity she saw in his gaze, but he was reaching across her to open her door and Susan was getting out of the car.

Susan had brushed her hair until it shone, and wore a pale pink suit that highlighted her fair features and underscored her willowy beauty. "Do I look okay?" she asked, fluffing her hair. Leah noticed that her hand shook. Her own was wrapped firmly around the strap of her purse because her hand also seemed to have a mind of its own.

"You look beautiful," Leah said.

Susan reached out to pat Leah's hair into place and give her a frail smile. "You do, too." She pulled up the collar of the white shirt under Leah's teal-blue coat-dress.

Leah took Susan's arm and started up the walk. She stopped halfway, succumbing to panic, and looked back at the car. Jeff and Charlie were leaning against the rear fender. They waved encouragingly.

Leah walked on, now almost dragging Susan. They went up the few steps and stopped in front of the door.

"Do you want to knock?" Leah asked.

Susan shook her head. "You knock. My hands aren't working this morning."

Without giving herself time to think Leah rapped firmly on the door. She listened for the vibration, the sound of life behind the door—and heard it. Foot-steps developed and grew louder, followed by the turn of the doorknob. With a gasp Susan ducked behind her smaller sister.

The door opened, and Leah was nose to chest with a very tall, broad man wearing gray dress slacks and a long-sleeved white shirt. She looked up into his mildly curious expression, at a complete loss for words. They'd apparently caught him fresh out of the shower, because his graying blond hair was wet and he smelled of a subtle after-shave. A gray-and-burgundy tie lay under his collar like a scarf, still unknotted.

Leah looked into the prominent but elegant angles of his face and his dark blue eyes and saw Susan. She opened her mouth to grope for words but found none. Instead, eloquent tears began to fall.

While she watched him, the curiosity in the man's eyes changed to sharp attention, then slowly, fright-eningly, to shock. He, too, opened his mouth. No sound came from it, but his eyes spoke of disbelief and his mouth formed the name "Iliana." Then he shook his head, as though forcing himself to put a realistic answer to what he saw. His eyes went over her face, widening further in deepening disbelief. "Leah?" he whispered.

Her eyes still spilling tears, her heart still unsure of his reaction, Leah reached behind her to pull Susan forward. She, too, wept silently. Leah put an arm around her. "Yes. And this is Susan."

Janos Nagy continued to stare at them for one agonizing moment. Then he opened his arms and with a loud, unashamed, primitive scream that spoke of a long agony and a joy too profound for words crushed them both to his chest.

Leah clung to him and to Susan, his grip on her so fierce, her own emotions so strong, that she was afraid she would faint. Then he held them both away from him, his hands cupping the backs of their heads. He looked deeply into Leah's eyes and shook his head, something sad but sweet crossing his tear-filled gaze. "You are your mother, to that brave but uncertain look in your eyes, and you..." He turned to Susan and laughed softly. "And you, poor child, are me with a pretty face. Ah. God!" He pulled them back into his embrace, his grip even stronger than before. "I can't believe it. I have dreamed of this so many times, but I tried to remember that you had your own lives, your own family. But in my dreams I always found you. I never dreamed—" His voice broke and he wept. "I never dreamed," he went on finally, "that you would come to look for me. How... how did you find me?"

It was such a long story, but Leah said briefly, "Through Gerda Szabo and Marilyn White."

"Gerda," he began in amazement, "she is still alive?"

"Yes. My husband—"

"Husband?" Janos looked up and beyond his daughters. He nodded, smiling. "That must be the man watching me as though one wrong move will land me in my rosebushes. Come!" he shouted, reaching a long arm up to wave.

Jeff and Charlie sprinted up the walk, then up the few steps to the porch. Janos freed Leah to offer Jeff his hand.

Jeff was mildly amused that they had worried about the man's health. He was big shouldered and flat-stomached and had a grip that could have splintered oak. There were lines in his handsome face that were proof of grief and suffering, but his smile was warm and genuine, as though it came from a constant well-spring of hope.

Leah made the introductions.

"So," Janos said, still gripping Jeff's hand. "If she is as much like her mother as she appears, you are a man of great strength and patience."

Jeff grinned, catching Leah's quick, rueful glance before turning back to her father. "No," he said, "but I manage, anyway."

Susan drew Charlie forward. "This is Jeff's associate and my friend, Charlie Barrett."

Janos took Charlie's outstretched hand. "If she is as much like *me* as she appears, you must be a veritable saint."

Charlie laughed. "No, sir. She's put me in purgatory, not in heaven."

"Charlie!" Susan complained as everyone laughed their endorsement. Janos drew them into a chande-liered hallway, then down into a sunken living room furnished eclectically with large, comfortable pieces. A wall of windows looked out onto a green lawn and a tall poplar tree in gold autumn dress. Beyond the lawn was a steep slope to the crest of the hill.

"Ella!" Janos shouted.

A small dark-haired woman in a cobbler apron entered the room, drying her hands on a tea towel. Her hair was obviously dyed and intended to sport a casual, contemporary style, but instead it simply stuck up—and out—in almost comic abandon. She took one look at the four young people standing in the middle of the room and smiled. "Guests," she said almost to herself. "How nice." Her smile turned to Janos. "Coffee. Right, Mr. Nagy?" And before he could say anything she bustled off.

"Ella!" he shouted after her.

"And pastry," she called back without turning around. "I know."

Janos laughed gently, directing his guests to chairs. "My housekeeper. She likes to think she reads my mind, but in truth I've often gotten coffee when I wanted brandy, or fish for dinner when I've wanted beef, but if she didn't come in twice a week to clean up after me and replenish the freezer, I'd be lost."

"If she's bringing pastry," Susan said, "she read my mind."

Janos turned to her, staring at her until she glanced nervously at Leah and hunched a shoulder apologetically. "I'm sorry. I—"

"No, no," he said quickly. "It is not that. I cannot believe you are here. After all these years."

"Susan found a photo of a baby and Gerda Szabo in our mother's things," Leah explained, telling him how it had been identified on the back. She went on to detail Susan's determination to find her natural parents, the accident that prevented her from accompanying Jeff and Leah on the search, then the circuitous route that had led to him.

Ella returned with coffee and a platter of home-made pastries. When she turned to take the empty tray back to the kitchen, Janos called, "Oh, Ella?"

"Call the restaurant," she said without turning. "I already have."

Janos shook his head, then turned his attention back to Leah. "How did your adoptive parents feel about your looking for me."

"They're both gone now," Leah said. "Mom died two years ago, and Dad just a few months ago. We were packing things up to prepare to sell the house when we found the photo."

"I'm sorry," he said. "I never met them. Although Iliana assured me they were fine people, I was always a little jealous because they had you and I didn't." He drew a breath, his light eyes darkening with remembered grief. "When I came home from Vietnam to learn that...that your mother had died...and that the Blakes had opened their home to Susan, as well, I decided to take you back. You were *mine!*" He winced, the memory apparently growing more difficult to bear. "I'd lost your mother and several years of my life, and I wanted the two of you more than I've ever wanted anything. More, even, than I wanted to live during those years of hell."

He drew a ragged breath and shook his head. "Then I began to think that you, Leah, were already twelve years old and the Blakes were the only parents you'd ever known. I knew what my trying to take you from them would do to you. In my torment I even considered just asking for Susan. But your mother's dying wish was that the two of you be together. And that would still have killed me—to have one of you and not the other. God!" He rubbed a hand over his forehead. "I almost weakened so many times. The only thing that gave me peace was Miss White's assurance that you were happy and healthy." He straightened and smiled sympathetically at his daughters. "I feel such gratitude for the Blakes' kindness. I'm sorry for your loss."

Leah smiled at him. "It's not a loss. They were wonderful parents, and we were happy children. And now we've found you."

He stared at her, still trapped in wonder. "You are so like your mother. I thought for a moment…she had come for me." He gave Leah a smile she would remember until she died. "But it is my daughter who has come for me. My daughters." His gaze swung to Susan, then to Jeff and Charlie. "Tell me, please, that you can stay for a while."

Jeff put his coffee cup on the table. "The girls can stay, of course, but Charlie and I have to go back tonight."

"Jeff," Leah said in surprise. She hadn't thought as far as what they would do once she and Susan had found their father. Leaving him after a brief visit was unthinkable, but watching Jeff leave without knowing where she stood with him held as little appeal.

Jeff looked into the distress in her eyes and forced himself to stay with the plan. She needed time with her father, time to put together that part of her life before she could give thought to him.

"The three of you need time alone," he said. "And I have to get back to work." He smiled at Janos. "You understand."

Janos looked from Leah's expression to Jeff's and nodded. "Yes, I think so. But Leah seems upset that you're leaving. My first duty as her newly discovered father is to minimize her distress. I will show you my place of business, you will have the best *Magyar gulyas* you have ever tasted, then you will go."

Jeff nodded. He'd wanted to be sure of the kind of man with whom he was leaving Leah and Susan. He was satisfied. "All right."

JEFF AND HIS COMPANIONS discovered that *Magyar gulyas* was Hungarian goulash. At a table in the Danube, the flagship restaurant in a chain of five, Janos explained, they were fed and fussed over by Janos and his partner, George Lawford.

Leah shook her head in wonder as she looked around. "This is quite a leap from cook on a fishing boat."

The large restaurant was decorated with old-world, Eastern European warmth, with tambourines and brightly woven scarves on the wall for ethnic flavor.

"My father started this restaurant in the fifties," George explained, pouring wine. George was an enormous man, as tall as Janos and with a girth as large as his smile. He had a thick shock of white hair. He seemed as thrilled by Janos's daughters as Janos himself, and brought dish after dish out of the kitchen. "We served good all-American food. When Janos came home with me after the war, he introduced a few Hungarian dishes. It was just the spark we needed. By the time my father retired twelve years ago, we were as Hungarian as Janos, and the Danube was the most popular restaurant for a hundred miles. It still is." He clapped his friend on the shoulder with cheerful affection. "There's not a better man or a better friend—"

"Where's the *csirke paprikas?*" Janos interrupted, glancing over the dishes on the table in a deliberate attempt to change the subject.

"Or a better friend anywhere," George went on, ignoring him. "I wouldn't have made it back from Vietnam without him."

"Our chicken paprika," Janos confided to his guests as though he hadn't heard George, "is the best you will ever eat. The paprika, you know, must never be added to the boiling fat, but always to the dish."

"I was very ill and he—"

"George, you are boring my daughters," Janos said, pushing him toward the kitchen. "The chicken paprika, if you please, and some green pepper salad."

With a reluctant shake of his head George headed for the kitchen. "*Cseresznye* for dessert or strudel?" he asked over his shoulder.

"Both!" Janos ordered. He turned to his guests with a proud smile. "Our deep-fried cherries are magnificent!" He ladled more food on Jeff's and Charlie's plates. "Come, gentlemen. You must stoke up for the ride home."

THE MIDAFTERNOON SUN was bright, and Leah squinted against it as she looked up into Jeff's eyes.

"I'll come back for you in two weeks," he said, pulling her close for a quick kiss. Charlie and Susan stood several feet away, locked in an embrace, and Janos waited on the veranda.

Leah held his head down when he tried to straighten. She kissed him again, thinking his kiss had been perfunctory, unsatisfactory. He responded willingly, but without the ardor she remembered longingly. Perhaps he simply didn't care anymore, she thought, looking into his eyes, trying to read his thoughts. He'd come with them out of his love for Susan, not for her.

Jeff framed her face in his hands and smiled. "Didn't I tell you it would be all right?"

Leah put her hands on his wrists, words of love and need on the tip of her tongue, unable to spill out. She tried to tell him with her eyes.

Jeff read what was trapped in her gaze. Having to leave her made him humble enough to settle for knowing how she felt even though she couldn't say it. But he knew she had to learn to say the words, or the new Leah would never have a chance. He kissed her again, then pulled free of her.

"We have to go," he said. He turned to hug Susan while Charlie gave Leah a fraternal pat on the shoulder. He saw her pull Charlie toward her, wrap her arms around him and say something quietly in his ear.

Janos joined them to shake Jeff's hand, then gathered his daughters close. "Don't worry about them. I've missed so many years of spoiling them. Drive safely."

THEY WERE ONLY fifty miles from home, on a winding stretch of road that followed the Columbia River to Astoria. It was dark and rainy, and Jeff couldn't remember ever having felt so empty. Leah had been able to open up to her father, but not to him. For the past two hundred miles he'd been dealing with the possibility that he simply didn't have what she needed.

"What are you thinking?" Charlie asked from the passenger seat.

Jeff stared bleakly ahead, guiding the car almost by rote. "Nothing," he lied.

There was silence for a moment. "I thought maybe you were thinking this was the Indianapolis 500," Charlie said.

Jeff gave him a blank glance.

"You must be doing ninety, Jeff," Charlie clarified.

Jeff glanced at the speedometer and immediately lifted his foot. Close enough. Eighty-six. "Sorry." He glanced at Charlie again, with a grin this time. "Scare ya?"

"No, I'm always green," Charlie replied. "She loves you, so chill out. You'll have her back in two weeks."

Jeff shook his head and turned the windshield wipers to fast. "Only a man who's never been married thinks you can ever be that sure of a woman."

Charlie relaxed against the headrest, apparently more at ease now that Jeff had slowed to sixty. "I've never been married, but I did have a woman named Leah put her arms around my neck. She nearly choked me with her desperation when she said, 'Take care of him for me, Charlie.' "

Jeff glanced at his companion, finding it impossible to tell in the shadowy interior of the car if he'd made that up for his benefit. Sensing the unspoken question, Charlie raised his hand. "I swear. So don't splatter us all over the pavement, okay? She'll be mad at me."

It was a glimmer of hope. Small maybe, but at this point he'd grasp at anything.

IT WAS AFTER MIDNIGHT when Jeff picked up the telephone. He stared at it for a moment, close to changing his mind. Then he downed the last of his Bloody Mary and stabbed out the number.

It was late to be making a call. Possibly too late—too late for everything. But he'd become convinced over the past few weeks, and today particularly, that in the presence of love and a willingness to give, time could be made to stand still—not forever, but long enough for people to catch up with it.

The connection was made at the other end of the line and a deep voice that sounded awake and alert despite the hour said, "Hello?"

Jeff swallowed and answered, "Dad? It's Jeff."

There was a surprised silence, then Adam Alden said with undisguised delight, "Son! I've been wondering how you were."

"YOU'RE SURE everything's okay?" Leah asked.

"Everything's fine," Milly responded.

"There are no problems you're not telling me about?"

"None."

"Do you swear?"

"Leah!" Milly's voice came through the telephone connection with loud impatience. "I'm doing fine. The new girl's working out beautifully. There are no big jobs due until the first week in December. And Sandy's madly in love with Jack again and working like a fiend, whistling all the while. It's disgusting. I'm glad you're not here to see it. So go back to your father and sister, and I don't want to hear from you again until you come home. Bye."

Leah listened in disbelief to the broken connection. She smiled at Susan, who lay on her stomach on the bed, polishing her fingernails.

"Hung up on you?" Susan guessed. "You're good, Lee, but you're not indispensable. That's not the reason you're restless, anyway."

Leah lifted an eyebrow at Susan as she crossed to the closet. "Who says I'm restless?"

"Father does."

Knowing what to call Janos had become a problem after several days. When Susan had stumbled over using his given name, and admitted to him honestly that Ed Blake would always be "Dad," she asked if he would find "Father" too formal. His eyes had filled, and he'd replied quietly, "I've waited for that for a lifetime."

"Well, I'm *not* restless. Father's mistaken," Leah said, crossing to the closet and pulling out a hooded sweatshirt. "I'm going for a walk. Try to be off my bed by the time I come home so I can get my beauty sleep before we go out to dinner."

Susan glanced at her watch, then blew on her fingernails. "We're going in four hours, sweetie. There simply isn't time for you to get even passably pretty."

Leah spun around, swatting Susan with her sweatshirt.

"My nails are wet!" Susan screamed.

"Ladies! Ladies." Janos appeared in the doorway, smiling indulgently over their playful quarrel. "You're lucky I haven't had a lot of practice and don't know how to punish such behavior."

Susan groaned over a waffled nail and wiped off the wet polish. She looked up to smile at him. "You scold a little. Then you buy us something so that our feelings aren't hurt."

Biting back a smile, he turned to Leah. "Is this true?"

Leah shook her head, coming to tuck her arm in his. "You send the bad one to bed without dinner—" she indicated Susan "—and you buy something for the good one." She pointed to herself over Susan's gasp of indignation.

He patted Leah's hand. "You are telling me that the one who struck the first blow is considered the good one?"

"Ah...yes," she said. "I was only defending myself against the suggestion that there wasn't enough time between now and dinner for me to get my beauty sleep."

"But she's the one," Susan said, waving her brush of pink polish, "who said that you didn't know what you were talking about."

Janos looked at Leah. "Oh?"

Leah cast Susan a quelling glance, and Susan stuck her tongue out at her. "She said that you'd said I was restless," Leah explained. "I said you were mistaken." She smiled at him. "I'm sorry, but you are."

He pinched the fabric of her sweatshirt. "Then where are you going?"

"For a walk."

"Why?"

"Because I'm...I need to..." She sighed, trapped. "I need to get some exercise."

He tipped her face up to him. "Why?" he insisted.

She sighed. "Because I'm restless."

He gave her a teasingly superior look. "Then I'm better at this fathering business than it seems."

Leah put her arms around him without hesitation or restraint. In the week she and Susan had spent with him he'd been the epitome of kindness and concern. He'd shared his memories of their mother with them and eagerly listened to their stories of their childhood and their adoration of their adoptive parents.

He'd taken two weeks off from work and spent most of his time taking them places or doing things for them. He bought them everything they exclaimed over until neither dared admire anything for fear he'd buy it. He never asked anything of them, and he accepted their gestures of affection and acceptance as though they were gold.

Susan's fear that he'd blame her for Iliana's death had proven foolish. Even Leah's guilt-ridden admission one night after Susan had gone to bed that she'd been reluctant to embark on the search because she'd always felt antagonistic toward her natural parents had been met with an understanding nod. She'd shown him Iliana's letters, and they had held each other and wept. He was everything they could have ever hoped to find at the end of their search.

"You're wonderful at fathering," Leah said sincerely.

"I'm going to be even better," he said cryptically. "I will accompany you on your walk and we will talk." He smiled at Susan. "And you will rest your leg and get *your* beauty sleep. Ella is still downstairs if you need anything."

Arm in arm, Janos and Leah walked down the steep slope to the beach. He talked about how wonderful the week had been for him, like a gift he'd never imagined having.

"Had you never considered remarrying?" Leah asked.

He shook his head, squinting his eyes against the reflection of bright sunlight on the water. "I spent so much of my life with your mother in my mind and so little time with her in my arms that I've grown used to living with the dream." He hugged her closer. "But now I have more than that. The beautiful children we made together will now be just a phone call or a half-day's drive away." He kissed the top of her head. "It is time for you to go home, Leah."

Leah kicked at a piece of driftwood as they crossed the soft sand to the hard-packed strand at the water's edge. "You don't understand, Father."

"Susan told me you've been separated."

Leah nodded. "Jeff's always been like a brother to Susan. He agreed to help us with the search for Mother and you because he cared for her, not for me."

Janos laughed softly. "That's nonsense. I saw his love for you immediately. You've hurt him?"

Leah nodded. "The Blakes were wonderful to Susan and me, but I...I like to understand things, to know every detail so that I can organize and plan. The most complex job of my life—being me—was without detail. I didn't know who I came from or what I was. So I tried to create a perfect person. Instead I made only a rigid, organized one. I was afraid of what I was, or what I wasn't, and covered up the fear with work. Oh, Father." She leaned against him wearily. "I tried to tell Jeff how much I love him before he left, but he didn't make it easy for me, and I couldn't say the words. I don't think he's waiting for me to come home."

Janos tugged her toward the burned-out root of a tree tossed onto the sand. He found a flat place on it and sat her down, leaning beside her. His eyes were dark and grave.

"A lover should never have to guess how you feel," he said. "You have to say the words. When your mother found me after two lonely years in which she'd lived in poverty and loneliness and had to give you up, we stared at each other, each afraid the other couldn't feel what we were feeling.

"I held back because I didn't know her mother had intercepted my letters or that her parents had abandoned her. I thought she'd rejected me, then changed her mind because life was difficult, and came to find me." He swallowed convulsively and swiped at his eyes. "Then she ran at me, crying her love for me, spilling the ugly story of the past two years, sobbing uncontrollably when she told me about you and what she'd had to do. Though I tried to make it up to her in the years that followed, that will always be my grief—that I made her come to me."

Leah touched his arm in silent sympathy. Janos and Iliana had suffered so much. Her insecurities seemed petty in comparison.

"But you're asking yourself," he said, "what you will do if you go to Jeff and he doesn't want you?"

She nodded grimly.

"He wants you," Janos said with conviction, "but he wants to know you want him. Does he make you happy?"

"Yes," she replied quickly, "but I think I make him miserable."

"When you are organized and compulsive about work, perhaps," he said with a smile, "but now you have the details, is that not right? Now you know who you are. The daughter of a woman who gave up her own happiness so that you could have yours, the daughter of a man who's loved you for a lifetime without ever having seen you until a week ago. We lived without you so that you would be happy. Please—" he paused, then went on with a desperate quality in his deep voice "—be happy now, or it has all been for nothing."

Leah smiled at him sadly. "I guess I am like my mother. When I look at the picture Gerda gave me, I see that she was afraid of things. So am I. Loving Jeff has made me open up. I've been happy, but pain has also hurt more. I'm afraid if he rejects me now the pain will be so strong I'll shut down for good and be of no more use to anyone, particularly myself."

Janos put an arm around her and held her close. "Your mother did fear a lot of things," he said, "but she was never afraid to care. Every time she loved, she was hurt—loving me, loving you, loving Susan—yet the last thing she did in her life was to try to put those she loved together. If you are like her, Leah—" he turned her to face him, looking into her eyes, his own gentle but firm "—then you will take the chance."

Leah leaned against his shoulder, absorbing his love and his strength. The image of Iliana's face formed in her mind. She saw clearly the wide eyes of the young girl filled with fears, then those of the young woman filled with love—even though she'd already made a great sacrifice, and would be called upon to make another. Leah remembered the letters, and felt Iliana's love as though she'd put her arms around her.

She thought of the years of love Ed and Selena Blake had given her as a child, and how they'd selflessly made room in their lives so that she and Susan could be together.

Love, it seemed, ran in the family. She had a responsibility to carry it on.

CHAPTER SEVENTEEN

JEFF PULLED into his driveway, turned the engine off and sat. He'd just won a custody case for his client, the children's father, by being smart enough to let the man's brash and simple honesty argue the case. He thought wryly that fathers were certainly figuring prominently in his life lately.

Winning always gave him a sense of personal satisfaction and of professional pride, but tonight he was hard put to feel either. Positive emotions of any kind had been out of his reach since he'd left Leah with her father.

At the time he'd experienced a flicker of hope that she would come back to him. In the long, rainy days since then he'd been unable to keep the flicker alive. She had the father who was the answer to all her questions about her mother and herself. She no longer needed the support and comfort of the husband to whom she could never quite open her heart.

Grabbing his briefcase, he got out of the car and locked it, hunching his shoulder against the cold rain that pelted down. Walking to the door, he pulled at his tie, then flipped his key ring over his finger to find the house key. If it wasn't for the rain, he thought grimly, he'd almost prefer to stand outside than spend one more night in the empty house. He'd been alone in it for a year—he didn't understand why it had seemed so particularly lifeless the past week. A corner of his mind he hadn't indulged in the past seven days realized that it was because he'd had those two weeks with Leah in the house they'd shared as newlyweds. His adjustment to life without her just wouldn't take again.

Telling himself firmly that he didn't have a choice, Jeff moved to fit his key in the lock when the door opened. Smythe sailed out at him, barking and whining a welcome.

Leah appeared in the doorway wearing an apron Alan had given him on his last birthday. The entire apron was painted to look like a fish standing on its tail. She had a wooden spoon in one hand and a hot pad in the other. "Hi," she said. "You're just in time. Don't forget to wipe your feet." She disappeared inside. Smythe did a quick turn around his ankles, then ran after her.

Jeff was still standing there, staring, when Leah poked her head back around the door. "Forget what I said about your feet. Just come on in."

Since she held the door open for him, he had to comply. But the effort required to place one foot in front of the other was almost more than he could manage. He was concentrating all his energy on holding down the joy the sight of her brought. She took his briefcase and set it near the closest chair, then reached up to help him off with his jacket. "This is drenched!" she said. "I'll hang it up over the tub. There's a gin and tonic for you on the table."

She hurried away, and he stared after her for a moment, fighting off the powerful emotions threatening to choke him. Joy and desire washed over him, urging him to believe that the sweet domesticity of this little scene meant she was back. Yet, despite the sweetness of her smile and all the little attentions, she looked nervous, uncertain, not quite open. If that was the only way he could have her, he'd take it. But until he knew for certain he intended to fight for more.

He went into the kitchen and found the table set for two with a red taper in a crystal holder she'd brought from home. He picked up the gin and tonic and sipped at it, walking to the stove to investigate the wonderful aromas filling the kitchen. Pork roast with prunes and apples, cauliflower au gratin, green beans almondine and roasted potatoes—a dietician's nightmare, but his favorite meal. He couldn't decide if the feast was a sign of their reconciliation or her way of letting him down easy.

She came back into the kitchen, looking more nervous than when she left. But she had a bright smile pasted on, and he tried to concentrate on that.

"You're back early," he said, stepping away from the stove as she reached into the oven. "Everything okay with your father?"

"Yes." She carried the roast to the table. He put his drink down, folded up a towel to use as a hot pad, then followed her with the cauliflower. "I can't believe how wonderful he is. Susan and I had a great time. He's going to bring her home for Thanksgiving and stay a few days."

"Good." Jeff followed her back to the stove, then back to the table with the last two bowls of food. "So all your fears of rejection were unfounded."

She looked up at him with an expression he couldn't quite analyze, except to recognize uncertainty in it. "Most of them," she said cryptically. "Would you like wine with dinner or another gin and tonic?"

He held up his half-full glass. "I'm okay." He had a feeling he was going to need a clear mind for this.

He wanted to tell her how happy he was to see her, how lonely he'd been without her, how much he appreciated the time and trouble she'd taken to prepare his meal. But she sliced the roast and spooned up the trimmings, keeping up a running patter about what she and Susan and their father had done during their visit.

When she exhausted that subject, she asked question after question about Smythe, Charlie, Alan, the office. Silence fell as she cleared away their plates. He stood to help her, but she took the bowl from him, pointing at the living room. "Go sit down. I'll bring coffee in a minute."

That was it. He pushed his chair away and grabbed her wrist. "Will you please stop acting like Harriet!" he demanded.

She frowned at him, forced to put down the platter she was holding. "Who?"

"Harriet," he repeated sharply. "Aren't we playing Ozzie and Harriet? Did you train Smythe to bring my slippers?"

The dog, hearing his name spoken in a tone he didn't care for, crawled under the table and lay down.

Now she looked hurt, and he considered falling on the serving fork. "I'm not playing anything," she said, very close to tears. He saw her swallow and straighten her shoulders. "I made your favorite things because I thought you'd like them, because I realized while I was in Heron Harbor that you've done a lot of things for me in the past month and I haven't done much for you."

"I wasn't looking for paybacks," he said more quietly.

She yanked away from him and her voice rose. "What were you looking for?"

"Just my wife."

She blinked, as though that wasn't the answer she'd expected. "Well, you've got me," she said with mild belligerence. "So what are you angry about?"

He took her by both shoulders, suddenly so frustrated that he shook her. "I'm angry because I don't get it!" he explained with desperation. "Why did you look so stricken when I left you at your father's? Why did you come back a week early, wait like the loving little wife for me to come home, and then stare at me across the table with that same damn look of confusion you used to give me before we broke up? I would presume a woman who takes that kind of action should be certain of what she's doing!"

Tears puddled in her lower lids, and her look of uncertainty turned to one of misery. "I was sure of what I was doing," she said quietly. "My father wanted to drive me back, but I took the bus because I wanted time to think and plan. By the time I got home I convinced myself that even though I'd been such a jerk, you'd want me back if I could make you understand that I'm different now. I couldn't wait to see you." She shook her head, and a tear spilled over. "I went to your office. Charlie was there and he told me you were in court this afternoon. He offered to drive me here and let me in with his key." More tears fell. "And then I found the boxes."

He tried to think. He knew he was upset, but he couldn't make sense of that. "Boxes," he repeated, waiting for the significance to register.

"In your bedroom," she said stiffly. "They're all over the floor, filled with your clothes. You're leaving, aren't you?"

Boxes. God. He smiled, beginning to understand. Infuriated, she pulled away from him, dashing away the tears with the side of her hand. "Well, if you think you can just file for divorce," she said, "and walk away, you're mistaken. I'll contest it. I'll drag it on so long and make everything so difficult for you you'll wish you were dealing with Sylvia Dunwiddie!"

His smile broadened. "Lee..." he began, reaching for her arm.

"You promised nothing would drive you away from me," she reminded him, dancing out of his reach. She backed toward the living room and he followed. "And what do you do at the first opportunity? You file for divorce! And like a dummy, I spent a whole afternoon making you Hussar's Kisses!"

"No, I didn't," he said.

"I stay with my father for a week and you pack up and try to leave!" Finally hearing what he'd said, she stopped her retreat and frowned. "What?"

He took her arm and pulled her toward the sofa, pushing her into its corner and sitting beside her, blocking her escape. "I said I didn't file for divorce. I was hurt and I wanted to hurt you. When I saw that I had, I realized divorce wasn't what either of us wanted, and there had to be another way."

Now she truly looked confused. "So you're... leaving to think things over... or something?"

"I'm not leaving at all," he said patiently. "My father's coming to visit, so I cleared out the closet and the dresser in the spare bedroom to make it more comfortable for him. The boxes are going into the garage. I just haven't gotten around to moving them yet."

Her eyes widened. "Your dad's coming? Why?"

"Because I called him," he replied. "I kept telling you to open up. I decided maybe I should practice what I preach."

Leah subsided, studying him warily. "You want to make peace with your father?"

"Yes." He sighed and relaxed beside her, leaning his head against the back of the sofa. "Helping you with the search, I was reminded that things aren't always what they appear and that there are two sides to everything."

Leah smiled at him. "I'm glad, Jeff." So he wasn't leaving. But that didn't mean he'd been waiting for her.

She wanted desperately to know what he was thinking—to be certain how he'd take a declaration of love and a promise of devotion and support. Then she remembered her father's caution that one lover should never have to read another's mind. Love was fearless, and she was suddenly filled with it.

She turned sideways to look at Jeff and loop her arms around his neck. She watched him turn his head to look into her eyes and wait for her to speak. His expression was wary.

"I love you," she said without giving herself time to think through the words. "I'm sorry for all I've withheld from you, and I promise, if you'll take me back, that I'll do my best to share myself. But I warn you—" she sighed "—there are parts of me you'll wish I'd spared you."

He studied her for one long, agonizing moment, then enveloped her in his arms, pulling her into his lap. He crushed her against him, and she felt a long shudder go through him. "I love all of you, Leah," he said softly. "I don't need you to be perfect. I just need you to be open to me." He held her away from him to look into her eyes. His own were anguished. "As a boy I watched my family fall apart. I didn't want that to happen to us. I love you, Lee. I need all of you. But the truth is, I was ready to settle for whatever you'd give me."

She kissed his lips and smiled into his eyes. "Now that I know my father I'm no longer afraid of what's inside me. It isn't that I think I'm a better person than I used to be. It's just that now I know what I'm made of, and that I'm capable of being better than I am." She leaned against his shoulder with a contented sigh. "Let's have lots of babies and put an addition onto the house." She made a broad gesture with one arm. "I feel like sharing everything because everything and everyone in my life is so wonderful."

"*Lots* of babies," he agreed heartily, kissing her hair. Then he recalled something she'd said earlier and wove his fingers into her hair to pull her head back. "You spent a whole afternoon making me what?"

She smiled slowly. "Hussar's Kisses."

He considered her reply, then said threateningly, "If that means you practiced with a guy in uniform—"

Laughing, she slapped his chest. "They're cookies. My father and I made them." She tried to wriggle to her feet. "I'll get them for you."

"No." He held fast.

"Don't you want to try them?"

"Yes." He grinned and stood, still holding her in his arms. "But I don't want to let you go. Where are they?"

She tightened her grip around his neck and pointed at the kitchen. Jeff carried her to the counter where she'd dropped the bag. She freed an arm to pick it up, and he moved on through the kitchen. She didn't have to ask his destination.

He moved gingerly through the boxes around his bed. "You've been eating a lot of your father's cooking, haven't you?" he teased, grunting dramatically as he stepped over a box and fell with her onto the bed.

She struggled to her knees astride Jeff's waist, peering anxiously into the bag. She breathed a sigh of relief that the cookies were still whole. She withdrew one and held it up for his inspection. It was flat and covered with nuts, an indentation in the middle filled with jam.

"Thumbprints," he said, absently running his hands along her thighs. "Alan's wife makes those."

"In plain old English it's a thumbprint cookie." Leah smiled, her eyes sparkling. Her happiness made him feel as though he might burst with it himself. "But these were made for you by your Hungarian father-in-law and his wicked gypsy daughter." She fluttered her eyelashes provocatively and put the cookie to his lips. "That makes them Hussar's Kisses."

"Mmm." He raised an eyebrow and took a bite. He chewed and analyzed. "I taste the difference," he assured her gravely. "This is no ordinary cookie."

"That's right." Leah broke off another bite and put it in his mouth. "There are hussars in my blood, you know," she said, leaning her forearms on his chest. "They wore fur caps, tight breeches, bright tunics and fur-trimmed jackets over one shoulder." Jeff swallowed while he could. The way she looked at him was making it difficult. The way she leaned on him wasn't helping, either. "They were clever, fearless fighters with a reputation as devastating lovers."

He saw the amusement under the blatant seduction in her eyes and felt it ensnare him. "So one of those cookies," he theorized, "is like an injection of sexual prowess?"

She nodded seriously and popped the last bite into her mouth. "Oh, yes."

"Should we have another?"

"Well, they're pretty powerful stuff." She began to unbutton her blouse. "And, anyway, hussars are in my blood, and you're just sort of naturally gifted."

"Why, thank you." When she tossed the blouse aside, he pulled her down onto him and unhooked her bra. She made a long, soft sound of contentment and rubbed her cheek against his. He took a moment to simply hold her, closing his eyes and stroking up and down her slender back. He was too filled with love and gratitude to say anything.

After a moment Leah leaned up, unbuttoned his shirt, then pulled it and his T-shirt off. Then she lay back atop him, flesh to flesh, and looked languorously into his eyes. "How many babies?" she asked, tracing his lips with an index finger.

He caught it and kissed her knuckle. "I don't know. We don't have to decide now, do we? I mean, we can't make them all tonight?"

She grinned and bit his chin. "You forget how efficient I am. Triplets would save time."

Jeff held her to him and laughed, accepting that there were some things about Leah he simply couldn't change. And wouldn't want to.

Take 4 bestselling love stories FREE

Plus get a FREE surprise gift!

HARLEQUIN®
OFFICIAL SWEEPSTAKES RULES

NO PURCHASE NECESSARY

1. To enter, complete an Official Entry Form or 3" × 5" index card by hand-printing, in plain block letters, your complete name, address, phone number and age, and mailing it to: Harlequin Fashion A Whole New You Sweepstakes, P.O. Box 9056, Buffalo, NY 14269-9056.

   No responsibility is assumed for lost, late or misdirected mail. Entries must be sent separately with first class postage affixed, and be received no later than December 31, 1991 for eligibility.

2. Winners will be selected by D.L. Blair, Inc., an independent judging organization whose decisions are final, in random drawings to be held on January 30, 1992 in Blair, NE at 10:00 a.m. from among all eligible entries received.

3. The prizes to be awarded and their approximate retail values are as follows: Grand Prize — A brand-new Mercury Sable LS plus a trip for two (2) to Paris, including round-trip air transportation, six (6) nights hotel accommodation, a $1,400 meal/spending money stipend and $2,000 cash toward a new fashion wardrobe (approximate value: $28,000) or $15,000 cash; two (2) Second Prizes — A trip to Paris, including round-trip air transportation, six (6) nights hotel accommodation, a $1,400 meal/spending money stipend and $2,000 cash toward a new fashion wardrobe (approximate value: $11,000) or $5,000 cash; three (3) Third Prizes — $2,000 cash toward a new fashion wardrobe. All prizes are valued in U.S. currency. Travel award air transportation is from the commercial airport nearest winner's home. Travel is subject to space and accommodation availability, and must be completed by June 30, 1993. Sweepstakes offer is open to residents of the U.S. and Canada who are 21 years of age or older as of December 31, 1991, except residents of Puerto Rico, employees and immediate family members of Torstar Corp., its affiliates, subsidiaries, and all agencies, entities and persons connected with the use, marketing, or conduct of this sweepstakes. All federal, state, provincial, municipal and local laws apply. Offer void wherever prohibited by law. Taxes and/or duties, applicable registration and licensing fees, are the sole responsibility of the winners. Any litigation within the province of Quebec respecting the conduct and awarding of a prize may be submitted to the Régie des loteries et courses du Québec. All prizes will be awarded; winners will be notified by mail. No substitution of prizes is permitted.

4. Potential winners must sign and return any required Affidavit of Eligibility/Release of Liability within 30 days of notification. In the event of noncompliance within this time period, the prize may be awarded to an alternate winner. Any prize or prize notification returned as undeliverable may result in the awarding of that prize to an alternate winner. By acceptance of their prize, winners consent to use of their names, photographs or their likenesses for purposes of advertising, trade and promotion on behalf of Torstar Corp. without further compensation. Canadian winners must correctly answer a time-limited arithmetical question in order to be awarded a prize.

5. For a list of winners (available after 3/31/92), send a separate stamped, self-addressed envelope to: Harlequin Fashion A Whole New You Sweepstakes, P.O. Box 4694, Blair, NE 68009.

PREMIUM OFFER TERMS

To receive your gift, complete the Offer Certificate according to directions. Be certain to enclose the required number of "Fashion A Whole New You" proofs of product purchase (which are found on the last page of every specially marked "Fashion A Whole New You" Harlequin or Silhouette romance novel). Requests must be received no later than December 31, 1991. Limit: four (4) gifts per name, family, group, organization or address. Items depicted are for illustrative purposes only and may not be exactly as shown. Please allow 6 to 8 weeks for receipt of order. Offer good while quantities of gifts last. In the event an ordered gift is no longer available, you will receive a free, previously unpublished Harlequin or Silhouette book for every proof of purchase you have submitted with your request, plus a refund of the postage and handling charge you have included. Offer good in the U.S. and Canada only.   HOFW-SWPR

HARLEQUIN® OFFICIAL
SWEEPSTAKES ENTRY FORM

4-FWHSS-2

Complete and return this Entry Form immediately – the more entries you submit, the better your chances of winning!

- Entries must be received by **December 31, 1991.**
- A Random draw will take place on **January 30, 1992.**
- No purchase necessary.

Yes, I want to win a FASHION A WHOLE NEW YOU Classic and Romantic prize from Harlequin:

Name _____ Telephone _____ Age _____

Address _____

City _____ State _____ Zip _____

Return Entries to: Harlequin FASHION A WHOLE NEW YOU,
P.O. Box 9056, Buffalo, NY 14269-9056   © 1991 Harlequin Enterprises Limited

PREMIUM OFFER

To receive your free gift, send us the required number of proofs-of-purchase from any specially marked FASHION A WHOLE NEW YOU Harlequin or Silhouette Book with the Offer Certificate properly completed, plus a check or money order (do not send cash) to cover postage and handling payable to Harlequin FASHION A WHOLE NEW YOU Offer. We will send you the specified gift.

OFFER CERTIFICATE

Item	A. ROMANTIC COLLECTOR'S DOLL	B. CLASSIC PICTURE FRAME
	(Suggested Retail Price $60.00)	(Suggested Retail Price $25.00)
# of proofs-of-purchase	18	12
Postage and Handling	$3.50	$2.95
Check one	☐	☐

Name _____

Address _____

City _____ State _____ Zip _____

Mail this certificate, designated number of proofs-of-purchase and check or money order for postage and handling to: Harlequin FASHION A WHOLE NEW YOU Gift Offer, P.O. Box 9057, Buffalo, NY 14269-9057. Requests must be received by December 31, 1991.

ONE
PROOF-OF-PURCHASE

4-FWHSP-2

To collect your fabulous free gift you must include the necessary number of proofs-of-purchase with a properly completed Offer Certificate.

© 1991 Harlequin Enterprises Limited

See previous page for details.

THE NEW INTERNATIONAL
WEBSTER'S
VEST POCKET
ENGLISH/SPANISH

D0696390

TRIDENT
PRESS

Published by
Trident Press International
2001 EDITION

Cover Design Copyright • Trident Press International
Copyright © 2001 Trident Press International

ISBN 1582792178

SPANISH PRONUNCIATION

The Spanish alphabet has twenty–eight letters. Note that ch, ll, and ñ are considered to be separate single letters and are so treated in the alphabetization of Spanish words. While rr is considered to be a distinct sign for a particular sound, it is not included in the alphabet and except in syllabification (notably for the division of words at the end of a line) is not treated as a separate letter, perhaps because words never begin with it.

Letter	Name	Sound
a	a	Like **a** in English **father**, e.g. **casa**, **fácil**.
b	be	When initial or preceded by **m**, like **b** in English **book**, e.g., **boca**, **combate**. When standing between two vowels and when preceded by a vowel and followed by **l** or **r**, like **b** in English **voodoo** except that it is formed with both lips, e.g., **saber**, **hablar**, **sobre**. It is generally silent before **s** plus a consonant and often dropped in spelling, e.g., **oscure** for **obscuro**.
c	ce	When followed by **e** or **i**, like **th** in English **think**, in Castilian, and like **c** in English **cent** in American Spanish, e.g., **acento**, **cinco**. When followed by **a**, **o**, **u**, or a consonant, like c in English **come**, e.g., **cantar**, **como**, **cubo**, **acto**, **creer**.
ch	che	Like **ch** in English **much**, e.g., **escuchar**
d	de	Generally, like **d** in English **dog**, e.g., **diente**, **rendir**. When standing between two vowels, when preceded by a vowel and followed by **r**, and when final, like **th** in English **this**, e.g., **miedo**, **piedra**, **libertad**.
e	e	At the end of a syllable, like **a** in English **fate**, but without the glide the English sound sometimes has, e.g., **beso**, **menos**. When followed by a consonant in the same syllable, like **e** in English **met**, e.g., **perla**, **selva**.
f	efe	Like **f** in English **five**, e.g., **flor**, **efecto**.

Letter	Name	Sound
g	ge	When followed by **e** or **i**, like **h** in English home, e.g., **gente**, **giro**. When followed by **a**, **o**, **u**, or a consonant, like **g** in English go, e.g., **gato**, **gota**, **agudo**, **grande**.
h	hache	Always silent, e.g., **hombre**, **alcohol**.
i	i	Like **i** in English machine, e.g., **comain**, **ida**. When preceded or followed by another vowel, it has the sound of English **y**, e.g., **tierra**, **reina**.
j	jota	Like **h** in English home, e.g., **jardín**, **junto**.
k	ka	Like English **k**, e.g., **kilociclo**.
l	ele	Like **l** in English laugh, e.g., **lado**, **ala**.
ll	elle	Somewhat like **lli** in William in Castilian and like **y** in English yes in American Spanish, e.g., **silla**, **llamar**.
m	eme	Like **m** in English man, e.g. **mesa**, **amar**.
n	ene	Generally, like **n** in English name, e.g., **andar**, **nube**. Before **v**, like **m** in English man, e.g., **invierno**, **enviar**. Before **c** (k) and **g** (g), like **n** in English drink, e.g., **finca**, **manga**.
ñ	eñe	Somewhat like **ni** in English onion, e.g., **año**, **enseñar**.
o	o	At the end of a syllable, like **o** in English note, but without the glide the English sound sometimes has, e.g., **boca**, **como**. When followed by a consonant in the same syllable, like **o** in English organ, e.g., **poste**, **norte**.
p	pe	Like **p** in English pen, e.g., **poco**, **aplicar**. It is often silent in **septiembre** and **séptimo**.
q	cu	Like **c** in English come. It is always followed by **ue** or **ui**, in which the **u** is silent, e.g., **querer**, **quitar**. The sound of English **qu** is represented in Spanish by **cu**, e.g., **frecuente**.

Letter	Name	Sound
r	ere	Strongly trilled when initial and when preceded by **l**, **n**, or **s**, e.g., **rico**, **alrededor**, **honra**, **israelí**. Pronounced with a single tap of the tongue in all other positions, e.g., **caro**, **grande**, **amar**.
rr	erre	Strongly trilled, e.g., **carro**, **tierra**.
s	ese	Generally, like **s** in English **say**, e.g., **servir**, **casa**, **este**. Before a voiced consonant (**b**, **d**, **g** (g), **l**, **r**, **m**, **n**), like **z** in English **zero**, e.g., **esbelto**, **desde**, **rasgar**, **eslabón**, **mismo**, **asno**.
t	te	Like **t** in English **stamp**, e.g., **tiempo**, **matar**.
u	u	Like **u** in English **rude**, e.g., **mudo**, **puño**. It is silent in **gue**, **gui**, **que**, and **qui**, but not in **güe**, and **güi**, e.g., **guerra**, **guisa**, **querer**, **quitar**, but **agüero**, **lingüístico**. When preceded or followed by another vowel, it has the sound of English **w**, e.g., **fuego**, **deuda**.
v	ve *or* uve	Like Spanish in all positions, e.g., **vengo**, **invierno**, **uva**, **huevo**.
x	equis	When followed by a consonant, like **s** in English **say**, e.g., **expresar**, **sexto**. Between two vowels, pronounced like **gs**, e.g., **examen**, **existencia**, **exótico**; and in some words, like **s** in **say**, e.g., **auxilio**, **exacto**. In **México** (for **Méjico**), like Spanish **j**.
y	ye *or* i griega	In the conjunction **y**, like **i** in English **machine**. When standing next to a vowel or between two vowels, like **y** in English **yes**, e.g., **yo**, **hoy**, **vaya**.
z	zeda *or* zeta	Like **th** in English **think** in Castilian and like **c** in English **cent** in American Spanish, e.g., **zapato**, **zona**.

Diphthong	Sound
ai, ay	Like **i** in English **might**, e.g., **baile, hay**
au	Like **ou** in English **pound**, e.g., **causa**
ei, ey	Like **ey** in English **they**, e.g., **reina, ley**
eu	Like **ayw** in English **hayward**, e.g., **deuda**
oi, oy	Like **oy** in English **boy**, e.g., **estoy**

SPANISH GRAMMAR

Stress, Punctuation, Capitalization

All Spanish words, except compound words and adverbs ending in **mente**, have only one stress. The position of this stress is always shown by the spelling in accordance with the following rules:

(a) Words ending in a vowel sound or in **n** or **s** are stressed on the syllable next to the last, e.g., **ca´sa, a´gua, se´rio, ha´blan, co´sas**.

(b) Words ending in a consonant except **n** or **s** are stressed on the last syllable, e.g., **se-ñor´, pa-pel´, fe-liz´, U-ra-guay´, es-toy´**.

(c) If the stress does not fall in accordance with either of the above rules, it is indicated by an acute accent placed above the stressed vowel, e.g., **ca-fé, a-pren-dí, na-ción, lá-piz, fá-cil, re-pú-bli-ca**. The acute accent is also used to distinguish between words spelled alike but having different meanings or parts of speech, e.g. **aun** (even) and **aún** (still, yet), **donde** (conj.) and **dónde** (adv.), **el** (def. art.) and **él** (pron.).

Question marks and exclamation points are placed both before and after a word or sentence, and the first is inverted, e.g. **¿Que tal?** (How's everything?), **¡Que lástima!** (What a pity!).

Capital letters are used less in Spanish than in English, e.g., **un inglés** (an Englishman), **el idioma español** (the Spanish language), **domingo** (Sunday), **enero** (January).

Gender of Nouns

A noun is either masculine or feminine. With few exceptions, nouns ending in **o** are masculine, e.g., **el libro** (the book); and nouns ending in **a**, **d**, and **ez** are feminine, e.g., **la ventana** (the window), **la ciudad** (the town), **la nuez** (the nut). There are no definitive rules for nouns that end in letters other than **o**, **a**, **d**, or **ez**.

Plural of Nouns

The plural of a noun is formed by adding **s** to those ending in an unstressed vowel or a stressed **é**; and **es** to those ending in a consonant. Nouns that end in **es** or representing a family name remain unchanged from the singular.

Definite Articles

The definite article corresponds to the gender of the noun it specifies.

The singulars of the definite article are **el** (masculine) and **la** (feminine). Plurals are **los** (masculine) and **las** (feminine).

The definite article is omitted before nouns in apposition, e.g., **Madrid, capital de España** (Madrid, the capital of Spain), and in the numbered names of rulers and popes, e.g., **Luis catorce** (Louis the Fourteenth).

Indefinite Articles

The singulars of the indefinite article are **un** (masculine) and **una** (feminine); the plurals are **unos** (masculine) and **unas** (feminine), e.g. **un mes** (a month), **unos meses** (some months); **una calle** (a street), **unas calles** (some streets).

The form **un** is also commonly used before feminine singular nouns beginning with a stressed **a** or **ha**, e.g., **un arma** (a weapon).

The plural forms **unos** and **unas** when followed by a cardinal number, mean *about*, e.g., **unos cinco años** (about five years).

The indefinite article is not used before a noun of nationality, religion, occupation, and the like, e.g., **Mi amigo es abogado** (My friend is a lawyer). If the noun is modified, the indefinite article is generally used, e.g., **Mi hermano es un abogado excelente** (My brother is an excellent lawyer). The indefinite article is omitted before **otro**, which therefore means both *other* and *another*, e.g., **Quiero otro libro** (I want another book).

Gender of Adjectives

Adjectives agree in gender and number with the noun they modify.

Adjectives ending in **o** become feminine by changing **o** to **a**, e.g., **alto** and **alta** (high). Adjectives ending in any other letter have the same form in the masculine and the feminine, e.g., **constante** (constant), **fácil** (easy), **belga** (Belgian), except adjectives of nationality ending in **l**, **s**, or **z** and adjectives ending in **or**, **án** and **ón**, which add **a** to form the feminine, e.g.,

español and **española** (Spanish), **inglés** and **inglesa** (English), **conservador** and **conservadora** (preservative), **barrigón** and **barrigona** (big–bellied).

Comparatives ending in **or** have the same form in the masculine and the feminine, e.g., **mejor** (better), **superior** (upper, superior).

Plural of Adjectives

Adjectives ending in a vowel form their plurals by adding **s**, e.g., **alto** and **altos**, **alta** and **altas** (high), **constante** and **constantes** (constant).

Adjective ending in a consonant form their plurals by adding **es**, e.g., **fácil** and **fáciles** (easy), **barrigón** and **barrigones** (big-bellied). Those ending in **z** change the **z** to **c** and add **es**, e.g., **feliz** and **felices** (happy).

The acute accent found on the last syllable of the masculine singular of some adjectives ending in **n** and **s** is omitted in the feminine singular and in the plural, e.g., **inglés** and **inglesa**, *pl.* **ingleses** (English).

Position of Adjectives

Adjectives generally follow the nouns they modify, e.g., **vino italiano** (Italian wine). However, they precede the noun they modify when used in a figurative, derived or unemphatic sense, e.g., **pobre hombre** (poor or pitiable man), but **un hombre pobre** (a poor man), **cierta ciudad** (a certain city), but **cosa cierta** (sure thing).

Shortening of Adjectives

When **bueno** (good), **malo** (bad), **primero** (first), **tercero** (third), **alguno** (some, any), and **ninguno** (none, no) are used before a masculine singular noun, they drop their final **o**, e.g., **buen libro** (good book), **mal olor** (bad odor), **primer capítulo** (first chapter), **algun muchacho** (some boy), **ningun soldado** (no soldier).

When **grande** (large, great) is used before a masculine or feminine singular noun, it drops **de**, e.g., **gran nación** (great nation). If the noun begins with a vowel or **h**, either **gran** or **grande** may be used, e.g., **grande amigo** or **gran amigo** (great friend).

Ciento (hundred) drops **to** before a noun, e.g., **cien años** (a hundred years), **cien dólares** (a hundred dollars).

The masculine **santo** (saint) becomes **san** before all names of saints except **Domingo** and **Tomás**, e.g., **San Francisco** (Saint Francis). Before common nouns it is not shortened, e.g., **el santo papa** (the Holy Father).

Formation of Adverbs

Adverbs are formed from adjectives by adding **mente** to the feminine form, e.g., **perfecto** (perfect), **perfectamente** (perfectly); **fácil** (easy), **fácilmente** (easily); **constante** (constant), **constantemente** (constantly). With two or more such adverbs in a series, **mente** is added only to the last one, e.g., **Escribe clara y correctamente** (He writes clearly and correctly).

Comparison of Adverbs

As with adjectives, the comparative and superlative of an adverb is formed by placing **más** (more) or **menos** (less) before the adverb, e.g., **despacio** (slowly), **más despacio** (more slowly).

The following adverbs have irregular comparatives and superlatives:

Positive	Comparative and Superlative
bien (well)	**mejor** (better, best)
mal (bad, badly)	**peor** (worse, worst)
mucho (much)	**más** (more, most)
poco (little)	**menos** (less, least)

Subject Pronouns

	Singular	Plural
1st person	**yo** (I)	**nosotros, nosotras** (we)
2nd person (familiar)	**tu** (thou, you)	**vosotros, vosotras** (you)
2nd person (formal)	**usted** (you)	**ustedes** (you)
3rd person masculine	**él** (he, it)	**ellos** (they)
3rd person feminine	**ella** (she, it)	**ellas** (they)
3rd person neuter	**ello** (it)	

With the exception of **usted** and **ustedes**, which are regularly expressed, these pronouns are used only for emphasis, for contrast, or to avoid ambiguity, and when no verb is expressed, e.g., **Yo trabajo mucho** (*I* work hard), **Él es aplicado pero ella es perezosa** (He is diligent, but she is lazy), **¿Quién llama? Yo** (Who is calling? I or me).

When the 3rd person subject is not a person, it is rarely expressed by a pronoun, e.g., **es larga** ((it) is long) and it is never expressed with impersonal verbs, e.g., **llueve** ((it is) raining).

The adjective **mismo**, *fem.* **misma** (self) is used with the subject pronouns to form the intensive subject pronoun, e.g., **yo mismo, yo misma** (I myself); **tú** (or **usted**) **mismo, tú** (or **usted**) **misma** (you yourself); **él mismo** (he himself), **ella misma** (she herself), **nosotros mismos, nosotras mismas** (we ourselves), **vosotros mismos, vosotras mismas** (you yourselves), **ellos mismos,** *fem.* **ellas mismas** (they themselves), **ustedes mismos, ustedes mismas** (you yourselves).

Prepositional Pronouns

	Singular	Plural
1st person	**mí** (me)	**nosotros, nosotras** (us)
2nd person (familiar)	**ti** (thee, you)	**vosotros, vosotras** (you)
2nd person (formal)	**usted** (you)	**ustedes** (you)
3rd person masculine	**él** (him, it)	**ellos** (them)
3rd person feminine	**ella** (her, it)	**ellas** (them)
3rd person neuter	**ello** (it)	
3rd person reflexive	**sí** (himself, herself, itself)	**sí** (themselves, yourselves, yourself)

These pronouns are used as objects of prepositions, e.g., **Compró un libro para mí** (He bought a book for me), **Compró un libro para sí** (He bought a book for himself), **Vd. compró un libro para sí** (You bought a book for yourself).

Relative Pronouns

The form **que**, meaning *that, which, who, whom*, is the most frequent relative pronoun and is invariable. It is used as both subject and object of the verb and refers to persons and things. For example, **El hombre que me conoce...** (The man *who* knows me...), **El hombre que conozco...** (The man *whom* I know...), **El libro que lee...** (The book *that* he is reading...), **El trabajo a que dedico mi tiempo...** (The work to *which* I devote my time...).

The form **quien**, *pl.* **quenes** (who, whom) is inflected for number, refers only to persons, and takes the personal **a** as direct object, e.g. **El amigo con quien viajé por España...** (The friend with *whom* I traveled in Spain...), **La señora a quien ví en la estación...** (The lady *whom* I saw at the station), **Los señores para quienes he traido estos libros...** (The gentlemen for *whom* I brought these books...).

The forms **el que** (*fem.* **la que,** *pl.* **los que, las que**) and **el cual** (*fem.* **la cual,** *pl.* **los cuales, las cuales**), both meaning *who, which, that*, agree in gender and number with their antecedent and are therefore used to replace **que** where the reference might be ambiguous, e.g., **El hijo de aquella señora, el cual vive en Nueva York...** (the son of that lady who (i.e., the son) lives in New York).

The forms **lo que** and **lo cual**, both meaning *what, which*, are invariable and refer to a previous statement, e.g., **No entiendo lo que él dice** (I don't understand what he is saying), **Llegó a medianoche, lo que indicaba que habia trabajado mucho** (He arrived at midnight, which indicated that he had worked hard).

The form **cuanto** (*fem.* **cuanta**, *pl.* **cuantos, cuantas**) contains its own antecedent and it means *all that which, all those which, all those who* or *whom, as much as, as many as*. For example, **Eso es cuanto quiero decir** (This is all that I want to say), **Dijo algo a cuantas personas se hallaban alli** (He said something to all the people who were there).

Regular Verbs

Spanish verbs are classified into three conjugations: those ending in **ar**, those ending in **er**, and those ending in **ir**, e.g., **hablar, comer, vivir**

First Conjugation	Second Conjugation	Third Conjugation
	Infinitive:	
hablar to speak	**comer** to eat	**vivir** to live
	Gerund:	
hablando speaking	**comiendo** eating	**viviendo** living
	Past Participle:	
hablado spoken	**comido** eaten	**vivido** lived
Present:	*Indicative:*	
hablo I speak	**como** I eat	**vivo** I live
hablas	**comes**	**vives**
habla	**come**	**vive**
hablamos	**comemos**	**vivimos**
habláis	**coméis**	**vivís**
hablan	**comen**	**viven**

First Conjugation	Second Conjugation	Third Conjugation
Imperfect:		
hablaba I was speaking	**comía** I was eating	**vivía** I was living
hablabas	**comías**	**vivías**
hablaba	**comía**	**vivía**
hablábamos	**comíamos**	**vivíamos**
hablabals	**comíais**	**vivíais**
hablaban	**comían**	**vivían**
Preterit:		
hablé I spoke	**comí** I ate	**viví** I lived
hablaste	**comiste**	**viviste**
habló	**comió**	**vivió**
hablamos	**comimos**	**vivimos**
hablasteis	**comisteis**	**vivisteis**
hablaron	**comieron**	**vivieron**
Future:		
hablaré I shall speak	**comeré** I shall eat	**viviré** I shall live
hablarás	**comerás**	**vivirás**
hablará	**comerá**	**vivirá**
hablaremos	**comeremos**	**viviremos**
hablaréis	**comeréis**	**vlviréis**
hablarán	**comerán**	**vivirán**
Conditional:		
hablaría I should speak	**comería** I should eat	**viviría** I should live
hablarías	**comerías**	**vivirías**
hablaría	**comería**	**viviría**
hablaríamos	**comeríamos**	**viviríamos**
hablaríais	**comeríais**	**viviríais**
hablarían	**comerían**	**vivirían**

Irregular Verbs

All simple tenses are shown in these tables if they contain one irregular form or more, except the conditional, and the imperfect and future subjunctive.

The letters (a) to (h) identify the tenses as follows:

        (a) gerund   (e) present subjunctive
        (b) past participle   (f) imperfect indicative
        (c) imperative   (g) future indicative
        (d) present indicative   (h) preterit indicative

abolir: defective verb used only in forms whose endings contain the vowel **i**.

acertar
- (c) **acierta**, acertad
- (d) **acierto, aciertas, acierta**, acertamos, acertáis, **aciertan**
- (e) **acierte, aciertes, acierte**, acertemos, acertéis, **acierten**

agorar
- (c) **agüera**, agorad
- (d) **agüero, agüeras, agüera**, agoramos, agoráis, **agüeran**
- (e) **agüere, agüeres, agüere**, agoremos, agoréis, **agüeren**

airar
- (c) **aíra**, airad
- (d) **aíro, aíras, aíra**, airamos, airáis, **aíran**
- (e) **aíre, aíres, aíre**, airemos, airéis, **aíren**

andar
- (h) **anduve, anduviste, anduvo, anduvimos, anduvisteis, anduvieron**

argüir
- (a) **arguyendo**
- (b) **argüido**
- (c) **arguye**, argüid
- (d) **arguyo, arguyes, arguye**, argüimos, argüis, **arguyen**
- (e) **arguya, arguyas, arguya**, arguyamos, arguyáis, **arguyan**
- (h) **argüi, argüiste, arguyó**, argüimos, argüisteis, **arguyeron**

asir
- (d) **asgo**, ases, ase, asimos, asis, asen
- (e) **asga, asgas, asga, asgamos, asgáis, asgan**

aunar
- (c) **aúna**, aunad
- (d) **aúno, aúnas**, aunamos, aunáis, **aúnan**
- (e) **aúne, aúnes**, aunemos, aunéis, **aúnen**

avongonzar
- (c) **avergüenza**, avergonzad
- (d) **avergüenzo, avergüenzas, avergüenza**, avergonzamos, avergonzáis, **avergüenzan**
- (e) **avergüence, avergüences, avergüence, avergoncemos, avergoncéis, avergüencen**
- (h) **avergonce**, avergonzaste, avergonzó, avergonzamos, avergonzasteis, avergonzaron

averiguar
- (e) **averigüe, averigües, averigüe, averigüeis, averigüen**
- (h) **averigüé**, averiguaste, averiguó, averiguamos, averiguasteis, averiguaron

bendecir
- (a) **bendiciendo**
- (c) **bendice**, bendecid
- (d) **bendigo, bendices, bendice**, bendecimos, bendecís, **bendicen**
- (e) **bendiga, bendigas, bendiga, bendigamos**, bendigáis, **bendigan**
- (h) **bendije, bendijiste, bendijo, bendijimos, bendijisteis, bendijeron**

bruñir
- (a) **bruñendo**
- (h) **bruñí, bruñiste, bruñó**, bruñimos, bruñisteis, **bruñeron**

bullir
- (a) **bullendo**
- (h) **bullí, bulliste, bulló**, bullimos, bullisteis, **bulleron**

caber
- (d) **quepo**, cabes, cabe, cabemos, cabéis, caben
- (e) **quepa, quepas, quepa, quepamos, quepáis, quepan**
- (g) **cabré, cabrás, cabrá, cabremos, cabréis, cabrán**
- (h) **cupe, cupiste, cupo, cupimos, cupisteis, cupieron**

caer
- (a) **cayendo**
- (b) **caido**
- (d) **caigo**, caes, cae, caemos, caéis, caen
- (e) **caiga, caigas, caiga, caigamos, caigáis, caigan**
- (h) **caí, caíste, cayó, caímos, caísteis, cayeron**

cocer
- (c) **cuece**, coced
- (d) **cuezo, cueces, cuece**, cocemos, cocéis, **cuecen**
- (e) **cueza, cuezas, cueza, cozamos, cozáis, cuezan**

coger
    (d) **cojo**, coges, coge, cogemos, cogéis, cogen
    (e) **coja, cojas, coja, cojamos, cojáis, cojan**

comenzar
    (c) **comienza**, comenzad
    (d) **comienzo, comienzas, comienza**, comenzamos,
        comenzáis, **comienzan**
    (e) **comience, comiences, comience, comencemos,
        comencéis, comiencen**
    (h) **comencé**, comenzaste, comenzó, comenzamos,
        comenzasteis, comenzaron

conducir
    (d) **conduzco**, conduces, conduce, conducimos, conducis,
        conducen
    (e) **conduzca, conduzcas, conduzca, conduzcamos,
        conduzcáis, conduzcan**
    (h) **conduje, condujiste, condujo, condujimos,
        condujisteis, condujeron**

construir
    (a) **construyendo**
    (b) **construído**
    (c) **construye**, construid
    (d) **construyo, construyes, construye**, construimos,
        construis, **construyen**
    (e) **construya, construyas, construya, construyamos,
        construyáis, construyan**
    (h) construi, construiste, **construyó**, construimos,
        construisteis, **construyeron**

continuar
    (c) **continúa**, continuad
    (d) **continúo, continúas, continúa**, continuamos,
        continuáis, **continúan**
    (e) **continúe, continúes, continúe**, continuemos, continuéis,
        continúen

crecer
    (d) **crezco**, creces, crece, crécemos, crecéis, crecen
    (e) **crezca, crezcas, crezca, crezcamos, crezcáis, crezcan**

dar
    (d) **doy**, das, da, damos, dais, dan
    (e) **dé**, des, **dé**, demos, deis, den
    (h) **dí, diste, dio, dimos, disteis, dieron**

decir
- (a) **diciendo**
- (b) **dicho**
- (c) **di**, decid
- (d) **digo, dices, dice**, decimos, decís, **dicen**
- (e) **diga, digas, diga, digamos, digáis, digan**
- (g) **diré, dirás, dirá, diremos, diréis, dirán**
- (h) **dije, dijiste, dijo, dijimos, dijisteis, dijeron**

delinquir
- (d) **delinco**, delinques, delinque, delinquimos, delinquis, delinquen
- (e) **delinca, delincas, delinca, delincamos, delincáis, delincan**

desosar
- (c) **deshuesa**, desosad
- (d) **deshueso, deshuesas, deshuesa**, desosamos, desosáis, **deshuesan**
- (e) **deshuese, deshueses, deshuese**, desosemos, desoséis, **deshuesen**

dirigir
- (d) **dirijo**, diriges, dirige, dirigimos, dirigis, dirigen
- (e) **dirija, dirijas, dirija, dirijamos, dirijáis, dirijan**

discernir
- (c) **discierne**, discernid
- (d) **discierno, disciernes, discierne**, discernimos, discernís, **disciernen**
- (e) **discierna, disciernas, discierna, discernamos, discernáis, distingan**

distinguir
- (d) **distingo**, distingues, distingue, distinguimos, distinguis, distinguen
- (e) **distinga, distingas, distinga, distingamos, distingáis, distingan**

dormir
- (a) **durmiendo**
- (c) **duerme**, dormid
- (d) **duermo, duermes, duerme**, dormimos, dormis, **duermen**
- (e) **duerma, duermas, duerma, durmamos, durmáis, duerman**
- (h) dormi, dormiste, **durmió**, dormimos, dormisteis, **durmieron**

empeller
- (a) **empellendo**
- (h) empellí, empelliste, **empelló**, empellimos, empellisteis, **empelleron**

enraizar
- (c) **enraíza**, enraizad
- (d) **enraízo**, **enraízas**, **enraíza**, enraizamos, enraizáis, **enraízan**
- (e) **enraíce**, **enraíces**, **enraíce**, **enraicemos**, **enraicéis**, **enraícen**
- (h) **enraicé**, enraizaste, enraizó, enraizamos, enraizasteis, enraizaron

erguir
- (a) **irguiendo**
- (c) **irgue** or **yergue**, erguid
- (d) **irgo, irgues, irgue, yergo, hergues, yergue** } erguimos, erguis { **irguen yerguen**
- (e) **irga, irgas, irga, yerga, yergas, yerga,** } erguimos, erguis { **irgan yergan**
- (h) erguí, erguiste, **irguió**, erguimos, erguisteis, **irguieron**

errar
- (c) **yerra**, errad
- (d) **yerro, yerras, yerra**, erramos, erráis, **yerran**
- (e) **yerre, yerres, yerre**, erremos, erréis, **yerren**

esforzar
- (c) **esfuerza**, esforzad
- (d) **esfuerzo, esfuerzas, esfuerza**, esforzamos, esforzáis, **esfuerzan**
- (e) **esfuerce, esfuerces, esfuerce, esforcemos, esforcéis, esfuercen**
- (h) **esforcé**, esforzaste, esforzó, esforzamos, esforzasteis, esforzaron

esparcir
- (d) **esparzo**, esparces, esparce, esparcimos, esparcís, esparcen
- (e) **esparza, esparzas, esparza, esparzamos, esparzáis, esparzan**

estar
- (c) **está**, estad
- (d) **estoy, estás, está**, estamos, estáis, **están**
- (e) **esté, estés, esté**, estemos, estéis, **estén**
- (h) **estuve, estuviste, estuvo, estuvimos, estuvisteis, estuvieron**

haber
- (c) **hé,** habed
- (d) **he, has, ha, hemos,** habéis, **han** (v. impers.), **hay**
- (e) **haya, hayas, haya, hayamos,** hayáis, **hayan**
- (g) **habré, habrás, habrá, habremos, habréis, habrán**
- (h) **hube, hubiste, hubo, hubimos, hubisteis, hubieron**

hacer
- (b) **hecho**
- (c) **haz,** haced
- (d) **hago,** haces, hace, hacemos, hacéis, hacen
- (e) **haga, hagas, haga, hagamos, hagáis, hagan**
- (g) **haré, harás, hará, haremos, haréis, harán**
- (h) **hice, hiciste, hizo, hicimos, hicisteis, hicieron**

inquirir
- (c) **inquiere,** inquirid
- (d) **inquiero, inquieres, inquiere,** inquirimos, inquiris,
  inquieren
- (e) **inquiera, inquieras, inquiera,** inquiramos, inquiráis,
  inquieran

ir
- (a) **yendo**
- (c) **vé, vamos,** id
- (d) **voy, vas, va, vamos, vais, van**
- (e) **vaya, vayas, vaya, vayamos, vayáis, vayan**
- (f) **iba, ibas, iba, íbamos, ibais, iban**
- (h) **fui, fuiste, fue, fuimos, fuisteis, fueron**

jugar
- (c) **juega,** jugad
- (d) **juego, juegas, juega,** jugamos, jugáis **juegan**
- (e) **juegue, juegues, juegue, juguemos, juguéis, jueguen**
- (h) **jugué,** jugaste, jugó, jugamos, jugasteis, jugaron

leer
- (a) **leyendo**
- (b) **leído**
- (h) **leí, leíste, layó, leímos, leísteis, leyeron**

ligar
- (e) **ligue, ligues, ligue, liguemos, liguéis, liguen**
- (h) **ligué,** ligaste, ligó, ligamos, ligasteis, ligaron

lucir
- (d) **luzco,** luces, luce, lucimos, lucís, lucen
- (e) **luzca, luzcas, luzca, luzcamos, luzcáis, luzcan**

mecer
  (d) **mezo**, meces, mece, mecemos, mecéis, mecen
  (e) **meza, mezas, meza, mezamos, mezáix, mezan**

mover
  (c) **mueve**, moved
  (d) **muevo, mueves, mueve**, movemos, movéis, **mueven**
  (e) **mueva, muevas, mueva**, movamos, mováis, **muevan**

oir
  (a) **oyendo**
  (b) **oído**
  (c) **oye, oíd**
  (d) **oigo, oyes, oye, oímos**, oís, **oyen**
  (e) **oiga, oigas, oiga, oigamos, oigáis, oigan**
  (h) oí, **oíste, oyó, oímos, oísteis, oyeron**

oler
  (c) **huele**, oled
  (d) **huelo, hueles, huele**, olemos, oléis, **huelen**
  (e) **huela, huelas, huela**, olamos, oláis, **huelan**

pedir
  (a) **pidiendo**
  (c) **pide**, pedid
  (d) **pido, pides, pide**, pedimos, pedís, **piden**
  (e) **pida, pidas, pida, pidamos, pidáis, pidan**
  (h) pedí, pediste, **pidió**, pedimos, pedisteis, **pedeiron**

perder
  (c) **pierde**, perded
  (d) **pierdo, pierdes, pierde**, perdemos, perdéis, **pierden**
  (e) **pierda, pierdas, pierda**, perdamos, perdáis, **pierdan**

placer
  (d) **plazco**, places, place, placemos, placeis, placen
  (e) **plazca, plazcas, plazca, plazcamos, plazcáis, plazcan**
  (h) plací, placiste, plació (or **plugo**), placimos, placisteis,
      placieron

poder
  (a) **pudiendo**
  (c) (**puede**, poded)
  (d) **puedo, puedes, puede**, podemos, podéis, **pueden**
  (e) **pueda, puedas, pueda**, podamos, podáis, **puedan**
  (g) **podré, podrás, podrá, podremos, podréis, podrán**
  (h) **pude, pudiste, pudo, pudimos, pudisteis, pudieron**

poner
- (b) **puesto**
- (c) **pon**, poned
- (d) **pongo**, pones, pone, ponemos, ponéis, ponen
- (e) **ponga, pongas, ponga, pongamos, pongáis, pongan**
- (g) **pondré, pondrás, pondrá, pondremos, pondréis, pondrán**
- (h) **puse, pusiste, puso, pusimos, pusisteis, pusieron**

querer
- (c) **quiere**, quered
- (d) **quiero, quieres, quiere**, queremos, queréis, **quieren**
- (e) **quiera, quieras, quiera**, queramos, queráis, **quieran**
- (g) **querré, querrás, querrá, querremos, querréis, querrán**
- (h) **quise, quisiste, quiso, quisimos, quisisteis, quisieron**

raer
- (a) **rayendo**
- (b) **raído**
- (d) **raigo** (or **rayo**), raes, rae, raemos, raéis, raen
- (e) **raiga** (or **raya**), **raigas, raiga, raigamos, raigáis, raigan**
- (h) **raí, raíste, rayó, raímos, raísteis, rayeron**

regir
- (a) **rigiendo**
- (c) **rige**, regid
- (d) **rijo, riges, rige**, regimos, regís, **rigen**
- (e) **rija, rijas, rija, rijamos, rijáis, rijan**
- (h) regí, registe, **rigió**, regimos, registeis, **rigieron**

reír
- (a) **riendo**
- (b) **reído**
- (c) **ríe, reíd**
- (d) **río, ríes, ríe, reímos**, reís, **ríen**
- (e) **ría, rías, ría, ríamos, ríáis, rían**
- (h) reí, **reíste, rió, reímos, reísteis, rieron**

reunir
- (c) **reúne**, reunid
- (d) **reúno, reúnes, reúne**, reunimos, reunís, **reúnen**
- (e) **reúna, reúnas, reúna**, reunamos, reunáis, **reúnan**

rezar
- (e) **rece, reces, rece, recemos, recéis, recen**
- (h) **recé**, rezaste, rezó, rezamos, rezasteis, rezaron

rodar
- (c) **rueda**, rodad
- (d) **ruedo, ruedas, rueda**, rodamos, rodáis, **ruedan**
- (e) **ruede, ruedes, ruede**, rodemos, rodéis, **rueden**

roer
- (a) **royendo**
- (b) **roído**
- (d) **roo** (**roigo**, or **royo**), roes, roe, roemos, roéis, roen
- (e) **roa** (**roiga**, or **roya**), roas, roa, roamos, roáis, roan
- (h) roí, **roíste, royó, roímos, roísteis, royeron**

rogar
- (c) **ruega**, rogad
- (d) **ruego, ruegas, ruega**, rogamos, rogáis, **ruegan**
- (e) **ruegue, ruegues, ruegue, roguemos, roguéis, rueguen**
- (h) **rogué**, rogaste, rogó, rogamos, rogasteis, rogaron

saber
- (d) **sé**, sabes, sabe, sabemos, sabéis, saben
- (e) **sepa, sepas, sepa, sepamos, sepáis, sepan**
- (g) **sabré, sabrás, sabrá, sabremos, sabréis, sabrán**
- (h) **supe, supiste, supo, supimos, supisteis, supieron**

salir
- (c) **sal**, salid
- (d) **salgo**, sales, sale, salimos, salís, salen
- (e) **salga, salgas, salga, salgamos, salgáis, salgan**
- (g) **saldré, saldrás, saldrá, saldremos, saldréis, saldrán**

segar
- (c) **siega**, segad
- (d) **siego, siegas, siega**, segamos, segáis, **siegan**
- (e) **siegue, siegues, siegue, seguemos, seguéis, sieguen**
- (h) **segué**, segaste, segó, segamos, segasteis, segaron

seguir
- (a) **siguiendo**
- (c) **sigue**, seguid
- (d) **sigo, siegues, sigue**, seguimos, seguís, **siguen**
- (e) **siga, sigas, siga, sigamos, sigáis, sigan**
- (h) seguí, seguiste, **siguió**, seguimos, seguisteis, **siguieron**

sentir
- (a) **sintiendo**
- (c) **siente**, sentid
- (d) **siento, sientes, siente**, sentimos, sentís, **sienten**
- (e) **sienta, sientas, sienta**, sentamos, sentáis, **sientan**
- (h) sentí, sentiste, **sintió**, sentimos, sentisteis, **sintieron**

ser
- (c) **sé**, sed
- (d) **soy, eres, es, somos, sois, son**
- (e) **sea, seas, sea, seamos, seáis, sean**
- (f) **era, eras, era, éramos, erais, eran**
- (h) **fui, fuiste, fue, fuimos, fuisteis, fueron**

tañer
- (a) **tañendo**
- (h) tañí, tañiste, **tañó**, tañimos, tañisteis, **tañeron**

tener
- (c) **ten**, tened
- (d) **tengo, tienes, tiene**, tenemos, tenéis, **tienen**
- (e) **tenga, tengas, tenga, tengamos, tengáis, tengan**
- (g) **tendré, tendrás, tendrá, tendremos, tendréis, tendrán**
- (h) **tuve, tuviste, tuvo, tuvimos, tuvisteis, tuvieron**

teñir
- (a) **tiñendo**
- (c) **tiñe**, teñid
- (d) **tiño, tiñes, tiñe**, teñimos, teñis, **tiñen**
- (e) **tiña, tiñas, tiña, tiñamos, tiñáis, tiñan**
- (h) teñí, teñiste, **tiñó**, teñimos, teñisteis, **tiñeron**

tocar
- (e) **toque, toques, toque, toquemos, toquéis, toquen**
- (h) **toqué**, tocaste, tocó, tocamos, tocasteis, tocaron

torcer
- (c) **tuerce**, torced
- (d) **tuerzo, tuerces, tuerce**, torcemos, torcéis, **tuercen**
- (e) **tuerza, tuerzas, tuerza, torzamos, torzáis, tuerzan**

traer
- (a) **trayendo**
- (b) **traído**
- (d) **traigo**, traes, trae, traemos, traéis, traen
- (e) **traiga, traigas, traiga, traigamos, traigáis, traigan**
- (h) **traje, trajiste, trajo, trajimos, trajisteis, trajeron**

valer
- (d) **valgo**, vales, vale, valemos, valéis, valen
- (e) **valga, valgas, valga, valgamos, valgáis, valgan**
- (g) **valdré, valdrás, valdrá, valdremos, valdréis, valdrán**

variar
- (c) **varía**, variad
- (d) **varío, varías, varía**, variamos, variáis, **varían**
- (e) **varíe, varíes, varíe**, variemos, variéis, **varíen**

vencer
- (d) **venzo**, vences, vence, vencemos, vencéis, vencen
- (e) **venza, venzas, venza, venzamos, venzáis, venzan**

venir
- (a) **viniendo**
- (c) **ven**, venid
- (d) **vengo, vienes, viene**, venimos, venís, **vienen**
- (e) **venga, vengas, venga, vengamos, vengáis, vengan**
- (g) **vendré, vendrás, vendrá, vendremos, vendréis, vendrán**
- (h) **vine, viniste, vino, vinimos, vinisteis, vinieron**

ver
- (b) **visto**
- (d) **veo**, ves, ve, vemos, veis, ven
- (e) **vea, veas, vea, veamos, veáis, vean**
- (f) **veía, veías, veía, veíamos, veíais, veían**

volcar
- (c) **vuelca**, volcad
- (d) **vuelco, vuelcas, vuelca**, volcamos, volcáis, **vuelcan**
- (e) **vuelque, vuelques, vuelque, volquemos, volquéis, vuelquen**
- (h) **volqué**, volcaste, volcó, volcamos, volcasteis, volcaron

yacer
- (c) **yaz** (or yace), yaced
- (d) **yazco** (**yazgo**, or **yago**), yaces, yace, yacemos, yacéis, yacen
- (e) **yazca** (**yazga**, or **yaga**), **yazcas, yazca, yazcamos, yazcáis, yazcan**

The following verbs, some of which are included in the foregoing table, and their compounds have irregular past participles:

abrir	cubierto	proveer	puesto
cubrir	dicho	pudrir	provisto
decir	escrito	romper	podrido
escribir	frito	solver	roto
freir	hecho	ver	suelto
hacer	impreso	volver	visto
imprimir	morir	muerto	vuelto
abierto	poner		

A

a, *prep.* to, at
abadía, *f.* abbey; abbacy
abajo, *adv.* under, below; downstairs
abanderado, *m.* (mil.) ensign; standard bearer
abandonar, *va.* to abandon
abandono, *m.* abandonment; carelessness
abanicar, *va.* to fan
abanico, *m.* fan; derrick
abarcar, *va.* to comprise
abarrotes, *m. pl.* groceries
abastecer, *va.* to supply
abatimiento, *m.* low spirits, depression
abdicar, *va.* to abdicate
abdomen, *m.* abdomen
abecé, *m.* alphabet
abecedario, *m.* alphabet
abedul, *m.* birch tree
abeja, *f.* bee
abejarrón or **abejorro,** *m.* bumblebee
abejón, *m.* drone; hornet
abertura, *f.* cleft, opening
abierto, *adj.* open; sincere
abismo, *m.* chasm, abyss
ablandar, *va., vn.* to soften
abnegar, *va.* to renounce
abochornar, *va., vr.* to shame, be embarrassed
abofetear, *va.* to slap one's face
abogacía, *f.* profession of law
abogado, *m.* lawyer; advocate
abogar, *vn.* to advocate; intercede
abolengo, *m.* ancestry
abolir, *va. def.* to abolish
abominable, *adj.* abominable
abominar, *va.* to detest
abonar, *va.* to manure; to credit with; to pay on an account; **abonarse,** to subscribe to
abono, *m.* fertilizer; payment; season ticket
abordar, *va.* to board a ship; approach (a subject)
aborrecer, *va.* to hate, abhor
abortar, *vn.* to miscarry, abort
aborto, *m.* abortion; monstrosity

abotonar, *va.* to button
abr., abreviatura, abbr, abbreviation
abrasar, *va.* to burn; to scorch
abrazar, *va.* to embrace
abrazo, *m.* embrace, hug
abrelatas, *m.* can opener
abreviar, *va.* to abbreviate
abrevistura, *f.* abbreviation
abridor, *m.* opener; **abridor de latas,** can opener
abrigar, *va.* to shelter; **abrigarse,** to wrap, cover up
abrigo, *m.* shelter; wrap, overcoat
abril, *m.* April
abrir, *va., vr.* to open
abrochar, *va.* to hook, clasp on
abrumar, *va.* to overwhelm
absceso, *m.* abscess
absorto, *adj.* absorbed; amazed
abstemio, *adj.* abstemious; *m.* teetotaler
abstenerse, *vr.* to abstain
abstinencia, *f.* abstinence
abstracto, *adj.* abstract
abstraer, *va.* to abstract; **abstraerse,** to be lost in thought
absuelto, *adj.* absolved, acquitted
absurdo, *adj.* absurd; *m.* absurdity
abuela, *f.* grandmother
abuelo, *m.* grandfather; **abuelos,** *pl.* ancestors
abundancia, *f.* abundance
abundar, *vn.* to abound
aburrido, *adj.* bored; boresome
aburrir, *va.* to bore; **aburrirse,** to be bored
abusar, *va., vn.* to abuse; to impose upon
abuso, *m.* abuse, misuse
a/c, a cuenta, on account, in part payment; **a cargo,** drawn on; in care of
A.C. or **A. de C., Anio de Cristo,** A.D. in the year of Our Lord
acá, *adv.* here, hither

acabar, *va.*, *vn.* to finish, complete; to die

academia, *f.* academy

académico, *adj.* academic

acalorar, *va.* to heat; **acalorarse**, to get excited, to become warm

acamper, *va.* to camp

acantonar, *va.* to quarter troops

acaparar, *va.* to monopolize

acariciar, *va.* to caress

acarrear, *va.* to transport; to occasion, cause

acarreo, *m.* cartage

acaso, *m.* chance, haphazard; **por si acaso**, just in case

acatar, *va.* to respect, obey (orders)

acatarrarse, *vr.* to catch cold

acaudalado, *adj.* rich, wealthy

acceder, *vn.* to accede, agree

accesible, *adj.* accessible

acceso, *m.* access, approach

accesorio, *adj.* accessory

accidental, *adj.* accidental

accidente *m.* accident

acción, *f.* act, action; share, stock

accionar, *vn.* to gesticulate

accionista, *m., f.* stockholder

aceitar, *va.* to oil

aceite, *m.* oil

aceituna, *f.* olive

acelerador, *m.* accelerator

acelerar, *va.* to accelerate

acento, *m.* accent

acentuar, *va.* to accentuate; to emphasize

acepción, *f.* meaning

aceptable, *adj.* acceptable

aceptación, *f.* acceptance

aceptar, *va.* to accept; to admit

acera, *f.* sidewalk

acerca de, *prep.* about

acercar, *va.*, *vr.* to bring together; to approach

acérrimo, *adj.* very vigorous; **enemigo acérrimo**, bitter enemy

acertado, *adj.* accurate

acertar, *va.* to conjecture right

acertijo, *m.* riddle, conundrum

acicalarse, *vr.* to dress meticulously; to paint one's face

ácido, *m.* acid; *adj.* acid, sour

acierto, *m.* accuracy; ability

aclamación, *f.* acclamation

aclamar, *va.* to applaud

aclaración, *f.* explanation

aclarar, *va.* to clarify; **aclararse**, to clear up

aclimatar, *va.* to acclimatize

acne, *m.* (med.) acne

acogedor, *adj.* cozy, inviting

acoger, *va.* to receive; to protect; **acogerse**, to resort to

acogida, *f.* reception; welcome

acólito, *m.* acolyte; assistant

acometida, *f.* attack, assault

acomodado, *adj.* wealthy

acomodador, *m.* usher

acomodar, *va.* to accomodate, arrange; *vn.* to fit, suit

acompañamiento, *m.* accompaniment

acompañante, *m.* companion; accompanist

acompañar, *va.* to accompany

acongojarse, *vr.* to become sad

aconsejable, *adj.* advisable

aconsejar, *va.* to advise

acontecer, *vn. def.* to happen

acontecimiento, *m.* event, incident

acopiar, *va.* to gather, to store up

acorazado, *m.* battleship

acordar, *va.* to resolve; *vn.* to agree; **acordarse**, to remember

acorde, *m.* accord; chord

acortar, *va.* to abridge, shorten

acosar, *va.* to molest, harass

acostar, *va.* to put to bed; **acostarse**, to lie down; go to bed

acostumbrar, *va.*, *vn.* to accustom; to be accustomed

acre, *adj.* acid; *m.* acre

acreditado, *adj.* accredited

acreditar, *va.* to assure, authorize; to credit; to accredit

acreedor, *m.* creditor; *adj.* worthy; **saldo acreedor**, credit balance

acrílico, *adj.* acrylic

acta, *f.* minutes of proceeding;
acta de venta, bill of sale

ACTH, (med.) ACTH

actitud, *f.* attitude, posture

activar, *va.* to activate

actividad, *f.* activity; liveliness

activo *adj.* active, diligent; *m.*
(com.) assets

acto, *m.* act; action

actuación, *f.* performance

actual, *adj.* actual, present

actualidad, actuality, current
event

actuar, *vn.* to act

acuario, *m.* aquarium

acuático, *adj.* aquatic

acudir, *vn.* to assist, to be
present; **acudir a,** to resort
to

acueducto, *m.* aqueduct

acuerdo, *m.* agreement; resolution

acumulador, *m.* battery

acumular, *va.* to accumulate

acurrucarse, *vr.* to huddle

acusación, *f.* accusation

acusar, *va.* to accuse; to reproach; **acusar recibo de,**
acknowledge receipt of

acusativo, *m.* accusative

acústica, *f.* acoustics

achacar, *va.* to impute, blame

achaque, *m.* ailment

achicar, *va.* to diminish; to
bail a boat

adaptable, *adj.* adaptable

adaptar, *va.* to adapt

**A. de J.C., antes de Jesucris-
to,** B.C. Before Christ

adefesio, *m.* ridiculous attire

adelantado, *adj.* anticipated;
por adelantadodo, in advance

adelantar, *va., vn.* to advance;
adelantarse, to take the lead

adelanto, *m.* progress, advance

adelgazarse, *vr.* to lose weight

ademán, *m.* gesture; attitude

además, *adv.* moreover, also;
además de, besides

adentro, *adv.* within; inwardly

adepto, *adj.* adept; *m.* follower

adeudar, *va.* to owe

adherencia, *f.* adhesion, adherence

adherir, *vn., vr.* to adhere

adhesión, *f.* adherence

adición, *f.* addition

adicto, *m.* addict; *adj.* addicted

adiós, *interj.* good-by, adieu

adivinanza, *f.* riddle

adivinar, *va.* to guess

adj., adjetivo, *adj.* adjective

adjetivo, *m.* adjective

adjuntar, *va.* to enclose, attach

administración, *f.* administration

administrar, *va.* to administer

admirable, *adj.* admirable

admiración, *f.* admiration;
wonder; (gram.) exclamation
point

admirar, *va.* to admire; **admi-
rarse,** to be surprised

admisión, *f.* admission

admitir, *va.* to admit

adobar, *va.* to stew

adobo, *m.* stew

adolescencia, *f.* adolescence,
youth

adolescente, *adj., m., f.* adolescent; bobby soxer

adonde, *adv.* whither, where

adopción, *f.* adoption

adoptar, *va.* to adopt

adoptivo, *adj.* adoptive;
adopted

adormecer, *va.* to put to sleep

adornar, *va.* to embellish

adquirir, *va.* to acquire

adrede, *adv.* purposely

aduana, *f.* customhouse

adular, *va.* to flatter; to fawn

adulterar, *va.* to adulterate

adulto, *adj.* adult

adv., adverbio, *adv.* adverb

**ad val., ad valórem, en pro-
porción al valor,** ad val. ad
valorem, in proportion to the
value

adverbio, *m.* adverb

adversario, *m.* adversary

adversidad, *f.* adversity

adverso, *adj.* adverse

advertencia, *f.* warning

advertir. *va.* to warn

aéreo, *adj.* air, aerial

aerógrafo, *m.* air brush

aeronáutica, *f.* aeronautics

aeroplano, *m.* airplane

aeropuerto, *m.* airport

afable, *adj.* affable

afamado, *adj.* famous

afán, *m.* anxiety, worry

afanarse, *vr.* to toil, labor

afección, *f.* disease

afectación, t. affectation

afectar, *va.* to affect

afectísimo, *adj.* devoted; yours truly

afecto, *m.* affection, love

afectuoso, *adj.* affectionate

afeitar, *va., vr.* to shave

afeminado, *adj.* effeminate

aferrado, *adj.* stubborn

afianzar, *va.* to bail, guarantee; to prop, fix

afición, *f.* preference; hobby

aficionado, aficionada, n. amateur

afilar, to sharpen

afiliado, *adj.* affiliated

afinar, *va.* to tune (musical instruments), to refine

afirmar, *va.* to secure, fasten; to affirm

afirmativo, *adj.* affirmative

aflicción, *f.* affliction, grief

afligirse, *vr.* to grieve

aflojar, *va.* to loosen

afmo. or **af.mo, afectísimo,** idiomatic expression for "Cordially yours," etc.

afortunadamente, *adv.* fortunately, luckily

afortunado, adj. fortunate

afrenta, *f.* outrage; insult

afro, *adj.* Afro

afrontar, *va.* to confront

aftosa, *adj.* (vet.) hoof-and-mouth disease

afuera, *adv.* out, outside

afueras, *f. pl.* outskirts

ágape, *m.* banquet; testimonial dinner

agarrar, *va.* to grasp

agasajar, *va.* to entertain

agente, *m.* agent

agitado, *adj.* excited

agitar, *va.* to shake; **agitarse,** to become excited

aglomerar, *va., vr.* to conglomerate

agobiar, *va., vr.* to oppress, burden

agonía, t. agony, anguish

agonizar, *vn.* to be dying

agosto, *m.* August (month); harvest time

agotado, *adj.* sold out; exhausted

agotar, *va.* to exhaust; **agotarse,** to run out of

agraciado, *adj.* graceful; gifted

agradable, *adj.* pleasant

agradar, *va.* to please, gratify

agradecer, *va.* to appreciate (a favor)

agradecido, *adj.* grateful

agradecimiento, *m.* gratitude, gratefulness

agrandar, *va.* to enlarge

agrario, *adj.* agrarian

agravar, *va.* to aggravate

agraviar, *va.* to wrong; **agraviarse,** to take offense

agregar, *va.* to add

agresión, *f.* aggression

agresivo, *adj.* aggressive

agriar, *va., vr.* to sour

agrícola, *adj.* agricultural

agricultor, *m.* agriculturist, farmer

agricultura, *f.* agriculture

agridulce, *adj.* bittersweet

agrietarse, *vr.* to crack

agrimensor, *m.* land surveyor

agrio, *adj.* sour; rude

agrónomo, *m.* agronomist

agrupar, *va., vr.* to group (in a picture); to crowd

agto. or **ag.to, agosto,** Aug. August

agua, *f.* water, liquid; rain

aguacate, *m.* avocado, alligator pear

aguacerol, *m.* shower of rain

aguado, *adj.* watery

aguafuerte, *f.* etching

aguantar, *va.* to endure, bear

aguar, *va., vr.* to thin out with water; to spoil (a party, etc.)

aguardar, *va.* to expect, wait for

aguardiente, *m.* distilled liquor

aguarrás, _m._ turpentine
agudo, _adj._ acute; sharp-pointed
aguijón, _m._ sting of a bee, wasp, etc.; stimulation
águila, _f._ eagle
aguileño, _adj._ aquiline
aguinaldo, _m._ Christmas gift
aguja, _f._ needle; switch; **aguja de coser**, sewing needle
agujero, _m._ hole
aguzar, _va._ to whet; to stimulate
ahí, _adv._ there; **de ahí (que)**, for this reason; **por ahí**, that way, more or less
ahijada, _f._ goddaughter
ahijado, _m._ godson
ahinco, _m._ zeal, earnestness
ahogar, _va. vr._ to drown; to suffocate
ahondar, _va._ to deepen; _vn._ to penetrate
ahora, _adv._ now, at present; _co·ij._ whether, or
ahorcar, _va., vr._ to kill by hanging
ahorita, _adv._ (Sp. Am.) just now, in just a minute
ahorrar, _va._ to save, economize
ahorro, _m._ saving, thrift
ahumar, _va._ to cure in smoke
ahuyentar, _va._ to put to flight
aire, _m._ air, wind
airear, _va._ to air, ventilate
airoso, _adj._ airy; graceful; successful
aislado, _adj._ insulated, isolated
aislador, _m._ (elec.) insulator
aislamiento, _m._ isolation; insulation; (fig.) solitude
aislar, _va._ to isolate; to insulate
ajar, _va._ to crumple
ajedrez, _m._ chess (game)
ajeno, _adj._ another's; contrary to
ají, _m._ chili pepper, chili
ajo, _m._ garlic; **¡ajo!** _interj._ darn!
ajustar, _va._ to regulate; to adjust; to tighten
ajuste, _m._ adjustment

al, contraction for **a el; al fin**, at last
ala, _f._ wing; brim of the hat
alabanza, _f._ praise, applause
alabar, _va._ to praise, extol
alabastro, _m._ alabaster; gypsum
alacena, _f._ cupboard
alacrán, _m._ scorpion
alambrado, _m._ wire fence
alambre, _m._ wire, copper wire; **alambre de púas**, barbed wire
alameda, _f._ poplar grove; tree-lined promenade
álamo, _m._ poplar, poplar tree; cottonwood tree
alarde, _m._ display; **hacer alarde**, to boast
alardear, _vn._ to brag, boast
alargar, _va._ to lengthen; to extend
alarido, _m._ outcry, howl
alarma, _f._ alarm
alarmante, _adj._ alarming
alarmar, _va., vr._ to alarm
a la v/, a la vista, (com.) at sight
alba, _f._ daybreak
albacea, _m._ executor; _f._ executrix
albañil, _m._ mason, bricklayer
albaricoque, _m._ apricot
albedrío, _m._ free will
alberca, _f._ reservoir; swimming pool
albergar, _va._ to lodge, house, harbor; **albergarse**, to take shelter
albergue, _m._ shelter
albóndiga, _f._ meat ball
alborada, _f._ early dawn; (mil.) morning watch
alborotar, _va._ to make a disturbance, stir
¡albricias! _interj._ good news!
álbum, _m._ album
albumen, _m._, **albúmina**, _f._ albumen
alcachofa, _f._ artichoke
alcaide, _m._ jailer, warden
alcalde, _m._ mayor
alcaldía, _f._ mayor's office
alcance, _m._ reach, scope
alcancía, _f._ money box; sav-

ings bank

alcanfor, *m.* camphor

alcantarillado, *m.* sewage system

alcanzar, *va.* to overtake, to reach

alcaparra, *f.* caper

alcoba, *f.* alcove; bedroom

aldaba, *f.* knocker, door latch

aldea, *f.* village

aldeano, *m.* peasant

alegar, *va.* to allege, affirm

alegato, *m.* (law) allegation, pleading; (Sp. Am.) quarrel

alegrar, *va.* to gladden; **alegrarse,** to rejoice

alegría, *f.* mirth, cheer

alejamiento, *m.* distance, remoteness; aloofness

alejar, *va.* to remove to a greater distance; to separate; **alejarse,** to withdraw, move away

alemán, alemana, *adj., n.* German

Alemania, *f.* Germany

alentador, *adj.* encouraging

alentar, *va.* to animate; to cheer, encourage

alergeno, *m.* allergen

alergia, *f.* allergy

alerta, *adv.* vigilantly, **estar alerta,** to be alert

alerto, *adj.* alert, vigilant

aletear, *vn.* to flutter

alevosía, *f.* treachery

alfabético, *adj.* alphabetical

alfabeto, *m.* alphabet

alfiler, *m.* pin; **alfiler imperdible,** safety pin

alfiletero, *m.* pincushion

alfombra, *f.* carpet; rug

alfombrilla, *f.* (med.) measles

algarabía, *f.* clamor, din

álgebra, *f.* algebra

algo, *pron.* some, something; anything; *adv.* a little, rather

algodón, *m.* cotton

algodonero, *m.* cotton plant

alguno (algún), alguna, *pron.* somebody, someone, anyone; *adj.* some, any

alhaja, *f.* jewel, gem

aliado, *adj.* allied; *n.* ally

alianza, *f.* alliance, league

alias, *adv.* alias; otherwise

aliciente, *m.* attraction, incitement, inducement

aliento, *m.* breath; encouragement

aligerar, *va.* to lighten; to hasten

alimentación, *f.* food, nourishment, meals

alimentar, *va.* to feed, nourish

alimenticio, *adj.* nutritious

alimento, *m.* nourishment, food

alinear, *va.* to align

alistar, *va., vr.* to enlist; to get ready, make ready

aliviar, *va.* to lighten; to ease

alma, *f.* soul; heart

almacén, *m.* department store; warehouse

almacenar, *va.* to store, lay up

almanaque, *m.* almanac

almeja, *f.* clam

almendra, *f.* almond

almíbar, *m.* syrup

almidón, *m.* starch

almidonar, *va.* to starch

almirante, *m.* admiral

almohada, *f.* pillow

almohadón, *m.* large cushion

almorranas, *f. pl.* hemorrhoids, piles

almorzar, *vn.* to breakfast; to eat lunch

almuerzo, *m.* breakfast; lunch

alocado, *adj.* crack-brained

alojamiento, *m.* lodging accommodation

alojar, *va., vr.* to lodge

alondra, *f.* lark

Alpes, *m. pl.* Alps

alpiste, *m.* canary seed

alquilar, *va.* to let, hire, rent

alquiler, *m.* hire; house rent

alquitrán, *m.* tar

alrededor, *adv.* around

alrededores, *m. pl.* environs; neighborhood

alt., altitud, alt., altitude; **altura,** ht., height

alta, *f.* new member

altanero, *adj.* haughty

altar, *m.* altar

altavoz, *m.* loudspeaker

alterar, *va.* to alter, change; to

disturb; **alterarse**, to become angry

altercar, *va.* to dispute, quarrel

alternar, *va.*, *vn.* to alternate

altiplano, *m.* high plateau

altísimo, *adj.* extremely high; **el Altísimo**, *m.* the Most High, God

altisonante, *adj.* high-sounding, pompous

altitud, *f.* altitude

altivo, *adj.* haughty, proud

alto, *adj.* high, elevated; loud; tall; *m.* height; story, floor; highland; (mil.) halt; (mus.) tenor

altoparlante, *m.* loudspeaker

altruismo, *m.* altruism

altura, *f.* height; highness; altitude; **alturas**, *pl.* the heavens

aludido, *adj.* referred to

aludir, *vn.* to allude, refer

alumbrado, *adj.* illuminated; *m.* lighting; **alumbrado fluorescente**, fluorescent lighting

alumbramiento, *m.* illumination; childbirth

alumbrar, *va.* to illuminate

alumbre, *m.* alum

aluminio, *m.* aluminum

alumno, *m.* disciple pupil

alusión, *f.* allusion, hint

alverjas, *f. pl.* peas

alza, *f.* advance in price; lift

alzar, *va.* to raise, lift up; to build; **alzarse**, to rise in rebellion

allá, *adv.* there; thither; **mas allá**, beyond

allanar, *va.* to level, flatten; to overcome (difficu lties)

allegado, *adj.* near; related; *n.* follower, ally

allí, *adv.* there, in that place

A.M., antemeridiano, A.M. or a.m., before noon

ama, *f.* mistress; **ama de casa**, housewife; **ama de llaves**, housekeeper

amable, *adj.* amiable, kind

amado, *n.* beloved, darling

amaestrar, *va.* to teach, to train

amamantar, *va.* to suckle, nurse

amanecer, *m.* dawn, daybreak; *vn.* to dawn; to appear at daybreak

amanerado, *adj.* affected, overrefined

amansar, *va.* to tame, domesticate; to soften, pacify

amante, *m.*, *f.* lover

amañarse, *vr.* to adapt oneself

amapola, *f.* (bot.) poppy

amar, *va.* to love

amargar, *va.* to make bitter; *vn.*, *vr.* to be bitter

amargo, *adj.* bitter, acrid; painful

amargura, *f.* bitterness

amarillo, *adj.* yellow

amarrar, *va.* to tie, fasten

amasar, *va.* to knead

amatista, amethyst

amazona, amazon, masculine woman

ámbar, *m.* amber

Amberes, *f.* Antwerp

ambición, *f.* ambition

ambicioso, *adj.* ambitious

ambiental, *adj.* environmental; **contaminación ambiental**, environmental pollution

ambiente, *m.* environment

ambiguo, *adj.* ambiguous

ambos, *adj. pl.* both

ambulancia, *f.* ambulance

ambulante, *adj.* ambulatory; roving; **vendedor ambulante**, *adj.* peddler

amedrentar, *va.* to intimidate

amén, *m.* amen; acquiescence; **amén de**, besides; except.

amenaza, *f.* threat, menace

amenazar, *va.* to threaten

amenizar, *va.* to render pleasant; to adorn (a speech)

ameno, *adj.* pleasant, entertaining.

América del Norte, *f.* North America.

Amiérica del Sur, *f.* South America.

América Latina, *f.* Latin America.

americanismo, *m.* Americanism; an expression or word used in the Spanish of Spanish America

americano, americana, *n., adj.* American

amiga, *f.* female friend

amigable, *adj.* friendly

amígdala, *f.* tonsil

amigo, amiga, *n.* friend.

aminoácido, *m.* amino acid.

amistad, *f.* friendship

amistoso, *adj.* friendly

amo, *m.* master, proprietor

amolar, *va.* to grind, sharpen

amoldar, *va., vr.* to mold; to adjust

amonestación, *f.* admonition; publication of marriage bans

amonestar, *va.* to admonish

amontonar, *va.* to heap together; to accumulate

amor, *m.* love; the object of love; **por amor de,** for the sake of; **amor propio,** pride

amoroso, *adj.* affectionate

amortiguador, *m.* shock absorber

amortiguar, *va.* to mitigate; to deaden, absorb

amortizar, *va.* to amortize

amotinarse, *vr.* to mutiny

amparar, *va.* to shelter, favor, protect; **ampararse,** to claim protection

amparo, *m.* protection, help, support; refuge, asylum

amperio, *m.* (elec.) ampere

ampliación, *f.* amplification, enlargement

ampliar, *va.* to amplify; expand, increase

amplificador, *m.* amplifier

amplio, *adj.* ample

ampolla, *f.* blister; vial

amputar, *va.* to amputate

amueblar, *va.* to furnish

anales, *m. pl.* annals

analfabetismo, *m.* illiteracy

analfabeto, analfabeta, *n.* illiterate person

análisis, *m.* or *f.* analysis

analizar, *va.* to analyze

análogo, *adj.* analogous

anaquel, *m.* shelf in a bookcase

anaranjado, *adj.* orange colored

anatomía, *f.* anatomy

anatómico, *adj.* anatomical

anca, *f.* buttock; hindquarters (of a horse)

anciano, *adj.* aged, old; ancient.

ancla, *f.* anchor

anclar, *vn.* to anchor

ancho, *adj.* broad, wide; *m.* breadth, width

anchoa, *f.* anchovy

anchura, *f.* width, breadth

andamiaje, *m.* scaffolding

andamio, *m.* scaffold

andante, *adj.* walking, errant; (mus.) andante

andar, *vn.* to go, walk; to fare; to proceed; to function, (as a machine)

andén, *m.* (rail.) platform

andrajoso, *adj.* ragged

anécdota, *f.* anecdote

anegar, *va.* to inundate; **anegarse,** to be flooded

anémico, *adj.* anemic

anestesia, *f.* (med.) anesthesia

anestésico, *m., adj.* anesthetic

anexo, *adj.* annexed; *m.* attachment on a letter

anfitrión, *m.* host

ángel, *m.* angel

anglosajón, anglosajona, *n., adj.* Anglo-Saxon

angosto, *adj.* narrow, close

anguila, *f.* (zool.) eel

angular, *adj.* angular; **piedra angular,** cornerstone

angustia, *f.* anguish

anhelo, *m.* longing

anillo, *m.* ring, small circle

ánima, *f.* soul

animación, *f.* animation, liveliness

animado, *adj.* lively; animated

animal, *m., adj.* animal brute

animar, *va., vr.* to animate, enliven; to encourage

ánimo, *m.* soul, spirit; courage; mind; intention

animoso, *adj.* courageous, spirited

aniquilar, *va., vr.* to annihilate, destroy

aniversario, *m.* anniversary

ano, *m.* anus

anoche, *adv.* last night

anochecer, *vn.* to grow dark

anónimo, *adj.* anonymous

anormal, *adj.* abnormal

anotación, *f.* annotation, note

anotar, *va.* to comment, note

ansia, *f.* anxiety, eagerness, yearning; worry

ansiar, *va.* to long for

ansioso, *adj.* anxious eager

antagonista, *m., f.* antagonist

antaño, *adv.* long ago; yore

antártico, *adj.* Antarctic

anteayer, *adv.* day before yesterday

antecesor, antecesora, *n.* predecessor; forefather

antedicho, *adj.* aforesaid

antemano, de antemano, *adv.* beforehand, in advance

antemeridiano, *adj.* in the forenoon

antena, *f.* feeler; antenna, aerial

antenoche, *adv.* night before last

anteojo, *m.* spyglass, eyeglass; **anteojos,** *pl.* eyeglasses

antepasado, *adj.* elapsed; **semana antepasada,** week before last; **antepasados,** *m. pl.* ancestors

anterior, *adj.* anterior, fore; previous

anterioridad, *f.* priority; preference

antes, *adv.* first; formerly; before; rather

antibiótico, *m.* antibiotic

anticipación, *f.* anticipation; **con anticipación,** in advance

anticipado, *adj.* in advance

anticipar, *va.* to anticipate, to forestall

anticuado, *adj.* antiquated; obsolete

antidetonante, *m., adj.* antiknock

antídoto, *m.* antidote

antier, *adv.* (contraction) day before yesterday

antiguamente, *adv.* formerly

antigüedad, *f.* antiquity; ancient times; **antigüedades,** *f. pl.* antiques

antigum, *adj.* antique, old

antihigiénico, *adj.* unsanitary

antihistamina, *f.* antihistamine

antílope, *m.* antelope

antimateria, *f.* antimatter

antipatía, *f.* antipathy

antipático, *adj.* disagreeable, displeasing

antiséptico, *adj.* antiseptic

antojarse, *vr.* to have a yen for

antojo, *m.* whim; longing

antorcha, *f.* torch, taper

anual, *adj.* annual

anualidad, *f.* anuity

anuario, *m.* annual; vearbook.

anular, *va.* to annul; *adj.* anular; **dedo anular,** ring finger

anunciador, *m.* announcer

anunciante, *m.* advertiser

anunciar, *va.* to announce; to advertise

anzuelo, *m.* fishhook; allurement

añadir, *va.* to add; to join

añejo, *adj.* old, age(wines)

añicos, *m. pl.* bits; **hacer añicos,** to break into bits

añil, *m.* indigo; bluing

año, *m.* year; **año bisiesto,** leap year; **cumplir años,** to have a birthday; **tener . . . años,** to be . . . years old.

apaciguar, *va., vr.* to appease, pacify; calm down

apachurrar, *va.* to crush, flatten.

apagado, *adj.* low, muffled

apañar, *va.* to grasp; to catch

aparador, *m.* buffet, sideboard; window, showcase

aparato, *m.* apparatus, appliance; ostentation, show

aparatoso, *adj.* pompous, showy

aparecer, *vn.* to appear

aparentar, *va.* to pretend, deceive

aparente, *adj.* apparent; suitable; evident

apariencia, *f.* appearance.

looks

apartado, m. post-office box

apartamento, or **apartamiento**, m. apartment

apartar, va. to separate; to remove; **apartarse**, to withdraw

aparte, m. new paragraph; adv. apart, separately

apasionado, adj. passionate; impulsive; fond of

apasionarse, vr. to be prejudiced (about)

apatía, f. apathy, indifference

apego, m. attachment, fondness.

apelación, f. appeal; court appeal.

apellido, m. surname

apenarse, vr. to grieve; become embarrassed

apenas, adv. scarcely, hardly.

apéndice, m. appendix; supplement.

apendicitis, f. appendicitis

aperitivo, m. appetizer

apertura, f. opening, cleft

apestar, vn. to otink

apetito, m. appetite

apetitoso, adj. appetizing

ápice, m. summit point

apiñar, va. to press things close together; **apiñarse**, to clog, crowd

apisonadora, f. steam roller

aplacar, va. to placate

aplanar, va. to level, smooth

aplaudir, va. to applaud

aplauso, m. applause, praise

aplazar, va. to defer, postpone

aplicado, adj. studious, industrious

aplicar, va. to apply; to attribute

aplomo, m. poise, composure

apócope, m. shortening, cutting off

apoderado, adj. authorized, empowered; m. (law) proxy, attorney in fact

apoderar, va. to empower; to grant power of attorney; **apoderarse**, to take possession

apodo, m. nickname

apoplejía, f. apoplexy

aportar, va. to bring, contribute

aposento, m. room, abode

aposición, f. (gram.) apposition

apostar, va. to bet

apóstol, m. apostle

apoyar, va. to favor; to support; **apoyarse**, to lean upon

apoyo, m. prop, support; protection

apreciable, adj. appreciable, valuable, respectable; (com.) **su apreciable**, your favor (letter)

apreciar, va. to appreciate, value

aprecio, m. appreciation, esteem, regard

apremiar, va. to press, compel; to hurry

aprender, va. to learn

aprendiz, aprendiza, n. apprentice

aprensión, f. apprehension, fear, misgiving

apresurado, adj. hasty

apresurar, va. to accelerate, expedite; **apresurarse**, to hurry, hasten

apretado, adj. tight

apretar, va. to compress, tighten, squeeze; to pinch (of shoes)

apretón, m. sudden pressure; **apretón de manos** handshake.

aprieto, m. predicament

aprisa, adv. in a hurry

aprobación, f. approval

aprobar, va. to approve

apropiación, f. appropriation

apropiado, adj. appropriate, adequate

apropiar, va. to appropriate; **apropiarse**, take possession of

aprovechable, adj. available, usable

aprovechar, va. to avail, make use of; vn. to progress in studies,art, etc.; **aprovecharse de**, to take advantage of

aproximar, va., vr. to approach; to move near, approximate

aptitud, f. aptitude, fitness, ability; talent

apto, adj. apt, fit, able

apuesta, f. bet, wager

apuesto, adj. elegant

apuntador, m. observer; prompter; (naut.) gunner

apuntar, va. to aim; to level, point out; to note; to write down; (theat.) to prompt

apunte, m. annotation; note, sketch

apurado, adj. poor, destitute; to be in a hurry

apurar, va. to rush, hurry; **apurarse**, to hurry; to worry

apuro, m. want, indigence; embarrassment; **salir de un apuro**, to get out of a difficulty.

aquel, aquella, adj. and **aquél, aquélla**, pron. that

aquello, pron. that, the former

aquí, adv. here, in this place

aquietar, va. to quiet, appease, lull; **aquietarse**, to become calm

árabe, n., adj. Arabic, the Arabic language; an Arab

arado, m. plow

arancel, m. tariff

arañar, va. to scratch; to scrape.

arar, va. to plow the land

arbitraje, m. arbitration

arbitrar, va. to arbitrate

arbitrario, adj. arbitrary

árbol, m. tree; shaft; (naut.) mast

arca, f. chest, wooden box

arcángel, m. archangel

arce, m. maple tree

arcilla, f. argil, clay

arco, m. arc; arch; fiddle bow; hoop; **arco iris**, rainbow

arcón, m. large chest; bin

archipiélago, m. archipelago

archivar, va. to file, place in archives

archivo, m. archives, file

arder, vn. to burn, blaze

ardid, m. stratagem, trick

ardiente, adj. ardent, intense

ardilla, f. squirrel

ardor, m. great heat; fervor, zeal

arduo, adj. arduous

área, f. area

arenoso, adj. sandy

arenque, m. herring

aretes, m. pl. earrings

argentino, adj. silvery; Argentine

argolla, f. large iron ring

argüir, vn. to argue

argumento, m. argument; plot of a play

aria, f. (mus.) aria, air

árido, adj. arid; barren

arisco, adj. fierce, surly

aristocracia, f. aristocracy

aristócrata, m., f. aristocrat

aristocrático, adj. aristocratic

aritmética, f. arithmetic

arma, f. weapon, arm

armamento, m. armament

armar, va. to furnish with arms; to man; to arm, fit up; to assemble

armario, m. clothes closet; cupboard; bookcase

armazón, f. framework, skeleton; m. skeleton of the body.

armiño, m. ermine

armisticio, m. armistice

armonía, f. harmony

armonioso, adj. harmonious

armonizar, va. to harmonize

aro, m. hoop

aroma, m. aroma, fragrance

arpa, f. (mus.) harp

arqueado, adj. arched, bent

arqueología, f. archaeology

arquitecto, m. architect

arquitectura, f. architecture

arraigar, vn. to take root; to become deep-seated

arrancar, va. to pull up by the roots; to wrest; vn. to start out

arranque, m. sudden start; extirpation; tantrum; (auto.) ignition, starter

arrasar va. to demolish, destroy

arrastrado, adj. dragged along; miserable, destitute.

arrear, va. to drive horses, mules, etc.; to urge on

arrebatado, *adj.* impetuous, rash, inconsiderate

arrebatar, *va.* to carry off, snatch; to enrapture

arrebato, *m.* sudden attack, rage, fit; rapture

arreciar, *vn.* to increase in intensity

arrecife, *m.* reef

arreglado, *adj.* moderate; neat

arreglar, *va.* to regulate; to adjust; to arrange; **arreglarse,** to dress; to manage

arreglo, *m.* arrangement, settlement

arrendamiento, *m.* leasing; rental

arrendar, *va.* to rent, lease

arreos, *m. pl.* appurtenances, accessories

arrepentimiento, *m.* remorse

arrepentirse, *vr.* to repent

arrestar, *va.* to arrest

arriba, *adv.* above, over, up, high, overhead, upstairs

arribo, *m.* arrival

arriendo, *m.* lease, farm rent

arriesgado, *adj.* risky, dangerous

arriesgar, *va., vr.* to risk, hazard.

arrimar, *va.* to approach, draw near; **arrimarse a,** to lean against, seek shelter under; to join

arroba, *f.* weight of twenty-five pounds; measure (thirty-two pints)

arrodillarse, *vr.* to kneel

arrogancia, *f.* arrogance

arrogante, *adj.* haughty, proud

arrojado, *adj.* rash, bold

arrojar, *va.* to dart, fling; to dash; to shed (a fragrance); to emit (light); to throw out; **arrojar un saldo,** to show a balance

arrojo, *m.* boldness; fearlessness

arrollar, *va.* to wind, coil

arropar, *va.* to clothe, dress; to cover (with blankets, etc.)

arroyo, *m.* gully, creek

arroz, *m.* rice

arruga, *f.* wrinkle; rumple

arrugar, *va.* to wrinkle; to rumple, fold; **arrugar el ceño,** to frown; **arrugarse,** to shrivel

arruinar, *va.* to demolish; to ruin; **arruinarse,** to lose one's fortune

arte, *m., f.* art; skill; **bellas artes,** fine arts

arteria, *f.* artery

arterial, *adj.* arterial; **tensión arterial,** blood pressure

artesano, *m.* artisan, workman.

ártico, *adj.* arctic

articular, *va.* to articulate.

artificial, *adj.* artificial

artillería, *f.* gunnery; artillery

artimaña, *f.* stratagem, deception

artista, *m.f.* artist

artístico, *adj.* artistic

artritis, *f.* (med.) arthritis

arveja, *f.* (bot.) vetch; (Sp. Am.) green pea

arzobispo, *m.* archbishop

as, *m.* ace

asa, *f.* handle, haft, hold

asado, *adj.* roasted; *m.* roast

asaltar, *va.* to attack; to assail

asalto, *m.* assault

asamblea, *f.* assembly, meeting

asar, *va.* to roast

asbesto, *m.* asbestos

ascendencia, *f.* ancestry; line of ancestors

ascendente, *adj.* ascending

ascender, *va., vn.* to ascend, climb; to be promoted; to amount to

ascendiente, *m.* ascendant, forefather; influence

ascenso, *m.* ascent; promotion

ascensor, *m.* elevator, lift

asco, *m.* nausea; loathing

aseado, *adj.* clean, neat

asear, *va.* to clean, make neat

asediar, *va.* to besiege

asegurado, *adj.* assured, secured, insured; *n.* policyholder

asegurar, *va.* to secure, insure; to assure; to affirm

asemejarse, *vr.* to resemble

asentimiento, *m.* assent

asentir, *vn.* to acquiesce, concede

aseo, *m.* cleanliness

aserción, *f.* assertion

aserrar, *va.* to saw

asesinar, *va.* to assassinate

asesinato, *m.* assassination

asesino, *m.* assassin

asesorar, *va.* to give legal advice to; **asesorarse,** to employ counsel; to take advice

asfalto, *m.* asphalt

asfixiar, *va., vr.* to asphyxiate, suffocate

así, *adv.* so, thus, in this manner; therefore, so that

asiático, asiática, *n., adj.* Asiatic

asiento, *m.* chair, stool; seat; entry

asignar, *vt.* to allocate, apportion, assign

asignatura, *f.* subject of a school course

asilo, *m.* asylum, refuge

asimismo, *adv.* similarly; likewise

asistencia, *f.* actual presence; attendance; assistance; help

asistir, *vn.* to be present; to attend; *va.* assist

asma, *f.* asthma

asno, *m.* ass; stupid fellow

asociado, asociada, *n.* associate

asociar, *va., vr.* to associate

asolar, *va.* to destroy, devastate

asolear, *va., vr.* to expose to the sun

asomar, *vn.* to begin to appear; to peep; to show; **asomarse,** to lean out

asombrar, *va.* to frighten, amaze; to astonish

asombroso, *adj.* astonishing, marvelous

aspecto, *m.* appearance; aspect

áspero, *adj.* rough, rugged; austere, gruff

aspiración, *f.* aspiration; ambition

aspiradora, *f.* vacuum sweeper

aspirar, *va.* to inhale; to aspire

aspirina, *f.* aspirin

asqueroso, *adj.* loathsome; dirty

asta, *f.* staff, pole

asterisco, *m.* asterisk

astilla, *f.* chip; splinter

astillero, *m.* dockyard

astringente, *adj., m.* astringent

astro, *m.* star

astrólogo, *m.* astrologer

astronave, *f.* space ship

astronomía, *f.* astronomy

astrónomo, *m.* astronomer

asueto, *m.* holiday, vacation

asumir, *va.* to assume

asunto, *m.* subject; matter; affair, business

asustar, *va., vr.* to frighten

atacar, *va.* to attack, ram

atajo, *m.* by-path; short cut

ataque, *m.* attack

atar, *va.* to tie, fasten

atarantado, *adj.* dazed

atareado, *adj.* busy

atarearse, *vr.* to work hard on a task

atascarse, *vr.* to become bogged

ataúd, *m.* coffin

atavío, *m.* dress, ornament

Atenas, *f.* Athens

atender, *vn.* to be attentive; to heed; *va.* to look after

atenerse, *vr.* to depend or rely (on)

atentado, *m.* attempt, transgression; attack, assault

atentar, *va.* to try; to attempt crime

atento, *adj.* attentive; mindful; courteous

atenuar, *va.* to diminish

ateo, atea, *n., adj.* atheist, atheistic

aterrar, *va., vr.* to terrify

aterrizaje, *m.* (avi.) landing

aterrizar, *vn.* (avi.) to land

atesorar, *va.* to treasure or hoard up riches

atestar, *va.* to attest, witness; to cram, crowd; **atestarse de,** to stuff oneself with

atestiguar, *va.* to witness, attest

atinar, *va.,* *vn.* to touch the mark; to conjecture rightly

atisbar, *va.* to pry

Atlántico, *n.,* *adj.* Atlantic

atlas, *m.* atlas

atleta, *m.,* *f.* athlete

atlético, *adj.* athletic

atmósfera, *f.* atmosphere

atmosférico, *adj.* atmospheric

atole, *m.* corn-flour gruel

atolondrar, *va.,* *vr.* to stun, daze

atollar, *vn.* to fall in the mud

atómico, *adj.* atomic

atomo, *m.* atom

atónito, *adj.* astonish

atontar, *va.,* *vr.* to stun, stupefy

atorar, *va.* to obstruct; **atorarse,** *vr.* to choke; to be stalled in the mud

atormentar, *va.* to torment

atornillar, *va.* to screw

atracar, *va.* to overhaul a ship; to glut; *vn.* (naut.) to make ahore

atracción, *f.* attraction

atractivo, *adj.* attractive; *m.* charm, grace

atraer, *va.* to attract

atrapar, *va.* to trap; to overtake; to deceive

atrás, *adv.* backwards; behind; past

atrasado, *adj.* backward, behind the times; tardy; in arrears

atrasar, *va.* to postpone; to delay; **atrasarse,** to be in arrears

atraso, *m.* delay, backwardness; arrears

atravesar, *va.* to cross; to pass over; **atravesarse,** to get in the way; to thwart one's purpose

atreverse, *vr.* to dare, venture

atrevido, *adj.* bold, daring; impudent

atrevimiento, *m.* audacity

atribuir, *va.* to attribute, ascribe; to impute; **atribuirse,** to assume

atribular, *va.* to vex, afflict

atributo, *m.* attribute

atrio, *m.* porch; portico

atrocidad, *f.* atrocity

atropellar, *va.* to trample; to run over; **atropellarse,** to hurry, flurry

atropello, *m.* trampling; outrage, insult; **atropello de automóvil,** automobile collision

attmo. or **att.**^{mo.} **atentísimo,** very kind, very courteous

atto. or **att.**^o **atento,** kind, courteous

atuendo, *m.* attire, garb; pomp, ostentation

atun, *m.* tunny fish, tuna

aturdir, *va.* to bewilder, confuse; to stupefy

audacia, *f.* audacity, boldness

audición, *f.* broadcasting; audition

audiencia, *f.* audience; hearing; a high court

audífono, *m.* earphone

audio-visual, *adj.* audio-visual

auditorio, *m.* assembly; audience.

auge, *m.* the pinnacle of power

augurar, *va.* to predict

aula, *f.* classroom

aullar, *vn.* to howl

aumentar, *va.,* *vn.* to augment, increase

aumento, *m.* increase, growth

aun, *adv.* still, even; **aún,** *adv.* yet

aunque, *conj.* though, notwithstanding

aurora, *f.* first dawn of day

ausencia, *f.* absense

ausente, *adj.* absent

austero, *adj.* austere, severe

australiano, australiana, *n.,* *adj.* Australian

austriaco, austriaca, *n.,* *adj.* Austrian

autentico, *adj.* authentic

auto, *m.* judicial sentence; edict; auto, automobile

autobús, *m.* motorbus

autógrafo, *m.* autograph

autómata, *m.* automation; robot

automático, *adj.* automatic

automatización, *f.* automation

automatizar, *va.* to automate

automóvil, *m.* automobile

autonomía, *f.* autonomy

autónomo, *adj.* autonomous

autopista, *f.* expressway, superhighway

autor, *m.* author; maker

autoridad, *f.* authority

autorización, *f.* authorization

autorizado, *adj.* competent, reliable

autorizar, *va.* to authorize

auxiliar, *va.* to aid, help, assist; *adj.* auxiliary

auxilio, *m.* aid, help, assistance; **primeros auxilios**, first aid

a/v., a la vista, (com.) at sight

avaluar, *va.* to estimate, evaluate, appraise

avanzada, *f.* (mil.) vanguard

avanzar, *va., vn.* to advance

avaricia, *f.* avarice

avaro, *adj.* avaricious; *m.* miser

ave, *f.* bird; **ave de corral**, fowl

avellana, *f.* filbert, hazelnut

avemaría, *f.* Ave Maria, salutation to the Virgin Mary

avena, *f.* oats; oatmeal

avenida, *f.* avenue, boulevard

avenir, *va., vr.* to reconcile; to adapt (to circumstances)

aventajar, *va.* to have the advantage

aventar, *va.* to fan; to expel; to scatter; **aventarse**, to be puffed up

aventura, *f.* adventure

aventurar, *va.* to venture, risk

aventurero, *adj.* adventurous; *m.* adventurer

avergonzar, *va., vr.* to shame; be ashamed

aversión, *f.* aversion, dislike

avestruz, *m.* ostrich

aviación, *f.* aviation

aviador, *n.* aviator

aviar, *va.* to provision, equip

avión, *m.* airplane

avisar, *va.* to inform, give notice

aviso, *m.* information; notice; advertisement; warning

avispa, *f.* wasp

axila, *f.* armpit

¡ay! *interj.* alas!

aya, *f.* governess

ayer, *adv.* yesterday; lately

ayuda, *f.* help, aid

ayudante, *m.* assistant

ayudar, *va.* to help, assist

ayunar, *vn.* to fast

ayunas, en ayunas, *adv.* fasting, without food; ignorant (of an affair)

ayuntamiento, *m.* town council; city hall

azabache, *m.* jet

azada, *f.* spade, hoe

azadón, *m.* pickax; hoe

azafrán, *m.* saffron

azahar, *m.* orange blossom

azar, *m.* hazard; unforeseen disaster; **al azar**, at random

azogue, *m.* mercury

azorar, *va., vr.* to frighten, terrify

azote, *m.* whip, lash; scourge

azotea, *f.* roof garden

azteca, *n.* Aztec

azúcar, *m.* or *f.* sugar

azucarera, *f.* sugar bowl

azucena, *f.* white lily

azufre, *m.* sulphur, brimstone

azul, *adj.* blue

azulejo, *m.* tile; bluebird

B

baba, *f.* drivel; drool

babel, *m.* babel, confusion

babero, *m.* bib

baboso, *adj.* driveling, silly; *n.* (Sp. Am.) fool, idiot

bacalao, *m.* codfish

bacinica or **bacinilla**, *f.* chamber pot

bacteria, *f.* bacteria

bacteriólogo, *m.* bacteriologist

bachiller, *m.* bachelor (degree); a college graduate

bachillerato, *m.* bachelor's degree

bahía, *f.* bay

bailar, *vn.* to dance

bailarín, bailarina, *n.* dancer,

ballerina

baile, *m.* dance, ball

baja, *f.* fall, diminution; fall in prices; loss in membership

bajada, *f.* descent; downgrade

bajar, *va.* to lower; to decrease (the price); *vn.* to descend

bajeza, *f.* meanness; lowliness

bajo, *adj.* low; under; short; despicable; (mus.) bass

bala, *f.* bullet; bale of paper

balada, f. ballad

balance, *m.* fluctuation; rolling of a ship; balance; balance of accounts

balancear, *va., vn.* to balance; to roll; **balancearse**, to rock, to sway

balanza, *f.* scale; comparative estimate

balazo, *m.* shot; bullet wound

balboa, *m.* a coin of Panama

balbucear, *va., vn.* to stammer

balcón, *m.* balcony

baldar, *va.* to cripple

balde, *m.* bucket, pail; **de balde**, gratis; **en balde**, in vain

balístico, balístics, *adj.* ballistic

balneario, *m.* bathing resort

balon, *m.* ball; bale

baloncesto, *m.* basketball

balonvolea, *m.* volleyball

balsa, *f.* raft, float; ferry

bálsamo, *m.* balsam, balm

ballena, *f.* whale; whalebone

bambolear, *vn., vr.* to reel, sway

bambú *m.* bamboo

banano, *m.* banana plant or fruit

bancario, *adj.* banking

bancarrota, *f.* bankruptcy

banco, *m.* bench; bank; **banco de sangre**, blood bank

banda, *f.* sash; band; gang; border

bandeja, *f.* tray

banderera, *f.* banner, flag

bandido, *m.* bandit, robber

bando, *m.* faction, team

banquero, banquera, *n.* banker

banqueta, *f.* sidewalk; three-legged stool

banquete, *m.* banquet; feast

bañar, *va.* to bathe; to water; to dip; **bañarse**, to take a bath.

bañera, *f.* bathtub

baño, *m.* bath; bathtub, bathroom; varnish; coat (of paint)

baraja, *f.* playing card; pack of cards; game of cards

baranda, *f.* banister, railing

barandal, *m.* railing

baratillo, *m.* bargain counter

barato, *adj.* cheap, lowpriced

barbacoa, *f.* barbecue

barbaridad, *f.* barbarity; rudeness; (coll.) ridiculous act; **una barbaridad**, a piece of nonsense; an "awful" lot; ¡que barbaridad! how terrible!

bárbaro, *adj.* barbarous, savage; rash, daring; rude

barbería, *f.* barbershop

barbero, *m.* barber

barca, *f.* boat; barge

barítono, *m.* (mus.) baritone

barniz, *m.* varnish

barnizar, *va.* to varnish

barómetro, *m.* barometer

barón, *m.* baron

baronesa, *f.* baroness

barquillo, *m.* cone-shaped wafer

barra, *f.* crowbar, lever

barraca, *f.* barrack; hut

barranca, *f.* cliff; gorge

barranco, *m.* ravine; gorge

barrera, *f.* clay pit; barrier

barriga, *f.* abdomen, belly

barril, *m.* barrel; cask; jug

barrio, *m.* district or section of a town; quarter; **barrios bajos**, slums

basar, *va.* to base

báscula, *f.* platform scale

base, *f.* base, basis

básico, *adj.* basic

basílica, *f.* basilica (cathedral)

basketbol, *m.* basketball

basta, *f.* basting; ¡basta! *interj.* enough!

bastante, *adj.* sufficient; quite, considerable; *adv.* enough; rather

bastar, *vn.* to suffice

bastardilla, f. italic

bastardo, adj., m. bastard

bastidor, m. embroidery frame; **bastidores**, pl. stage scenery; wings; **tras bastidores**, backstage

bastilla, f. hem

bastón, m. cane, stick

bastos, m. pl. clubs (suit in cards)

basura, f. sweepings; garbage

basurero, n. dustpan; dunghill

bata, f. dressing gown

batalla, f. battle, combat

batallar, vn. to battle, dispute

batallón, m. (mil.) battalion

batata, f. sweet potato

batea, f. round wooden tray

batería, f. battery; (mus.) percussion section

batidor, m. beater

batir, va., vn. to beat

batista, f. batiste, cambric

batuta, f. baton; **llevar la batuta**, to lead, to preside

baúl, m. trunk, chest

bautismo, m. baptism

bautizar, va. to baptize, christen

bautizo, m. baptism

baya, f. berry

bayo, adj. bay (of a horse)

bayoneta, f. bayonet

bazar, m. bazaar

beata, f. overly pious woman; hypocrite

beato, adj. devout

bebedor, bebedora, n. drunkard, drinker

beber, va., vn. to drink; drinking

bebida, f. drink, beverage; **bebida alcohólica**, intoxicant

beca, f. scholarship, fellowship

becerro, m. calf; calfskin

beldad, f. beauty

Belén, m. Bethlehem; **estar en Belén**, to be absentminded

belga, adj., n. Belgian.

Bélgica, f. Belgium

bélico, adj. warlike, martial

beligerante, n., adj. belligerent

belleza, f. beauty

bello, adj. beautiful, handsome; **bellas artes**, fine arts

bemol, m.(mus.) flat

bencina, f. (chem.) benzine

bendecir, va. to bless

bendición, f. benediction; blessing

bendito, adj. sainted, blessed; simple

benefactor, m. benefactor

beneficencia, f. beneficence, charity

beneficiado, beneficiada, n. beneficiary

beneficiar, va. to profit; to benefit

beneficiario, m. beneficiary

beneficio, m. benefit; profit

benemérito, adj. worthy

benévolo, adj. benevolent

berenjena, f. eggplant

berrear, vn. to low, bellow

berrinche, m. fit of anger; sulkiness

besar, va. to kiss

beso, m. kiss

bestia, f. beast; animal; dunce, idiot.

bestial, adj. bestial, brutal

betabel, m. (Mex.) beet

betarraga or **betarrata**, (bot.) beet

betatrón, m. betatron

bevatrón, m. bevatron

biberón, m. nursing bottle

Biblia, f. Bible

bíblico, adj. Biblical

bibliografía, f. bibliography

biblioteca, f. library

bibliotecario, bibliotecaria, n. librarian

bicarbonato, m. bicarbonate

biceps, m. (anat.) biceps

bicicleta, f. bicycle

bicho, m. vermin; insect

bien, m. good; benefit; **bienes**, pl. property; riches; land; adv. well; right; all right; **¡bienes!** interj. fine! all right!

bienal, adj. biennial

bienaventurado, adj. blessed, happy, fortunate

bienestar, m. well-being

bienhechor, m. benefactor

bienio, m. space of two years

bienvenida, *f.* welcome

bienvenido, *adj.* welcome

bifocal, *adj.* bifocal

biftec, *m.* beefsteak

bigamo, bigama, *n.* bigamist

bigote, *m.* mustache

bilingüe, *adj.* bilingual

bilis, *f.* bile

billar, *m.* billiards

billete, *m.* ticket; billet, label; note, short letter; love letter; banknote bill

billetera, *f.* billfold

billetero, billetera, *n.* (Sp. Am.) vendor of lottery tickets

billón, *m.* billion

billonario, billonaria, *n.* billionaire

bimestral, *adj.* bimonthly

bimestre, *m.* space of two months; bimonthly rent, salary, etc.

bimotor, *adj.* two-motored

binóculo, *m.* opera glass

bioastronáutica, *f.* bioastronautics

biografía, *f.* biography

biología, *f.* biology

biombo, *m.* screen

biopsia, *f.* biopsy

bioquímico, *adj.* biochemical; *m.* biochemist

biosfera, *f.* biosphere

bisabuela, *f.* great-grandmother

bisabuelo, *m.* great-grandfather.

bisagra, *f.* hinge

bisel, *m.* bevel

bisemanal, *adj.* semiweekly.

bisonte, *m.* bison

bisoño, *adj.* inexperienced; *n.* novice

bistec, *m.* beefsteak

bizcocho, *m.* cake, ladyfinger

biznieta, *f.* great-granddaughter

biznieto, *m.* great-grandson

blanco, blanca, *f.* white, blank; *m.* blank; target

blancura, *f.* whiteness

blando, *adj.* soft, smooth; mellow; mild, gentle

blanquear, *va., vn.* to bleach; to whitewash

blasfemia, *f.* blasphemy; oath

bledo, *m.* (bot.) wild amaranth; **no me importa un bledo,** I don't give a rap, I don't care

bloc, *m.* bloc, political group; pad (of paper)

bloqueo, *m.* blockade

blusa, *f.* blouse

boa, *f.* (zool.) boa

bobería, *f.* folly, foolishness

bobina, *f.* bobbin; coil; spool; (elec.) coil; **bobina de reacción (nuclear),** reactor (nuclear)

bobo, boba, *n.* dunce, fool; *adj.* stupid; silly

boca, *f.* mouth; entrance, opening; mouth of a river

bocacalle, *f.* street intersection or opening

bocamanga, *f.* armhole

boceto, *m.* sketch

bocina, *f.* bugle horn; speaking trumpet; automobile horn

bocio, *m.* goiter

bochornoso, *adj.* shameful; sultry (weather)

boda, *f.* wedding; **bodas de plata** or **de oro,** silver or golden anniversary

bodega, *f.* wine cellar; warehouse

bofetada, *f.* slap on the face

bofetón, *m.* box on the ear

boga, *f.* vogue, fad, popularity

bogar, *vn.* to row, paddle

boicotear, *va., vn.* to boycott

boina, *f.* beret

bola, *f.* ball; globe; marble; (coll.) lie, fib; disturbance

bolear, *vn.* to knock the balls about (billiards); (Mex.) to shine shoes

bolero, *m.* Spanish dancer; Andalusian dance; (Mex.) top hat; bootblack

boletín, *m.* bulletin

boleto, *m.* ticket; **boletode ida y vuelta,** round-trip ticket; **boleto sencillo,** one-way ticket

boliche, *m.* bowling

bolillo, *m.* (Mex.) kind of bread roll

boliviano, boliviana, adj., n. Bolivian; m. a Bolivian coin

bolo, m. bowling pin; bolo (knife); **bolos,** pl. bowling

bolsa, f. purse, pouch; case; money exchange; stock exchange

bolsillo, m. pocket

bomba, f. pump; bomb; **bomba atómica,** atomic bomb; **bomba de aerosol,** aerosol bomb; **bomba de hidrógeno,** hydrogen bomb; **bomba de neutrón,** neutron bomb

bombardeo, m. bombardment

bombear, va. to pump (water)

bombero, m. fireman

bombilla, f. light bulb; (Sp. Am.) a tube to sip maté

bombón, m. bonbon, candy

bonanza, f. bonanza

bondad, f. kindness

bondadoso, adj. kind

bonito, adj. pretty

bono, m. (com.) bond, certificate

boquiabierto, adj. open-mouthed

boquilla, f. mouthpiece

borbotón, m. bubbling; **hablar a borbotones,** to speak in torrents, babble

bordado, m. embroidery

bordar, va. to embroider

bordo, m. board; the side of a ship; (naut.) **a bordo,** on board; **franco a bordo,** free on board (f.o.b.)

borinqueño, borinqueña, n., adj. Puerto Rican

borrachera, f. drunkenness

borracho, adj. intoxicated

borrador, m. eraser; rough draft

borrar, va. to erase

borrasca, f. storm, squall

borrego, borrega, n. yearling lamb

borrico, m. ass; blockhead

borrón, m. ink blot, splotch

borronear, va. to sketch, scribble

borroso, adj. blurred

bosque, m. forest, woods

bosquejo, m. outline, sketch

bostezar, vn. to yawn; to gape

bostezo, m. yawn, yawning

bota, f. cask; boot

botánica, f. botany

botar, va. to cast, throw; to launch

botarate, m., f. fool

bote, m. small boat, rowboat; jar, bottle; **bote de salvamento,** lifeboat

botella, f. bottle, flask

botica, f. drugstore, pharmacy

boticario, m. druggist

botiquín, m. first-aid kit

botón, m. button; bud

bóveda, f. arch; vault

bovino, adj. bovine

boxeador, m. boxer, pugilist

boxear, vn. to box

boxeo, m. boxing, pugilism

boya, f. buoy

bozal, m. muzzle

bracero, m. day laborer

bragazas, m. milksop

bragueta, f. trousers fly

brama, f. rut, mating time

bramar, vn. to roar, bellow

brasa, f. live coal

brasero, m. brazier, hearth.

Brasil, m. Brazil

brasileño, brasileña, n., adj. Brazilian

brasilero, adj. (Sp. Am.) Brazilian

bravío, adj. savage, wild

bravo, adj. brave, valiant; fierce; excellent, fine; ¡bravo! interj. bravo!

bravura, f. bravery; courage; bravado, boast

brazalete, m. bracelet

brazo, m. arm; **brazos,** pl. hands, man power

brea, f. pitch, tar

brecha, f. breach; gap

bregar, vn. to contend, struggle

Bretaña, f. Brittany; **Gran Bretaña,** Great Britain

breve, adj. brief, short; **en breve,** shortly

brevedad, f. brevity

bribón, bribóna, adj. rascally; n. rogue

brida, f. bridle; check, curb

brigada, *f.* brigade

brillante, *adj.* bright, shining; *m.* brilliant, diamond

brincar, *vn.* to leap, jump

brinco, *m.* leap, jump, **dar brincos**, to leap

brindar, *vn.* to drink one's health, toast; *va.* to offer

brindis, *m.* health, toast

brio, *m.* strength, vigor

brioso, *adj.* vigorous, fiery

brisa, *f.* breeze

británico, británica, *adj., n.* British, Britisher

brocado, *m.* brocade

brocha, *f.* painter's brush

broche, *m.* clasp; brooch

broma, *f.* joke, jest

bromear, *vn.* to jest, joke

bromuro, *m.* bromide

bronce, *m.* bronze, brass

bronco, *adj.* rough, coarse

bronquio, *m.* bronchial tube

bronquitis, *f.* bronchitis

brotar, *vn.* to bud, germinate, to break out, appear (said of a disease)

bruja, *f.* witch, hag; *adj.* (coll.) broke, short of funds

brujo, *m.* sorcerer

brújula, *f.* compass; magnetic needle

bruma, *f.* mist, haze

brumoso, *adj.* misty, hazy

brusco, *adj.* rude, gruff

Bruselas, *f.* Brussels

brutal, *adj.* brutal, brutish

bruto, *m.* brute, blockhead; **bruto, bruta**, *adj.* brutal, stupid; crude (ore, oil, etc.); gross (profits, etc.); **en bruto**, in a raw (unmanufactured) state

bucear, *vn.* to dive

bucle, *m.* curl

buche, *m.* craw, crop; mouthful

buen, *adj.* good; **hacer buen tiempo**, to be good weather

buenaventura, *f.* fortune, good luck

bueno, *adj.* good, perfect; proper; healthy; useful

buey, *m.* ox, bullock

búfalo, *m.* buffalo

bufanda, *f.* scarf

bufete, *m.* desk, lawyer's office

bufo, *m.* buffoon; **bufo, bufa,** *adj.* comic

bufón, *m.* buffoon; jester; *adj.* funny, comical

buho, *m.* owl

buitre, *m.* vulture

bujía, *f.* spark plug; candle

bulbo, *m.* (bot.) bulb

bulevar, *m.* boulevard

bulla, *f.* clatter; crowd

bullicio, *m.* bustle; uproar

buque, *m.* boat, ship, vessel

burdo, *adj.* coarse (of cloth); ordinary

burla, *f.* scoff, sneer; hoax

burlar, *va.* to mock, deceive; to frustrate; **burlar se de,** to make fun of

buró, *m.* bureau, chest of drawers

burocracia, *f.* bureaucracy

busca, *f.* search

busto, *m.* bust

buzo, *m.* diver

buzón, *m.* mailbox, letter drop

C

C., centígrado, C. Centigrade

c/, cargo, (com.) cargo, charge

C.A., corriente alterna, A.C. alternating current

cabal, *adj.* just, exact; complete, accomplished

caballería, *f.* cavalry; knighthood

caballeriza, *f.* stable

caballero, *m.* knight; gentleman

caballete, *m.* easel

caballo, *m.* horse; knight (in chess); **a caballo**, on horseback

cabaña, *f.* hut, shack; cottage, cabin; cabana

cabaret, *m.* cabaret, night club

cabecear, *vn.* to nod with sleep

cabecera, *f.* upper end; head (of a bed or a table); headwaters; **médico de cabecera**, attending physician

cabecilla, *m.* ringleader

cabellera, *f.* head of hair

cabello, *m.* hair of the head

cabelludo, *adj.* hairy; **cuero cabelludo**, scalp

caber, *va., vn.* to contain, include; to fit; to be possible

cabeza, *f.* head; top; leader

cabezudo, *adj.* headstrong, obstinate

cabida, *f.* content, capacity

cabildo, *m.* town council

cabina, *f.* (avi.) cockpit

cabizbajo, *adj.* pensive

cable, *m.* cable; rope

cablegrafiar, *va.* to cable

cablegráfico, *adj.* cable; **dirección cablegráfica**, cable address

cablegrama, *m.* cablegram

cabo, *m.* extremity cape, headland; end, tip; (mil.) corporal

Cabo de Buena Esperanza, Cape of Good Hope

Cabo de Hornos, Cape Horn

cabra, *f.* goat

cabria, *f.* hoist

cabritilla, *f.* kidskin

cabrito, *m.* kid

cacahuate or **cacahuete**, *m.* peanut

cacao, *m.* (bot.) cacao, cocoa seed

cacerola, *f.* casserole, pan

cacto, *m.* cactus

cacha, *f.* knife handle

cachete, *m.* cheek

cachorro, cachorra, *n.* cub (of any animal)

cachucha, *f.* man's cap

cada, *adj.* each, every;

cada uno, everyone; each

cadena, *f.* chain; series; network

cadencia, *f.* cadence

cadera, *f.* hip

cadete, *m.* (mil.) cadet

caducar, *vn.* to dote; to lapse (of a legacy, etc.)

C.A.E., cóbrese al entregar, C.O.D. or c.o.d. cash or collect on delivery

caer, *vn.* to fall; to befall, happen

café, *m.* coffee; café

cafetera, *f.* coffee pot; (Arg.) a noisy motorcycle; a jalopy

cafetería, *f.* coffee store; coffeehouse

cafeto, *m.* coffee tree

caída, *f.* fall, falling

caído, *adj.* fallen

caimán, *m.* caiman; (fig.) fox, sly individual

cajero, cajera, *n.* cashier

cajeta, *f.* (Mex.) confection made of goat's milk

cajón, *m.* drawer; locker; coffin; **ser de cajón**, (coll.) to be customary

calabaza, *f.* pumpkin, gourd; **dar calabazas**, to jilt; to flunk.

calabozo, *m.* dungeon; jail

calamar, *m.* squid

calambre, *m.* cramp

calamidad, *f.* misfortune

calar, *va.* to penetrate, pierce

calavera, *f.* skull; madcap

calcetín, *m.* sock

calcio, *m.* calcium

calculador, *adj.* calculating; **calculador electrónico**, electronic computer

calculadora, *f.* adding machine

calcular, *va.* to calculate

cálculo, *m.* calculation; **cálculo biliario**, gallstone

caldera, *f.* caldron, kettle, boiler

calefacción, *f.* heating

calendario, *m.* almanac, calendar

calentador, *m.* heater

calentar, *va.* to warm, heat; **calentarse**, to grow hot; to dispute warmly

calentura, *f.* fever

calibre, *m.* caliber, gauge; (fig.) sort, kind

calicanto, *m.* stone masonry

cálido, *adj.* hot, warm

caliente, *adj.* hot; fiery

calificación, *f.* qualification; mark (in school)

calificar, *va.* to qualify; to rate

calisténica, *f.* calisthenics

cáliz, *m.* chalice; goblet

calma, f. calm; calmness
calmante, m. (med.) sedative
calmar, va., vr. to calm, quiet, pacify
calor, m. heat, ardor; **hacer** or **tener calor,** to be warm
calorífero, m. heater; **calorífero de aire caliente,** hot air heater
calumnia, f. slander
caluroso, adj. warm, hot
calva, f. bald spot
calvo, adj. bald
calzada, f. roadway, street
calzado, m. footwear
calzar, va. to put on, to block with a wedge
calzoncillos, m. pl. shorts
calzones, m. pl. trousers
callado, adj. silent; quiet
callar, vn. to be silent; to hush
calle, f. street
callejero, adj. fond of loitering in streets
callejón, m. alley, narrow pass
callo, m. corn; callus
cama, f. bed, couch; litter
cámara, f. hall; chamber; camera; cockpit; chamber of a firearm
camarada, n. comrade, companion
camarera, f. waitress; chambermaid
camarero, m. waiter; steward
camarilla, f. clique
camarón, m. (zool.) shrimp
camarote, m. berth, cabin
cambiar, va. to barter, exchange; to change; to alter; to make change (money)
cambio, m. exchange, barter; change
camelia, f. camellia
camilla, f. pallet, stretcher
caminante, m. traveler, walker
caminar, vn. to walk; travel
camino, m. road, way
camión, m. truck, bus
camioneta, f. station wagon, small truck
camisa, f. shirt
camiseta, f. undershirt
camisón, m. nightgown
camote, m. (Sp. Am.) sweet potato

campamento, m. (mil.) encampment, camp
campana, f. bell
campanada, sound of a bell
campanario, m. belfry, steeple
campanilla, f. hand bell; (anat.) uvula
campaña, f. campaign, expedition
campechano, adj. frank; hearty
campeón, m. champion
campeonato, m. championship
campesino, adj. rural; n. peasant
campestre, adj. rural, rustic
campo, m. country; countryside; field; camp; ground
cana, f. gray hair
Canadá, m. Canada
canadiense, n., adj. Canadian
canal, m. channel, canal; gutter
Canal de la Mancha, m. English Channel
canalla, f. mob, rabble, populace; m. scoundrel
canallada, despicable act
canario, m. canary bird
canasta, f. basket, hamper; canasta (card game)
canastilla, f. small basket; layette
cancelar, va. to cancel, erase
cáncer, m. (med.) cancer
canceroso, adj. cancerous
canciller, m. chancellor; consular assistant
candado, m. padlock
candela, f. fire; light
candelabro, m. candelabrum
candelero, m. candlestick
candidato, candidata, n. candidate
cándido, adj. candid
candor, m. candor, frankness
cangrejo, m. crawfish, crab
canguro, m. kangaroo
caníbal, m. cannibal
canilla, f. shinbone
canjear, va. to exchange
cano, adj. gray-headed
canoa, f. canoe

canoso, *adj.* white-haired
cansado, *adj.* tired; tiresome
cansancio, *m.* weariness
cantaleta, *f.* singsong
cantante, *m.*, *f.* singer
cantar, *va.*, *vn.* to sing
cántaro, *m.* pitcher; **llover a cántaros**, to rain heavily
cantera, *f.* quarry
cantidad, *f.* quantity, number
cantina, *f.* canteen; barroom
cantinero, *m.* bartender
canto, *m.* song; singing; stone; edge
cantor, cantora, *f.* singer
caña, *f.* cane, reed; sugar cane; stalk
cáñamo, *m.* hemp; hempen cloth
cañaveral, *m.* sugar-cane field
cañería, *f.* pipe line
caño, *m.* tube; pipe line
cañón, *m.* pipe; canyon; cannon; gun barrel; **cañón antiaéreo**, antiaircraft gun; **cañón anticarro** or **antitanque**, antitank gun
caoba, *f.* mahogany
caos, *m.* chaos; confusion
capa, *f.* cloak; layer, coating
capacidad, *f.* capacity
capacitar, *va.*, *vr.* to enable, qualify; to delegate
capataz, *m.* overseer; foreman
capellán, *m.* chaplain, minister
caperuza, *f.* hood; **Caperucita Roja**, Little Red Riding Hood
capilla, *f.* hood; chapel
capital, *m.* capital, stock; *f.* capital, metropolis; *adj.* capital; principal
capitalismo, *m.* capitalism
capitalista, *n.*, *adj.* capitalist
capitán, *m.* captain
capitolio, *m.* capitol
capítulo, *m.* chapter (of a book)
caporal, *m.* chief, ringleader
capota, *f.* cape; top (of vehicles)
capote, *m.* cape, cloak; raincoat; **decir para su capote**, to say to oneself
capricho, *m.* caprice, whimsi-

cal; obstinate
capturer, *va.* to capture
capullo, *m.* pod of silkworm; bud
caqui, *m.*, *adj.* khaki
cara, *f.* face, front; surface
carabina, *f.* carbine; **ser como la carabina de Ambrosio** to be good for nothing, to be worthless
¡caracoles! *interj.* Blazes! Confound it!
carácter, *m.* character, nature, disposition
característica, *f.* trait, characteristic
característico, *adj.* characteristic
¡caramba! *interj.* Heavens!
carambola, *f.* carom (in billiards); trick; **por carambola**, indirectly, by chance
carátula, *f.* mask; title page
caravana, *f.* caravan; (Mex.) bow, curtsy
carbónico, *adj.* carbonic
carbono, *m.* (chem.) carbon
carbunclo, *m.* carbuncle
carburador, *m.* carburetor
cárcel, *f.* prison; jail
carcomido, *adj.* wormeaten
cardán, *m.* universal joint
cardenal, *m.* cardinal
cardiaco, *m.* cardiac
cardinal, *adj.* cardinal (point); principal, fundamental
cardo, *m.* thistle
carecer, *vn.* to want, lack
carencia, *f.* lack; scarcity
carestía, *f.* scarcity, want; famine; high price
careta, *f.* mask
carey, *m.* tortoise, shell turtle; tortoise shell
carga, *f.* load, burden; freight; cargo; load (of a firearm)
cargado, *adj.* loaded, full
cargador, *m.* freighter; loader
cargamento, *m.* load, cargo
cargar, *va.* to load, carry; to freight; to attack; to load a gun; to charge (on account)
cargo, *m.* debit; office; charge; care; accusation
caribe, *adj.* Caribbean

caricia, f. caress
caridad, f. charity
caries, f. (med.) caries, decay
cariño, m. fondness, love
cariñoso, adj. affectionate
carmesí, m. crimson
carnada, f. bait, lure
carnal, adj. related by blood; **primo carnal,** first cousin
carnaval, m. carnival
carne, f. flesh, meat; pulp of fruit
carnero, m. sheep, mutton
carnicería, f. meat market; slaughter
carnicero, m. butcher; adj. carnivorous
carnívoro, adj. carnivorous
caro, adj. expensive; dear
carpa, f. carp (fish); (Sp. Am.) a camping tent
carpeta, f. table cover; portfolio
carpintería, f. carpentry; carpenter's shop
carpintero, m. carpenter
carraspera, f. hoarseness
carrera, f. running; career; race; course, **carrera de relevos,** relay race; **carrera de vallas,** hurdles
carreta, f. cart; wagon
carretada, f. wagonload
carretaje, m. cartage
carretera, f. highway
carro, m. cart, freight car, car; wagon
carruaje, m. carriage, vehicle
carta, f. letter; charter
cartel, m. placard; handbill
cartera, f. brief case, letter case; pocketbook
cartero, postman
cartílago, m. cartilage
cartucho, m. cartridge
cartulina, f. Bristol board, fine cardboard
casa, f. house; concern; home
casamiento, m. marriage, wedding
casar, va., vr. to marry
cascabel, m. rattle; sleigh bell; (zool.) rattlesnake
cascajo, m. gravel
cascanueces, m. nutcracker

cascar, va., vr. to crack, break into pieces
cáscara, f. rind, peel, husk
casco, m. skull, cranium; helmet; hulk (of a ship); crown (of a hat); hoof
casero, casera, n. landlord or landlady; adj. domestic, familiar; homemade
casi, adv. almost, nearly
casilla, f. hut, booth, cabin; ticket office; **casilla de correos,** P.O. Box
casimir, m. cashmere
caso, m. case; event; occasion; (gram.) case
casta, f. caste, race, lineage; breed; kind, quality
castaña, f. chestnut
castaño, m. chestnut tree; adj. hazel; brown
castañuela, f. castanet
castellano, castellana, n., adj. Castilian; Spanish language
castidad, f. chastity
castigar, va. to punish
castigo, m. punishment
Castilla, f. Castile
castillo, m. castle; fortress
castizo, adj. pure, correct (as to language)
casto, adj. pure, chaste
castrar, va. to geld, castrate
casual, adj. casual, accidental
casualidad, f. casualty, accident; chance, coincidence; **por casualidad,** by chance
catalán, catalana, n., adj. Catalan, Catalonian
catálogo, m. catalogue; list
cataplasma, f. poultice, plaster
catar, va. to taste; to judge
catarata, f. cataract, waterfall; (med.) cataract
catarro, m. catarrh, cold
catástrofe, f. catastrophe, disaster
cátedra, f. professorship, subject taught by a professor
catedral, adj., f. cathedral
catedrático, m. professor of a university
categoría, f. category; rank
caterva, f. mob, throng

catolicismo, *m.* Catholicism
católico, *adj.*, *n.* Catholic
catorce, *m.*, *adj.* fourteen
catre, *m.* cot
cauce, *m.* trench, ditch, drain; bed of a river
caucho, *m.* rubber
caudal, *m.* property, wealth; abundance, plenty
caudaloso, *adj.* carrying much water (of rivers)
caudillo, *m.* chief, leader, dictator
causa, *f.* cause; occasion; motive, case, lawsuit; **a causa de**, on account of
causar, *va.* to cause, occasion
cautela, *f.* caution
cauterizar, *va.* to cauterize
cautivar, *va.* to captivate, charm, attract
cautivo, cautiva, *n.* captive, prisoner
caverna, *f.* cavern, cave
cavidad, *f.* cavity, hollow
cayo, *m.* cay, key
caza, *f.* game; hunting; *m.* (avi.) fighter plane
cazador, *m.* hunter, huntsman
cazar, *va.* to chase, hunt
cazuela, *f.* stewing pan; crock
C.C., corriente continua, D.C. or d.c., direct current
cebada, *f.* barley
cebo, *m.* food; bait, lure; priming
cebolla, *f.* onion
cebra, *f.* zebra
ceder, *va.* to grant, yield; *vn.* to submit, comply
cédula, *f.* charter, patent; ticket; permit, license; **cédulas hipotecarias,** mortgage, bank stock
céfiro, *m.* zephyr, breeze
cegar, *vn.* to become blind; *va.* to deprive of sight
ceguera, *f.* blindness
ceja, *f.* eyebrow
celda, *f.* cell
celebración, *f.* celebration
celebrar, *va.* to celebrate
celeste, *adj.* celestial, sky blue
celestial, *adj.* celestial; heav-

enly; perfect
célibe, *m.* unmarried person; bachelor
celo, *m.* zeal; rut (in animals); **celos,** *pl.* jealousy; **tener celos de,** to be jealous of
celosía, *f.* lattice of a window; Venetian blind
celoso, *adj.* jealous, zealous
célula, *f.* cell
cementar, *va.* to cement
cementerio, *m.* cemetery
cemento, *m.* cement; putty
cena, *f.* supper
cenagal, *m.* slough; swamp
cenar, *vn.* to have supper
cenicero, *m.* ash tray
ceniciento, *adj.* ash-colored; **Cenicienta**, *f.* Cinderella
cenit, *m.* zenith
censo, *m.* census
censor, *m.* censor, critic
censura, *f.* critical review censure, blame
censurar, *va.* to to censure, blame
centavo, *m.* a cent
centena, *f.* hundred
centenar, *m.* hundred
centenario, *adj.* centenary; *m.* centennial
centeno, *m.* (bot.) rye
centésimo, *adj.* centesimal, hundredth
centígrado, *adj.*, *m.* centigrade
centigramo, *m.* centigram
centímetro, *m.* centimeter
céntimo, *m.* centime; cent
central, *adj.* central, centric; *f.* central or main station; powerhouse; (Sp. Am.) sugar mill
centralizar, *va.* to centralize
céntrico, *adj.* central
centro, *m.* center
Centroamérica, *f.* Central America
cénts., céntimos, ¢ or c., cents
ceño, *m.* frown
cepillo, *m.* brush; **cepillo de dientes,** toothbrush; **cepillo de carpintero,** plane
cera, *f.* wax; wax taper
cerámica, *f.* ceramics

cerca, *f.* enclosure, fence; *adv.* near, close by

cercanía, *f.* proximity

cercano, *adj.*, *adv.* near, close by

cercar, *va.* to inclose; to fence

cerciorar, *va.*, *vr.* to ascertain, affirm

cerdo, *m.* hog, pig

cereal, *m.* cereal; grain

cerebral, *adj.* cerebral

cerebro, *m.* brain

ceremonia, *f.* ceremony

cerezo, *m.* cherry tree

cerillo, *m.* (Mex.) wax match

cernir, *va.* to sift, strain

cero, *m.* zero

cerrado, *adj.* closed; stupid, dense

cerradura, *f.* lock

cerrajero, *m.* locksmith

cerrar, *va.*, *vn.* to close, shut; to lock; **cerrarse**, to be obstinate

cerro, *m.* hill

cerrojo, *m.* latch (of a door)

certeza, *f.* certainty, assurance

certidumbre, *f.* certainty, conviction

certificado, *m.* certificate; *adj.* certified, registered (as a letter)

certificar, *va.* to certify, affirm; to register (a letter)

cerveza, *f.* beer, ale, lager

cesante, *adj.* jobless

cesáreo, *adj.* Caesarian

cesión, *f.* cession, transfer; concession

cesionario, cesionaria, *n.* assignee, indorsee (of negotiable instrument)

césped, *m.* sod, lawn

cesta, *f.* basket

cesto, *m.* hand basket

cetro, *m.* scepter

cf, costo de flete, freight cost; **caballo de fuerza**, h.p. horsepower; **confesor**, confessor

cg., centigramo, cg. centigram

cía, or **C.ía: Compañía**, Co. or co. Company; Soc., Society

cicatriz, *f.* scar

ciclista, *m., f.* cyclist

ciclo, *m.* cycle

ciclón, *m.* cyclone

ciclotrón, *m.* cyclotron

cidra, *f.* citron

ciego, *adj.* blind; *n.* blind person

cielo, *m.* sky, heaven

ciempiés, *m.* centipede

cien, *adj.* one hundred (used before a noun)

ciencia, *f.* science

cieno, *m.* mud, mire

científico, *adj.* scientific

ciento, *adj.* one hundred; *m.* a hundred

cierto, *adj.* certain, true

ciervo, *m.* deer, hart, stag

c.i.f., costo, seguro y flete, c.i.f., (com.) cost, insurance and freight

cifra, *f.* cipher, number

cigarra, *f.* katydid, cricket

cigarrera, *f.* cigarette case

cigarrillo, *m.* cigarette

cigarro, *m.* cigar; cigarette

cigüeña, *f.* (orn.) stork; (mech.) crank

cigüeñal, *m.* crankshaft

cilíndrico, *adj.* cylindrical

cilindro, *m.* cylinder; barrel

cima, *f.* summit, peak

cimentar, *va.* to lay a foundation, to establish fundamental principles

cimiento, *m.* groundwork of a building; basis, origin

cinc, *m.* zinc

cincel, *m.* chisel

cincelar, *va.* to chisel, engrave

cinco, *adj.*, *m.* five

cincuenta, *m.*, *adj.* fifty

cincha, *f.* girth, cinch

cine, cinema, cinematógrafo, *m.* moving-picture play or show

cinta, *f.* ribbon, tape, band

cintura, *f.* waistline

cinturón, *m.* belt; **cinturón de asiento, cinturón de seguridad**, seat belt, safety belt; **cinturón salvavidas**, life belt

ciprés, *m.* cypress tree

circo, *m.* circus

circuito, m. circuit
circulación, f. circulation
circular, adj. circular; vn. to circulate
círculo, m. circle; circumference; district; orb; club
circundar, va. to surround, encircle
circunferencia, f. circumference
circunspecto, adj. circumspect, cautious
circunstancia, f. circumstance, incident
ciruela, f. plum; **ciruela pasa**, prune
ciruelo, m. plum tree
cirugía, f. surgery
cirujano, m. surgeon
cisne, m. swan
cisterna, f. cistern; reservoir.
cita, f. citation, quotation; appointment, date
citación, f. quotation; summons.
citar, va. to make an appointment to meet a person; to convoke; to cite; to quote; to summon
cítrico, adj. (chem.) citric
ciudad, f. city
ciudadanía, f. citizenship; citizens
ciudadano, ciudadana, n. citizen
cívico, adj. civic
civil adj. civil, polite
civilización, f. civilization culture
civilizar, va. to civilize
civismo, m. patriotism
cizalla, f. metal shears
clamor, m. clamor, outcry
clamoroso, adj. clamorous; **exito clamoroso**, howling success
clandestino, adj. clandestine
clara, f. egg white
claraboya, f. skylight
claridad, f. light, brightness, clearness
clarificar, va. to brighten; to clarify
clarín, m. horn, bugle; trumpet; trumpeter

clarinete, m. clarinet; clarinet player
claro, adj. clear, bright; intelligible; light, evident, manifest; **¡claroro!** interj. of course!
clase, f. class, rank; kind
clásico, adj. clássical, classic
clasificar, va. to classify, class
clausura, f. closing; ad- journment
clausurar, va. to close; to adjourn
clave, f. key, code; (mus.) clef; m. harpsichord, clavichord
clavel, m. (bot.) pink, carnation
clavícula, f. clavicle, collarbone
clavija, f. pin, peg; plug, key
clavo, m. nail; **clavo de especia**, clove; **clavo de rosca**, screw
clemencia, f. clemency, mercy
clérigo, m. clergyman
clero, m. clergy
clima, m. climate.
clínica, f. clinic.
clínico, adj. clinical
clisé, m. plate, mat, cut
cloaca, f. sewer
cloro, m. (chem.) chlorine
clorofila, f. chlorophyll
cloroformo, m. chloroform
cloruro, m. (chem.) chloride
club, m. club, association
clueca, f. clucking (of a hen)
clueco, adj. decrepit; (Sp. Am.) presumptuous, vain
cm. or **c/m, centímetro**, cm., centimeter
Co., Compañia, Co., Company; Soc., Society
c/o, a cargo de, c/o or c.o., in care of
coagular, va., vr. to coagulate, curd
coartar, va. to limit, restrain
cobarde, adj. cowardly, timid; m. coward
cobardía, f. cowardice
cobertizo, m. small shed
cobija, f. bed cover, blanket
cobijar, va. to cover; to shelter
cobra, f. (zool.) cobra
cobrador, m. collector; street-

car or train conductor

cobrar, *va.* to collect; to recover; to receive; to charge (price, fee)

cobre, *m.* copper

cóbrese al entregar, cash on delivery, C.O.D.

cobro, *m.* collection; payment

cocaína, *f.* cocaine

cocer, *va.* to boil, cook; *vn.* to boil; to ferment

cocido, *adj.* cooked, boiled; *m.* kind of beef stew

cociente, *m.* quotient

cocina, *f.* kitchen, cuisine; **cocina económica,** cooking range

cocinar, *va., vn.* to cook

cocinero, cocinera, *n.* cook

coco, *m.* coconut, coconut tree; bogey, bugaboo

cocodrilo, *m.* crocodile; faithless person

cocuyo or **cucuyo,** *m.* firefly

coche, *m.* coach; carriage; car; **coche de alquiler,** cab

cochino, *adj.* dirty, nasty; *m.* pig

coctelera, *f.* cocktail shaker

codicia, *f.* lust, greed

codicioso, *adj.* covetous

código, *m.* code of laws

codorniz, *f.* (orn.) quail

coerción, *f.* coercion

cofre, *m.* trunk; box, chest; hood (of an automobile)

coger, *va.* to catch; to surprise

cohecho, *m.* bribery

coherente, *adj.* coherent, cohesive

cohesión, *f.* cohesion

cohete, *m.* skyrocket; **cohete especial de combustible sólido,** solid-fuel space rocket

cohibir, *va.* to restrain

coincidencia, *f.* coincidence

coincidir, *vn.* to coincide

cojear, *vn.* to limp, hobble

cojera, *f.* lameness, limp

cojín. *m.* cushion

cojinete, *m.* bearing (of an axle, etc.)

cojo, *adj.* lame, cripple

col, *f.* cabbage

cola, *f.* tail; train (of a gown);

line; glue; **hacer cola,** to stand in line

colaboración, *f.* collaboration

colaborar, *vn.* to collaborate

colador, *m.* colander, strainer

colapso, *m.* prostration, collapse

colar, *va., vn.* to strain, filter; **colarse,** (coll.) to squeeze (into a party) uninvited

colchón, *m.* mattress

colección, *f.* collection; set

colecta, *f.* collection of offerings

colectividad, *f.* collectivity; community

colectivización, *f.* collectivization

colectivizar, *va.* collectivize

colectivo, *adj.* collective; **contrato colectivo,** closed shop

colector, *m.* collector, gatherer

colegial, *m.* collegian; *adj.* collegiate

colegio, *m.* school; boarding school; college

cólera, *f.* anger, rage, fury; *m.* (med.) cholera

colérico, *adj.* enraged

colgante, *adj.* pendulous, hanging; **puente colgante,** suspension bridge

colgar, *va.* to hang; *vn.* to be suspended

colibrí, *m.* hummingbird

coliflor, *f.* cauliflower

colina, *f.* hill, hillock

colinabo, *m.* turnip

coliseo, *m.* opera house, theater

colmar, *va.* to heap up, fill up; **colmarse,** to reach the limit

colmena, *f.* hive, beehive

colmillo, *m.* eyetooth; long tusk

colmo, *m.* heap; completion; fill; limit

colocación, *f.* employment; situation, place; allocation

colocar, *va.* to arrange; to lay, place; to give employment to

colon, *m.* (anat.) colon

Colón, Columbus

colón, *m.* monetary unit of Costa Rica

colonia, *f.* colony; (Cuba) sugar-cane plantation; (Mex.) urban subdivision

colonial, *adj.* colonial

colonizar, *va.* to colonize

color, *m.* color, hue, dye; pretext

colorado, *adj.* ruddy, red

colorear, *va.* to color; to palliate, excuse; *vn.* to grow red

colorido, *m.* color; coloring

colorín, *m.* (orn.) linnet; vivid color; (Chile) a redheaded person

colosal, *adj.* colossal, great

coloso, *m.* colossus

columna, *f.* column; **columna vertebral,** spinal column

columpio, *m.* swing

collar, *m.* necklace

coma, *f.* comma (punctuation mark); (med.) coma

comadre, *f.* midwife; title given godmother of one's child; intimate woman friend, pal

comadrona, *f.* midwife

comandante, *m.* commander, chief; warden

comandita, *f.* (com.) silent partnership

comarca, *f.* territory, district; boundary, limit

combate, *m.* combat

combatiente, *m.* combatant

combatir, *va., vn.* to combat, fight; to attack; to contradict

combinar, *va., vr.* to combine

combustible, *adj.* combustible; *m.* fuel

comedia, *f.* comedy, play

comediante, *m., f.* actor, comedian

comedido, *adj.* eager to help

comedor, *m.* dining room

comején, *m.* white ant, termite

comentador, comentadora, *n.* commentator

comentar, *va.* to comment; to remark; to expound

comentario, *m.* comment, commentary

comer, *va.* to eat, chew; to dine; to take a piece in chess

comercial, *adj.* commercial

comerciante, *m.* trader, merchant, businessman

comerciar, *va.* to trade, have business intercourse with; **comerciar en,** to deal in

comercio, *m.* trade, commerce, business; communication, intercourse

comestable, *adj.* edible; **comestables,** *m. pl.* provisions, groceries

cometer, *va.* to commit

cometido, *m.* task, mission

comezón, *f.* itch

comicios, *m. pl.* elections; polls

cómico, *adj.* comic, comical; **cómico, cómica,** *n.* actor, actress

comida, *f.* food; dinner; meal

comienzo, *m.* beginning

comilón, comilona, *n., adj.* glutton

comillas, *f. pl.* quotation marks

comino, *m.* cumin (plant or seed); **no valer un comino,** to be worthless

comisario, *m.* commissary; deputy

comisión, *f.* trust, commission; committee

comisionado, *m.* commissioner

comisionar, *va.* to commission, depute

comité, *m.* committee

comitiva, *f.* retinue

como, *adv.* (interrogative, **cómo)** how, in what manner; as; like; **¿a cómo estamos?** what is the date?

cómoda, *f.* chest of drawers

comodidad, *f.* comfort; convenience

cómodo, *adj.* convenient, commodious; comfortable

compacto, *adj.* compact

compadecer, *va., vr.* to pity, sympathize with

compadre, *m.* godfather of one's child; friend, old pal

compañero, compañera, *n.* companion, comrade, friend, partner; pal

compañía, *f.* company, society; partnership

comparación, *f.* comparison

comparar, *va.* to compare

compartir, *va.* to share

compás, *m.* compass; (mus.) measure, time; beat

compasión, *f.* compassion, pity

compasivo, *adj.* compassionate

compatible, *adj.* compatible

compatriota, *m., f.* countryman; countrywoman; fellow citizen

compeler, *va.* to compel, constrain

compendio, *m.* summary

compensación, *f.* compensation

compensar, *va., vn.* to compensate

competencia, *f.* competition, rivalry; competence

competente, *adj.* competent

competidor, competidora, *n.* competitor

compilar, *va.* to compile

complacer, *va.* to please another; **complacerse,** to be pleased with

complaciente, *adj.* pleasing; accommodating

complejo, *m.* complex; **complejo, compleja,** *adj.* complex, intricate

complementario, *adj.* complementary

complemento, *m.* complement; (gram.) object

completar, *va.* to complete

completo, *adj.* complete

complexión, *f.* constitution, physique

complicación, *f.* complication

complicar, *va.* to complicate

cómplice, *m., f.* accomplice

complot, *m.* plot, conspiracy

componer, *va.* to compose; to repair; to settle; **componerse,** to arrange one's hair, clothes, etc., **componerse de,** to be composed of

comportarse, *vr.* to comport oneself

compositor, compositora, *n.* composer; compositor

compostura, *f.* composition; mending, repairing; composure

compota, *f.* preserves

compra, purchase

comprar, *va.* to buy, purchase

comprender, *va.* to include, comprise; to understand

comprensible, *adj.* comprehensible

comprensión, *f.* understanding

comprensivo, *adj.* understanding

compresión, *f.* compression

compresor, *m.* compressor

comprimir, *va.* to compress; to condense; to repress

comprobante, *m.* voucher

comprobar, *va.* to verify, check; to confirm

comprometer, *va.* to compromise; to put in danger; **comprometerse,** to commit oneself; to become engaged

comprometido, *adj.* betrothed

compromiso, *m.* compromise; commitment; engagement

compuerta, *f.* lock, floodgate

compuesto, *m.* compound; *adj.* composed; repaired

compulsorio, *adj.* compulsory

computar, *va.* to compute

cómputo, *m.* computation

comulgar, *vn.* to take communion

común, *adj.* common, usual; *m.* watercloset

comunicación, *f.* communication

comunicar, *va.* to communicate

comunidad, community

comunión, communion; fellowship; common possession

comunismo, *m.* communism

comunista, *m., f.* communist

con, *prep.* with; by

conato, *m.* endeavor; crime attempted but not executed

concebir, va., vn. to conceive
conceder, va. to concede
concejal, m. councilman
concejo, m. town hall
concentración, f. concentration
concentrar, va., vr. to concentrate
concepción, f. conception
concepto, m. conception, concept; opinion
concerniente, adj. concerning
concernir, v. imp. to concern
concertar, va. to settle; vn. to agree, accord
concertista, m., f. concert performer or manager
concesión, f. concession, grant
conciencia, f. conscience
concienzudo, adj. conscientious
conciliación, f. conciliation
conciliar, va. to conciliate, reconcile
concilio, m. council
conciso, adj. concise, brief
conciudadano, **conciudadana**, n. fellow citizen; countryman
concluir, va. to conclude, complete; to infer
conclusión, f. conclusion, consequence
concluyente, adj. conclusive
concordancia, f. concordance, concord; harmony
concordar, va. to accord; vn. to agree
concordia, f. conformity, union, harmony
concretar, va. to combine, unite; to limit; to sum up
concreto, adj. concrete
concubina, f. concubine, mistress
concurrencia, f. audience
concurrentes, m. pl. attendants, guests
concurrido, adj. crowded, well-attended
concurrir, vn. to concur, agree; to attend
concurso, m. competition, contest

concusión, f. concussion
concha, f. shell; tortoise shell
condado, m. county
conde, m. earl, count
condecorar, va. to confer a decoration on
condensación, f. condensation
condensar, va., vr. to condense
condesa, f. countess
condescendencia, f. condescension, compliance
condescender, vn. to condescend
condición, f. condition, quality; stipulation
condimentar, va. to season (food)
condimento, m. condiment
condiscípulo, **condiscípula**, n. fellow-student
condolerse, vr. to condole, to sympathize
cóndor, m. (orn.) condor
conducente, adj. conducive
conducta, f. conduct; behavior
conducto, m. conduit; channel; **por conducto de**, through (agent)
conductor, m. conductor, guide
conectar, va. to connect
conejo, **coneja**, n. rabbit
conejillo, m. small rabbit; **conejillo de Indias**, guinea pig
conexión, f. connection
confección, f. (med.) compound; confection
confeccionar, va. to make, put together
confederación, f. confederacy, confederation
confederado, **confederada**, n., adj. confederate
conferenciante, m., f. public lecturer
conferenciar, vn. to hold a conference; to consult together
conferencista, m., f. lecturer, speaker
conferir, va. to confer, grant
confesar, va. to confess

confesión, *f.* confession

confesor, *m.* confessor

confiado, *adj.* confident; arrogant, forward

confianza, *f.* confidence, boldness; assurance; intimacy; trust; **digno de confianza**, reliable, trustworthy

confiar, *va.*, *vn.* to confide, trust in; to hope, count on

confidencia, *f.* confidence

confidencial, *adj.* confidential

confidente, *m.*, *f.* confidant

confín, *m.* limit, boundary

confinar, *va.*, *vn.* to confine, limit; to border upon

confirmación, *f.* confirmation

confirmr, *va.* to confirm

confiscar, *va.* to confiscate

confite, *m.* candy, bonbon

conflicto, *m.* conflict

conformar, *va.* to conform; *vn.* to suit, fit; **conformarse**, to resign oneself

conforme, *adj.* conformable, suitable; **estar conforme**, to be in agreement; *adv.* according to

conformidad, *f.* conformity; patience, resignation

confort, *m.* comfort

confortante, *adj.* comforting; *m.* sedative

confortar, *va.* to comfort

confraternidad, *f.* confraternity, brotherhood

confrontar, *va.* to confront; to compare

confundir, *va.*, *vr.* to confound; to perplex

confusión, *f.* confusion, disorder; perplexity

confuso, *adj.* confused; perplexed

conga, *f.* conga

congelación, *f.* freezing

congelador, *m.* freezer

congeladora, *f.* deep freezer

congelar, *va.*, *vr.* to freeze, congeal

congeniar, *vn.* to be congenial

congénito, *adj.* congenital

conglomeración, *f.* conglomeration

congoja, *f.* anguish, grief

congratular, *va.* to congratulate

congregar, *va.* to assemble, meet

congreso, *m.* congress

congruencia, *f.* congruency

cónico, *adj.* conical

conjetura, *f.* conjecture

conjugar, *va.* to conjugate

conjunción, *f.* conjunction

conjunto, *adj.* united, conjunct; *m.* the whole, the ensemble

conjurar, *va.*, *vn.* to conjure; to cospire

conmemoración, *f.* commemoration

conmemorar, *va.* to commemorate

conmemorativo, *adj.* memorial

conmigo, *pron.* with me, with myself

conmiseración, *f.* commiseration, pity

conmovedor, *adj.* affecting, moving, touching

conmover, *va.*, *vr.* to disturb, move, stir

conmutador, *m.* electric switch

connivencia, *f.* connivance

conocedor, conocedora, *n.* expert; connoisseur

conocer, *va.* to know, to be acquainted; to understand

conocido, conocida, *n.* acquaintance

conocimiento, *m.* knowledge, understanding; consciousness; (com.) bill of lading; **poner en conocimiento**, to inform, to advise

conque, *conj.* so then

conquista, *f.* conquest

conquistador, *m.* conqueror

conquistar, *va.* to conquer

consagrar, *va.* to consecrate, dedicate

consciente, *adj.* conscious, aware

consecución, *f.* attainment

consecuencia, *f.* consequence; result

consecuente, *adj.* consequent, logical

consecutivo, *adj.* consecutive

conseguir, *va.* to attain, get

consejero, *m.* counselor; councilor; advisor

consejo, *m.* counsel, advice; council; advisory board

consentido *adj.* pampered

consentimiento, *m.* consent, assent

consentir, *va.* to consent, to agree; to comply, acquiesce; to coddle

conserje, *m.* concierge, janitor

conserva, *f.* conserve, preserve; **conservas**, canned goods

conservador, *adj.* conservative

conservar, *va.* to conserve; to keep, maintain

couservatorio, *m.* conservatory

considerable, *adj.* considerable

consideración, *f.* consideration, regard

considerado, *adj.* prudent, considerate; esteemed

considerando, *conj.* whereas

considerar, *va.* to consider, think over; to respect

consigna, (mil.) watchword

consignación, *f.* consignation; consignment

consignar, *va.* to consign

consignatario, *m.* trustee; consignee

consigo, *pron.* with oneself

consiguiente, *adj.* consequent, consecutive; **en consequence**, effect; **por consiguiente**, consequently

consistencia, *f.* consistence

consistente, *adj.* consistent; firm, solid

consistir, *vn.* to consist

consocio, *m.* partner, fellow member

consolación, *f.* consolation

consolar, *va.* to console, to cheer

consolidar, *va., vr.* to consolidate, strengthen

consorte, *m., f.* consort, companion

conspicuo, *adj.* conspicuous; prominent

conspiración, *f.* conspiracy, plot

conspirar, *vn.* to conspire, plot

constancia, *f.* constancy

constante, *adj.* constant, firm

constar, *v. imp.* to be evident or certain; to be composed of, consist of; **hacer constar**, to state; **me consta**, I know positively

constelación, *f.* constellation

consternar, *va.* to confound, dismay

constipación, *f.* cold; constipation

constipado, *m.* cold in the head

constitución, *f.* constitution

constitucional, *adj.* constitutional

constituir, *va., vr.* to constitute

construcción, *f.* construction

constructor, constructora, *n.* builder

construir, *va.* to build, construct; to construe

consuelo, *m.* consolation, comfort

cónsul, *m.* consul

consulado, *m.* consulate

consulta, *f.* consultation

consultar, *va.* to consult

consultivo, *adj.* advisory

consultor, consultora, *n.* adviser, counselor; *adj.* advisory, consulting

consultorio, *m.* doctor's office; clinic

consumar, *va.* to consummate, finish, perfect

consumidor, consumidora, *n.* consumer; *adj.* consuming

consumir, *va.* to consume; **consumirse**, to languish

consumo, *m.* consumption of provisions; demand (for merchandise)

consunción, (med.) consumption

contabilidad, *f.* accounting, bookkeeping

contacto, *m.* contact, touch

contado, *adj.* scarce, rare; **al contado,** cash, ready money

contador, *m.* accountant; counter; **contador de agua,** water meter; **contador Geiger,** Geiger counter

contagiar, *va.* to infect

contagio, *m.* contagion

contagioso, *adj.* contagious

contaminar, *va.* to contaminate

contante, *adj.* fit to be counted; **dinero contante y sonante,** ready cash

contar, *va.* to count, calculate; to relate

contemplar, *va.* to contemplate, to coddle

contender, *vn.* to contend; to contest

contendiente, *m., f.* competitor; contender

contener, *va.* to contain, comprise; **contenerse,** to repress

contenido, *m.* contents

contentar, *va., vr.* to content

contento, *adj.* glad, pleased; content; *m.* contentment

conteo, *m.* countdown

contestación, *f.* answer, reply

contestar, *va.* to answer

contienda, *f.* contest, dispute

contigo, *pron.* with you (sing.)

continental, *adj.* continental

continente, *m.* continent, mainland

contingente, *adj.* accidental; *m.* contingent; share

continuación, *f.* continuation, continuance, continuity

continuamente, *adv.* continuously, continually

continuar, *va., vn.* to continue

continuidad, *f.* continuity

continuo, *adj.* continuous, continual

contorno, *m.* environs; contour, outline

contrabajo, *m.* bass viol

contrabandista, *m.* smuggler

contracción, *f.* contraction

contradecir, *va.* to contradict

contradicción, *f.* contradiction

contradictorio, *adj.* contradictory

contraer, *va., vn.* to contract; to reduce; **contraerse,** to shrink up

contrahecho, *adj.* deformed

contralor, *m.* controller

contralto, *m., f.* contralto

contraorden, *f.* countermand

contrapeso, *m.* counterweight; (Chile) uneasiness; **hacer contrapeso a,** to counterbalance

contrapunto, *m.* (mus.) counterpoint, harmony

contrariar, *va.* to contradict, oppose; to vex

contrariedad, *f.* opposition; disappointment

contrario, contraria, *n.* opponent, antagonist; *adj.* contrary, opposite; hostile; **al contrario,** on the contrary

contrarrestar, *va.* to counteract

contraseña, *f.* countersign; (mil.) watchword, password

contrastar, *va.* to contrast; to assay metals

contraste, *m.* contrast; opposition

contratar, *va.* to engage, hire; to contract

contratiempo, *m.* disappointment; mishap

contratista, *m.* contractor

contrato, *m.* contract, pact

contraveneno, *m.* antidote

contravenir, *va.* to contribute

contribuyente, *m., f.* contributor; taxpayer

contrincante, *m.* competitor

contrito, *adj.* contrite

control, *m.* control, check

contusión, *f.* contusion

convalecencia, *f.* convalescence

convalecer, *vn.* to convalesce

convencer, *va.* to convince

convencimiento, *m.* conviction

convención, *f.* convention

convencional, *adj.* conventional

convenido, *adj.* agreed

conveniencia, *f.* utility, profit; convenience; ease; desirability

conveniente, *adj.* convenient, advantageous; desirable

convenio, *m.* pact

convener, *vn.* to agree, coincide; to compromise; to fit, suit

convento, *m.* convent

conversación, *f.* conversation

conversar, *vn.* to converse, talk

converso, *m.* convert

convertir, *va.* to transform, convert; to reform; **convertirse,** to become

convicción, *f.* conviction

convidado, *adj.* invited; **convidado, convidada,** *n.* invited guest

convidar, *va.* to invite

convincente, *adj.* convincing

convocar, *va.* to convoke, assemble

convoy, *m.* convoy, escort

convulsión, *f.* convulsion

conyugal, *adj.* conjugal

cónyuges, *m. pl.* married couple, husband and wife

coñac, *m.* cognac, brandy

cooperación, *f.* cooperation

cooperar, *vn.* to cooperate

cooperativo, *adj.* cooperative; **cooperativa,** cooperative society

coordinación, *f.* coordination

coordinar, *va.* to coordinate

copa, *f.* cup; goblet; top of a tree; crown of a hat; **copas,** *pl.* hearts (at cards)

Copenhague, *f.* Copenhagen

copete, *m.* toupee; pompadour; top, summit

copia, *f.* copy, transcript; imitation

copiar, *va.* to copy; to imitate

copioso, *adj.* abundant

copla, *f.* couplet; popular ballad, folksong

coqueta, *f.* coquette, flirt

coquetear, *vn.* to flirt

coquetería, *f.* coquetry, flirtation

coquetón, coquetona, *adj.* flirtatious

coraje, *m.* anger

corajudo, *adj.* ill-tempered

coral, *m.* coral; *adj.* choral

coraza, *f.* cuirass; armor plate; shell of a turtle

corazón, *m.* heart; core; benevolence; center

corazonada, *f.* sudden inspiration; presentiment, hunch

corbata, *f.* necktie

corcovado, *adj.* humpbacked, crooked

corcho, *m.* cork

cordel, *m.* cord, rope

cordero, *m.* lamb; meek, gentle man

cordial, *adj.* cordial, affectionate; *m.* cordial

cordialidad, *f.* cordiality

cordillera, range of mountains

cordón, *m.* cord, string; military cordon

cordura, *f.* prudence, sanity, good judgment

corista, *m.* chorister; *f.* chorus girl

cornada, *f.* thrust with horns

córnea, cornea

corneta, *f.* cornet; *m.* bugler

coro, *m.* choir, chorus

corona, *f.* crown; coronet; top of the head; crown (English silver coin); monarchy; halo

coronar, *va.* to crown; to complete, perfect

coronel, *m.* (mil.) colonel

coronilla, *f.* crown of the head

corporación, *f.* corporation

corporal, *adj.* corporal, bodily

corpulento, *adj.* corpulent

Corpus, *m.* Corpus Christi (religious festival)

corral, *m.* poultry yard; **aves de corral,** poultry

correa, *f.* leather strap, belt; **tener correa,** to bear teasing good-humoredly

corrección, *f.* correction; proper demeanor

correcto, *adj.* correct

corredor, *m.* runner; corridor; broker

corregidor, *m.* corregidor

(Spanish magistrate)

corregir, *va.* to correct, amend; to reprehend

correo, *m.* mail; mailman; post office

correoso, *adj.* leathery

correr, *vn.* to run; to race; to flow; to blow (applied to the wind); to pass away (applied to time); *va.* to race (an animal); **correrse,** to become disconcerted

correría, *f.* excursion, incursion; **correrías,** youthful escapades

correspondencia, *f.* correspondence; proportion

corresponder, *va.* to reciprocate; to correspond; to agree

correspondiente, *adj.* corresponding; suitable

corresponsal *m.* correspondent

corretear, *vn.* to run around (as children)

corrida, *f.* course, race; **corrida de toros,** bullfight

corrido, *m.* (mus.) a special rhythm

corriente, *f.* current (of water, electricity, etc.); stream; **tener al corriente,** to keep advised; *adj.* current; ordinary

corromper, *va., vr.* to corrupt

corrupción, *f.* corruption

cortapapel, *m.* paper knife

cortaplumas, *m.* penknife

corte, *m.* cutting; cut; felling of trees; cut goods to make a garment; *f.* (royal) court, the court of chancery; retinue; courtship, flattery; **hacer la corte,** to woo; **Cortes,** *f. pl.* Cortes, Spanish Parliament

cortejar, *va.* to make love, court

cortejo, *m.* cortege, procession

cortés, *adj.* courteous, polite

cortesano, *m.* courtier; **cortesana,** *f.* courtesan

cortesía, *f.* courtesy

cortina, *f.* curtain

corto, *adj.* short; shy

cortocircuito, *m.* short circuit

corva, *f.* bend of the knee

cosa, *f.* thing; matter

cosecha, *f.* harvest; crop

cosechar, *va.* to crop, reap

coser, *va.* to sew; **máquina de coser,** sewing machine

cosmético, *m.* cosmetic

cosmopolita, *n., adj.* cosmopolite, cosmopolitan

cosquillas, *f. pl.* tickling; **hacer cosquillas,** to tickle

costa, *f.* cost, price; expense; coast, shore

costado, *m.* side; (mil.) flank

costal, *m.* sack, large bag

costar, *vn.* to cost

coste, *m.* cost, expense

costear, *va.* to pay the cost; *vn.* to sail along the coast

costero, *adj.* coastal

costilla, *f.* rib; (coll.) wife

costo, *m.* cost, price

costoso, *adj.* costly, expensive

costra, *f.* crust

costura, *f.* seam; needlework; sewing

costurera, *f.* seamstress

cotidiano, *adj.* daily

cotización, *f.* (com.) quotation

cotizar, *va.* to quote (a price)

coto, *m.* (med.) goiter

cotorra, *f.* magpie; (coll.) talkative woman

coyote, *m.* coyote

coyuntura, *f.* joint, articulation

C.P.T., Contador Público Titulado, C.P.A. Certified Public Accountant

cráneo, *m.* skull, cranium

cráter *m.* crater

creación, *f.* creation

Creador, *m.* the Creator, God

creador, *adj.* creative

crear, *va.* to create, make; to establish

crecer, *vn.* to grow; to increase; to swell

creces, *f. pl.* increase; **pagar con creces,** to pay back generously

creciente, *f.* swell; leaven; crescent (of the moon); (naut.) flood tide; *adj.* growing, increasing; crescent

(moon)
crecimiento, m. growth
credencial, f. credential
crédito, m. credit; reputation
crédulo, adj. credulous
creer, va. to believe; to think; **¡ya lo creo!** you bet! of course!
crema, f. cream
cremallera, f. (mech.) rack; zipper
crepúsculo, m. twilight
crespo, adj. crisp; curly; m. (Sp. Am.) a curl
crespón, m. crepe
cresta, f. cockscomb; crest of some birds; top, summit of a mountain; (Col.) a thing one loves; love
cría, f. breed or brood of animals; hatch; (coll.) child reared by a nurse
criada, f. maid servant
criadilla, f. testicle; small loaf; truffle
criado, m. servant
criador, m. creator; breeder
crianza, f. breeding, education
criar, va. to create, produce; to breed; to nurse; to suckle; to bring up
crimen, m. crime
criminal, adj., n. criminal
crin, f. mane, horsehair
criollo, criolla, n. born in Latin America of European parents; peasant; adj. native, typical of the region
crisis, f. crisis
crisma, f. (coll.) head
crisol, m. crucible; melting pot
cristal, m. crystal; crystal glass; **cristal tallado**, cut crystal
cristalería, f. glassware
cristalino, adj. crystalline, clear
cristalizar, va. to crystallize
cristianismo, m. Christianism
cristiano, cristiana, n., adj. Christian
Cristo, m. Christ
Cristóbal Colón, Christopher Columbus
criterio m. criterion, judgment

crítica, f. criticism
criticar, va. to criticize
crítico, m. critic, censurer; adj. critical
cromo, m. chromium, chrome
crónico, adj. chronic
cronista, m., f. chronicler; reporter
croqueta, f. croquette
cruce, m. crossing; crossroads
crucificar, va. to crucify; to torment
crucifijo, m. crucifix
crucigrama, m. crossword puzzle
crudo, adj. raw, crude; green unripe; rude, cruel
cruel, adj. cruel
crueldad, f. cruelty
crujido, m. crack, creak
crujir, vn. to crackle, rustle; **crujir los dientes**, to grind the teeth
cruz, f. cross
cruzada, f. crusade
cruzado, adj. crossed; of crossed breed, etc.
cruzar, va. to cross
c.s.f.; costo, seguro y flete, c.i.f.; cost, insurance, and freight
cta. or **c.ta, cuenta**, (com.) a/c or acc., account
cta., cte. or **cta., corr.te , cuenta corriente**, (com.) current account
cte. or **corr.te, corriente**, current, usual, common
c/u, cada uno, each one, every one
cuaderno, m. memorandum book
cuadra, f. block of houses
cuadrado, adj. square; (Cuba) rude and stupid; m. square
cuadragésimo, adj. fortieth
cuadrángulo, m. quadrangle
cuadrilátero, adj. quadrilateral
cuadrilla, f. gang, crew, troop; matador and his assistants
cuadro, m. square; picture; picture frame
cuadrúpedo, adj. quadruped
cuajar, va. to coagulate; vn. to

succeed; to please; **cuajarse,** to coagulate

cual, *pron., adj.* which; such as; *adv.* as; how; like; **¿cuál?** *interr.* which (one)?

cualidad *f.* quality

cualquiera, *adj., pron.* any; anyone, anybody, somebody

cuan, *adv.* how, as (used only before adj. or adv.); **cuán,** *adv.* how, what

cuando (*interr.* **cuándo**), *adv.* when; in case that; if; although; even; sometimes

cuanto, *adj.* as many as, as much as; **¿cuánto?** how much?; **¿cuántos?** how many?; *adv.* as; the more; **cuanto antes,** at once; **en cuanto a,** with regard to

cuarenta, *adj.* forty

cuarentena, *f.* quarantine

cuaresma, *f.* Lent

cuartel, *m.* barracks; **cuartel general,** headquarters

cuarteto, *m.* quartet

cuarto, *m.* fourth part, quarter; dwelling, room; *adj.* fourth

cuate, *m., adj.* (Mex.) twin; (coll.) pal

cuatro, *adj.* four; *m.* figure four; (mus.) quartet ; **las cuatro,** *f. pl.* four o'clock

cubano, cubana, *adj., n.* Cuban

cúbico, *adj.* cubic

cubierta, *f.* cover; envelope; wrapping; deck of a ship; (auto.) hood

cubierto, *m.* place for one at the table; regular dinner

cubil, *m.* lair of wild beasts

cubo, *m.* cube; pail; hub (of a wheel)

cubrir, *va.* to cover; to disguise; to cover a mare; **cubrirse,** to put on one's hat

cucaracha, *f.* cockroach

cucurucho, *m.* paper cone

cuchara, *f.* spoon

cucharada, *f.* spoonful

cucharita, *f.* teaspoon

cucharón, *m.* ladle, dipper, large spoon; scoop

cuchicheo, *m.* whispering, murmur

cuchillo, *m.* knife

cuello, *m.* neck; neck of a bottle; collar of a garment; **cuello de estrangulación,** bottleneck

cuenca, *f.* valley, basin of a river; (anat.) eye socket

cuento, *m.* story, tale, narrative; **cuento de hadas,** fairy tale

cuerda, *f.* cord; string for musical instruments; spring of a watch or clock; **bajo cuerda,** underhandedly; **dar cuerda,** to wind

cuerdo, *adj.* prudent, judicious; in his senses

cuerno, *m.* horn; corn, callosity; **cuerno de abundancia,** horn of plenty

cuerpo, *m.* body; cadaver; corpse; staff, corps

cuervo, *m.* (orn.) crow, raven

cuesta, *f.* hill; **cuesta arriba,** uphill; with great trouble and difficulty

cuestión, *f.* question; dispute; problem; matter

cuestionario, *m.* questionnaire

cueva, *f.* cave, grotto, den

cuidado, *m.* care, attention; solicitude, anxiety; accuracy; **tener cuidado,** to be careful; **¡cuidado!** *interj.* watch out!

cuidadoso, *adj.* careful

cuidar, *va.* to heed, care; to mind, look after; **cuidarse,** to be careful of one's health

cuita, *f.* grief, affliction

culata, *f.* breech of a gun; butt

culebra, *f.* snake; **culebra de cascabel,** rattlesnake

culo, *m.* breech, backside; anus; bottom

culpa, *f.* misdemeanor; sin; guilt; **tener la culpa,** to be at fault

culpable, *adj.* guilty

culpar, *va.* to accuse, blame

cultivar,*va.* to cultivate

cultivo,*m.* cultivation; farming; culture (of bacteria)

culto, *adj.* elegant, correct; polished; civilized; culture; worship, cult, religion; homage

cultura, *f.* culture

cumbre, *f.* top, summit

cumpleaños, *m.* birthday

cumplido, *adj.* polished, polite; *m.* compliment

cumplimiento, *m.* compliment; accomplishment; fulfillment; expiration (of credit, etc.)

cumplir, *va.* to execute, carry out; to fulfil; **cumplir años,** to have a birthday; *vn.* to fall due

cúmulo, *m.* heap, pile

cuna, *f.* cradle; native country; lineage; origin

cuñado, cuñada, *n.* brother- or sister-in-law

cuociente, *m.* quotient

cuota, *f.* quota, fixed share; fee

cupé, *m.* coupé; cab

cupo, *m.* quota, share

cupón, *m.* coupon

cúpula, *f.* cupola, dome

cura, *m.* priest, parson; *f.* healing, cure, remedy

curandero, *m.* quack, medicaster

curar, *va.* to cure, heal

curiosidad, *f.* curiosity; neatness; rarity

curioso, *adj.* curious, strange; neat; diligent

cursar, *va.* to study (a course)

curtir, *va.* to tan leather; to sunburn; to inure to hardships

curva, *f.* curve, bend, curved line; **curva cerrada,** sharp bend; **curva doble,** s-curve

curvo, *adj.* curved, bent

cúspide, *f.* apex, peak

custodia, *f.* custody, keeping, hold; guard, escort; (rel.) monstrance

custodiar, *va.* to guard, watch

cutícula, *f.* cuticle

cuyo, cuya, *pron.* of which, of whom, whose, whereof

czar, *m.* czar

Ch

ch/, cheque, check

chabacano, *adj.* coarse, awkward; *m.* (Mex.) apricot

chacarero, *m.* (Arg. Urug.) farmer on small scale

chacra, *f.* (Arg. Urug.) small size farm

chal, *m.* shawl

chalán, *m.* hawker, huckster; (Mex.) **chalán de río,** river ferry

chaleco, *m.* waistcoat, vest

chalina, *f.* scarf

chalupa, *f.* (Mex.) small canoe

chamaco, chamaca, *n.* (Mex.) small boy or girl

chamarra, *f.* mackinaw coat

chambón, chambona, *adj.* awkward, bungling; *n.* bungler

champaña, *m.* champagne

champú, *m.* shampoo

chamuscar, *va.* to singe, scorch

chancear, *vn., vr.* to joke, jest

chancla, *f.* old shoe

chanza, *f.* joke, jest, fun

chapa, *f.* thin metal plate flush on cheek; veneer

chaparro, *adj.* (Mex.) small or short (of a person)

chaparrón, *m.* violent shower of rain

chapulín, *m.* grasshopper

chaqueta, *f.* jacket, coat

charada, *f.* charade

charca, *f.* pool of water, pond

charco, *m.* pool of standing water

charla, *f.* idle chitchat, prattle, talk

charlatán, charlatana, *n.* idle talker; quack

charol, *m.* varnish; lacquer; enamel; patent leather

charro, *m.* churl; Mexican cowboy; *adj.* gaudy

chasco, *m.* joke, jest; disappointment; **llevarse chasco,** to be disappointed

chasis, *m.* chassis

chasquido, *m.* crack of a whip

chato, *adj.* flat, flattish; flat-nosed

chaveta, *f.* bolt, pin, pivot; **perder la chaveta,** to become rattled

chelín, *m.* shilling

cheque, *m.* (com.) check

chicle, *m.* chewing gum

chico, *adj.* little, small; *n.* little boy or girl

chícharo, *m.* pea

chicharrón, *m.* crackling, pork rind or fat cooked until crisp

chichón, *m.* lump on the head occasioned by a blow

chiflar, *vn.* to whistle; **chiflarse,** (coll.) to become mentally unbalanced; to act silly

chile, *m.* (bot.) chili, red pepper

chileno, chilena, *n., adj.* Chilean

chillido, *m.* squeak, shriek

chimenea, *f.* chimney; smoke-stack; (naut.) funnel

chimpancé, *m.* chimpanzee

china, *f.* porcelain; pebble; (Cuba and P.R.) thin-skinned orange; **China,** China

chinche, *f.* bedbug; thumb-tack

chinchilla, *f.* chinchilla

chinela, *f.* house slipper

chino, china, *n., adj.* Chinese; *m.* Chinese language

chiquillo, chiquilla, *n.* child, youngster

chiquito, chiquita, *adj.* little, small; *n.* little boy or girl

chiripa, *f.* fluke (in billiards); (coll.) fortunate chance; **de chiripa,** by mere chance

chisme, *m.* misreport; gossip

chismear, *va., vn.* to tattle, gossip

chismoso, *adj.* tattling, tale-bearing

chispa, *f.* spark; very small diamond; small particle; **¡chispas!** *interj.* blazes! **echar chispas,** to rave

chiste, *m.* joke, jest

chistoso, *adj.* funny, comical

chivo, chiva, *n.* kid, goat

chocante, *adj.* repugnant

chocolate, *m.* chocolate

chochear, *vn.* to dote

chochera, *f.* second childhood

chofer or **chófer,** *m.* chauffeur, driver

choque, *m.* shock; collision; crash, clash

chorizo, *m.* pork sausage

chorrear, *vn.* to drip from a spout, gush, drip; trickle

chorro, *m.* gush; **a chorros,** abundantly

chotear, *va.* to rib, kid, poke fun at

choza, *f.* hut, cabin

chuleta, *f.* chop; **chuleta de puerco,** pork chop

chulo, chula, *n.* jester, clown; *adj.* (Sp. Am.) pretty, darling

chusco, *adj.* pleasant, droll

chuzo, *m.* spear or pike; **llover a chuzos,** to rain heavily

D

D., Dn. or **D.ⁿ, Don,** Don, title equivalent to Mr., but used before given name

Da. or **D.ª, Doña,** Donna, title equivalent to Mrs. or Miss but used before given name

dádiva, *f.* gift, present; handout

dado, *m.* die (*pl.* dice); (*p.p.* of **dar**) **dado que** or **dado caso que,** in case that, provided that, since

daga, dagger

dalia, (bot.) dahlia

dama, lady, mistress; king (in checkers (theat. leading lady; **damas,** *pl.* checkers

danés, danesa, *n., adj.* Danish

Danubio, *m.* Danube

danza, *f.* dance

danzar, *vn.* to dance

dañar, *va.* to damage; to injure; to spoil

dañino, *adj.* harmful

daño, *m.* damage, injury

dar, *va., vn.* to give; to supply. **dar a conocer,** to make known; **dar prestado,** to lend; **darse por vencido,** to give up; **darse cuenta de,** to realize: **darse prisa,** to hurry

data, *f.* date; item in an account

datar, *va.* to date

dátil, *m.* (bot.) date

dato, *m.* datum; **datos,** *pl.* data

D. de J.C., después de Jesucristo, A.D. After Christ

DDT, DDT (insecticide)

de, *prep.* of; from; for

debajo, *adv.* under, underneath, below

debate, *m.* debate, contest

debe, *m.* (com.) debit; **debe y haber,** debit and credit

deber, *m.* obligation, duty; debt; *va.* to owe; to be obliged

debido, debida, *adj.* due; proper

débil, *adj.* feeble, weak

débito, *m.* debt; duty

debutar, *vn.* to make one's debut

década, *f.* decade

decadencia, *f.* decay, decline

decaer, *vn.* to decay, decline

decaído, *adj.* crestfallen

decano, *m.* senior, dean

decencia, *f.* decency

decente, *adj.* decent, honest

decididamente, *adv.* decidedly

decigramo, *m.* decigram

decimal, *adj.* decimal

décimo, *adj.* tenth
va. to say, tell, speak; **querer decir,** to mean; *m.* familiar saying

decisión, *f.* decision, determination

decisivo, *adj.* decisive

declamar, *vn.* to harangue, recite

declaración, *f.* declaration, statement, explation; (law) deposition; railroad bill of lading

declarar, *va.* to declare, state; (law) to depose upon oath; **declararse,** to declare one's opinion; (coll.) to declare one's love

declinación, *f.* decline; (gram.) declension

declinar, *vn.* to decline; *va.* (gram.) to decline

declive, *m.* declivity, slope

decomisar, *va.* to confiscate

decoración, *f.* decoration, ornament; stage scenery

decorado, *m.* decoration, stage scenery

decorar, *va.* to decorate; to adorn; to illustrate

decoroso, *adj.* decorous, decent

decretar, *va.* to decree, decide; to determine

decreto, *m.* decree

dedal, *m.* thimble

dedicación, *f.* dedication; consecration

dedicado, *adj.* dedicated; destined

dedicar, *va.* to dedicate, devote, consecrate; **dedicarse,** to apply oneself to

dedicatoria, *f.* dedication

dedillo, *m.* little finger; **saber una cora al dedillo,** to know a thing perfectly

dedo, *m.* finger; toe; **dedo meñique,** little finger; **dedo pulgar,** thumb; **dedo del corazon,** middle finger; **dedo anular,** ring finger

deducción, *f.* deduction

deducir, *va.* to deduce, to subtract, deduct

defectivo, *adj.* defective

defectuoso, *adj.* defective

defender, *va.* to defend, uphold

defensa, *f.* defense, justification; apology; shelter, protection

defensiva, *f.* defensive

defensor, defensora, *n.* defender, supporter; lawyer

deferencia, *f.* deference

deficiencia, *f.* deficiency

deficiente, *adj.* deficient

déficit, *m.* deficit

definición, *f.* definition

definido, *adj.* definite

definir, *va.* to define, describe

definitivo, definitiva, *adj.* definitive, final; **en definiti-**

va, in short, definitely

deformado, *adj.* deformed

deformar, *va., vr.* to deform, disfigure

deforme, *adj.* deformed, ugly

deformidad, *f.* deformity

defraudar, *va.* to defraud

defunción, *f.* death

degenerar, *vn.* to degenerate

degollar, *va.* to behead

degradación, *f.* degradation

degradar, *va., vr.* to degrade

deidad, *f.* deity, divinity

dejado, *adj.* slovenly, indolent

dejar, *va.* to leave, let; to omit; to permit, allow; to forsake; to bequeath; **dejarse,** to abandon oneself (to)

del, of the (contraction of **de el)**

delantal, *m.* apron

delante, *adv.* ahead; **delante de,** *prep.* in front of

delantero, *adj.* foremost, first; **delantera,** *f.* forepart; lead, advantage; **tomar la delantera,** to take the lead

delatar, *va.* to accuse, denounce

delegación, *f.* delegation

delegado, delegada, *n.* delegate, deputy

delegar, *va.* to delegate, substitute

deleitar, *va.* to delight

deleite, *m.* pleasure, delight

deletrear, *va., vn.* to spell

delgado, *adj.* thin

deliberación, *f.* deliberation

deliberar, *vn.* to deliberate

delicadeza, *f.* delicacy, subtlety

delicado, *adj.* delicate, tender; fastidious; dainty

delicia, *f.* delight, pleasure

delicioso, *adj.* delicious, delightful

delincuencia, *f.* delinquency

delincuente, *m., f.* delinquent

delinquir, *vn.* to transgress the law

delirante, *adj.* delirious

delirar, *vn.* to be delirious

delirio, *m.* delirium; nonsense

delito, *m.* crime

delta, *f.* delta

demanda, *f.* demand, claim; lawsuit; request; **oferta y demanda,** supply and demand

demandado, demandada, *n.* defendant

demandar, *va.* to demand, petition, claim; to sue

demás, *adj.* other; **los** or **las demás,** the rest, the others; *adv.* besides; **y demás,** and so on; **por demás,** in vain, to no purpose

demasía, *f.* excess in the price; abundance, plenty

demasiado, *adj.* excessive, overmuch; *adv.* too much, excessively

demente, *adj.* mad, insane

democracia, *f.* democracy

demoler, *va.* to demolish

demonio, *m.* devil, demon; **¡demonio!** *interj.* the deuce!

demora, *f.* delay

demorar, *vn.* to delay, tarry

demostración, *f.* demonstration

demostrar, *va.* to prove, demonstrate, show

demostrativo, *adj.* demonstrative

denigrar, *va.* to blacken; to calumniate

denominación, *f.* denomination

denominador, *m.* (math.) denominator

denominar, *va.* to call, give a name to

denso, *adj.* dense, thick

dentadura, *f.* set of teeth

dental, *adj.* dental

dentición, *f.* dentition, teething

dentífrico, *m.* dentifrice; *adj.* for tooth cleaning

dentista, *m.* dentist

dentistería, *f.* dentistry

denuncia, *f.* denunciation

denunciar, *va.* to denounce

departamento, *m.* department; section, bureau; apartment; (rail.) compartment

dependencia, *f.* dependency; relation, affinity

depender, *vn.* to depend, be dependent on; **depender de,**

to count on

dependiente, *m.* dependent; subordinate; clerk

deplorable, *adj.* deplorable

deplorar, *va.* to deplore, regret

deponer, *va.* to depose, declare; to displace; *vn.* to evacuate the bowels

deportar, *va.* to deport, banish

deporte, *m.* sport, amusement

deportive, *adj.* sport, athletic

deposición, *f.* deposition; assertion, affirmation; evacuation of the bowels

depositar, *va.* to deposit

depósito, *m.* deposit; warehouse

depravar, *va.* to deprave, corrupt

depresión, *f.* depression

deprimir, *va.* to depress

derecha, *f.* right hand, right side; right wing (in politics)

derecho, *adj.* right, straight; *m.* right; law; just claim; tax duty; fee; **dar derecho** to entitle

derivado, *m.* by-product; (gram.) derivative; derived

derivar, *va., vn.* to derive; (naut.) to deflect from the course

derogar, *va.* to derogate, abolish

derramar, *va.* to drain off water; to spread; to spill; to shed; **derramarse**, to spill; to become scattered

derrame, *m.* leakage

derredor, *m.* circumference, circuit; **al derredor** or **en derredor**, about, around

derretir, *va., vr.* to melt

derribar, *va.* to demolish; to overthrow

derrocar, *va.* to overthrow; to demolish

derrochar, *va.* to squander

derrota, *f.* defeat, rout (of an army, etc.)

derrotar, *va.* to cause (a ship) to fall off her course; to defeat

derrotero, *m.* ship's course; (fig.) course, way

derrumbar, *va.* to demolish; **derrumbarse**, to crumble

derrumbe, *m.* landslide

desabotonar, *va.* to unbutton

desabrido, *adj.* tasteless, insipid

desabrigar, *va.* to uncover, to

deprive of clothes or shelter

desabrochar, *va.* to unclasp, unbutton, unfasten

desacierto, *m.* error, blunder

desacomodar, *va.* to incommode, inconvenience; **desacomodarse**, to lose one's place

desacreditar, *va.* to discredit

desacuerdo, *m.* disagreement

desafiar, *va.* to challenge; to defy

desafinar, *vn., vr.* get out of tune

desafortunado, *adj.* unfortunate

desagradable, *adj.* disagreeable, unpleasant

desagradar, *va.* to displease, offend

desagradecido, *adj.* ungrateful; *n.* ingrate

desagrado, *m.* displeasure

desagüe, *m.* drain outlet

desahogado, *adj.* in comfortable circumstances

desahogar, *va.* to relieve; **desahogarse**, to unbosom

desahogo, *m.* ease, relief; unbosoming

desahuciar, *va.* to declare (a patient) incurable

desaire, *m.* disdain; slight

desalentar, *va.* to discourage; **desalentarse**, to lose hope, be discouraged

desaliento, *m.* dismay, discouragement, dejection

desaliñado, *adj.* slipshod

desalojar, *va.* to dislodge, evict; to displace

desamarrar, *va.* to untie

desamparar, *va.* to forsake

desanimado, *adj.* downhearted

desanimar, *va., vr.* to discourage

desapacible, *adj.* disagreeable, unpleasant

desaparecer, *vn.* to disappear

desaparición, *f.* disappearance

desapercibido, *adj.* unprepared; unguarded

desaplicado, *adj.* indolent, careless

desaprovechar, *va.* to misspend

desarmador, *m.* screwdriver

desarmar, *va.* to disarm; to disassemble; (fig.) to pacify

desarme, *m.* disarmament

desarreglado, *adj.* immoderate in eating, drinking, etc.; disarranged; slovenly

desarreglar, *va.* to disarrange

desarrollar, *va.*, *vr.* to develop, unfold

desarrollo, *m.* development; evolution; developing of a photo

desarropar, *va.* to take off covers or blankets

desaseo, *m.* uncleanliness

desastrado, *adj.* wretched, miserable; ragged

desastre, *m.* disaster

desastroso, *adj.* disastrous

desatar, *va.* to untie, separate; **desatarse**, to lose all reserve

desatender, *va.* to pay no attention; to disregard, neglect

desatento, *adj.* inattentive, rude, uncivil

desatinado, *adj.* extravagant; tactless

desatino, *m.* extravagance, folly; nonsense, blunder

desavenencia, *f.* discord, disagreement

desayunarse, *vr.* to breakfast

desayuno, *m.* breakfast

desbandarse, *vr.* to disband

desbaratar, *va.* to destroy; to dissipate; **desbaratarse**, to break to pieces

desbocado, *adj.* wild (applied to a horse); foul-mouthed, indecent

desbordar, *vn.*, *vr.* to overflow; to give vent to one's temper or feelings

desbordamiento, *m.* overflowing

descabellado, *adj.* disorderly; wild, unrestrained

descalabro, *m.* calamity, considerable loss

descalificar, *va.* to disqualify

descalzo, *adj.* barefooted

descansado, *adj.* rested, refreshed; quiet

descansar, *vn.* to rest; to repose, sleep

descanso, *m.* rest, repose

descarado, *adj.* bold, impudent

descaro, *m.* impudence

descarriar, *va.* to lead astray; **descarriarse**, to go astray; to deviate from justice or reason

descarrilar, *vn.*, *vr.* (rail.) to jump the track; *va.* to derail

descartar, *va.* to discard; to dismiss

descendencia, *f.* descent, offspring

descender, *vn.* to descend; to be derived from

descendiente, *adj.*, *m.* descending; descendant

descifrar, *va.* to decipher; to decode

descolgar, *va.* to unhang, take down

descolorido, *adj.* pale, colorless, faded

descollar, *vn.* to stand out; to excel, to surpass

descomponer, *va.* to spoil; to set at odds, disconcert; (chem.) to decompose; *vn.* to be indisposed; to change for the worse (of the weather); **descomponerse**, to get out of order; to become spoiled

descompuesto, *adj.* slovenly; out of order; spoiled (applied to food)

desconcertado, *adj.* baffled

desconcertar, *va.*, *vr.* to disturb; to confound; to embarrass, disconcert

desconectar, *va.*, *vr.* to disconnect

desconfiado, *adj.* suspicious, mistrustful

desconfianza, *f.* distrust, lack of confidence

desconfiar, *vn.* to mistrust, suspect

desconforme, *adj.* discordant; unlike; unsatisfied

desconocer, *va.* to disown, to disavow; to be ignorant of a thing; not to know a person; not to acknowledge (a favor)

desconocido, *adj.* unknown, unrecognizable; *n.* stranger

desconsiderado, *adj.* inconsiderate, imprudent

desconsolado, *adj.* disconsolate, dejected

desconsolador, *adj.* lamentable; disconsolate; disconcerting

desconsuelo, *m.* affliction; dejection, grief

descontar, *va.* to discount; to deduct

descontento, *m.* discontent, disgust; *adj.* unhappy, discontented

descontinuar, *va.* to discontinue

descorazonado, *adj.* depressed (in spirit)

descortés, *adj.* impolite

descortesía, *f.* discourtesy

descotado, *adj.* décolleté, low cut

descote, *m.* exposure of neck and shoulders

descrédito, *m.* discredit

describir, *va.* to describe

descripción, *f.* description

descriptivo, *adj.* descriptive

descrito, *adj.* described

descuartizar, *va.* to quarter to divide the body into four parts); to carve

descubierto, *adj.* uncovered; bareheaded

descubrimiento, *m.* discovery, disclosure

descubrir, *va.* to discover, disclose; to uncover; to reveal; **descubrirse,** to take off one's hat

descuento, *m.* discount; decrease, rebate

descuidado, *adj.* careless, negligent

descuidar, *va., vn.* to neglect; **descuidarse,** to become negligent

descuido, *m.* indolence, negligence, forgetfulness

desde, *prep.* since, after, from; **desde luego,** of course

desdecirse, *vr.* to retract

desdén, *m.* disdain, scorn, contempt

desdeñar, *va.* to disdain

desdicha, *f.* misfortune

desdichado, *adj.* unfortunate, miserable

deseable, *adj.* desirable

desear, *va.* to desire, wish

desecar, *va.* to dry; to desiccate

desechar, *va.* to reject, refuse; to exclude

desembarcar, *va., vn.* to disembark

desembarque, *m.* landing

desembocar, *vn.* to flow into (as a river)

desembolso, *m.* disbursement, expenditure

desembuchar, *va.* to disgorge; (coll.) to unbosom

desempacar, *va.* to unpack

desempeñar, *va.* to perform (a duty); to discharge (any office)

desempeño, *m.* performance of an obligation

desempleo, *m.* unemployment

desencanto, *m.* disillusion

desenfrenado, *adj.* licentious, wanton

desenfrenar, *va.* to unbridle; **desenfrenarse,** to give full play to one's desires; to fly into a rage

desenfreno, *m.* licentiousness; unruliness

desengañar, *va., vr.* to disillusion, disappoint; to set right

desengaño, *m.* disillusion, disappointment

desenlace, *m.* denouement, outcome, conclusion

desenlazar, *va.* to unravel (a plot)

desenredar, *va.* to disentangle; **desenredarse,** to extricate oneself

desenterrar, *va.* to disinter, to dig up

desenvoltura, *f.* poise

desenvolver, *va.* to unwrap; to unroll; to develop; **desenvolverse,** to get along with assurance

desenvuelto, *adj.* poised

deseo, *m.* desire, wish

deseoso, *adj.* desirous

desequilibrio, *m.* unsteadiness, lack of balance

deserción, *f.* desertion

desertar, *va.* to desert; (law) to abandon a cause

desertor, *m.* deserter, fugitive

desesperación, *f.* despair, desperation; anger, fury

desesperadamente, *adv.* desperately

desesperado, *adj.* desperate, hopeless

desesperar, *vn., vr.* to despair; vex; *va.* to make desperate

desfalco, *m.* ebezzlement

desfallecer, *vn.* to pine, fall away, weaken

desfallecido, *adj.* faint, languid

desfallecimiento, *m.* languor, fainting, swoon

desfavorable, *adj.* unfavorable

desfigurar, *va.* to disfigure, deform; **desfigurarse**, to become disfigured or distorted

desfigurado, *adj.* deformed

desfile, *m.* parade

desganado, *adj.* having no appetite

desgano, *m.* lack of appetite; reluctance

desgarbado, *adj.* ungraceful, uncouth, gawky

desgarrado, *adj.* ripped, torn

desgarrador, *adj.* piercing; heartrending

desgarrar, *va.* to rend, tear

desgaste, *m.* wearing out, wastage

desgonzar, *va.* to separate; to unhinge; to disjoint

desgracia, *f.* misfortune, grief; disgrace; unpleasantness; **por desgracia**, unfortunately

desgraciado, *adj.* unfortunate, unhappy

desgreñar, *va.* to dishevel the hair

deshabitado, *adj.* deserted, desolate

deshecho, *adj.* undone, destroyed, wasted; melted; in pieces

deshelar, *va., vr.* to thaw

deshilachar, *va.* to ravel

deshilar, *va.* to ravel

deshojar, *va.* to strip off the leaves

deshonor, *m.* dishonor; insult

deshonra, *f.* dishonor; seduction of a woman

deshonroso, *adj.* dishonorable, indecent

deshuesar, *va.* to bone; to stone (fruit)

desidia, *f.* idleness, indolence

desidioso, *adj.* indolent, lazy, idle

desierto, *adj.* deserted, solitary; *m.* desert, wilderness

designación, *f.* designation

designar, *va.* to appoint; to name; to designate

designio, *m.* design, purpose

desigual, *adj.* unequal, unlike; uneven

desigualdad, *f.* inequality, dissimilitude; unevenness

desilusión, *f.* disillusion

desilusionar, *va., vr.* to disillusion

desinfectante, *m.* disinfectant

desinflamar, *va.* to cure an inflammation

desintegración, *f.* disintegration; fission

desintegrar, *vt., vi.* to disintegrate

desinterés, *m.* disinterestedness, unselfishness

desinteresado, *adj.* disinterested, unselfish

desistir, *vn.* to desist, cease, stop

deslave, *m.* washout

desleal, *adj.* disloyal; perfidious

deslealtad, *f.* disloyalty

desleír, *va.* to dilute, dissolve

deslenguado, *adj.* foulmouthed

desligar, *va.* to loosen, unbind, to extricate

desliz, *m.* slip, sliding; (fig.) slip, false step

deslizar, *vn., vr.* to slip, slide; to speak carelessly

deslucido, *adj.* unadorned; gawky; useless

deslumbrador, *adj.* dazzling

deslumbrar, *va.* to dazzle

desmantelado, *adj.* dismantled, stripped

desmañado, *adj.* clumsy, awkward

desmayar, *vn.* to be dispirited or fainthearted; **desmayarse,** to faint

desmayo, *m.* swoon; dismay, discouragement

desmedido, *adj.* out of proportion; excessive

desmejorar, *va.* to debase, make worse

desmembrar, *va.* to dismember; to curtail; to separate

desmemoriado, *adj.* forgetful

desmentir, *va.* to contradict

desmenuzar, *va.* to crumble, chip, to fritter; to examine minutely

desmerecer, *va., vn.* to become undeserving of; to compare unfavorably

desmesurado, *adj.* excessive; huge; immeasurable

desmoralizar, *va., vr.* to demoralize

desmoronar, *va.* to destroy little by little; **desmoronarse,** to decay, crumble

desnatar, *va.* to skim milk

desnivel, *m.* unevenness of the ground

desnudar, *va.* to denude, strip of clothes; to discover, reveal; **desnudarse,** to undress

desnudo, *adj.* naked, bare

desnutrición, *f.* malnutrition

desnutrido, *adj.* undernourished

desobedecer, *va.* to disobey

desobediencia, *f.* disobedience

desobediente, *adj.* disobedient

desocupar, *va.* to quit, empty; **desocuparse,** to quit an occupation

desodorante, *m.* deodorant

desolación, *f.* destruction; affliction

desolado, *adj.* desolate; lonely

desorden, *m.* disorder, confusion

desordenado, *adj.* disorderly, unruly

desordenar, *va., vr.* to disorder, disarrange

desorganización, *f.* disorganization

desorganizar, *va.* to disorganize

desorientado, *adj.* confused, having lost one's bearings

despacio, *adv.* slowly, leisurely

despacito, *adv.* gently, leisurely

despachar, *va.* to dispatch; to expedite; to dismiss

despacho, *m.* dispatch, expedition; cabinet; office

desparejar, *va.* to make unequal or uneven

desparpajo, *m.* pertness of speech or action

desparramar, *va.* to disseminate; to scatter, overspread; to squander

despavorido, *adj.* frightened, terrified

despecho, *m.* indignation, displeasure; despite, spite; **a despecho de,** in spite of

despedazar, *va.* to tear into pieces, cut asunder; to mangle

despedida, *f.* farewell, dismissal, leavetaking; close (of letter)

despedir, *va.* to discharge, dismiss from office; **despedirse,** to take leave

despegar, *va.* to unglue, detach; (avi.) to take off

despego, *m.* lack of love, coolness

despeinar, *va.* to entangle the hair

despejado, *adj.* sprightly, vivacious; clear, cloudless

despejar, *va.* to clear away obstructions; **despejarse,** to cheer up; to become clear weather

despejo, *m.* sprightliness; grace

despellejar, *va.* to skin

despensa, *f.* pantry, larder; provisions

despepitar, *va.* to remove the seeds from; **despepitarse,** to give vent to one's tongue

desperdiciar, *va.* to squander; not to avail oneself of

desperdicio, *m.* prodigality, profusion; remains; refuse

despertador, *m.* alarm clock

despierto, *adj.* awake; vigilant; brisk, sprightly

despilfarrar, *va.* to squander

despilfarro, *m.* slovenliness; waste

desplante, *m.* arrogant attitude

desplazado, *adj.* displaced

desplegar, *va.* to unfold, display; to explain, elucidate; to unfurl

desplomar, *va.* to make a wall bulge out; **desplomarse,** to bulge out; to collapse

desplome, *m.* downfall, collapse, tumbling down

despoblado, *m.* desert, uninhabited place; *adj.* depopulated

despoblar, *va., vr.* to depopulate; to desolate

despojar, *va.* to despoil; to deprive of, to strip; **despojarse,** to undress

despojos, *m. pl.* remains; debris, waste

desposado, *adj.* newly married; handcuffed

déspota, *m., f.* despot, tyrant

despótico, *adj.* despotic

despreciable, *adj.* contemptible, despicable, worthless

despreciar, *va.* to despise; to reject

desprecio, *m.* scorn, contempt

desprender, *va.* to unfasten, loosen, to separate; **desprenderse,** to give way, fall down; to extricate oneself; to be inferred

desprendimiento, *m.* alienation; unselfishness

despreocupado, *adj.* unconcerned, unconventional

desprestigio, *m.* loss of prestige

desprevenido, *adj.* unprepared

desproporción, *f.* disproportion

despropósito, *m.* absurdity, nonsense

desprovisto, *adj.* unprovided; devoid

después, *adv.* after, afterward, later; then; **después de J.C.** A.D., after Christ

desquitar, *va.* to retrieve a loss; **desquitarse,** to recoup; to retaliate, take revenge

desquite, *m.* revenge, retaliation

destacamento, *m.* (mil.) detachment

destacar, *va.* to build up, highlight; (mil.) to detach (a body of troops); **destacarse,** to stand out, be conspicuous

destapar, *va., vr.* to uncover

destartalado, *adj.* shabby; jumbled

destello, *m.* trickle; sparkle; gleam

destemplado, *adj.* inharmonious, out of tune; intemperate

destemplar, *va.* to distemper, alter, disconcert; to untune; **destemplarse,** to be ruffled; to be out of tune

desteñir, *va., vr.* to discolor, fade

desterrado, desterrada, *n.* exile; *adj.* exiled, banished

desterrar, *va.* to banish, exile

destierro, *m.* exile, banishment

destinar, *va.* to destine for, intend for

destinatario, destinataria, *n.* addressee, assignee

destino, *m.* destiny; fate, doom; destination; **con destino a,** bound for

destitución, *f.* destitution, abandonment

destituir, *va.* to deprive; to dismiss from office

destornillador, *m.* screwdriver

destornillar, *va.* to unscrew

destronar, *va.* to dethrone, to

depose

destrozado, *adj.* tattered, torn

destrozar, *va.* to destroy

destrucción, *f.* destruction, ruin

destructivo, *adj.* destructive

destruir, *va.* to destroy, ruin

desunir, *va.* to separate, to disunite

desuso, *m.* disuse; obsoleteness

desvalido, *adj.* helpless, destitute

desvanecer, *va.* to cause to vanish; to remove; *vn.*, *vr.* to faint ; to become insipid; to vanish

desvarío, *m.* delirium, raving; giddiness; extravagance

desvelar, *va.* to keep awake; **desvelarse**, to be watchful, spend a sleepless night

desvelo, *m.* lack of sleep; watchfulness; care

desventaja, *f.* disadvantage

desventura, *f.* misfortune, calamity

deoventurado, *adj.* unfortunate

desvergonzado, *adj.* impudent, shameless

desvergüenza, *f.* shame; impudence

desvestir, *vt.* to undress

desviar, *va.*, *vr.* to deviate; to dissuade

detallar, *va.* to detail, relate minutely; to itemize

detalle, *m.* detail; retail

detallista, *m.* retailer

detención, *f.* detention, delay

detener, *va.* to stop, detain; to arrest; to withhold; **detener**, to tarry; to stop

detenido, *adj.* under arrest

deteriorar, *va.*, *vr.* to deteriorate

deterioro, *m.* deterioration

determinación, *f.* determination; boldness

determinado, *adj.* determinate; specific; resolute

determinar, *va.*, *vr.* to determine; to resolve

detestable, *adj.* detestable

detester, *va.* to detest, hate

detonador, *m.* detonator, fuse, blasting cap

detrás, *adv.* behind; behind one's back

detrimento, *m.* detriment, damage, loss

deuda, *f.* debt

deudor, deudora, *n.* debtor

devastar, *va.* to desolate, lay waste

devengar, *va.* to earn or draw (as salary, interest, etc.)

devoción, *f.* devotion, piety; strong affection

devolución, *f.* (law) devolution; restitution, return

devolutivo, *adj.* returnable

devolver, *va.* to return; to restore; to refund, repay; (coll.) to vomit

devoto, *adj.* devout, pious; devoted

D. F., Distrito Federal, Federal District

dia, *m.* day, daylight; **al día**, up to date

diabetes, *f.* diabetes

diabético, *adj.* diabetic

diablo, *m.* devil, Satan

diablura, devilishness

diabólico, *adj.* diabolical, devilish

diadema, diadem

diagnóstico, *m.* diagnosis

diagonal, *adj.* diagonal

diagrama, *m.* diagram

dialecto, *m.* dialect

diamante, *m.* diamond

diámetro, *m.* diameter

diana, *f.* (mil.) reveille

diantre, *m.* deuce, devil

diapasón, *m.* (mus.) diapason, octave; tuning fork

diario, *m.* journal, diary; daily newspaper; daily expense; *adj.* daily

diarrea , diarrhea

dibujante, *m.* draftsman; one who draws

dibujar, *va.* to draw, design

dibujo, *m.* drawing, sketch, draft

dicción, *f.* diction

diccionario, m. dictionary

diciembre, m. December

dictado, m. dictate; dictation

dictador, m. dictator

dictadura, f. dictatorship

dictáfono, m. dictaphone

dictamen, m. opinion, notion; suggestion

dictar, va. to dictate

dicha, f. happiness, good fortune; **por dicha,** by chance, luckily

dicho, m. saying, sentence, proverb; declaration; adj. said; **dejar dicho,** to leave word

dichoso, adj. happy, prosperous, lucky

diecinueve or **diez y nueve,** m., adj. nineteen

dieciocho or **diez y ocho,** m., adj. eighteen

dieciseis or **diez y seis,** m., adj. sixteen

diecisiete or **diez y siete,** m., adj. seventeen

Diego, m. James

diente, m. tooth, fang, tusk, jag; **dientes postizos,** false teeth; **hablar** or **decir entre dientes,** to mumble, mutter

diestra, f. right hand

diestro, adj. clever, handy

dieta, f. diet, regimen

dietética, f. dietetics

diez, adj., m. ten

difamar, va. to defame, libel

diferencia, f. difference; **diferencias,** pl. controversies, disputes

diferencial, adj. differential, different; m. (auto.) differential

diferenciar, va., vr. to differ, differentiate

diferente, adj. different, unlike

diferir, va. to defer, put off; to differ

difícil, adj. difficult

dificultad, f. difficulty

dificultar, va. to raise difficulties; to render difficult

difteria, f. diphtheria

difundir, va. to diffuse, outspread; to divulge

difunto, adj. dead, deceased; late; **difunta,** n. deceased person

difusión, diffusion, extension

difusora, (rad.) broadcasting station

digerible, adj. digestible

digerir, va. to digest; to think over, to examine carefully

digestión, f. digestion

digestivo, adj. digestive

digital, f. (bot.) digitalis, foxglove; adj. pertaining to the fingers; **impresiones** or **huellas digitales,** fingerprints

dignarse, vr. to condescend, deign

dignidad, f. dignity, rank

digno, adj. meritorious, worthy, deserving; **digno de confianza,** trustworthy, reliable

dije, m. charm, amulet; jewel

dilación, f. delay

dilatado, adj. large, extended; long delayed

dilatar, va. to dilate, expand; to spread out; to defer, to protract; **dilatarse,** to dilate, to delay

dilecto, adj. loved, beloved

diligencia, f. diligence; industriousness; errand; stagecoach

digente, adj. diligent, industrious

dilucidar, va. to elucidate

diluvio, m. deluge

dimanar, vn. to spring from; to originate; to flow

dimensión, f. dimension

dimes, m. pl. **andar en dimes y diretes,** (coll.) to contend, to argue back and forth

diminutivo, m., adj. diminutive

diminuto, adj. tiny, minute

dimitir, va. to resign; to abdicate

Dinamarca, f. Denmark

dinámica, f. dynamics

dinámico, adj. dynamic

dinamita, f. dynamite

dínamo, f. dynamo

dinastia, f. dynasty

dineral, *m.* large sum of money

dinero, *m.* coin, money, currency

dintel, *m.* doorframe

Dios, *m.* God; **Dios mediante**, God willing; **Dios quiera, Dios lo permita**, God grant

dios, diosa, *m., f.* god, goddess

diploma, *m.* diploma

diplomacia, *f.* diplomacy

diplomarse, *vr.* to be graduated

diplomático, *adj.* diplomatic; *m.* diplomat

diputado, *m.* delegate, representative

diputar, *va.* to depute

dique, *m.* dike, dam

dirección, *f.* direction; guidance, administration; management; manager's office; address, addressing

directivo, *adj.* managing; **directiva**, *f.* governing body

directo, *adj.* direct, straight, nonstop; apparent, evident

director, *m.* director; conductor; editor (of a publication); manager

directora, *f.* directress; principal (of a school)

directorio, *m.* directory; board of directors

dirigente, *adj.* directing, ruling

dirigible, *m.* airship, dirigible

dirigir, *va.* to direct; to conduct; to govern; **dirigir la palabra**, to address (someone); **dirigirse**, to turn, to go; to address; **dirigirse a**, to speak to, to turn to

discernir, *va.* to discern, to distinguish

disciplina, *f.* discipline

disciplinar, *va.* to discipline

discípulo, discípula, *n.* disciple, scholar, pupil

díscolo, *adj.* ungovernable; peevish

discordancia, *f.* disagreement, discord

discordante, *adj.* dissonant, discordant

discoteca, *f.* discotheque; record shop or library

discreción, *f.* discretion

disculpa, *f.* apology, excuse

disculpar, *va., vr.* to excuse, acquit, absolve

discurrir, *vn.* to discourse upon a subject; to discuss; *va.* to invent, to contrive

discurso, *m.* speech

discusión, *f.* discussion

discutir, *va., vn.* to discuss, argue

disección, *f.* dissection, anatomy

diseminar, *va.* to scatter as seed; to disseminate, propagate

disensión, *f.* dissension, strife

disentería, *f.* dysentery

diseñar, *va.* to draw, design

diseño, *m.* design, draft

disertar, *vn.* to discourse, debate

disfraz, *m.* mask, disguise; masquerade

disfrazar, *va., vr.* to disguise, conceal; to mask

disfrutar, *va.* to enjoy

disgustar, *va.* to displease; to offend; **disgustarse**, to be displeased, to be worried

disgusto, *m.* sorrow, grief; aversion

disimular, *va.* to dissemble; to pretend; to tolerate

disimulo, *m.* dissimulation; pretence

disipación, *f.* dissipation

disipar, *va., vr.* to dissipate

dislocación, *f.* dislocation

disminuir, *va.* to diminish

disoluto, *adj.* dissolute

disolver, *va.* to loosen, untie; to dissolve; to melt, liquefy; **disolverse**, to dissolve, to break up

disonante, *adj.* dissonant, inharmonious; (fig.) discordant

disparar, *va., vn.* to shoot

disparate, *m.* nonsense, absurdity; blunder

disparejo, *adj.* unequal, uneven

disparidad, f. disparity

disparo, m. shot, discharge, explosion

dispensar, va. to dispense; to excuse, absolve; to grant

dispensario, m. dispensary of drugs; clinic

dispersar, va. vr. to scatter

displicente, adj. disagreeable, peevish

disponer, va. vn. to arrange; to dispose, prepare; to dispose of; to resolve

disposición, f. disposition, arrangement; resolution; disposal, command

dispuesto, adj. disposed, fit, ready; **bien dispuesto**, favorably inclined; **mal dispuesto**, unfavorably disposed

disputar, va. vn. to dispute, question; to argue

distancia, f. distance

distante, adj. distant, far off

distinción, f. distinction; difference; prerogative

distinguido, adj. distinguished, prominent, conspicuous

distinguir, va. to distinguish; to show regard for; **distinguirse**, to distinguish oneself; to excel

distintivo, m. insignia

distinto, adj. distinct, different; clear

distracción, f. distraction; amusement, pastime

distraer, va. to distract; to amuse, entertain; **distraerse**, to be absent-minded; to enjoy oneself

distraído, adj. absentminded; inattentive

distribuidor, m. distributor

distribuir, va. to distribute, divide; to sort

distrito, m. district

disturbio, m. disturbance, interruption

disuadir, va. to dissuade

diurno, adj. diurnal, by day

diva, f. prima donna

divagación, f. wandering, digression

diván, m. sofa

divergencia, f. divergence

diversidad, f. diversity; variety of things

diversión, f. diversion, pastime, sport

diverso, adj. diverse, different; several, sundry

divertido, adj. amused; amusing

divertir, va. to divert (the attention); to amuse, entertain; **divertirse**, to have an enjoyable time

dividendo, m. (math., com.) dividend

dividir, va. vr. to divide, separate; to split, break up

divinidad, f. god; divinity; woman of exquisite beauty; **la Divinidad**, the Deity

divino, adj. divine, heavenly

divisa, f. motto, badge

divisar, vn. to perceive indistinctly

división, f. division; partition; separation; (gram.) hyphen

divociar, va. vr. to divorce, separate

divorcio, m. divorce

dls., dólares, $ or dol., dollars

dm., decímetro, dm. decimeter

do, m. (mus.) do

doblar, va. vn. to double, fold; to bend; to toll; **doblarla esquina**, to turn the corner; **doblarse**, to bend, submit

doblez, m. crease, fold; m., f. duplicity in dealing

doce, adj., m. twelve

docena, f. dozen

docente, adj. teaching; **personal docente**, teaching staff

dócil, adj. docile, obedient

docto, adj. learned

doctor, m. doctor; physician

doctrina, f. doctrine

documento, m. document

dogma, m. dogma

dogmático, adj. dogmatic

dólar, m. dollar

dolencia f. disease, affliction

doler, vn. vr. to feel pain; to ache; to be sorry; to repent

doliente, *adj.* suffering; sorrowful; *m.,* mourner

dolor, *m.* pain, aching, ache; grief; regret

doloroso, *adj.* sorrowful; painful

domar, *va.* to tame, subdue, master

domesticar, *va.* to domesticate, tame

doméstico, *adj.* domestic; *n.* domestic, menial

domicilio, *m.* domicile, home, abode

dominación, *f.* domination

dominante, *adj.* dominant, domineering

dominar, *va.* to dominate; to control; to master (a language or a subject); **dominarse,** to control oneself

domingo, *m.* Sunday

dominio, *m.* dominion, domination, power, authority; domain

dominó, *m.* domino (a masquerade garment); game of dominoes

don, *m.* Don, the Spanish title for a gentleman (used only before given name)

don, *m.* gift, quality; **el don de la palabra,** the gift of speech; **don de gentes,** savoir-faire, courteous, pleasant manners

donación, *f.* donation, gift

donaire, *m.* grace, elegance

donativo, *m.* free contribution

doncella, *f.* virgin, maiden; lady's maid

donde, *adv.* where

dondequiera, *adv.* anywhere; wherever

doña, *f.* lady, mistress; title, equivalent to Mrs. or Miss, used only before given name

doquier or **doquiera,** *adv.* anywhere

dorado, *adj.* gilded; *m.* gilding

dorar, *va.* to gild; to palliate

dormido, *adj.* asleep

dormilón, dormilona, *n.* (coll.) sleepyhead; *adj.* fond of sleeping

dormir, *vn.* to sleep; **dormir-**

se, to fall asleep

dormitar, *vn.* to doze, to be half asleep

dormitorio, *m.* dormitory, bedroom

dorsal, *adj.* dorsal; **espina dorsal,** spinal column

dorso, *m.* back

dos, *adj., m.* two; **de dos en dos,** by two's, two abreast

doscientos, doscientas, *m., adj.* two hundred

dotar, *va.* to endow, to give a dowry to

dragón, *m.* dragon; dragoon

drama, *m.* drama

dramático, *adj.* dramatic

dramatizar, *va.* to dramatize

drástico, *adj.* drastic

drenaje, *m.* drainage

droga, *f.* drug; (coll.) nuisance

droguería, *f.* drugstore

ducha, *f.* shower bath; douche

duda, *f.* doubt, suspense, hesitation; **poner en duda,** to question; **no cabe duda,** there is no doubt

dudable, *adj.* dubious

dudar, *va., vn.* to doubt, waver

duelo, *m.* duel; grief; mourning

duende, *m.* elf, goblin

dueño, dueña, *n.* owner, master, proprietor; **dueño de sí mismo,** self-controlled

dueto, *m.* duet

dulce, *adj.* sweet; mild, soft, meek; *m.* candy, sweetmeat

dulcería, *f.* confectionery store

dulcificar, *va.* to sweeten

dulzura, *f.* sweetness; gentleness

duodeno, *m.* duodenum

duplicado, *m.* duplicate

duplicar, *va.* to double, duplicate

duque, *m.* duke

durable, *adj.* durable, lasting

duración, *f.* duration, term

duradero, *adj.* lasting, durable

durante, *pres. p.* of **durar,** during

durar, *vn.* to last, endure; to wear well (as clothes)

durazno, *m.* peach; peach tree

dureza, *f.* hardness

durmiente, *adj.* sleeping; *m.* (Sp. Am.) (rail.) cross tie

duro, *adj.* hard, solid; unjust; rigorous, cruel; stubborn; stale (of bread); *m.* peso, dollar

d/v., dias vista, (com.) days' sight

E

e, *conj.* and (used only before words beginning with *i* or *hi,* when not followed by *e*)

ebanista, *m.* cabinetmaker

ébano, *m.* ebony

ebrio, *adj.* inebriated, drunk

eclesiástico, *m.* clergyman, ecclesiastic; *adj.* ecclesiastical

eclipsar, *va.* (ast.) to eclipse; to outshine; **eclipsarse,** to disappear

eclipse, *m.* eclipse

eco, *m.* echo

ecología, *f.* ecology

ecológico, *adj.* ecological

economía, *f.* economy

económico, *adj.* economic; economical

economista, *m.* economist

economizar, *va.* to economize

ecuación, *f.* equation

ecuador, *m.* equator

ecuatorial, *adj.* equatorial

ecuestre, *adj.* equestrian

echar, *va.* to cast, throw, dart; to cast away; **echar a perder,** to spoil; **echar de menos,** to miss; **echarse,** to lie, stretch at full length

edad, *f.* age, era, time; **mayor de edad,** of age

Edén, *m.* Eden, paradise

edición, *f.* edition

edificar, *va.* to build

edificio, *m.* building, structure

editor, editora, *n., adj.* publisher; publishing

educación, *f.* education; bringing up

educado, *adj.* educated

educando, educanda, *n.* pupil, scholar

educar, *va.* to educate, instruct

educative, *adj.* educational

EE. UU., E.U., E.U.A. or E.U. de A., Estados Unidos, Estados Unidos de América, U.S., United States, U.S.A., United States of America

efectivamente, *adv.* in effect, truly

efectivo, *adj.* effective, true, certain; *m.* cash; **hacer efectivo,** to cash

efecto, *m.* effect, consequence, purpose; **efectos,** *pl.* merchandise, wares, goods, belongings

efectuar, *va.* to effect, accomplish

efervescencia, *f.* effervescence

eficacia, efficacy

eficaz, *adj.* efficacious, effective

eficiente, *adj.* efficient, effective

efigie, *f.* effigy, image

efímero, *adj.* ephemeral, passing

egipcio, egipcia, *n., adj.* Egyptian

Egipto, *m.* Egypt

egoísmo, *m.* selfishness, egoism

egoísta, *adj.* egoistic, selfish; *m., f.* self-seeker

egreso, *m.* debit, expense

eje, *m.* axle tree, axle, axis, shaft

ejecución, *f.* execution; performance

ejecutante, *m.* performer

ejecutar, *va.* to execute, perform, carry out; to put to death

ejecutivo, *adj., m.* executive

ejemplar, *m.* copy; sample; *adj.* exemplary; excellent

ejemplo, *m.* example; comparison; pattern, copy; **por ejemplo,** for instance

ejercicio, *m.* exercise, practice; (mil.) drill

ejercitar, *va.* to exercise, to put into practice

ejército, *m.* army

ejido, *m.* common land

el, *art. m.* the

él, *pron.* he

elaborar, *va.* to elaborate: to manufacture

elasticidad, *f.* elasticity; resilience

elección, *f.* election; choice

electivo, *adj.* elective

electo, *adj.* elect

elector, *m.* elector

electorado, *m.* electorate

electoral, *adj.* electoral

electricidad, *f.* electricity

electricista, *m.* electrician

eléctrico, *adj.* electric, electrical

electrizar, *va.* to electrify

electrónica, *f.* electronics

electrotipo, in electrotype

elefante, *m.* elephant

elegancia, *f.* elegance

elegible, *adj.* eligible

elegir, *va.* to choose, elect

elemental, *adj.* elemental, elementary

elemento, *m.* element; ingredient; **elementos,** *pl.* elements; rudiments, first principles

elenco, *m.* catalogue, list, index

elevación, *f.* elevation; highness; exaltation, pride; height; (avi.) altitude

elevado, *adj.* elevated, lofty, high

elevador, *m.* elevator, hoist

elevar, *va.* to raise; to elevate; to heave; **elevarse,** to be enraptured; to be puffed up, to rise

eliminación, *f.* elimination

eliminar, *va.* to eliminate

elixir or **elíxir,** *m.* elixir

elocución, *f.* elocution

elocuencia, *f.* eloquence

elocuente, *adj.* eloquent

elogiar, *va.* to praise, eulogize

elogio, *m.* eulogy, praise, compliment

elucidar, *va.* to elucidate, explain

eludir, *va.* to elude

ella, *pron.* she

ello, *neut. pron.* it, that

ellos, ellas, *pron. pl.* they (*masc.* and *fem.*)

emanar, *vn.* to emanate

emancipar, *va.* to emancipate

embajada, *f.* embassy

embajador, *m.* ambassador

embarazada, *adj.* pregnant

embarazo, *m.* embarrassment; obstacle; pregnancy

embarazoso, *adj.* difficult, intricate

embarcación, *f.* embarkation; any vessel or ship

embarcar, *va.* to embark, ship; **embarcarse,** to go on shipboard, embark; (fig.) to engage in any affair

embargar, *va.* to lay an embargo; to impede, restrain

embargo, *m.* embargo on shipping; **sin embargo,** however, nevertheless

embarque, *m.* shipment

embaucar, *va.* to deceive, to trick

embeberse, *vr.* to become absorbed

embelesar, *va., vr.* to amaze, astonish; to charm

embeleso, *m.* rapture, bliss, amazement

embellecer, *va.* to embellish, beautify, adorn

emblanquecer, *va., vr.* to whiten

emblema, *m.* emblem, symbol

embobar, *va.* to amuse, to distract; **embobarse,** to stand gaping

émbolo, *m.* (mech.) wrist pin; piston

emborrachar, *va., vr.* to intoxicate

emboscada, *f.* ambush

embotellar, *va.* to bottle

embragar, *va.* to put in gear

embrague, *m.* clutch, coupling

embriagar, *va., vr.* to intoxicate; to enrapture

embriaguez, *f.* intoxication, drunkenness; rapture

embrollar, *va.* to entangle, embroil

embrollo, *m.* tangle, trickery; embroiling

embromado, *adj.* vexed, annoyed

embrujar, *va.* to bewitch

embrutecer, *va.* to make stupid; **embrutecerse**, to become stupid

embudo, *m.* funnel

embuste, *m.* lie; fraud

embustero, embustera, *n.* impostor, cheat, liar

emergencia, *f.* emergency; emergence

emersión, *f.* emersion

emigración, *f.* emigration

emigrante, *m., f.* emigrant

emigrar, *vn.* to emigrate

eminencia, *f.* eminence

eminente, *adj.* eminent

emisario, *m.* emissary

emisora, *f.* broadcasting station

emocionar, *va., vr.* to touch, move, arouse emotion

empacho, *m.* indigestion; overloading; **sin empacho**, without ceremony; unconcernedly

empalagoso, *adj.* cloying

empalme, *m.* (rail.) junction; (rad.) hookup

empanada, *f.* meat tart

empanizado, *adj.* breaded

empañar, *va.* to dim, blemish; **empañarse**, to become tarnished

empapar, *va.* to soak, drench; **empaparse**, to be soaked; to go deeply into a matter

empapelar, *va.* to paper (a room, etc.)

empaque, *m.* packing

empaquetar, *va.* to make into a package

emparedado, *m.* sandwich

emparejar, *va.* to level; to match, fit; to equalize

empatar, *va.* to equal; to be a tie (in voting, in a game, etc.)

empate, *m.* equality of votes, tie

empeine, *m.* groin; instep; hoof

empellón, *m.* push, heavy blow; **a empellones**, rudely, by dint of blows

empeñar, *va.* to pawn; **empeñarse**, to pledge himself; to persevere

empeño, *m.* obligation; perseverance; pawn

empeorar, *va.* to make worse; *vn.* to grow worse

emperador, *m.* emperor

emperatriz, *f.* empress

empero, *conj.* yet, however

empezar, *va.* to begin

empinar, *va.* to raise, lift; to exalt; **empinarse**, to stand on tiptoe

empleado, empleada, *n.* employee, clerk

emplear, *va.* to hire; to occupy; to use

empleo, *m.* employment, occupation

empobrecer, *va.* to reduce to poverty; *vn.* to become poor

empolvado, *adj.* powdered; dusty

empolvar, *va.* to powder; **empolvarse**, to become dusty

empollar, *va.* to brood, hatch

emprendedor, *adj.* enterprising

emprender, *va.* to undertake

empresa, *f.* enterprise, undertaking; business concern

empresario, *m.* impresario, contractor

empréstito, *m.* loan

empuje, *m.* impulsion, impulse, pushing

empujón, *m.* impulse, push; **a empujones**, pushingly, rudely

empuñar, *va.* to clinch, grip

emular, *va.* to emulate, rival

emulsión, *f.* emulsion

en, *prep.* in; for; on, upon

enagua, *f.*, **enaguas**, *pl.* underskirt, skirt

enaltecer, *va., vr.* to praise, exalt

enamorado, *adj.* in love, enamored, lovesick

enamorar, *va.* to inspire love; to woo; **enamorarse**, to fall in love

enano, *adj.* dwarfish; *n.* dwarf, midget

encabezamiento, *m.* headline; heading

encabezar, *va.* to head a list

encadenar, *va.* to chain, link together; to connect, unite

encajar, *va.* to enchase; to fit in; to push or force in; **encajarse,** to thrust oneself into some narrow place; (coll.) to intrude

encaje, *m.* chasing, inlaid work; lace; socket, groove

encallar, *vn.* (naut.) to run aground

encaminar, *va.* to guide, show the way; **encaminarse,** to take a road, to be on the way

encanecer, *vn.* to grow gray-haired

encantador, *adj.* charming, delightful, enchanting

encantar, *va.* to enchant, charm, delight; to cast a spell

encanto, *m.* enchantment, spell, charm; delightfulness

encapricharse, *vr.* to become stubborn

encaramarse, *vr.* to climb

encarar, *vn.* to face, come face to face

encarcelar, *va.* to imprison

encarecer, *va., vn.* to raise the price; to recommend strongly

encargar, *va.* to charge, commission; **encargarse,** to take upon oneself

encargo, *m.* charge, commission; order, request; responsibility; errand

encariñar, *va.* to inspire affection; **encariñarse con,** to become fond of

encarrilar, *va.,vr.* to place on the right track; to set right

encauzar, *va.* to channel, lead, direct

encendedor, *m.* lighter; cigarette lighter

encender, *va.* to kindle, light, to set on fire; to inflame, incite; **encenderse,** to fly into a rage

encendido, *adj.* inflamed,

high-colored; *m.* ignition

encerado, *m.* oilcloth; blackboard

encerrar, *va.* to shut up, confine; to contain; **encerrarse,** to withdraw, go behind closed doors

encía, (gum (of the teeth)

enciclopedia, *f.* encyclopedia

enciclopédico, *adj.* encyclopedic

encierro, *m.* confinement, enclosure; cloister; prison

encima, *adv.* above, over; at (the top);over and above, besides

encina, *f.* evergreen oak, live oak

encinta, *adj.* pregnant, expectant (mother)

enclenque, *adj.* feeble, sickly

encoger, *va.* to contract, shorten; to shrink; **encogerse,** to shrink

encogido, *adj.* shrunk; timid

encolerizar, *va., vr.* to provoke, to irritate

encomendar, *va.* to recommend; to instruct; **encomendarse,** to commit oneself to another's protection

encomiar, *va.* to praise

encomiástico, *adj.* complimentary, extolling

encomienda, *f.* commission, charge; message; **encomienda postal,** parcel post

encomio *m.* praise, commendation

encono, *m.* rancor, ill will

encontrar, *va., vn.* to meet, find, encounter; **encontrarse,** to clash; to be of contrary opinions; **encontrarse con,** to meet, come upon

encopetado, *adj.* presumptuous, boastful

encrespar, *va.* to curl, frizzle; **encresparse,** to become rough (as the sea)

encrucijada, *f.* crossroad; street intersection

encuadernador, *m.* book binder

encuadernar, *va.* to bind

books

encuentro, m. shock, jostle; encounter, meeting; **salir al encuentro,** to go to encounter; to go to meet a person

encumbrado, adj. high, elevated

encumbrar, va. to raise, elevate; to mount, ascend

encurtido, m. pickle

enchapar, va. to veneer, plate

enchilada, f. (Mex.) kind of pancake stuffed with various foods and chili

enchufe, m. socket joint

endemoniado, adj. possessed with the devil; devilish

enderezar, va. to rectify; to straighten; **enderezarse,** to stand upright

endiablado, adj. devilish, diabolical

endiosar, va. to deify; **endiosarse,** to be puffed up with pride

endorso, m. endorsement

endosar, va. to indorse a bill of exchange

endoso, m. endorsement.

endrogarse, vr. (Sp. Am.) to get into debt

endulzar, va. to sweeten; to soften

endurecer, va. to harden; **endurecerse,** to become cruel; to grow hard

endurecido, adj. inured, hardened

enemigo, adj. hostile, opposed; **enemiga,** n. enemy

enemistar, va. to make an enemy; vn. to become an enemy

energía, f. energy, power, vigor; **energía atómica,** atomic energy; **energía nuclear** or **nuclearia,** nuclear or atomic energy

enérgico, adj. energetic; expressive

enero, m. January

enfadar, va., vr. to vex, molest, trouble; to become angry

énfasis, m. emphasis.

enfático, adj. emphatic

enfermar, vn. to fall ill; va. to make sick

enfermería, f. infirmary

enfermero, enfermera, n. nurse; hospital attendant

enfermizo, adj. infirm, sickly

enfermo, adj. sick, diseased, indisposed; n. sick person, patient

enflaquecer, va. to make thin; **enflaquecerse,** to lose weight

enfocar, va. to focus

enfoque, m. focus

enfrenar, va. to bridle; to put on the brake; to curb, restrain

enfrentar, va. to encounter, face

enfrente, adv. opposite, in front

enfriamiento, m. refrigeration; cold, chin

enfriar, va. to cool, refrigerate; **enfriarse,** to cool down

enfurecer, va. to irritate, enrage; **enfurecerse,** to grow furious

engalanar, va. to adorn

enganchar, va. to hook; to hitch, connect; to ensnare

engañar, va. to deceive, cheat; **engañarse,** to be deceived; to make a mistake

engañoso, adj. deceitful, misleading

engatusar, va. to wheedle, coax

engendrar, va. to beget, engender

engordar, a. to fatten; to grow fat

engorroso, adj. troublesome, cumbrous

engranaje, m. gear, gearing

engrandecer, va. to augment; to exaggerate; to exalt

engrasar, va. to grease, oil

engreimiento, m. presumption, vanity; overindulgence

engreír, va. to make proud; to spoil, overindulge; **engreírse,** to become vain; to become spoiled or overindulged

enhebrar, va. to thread a needle

enhorabuena, *f.* congratulation; felicitation; *adv.* well and good

enhoramala, *adv.* in an evil hour

enigmático, *adj.* enigmatical

enjabonar, *va.* to soap, lather

enjambre, *m.* swarm of bees; crowd

enjaular, *va.* to shut up in a cage; to imprison

enjuagar, *va.* to rinse.

enjuague, *m.* rinsing; rinse

enjuiciar, *va.* to bring a lawsuit to trial; to pass judgment

enlace, *m.* link; kindred, affinity, wedding

enladrillar, *va.* to pave with bricks

enlazar, *va., vr.* to join, unite, connect; to be joined in wedlock

enlodar, *va.* to bemire

enloquecer, *va.* to madden; *vn.* to become insane; **enloquecerse,** to become insane; to become infatuated

enloquecido, *adj.* deranged

enmarañar, *va.* to entangle, involve in difficulties; to puzzle

enmendar, *va.* to correct reform

enmienda, *f.* correction, amendment

enmohecerse, *vr.* to grow moldy or musty; to rust

enmudecer, *vn.* to grow dumb; to become silent

enojado, *adj.* angry, cross

enojar, *va.* to irritate, make angry; to offend; **enojarse,** to become angry

enojo, *m.* peevishness; anger, displeasure

enorgullecer, *va., vr.* to fill with pride; to become proud

enorme, *adj.* enormous, vast, huge

enormidad, *f.* enormity

enredadera, *f.* climbing plant; vine

enredar, *va.* to entangle, ensnare; to puzzle; **enredarse,**

to fall in love (unlawful love); to become entangled or involved

enredo, *m.* entanglement; plot of a play

enrejado, *m.* grating; railing (as a fence); trellis-work

enriquecer, *va.* to enrich; *vn.* to grow rich

enrojecer, *va., vr.* to blush

enrollar, *va.* to wind, roll, coil

enronquecer, *va.* to make hoarse; *vn.* to grow hoarse

ensalada, *f.* salad

ensalzar, *va.* to exalt, praise

ensanchar, *va.* to widen, enlarge

ensanche, *m.* widening; gore (in garments); increase

ensangrentar, *va., vr.* to stain with blood

ensayar, *va.* to rehearse; to try

ensenada, *f.* small bay

enseñanza, *f.* teaching, instruction

enseñar, *va.* to teach, instruct; to show

enseres, *m. pl.* chattels; implements, fixtures; household goods

enseriarse, *vr.* (Sp. Am.) to become earnest or serious

ensuciar, *va., vr.* to stain, soil

ensueño, *m.* dream, reverie, illusion

entablar, *va.* to cover with boards; to start (a conversation, debate, etc.)

entapizar, *va.* to cover with tapestry, upholster

entenado, entenada, *n.* stepson, stepdaughter

entender, *va., vn.* to understand, comprehend

entendimiento, *vr.* understanding, knowledge

enterar, *va.* to inform thoroughly; to instruct; to let know. **enterarse (de),** to find out, inform oneself; to be told

entereza, *f.* entireness, integrity; fortitude; uprightness

enternecer, *va.* to soften; to move to compassion; **enternecerse,** to be moved to pity, to be touched

entero, *adj.* whole, entire; perfect, complete; sound

enterrar, *va.* to bury

entidad, *f.* entity, real being; (fig.) consideration, importance

entierro, *m.* burial; interment funeral

entonación, *f.* modulation; intonation, tone, voice

entonar, *va.* to tune, intonate, chant

entonces, *adv.* then, at that time

entorpecer, *va.* to benumb; to stupefy; to hinder

entrada, *f.* entrance, entry, admission; **eutradas y gastos,** receipts and expenses

entrañable, *adj.* intimate, affectionate

entrañas, *f. pi.* viscera, intestines; (fig.) heart

entrar, *va., vn.* to enter; to commence

entreacto, *m.* (theat.) intermissior

entrecejo, *m.* the space between the eyebrows; frowning, supercilious look

entrega, delivery; surrender; **entrega inmediata,** special delivery

entregar, *va.* to deliver; to restore

entremés, *m.* appetizer

entremeter, *va.* to put one thing between others; **entremeterse,** to intrude

eatremetido, entrometida, *n.* meddler, intruder; kibitzer; *adj.* meddling

entrenar, *va.* to train, coach

entrepaño, *m.* panel

entresacar, *va.* to sift, separate; to thin out (hair)

entresuelo, *m.* mezzanine; basement

entretanto, *adv.* meanwhile

entretela, *f.* interlining

entretener, *va.* to amuse; to entertain, divert; **entretenerse,** to amuse oneself

entretenido, *adj.* pleasant,

amusing

entretenimiento, *m.* amusement, entertainment

entretiempo, *m.* season between summer and winter (spring or autumn)

entrevista, *f.* interview

entronque, *m.* crossroads, junction

entumecer, *va.* to benumb; *vn.* to become numb; to swell

entusiasmar, *va.* to arouse enthusiasm,enrapture; **entusiasmarse,** to become enthusiastic

entusiasmo, *m.* enthusiasm

entusiasta, *m., f.* enthusiast; *adj.* enthusiastic

envanecer, *va.* to make vain; to swell with pride; **envanecerse,** to become proud or vain

envasar, *va.* to barrel; to bottle; to can

envase, *m.* packing, bottling; container

envejecer, *va.* to make old; *vn.* to grow old

envenenamiento, *m.* poisoning

envenenar, *va.* to poison

enviado, *m.* envoy, messenger

enviar, *va.* to send, transmit

enviciar, *va.* to corrupt; **enviciarse,** to become strongly addicted (to something)

envidia, *f.* envy; emulation

envidiable, *adj.* enviable

envidiar, *vn.* to envy; to grudge

envidioso, *adj.* envious, jealous

envío, *m.* sending, shipment, remittance

enviudar, *vn.* to become a widower or widow

envoltorio, *m.* bundle of goods

envoltura, *f.* wrapper

envolver, *va.* to involve; to wrap up

enyesar, *va.* to plaster; to put in a cast

epidemia, *f.* epidemic disease

epidermis, *f.* epidermis, cuticle

epigrama, *m.* epigram
epilepsia, *f.* epilepsy
epílogo, *m.* epilogue
episodio, *m.* episode
epístola, *f.* epistle, letter
epitafio, *m.* epitaph
época, *f.* epoch; age, era
epopeya, *f.* epic; epic poem
equidad, equity, honesty
equilátero, *adj.* equilateral
equilibrado, *adj.* balanced
equilibrar, *va.* to balance; to counterbalance
equilibrio, *m.* equilibrium, balance
equinoccio, *m.* equinox
equipaje, *m.* baggage, luggage; equipment
equipar, *va.* to fit out, equip
equipo, *m.* equipment; (sports) team
equitación, *f.* horsemanship
equitativo, *adj.* fair, equitable
equivalente, *adj.* equivalent
equivocación, *f.* error, misunderstanding
equivocar, *va., vr.* to mistake, misconceive, misunderstand
era, *f.* era, age
erigir, *va.* to erect, build
ermitaño, *m.* hermit; hermit crab
erosión, *f.* erosion
erradicación, *f.* extirpation
errante, *adj.* errant, erring, roving
errar, *va.* *vn.* to err, commit errors
errata, *f.* error in printing
erróneo, *adj.* erroneous
error, *m.* error, mistake
erudito, *adj.* learned, lettered, erudite; *m.* sage, scholar
erupción, *f.* eruption, rash
eructar, erutar, to belch
esbelto, *adj.* svelte
esbozo, *m.* outline, sketch
escabroso, *adj.* rough, uneven; scabrous
escafandra, *f.* diving suit; **escafandra autónoma,** Scuba
escala, *f.* ladder; scale
escalafón, *m.* seniority scale; grade scale

escalar, *va.* to climb, scale
escalera, *f.* stairway; **escalera mecánica,** escalator; **escalera de mano,** stepladder
escalofrío, *m.* (med.) chill
escalón, *m.* step of a stair; degree of dignity; (mil.) echelon
escama, *f.* fish scale
escampar, *vn.* to stop raining
escandalizar, *va., vr.* to scandalize, shock
escándalo, *m.* scandal
escandaloso, *adj.* scandalous
escapada, *f.* escape, flight
escapar, *vn., vr.* to escape, flee
escaparate, *m.* show window, showcase; cupboard, cabinet
escape, *m.* escape, flight; exhaust; **a todo escape,** at full speed
escapulario, *m.* scapulary
escarbadientes, *m.* toothpick
escarbar, *va.* to scratch the earth (as chickens do)
escarcha, *f.* white frost
escardar, *va.* to weed
escarlata, *f.* scarlet color; scarlet cloth
escarlatina, *f.* scarlet fever
escarmentar, *vn.* to profit by experience; to take warning; *va.* to punish severely
escarmiento, *m.* warning, chastisement
escasear, *vn.* to grow less, decrease
escasez, *f.* scantiness, want
escatimar, *va.* to curtail, lessen; to skimp
escena, *f.* stage; scene; incident, episode
escenario, *m.* scenario, stage
escéptico, *adj.* skeptic, skeptical
esclarecer, *va.* to lighten, clear up; to illustrate
esclarecido, *adj.* illustrious, noble
esclavizar, *va., vr.* to enslave
esclavo, esclava, *n.* slave, captive
esclusa, *f.* lock; sluice, floodgate
escoba, *f.* broom
escocés, escoesa, *n., adj.*

Scotsman, Scotswoman; Scotch, Scottish

escoger, *va.* to choose, select

escogido, *adj.* choice, selected

escolar, *m.* scholar, student; *adj.* scholastic

escolástico, *adj.* scholastic

escolta, *f.* (mil.) escort convoy

escollo, *m.* sunken rock; reef; difficulty

escombro, *m.* rubbish, debris; mackerel

esconder, *va., vr.* to hide conceal

escondidas or **escondidillas**, *adv.* in a secret manner

escondido, *adj.* hidden

escopeta, *f.* gun, shotgun

escorbuto, *m.* scurvy

escorial, *m.* dump pile

escorpión, *m.* scorpion

escotado, *adj.* low-necked

escote, *m.* low-cut in a garment

escribano, *m.* notary; clerk

escribiente, *m., f.* amanuensis, clerk

escribir, *va.* to write; **escribir a máquina**, to typewrite

escrito, *m.* writing, manuscript; communication; (law) writ, brief; *p.p.* of **escribir**, written; **por escrito**, in writing

escritor, **escritora**, *n.* writer, author

escritorio, *m.* writing desk

escritura, *f.* writing; deed; **Escritura**, Scripture

escrúpulo, *m.* doubt, scruple

escrupuloso, *adj.* scrupulous; exact

escrutinio, *m.* scrutiny, inquiry

escuadra, *f.* square; squadron

escuchar, *va.* to listen

escudo, *m.* shield, buckler; coat of arms; scutcheon of a lock; escudo (Sp. coin)

escudriñar, *va.* to search, pry into

escuela, *f.* school; **escuela de párvulos**, kindergarten

escueto, *adj.* devoid of trimmings; unencumbered

esculpir, *va.* to sculpture, carve

escultor, *m.* sculptor, carver

escultura, *f.* sculpture; work of a sculptor

escupidera, *f.* spittoon

escupir, *va.* to spit

escurrir, *va.* to drain to the dregs; *vn.* to drop; to slip, slide; **escurrirse**, to slip away

ESE: estesudeste, ESE or E.S.E., east southeast

ese, **esa**, *adj.* and **ése**, **ésa**, *pron.* that; **esos**, **esas**, *pl.* those

esencia, *f.* essence

esencial, *adj.* essential; principal

esfera, *f.* sphere; globe; dial

esférico, *adj.* spherical

esforzar, *va.* to strengthen; **esforzarse**, to exert oneself, to make an effort

esfuerzo, *m.* effort

esfumarse, *vr.* to disappear, fade away

esgrima, *f.* fencing

eslabón, *m.* link of a chain

esmalte, *m.* enamel; fingernail polish

esmerado, *adj.* painstaking, carefully done

esmerarse, *vr.* to do one's best, to take pains

esmero, *m.* elaborate effort; neatness

eso, *dem. pron. neuter,* that (idea or statement); **por eso**, for that reason, therefore

esófago, *m.* gullet; throat, esophagus

espacial, *adj.* relating to space

espacio, *m.* space, capacity; distance

espacioso, *adj.* spacious

espada, *f.* sword; spade (in cards)

espalda, *f.* back; shoulders; **a espaldas**, behind one's back

espaldar, *m.* back of a seat

espantajo, *m.* scarecrow; bugaboo

espantar, *va.* to frighten, daunt; to chase or drive away

espanto, *m.* fright; menace, threat; wonder, surprise; apparition, spook

España, *f.* Spain

español, española, *n., adj.* Spaniard; Spanish; *m.* Spanish language

esparcimiento, *m.* recreation, relaxation

esparcir, *va.* to scatter; to divulge

espárrago, *m.* asparagus.

espasmo, *m.* spasm

especial, *adj.* special, particular

especialidad, *f.* specialty

especialista, *m., f.* specialist

especializarse, *vr.* to specialize

especie, *f.* species; matter; motive; class, sort, kind

especificación, *f.* specification

especificar, *va.* to specify

específico, *adj.* specific; *m.* patented medicine

espécimen, *m.* specimen, sample

espectáculo, *m.* spectacle, sight; show

espectador, espectadora, *n.* spectator, onlooker

espectro, *m.* specter, phantom, apparition; spectrum

especulación, *f.* speculation

especular, *va.* to speculate

espejismo, *m.* mirage

espejo, *m.* looking glass, mirror

espera, *f.* stay, waiting; (law) adjournment, delay; **sala de espera,** waiting room

esperanto, *m.* Esperanto

esperanza, *f.* hope, expectation

esperar, *va.* to hope; to expect, to wait for

espesar, *va., vr.* to thicken, condense

espeso, *adj.* thick, dense

espía, *m., f.* spy

espiar, *va.* to spy, lurk

espiga *f.* ear (of grain)

espina *f.* thorn; thistle; backbone; fishbone; **estar en espinas,** to be on needles and pins

espinaca, *f.* (bot.) spinach

espinazo, *m.* spine, backbone

espinoso, *adj.* thorny

espiral, *adj.* spiral

espirar, *va.* to exhale; *vn.* to breathe

espiritismo, *m.* spiritualism; spiritism

espíritu, *m.* spirit, soul; genius; ardor; courage; (chem.) spirits; **el Espíritu Santo,** the Holy Ghost

espiritual, *adj.* spiritual

esplendidez, *f.* splendor, magnificence

espléndido, *adj.* splendid

esplendor, *m.* radiance

esplín, *m.* melancholy

esponjar, *va.* to sponge; **esponjarse,** to get fluffy; to be puffed up with pride

esponjoso, *adj.* spongy

esponsales, *m. pl.* espousals, betrothal

espontáneo, *adj.* spontaneous

esposa, *f.* wife; **esposas,** *pl.* handcuffs

esposo, *m.* husband; **esposos,** *pl.* married couple

espuela, *f.* spur; stimulus; (bot.) larkspur

espumoso, *adj.* frothy, foamy

esputo, *m.* spit, sputum, saliva

esquela, *f.* note, slip of paper

esqueleto, *m.* skeleton

esquema, *m.* diagram, plan

esquiar, *vn.* to ski

esquilar, *va.* to shear

esquina, *f.* corner, angle; **doblar la esquina,** to turn the corner

esquivar, *va.* to shun, avoid, evade

esquivo, *adj.* shy, reserved

estabilizar, *va.* to stabilize

estable, *adj.* stable

establecer, *va.* to establish, found; to decree

establecimiento, *m.* establishment; founding; household

establo, *m.* stable

estación, *f.* station; position,

situation; season (of the year)

estacionamiento, *m.* parking

estacionar, *va.* to park

estacionario, *adj.* stationary

estadía, *f.* stay, sojourn

estadio, *m.* stadium

estadista, *m.* statesman

estadística, *f.* statistics

estadístico, *adj.* statistical

estado, *m.* state, condition; **estado de cuenta,** statement of an account; **ministro de Estado,** Secretary of State

Estados Unidos de América, *m. pl.* United States of America

estadounidense, *adj.* of the United States of America; *m., f.* person from the U. S. A.

estafa, *f.* trick; swindle

estafar, *va.* to deceive, defraud; to swindle

estallar, *vn.* to burst, explode

estallido, *m.* crash; outburst

estambre, *m.* fine wool; stamen of flowers

estampa, *f.* print, stamp

estampar, *va.* to print; to stamp; to imprint

estampido, *m.* report of a gun, etc.; crack, crash; **estampida,** *f.* stampede

estampilla, *f.* signet, rubber stamp; (Sp. Am.) postage stamp

estancia, *f.* stay, sojourn; mansion; (Sp. Am.) cattle ranch; living room

estandarte, *m.* banner, standard

estanque, *m.* pond, pool

estanquillo, *m.* cigar store

estante, *m.* shelf; bookcase

estar, *vn.* to be; to be in a place; **estar de prisa,** to be in a hurry; **estar bien,** to be well; **estar malo,** to be ill

estaroide, *m.* steroid

estatua, *f.* statue

estatura, *f.* stature

estatuto, *m.* statute, law, bylaw

este, *m.* east

este, esta, *adj.* and **éste, ésta,** *pron.* this; **estos, estas,** *pl.*

these

estela de vapor, *f.* contrail

estenografía, *f.* stenography, shorthand

estenógrafo, estenógrafa, *n.* stenographer, shorthand writer

estenotipia, *f.* stenotyping

estera, *f.* mat.

estereofónico, estereofónica, *adj.* stereophonic

estereoscopio, *m.* stereoscope

estéril, *adj.* sterile; barren

esterilizar, *va.* to sterilize

esterlina, *adj.* sterling; **libra esterlina,** pound sterling

estero, *m.* estuary, firth; (Arg.) swamp

estética, *f.* aesthetics

estetoscopio, *m.* stethoscope

estiércol, *m.* dung; excrement, manure

estigma, *m.* birthmark; stigma, affront

estilo, *m.* stylus; style; use, custom

estima, *f.* esteem

estimable, *adj.* worthy of esteem

estimar, *va.* to estimate, value; to esteem; to judge

estimular, *va.* to encourage, stimulate

estímulo, *m.* stimulus, encouragement, inducement

estío, *m.* summer

estipular, *va.* to stipulate

estirado, *adj.* forced; taut

estirar, *va.* to dilate, stretch out

estirpe, *f.* race, origin, stock

esto, *pron. neuter* this; **en esto,** at this juncture; **por esto,** for this reason

estoico, *adj.* stoic, indifferent

estómago, *m.* stomach

estorbar, *va.* to hinder, obstruct; to molest

estorbo, *m.* hindrance, impediment

estornudar, *vn.* to sneeze

estornudo, *m.* sneeze

estrangulación, *f.* strangulation; **cuello de estrangulación,** bottleneck

estrategia, *f.* strategy
estratégico, *adj.* strategic
estrechar, *va.* to tighten: to contract, clasp
estrechez, *f.* tightness; narrowness; poverty
estrecho, *m.* strait; *adj.* narrow, close; tight; intimate
estrella, *f.* star
estrellado, *adj.* starry; dashed to pieces; **huevos estrellados**, fried eggs
estrellar, *va.* to dash to pieces; to crash, to hit against; to fry (eggs)
estremecer, *va.* to shake, make tremble; **estremecerse**, to shake; to thrill
estremecimiento, *m.* trembling, shaking, shiver, thrill
estrenar, *va.* to inaugurate; to use for the first time
estreno, *m.* début, first performance, premiere
estreñimiento, *m.* obstruction; constipation
estrépito, *m.* noise, clamor
estribar, *vn.* depend upon (a reason)
estricto, *adj.* strict; severe
estridente, *adj.* strident
estroboscopio, *m.* stroboscope
estrofa, *f.* (poet.) stanza
estropajo, *m.* dishrag; worthless thing
estropear, *va.* to spoil by rough usage
estructura, *f.* structure
estruendo, *m.* clamor, noise
estrujar, *va.* to press, squeeze
estuche, *m.* kit
estudiante, *m.* scholar, student
estudiar, *va.* to study
estudio, *m.* study; studio
estupefacto, *adj.* stupefied
estupendo, *adj.* stupendous
estupidez, *f.* stupidity
etapa, *f.* stage, station, step
etcétera, *f.* et cetera, and so on
éter, *m.* ether
etéreo, *adj.* ethereal
eternidad, *f.* eternity
eterno, *adj.* eternal

ético, *adj.* ethical, moral
etimología, *f.* etymology
etiqueta, *f.* etiquette, formality; label; **de etiqueta**, in formal dress
E.U.A., Estados Unidos de América, U.S.A., United States of America
eucalipto, *m.* eucalyptus
eufonía, euphony
Europa, Europe
europeo, europea, *n., adj.* European
evacuar, *va.* to evacuate, empty
evangelio, *m.* gospel
evaporar, *va., vn.* to evaporate
evasivo, *adj.* evasive, elusive
eventual, *adj.* eventual, fortuitous
evitable, *adj.* avoidable
evocar, *va.* to call out; to invoke
evolución, *f.* evolution; evolvement
exactitud, *f.* exactness
exacto, *adj.* exact; punctual
exageración, *f.* exaggeration
exagerar, *va.* to exaggerate
exaltado, *adj.* hot-headed
exaltar, *va.* to exalt, elevate; to praise; **exaltarse**, to become excited and angry
examen, *m.* examination
exasperar, *va.* to exasperate
excavadora, *f.* excavating machine, steam shovel
excavar, *va.* to excavate
excedente, *adj.* excessive, exceeding; *m.* surplus, excess
exceder, *va.* to exceed
Excelencia, *f.* Excellency (title)
excelencia, *f.* excellence
excelente, *adj.* excellent
excelso, *adj.* elevated, lofty
excentricidad, *f.* eccentricity
excéntrico, *adj.* eccentric
excepción, *f.* exception
excepcional, *adj.* exceptional
excepto, *adv.* excepting
exceptuar, *va.* to except, exempt
excesivo, *adj.* excessive
exceso, *m.* excess

excitar, *va.* to excite, arouse; to urge

exclamación, *f.* exclamation

exclamar, *va.* to exclaim, cry out

excluir, *va.* to exclude

exclusión, *f.* exclusion; preclusion

exclusivo, *adj.* exclusive, select

excomulgar, *va.* to excommunicate

excomunión, *f.* excommunication

excremento, *m.* exerement

excursión, excursion, outing

excusa, *f.* excuse, apology

excusado, *adj.* excused; exempted; *m.* toilet, water closet

excusar, *va.* to excuse, pardon; to exempt; **excusarse,** to decline a request

exento, *adj.* exempt, free

exhausto, *adj.* exhausted

exhibición, *f.* exhibition, exposition

exhibir, *va.* to exhibit, display

exigencia, *f.* exigency, demand

exigente, *adj.* demanding

exigir, *va.* to demand, require

eximir, *va.* to exempt, excuse

existencia, *f.* existence; **en-existencia,** in stock

existir, *vn.* to exist, be

éxito, *m.* outcome; **buen éxito,** success

exorbitante, *adj.* exorbitant

exótico, *adj.* exotic, foreign

expansión, *f.* expansion, extension

expansivo, *adj.* effusive

expedición, *f.* expedition; shipment

expediente, *m.* expedient; pretext; proceedings

expedir, *va.* to expedite, dispatch, forward; to issue

expeler, *va.* to expel, eject

experiencia, *f.* experience

experimentado, *adj.* experienced, expert

experimentar, *va.* to experience; to experiment

experimento, *m.* experiment, trial

experto, *adj.* expert, experienced; **experta,** *n.* expert, old hand

expirar, *vn.* to expire

explayar, *va.* to extend, dilate; **explayarse,** to dwell upon, enlarge upon

explicable, *adj.* explainable

explicación, *f.* explanation

explicar, *va.* to explain, expound; **explicarse,** to explain oneself

explícito, *adj.* explicit

exploración, *f.* exploration

explorador, exploradora, *n.* explorer; scout; *adj.* exploring

explorer, *va.* to explore; to inquire

explosión, *f.* explosion

exponente, *m., f.* exponent; *m.* (math.) exponent

exponer, *va.* to expose; to explain

exportación, *f.* exportation, export

exportador, *adj.* exporting; *m.* exporter

exportar, *va.* to export

expresión, *f.* expression

expresivo, *adj.* expressive

exprimir, *va.* to wring

exprofeso, *adv.* on purpose

expropiar, *va.* to expropriate

expuesto, *adj.* exposed; **lo expuesto,** what has been stated

expulsar, *va.* to expel

exquisito, *adj.* exquisite

éxtasis, *m.* ecstasy, enthusiasm

extender, *va.* to extend, spread; **extenderse,** to spread out

extensión, *f.* extension; extent

extenso, *adj.* extensive, vast

extenuar, *va.* to extenuate

exterior, *adj.* exterior, external; *m.* exterior; abroad

exterminar, *va.* to exterminate

extinguir, *va.* to extinguish

extirpar, *va.* to extirpate

extra, *inseparable prep.* out of, beyond, extra (as a prefix); *adj.* unusually good

extracción, *f.* extraction

extractar, *vn.* to extract, abridge

extracto, *m.* extract

extraer, *va.* to extract

extranjero, *adj.* foreign; **extranjera,** *n.* foreigner, alien; **ir al extranjero,** to go abroad

extrañar, *va.* to miss; **extrañarse,** to be surprised, wonder at

extraordinario, *adj.* extraordinary, uncommon, odd

extrasensorio, extrasensoria, *adj.* extrasensory

extravagancia, *f.* folly, freak

extravagante, *adj.* freakish; eccentric

extraviar, *va.* to mislead; **extraviarse,** to lose one's way

extremidad, *f.* extremity

F

f., franco, (com.) free

f/, fardo, bl. bale; bdl. bundle

f.a.b., franco a bordo, (com.) f.o.b., free on board

fábrica, *f.* factory

fabricación, *f.* manufacture; **fabricación en serie** or **en gran escala,** mass production

fabricante, *m.* manufacturer

fabricar, *va.* to build, construct

facción, *f.* faction; **facciones,** *pl.* features, physiognomy

fácil, *adj.* facile, easy

facilidad, *f.* facility; ability; **facilidades,** *pl.* opportunities; conveniences

factible, *adj.* feasible

factor, *m.* factor, element; (math.) factor

factura, *f.* invoice, bill

facturar, *va.* to invoice; to check (baggage)

facultad, *f.* faculty, authority; ability

facultar, *va.* to authorize

facha, *f.* appearance, aspect

fachada, *f.* facade, face, front

fachendear, *vn.* to brag, boast

faena, *f.* work; fatigue

faisán, *m.* pheasant

faja, *f.* band, belt, sash; girdle

fajar, *va.* to swathe; to girdle

fajina, *f.* toil, chore; bugle call to mess; **hacer fajina,** (coll.) to clean house thoroughly

falsete, *m.* falsetto voice

falso, *adj.* false, untrue

falta, *f.* fault; mistake; want; lack; flaw; **hacer falta,** to be necessary; to be lacking; **sin falta,** without fail; **no faltaba más,** (coll.) that's the last straw

faltar, *vn.* to lack

falto, *adj.* devoid

fallar, *va.* to give sentence, judge; *vn.* to fail, miss

fallecer, *vn.* to die

fallo, *m.* judgment, sentence

familia, *f.* family; species

familiar, *adj.* familiar; colloquial; informal; *m.* member of one's family

familiaridad, *f.* familiarity

familiarizar, *va., vr.* to familiarize

fango, *m.* mire, mud

fantasma, *m.* phantom, ghost

fantástico, *adj.* fantastic; (coll.) superb

farmacéutico, *adj.* pharmaceutical; *m.* pharmacist

farmacia, *f.* pharmacy

faro, *m.* (naut.) lighthouse

farol, *m.* lantern, light

farsa, *f.* farce; sham

farsante, *m.* charlatan; *adj.* boastful; deceitful

fascinador, *adj.* fascinating

fascinar, *va.* to fascinate; to charm

fase, *f.* phase, aspect

fastidiar, *va.* to bore, to annoy

fastidio, *m.* boredom, ennui

fatiga, *f.* fatigue, weariness

fatigar, *va., vr.* to tire, harass

fausto, *adj.* happy, fortunate

favor, *m.* favor

favorable, *adj.* favorable, advantageous, propitious

favorecer, *va.* to favor, protect

favoritismo, *m.* favoritism

favorito, *adj.* favorite, beloved

faz, *f.* face, front

F.C. or f.c., ferrocarril, R.R. or r.r., railway

fe, *f.* faith, belief; testimony; **dar fe**, to certify

Febo or feb.º, febrero, Feb. February

febrero, *m.* February

fecundar, *va.* to fertilize

fecundo, *adj.* fruitful, fertile

fecha, date (of letter, etc.)

fechar, *va.* to date (a letter, document, etc.)

federación, *f.* federation

federal, *adj.* federal

felicidad, *f.* felicity, happiness

felicitar, *va.* to congratulate

feliz, *adj.* happy, fortunate

felpa, *f.* plush

femenino, *adj.* feminine, female

feminista, *m., f.* feminist

fenómeno, *m.* phenomenon

feo, *adj.* ugly; deformed

feraz, *adj.* fertile, fruitful (of vegetation)

feria, *f.* fair, market

feriado, *adj.* suspended (applied to work); **día feriado**, holiday

fermentar, *vn.* to ferment

férreo, *adj.* iron, ferrous; **vía férrea**, railroad

ferretería, *f.* hardware store

ferrocarril, *m.* railroad

ferroviario, *adj.* railroad

fértil, *adj.* fertile, fruitful

fertilizar, *va.* to fertilize

ferviente, *adj.* fervent, ardent

fervor, *m.* fervor, ardor

festejar, *va.* to fete; to celebrate

festejo, *m.* feast, entertainment

festín, *m.* feast, banquet

festivo, *adj.* festive; gay, merry; **día festivo**, holiday

fétido, *adj.* fetid, stinking

feto, *m.* fetus

fiado, *adj.* on trust, on credit

fiador, fiadora, *n.* bondsman, surety (person); *m.* fastener; catch of a lock

fiambre, *m.* cold lunch

fianza, *f.* security, bail

fiar, *va.* to bail; to sell on credit; to commit to another; *vn.* to confide, to trust

fiasco, *m.* failure

ficción, *f.* fiction

ficticio, *adj.* fictitious

ficha, *f.* counter (at games), chip

fidedigno, *adj.* true; **fuente fidedigna**, reliable source

fideos, *m. pl.* vermicelli, spaghetti, noodles

fiebre, *f.* fever; **fiebre aftosa**, hoof-and-mouth disease

fiel, *adj.* faithful, loyal; **fieles**, *m. pl.* the faithful

fieltro, *m.* felt; felt hat

fiera, *f.* wild beast; fiendish person; (coll.) very able or shrewd person

fiero, *adj.* fierce, ferocious

fiesta, *f.* fiesta; feast; festivity, party; **día de fiesta**, holiday

fig., figura, fig. figure

figura, *f.* figure, shape

figurado, *adj.* figurative

figurar, *va.* to shape, fashion; *vn.* to figure, be conspicuous; **figurarse**, to fancy, imagine

figurín, *m.* fashion plate

fijar, *va.* to fix, fasten; to determine; to post; **se prohíbe fijar carteles**, post no bills; **fijarse**, to take notice(of)

fijo, *adj.* fixed, firm

fila, *f.* row, line (of soldiers, etc.)

filantrópico, *adj.* philanthropic

filántropo, *m.* philanthropist

filarmónico, *adj.* philharmonic

filatelia, *f.* philately

filete, *m.* loin, tenderloin

filial, *adj.* filial

filigrana, *f.* filigree

filipino, filipina, *n., adj.* Philippine

filo, *m.* edge (of a knife, etc.)

filosofía, *f.* philosophy

filosófico, *adj.* philosophical

filósofo, *m.* philosopher

filtrar, *va.* to filter, strain

filtro, *m.* filter

fin, *m.* end, conclusion; **al fin, por fin**, at last

finado, finada, *n., adj.* dead, deceased

final, *adj.* final; *m.* end, finale

finalidad, *f.* finality

finalizar, *va.* to finish, conclude

financiero, *adj.* financial

finca, *f.* land or house property; ranch

fineza, *f.* fineness, perfection; expression of courtesy; delicacy

fingido, *adj.* feigned, sham

fingir, *va., vr.* to feign

fino, *adj.* fine, perfect, pure; delicate; acute, sagacious

firma, *f.* signature; company, firm

firmar, *va.* to sign, subscribe

firme, *adj.* firm, secure; constant, resolute

firmeza, *f.* firmness

fiscal, *m.* attorney general, public prosecutor; *adj.* fiscal

fisco, *m.* exchequer

física, *f.* physics

físico, *adj.* physical; *m.* physicist; physique; (coll.) face, physiognomy

fisiología, *f.* physiology

flaco, *adj.* thin, meager

flamante, *adj.* flaming, bright; quite new

flautín, *m.* piccolo, fife

fleco, *m.* flounce, fringe; bangs (style of haircut)

flecha, *f.* arrow

flema, *f.* phlegm

flete, *m.* (naut.) freight; **flete aéreo**, air freight

flexible, *adj.* flexible

flojo, *adj.* loose; lazy

flor, *f.* flower; **echar flores**, to compliment, flatter

florecer, *vn.* to blossom, bloom

floreciente, *adj.* in bloom

florero, *m.* flower vase

florido, *adj.* florid, flowery

florista, *m., f.* florist

flota, *f.* fleet

flotador, *m.* float; **flotador de**

hidroavión, pontoon

flotar, *vn.* to float

flote, *m.* floating; **a flote**, buoyant, afloat

fluctuar, *vn.* to fluctuate

fluir, *vn.* to flow, run (as a liquid)

fluorización, *f.* fluoridation

fluorizar, *va.* to fluoridate

focal, *adj.* focal

foco, *m.* focus; center; bulb (electric light)

fogoso, *adj.* fiery, ardent, fervent; impetuous

follaje, *m.* foliage

folleto, *m.* pamplet

fomentar, *va.* to promote, encourage

fomento, *m.* promotion, fostering; improvement, development

fonda, *f.* hotel, inn

fondo, *m.* depth; bottom; rear; fund(s), capital, stock; essential nature; (art) background; **a fondo**, completely, fully

fonética, *f.* phonetics

fonógrafo, *m.* phonograph, gramophone

forastero, *adj.* strange, exotic; *n.* stranger, foreigner

forma, *f.* form, shape; way

formal, *adj.* formal; serious

formalidad, *f.* formality; punctuality; good behavior

formalizar, *va.* to make official; **formalizarse**, to settle down, become earnest

formar, *va.* to form, shape

formidable, *adj.* formidable; terrific

formón, *m.* chisel; punch

fórmula, *f.* formula

formular, *va.* to formulate, draw up

formulario, *m.* form (for filling in information)

foro, *m.* court of justice; bar; background of the stage; forum

forrar, *va.* to line (clothes, etc.); to cover (books, etc.)

fortalecer, *va.* to fortify, strengthen

fortaleza, *f.* fortitude,

strength, vigor; (mil. fortress
fortificar, *va.* to fortify
fortuna, *f.* fortune; **por fortuna**, fortunately
forzar, *va.* to force; to ravish
forzoso, *adj.* necessary
fosa, *f.* grave
fosforescente, *adj.* phosphorescent
fósforo, *m.* phosphorus; match
foso, *m.* pit; moat, ditch, fosse; **foso séptico**, septic tank
fotogénico, *adj.* photogenic
fotograbado, *m.* photoengraving, photogravure
fotografía *f.* photograph, picture
fotegrafiar, *va.* to photograph
fotógrafo, *m.* photographer
frac, *m.* evening coat, dress coat
fracasar, *vn.* to fail
fracaso, *m.* failure
fractura, fracture
fragancia, *f.* fragrance, perfume
fragante, *adj.* fragrant; flagrant
fragmento, *m.* fragment
frambuesa, *f.* raspberry
francés, francesa, *adj.* French; *m.* French language; Frenchman; *f.* Frenchwoman
Francia, *f.* France
franco, *adj.* frank, liberal, open, sincere; **franco a bordo**, free on board; **franco de porte**, postpaid; *m.* franc
franja, *f.* fringe; braid, border; stripe
franqueo, *m.* postage
franqueza, *f.* frankness
franquicia, *f.* franchise, grant; **franquicia postal**, free postage
frase, *f.* phrase, sentence
fraternal, *adj.* fraternal, brotherly
fraternidad, *f.* fraternity, brotherhood
fraudulento, *adj.* fraudulent
frazada, *f.* blanket
frecuencia, *f.* frequency; **con frecuencia**, frequently

frecuente, *adj.* frequent
freir, *va.* to fry
fréjol or **frijol**, bean
frenesí, *m.* frenzy
frente, *f.* face; forehead; **frente a frente**, face to face; *m.* (mil.) front line; **en frente**, in front, across the way
fresa,, *f.* strawberry
fresco *adj.* fresh, cool; new; bold; *m.* refreshing air; **tomar el fresco**, to enjoy the cool air
frescura, *f.* freshness, coolness; smart repartee
fresno, *m.* ash tree
frialdad, *f.* coldness; indifference
frijoles, *m. pl.* beans
frío, fría, *adj.* cold; indifferent; *m.* cold; **hacer frío** or **tener frío**, to be cold
frito, *adj.* fried
frívolo, *adj.* frivolous
frondoso, *adj.* leafy
frontera, *f.* frontier, border
frontón, *m.* wall of a handball court; pelota court
frotar, *va.* to rub
fructífero, *adj.* fruitful
frugal, *adj.* frugal, sparing
frugalidad, *f.* frugality
fruncir, *va.* to pleat; to gather, shirr; to pucker; to reduce to a smaller size: **fruncir las cejas**, to knit the eyebrows; **fruncir el ceño**, to frown
fruta, *f.* fruit
frutal, *adj.* fruit-bearing
frutera, *f.* fruit woman; fruit dish
frutería, *f.* fruit store
frutilla, *f.* small fruit; strawberry (in South America)
fruto, *m.* fruit; benefit
fuego, *m.* fire; skin eruption; ardor
fuelle, *m.* bellows, blower
fuente, *f.* fountain; source; issue; spring (of water); platter, dish
fuera, *adv.* outside; **fuera de sí**, frantic, beside oneself; **fuera de alcance**, beyond reach

fuerte, *m.* fortification; fort; *adj.* strong; loud; *adv.* strongly; loudly

fuerza, *f.* force, strength, vigor; violence, coercion; **a fuerza de**, by dint of; **fuerza mayor**, act of God

fuete, *m.* (Sp. Am.) horsewhip

fuga, *f.* flight, escape; leak; (mus.) fugue

fugarse, *vr.* to escape, flee

fugaz, *adj.* fugitive; volatile

fulano, fulana, or Fulano de Tal, *n.* John Doe, so-and-so

fulgor, *m.* glow, brilliancy

fulminante, *m.* percussion cap; *adj.* explosive

fumar, *va.*, *vn.* to smoke (cigars ,etc.)

fumigación, *f.* fumigation

funcionamiento, *m.* functioning

funcionar, *vn.* to function; to work, run (as machines)

funcionario, *m.* official, functionary

funda, *f.* case, sheath; slip cover; **funda de almohada**, pillowcase

fundación, *f.* foundation

fundador, fundadora, *n.* founder

fundamental, *adj.* fundamental

fundamento, *m.* foundation, base, groundwork; reason; good behavior

fundar, *va.* to found; to establish

fundir, *va.* to melt metals

fúnebre, *adj.* mournful, sad; funeral

funesto, *adj.* funereal dismal; disastrous

furgón, *m.* baggage, freight,or express car

furor, *m.* fury

fusil, *m.* musket, rifle

fusilar, *va.* to shoot, execute

fusión, *f.* fusion, union

futbol, *m.* football, soccer

futuro, *adj.*, *m.* future

G

g/, gramo, gr. gram

g/, giro, draft

gabardina, *f.* gabardine; raincoat

gabinete, *m.*, cabinet, study

gafas, *f. pl.* spectacles, goggles

galán, *m.* gallant, courtier; lover; actor

galante, *adj.* gallant, courtly; generous, liberal

galantear, *va.* to court, woo

galanteo, *m.* gallantry, courtship

galantería, *f.* gallantry; compliment

galera, *f.* galley

galería, *f.* gallery

galgo, *m.* greyhound

galón, *m.* braid; gallon

galope, *m.* gallop

galvanómetro, *m.* galvanometer

galleta, *f.* cracker; cookie

gallina, *f.* hen; coward

gallinero, *m.* hen coop

gallo, *m.* cock, rooster; **misa de gallo**, midnight mass

gama globulina, *f.* gamma globulin

gana, *f.* appetite; desire; mind; **tener gana**, to be willing; **de buena gana**, voluntarily; **de mala gana**, unwillingly

ganadería, *f.* cattle breeding

ganado, *m.* cattle

ganancia, *f.* gain, profit

ganar, *va.* to gain, win; to beat (in a game); to earn

ganga, *f.* bargain

ganso, gansa, *n.* gander; goose

garage or garaje, *m.* garage

garantía, *f.* guarantee, pledge

garantizar, *va.* to guarantee, warrant

garbanzo, *m.* chick-pea

garbo, *m.* gracefulness

garboso, *adj.* graceful

gardenia, *f.* gardenia

garganta, *f.* throat, gullet; gorge

gárgara, *f.* gargle

garrapata, *f.* tick (insect)

garrote, *m.* cudgel, club

gas, m. gas
gasolina, f. gasoline
gasolinera, f. gas station; motor launch
gasómetro, m. gas storage tank, gas holder
gastador, adj. extravagant
gastar, va. to spend; to wear out; to use up
gasto, m. expense, cost
gata, f. tabby; **a gatas**, on all fours
gatear, vn. to creep, crawl
gato, m. cat; tomcat; jack
gaucho, m. Argentine cowboy
gavilán, m. (orn.) hawk
gaviota, f. (orn.) gull, sea gull
gazapo, m. young rabbit; blunder
gelatina, f. gelatine, jelly
gemido, m. groan, moan
gemir, vn. to groan, moan
gen, m. gene
generación, f. generation
generador, m. generator
general, m. general; adj. general, usual; **por lo general**, as a rule
generosidad, f. generosity
generoso, adj. generous
Génesis, f. Genesis
genial, adj. outstanding
genio, m. genius; temper
genital, adj. genital
genocidio, m. genocide
gente, f. people
gentil, adj. courteous
gentileza, f. gentility; courteous gesture
gentío, m. crowd, multitude
gentuza, f. rabble, mob
genuino, adj. genuine
geografía, f. geography.
geográfico, adj. geographical
geología, f. geology
geólogo, m. geologist
geometría, f. geometry
gerencia, f. management
gerente, m. manager
germinar, vn. to germinate
gerundio, m. (gram.) gerund, present participle
gestión, f. action, step
gestionar, va. to take steps to obtain something

gesto, m. face, aspect; gesture
gigante, m. giant; adj. gigantic
gigantesco, adj. gigantic
gimnasia, f. gymnastics
gimnasio, m. gymnasium
ginebra, f. gin
ginecólogo, m. gynecologist
girafa, f. giraffe
girar, vn. to rotate, revolve; (com.) to draw on
girasol, m. sunflower
giro, m. turn, bend; (com.) draft; **giro a la vista**, sight draft; **giro postal**, money order
gitano, gitana, n. gypsy
glacial, adj. icy
gladiolo, m. (bot.) gladiolus
glicerina, f. glycerine
glóbulo, m. globule
gloria, f. glory
glorificar, va. to glorify
glorioso, adj. glorious
glosario, m. glossary
glotón, glotona, n., adj. glutton; gluttonous
glucosa, f. glucose
gobernación, f. government; governor's office or mansion
gobernador, m. governor
gobernar, va. to govern; to regulate; to direct
gobierno, m. government
golfo, m. gulf
golondrina, f. (orn.) swallow
golosina, f. dainty, titbit
goloso, adj. gluttonous
golpe, m. blow, stroke, hit; knock; **de golpe**, all at once
golpear, va., vn. to beat, knock; to bruise; to tap
goma, f. gum; rubber; eraser
gordo, adj. fat; thick
gordura, f. grease; fatness
gorgojo, m. grub, weevil
gorila, m. (zool.) gorilla
gorra, f. cap, bonnet; **de gorra**, (coll.) at others' expense, sponging
gorro, m. cap or hood
gota, f. drop; gout
gotear, vn. to drip
gotera, f. leak, leakage
gozar, va. to enjoy
gozoso, adj. joyful

gr., gramo, gr., gram
grabación, f. recording; enraving
grabado, m. engraving, illustration; **grabado al agua fuerte,** etching
gracia, f. grace; pardon; **gracias,** pl. thanks
gracioso, adj. graceful; funny, pleasing; m. clown, buffoon
grada, f. step of a staircase; **gradas,** pl. seats of a stadium
grado, m. step; degree; grade. .
graduación, f. graduation
gradual, adj. gradual
graduar, va., vr. to graduate; to grade
gráfico, adj. graphic; vivid
Gral. General, Gen. General
gramática, f. grammar
gramatical, adj. grammatical
gramo, m. gram
gran, adj. contraction of **grande,** great, large, big
granada, f. grenade, shell, pomegranate
Gran Bretaña, f. Great Britain
grande, adj. great; large, big
grandioso, adj. grand, magnificent
granero, m. granary
granito, m. granite
granizo, m. hail
granja, f. grange, farm
grano, m. grain, kernel; pimple; **ir al grano,** to get to the point
grasa, f. suet, fat, grease; shoe polish
gratificación, f. gratification; gratuity
gratificar, va. to gratify, reward
gratitud, f. gratitude
grato, adj. pleasant, pleasing; **su grata,** your favor (letter)
gratuito, adj. free
gravamen, m. charge, tax
gravar, va. to burden; to tax
grave, adj. grave, serious
Grecia, f. Greece
gremio, m. guild, trade union
griego, adj. Greek
grieta, f. opening, crack
grillo, m. cricket

gringo, gringa, n. (Sp. Am.) (coll.) foreigner (especially an Anglo-Saxon)
gripe, f. grippe, influenza
gris, adj. gray
gritar, vn. to scream
grito, m. cry, scream
grosería, f. insult; coarseness
grosero, adj. coarse, rude
grúa, f. crane, derrick
gruesa, f. gross
grueso, adj. thick, coarse
gruñido, m. grunt, growl
grupo, m. group
gruta, f. grotto
gsa., gruesa, gro., gross
gte., gerente, mgr., manager
guacamayo, m., **guacamaya,** f. macaw
guante, m. glove
guapo, adj. courageous; bold; elegant, handsome
guarda, m., f. guard, keeper
guardabrisa, m. windshield
guardafango, m. fender; dashboard
guardar, va. to keep; to guard
guardarropa, m., f. keeper of a wardrobe; m. coatroom
guardia, f. guard; watch; m. guardsman
guasa, f. (coll.) fun, jest
guasón, guasona, adj. (coll.) fond of teasing
guatemalteco, guatemalteca, n., adj. Guatemalan
guayaba, f. guava (fruit); **guayabo,** m. guava (tree)
güero, güera, n., adj. (Mex.) blond, light-haired. See **huero**
guerra, war; **dar guerra,** to be a nuisance (usually a child)
guerrero, m. warrior; **guerrera,** adj. martial, warlike
guía, m., f. guide; guidebook
guiar, va. to guide, lead; to drive
Guillermo, William
guillotina, f. guillotine
guindar, va. to hang
guiñar, va. to wink
guión, m. hyphen; (rad.) script
guisado, m. stew
guisante, m. (bot.) pea

guisar, va. to cook, stew
guiso, m. any edible concoction
guitarra, f. guitar
gusano, m. maggot, worm
gustar, va., vn. to like, be fond of
gusto, m. taste; pleasure, delight; choice
gustoso, adj. tasty; willing

H

h., **habitantes**, pop., population
haba, f. (bot.) navy bean
Habana, f. Havana
habanero, **habanera**, n., adj. native of Havana; of Havana
habano, m. Havana cigar
haber, va. to have (as an auxiliary verb); to exist; m. (com.) credit; **haberes**, m. pl. property
habichuela, f. kidney bean; **habichuela verde**, string bean
hábil, adj. able, skillful
habilidad, f. ability, dexterity, aptitude
habilitar, va. to qualify, enable; to equip
habitación, f. dwelling
habitante, m., f. inhabitant
habitar, va. to inhabit, reside
hábito, m. custom
habituarse, vr. to accustom oneself
habla, f. speech; language; **sin habla**, speechless
hablador, adj. talkative
hablar, va., vn. to speak, talk
hacendado, m. landholder, farmer
hacendoso, adj. industrious, diligent
hacer, va., vn. to make, do; to manufacture; **hacer alarde**, to boast; **hacer calor**, to be warm; **hacer frío**, to be cold
hacia, prep. toward; about
hacienda, f. landed property; farmstead
hada, f. fairy
halagar, va. to please; to flat-

ter
halago, m. caress; flattery
halagüeño, adj. pleasing; flattering
halcón, m. falcon, hawk
haltera, f. barbell
hallar, va. to find; to discover; to come upon; **hallarse**, to be; **no hallarse**, to be out of sorts
hallazgo, m. finding, discovery
hambre, f. hunger; famine; **tener hambre**, to be hungry
hambriento, adj. hungry; starved
haragán, **haragana**, n. idler; adj. lazy
harapo, m. rag, tatter
harén, m. harem
harina, f. flour
harinoso, adj. mealy, starchy
harmonía, f. harmony
hartar, va., vr. to cloy, satiate
harto, adj. satiated; sufficient; adv. enough
hasta, prep. till, until; conj. also, even
hazaña, f. exploit, feat
hazmerreír, m. laughingstock
he, adv. behold, look here (generally followed by **aquí** or **allí**); **he aquí**, here it is
hebilla, f. buckle
hebra, f. thread, filament
hebreo, hebrea, n. Hebrew; m. Hebrew language; adj. Hebraic, Judaical
hecatombe, f. massacre, slaughter
hectárea, f. hectare
hecho, adj. made, done; accustomed; m. fact; act, deed
hechura, f. making; workmanship
hediondo, adj. ill-smelling
helada, f. frost; nip
heladería, f. ice-cream parlor
helado, adj. frozen; icy; m. ice cream
helar, va., vn. to congeal; to freeze, ice; to astonish, amaze; **helarse**, to be frozen; to congeal
hélice, f. propeller
helicóptero, helicopter

hembra, *f.* female; eye of hook; nut of a screw

hemisferio, *m.* hemisphere

hemorragia, *f.* (med.) hemorrhage

hemorroides, *f. pl.* piles, hemorrhoids

heno, *m.* hay

heredar, *va.* to inherit

hereditario, *adj.* hereditary

heredero, heredera, *n.* heir, heiress

hereje, *m., f.* heretic

herencia, *f.* inheritance, heritage; heirship

herida, *f.* wound, hurt

herir, *va.* to wound, to hurt; to offend

hermanastra, *f.* stepsister

hermanastro, *m.* stepbrother

hermano, hermana, *n.* brother, sister; **primo hermano,** or **prima hermana,** first cousin

hermético, *adj.* airtight

hermoso, *adj.* beautiful, handsome

hermosura, *f.* beauty

héroe, *m.* hero

heroico, *adj.* heroic

heroína, *f.* heroine

heroísmo, *m.* heroism

herradura, *f.* horseshoe

herramienta, *f.* tool, implement

herrería, *f.* ironworks

herrero, *m.* blacksmith

hervir, *vn.* to boil

hervor, *m.* boiling; fervor

hidroavión, *m.* seaplane

hidrógeno, *m.* hydrogen

hidropesía, *f.* dropsy

hidroplano, *m.* hydroplane (boat)

hiedra, *f.* ivy

hiel, *f.* gall, bile

hielo, *m.* frost, ice

hiena, *f.* hyena

hierba or **yerba,** *f.* herb; grass; weed

hierbabuena, *f.* (bot.) mint

hierro, *m.* iron; **hierros,** *pl.* fetters

hígado, *m.* liver

higiene, *f.* hygiene

hija, *f.* daughter; child

hijastra, *f.* stepdaughter

hijastro, *m.* stepson

hijo, *m.* son; child

hilar, *va.* to spin

hilera, *f.* row; ridgepole; (mech.) wire drawer

hilo, *m.* thread; linen; wire

hilvanar, *va.* to baste

himno, *m.* hymn; anthem

hincapié, *m.* stress; **hacer hincapié,** to emphasize

hincarse, *vr.* to kneel

hinchado, *adj.* swollen

hinchar, *va., vr.* to swell

hindú, *m., f.* Hindu

hipnotismo, *m.* hypnotism

hipnotizar, *va.* to hypnotize

hipo, *m.* hiccough

hipócrita, *adj., n.* hypocritical; hypocrite

hipopótamo, *m.* hippopotamus

hipoteca, *f.* mortgage

hirviente, *adj.* boiling

hispano, *adj.* Hispanic, Spanish

Hispanoamérica, *f.* Spanish America

hispanoamericano, hispanoamericana, *adj., n.* Spanish-American

histérico, *adj.* hysterical

historia, *f.* history; story

historisdor, historisdora, *n.* historian

histórico, *adj.* historical

hocico, *m.* snout, muzzle

hogar, *m.* home; hearth

hoguera, *f.* bonfire; blaze

hoja, *f.* leaf; blade (of knife, sword, etc.); sheet (of paper or metal), **hoja de trébol,** cloverleaf

hohalata, *f.* tin plate

hojear, *va.* to turn the leaves of a book

Holanda, *f.* Holland

holandés, holandésa, *n., adj.* Dutch

holgado, *adj.* loose; in easy circumstances

holgazán, holgazana, *n.* idler

hollín, *m.* soot

hombre, *m.* man, human being

hombro, m. shoulder

homenaje, m. homage, tribute

homicida, m., f. murderer; adj. homicidal

homicidio, m. murder

hondo, adj. profound, deep

hondureño, hondureña, n., adj. Honduran

honesto, adj. honest; modest

hongo, m. mushroom; fungus

honor, m. honor

honorable, adj. honorable

honorario, adj. honorary; m. honorarium, fee

honra, f. honor; chastity (in women); **honras,** pl. funeral honors

honrado, adj. honest, honorable

honrar, va. to honor; **honrarse,** to deem it an honor

hora, f. hour; time

horario, m. hour hand; time table; hours; schedule

horma, f. mold; **horma de zapatos,** shoe last

hormiga, f. ant

hormigón, m. concrete

hormigonera, f. concrete mixer

horno, m. oven; furnace; **alto horno,** blast fumace

horquilla, f. hairpin

horrible, adj. horrible

horror, m. horror, fright

horrorizar, va., vr. to horrify

hortaliza, f. vegetables

hospedaje, m. lodging

hospedar, va., vr. to lodge, board

hospicio, m. orphanage; old peoples home

hospital, m. hospital

hospitalidad, f. hospitality

hospitalización, f. hospitalization

hospitalizar, va. to hospitalize

hostia, f. host; wafer

hotel, m. hotel

hoy, adv. today

hoyo, m. hole, pit

hoz, f. sickle

huelga, f. strike of workmen

huella, f. track, trace

huérfano, huérfana, n., adj. orphan

huero, adj. empty, addle; **huevo huero,** rotten egg

huerta, orchard, vegetable garden

huerto, m. fruit garden

hueso, m. bone; stone, core

huésped, huéspeda, n. guest; boarder

huevo, m. egg

huida, f. flight, escape

huir, vn. to flee, escape

hule, m. rubber; oilcloth

humanidad, f. humanity, mankind; **humanidades,** pl. humanities, human learning

humanitario, humanitaria, n., adj. humanitarian

humano, adj. human; humane, kind

humedad, f. humidity, moisture, wetness

humedecer, va. to moisten, wet, soak

húmedo, adj. humid, wet

humildad, f. humility, humbleness

humilde, adj. humble, meek

humillar, va., vr. to humble; to humiliate

humo, m. smoke; fume

humor, m. humor, disposition

hundir, vn., vr. to submerge; to sink

húngaro, húngara, adj., n. Hungarian

Hungría, f. Hungary

huracán, m. hurricane, storm

hurtar, va. to steal, rob

I

ibérico, adj. Iberian

id., idem, id., same, ditto

ida, f. departure; **idas y venidas,** comings and goings

idea, f. idea; scheme

ideal, m., adj. ideal

idealismo, m. idealism

idealista, n., adj. idealist; idealistic

idealizar, va., vn. to idealize

idear, va. to conceive; to think, to contrive, to plan

idem, item, the same, ditto

idéntico, *adj.* identical

identificar, *va., vr.* to identify

idioma, *m.* language

idiosincrasia, *f.* idiosyncrasy

idiota, *m., f.* idiot; *adj.* idiotic

idolatrar, *va.* to idolize

idolo, *m.* idol

iglesia, *f.* church

ignorancia, *f.* ignorance

ignorante, *adj.* ignorant

ignorar, *va.* to be ignorant of

igual, *adj.* equal, similar

igualar, *va.* to equalize; equal; **igualarse**, to place oneself on a level (with)

igualdad, *f.* equality

igualmente, *adv.* equally

ilegal, *adj.* illegal, unlawful

ilegítimo, *adj.* illegitimate

ileso, *adj.* unhurt

iluminación, *f.* illumination, lighting

iluminar, *va.* to illumine, illuminate

ilustración, *f.* illustration

ilustrar, *va.* to illustrate; to enlighten

ilustre, *adj.* illustrious

imagen, *f.* image

imaginación, *f.* imagination

imaginar, *va., vn.* to imagine

imaginario, *adj.* imaginary, fancied

imán, *m.* magnet

imbécil, *m., f.* imbecile, idiot; *adj.* feeble minded

imitación, *f.* imitation

imitar, *va.* to imitate

impaciencia, *f.* impatience

impaciente, *adj.* impatient

impar, *adj.* unequal, odd

imparcial, *adj.* impartial

impartir, *va.* to impart

impávido, *adj.* calm in the face of danger

impecable, *adj.* impeccable

impedir, *va.* to impede, prevent

imperar, *vn.* to rule, command; to reign; to prevail

imperativo, *adj.* imperative, pressing; *m.* (gram.) imperative (case)

imperdible, *m.* safety pin

imperdonable, *adj.* unpardonable

imperfecto, *adj.* imperfect

imperial, *adj.* imperial

imperialismo, *m.* imperialism

imperio, *m.* empire

imperioso, *adj.* imperious, pressing; arrogant

impermeable, *adj.* waterproof; *m.* raincoat

impersonal, *adj.* impersonal

impertinente, *adj.* impertinent; importunate

impertinentes, *m. pl.* lorgnette

ímpetu, *m.* impetus; impetuosity

impetuoso, *adj.* impetuous

implicar, *va. vn.* to impliclite, involve

implícito, *adj.* implicit

implorar, *va.* to implore

imponderabilidad, *f.* weightlessness

imponer, *va.* to impose; **imponerse**, to assert oneself

importador, **importadora**, *n.* importer

importancia, *f.* importance, import

importante, *adj.* important

importar, *vn.* to matter; to mind; to import

importe, *m.* amount, cost

imposibilidad, *f.* impossibility

imposible, *adj.* impossible

imposición, *f.* imposition

impostor, **impostora**, *n.* impostor

impotente, *adj.* impotent; helpless

impracticable, *adj.* impracticable

imprenta, *f.* printing; printing office

imprescindible, *adj.* indispensible, essential

impresión, *f.* impression; edition; presswork

impresionar, *va.* to impress

impresos, *m. pl.* printed matter

impresor, **impresora**, *n.* printer

imprevisto, *adj.* unforeseen

imprimir va. to print
impropio, adj. improper, unfit
improvisar, va. to improvise
improviso, adj. unforeseen; **de improviso,** unexpectedly
impuesto, m. tax, impost, duty; **impuesto sobre rentas,** income tax
impulsar, va. to further, impel; (mech.) to drive
impulso, m. impulse, impulsion, spur
impureza, f. impurity
inaccesible, adj. inaccessible
inaceptable, adj. unacceptable
inagotable, adj. inexhaustible
inalámbrico, adj. wireless
inaudito, adj. unheard of, unusual
inauguración, f. inauguration
inaugurar, va. to inaugurate
inca, m. Inca; Peruvian gold coin
incansable, adj. untiring
incapaz., adj. incapable, unable
incendiar, va., vr. to set on fire
incendio, m. fire, conflagration
incentivo, m. incentive
incertidumbre, f. uncertainty
incidente, m. incident
incienso, m. incense
incierto, adj. uncertain
incitar, va. to incite, stir
inclinar, va., vn. to incline, slope; **inclinarse por,** to be favorably disposed to
incluir, va. to include, comprise; to inclose
inclusive, adv. inclusive, including
incluso, inclosed
incógnito, adj. unknown
incoherente, adj. incoherent
incomodar, va. to inconvenience, disturb
incomodidad, f. inconvenience, annoyance
incómodo, adj. uncomfortable, inconvenient
incomparable, adj. incomparable

incompatible, adj. incompatible
incompetente, adj. incompetent
incompleto, adj. incomplete
incomprensible, adj. incomprehensible
inconcebible, adj. inconceivable
inconsciente, adj. unconscious
inconstante, adj. inconstant, fickle
inconveniencia, f. inconvenience
inconveniente, adj. inconvenient; inadvisable; m. obstacle; objection
incorporar, va. to incorporate; to join; **incorporarse,** to become incorporated; to sit up (in bed)
incorrecto, adj. incorrect
incorregible, adj. incorrigible
incrédulo, adj. incredulous
increíble, adj. incredible
incremento, m. increment, increase
incubar, va. to hatch
inculcar, va. to inculcate
incurable, adj. incurable
incurrir, vn. to incur
indagar, va. to investigate
indecente, adj. indecent
indeciso, adj. undecided
indefinido, adj. indefinite
indemnizar, va. to indemnify
independencia, f. independence
independiente, adj. independent
indescriptible, adj. indescribable
indicación, f. indication
indicar, va. to indicate
indicativo, adj. indicative; m., adj. (gram.) indicative
índice, m. mark, sign; hand of a watch or clock; index; forefinger
índico, adj. pertaining to the East Indies; **Océano Índico** or **Mar de las Indias,** Indian Ocean
indiferencia, f. indifference

indiferente, *adj.* indifferent

indígena, *adj., n.* indigenous, native

indigente, *adj.* indigent,

indigestión, *f.* indigestion

indigesto, *adj.* indigestible

indignación, *f.* indignation, anger

indio, india, *n., adj.* Indian

indirecta, *f.* hint, cue

indirecto, *adj.* indirect

indispensable, *adj.* indispensable

individual, *adj.* individual

individuo, *m.* individual

índole, *f.* disposition, temper; kind; nature

inducir, *va.* to induce

indudable, *adj.* undeniable; evident, certain

indulgencia, *f.* indulgence, forgiveness

industria, *f.* industry

industrial, *adj.* industrial

industrialización, *f.* industrialization

industrializer, *va.* to industrialize

industrioso, *adj.* industrious

inédito, *adj.* not published, unedited

inepto, *adj.* inept, unfit

inercia, *f.* inertia; inactivity

inesperado, *adj.* unexpected

inevitable, *adj.* inevitable

infame, *adj.* infamous, bad; *m., f.* wretch, scoundrel

infancia, *f.* infancy

infante, *m.* infant; any son of the king of Spain, except the heir apparent

infantil, *adj.* infantile

infección, *f.* infection

infectar, *va.* to infect

infeliz, *adj.* unhappy, unfortunate

inferior, *adj.* inferior; lower

inferioridad, *f.* inferiority

inferir, *va.* to infer; to inflict

infiel, *adj.* unfaithful

infierno, *m.* hell

ínfimo, *adj.* lowest

infinidad, *f.* infinity

infinitivo, *m.* (gram.) infinitive

infinito, *adj.* infinite, im-

mense; *adv.* infinitely, immensely; *m.* infinity

inflación, *f.* inflation

inflamable, *adj.* inflammable

intramar, *va.* to inflame; **intramarse**, to catch fire

inflar, *va., vr.* to inflate

influencia, *f.* influence

influenza, *f.* influenza

influir, *va.* to influence

influyente, *adj.* influential

información, *f.* information

informal, *adj.* not punctual; unreliable

informar, *va.* to inform, report

informe, *m.* information; report, account

infortunio, *m.* misfortune

infracción, *f.* violation

infructuoso, *adj.* fruitless

infundado, *adj.* groundless

infundir, *va.* to infuse; to instill

ingeniar, *va.* to conceive; to contrive

ingeniero, *m.* engineer

ingenio, *m.* wit, ingenuity; **ingenio de azúcar**, sugar mill

ingenioso, *adj.* ingenious, witty; resourceful

ingenuidad, *f.* candor, naiveté

ingenuo, *adj.* candid, naive

Inglaterra, *f.* England

inglés, inglesa, *n., adj.* Englishman, Englishwoman; English; *m.* English language

ingratitud, *f.* ingratitude

ingrato, *adj.* ungrateful

ingrediente, *m.* ingredient

ingreso, *m.* (com.) receipts, revenue; entrance

inhumano, *adj.* inhuman

inicial, *f., adj.* initial

iniciar, *va.* to initiate, begin; **iniciarse**, to be initiated

iniciativa, *f.* initiative

injusticia, *f.* injustice

inmaculado, *adj.* immaculate

inmediato, *adj.* immediate, next

inmejorable, *adj.* unsurpassable

inmenso, *adj.* immense, infinite

inmersión, immersion, dip

inmigración, _f._ immigration

inmigrar, _vn._ to immigrate

inmoral, _adj._ immoral

inmoralidad, _f._ immorality

inmortal, _adj._ immortal

inmortalidad, _f._ immortality

inmóvil, _adj._ immovable, stable; death-like

inmueble, _adj._ (law) immovable (property); **bienes inmuebles**, real estate

inmundo, _adj._ filthy, dirty

inmune, _adj._ immune

innato, _adj._ inborn, natural

innovación, _f._ innovation

inocencia, _f._ innocence

inocente, _adj._ innocent

inodoro, _m._ water closet

inofensivo, _adj._ harmless

inolvidable, _adj._ unforgettable

inquietud, _f._ restlessness

inquilino, inquilina, _n._ tenant, renter

inquisición, _f._ inquisition

insaciable, _adj._ insatiable

inscribir, _va., vr._ register

inscripción, _f._ inscription

insecto, _m._ insect

inseguro, _adj._ uncertain

inseparable, _adj._ inseparable

inserción, _f._ insertion

insertar, _va._ to insert

inservible, _adj._ useless

insignia, _f._ badge, insignia

insignificante, _adj._ insignificant

insinuación, _f._ insinuation, hint

insinuar, _va._ to insinuate, hint; **insinuarse**, to ingratiate oneself

insistencia, _f._ persistence

insistir, _vn._ to insist

insolente, _adj._ insolent

insomnio, _m._ insomnia

inspección, _f._ inspection

inspector, _m._ inspector

inspiración, _f._ inspiration

inspirar, _va._ to inspire

instalación, _f._ installation

instalar, _va._ to install; **instalarse**, to settle

instantáneo, _adj._ instantaneous; **instantánea**, _f._ snapshot

instigar, _va._ to instigate

instintivo, _adj._ instinctive

instinto, _m._ instinct

institución, _f._ institution

instituto, _m._ institute

institutriz, _f._ governess

instrucción, _f._ instruction; education

instructor, _m._ instructor

instruido, _adj._ well-educated

instruir, _va._ to instruct

instrumento, _m._ instrument; machine

insubordinado, _adj._ insubordinate

insuficiente, _adj._ insufficient

insufrible, _adj._ insufferable

insuperable, _adj._ insurmountable

insurrecto, insurrecta, _n., adj._ insurgent, rebel

intachable, _adj._ blameless; irreproachable

integridad, _f._ integrity, whole

íntegro, _adj._ entire

intelectual, _adj., n._ intellectual

inteligencia, _f._ intelligence; understanding

inteligente, _adj._ intelligent

intemperie, _f._ rough or bad weather; **a la intemperie**, outdoors

intempestivo, _adj._ inopportune

intención, intention

intensidad, intensity

intensificar, _va._ to intensify

intenso, _adj._ intense, ardent

intentar, _va._ to try; to intend

intento, _m._ intent, purpose

intercambio, _m._ interchange

interceder, _vn._ to intercede

interés, _m._ interest

interesante, _adj._ interesting

interesar, _vn., vr._ to be concerned or interested in; _va._ to interest

interino, _adj._ provisional, acting (of an employ or office)

interior, _adj._ interior, internal; **ropa interior**, underwear; _m._ interior

interjección, _f._ (gram.) interjection

intermediar, *va.* to interpose

intermedio, *adj.* intermediate; *m.* intermission; interlude, recess; **por intermedio de,** through, by means of

internacional, *adj.* international

internar, *va.* to intern; to place in a boarding school or asylum; *vn.* to pierce

interno, *adj.* interior, internal, inside; *n.* boarding-school student

interplanetario, interplanetaria, *adj.* interplanetary

interpretación, *f.* interpretation

interpretar, *va.* to interpret, explain; to translate

intérprete, *m.* interpreter

interrogación, *f.* interrogation

interrogar, *va.* to interrogate

interrumpir, *va.* to interrupt

interrupción, *f.* interruption

interruptor, *m.* (elec.) switch

intervalo, *m.* interval

intervención, *f.* intervention

intervenir, *vn.* to intervene, mediate

intestino, *m.* intestine

intimidad, *f.* intimacy

intolerable, *adj.* intolerable

intolerancia, *f.* intolerance

intranquilo, *adj.* restless

intransitive, *adj.* (gram.) intransitive

intriga, *f.* intrigue, plot

intrigante, *adj.* intriguing, scheming

intrínseco, *adj.* intrinsic

introducción, *f.* introduction

introducir, *va.* to introduce; **introducirse,** to gain access (to)

intruso, *adj.* intrusive, obtrusive; *n.* intruder

intuición, *f.* intuition

inundación, *f.* inundation, flood

inundar, *va.* to inundate

inútil, *adj.* useless

invadir, *va.* to invade

inválido, *adj.* invalid, null; *n.* invalid

invariable, *adj.* invariable

invasión, *f.* invasion

invencible, *adj.* invincible

invención, *f.* invention

inventar, *va.* to invent

inventario, *m.* inventory

invento, *m.* invention

invernadero, *m.* (mil.) greenhouse

inverosímil, *adj.* unlikely, improbable

inversión, *f.* inversion; investment

invertir, *va.* to invert; (com.) to invest

investigación, *f.* investigation, research

investigar, *va.* to investigate

invierno, *m.* winter

invisible, *adj.* invisible

invitación, *f.* invitation

invitado, invitada, *n.* guest

invitar, *va.* to invite

invocar, *va.* to invoke

involuntario, *adj.* involuntary

inyección, *f.* injection

inyectar, *va.* to inject

ir, *vn.* to go; to walk; to progress; **irse,** to go away, depart

ira, *f.* anger, wrath

iris, *m.* rainbow; iris (of the eye)

Irlanda, *f.* Ireland

irlandés, irlandésa, *n.,* *adj.* Irishman, Irishwoman; Irish

ironía, *f.* irony

irónico, *adj.* ironical

irregular, *adj.* irregular

irremediable, *adj.* irremediable, helpless

irreparable, *adj.* irreparable

irresistible, *adj.* irresistible

irresponsable, *adj.* irresponsible

irrevocable, *adj.* irrevocable

irritación, *f.* irritation; wrath

irritar, *va.* to irritate

isla, *f.* isle., island

israelita, *n.* *adj.* Israelite, Jew, Jewish

istmo, *m.* isthmus

Italia, *f.* Italy

italiano, italiana, *n.,* *adj.* Italian; *m.* Italian language

itinerario, *adj.,* *m.* itinerary

izar, *va.* (naut.) to hoist

izquierdo, *adj.* left; left-handed; **izquierda**, *f.* left wing in politics; left, left hand

J

jabalí, *m.* wild boar

jabón, *m.* soap

jacinto, *m.* hyacinth

jactarse, *vr.* to boast

jadeante, *adj.* panting

jal lai, *m.* Basque ball

jaiba, *f.* (Sp. Am.) crab

jalea, *f.* jelly

jamás, *adv.* never

jamón, *m.* ham

Japón, *m.* Japan

japonés, japonesa, *adj., n.* Japanese; *m.* japanese language

jaqueca, *f.* headache

jarabe, *m.* sirup; **jarabe tapatío**, Mexican regional dance

jardín, *m.* garden

jardinero, jardinera, *n.* gardener

jarra, *f.* jug, jar, pitcher

jarro, *m.* pitcher, jug

J.C., **Jesucristo**, J.C., Jesus Christ

jefatura, *f.* leadership; **jefatura de policía**, police headquarters

jeringa, *f.* syringe

Jesucristo, *m.* Jesus Christ

jesuita, *m., adj.* Jesuit

Jesús, *m.* Jesus; *interj.* goodness!

jinete, *m.* horseman, rider

jira, *f.* strip of cloth; tour; **jira campestre**, picnic

jirafa, *f.* giraffe

jocoso, *adj.* comical

jornada, *f.* one-day march; journey

joroba, *f.* hump

jorobado, *adj.* hunchbacked

jota, *f.* the letter j; Spanish dance; **no saber ni jota**, not to know a thing

joven, *adj.* young; *m., f.* young man, young woman

jovial, *adj.* jovial, gay

joya, *f.* jewel

joyería, *f.* jewelry store

joyero, *m.* jeweler

juanete, *m.* bunion

jubilar, *va., vr.* to pension off; to retire

júbilo, *m.* joy

judía, *f.* kidney bean; string bean; Jewess

judicial, *adi.* judicial,juridical

judío, *adj.* Jewish; *m.* Jew

jueves, *m.* Thursday

juez, *m.* judge

jugada, *f.* move (in a game); mean trick

jugar, *va., vn.* to play; to gamble

jugo, *m.* sap, juice

jugoso, *adj.* juicy

juguete, *m.* toy, plaything

juguetón, *adj.* playful

juicio, *m.* judgment, reason; trial

juicioso,*adj.* wise, prudent

julio, *m.* July

junio, *m.* June

junta, *f.* session, meeting; board; **junta directiva**, board of directors

juntar, *va.* to unite; to collect, gather; **juntarse**, to assemble

junto, *adv.* near, close; **junto, junta**, *adj.* united; **juntos**, *pl.* together, side by side

jurado, *m.* jury; juror, juryman

juramento, *m.* oath

jurar, *va., vn.* to swear, make oath; to curse

jurisdicción, *f.* jurisdiction

justicia, *f.* justice; fairness; **la justicia**, the police

justificación, *f.* justification

justificar, *va.* to justify

justo, *adj.* just; fair, upright; tight

juvenil, *adj.* juvenile,youthful

juventud, *f.* youthfulness, youth

juzgado, *m.* tribunal; court

juzgar, *va., vn.* to judge

K

kaki, *m., adj.* khaki

karate, _m._ karate

Kc., Kilociclo, kc., kilocycle

Kg. or **kg., kilogramo,** k. or kg., kilogram

kilo, _m._ kilo, kilogram

kilociclo, _m._ kilocycle

kilogramo, _m._ kilogram

kilométrico, kilométrica, _adj._ kilometric; (coll.) too long

kilómetro, _m._ kilometer

kilotón, _m._ kiloton

kilovatio, _m._ kilowatt

kiosco, _m._ kiosk, booth

Km. or **km., kilómetro,** km., kilometer

kodak, _m._ kodak

kv. or **k.w., kilovatio,** kw., kilowatt

L

l., ley, law; **libro,** bk., book; **litro,** l., liter

L/, l.ª, l.: **letra,** bill, draft, letter

£, libra esterlina, £, pound sterling

la, _art._ (fem. sing.) the _pron._ (acc. fem. sing.) her, it, as **la vio,** he saw her, **la compré,** I bought it (casa)

laberinto, _m._ labyrinth, maze

labia, _f._ (coll.) gift of gab

labio, _m._ lip; edge of anything

labor, _f._ labor, task; needlework

laborar, _va., vn._ to work; to till

laboratorio, _m._ laboratory

laborioso, _adj._ industrious

labrador, labradora, _n._ farmer; peasant

labrar, _va._ to work; to labor, to cultivate the ground

laca, _f._ lac; lacquer

lacio, _adj._ straight (applied to hair)

lacónico, _adj._ laconic

lactancia, _f._ time of suckling

lácteo, _adj._ lacteous, milky

ladino, _adj._ cunning, crafty

lado, _m._ side; party

ladrar, _vn._ to bark

ladrillo, _m._ brick

ladrón, _m._ thief, robber

lagartija, _f._ (zool.) eft, newt

lagarto, _m._ lizard; alligator; (coll.) sly person

lago, _m._ lake

lágrima, _f._ tear

laguna, _f._ lagoon, pond; blank space (as in a text), hiatus; gap

lamentar, _va._ to lament, regret; _vn., vr._ to lament, complain, cry

lamer, _va._ to lick, to lap

lámina, _f._ plate, sheet of metal; copper plate; print, picture

lana, _f._ wool

lanar, _adj._ woolly; **ganado lanar,** sheep

lance, _m._ cast, throw; critical moment; quarrel

lancha, _f._ barge, launch

langosta _f._ locust; lobster

lánguido, _adj._ languid

lanudo, _adj._ woolly, fleecy

lanza, _f._ lance, spear

lanzacohetes, _m._ rocket launcher

lanzar, _va._ to throw, fling; to launch

lapicero, _m._ pencil case

lápida, _f._ tombstone

larga, _f._ delay; **a la larga,** in the long run

largar, _va._ to slacken; to let go; **largarse,** (coll.) to get out, leave

largo, _adj._ long; **larga ejecución (discos),** long-playing (records); _m._ length

laringe, _f._ larynx

lástima, _f._ pity

lastimar, _va._ to hurt; to wound; **lastimarse,** to be hurt

lata, _f._ tin can; (coll.) nuisance annoyance

latente, _adj._ dormant

lateral, _adj._ lateral

latido, _m._ pant, palpitation; barking

latigazo, _m._ crack of a whip

látigo, _m._ whip

latín, _m._ Latin language

latino, latina, _adj., n._ Latin

Latinoamérica, _f._ Latin America

latinoamericano, latinoamericana, *adj.* Latin American

latir, *vn.* to palpitate; to howl (as dogs)

latitud, *f.* latitude

latón, *m.* brass; brassie

latoso, *adj.* boring; **latosa,** *n.* bore

laurel, *m.* (bot.) laurel; laurel crown

lavado, *m.* washing, wash

lavamanos, *m.* wash bowl

lavandería, *f.* laundry

lavar, *va.* to wash

lavativa, *f.* enema

lavatorio, *m.* lavatory

laxante, *m., adj.* (med.) laxative

lazarillo, *m.* blind man's guide

lazo, *m.* lasso, lariat; tie; bond

lb., libra, lb., pound

Ldo., L.do, or l.do, Licenciado, (Sp. Am.) lawyer

le, *pron.* dative case of **él** or **ella**

leal, *adj.* loyal, faithful

lealtad, *f.* loyalty

lección, *f.* lesson

lector, lectora, *n.* reader

leche, *f.* milk

lechería, *f.* dairy

lechero, *m.* milkman, dairyman; *adj.* pertaining to milk

lecho, *m.* bed; litter

lechuga, *f.* lettuce

lechuza, *f.* owl

leer, *va.* to read

legación, *f.* legation, embassy

legal, *adj.* legal, lawful

legalizar, *va.* to legalize

legar, *va.* to depute; to bequeath

legendario. *adj.* legendary

legible, *adj.* legible

legión, *f.* legion

legislación, *f.* legislation

legislativo, *adj.* legislative

legislatura, *f.* legislature

legítimo, *adj.* legitimate

legumbre, *f.* legume; vegetable

leído, *adj.* well-read

lejano, *adj.* distant

lejos, *adv.* far off

lengua, *f.* tongue; language

lenguaje, *m.* language

lente, *m.* or *f.* lens; monocle; **lentes,** *m. pl.* eye glasses; **lentes de contacto,** contact lenses

lenteja, *f.* (bot.) lentil

lentitud, *f.* slowness

lento, *adj.* slow, lazy

leña, *f.* kindling wood

león, *m.* lion

leona, *f.* lioness

leopardo, *m.* leopard

lerdo, *adj.* slow, heavy

lesbiano, *adj.* lesbian

lesion, *f.* wound; injury

letargo, *m.* drowsiness

letra, *f.* letter; handwriting; (com.) draft; words in a song; **al pie de la letra,** literally; **letras,** *pl.* learning, letters

letrado, *adj.* learned, lettered; *m.* lawyer, jurist

letrero, *m.* inscription, label; poster

levadura, *f.* yeast

levantar, *va.* to raise; to impute falsely; **levantarse,** to rise, to get up

leve, *adj.* light; trifling

ley, *f.* law

liberal, *adj.* liberal, generous

libertad, *f.* liberty, freedom

libertinaje, *m.* licentiousness

libra, *f.* pound (weight); **libra esterlina,** pound sterling

librar, *va.* to free, rid

libre, *adj.* free; exempt; *m.* (Mex.) taxicab

librería, *f.* bookstore

librero, *m.* bookseller; bookcase

libreta, *f.* memorandum book

libro, *m.* book

Lic. or **Licdo., licenciado,** (Sp. Am.) lawyer

licencia, *f.* permission, license

licenciado, *m.* licentiate, title given a lawyer

liceo, *m.* lyceum, high school

lícito, *adj.* lawful, licit

licor, *m.* liquor

líder, *m., f.* leader; (labor) instigator, agitator; chief

liebre, *f.* hare

ligar, *va., vr.* to tie, bind; to alloy; to confederate

ligereza, *f.* lightness; levity; swiftness

ligero, *adj.* light, swift

lija, *f.* sandpaper

lima, *f.* file; sweet lime (fruit)

limar, *va.* to file; to polish

limeño, limeña, *n.* native of Lima; *adj.* from Litna

limitación, *f.* limitation

limitar, *va.* to limit

límite, *m.* limit, boundary

limón, *m.* lemon

limonada, *f.* lemonade

limosna, *f.* alms, charity

limosnero, limosnera, *n.* beggar

limpiabotas, *m.* boot-black

limpiar, *va.* to clean

limpieza, *f.* cleanliness

limpio, *adj.* clean

linaza, *f.* linseed

lindo, *adj.* pretty

lino, *m.* flax; linen

linóleo, *m.* linoleum

linotipo, *m.* linotype

linterna, *f.* lantern; **linterna de proyección**, slide projector

lío, *m.* bundle; mess; **armar un lío**, to cause trouble

liquidación, *f.* liquidation, settlement; clearance sale

liquidar, *va.* to liquidate; to settle, clear accounts

líquido, *adj.* liquid, net; *m.* liquid

lira, *f.* lyre

lírico, *adj.* lyrical, lyric

lirio, *m.* iris (flower); lily

Lisboa, *f.* Lisbon

lisiado, *adj.* crippled

liso, *adj.* flat, smooth

lisonja, *f.* flattery

lista, *f.* list; stripe; **pasar lista**, to call the roll

listo, *adj.* ready; alert

literal, *adj.* literal

literario, *adj.* literary

literato, literata, *n.* literary person, writer; *adj.* learned

literatura, *f.* literature

litografía, *f.* lithography

litro, *m.* liter

liviano, *adj.* light; unchaste

lo, *pron.* (acc. case third pers.

sing.) him, it; *art.* the (used before an adjective)

lobo, *m.* wolf

local, *adj.* local; *m.* place

localidad, *f.* locality; **localidades**, *pl.* accommodations, tickets, seats

localizar, *va.* to localize

loción, *f.* lotion, wash

loco, loca, *adj.*, *n.* mad, crackbrained

locomotora, *f.* locomotive

locura, *f.* madness, folly; absurdity

locutor, locutora, *n.* (radio) announcer

lodo, *m.* mud, mire

lógico, *adj.* logical

lograr, *va.* to gain, obtain

loma, *f.* hillock

lombriz, *f.* earthworm

lomo, *m.* loin

lona, *f.* canvas; sailcloth

Londres, *m.* London

longitud, *f.* length; longitude

loro, *m.* parrot

losa, *f.* flagstone; slab

lote, *m.* lot; share

lotería, *f.* lottery; lotto

loza, *f.* chinaware

Ltda., Sociedad Limitada, (Sp. Am.) Inc., Incorporated

lubricante, *adj.*, *m.* lubricant

lubricar, lubrificar, *va.* to lubricate

luciérnaga, *f.* firefly

lucir, *vn.*, *vr.* to shine, be brilliant; show off

lucrativo, *adj.* lucrative

lucha, *f.* struggle; wrestling

luchar, *vn.* to struggle; to wrestle

luego, *adv.* presently; soon afterwards; **desde luego**, of course; **hasta luego**, good-by

lugar, *m.* place; space; cause, motive

lujo, *m.* luxury; **de lujo**, de luxe

lujoso, *adj.* luxurious

lumbre, *f.* fire; light

lumbrera, *f.* luminary

luna, *f.* moon; glass plate for mirrors; **luna de miel**, honeymoon

lunar, m. mole; blemish
lunes, m. Monday
luneta, f. orchestra seat
lustre, m. luster; splendor
lustroso, adj. bright
luto, m. mourning
luz, f. light; **dar a luz,** to give birth

LL

llaga, f. wound, sore
llama, f. flame; (zool.) llama
llamada, f. call
llamar, va. to call; to invoke; **¿como se llama Ud.?** What is your name?
llamativo, adj. showy
llano, m. field, plain
llanta, f. tire
llanto, m. flood of tears
llanura, f. plain, field
llave, f. key; **llave inglesa,** monkey wrench
llavero, m. key ring
llegada, f. arrival
llegar, vn. to arrive; **llegar a ser,** to become
llenar, va. to fill
lleno, adj. full, replete
llevar, va. to carry, bear, take away; to wear (clothes)
llover, v. imp. to rain
llovíznar, v. imp. to drizzle
lluvia, f. rain
lluvioso, adj. rainy

M

m., masculino, m. masculine; **metro,** m. meter; **milla,** m. mile
maceta, f. flowerpot
macizo, adj. massive, solid
machacar, va. to pound, crush
macho, m. male animal; hook (of hook and eye); adj. masculine, male; vigorous
madrastra, f. stepmother
madre, f. mother
madreperla, f. mother of pearl
madreselva, f. honey-suckle
madrileño, madrileña, n., adj. inhabitant of Madrid; from

Madrid
madrina, f. godmother
madrugada, f. dawn
madrugar, vn. to get up early; to anticipate, beforehand
madurar, va., vn. to ripen; to mature
madurez, f. maturity
maduro, adj. ripe; mature
maestra, f. woman teacher
maestría, f. mastership skill
maestro, m. master; expert; teacher; **maestro, maestra,** adj. masterly; **obra maestra,** masterpiece
magia, f. magic
mágico, adj. magical
magnánimo, adj. magnanimous
magnetismo, m. magnetism
magnetófono, m. tape recorder
magnífico, adj. magnificent
magnitud, f. magnitude
maguey, m. (bot.) maguey, century plant
mahometano, mahometana, n., adj. Mohammedan
maíz, m. corn, maize
majar, va. to pound; to mash
majestad, f. majesty
mal, m. evil, hurt, injury; illness; adj. (used only before masculine nouns) bad
malaria, f. malaria
malcriado, adj. ill-bred
maldad, f. wickedness
maldecir, va. to curse
maldición, f. curse
maldito, adj. wicked; damned; cursed
malestar, m. indisposition
maleta, f. suitcase, satchel
malgastar, va. to misspend
malicioso, adj. malicious
maligno, adj. malignant
malnutrido, adj. undernourished
malsano, adj. unhealthful
maltratar, va. to mistreat
mamá, f. mamma
mamar, va., vn. to suck
manada, f. flock, drove
manantial, m. source, spring
manar, vn. to spring from

manco, *adj.* one-handed

mandamiento, *m.* commandment

mandar, *va.* to command; to send; *va., vn.* to govern

mandíbula, *f.* jawbone

mando, *m.* authority, power

mandolina, *f.* mandolin

manecilla, *f.* hand of a clock

manejar, *va.* to manage, handle; to drive (a car, etc.); manejarse, to behave

manera, *f.* manner, mode

manga, *f.* sleeve

mango, *m.* handle, heft; mango (a fruit)

manguera, *f.* hose, hose pipe

maní, *m.* (Sp. Am.) peanut

manía, *f.* frenzy, madness

manicero, *m.* peanut vendor

manicomio, *m.* insane asylum

manifestar, *va.* to manifest, show

maniobra, *f.* maneuver

maniquí, *m.* mannikin

manjar, *m.* food; choic morsel

mano, *f.* hand; coat, layer

manómetro, *m.* pressure guage

manosear, *va.* to handle; to muss

mansión, *f.* mansion

manta, *f.* blanket

manteca, *f.* lard

mantel, *m.* tablecloth

mantener, *va., vr.* to maintain, support

mantequilla, *f.* butter

mantilla, *f.* mantilla, head-shawl

manual, *adj.* manual, handy; manual

manubrio, *m.* handle bar

manufacturar, *va.* to manufacture

manuscrito, *m.* manuscript; manuscrita, manuscrita, *adj.* written by hand

manutención, *f.* maintenance

manzana, *f.* apple; block of houses

manzano, *m.* apple tree

maña, *f.* dexterity; skill, trick; evil habit

mañana, *f.* morning, pasado

mañana, day after tomorrow

maoísmo, *m.* Maoism

mapa, *m.* map

maquillaje, *m.* make-up

máquina, *f.* machine, engine; máquina de escribir, typewriter

maquinalmente, *adv.* mechanically

maquinaria, *f.* machinery

maquinista, *m.* machinist

mar, *m.* or *f.* sea

maravilla, wonder; a las mil maravillas, uncommonly well; exquisitely

maravillarse, *vr.* to wonder, be astonished

maravilloso, *adj.* marvelous

marcar, *va.* to mark

marco, *m.* frame

marcha, *f.* march; ponerse en marcha, to proceed, to start off

marchar, *vn.* to march; marcharse, to go away, leave

marchitar, *va., vn.* to wither

marchito, *adj.* faded, withered

marea, *f.* tide

marear, *va.* to molest, annoy. marearse, to become seasick

mareo, *m.* seasickness

marfil, *m.* ivory

margarita, *f.* daisy

margen, *m.* or *f.* margin; border

mariano, mariana, *adj.* marian, pertaining to the Virgin Mary

marido, *m.* husband

marimba, *f.* marimba

marina, *f.* navy; shipping

marinero, *m.* sailor

marino, *adj.* marine; *m.* seaman, sailor

mariposa, *f.* butterfly; braza mariposa, butterfly stroke

mariscal, *m.* marshal

marisco, *m.* shellfish

mármol, *m.* marble

marqués, *m.* marquis

marquesa, *f.* marchioness

marrano, *m.* pig, hog

marta, *f.* marten, marten fur

martes, *m.* Tuesday

martillo, *m.* hammer

marzo, *m.* March

mas, *conj.* but, yet

más, *adv.* more

masa, *f.* dough, paste; mass:

masaje, *m.* massage

mitscara, *m.* or *f.* masquerader; *f.* mask

mascota, *f.* mascot

masculino, *adj.* masculine, male

masonería, *f.* freemasonry

masticar, *va.* to chew

mata, *f.* plant, shrub

matadero, *m.* slaughterhouse

matanza, *f.* slaughtering; cattle to be slaughtered; massacre

matar, *va., vr.* to kill

matemática, or **matemáticas,** *f.* mathematics

matemático, *adj.* mathematical; *m.* mathematician

materia, matter, material; subject; matter (pus)

material, *adj.* material; *m.* ingredient; cloth; material

maternal, *adj.* maternal

maternidad, *f.* motherhood

materno, *adj.* maternal, motherly

matiné, *f.* matinée

matiz, *m.* shade of color; shading

matorral, *m.* shrub, thicket

matrícula, *f.* register; license number; roster; entrance fee in a school

matricular, *va., vr.* to matriculate, register

matrimonio, *m.* marriage, matrimony

matriz, *f.* uterus, womb; mold, die; *adj.* main, parent; **casa matriz,** head or main office

matrona, *f.* matron

máxima, *f.* maxim, rule

máxime, *adv.* principally

máximo, *adj.* maximum

mayo, *m.* May

mayonesa, *f., adj.* mayonnaise

mayor, *adj.* greater, larger; elder; **estado mayor,** military staff; *m.* superior; major; **al por mayor,** wholesale

mayordomo, *m.* steward, ma-

jordomo

mayoría, *f.* majority

mayúscula, *f.* capital letter

m/cta., mi cuenta, (com.) my account

m/cte., m/co., moneda corriente, cur., currency

me, *pron.* me (dative case)

mear, *vn.* to urinate

mecánicamente, *adv.* mechanically; automatically

mecánica, *f.* mechanics

mecánico, *adj.* mechanical; *m.* mechanic

mecanismo, *m.* mechanism

mecanografía, *f.* typewriting

mecanógrafo, mecanógrafa, *n.* typist

mecedora, *f.* rocking chair

mecer, *va.* to rock

medalla, *f.* medal

mediados, a mediados de, *adv.* about the middle of

mediano, *adj.* moderate; medium

medianoche, *f.* midnight

mediante, *adv.* by means of, through; **Dios mediante,** God willing

mediar, *vn.* to mediate

medicina, *f.* medicine

médico, *m.* physician; **médica,** *adj.* medical

medida, *f.* measure

medidor, *m.* meter; gauge

medio, *adj.* half, halfway; medium, average; **a medias,** by halves; *m.* way, method; medium; middle; **medios,** *m. pl.* means

mediodía, *m.* noon, midday

medir, *va.* to measure; **medirse,** to be moderate

meditación, *f.* meditation

meditar, *va., vn.* to meditate

Mediterráneo, *m.* Mediterranean

megatón, *m.* megaton

mejicano, mejicana, or **mexicano, mexicana,** *n., adj.* Mexican

mejilla, *f.* cheek

mejor, *adj., adv.* better, best; **a lo mejor,** when least expected

mejora, f. improvement

mejorar, va. to improve; vn., vr. to improve (as to health)

mejoría, f. improvement

melancólico, adj. melancholy, sad

melocotón, m. peach

melodía, f. melody

melodioso, adj. melodious

melodrama, m. melodrama

melón, m. melon

mella, f. gap; **hacer mella,** to affect

mellizo, melliza, n., adj. twin

membrete, m. letterhead

membrillo, m. quince

memorable, adj. memorable

memorándum, m. memorandum

memoria, f. memory; memoir; report (of a conference, etc.)

memorial, m. memorial, brief

mencionar, va. to mention

mendigo, m. beggar

menear, va. to stir; **menearse,** (coll.) to wriggle, waddle

menester, m. necessity; **ser menester,** to be necessary

menor, m., f. minor (one under age); adj. less, smaller, minor

menos, adv. less; with exception of; **a lo menos,** or **por lo menos,** at least, however; **venir a menos-,** to grow poor; **a menos que,** unless; **echar de menos** to miss

mensaje, m. message, errand

mensajero, mensajera, n. messenger

menstruación, f. menstruation

mensual, adj. monthly

mensualidad, f. month's allowance; monthly installment

menta, f. (bot.) mint

mental, adj. mental

mentalidad, f. mentality

mentar, va. to mention

mente, f. mind

mentira, f. lie, falsehood; **parecer mentira,** to seem impossible

mentiroso, adj. lying, deceit-ful; **mentiroso, mentirosa,** n. liar

menú, m. bill of fare

menudeo, m. retail

menudo, adj. small; minute; **a menudo,** repeatedly, often; m. small change (money); tripe, entrails

meñique, m. little finger

mercado, m. market

mercancía, f. merchandise

merced, f. favor, mercy; will, pleasure

mercenario, adj. mercenary

mercurio, m. mercury, quicksilver

merendar, vn. to lunch

merengue, m. meringue

meridiano, m. meridian; **pasado meridiano,** afternoon

meridional, adj. southern

merienda, f. luncheon, light repast

mérito, m. merit, desert

merma, f. decrease; waste, leakage; shortage

mes, m. month

mesa, f. table

mesada, f. monthly allowance

meseta, f. landing (of a staircase); tableland, plateau

Mesías, m. Messiah

mestizo, mestiza, adj., n. of mixed blood

meta, f. goal

metáfora, f. metaphor

metal, m. metal; voice timbre

metálico, adj. metallic, metal

metate, m. (Mex.) grinding stone

meter, va. to place, put; to introduce, to insert; **meterse,** to meddle, interfere

meticuloso, adj. conscientious

metiche, m., f. (coll.) prier, meddler

método, m. method

métrico, adj. metrical

metro, m. meter; verse; (Spain, coll.) subway

metrópoli, f. metropolis

Mex. or **Mej., Méjico,** Mex., Mexico

mg., miligramo, mg., milligram

m/g, mi giro, (com.) my draft

mi, *pron.* my; *m.* (mus.) mi

mi, *pron.* me (objective case of the pronoun yo)

microbio, *m.* microbe

micrófono, *m.* microphone

microscopio, *m.* microscope; **microscopio electrónico,** electron microscope

miedo, *m.* fear, dread; **tener miedo,** to be afraid

miel, *f.* honey; **luna de miel,** honeymoon

miembro, *m.* member; limb

mientras, *adv.* in the meantime; while; **mientras tanto,** meanwhile

miércoles, *m.* Wednesday

mierda, *f.* excrement, ordure

miga, *f.* crumb

migaja, *f.* scrap, crumb

mil, *m.* one thousand

milagro, *m.* miracle, wonder

milagroso, *adj.* miraculous

milésimo, *adj.* thousandth

milicia, *f.* militia

miligramo, *m.* milligram

milímetro, *m.* millimeter

militar, *adj.* military

milreis *m.* milreis (Portuguese and Brazilian coin)

milla, *f.* mile

millar, *m.* thousand

millón, *m.* million

millonario, millonaria, *n.* millionaire

mimar, *va.* to flatter, spoil; to fondle, caress

mimbre, *m.* wicker

mimeógrafo, *m.* mimeograph

mina, *f.* mine

mineral, *adj.* mineral

minero, *m.* miner

miniatura, *f.* miniature

mínimo, *adj.* least, smallest

ministerio, *m.* ministry (office), cabinet

ministro, *m.* minister; **Ministro de Estado,** Secretary of State

minoría, minoridad, minority

minucioso, *adj.* meticulous

minúscula, *adj.* small (applied to letters)

minutero, *m.* minute hand

minuto, *m.* minute

mío, mía, *pron.* mine

miope, *n., adj.* nearsighted; near-sighted person

miopía, *f.* nearsightedness

mirada, *f.* glance; gaze

mirar, *va.* to behold, look; to observe; **mirarse,** to look at oneself; to look at one another

mirlo, *m.* blackbird

misa, *f.* mass

misceláneo, *adj.* miscellaneous

miserable, *adj.* miserable, wretched; avaricious

miseria, misery; trifle

misericordia, *f.* mercy

misión, *f.* mission

misionero, *m.* missionary

misterio, *m.* mystery

misterioso, *adj.* mysterious

mitad, *f.* half; middle

mitigar, *va.* to mitigate

mitología, *f.* mythology

mixto, *adj.* mixed, mingled

m/l or **m/L, mi letra,** my letter, my draft

ml., mililitro, ml., milliliter

mm, milímetro, mm., millimeter

m/n, moneda nacional, national currency

moco, *m.* mucus

mocoso, *adj.* sniveling, mucous; **mocoso, mocosa,** *n.* brat

mochila, *f.* knapsack

moda, *f.* fashion, mode

modales, *m. pl.* manners, breeding

moderación, *f.* moderation

moderado, *adj.* moderate

modernista, *adj.* modernistic

modernizar, *va.* to modernize

moderno, *adj.* modern

modestia, *f.* modesty; humility

modesto, *adj.* modest; unassuming

módico, *adj.* moderate, reasonable (as price)

modo, *m.* mode, manner;

mood; **de ningún modo**, by no means

mofa, *f.* mockery

mohoso, *adj.* musty; rusty

mojado, *adj.* wet

molar, *va., vr.* to wet, moisten

molde, *m.* mold; pattern (for a dress. etc.); matrix, cast

moldura, *f.* molding

mole, *m.* (Mex.) spicy sauce for fowl and meat

moler, *va.* to grind

molestar, *va.* to vex, tease; to trouble

molestia, *f.* trouble; inconvenience

molino, *m.* mill; **molino de viento**, windmill

momento, *m.* moment, while

mona, *f.* female monkey

monada, *f.* (coll.) pretty child or thing

monarca, *m.* monarch

monarquía, *f.* monarchy

mondongo, *m.* tripe

moneda, *f.* money, currency

monja, *f.* nun

monje, *m.* monk

monograma, *m.* monogram

monólogo, *m.* monologue

monopolio, *m.* monopoly

monosílabo, *m.* monosyllable

monstruo, *m.* monster

montaña, *f.* mountain

montar, *vn.* to mount (on horseback); to amount to; *va.* to set (as diamonds)

monto, *m.* amount, sum

montón, *m.* heap, pile; **a montones**, abundantly, by heaps

monumento, *m.* monument

mora, *f.* blackberry, mulberry

morada, *f.* abode, residence

morado, *adj.* violet, purple

moral, *f.* morals, ethics; *adj.* moral

moralidad, *f.* morality, morals

moratorio, *f.* moratorium

mórbido, *adj.* morbid

mordaz, *adj.* sarcastic

morder, *va.* to bite

moreno, *adj.* brown, swarthy; brunet

moribundo, *adj.* dying

morir, *vn., vr.* to die, expire

moroso, *adj.* slow, tardy

mortal, *adj.* mortal; deadly

mosaico, *m.* tile

mosca, *f.* fly

mosquitero, *m.* mosquito net

mosquito, *m.* mosquito

mostaza, *f.* mustard

mostrador, *m.* counter

mostrar, *va.* to show, exhibit; **mostrarse**, to appear, show oneself

mota, *f.* powder puff

motín, *m.* mutiny, riot

motocicleta, *f.* motorcycle

motor, *m.* motor, engine

motriz, *adj.* motor, moving

mover, *va.* to move; to stir up

móvil, *m.* motive, incentive

movilizar, *va.* to mobilize

moza, *f.* girl, lass; maidservant

mozo, *m.* youth, lad; waiter

muchacha, *f.* girl, lass

muchacho, *m.* boy, lad

muchedumbre, *f.* crowd

mucho, *adj., adv.* much, abundant

mudar, *va.* to change; to molt; **mudarse**, to change residence

mudo, *adj.* dumb; silent, mute

mueble, *m.* piece of furniture; **muebles**, *pl.* furniture

mueca, grimace

muela, molar tooth

muerte, *f.* death

muerto, *m.* corpse; *adj.* dead

mugre, *f.* dirt

mujer, *f.* woman; wife

mula, *f.* she-mule

mulato, mulata, *n., adj.* mulatto

muleta, *f.* crutch

multa, *f.* fine, penalty

multar, *va.* to fine

multiplicar, *va.* to multiply

mundial, *adj.* world-wide

mundo, *m.* world

municipal, *adj.* municipal

muñeca, *f.* wrist; doll

muralla, *f.* rampart, wall

murciélago, *m.* (zool.) bat

murmullo, *m.* murmur, mutter

murmurar, *vn.* to murmur; to gossip

muro, m. wall
muscular, adj. muscular
músculo, m. muscle
museo, m. museum
musgo, m. moss:
música, f. music
musical, adj. musical
músico, m. musician
mutación, f. mutation
mutuo, adj. mutual, reciprocal
muy, adv. very; greatly
Mzo. or **mzo., marzo,** Mar.,
March

N

N., norte, N., No. or no., north
n/, nuestro, our
nabo, m. turnip
Nac., nacional, nat., national
nácar, m. mother of pearl
nacer, vn. to be born
nacido, adj. born; m. tumor,
abscess
nacimiento, m. birth; Nativity
nación, f. nation
nacional, adj. national
nacionalidad, f. nationality
nada, f. nothing; **de nada,**
don't mention it
nadar, vn. to swim
nadie, pron. nobody, no one
nafta, f. naphtha; (Arg. Urug.)
gasoline
naipe, m. playing card
nalga, f. buttock, rump
Nápoles, m. Naples
naranja, f. orange
naranjada, f. orangeade
naranjado, adj. orange-col-
ored
naranjo, m. orange tree
narciso, m. daffodil
narcótico, adj., m. narcotic
nariz, f. nose
narrar, va. to narrate, tell
nasal, adj. nasal
nata, f. film formed on surface
of milk when boiled: **la tor y
nata,** the cream, the elite
natal, adj. natal, native
natalidad, f. birth rate
natalicio, m. birthday
natilla, f. pl. custard

natividad, f. nativity
nativo, adj. native
natural, adj. natural, native;
unaffected
naturaleza, f. nature
naturalmente, adv. naturally
náusea, f. nausea
navaja, f. razor
naval, adj. naval
navegable, adj. navigable
navegación, f. navigation,
shipping
navegar, vn. to navigate
navidad, f. nativity; **Navidad,**
Christmas
N.B., Nota Bene, (Latin) N.B.,
take notice
n/c., or **n/cta. nuestra cuenta,** (com.) our account
NE, nordeste, NE or N.E.,
northeast
neblina, f. fog; drizzle
nebuloso, adj. foggy, hazy
necedad, f. nonsense
necesario, adj. necessary
necesitar, va., vn. to need
necio, adj. ignorant, silly
néctar, m. nectar
negar, va., vr. to deny, refuse
negativo, adj. negative
negligencia, f. negligence
negociante, m., f. dealer, merchant
negocio, m. business; affair;
negotiation; **hombre de negocios,** businessman
negro, adj. black; n. Negro
nene, nena, n. baby
neoyorquino, neoyorquina,
n., adj. New Yorker
nervio, m. nerve
neto, adj. net
neumático, m. tire
neumonía, f. pneumonia
neutral, adj. neutral
neutralidad, f. neutrality
neutrino, m. neutrino
neutro, adj. neutral, neuter
nevada, f. snowfall
nevar, vn. imp. to snow
nevera, f. icebox
n/f., nuestro favor, our favor
n/g., nuestro giro, (com.) our
draft
niacina, f. niacin

nido, m. nest

niebla, f. fog, mist

nieta, f. granddaughter

nieto, m. grandson

nieve, f. snow

ninfa, f. nymph

ningún, adj. (contraction of **ninguno**), no, not any (used only before masculine nouns); **de ningún modo,** in no way, by no means

ninguno, adj. none, neither; **en ninguna parte,** no place, nowhere

niña, f. little girl; **niña del ojo,** pupil of the eye; **niña de los ojos,** (coll.) apple of one's eye

niñez, f. childhood

niño, adj. childish; m. child, infant

níquel, m. nickel

nítido, adj. neat; clear

nitrato, m. (chem.) nitrate

nitrógeno, m. nitrogen

nivel, m. level, plane

nivelar, va. to level

n/l. or **n/L.,** **nuestra letra,** (com.) our letter, our draft

NNE, **nornordeste,** NNE or N.N.E., north-northeast

NNO, **nornoroeste,** NNW or N.N.W., north-north-west

NO, **noroeste,** NW or N.W., northwest

No. or **N.º,** **número,** no., number

n/o., **nuestra orden,** (com.) our order

no, adv. no; not

noble, adj. noble; illustrious

nobleza, f. nobleness, nobility

noción, f. notion, idea

nocivo, adj. injurious

nocturno, adj. nightly; m. (mus.) nocturne

noche, f. night; **esta noche,** tonight; this evening; **Noche Buena,** Christmas Eve

nombramiento, m. nomination; appointment

nombrar, va. to name; to nominate; to appoint

nombre, m. name; reputation

nominativo, m. (gram.) nominative

non, adj. odd, uneven

nono, adj. ninth

non plus ultra, unexcelled, unsurpassed

nordeste, m. northeast

norma, f. standard, model, rule

nornoroeste, m. northnorthwest

noroeste, m. northwest

norte, m. north; guide

Norteamérica, f. North America

norteamericano, norteamericana, n., adj. North America, a native of U. S. A

Noruega, f. Norway

noruego, noruega, n., adj. Norwegian

nos, pron. dative of we

nosotros, nosotras, pron. we, ourselves

nostalgia, f. homesickess, nostalgia

nota, f. note, notice, remark; bill; **nota bene,** N. B. take notice

notable, adj. remarkable

notar, va. to note, observe, mark

notario, m. notary

noticia, f. notice; knowledge, information, news; **en espera de sus noticias,** (com.) awaiting your reply

noticiario, m. latest news, news report

notificar, va. to notify

notorio, adj. notorious;

Novbre., nov.ᵉ, noviembre, Nov., November

novecientos, novecientas, adj., m. nine hundred

novela, f. novel

novelista, m., f. novelist

novena, f. Novena

noveno, adj. ninth

noventa, m., adj. ninety

novia, f. bride; fiancée

noviembre, m. November

novillo, m. young bull

novio, m. bridegroom; fiancé, sweetheart (male); **viaje de novios,** honeymoon trip

n/r, nuestra remesa, (com.)

our remittance or our shipment

N.S., Nuestro Señor, Our Lord

N.S.J.C., Nuestro Señor Jesucristo, Our Lord Jesus Christ

nuclear, *adj.* nuclear

núcleo, *m.* nucleus, core

nudo, *m.* knot, gnarl

nuera, *f.* daughter-in-law

nuestro, nuestra, *adj., pron.* our, ours

nueva, *f.* news

nueve, *m., adj.* nine

nuez, *f.* walnut; **nuez moscada,** nutmeg

nulidad, *f.* nonentity

nulo, *adj.* null, void

núm., número, no., number

numerar, *va.* to number, numerate

número, *m.* number; cipher

numeroso, *adj.* numerous

nunca, *adv.* never

nupcial, *adj.* nuptial

nupcias, *f., pl.* nuptials, wedding

nutrición, *f.* nutrition, feeding

nutrir, *va.* to nourish

nutritivo, *adj.* nourishing

nylon, *m.* nylon

Ñ

ñame, *m.* (bot.) yam

ñato, ñata, (Sp. Am.) *n., adj.* pug-nosed

O

o, (**ó** when between numbers) *conj.* or

O., oeste, W., West

obedecer, *va.* to obey

obediencia, *f.* obedience

obediente, *adj.* obedient

obertura, *f.* (mus.) overture

obispo, *m.* bishop

objeción, *f.* objection

objetar, *va.* to object, oppose

objetivo, *adj.* objective; *m.* objective, purpose

objeto, *m.* object, thing; purpose

oblicuo, *adj.* oblique

obligación, *f.* obligation

obligado, *adj.* obliged to; obligated

oblongo, *adj.* oblong

obra, *f.* work, deed

obrar, *va.* to work; to operate, act; *vn.* to act; to ease nature

obrero obrera, *n.* day laborer

obsceno, *adj.* obscene

obsequiar, *va.* to regale; to fete; to make a present of

obsequio, *m.* gift

observación, *f.* observation; remark

observador, observadora, *n.* observer; *adj.* observing

observar, *va.* to observe, watch

obstáculo, *m.* obstacle; **obstáculo sónico,** sonic barrier

obstante, participle of **obstar;** **no obstante,** notwithstanding, nevertheless

obstar, *va.* to hinder

obstetricia, *f.* obstetrics

obstruir, *va., vr.* to obstruct

ocasión, *f.* occasion, chance; **de ocasión,** used, secondhand

ocasionar, *va.* to cause, occasion

occidental, *adj.* western

occidente, *m.* occident, west

océano, *m.* ocean

ocio, *m.* leisure; idleness

ocioso, *adj.* idle

octava, *f.* octave

octavo, *adj.* eighth

Octbre, oct.ᵉ, octubre, Oct., October

octubre, *m.* October

oculto, *adj.* hidden, concealed

ocupación, *f.* occupation

ocupado, *adj.* busy; occupied

ocupar, *va., vr.* to occupy, be occupied

ocurrencia, *f.* occurrence, event, incident; witty remark

ochenta, *adj., m.* eighty

ocho, *m., adj.* eight

odiar, *va.* to hate; **odiarse,** to hate one another

oeste, *m.* west; west wind

ofender, *va.* to offend; **ofen-**

derse, to take offense

ofensa, *f.* offensive, injury

oferta, *f.* offer; offering; **oferta y demanda,** supply and demand

oficial, *adj.* official; *m.* officer; official

oficiar, *va.* to officiate

oficina, *f.* office, bureau

oficio, *m.* employ, occupation; business; **oficios,** *pl.* divine service

ofrecer, *va.* to offer; **ofrecerse,** to offer one's services; to present itself

ofrecimiento, *m.* offering, promise

oído, *m.* hearing; ear

oír, *va.* to hear; to listen

ojal, *m.* buttonhole

¡ojalá! *interj.* God grant!

ojeada, *f.* glance, look

ojear, *va.* to eye, view; to glance

ojera, *f.* dark circle under the eye

ojo, *m.* eye; sight; eye of a needle

ola, *f.* wave, billow

oler, *va.* to smell, to scent; *vn.* to smell, to smack of

olivo, *m.* olive tree

olor, *m.* odor, scent

oloroso, *adj.* fragrant, odorous

olvidadizo, *adj.* forgetful

olvidar, *va., vr.* to forget

olla, *f.* kettle

ombligo, *m.* navel

omisión, *f.* omission

omitir, *va.* to omit

ómnibus, *m.* omnibus, bus

omnipotente, *adj.* omnipotent

once, *m., adj.* eleven

onceno, *adj.* eleventh

onda, *f.* wave

ondear, *va., vn.* to undu.late, wave

ondulado, *adj.* wavy

O.N.U., Organización de las Naciones Unidas, U.N., United Nations

onz., onza, oz., ounce

onza, *f.* ounce (weight)

opaco, *adj.* opaque, dark

ópalo, *m.* opal

opción, *f.* option, choice

ópera, *f.* opera

operación, *f.* operation; **operación cesarea,** Caesarean operation

operar, *va., vn.* to operate; **operarse,** (med.) to have an operation

opereta, *f.* operetta

opinar, *va., vn.* to give an opinion

opinión, *f.* opinion

opio, *m.* opium

oporto, *m.* port wine

oportunidad, *f.* opportunity

oportuno, *adj.* opportune

oposición, *f.* opposition

optar, *va.* to choose, elect

óptico, *adj.* optic, optical

optimismo, *m.* optimism

optimista, *m., f.* optimist; *adj.* optimistic

opuesto, *adj.* opposite, contrary

opulencia, *f.* wealth, riches

ora, *conj.* whether, either

oración, *f.* oration, speech; prayer; (gram.) sentence

orador, oradora, *n.* orator, speaker

oral, *adj.* oral

orar, *vn.* to pray

oratoria, *f.* oratory

orbe, *m.* earth, globe

orden, *m.* order, arrangement; *f.* order, command; **a sus órdenes,** at your service

ordenar, *va.* to arrange; to order, command

ordeñar, *va.* to milk

ordinario, *adj.* ordinary, usual, common; coarse

oreja, *f.* ear

orejón, *m.* preserved peach

organdí, *m.* organdy

orgánico, *adj.* organic

organismo, *m.* organism

organización, *f.* organization

organizar, *va.* to organize

órgano, *m.* organ

orgullo, *m.* pride, haughtiness

orgulloso, *adj.* proud, haughty

orientación, *f.* orientation; position

oriental, *adj.* oriental, eastern

orientar, *va.* to orient; **orientarse,** to find one's bearings

oriente, *m.* orient, east

original, *adj.* original, primitive; novel, new; *m.* original, first copy

originalidad, *f.* originality

orina, *f.* urine

orines, *m., pl.* urine

orinar, *vn.* to urinate

ornamento, *m.* ornament

ornar, *va.* to trim, adorn

oro, *m.* gold; money

orquesta, *f.* orchestra

orquídea, *f.* orchid

ortografía, *f.* orthography, spelling

ortopédico, *adj.* orthopedic

oruga, *f.* (bot.) rocket; caterpillar

os, *pron.* dative of you, to you

osa, *f.* she-bear; **Osa Mayor,** (ast.) Great Bear, the Dipper

oscurecer, *va., vn., vr.* to darken; to become dark

oscurecimiento, *m.* blackout; darkening

oscuridad, *f.* darkness; obscurity

oscuro, *adj.* obscure, dark; **a oscuras,** in the dark

oso, *m.* bear

ostentar, *va.* to show, display; *vn.* to boast

ostra, *f.* oyster

otoño, *m.* autumn, fall

otro,otra, adj. another, other; **otra vez,** another time, once again

ovación, *f.* ovation

ovalado, *adj.* oval-shaped

ovario, *m.* ovary

oveja, *f.* sheep

oxidar, *va., vr.* to rust

óxido, *m.* (chem.) oxide

oxígeno, *m.* oxygen; **oxígeno líquido,** liquid oxygen

oyente, *m., f.* listener; **oyentes,** audience

P

pabellón, *m.* pavilion; flag

paciencia, *f.* patience

paciente, *adj., m., f.* patient

pacífico, *adj.* pacific, peaceful

pacto, *m.* contract, pact

padecer, *va.* to suffer

padrastro, *m.* stepfather; hangnail

padre, *m.* father; **padres,** *pl.* parents; ancestors

padrenuestro, *m.* the Our Father, the Lord's Prayer

padrino, *m.* godfather; sponsor, protector

paella, *f.* rice, seafood and chicken dish

pagadero, *adj.* payable

pagano, *m.* heathen, pagan

pagaré, *m.* promissory note; I. O, U

página, *f.* page of a book

pago, *m.* pay, payment; (Arg., Urug.) rural home place

paila, *f.* kettle

país, *m.* country, region

paisaje, *m.* landscape

paisano, paisana, *n.* countryman (or woman)

pájaro, *m.* bird

paje, *m.* page

palabra, *f.* word; **de palabra,** by word of mouth; **tener la palabra,** to have the floor

palacio, *m.* palace

paladar, *m.* palate; taste

palco, *m.* box in a theater

pálido, *adj.* pallid, pale

palillo, *m.* toothpick

paliza, *f.* whipping

palma, *f.* palm of the hand

palmera, *f.* palm tree

palmotear, *vn.* to clap hands, applaud

palo, *m.* stick; cudgel; post; blow with a stick

paloma, *f.* dove, pigeon

palomilla, *f.* (Mex.) boys' gang; one's social crowd

palomita, *f.* squab; **palomitas de maíz,** popcorn

palomo, *m.* cock pigeon

palpar, *va.* to feel, touch; to grope

palpitante, *adj.* palpitating; **cuestión palpitante,** important, live issue

palpitar, *vn.* to palpitate, beat, throb

paludismo, *m.* malaria
pampa, *f.* great plain, prairie
pámpano, *m.* pompano (a fish)
pan, *m.* bread
panadería, *f.* bakery
panadero, panadera, *n.* baker
páncreas, *m.* pancreas
pandereta, *f.* tambourine
pandilla, *f.* gang
pando, *adj.* bulging, convex
pánico, *m.* panic, fright
panorama, *m.* panorama
pantalones, *m. pl.* trousers
pantalla, *f.* screen, fire screen;
lamp shade
panteón, *m.* cemetery
pantera, *f.* panther
pantorrilla, *f.* calf (of the leg)
pantufla, *f.* slipper, shoe
panza, *f.* belly, paunch
pañal, *m.* diaper
paño, *m.* cloth
pañoleta, *f.* bandanna
pañuelo, *m.* handkerchief
papa, *m.* Pope; *f.* potato; soft
food for babies; (coll.) fib, exaggeration
papá, *m.* papa, father
papada, *f.* double chin
papagayo, *m.* parrot
papaya, *f.* papaya
papel, *m.* paper; role, part
papelería, *f.* stationery; stationery store
papeleta, *f.* ballot
paquete, *m.* package, bundle
par, *adj.* par, equal; sin **par**,
matchless; *m.* pair; par
para, *prep.* for, to, in order to
parabién, *m.* congratulation,
felicitation
parabrisa, *m.* windshield
paracaídas, *m.* parachute
parada, *f.* halt; stop, pause;
(mil.) parade
paradero, *m.* whereabouts
parado, *adj.* stopped (as a
clock); (Sp. Am.) standing up
paradoja, *f.* paradox
paraguas, *m.* umbrella
paraíso, *m.* paradise
paralelo, *adj.*, *m.* parallel
parálisis, *f.* paralysis
paralizar, *va.* to paralyze;
stop, impede; **paralizarse**, to

become paralyzed
pararrayo, *m.* lightning rod
parásito, *m.* parasite
parasol, *m.* parasol
parche, *m.* patch; plaster
pardo, *adj.* brown
parecer, *m.* opinion, advice; **al
parecer**, apparently; *vn.* to
appear, seem; **parecerse**, to
resemble
parecido, *m.* resemblance
pared, *f.* wall
pareja, *f.* pair; couple
parentela, *f.* relatives
parentesco, *m.* kingship
pares o nones, *m. pl.* even or
odd
pariente, parienta, *n.* kins-
man, kinswoman
parir, *va.*, *vn.* to give birth
parisiense, *m.*, *f.*, *adj.* Parisian
parodia, *f.* parody
parpadear, *vn.* to blink
párpado, *m.* eyelid
parque, *m.* park
parra, *f.* grapevine
párrafo, *m.* paragraph
parranda, *f.* spree, revel
parrandear, *vn.* to go on a
spree
parrilla, *f.* gridiron, broiler
párroco, *m.* parson
parroquia, *f.* parish
parte, *f.* part; side
partera, *f.* midwife
partición, *f.* partition, division
participación, *f.* participation,
share
participar, *va.*, *vn.* to participate, partake; to communi-
cate
participio, *m.* participle
particular, *adj.* particular,
special; *m.* civilian; topic
partida, *f.* departure; item,
entry; game
partidario, partidaria, *n.* advocate
partido, *m.* party; match; **sa-
carle partido a**, to take advantage of
partir, *va.* to part, divide; *vn.*
to depart; **a partir de**, beginning with
parto, *m.* childbirth

párvulo, *m.* child; **escuela de párvulos,** kindergarten

pasa, *f.* raisin; **ciruela pasa,** prune

pasadero, *adj.* supportable, passable

pasaje, *m.* passage; fare

pasajero, *adj.* transient, transitory; *m.* traveler, passenger

pasaporte, *m.* passport

pasar, *va.* to pass; to suffer; *vn.* to spend (time); *v. imp.* to happen; **pasar por alto,** to overlook; **¿qué pasa?** what is the matter?

pasatiempo, *m.* pastime

Pascua, *f.* Christmas; Easter

pase, *m.* permit

pasear, *va., vn.* to stroll; to ride; **pasearse,** to go out for amusement

paseo, *m.* walk, stroll, ride

pasión, *f.* passion

pasivo, *adj.* passive, inactive; *m.* liabilities of a business house

pasmar, *va.* to benumb; to chill; **pasmarse,** to be astonished

paso, *m.* pace, step; passage

pasta, *f.* paste; dough; binding for books

pastar, *vn.* to pasture

pastel, *m.* pie, cake; cray

pastelero, pastelera, *n.* pastry cook

pasterizar, *va.* to pasteurize

pastilla, *f.* tablet, lozenge

pasto, *m.* pasture

pastor, *m.* shepherd; pastor, minister

pata, *f.* foot and leg of an animal; female duck; **patas arriba,** topsy-turvy

patada, *f.* kick

patán, *m.* yokel, churl

patata, *f.* potato

patear, *va., vn.* to kick, stamp the feet

patente, *adj.* patent, manifest, evident; *f.* patent

paternal, *adj.* paternal

paterno, *adj.* paternal

patético, *adj.* pathetic

patín, *m.* ice skate; **patín de**

ruedas, roller skate

patinar, *vn.* to skate; to skid; to spin

patineta, *f.* scooter

patio, *m.* yard, courtyard

pato, pata, *n.* duck

patria, *f.* native country

patriarca, *m.* patriarch

patriota, *m., f.* patriot

patriotismo, *m.* patriotism

patrocinar, *va.* to favor, sponsor

patrón, *m.* patron; employer; pattern

patrulla, *f.* patrol, squad

pausa, *f.* pause

pausar, *vn.* to pause

pauta, *f.* ruler; standard, model; (mus.) ruled staff

pavimentar, *va.* to pave

pavo, *m.* turkey; **pavo real,** peacock

pavor, *m.* fear, terror

payaso, *m.* clown

paz, *f.* peace

p/cta., por cuenta, (com.) on account, for account

P.D., posdata, P. S., postscript

pdo. or p.dⁿ, pasado, pt., past

peatón, *m.* pedestrian

peca, *f.* freckle, spot

pecado, *m.* sin

pecador, pecadora, *n.* sinner

pecar, *vn.* to sin

peculiar, *adj.* peculiar

pecuniario, *adj.* financial

pecho, *m.* breast; chest; teat; bosom

pechuga, *f.* breast of a fowl

pedagogía, *f.* pedagogy

pedal, *m.* pedal

pedante, *adj.* pedantic

pedazo, *m.* piece, bit

pedestal, *m.* pedestal

pedido, *m.* request, order

pedigüeño, *adj.* beggary

pedir, *va.* to ask, to beg; to demand;

pedir prestado, to borrow

pedrada, *f.* throw of a stone, blow

pegajoso, *adj.* sticky; contagious

pegar, *va.* to cement, stick, paste; to join, unite; to

spank; *vn.* to take root;
pegarse, to adhere

peinado, *m.* hairdressing, coiffure

peinadora, *f.* hairdresser

peinar, *va.*, *vr.* to comb (the hair)

peine, *m.* comb

pelado, pelada, *n.* (Mex.) person of the lower classes; ignorant peasant; *adj.* coarse, vulgar

pelea, *f.* fight, quarrel

pelear, *vn.*, *vr.* to fight

película, *f.* film

peligro, *m.* danger, peril

peligroso, *adj.* dangerous

pelo, *m.* hair; pile; **tomar el pelo,** to tease

pelota, *f.* pelota, ball; **en pelota,** entirely naked

pelotera, *f.* quarrel, brawl, free-for-all

pelotón, *m.* large ball; crowd; (mil.) platoon

peluquería, *f.* barbershop

peluquero, *m.* barber, hairdresser

pellejo, *m.* skin, hide; pelt

pellizcar, *va.* to pinch

pena, *f.* embarrassment; trouble, affliction; **a duras penas,** with difficulty

penal, *adj.* penal

penalidad, *f.* suffering, trouble; penalty

pendiente, *adj.* pending; **pendiente de pago,** unpaid; *m.* pendant; earring, eardrop; *f.* slope, incline

péndulo, *m.* pendulum

pene, *m.* (anat.) penis

península, *f.* peninsula

penitencia, *f.* penitence, penance

penoso, *adj.* distressing, embarrassing

pensar, *vn.* to think; to intend

pensión, *f.* pension; annuity; price of board and tuition; boarding house

pentagrama, *m.* musical staff

peña, *f.* rock, large stone

peón, *m.* laborer; pawn (in chess)

peor, *adj.*, *adv.* worse

pepino, *m.* cucumber

pepita, *f.* kernel; seed of some fruits; distemper in fowl

pequeño, *adj.* little, small; young

percal, *m.* percale

percance, *m.* misfortune

percepción, *f.* perception

percibir, *va.* to perceive, comprehend

percha, *f.* perch; clothes hanger

perder, *va.* to lose; **echar a perder,** to ruin; to spoil; **perderse,** to go astray

pérdida, *f.* loss, damage

perdiz, *f.* partridge

perdón, *m.* pardon, forgiveness

perdonar, *va.* to pardon, forgive

perecer, *vn.* to perish, die

pereza, *f.* laziness

perezoso, *adj.* lazy, idle

perfección, *f.* perfection

perfecto, *adj.* perfect

perfil, *m.* profile

perforadora, *f.* air drill

perforar, *va.* to perforate

perfumar, *va.* to perfume

perfume, *m.* perfume

pericia, *f.* skill, ability

perifonear, *va.* to broadcast (radio)

perilla, *f.* doorknob; goatee; **de perilla,** to the purpose, in time

periódico, *adj.* periodical; *m.* newspaper

periodismo, *m.* journalism

periodista, *m.*, *f.* journalist

periodo, *m.* period, term

periscopio, *m.* periscope

perito, perita, *n.*, *adj.* expert; skillful, experienced

perjudicar, *va.* to injure, hurt

perjudicial, *adj.* harmful, injurious

perjuicio, *m.* damage

perla, *f.* pearl; **de perlas,** just perfect

permanecer, *vn.* to remain, stay

permanente, *adj.* permanent

permiso, *m.* permission

permitir, *va.* to permit, allow; **permitirse**, to take the liberty; **Dios lo permita**, may God will it

perno, *m.* spike, bolt; (mech.) joint pin

pero, *conj.* but, yet, except; *m.* defect, fault; **poner peros**, to find fault

peróxido, *m.* peroxide

perpendicular, *adj.* perpendicular

perpetuo, *adj.* perpetual

perplejo, *adj.* perplexed

perra, *f.* female dog; bitch

perseguir, *va.* to pursue, persecute

perseverancia, *f.* perseverance, constancy

perseverante, *adj.* persevering

perseverar, *vn.* to persevere

persiana, *f.* venetian blind

persignarse, *vr.* to make the sign of the cross

persistente, *adj.* persistent, tenacious

persistir, *vn.* to persist

persona, *f.* person

personaje, *m.* personage; character (in a play)

personal, *adj.* personal; *m.* personnel, staff

personalidad, *f.* personality

perspectiva, *f.* perspective; prospect; sight, outlook

perspicaz, *adj.* perspicacious, keen

persuadir, *va.* to persuade

pertenecer, *vn.* to belong to

perturbar, *va.* to perturb, disturb

peruano, peruana, *adj., n.* Peruvian

perversidad, *f.* perversity

perverso, *adj.* perverse

pervertir, *va.* to pervert, corrupt

pesadez, *f.* heaviness, fatigue

pesadilla, *f.* nightmare

pesado, *adj.* heavy, weighty

pésame, *m.* message of condolence

pesar, *m.* sorrow, grief; regret, repentance; **a pesar de**, in spite of; *vn.* to weigh; to be heavy; *va.* to weigh

pesca, *f.* fishing, fishery

pescado, *m.* fish (when caught; in the water it is **pez**)

pescador, pescadora, *n.* fisher, fisherman (or woman)

pescar, *va.* to fish

pescuezo, *m.* neck

pesebre, *m.* manger

peseta, *f.* monetary unit of Spain

pesimista, *m., f.* pessimist; *adj.* pessimistic

pésimo, *adj.* very bad

peso, *m.* monetary unit of Sp. Am. countries with sign same as the U. S. dollar; weight, heaviness; balance; load

pestaña, *f.* eyelash

pestañear, *vn.* to wink, move the eyelids

peste, *f.* plague; stench

petaca, *f.* (Sp. Am.) suitcase

petate, *m.* straw sleeping mat

petición, *f.* petition, request, plea

petróleo, *m.* petroleum, oil, mineral oil

petunia, *f.* (bot.) petunia

pez, *m.* fish (in the water); *f.* pitch, tar

piadoso, *adj.* pious, merciful

pianista, *m., f.* pianist

piano, *m.* piano; **piano de cola**, grand piano

picadillo, *m.* mincemeat, hash

picadura, *f.* prick; puncture; bite (of an insect or snake)

picaflor, *m.* hummingbird; fickle person

picante, *adj.* sharp, pricking; hot, highly seasoned; piquant

picaporte, *m.* picklock; catch, bolt; doorlatch

picar, *va.* to prick; to sting; to mince; to itch; **picarse**, to be piqued; to be motheaten; to begin to rot (as fruit)

picardía, *f.* roguery; mischievousness

pícaro, *adj.* roguish; mischievous, malicious; *m.* rogue

picazón, f. itching

pico, m. beak; bill; peak; pickax; point; odd; a bit over; **cien dólares y pico,** one hundred and odd dollars; **la una y pico,** few minutes past one (o'clock)

picoso, adj. (Mex. coll.) hot, highly seasoned!

pichón, m. young pigeon; young bird

pie, m. foot; base, foundation; **al pie de la letra,** literally; **ponerse de pie,** to stand up

piedad, f. mercy, pity

piedra, f. stone; gem

pierna, f. leg

pieza, f. piece; piece of furniture; room

pijamas, m. pl. pajamas

pila, f. font; pile, battery; heap; holy water basin; **nombre de pila,** Christian name

pilar, m. pillar

piloto, m. pilot; first mate

pillo, adj. roguish; m. rogue

pimienta, f. pepper

pimpollo, m. sprout, bud

pincel, m. artist's brush

pinchazo, m. puncture; prick

pinta, f. spot, blemish; pint

pintar, va. to paint, picture; to describe; **pintarse,** to paint one's face

pintor, pintora, n. painter, artist

pintoresco, adj. picturesque

pintura, f. painting; picture

pinzas, f. pl. forceps, tweezers

piña, f. pineapple; fir cone

piñata, f. potful of goodies broken by blindfolded children at games

piojo, m. louse

pipa, f. wine cask; tobacco pipe

pirámide, f. pyramid

pirata, m. pirate

piropo, m. compliment, flattery

pisada, f. footstep; footprint; footfall

pisapapeles, m. paperweight

pisar, va. to step, tread, trample

piscina, f. swimming pool

piso, m. floor, story

pisotear, va. to trample

pista, f. trace, footprint; racetrack

pito, m. whistle; **no me importa un pito,** I don't care a straw

pizarrón, m. blackboard

pl., plural, pl. plural

placa, f. plaque; sheet of metal

placer, m. pleasure, delight

plan, m. plan; design, plot

plancha, f. plate; flatiron; slab

planchar, va. to iron

planeador, m. (avi.) glider

planear, vn. to glide

planeta, m. planet

piano, adj. plane, level; m. plane; floorplan; **de piano,** frankly, plainly

planta, f. sole of the foot; plant

plantar, va. to plant; (coll.) to jilt; **plantarse,** to stand firm

plasma, m. plasma

plástico, adj. plastic

plata, f. silver; money

plataforma, f. platform

plátano, m. banana; plantain; plane tree

plateado, adj. silvery; silverplated

platero, m. silversmith

plática f. chat, conversation

platicar, vn. to converse, chat

platillo, m. saucer; side dish; cymbal

Platino, m. platinum

plato, m. dish; plate; **lista de platos,** menu; **plato toca discos,** turntable.

playa, f. shore, beach

plaza, f. square, place; fortified place

plazo, m. term, date of payment; **a plazos,** on credit, on time

plegar, va. to fold; to pleat

plegaria, f. prayer

pleito, m. dispute; lawsuit

plenamente, adv. fully, completely

pliego, m. sheet of paper

plomero, m. plumber

plomo, m. lead (metal)

pluma, *f.* feather, plume; pen

plumaje, *m.* plumage

P.M. or **p.m.,** *pasado meridiano,* P.M., afternoon

p/o or **P.O., por orden,** (com.) by order

población, *f.* population; town

poblado, *m.* town, village

poblar, *va.* to populate, people

pobre, *adj.* poor, indigent; deficient

pobreza, *f.* poverty

poco, *adj.* little, scanty; *m.* a small part; **pocos,** *pl.* few; **poco,** *adv.* little; **hace poco,** a short time ago

podar, *va.* to prune

poder, *m.* power, authority; command; **en poder de,** in the hands of; **por poder,** by proxy; *vn.* to be able; *v. imp.* to be possible

poderoso, *adj.* powerful

podrir, *vn.* **pudrir**

poema, *m.* poem

poesía, *f.* poetry

poeta, *m.* poet

poético, *adj.* poetic

poetisa, *f.* poetess

polaco, polaca, *n.* Pole; *adj.* Polish; *m.* Polish language

polar, *adj.* polar

Polea, *f.* pulley

policía, *f.* police; *m.* policeman

polígamo, polígama, *n., adj.* polygamist

política, *f.* politics; policy

político, *adj.* political; polite; *m.* politician

póliza, *f.* insurance policy

polo, *m.* pole; polo; **polo acuático,** water polo

Polonia, *f.* Poland

polonio, *m.* polonium

polvera, *f.* compact; vanity case

polvo, *m.* powder; dust

pólvora, *f.* gunpowder

polla, *f.* pullet; pool; (coll.) young girl

pollera, *f.* hen-coop; (Sp. Am.) wide skirt; national costume of Panama

pollo, *m.* young chicken; (coll.) young man

pomo, *m.* small bottle

pompón, *m.* pompon

pómulo, *m.* cheekbone

ponche, *m.* punch (drink)

ponchera, *f.* punchbowl

ponderar, *va.* to ponder, consider, weigh; to exaggerate

poner, *va.* to put, to place; to lay eggs; **poner al corriente,** to acquaint (with), to inform; **ponerse,** to become: to set (as the sun, etc.)

poniente, *m.* west; west wind; *adj.* setting (as sun, etc.)

popa, *f.* (naut.) poop, stern

popular, *adj.* popular

popularidad, *f.* popularity

populoso, *adj.* populous

poquito, *adj.* very little; *m.* a little; **poquito a poquito,** little by little

por, *prep.* for, by, about; through; on account of

porcelana, *f.* porcelain, china

porcentaje, *m.* percentage

porción, *f.* part, portion

pordiosero, pordiosera, *n.* beggar

porfiado, *adj.* obstinate

porfiar, *vn.* to dispute obstinately

pormenor, *m.* detail

poro, *m.* pore

porque, *m.* cause, reason

¿por qué? *interr.* why?

portada, *f.* title page, frontispiece

portador, portadora, *n.* carrier, bearer

portal, *m.* porch; portico, piazza

portamonedas, *m.* purse, pocketbook

portar, *va.* to carry; to bear (arms, etc.); **portarse,** to behave, comport oneself

portátil, *adj.* portable

porte, *m.* portage, freight, postage; bearing, carriage

portero, portera, *n.* porter, janitor or janitress, concierge

portuario, portuaria, *adj.* relating to a seaport

porvenir, *m.* future

posada, *f.* boardinghouse; inn,

hotel; (Mex.) pre-Christmas party

posar, vn. to lodge; to sit down, repose

posdata, f. postscript

poseer, va. to possess, own

posesión, f. possession

posesivo, adj. possessive

posibilidad, f. possibility

posible, adj. possible

posición, f. position, place; posture; situation

positivo, adj. positive

posponer, va. to postpone

postal, adj. postal; **paquete postal,** parcel post

poste, m. post, pillar

postema, f. abscess, tumor

postergar, va. to defer, delay

posteridad, f. posterity

posterior, adj. back, rear

posteriormente, adv. later, subsequently

postizo, adj. artificial, false

postrarse, vr. to prostrate oneself; to kneel down

postre, adj. last in order; **a la postre,** at last; m. dessert

potasa, f. potash

pote, m. pot, jar; flowerpot

potencia, power; strength

potente, adj. potent, powerful, mighty

pozo, m. well; (min.) shaft, pit

P.P., porte pagado, p.p. postpaid

p. p., por poder, (law) by power of attorney or by proxy

ppdo., p.pdo or **p.ºp.ᵈº, próximo pasado,** in the past month

practicante, m., f. (med.) intern

practicar, va. to practice; to exercise

práctico, adj. practical; skillful

precaución, f. precaution

precaver, va. to prevent, guard against

precedente, adj. precedent, foregoing

preceder, va. to precede

preciar, va. to value, appraise; **preciarse de,** to take pride

in, boast

precio, m. price, value

precioso, adj. precious; beautiful

precipitación, f. inconsiderate haste

precipitar, va. to precipitate; **precipitarse,** to run headlong to one's destruction

precisar, va. to compel, oblige; to necessitate; to state

precisión, f. preciseness; **con toda precisión,** on time, very promptly

preciso, adj. necessary, requisite; precise

precoz, adj. precocious

precursor, precursora, n. forerunner; adj. preceding

predicado, m. predicate

predicador, m. preacher

predicción, f. prediction

predilecto, adj. favorite

predispuesto, adj. biased, predisposed

predominar, va., vn. to predominate, prevail

prefacio, m. preface

preferencia, f. preference; **de preferencia,** preferably

preferente, adj. preferred, preferable

preferible, adj. preferable

preferir, va. to prefer

pregunta, f. question, inquiry

preguntar, va. to question, inquire

preguntón, preguntona, n. inquisitive person; adj. inquisitive

prehistórico, adj. prehistoric

prejuicio, m. prejudice

preliminar, adj., m. preliminary

preludio, m. prelude

prematuro, adj. premature

premeditar, va. to premeditate

premiar, va. to reward, remunerate

premio, m. reward, prize, recompense; (com.) premium; interest

prenda, f. pledge, forfeit; pawn; piece of jewelry

prender, va. to seize, catch; to imprison; vn. to catch or take fire; to take root

prensa, f. press, newspapers

preocupar, va. to preoccupy; **preocuparse**, to care about, worry

prep., preposición, prep., preposition

preparación, f. preparation

preparar, va., vr. to prepare

preparativo, m. preparation

preposición, f. (gram.) preposition

prerrogativa, f. prerogative, privilege

presa, f. capture, seizure; prey; dike, dam

prescribir, va. to prescribe

presencia, f. presence

presenciar, va. to witness, see

presentación, f. presentation, introduction

presentar, va. to present, introduce; **presentarse**, to appear; to introduce oneself

presente, adj. present; m. present, gift; instant; **el 20 del presente**, the 20th instant; **hacer presente**, to call attention; **la presente**, the present writing; **tener presente**, to bear in mind

presentimiento, m. presentiment, misgiving

presentir, va. to have a presentiment

preservación, f. preservation

preservar, va. to preserve

presidencia, f. presidency; chairmanship

presidente, m. president; chairman

presidiario, m. convict

presidio, m. prison

presidir, va. to preside

presión, f. pressure, pressing; **presión arterial**, blood pressure

préstamo, m. loan

presto, adj. quick, prompt, ready; adv. soon, quickly

presumido, adj. presumptuous, arrogant

presupuesto, m. estimate; budget

pretender, va. to pretend, claim; to try, attempt

pretendiente, · m. pretender; suitor; candidate, office seeker

pretérito, adj. preterit, past

pretexto, m. pretext, pretense

prevención, f. prevention

prevenir, va. to prepare; to foresee; to prevent; to warn; **prevenirse**, to be prepared

preventivo, adj. preventive

prever, va. to foresee

previo, adj. previous

provisión, f. foresight

previsor, adj. foreseeing, farseeing

prieto, adj. brackish, very dark; **prieta**, n. very dark person

prima, f. (mus.) treble; (com.) premium; female cousin

primario, adj. first; **escuela primaria**, elementary school

primavera, f. spring (the season)

primeramente, adv. in the first place, mainly

primero, adj. first, prior, former; **primeros auxilios**, first aid

primitivo, adj. primitive, original

primo, prima, n. cousin

primogénito, primogénita, adj., n. first-born

primoroso, adj. exquisite

princesa, f. princess

principal, adj. principal, main

príncipe, m. prince

principiar, va. to begin

principio, m. beginning; principle

prioridad, f. priority

prisa, f. hurry; haste; **a toda prisa**, at full speed; **darse prisa**, to hurry; **tener prisa**, to be in a hurry

prisión, f. prison; duress

prisionero, prisionera, n. prisoner

privado, adj. private

privar, va., vr. to deprive; to prohibit

privilegiado, *adj.* privileged

pro, *m.* or *f.* profit, benefit, advantage; **en pro de**, in behalf of; **el pro y el contra**, the pro and con

proa, *f.* (naut.) prow, bow

probabilidad, *f.* probability

probable, *adj.* probable, likely

probar, *va.* to try; to prove; to taste; *vn.* to suit, agree; **probarse**, to try on (clothes)

problema, *m.* problem

problemático, *adj.* problematical

procedencia, *f.* origin, source

procedente, *adj.* coming from, proceeding from

proceder, *m.* procedure; *vn.* to proceed, go on; to issue

procesar, *va.* to prosecute; to indict

procesión, *f.* procession

proceso, *m.* process, lawsuit

proclamar, *va.* to proclaim

procurador, *m.* procurer; solicitor; attorney; **procurador publico**, attorney at law; **Procurador General**, Attorney General

prodigar, *va.* to waste, lavish

pródigo *adj.* prodigal

producción, *f.* production

producir, *va.* to produce, yield

productiveo, *adj.* productive, fertile; profitable

producto, *m.* product; amount

prof., profesor, prof., professor; **profeta**, prophet

profecía, *f.* prophecy

profesión, *f.* profession

profesor, profesora, *n.* professor, teacher

profesorado, *m.* body of teachers, faculty

profeta, *m.* prophet

profundidad, *f.* profoundness; depth; **carga de profundidad**, (mil.) ash can (depth charge)

progenitor, *m.* ancestor, forefather

programa, *m.* program

progresar, *vn.* to progress, to improve

progreso, *m.* progress, ad-

vancement

prohibición, *f.* prohibition

prohibir, *va.* to prohibit, forbid

prójimo, *m.* fellow creature; neighbor

prole, *f.* issue, offspring

prólogo, *m.* prologue

promedio, *m.* average

promesa, *f.* promise; pious offering

prometer, *va.* to promise, assure; *vn.* to be promising

prometido, prometida, *n.,* *adj.* betrothed

prominente, *adj.* prominent

promoción, *f.* promotion

premover, *va.* to promote, further

pronombre, *m.* pronoun,

pronosticar, *va.* to predict, foretell

prontitud, *f.* promptness

pronto, *adj.* prompt, ready; soon; *adv.* promptly; quickly

pronunciar, *va.* to pronounce; **pronunciarse**, to rebel

propaganda, *f.* propaganda; advertising

propagandista, *m., f., adj.* propagandist

propagar, *va., vr.* to propagate, spread, disseminate

propicio, *adj.* propitious favorable

propiedad, *f.* property; propriety

propietario, *adj.* proprietary; *m.* proprietor; **propietaria**, *f.* proprietress

propina, *f.* tip, gratuity

propio, *adj.* proper; own; characteristic

proponer, *va.* to propose, suggest; **proponerse**, to intend, plan, be determined

proporción, *f.* proportion

proporcionar, *va.* to proportion; to adjust, adapt; to provide, supply

proposición, *f.* proposition

propósito, *m.* purpose; **a propósito**, adequate, fitting; **de propósito**, on purpose; **a propósito de**, apropos of

propuesta, *f.* proposal, offer, proposition; nomination

prorrata, *f.* quota; **a prorrata**, in proportion

prórroga, *f.* extension, renewal

prosa, *f.* prose

prosaico, *adj.* prosaic

proseguir, *va.* to pursue, prosecute; to continue

prosperar, *vn.* to prosper, thrive

prosperidad, *f.* prosperity

próspero, *adj.* prosperous

prostituta, *f.* prostitute

protección, *f.* protection

protector, protectora, *n.* protector

proteger, *va.* to protect

protegido, protegida, *n.* protegé

proteína, *f.* protein

protesta, *f.* protest

protestante, *n., adj.* Protestant

protestar, *va.* to protest

protocolo, *m.* protocol

prototipo, *m.* prototype

protuberancia, *f.* bulge

provecho, *m.* profit, benefit

provechoso, *adj.* beneficial

proveer, *va.* to provide; to provision

proverbio, *m.* proverb

providencia, *f.* providence

provincia, *f.* province

provocar, *va.* to provoke

prox., próximo, next, nearest

próximamente, *adv.* very soon; shortly

próximo, *adj.* next, nearest, following

proyectar, *va.* to project, plan

proyectil, *m.* projectile

proyecto, *m.* project, plan

proyector, *m.* projector; spotlight

prudente, *adj.* prudent, cautious

P. S., posdata, P.S., postscript

psiquiatría, *f.* psychiatry

pte., presente, pres. present

pto., puerto, pt., port; **punto**, pt., point

publicación, *f.* publication

publicar, *va.* to publish, reveal

publicidad, *f.* publicity

público, *adj.* public; *m.* attendance, audience

pudiente, *adj.* rich, opulent

pudín, *m.* pudding

pudor, *m.* modesty, decorum

pudrir, *vn.* to rot

pueblo, *m.* town, village; populace

puente, *m.* bridge; **puente aéreo**, airlift

puerca, *f.* sow

pueril, *adj.* childish

puerta, *f.* door, gateway

pues, *conj.* as, since, because, for; *adv.* then, therefore

puesta, *f.* (ast.) set, setting; **puesta del sol**, sunset

puesto, *m.* place; post; employment; booth; **puesto, puesta**, *adj.* put, set, placed; **puesto que**, since

pujar, *va.* to outbid; to push ahead, push through

pulcro, *adj.* neat, tidy

pulga, *f.* flea

pulgada, *f.* inch

pulmón, *m.* lung; **pulmón de acero**, iron lung

pulmonía, *f.* pneumonia

púlpito, *m.* pulpit

pulsera, *f.* bracelet

pulverizador, *m.* atomizer

pulverizar, *va.* to pulverize, to spray

punta, *f.* point, tip; **punta de combate**, warhead

puntada, *f.* stitch

puntapié, *m.* kick

puntería, *f.* aiming (of firearms); marksmanship

puntiagudo, *adj.* sharp-pointed

puntilla, *f.* small point; **de puntillas**, on tiptoe

punto, *m.* period; point, end; dot; **estar a punto de**, to be about to; **son las dos en punto**, it is exactly two o'clock

puntual, *adj.* punctual

punzada, *f.* prick, sting; sharp pain

puñado, *m.* handful

puñal, *m.* poniard, dagger

puño, *m.* fist; cuff
pupila, *f.* eyeball, pupil
pupilo, *m.* pupil; scholar; boarder; orphan ward (boy)
pupitre, *m.* writing desk
purga, *f.* physic; purge
purgar, *va.* to purge, purify; to administer a physic; to atone
purgatorio, *m.* purgatory
pus, *m.* pus, matter
puta, *f.* whore
pza.: pieza, pc. piece

g

q.e.p.d., que en paz descanse, may (he, she) rest in peace
ql. or **q.**[1]**, quintal,** cwt., hundred-weight
qq., quintales, cwts., hundred-weights
que, *relative pron.* that, which, who, whom; **qué,** *interrogative and exclamatory pron.* what; how; **no hay de que,** don't mention it; *conj.* that; than; whether; because
quebrada, *f.* brook
quebrado, *m.* (math.) fraction; *adj.* broken; bankrupt
quebrar, *va., vr.* to break; *vn.* to fail
quedar, *vn.* to stay, remain; to be left
quedo, *adj.* quiet, still; *adv.* softly, gently
quehacer, *m.* occupation, work; task, chore
queja, *f.* complaint
quejarse, *vr.* to complain of; to moan
quejido, *m.* groan, moan
quemar, *va., vr.* to burn; to kindle; *vn.* to be too hot
querella, *f.* complaint; quarrel
querer, *va.* to wish, desire; to like, love; **querer decir,** to mean, signify; **sin querer,** unwillingly; **Dios quiera,** God grant
querido, *adj.* dear, beloved; *n.* darling, lover
quetzal, *m.* (orn.) quetzal; monetary unit of Guatemala

quiebra, *f.* bankruptcy
quien, *pron.* who, which; **¿quién?** who?
quienquiera, *pron.* whoever
quieto, *adj.* quiet, still
quietud, *f.* quietness, peace
quím., química, chem., chemistry
química, *f.* chemistry
químico, *m.* chemist; *adj.* chemical
quince, *adj., m.* fifteen
quincena, *f.* fortnight; semimonthly pay
quincenal, *adj.* semimonthly
quinientos, quinientas, *adj., m.* five hundred
quinina, quinine
quinta, country house; (mus.) fifth
quintal, *m.* hundredweight
quinto, *m., adj.* fifth
quintuplo, *adj.* quintuple, fivefold
quirófano, *m.* operating room
quirúrgico, *adj.* surgical
quitar, *va.* to remove, take away
quizá, *adv.* perhaps

R

R., Reverendo, Rev., Reverend; **Respuesta,** reply; **Reprobado,** not passing (in an examination)
rabia, *f.* rage, fury
rabioso, *adj.* rabid; furious
rabo, *m.* tail
racimo, *m.* bunch, cluster (of grapes, etc.)
raciocinio, *m.* reasoning
racional, *adj.* rational; reasonable
radar, *m.* radar
radiación, *f.* radiation
radiador, *m.* radiator
radical, *adj.* radical; *m.* (math.) radical; extremist
radicar, *vn.* to take root; **radicarse,** to take root; to settle, establish oneself
radio, *m.* or *f.* radio, receiver; radio broadcasting station; (math., anat.) radius; (chem.)

radium

radiodifusión, f. radio broadcasting

radiodifusora, f. broadcasting station

radioescucha, m., f. radio listener

radiorreceptor, m. radio receiving set

radiotelescopio, m. radio telescope

radioyente, m., f. radio listener

raja, f. splinter, chip of wood; slice (of fruit); fissure, crack

rajar, va. to split, chop

ralo, adj. thin, sparse

rama, f. branch (of a tree, of a family)

ramal, m. ramification

ramillete, m. bouquet

ramo, m. branch (of a tree); branch (of trade, art, etc.); bouquet

rampa, f. slope, ramp

rana, f. frog

rancio, adj. rank, rancid

ranchero, m. small farmer

rango, m. rank

ranura, f. groove

rapidez, f. rapidity, speed

rapiña, f. rapine, robbery; **ave de rapiña**, bird of prey

rapsodia, f. rhapsody

raqueta, f. racket; **de raqueta nieve**, snowshoe

raquítico, adj. rickety

rascacielos, m. skyscraper

rascar, va. to scratch, scrape

rasgado, adj. torn, open; **boca rasgada**, wide mouth; **ojos rasgados**, large eyes

rasgar, va. to tear, rend

rasgo, m. dash, stroke; kind gesture; feature, trait

rasguño, m. scratch

raso, m. satin, sateen; **raso, rasa**, adj. plain; flat

raspar, va. to scrape, rasp

rastrillo, m. hammer of a gun; rake

rastro, m. track; sledge; slaughterhouse; sign, token; trail

rata, f. (zool.) rat

ratero, adj. mean, vile; m. pickpocket

ratificar, va. to ratify

rato, m. while; moment

ratón, m. mouse

raya, f. stroke; stripe; streak; line; dash (in punctuation)

rayado, adj. striped

rayar, va. to draw lines, rule; to stripe; **rayar en**, to border on

rayo, m. ray, beam of light; flash of lightning; radius; **rayo equis**, X ray

rayón, m. rayon

raza, f. race, lineage

razón, f. reason; cause, motive; ratio, rate; **razón social**, firm name; **dar razón**, to inform, give account; **tener razón**, to be right

rezonable, adj. reasonable

razonamiento, m. reasoning

reacción, f. reaction; **propulsión por reacción**, jet propulsion

reaccionar, vn. to react

real, adj. real, actual; royal; **pavo real**, peacock

realce, m. luster, enhancement; **dar realce**, to highlight, give importance to

realidad, f. reality, fact

realismo, m. realism

realización, f. realization, fulfillment; bargain sale

realizar, va. to realize, fulfill

realmente, adv. really

realzar, va. to raise, elevate; to emboss; to heighten

reanudar, va. to renew, resume

rebaja, f. deduction; reduction, rebate

rebajar, va. to lessen, curtail; to lower (as price); **rebajarse**, to humble oneself

rebanada, f. slice

rebaño, m. flock of sheep, herd of cattle, drove

rebelarse, vr. to rebel

rebelde, m. rebel; adj. rebellious

rebotar, va. to repel; vn. to rebound

rebozo, *m.* woman's shawl

rebuznar, *vn.* to bray

recado, *m.* message

recaída, *f.* relapse

recalcar, *va.* to emphasize

recámara, *f.* boudoir, bed-room; chamber of a gun

recapacitar, *va.* to think over, meditate

recatado, *adj.* prudent, modest

recelo, *m.* suspicion, mistrust

recepción, *f.* reception

receptor, *m.* radio receiver

receso, *m.* withdrawal, retirement; recess

receta, *f.* recipe; prescription

recetar, *va.* to prescribe

recibir, *va.* to receive; to let in; to go to meet; **recibirse,** to graduate in a profession

recibo, *m.* receipt, voucher

recién, *adv.* recently, lately; **recién casado, recién casada,** newlywed

recio, *adj.* stout, strong; *adv.* loudly

recipiente, *m.* recipient, container

reciprocidad, *f.* reciprocity

recíproco, *adj.* reciprocal

recitar, *va.* to recite

reclamar, *va.* to claim, demand

recluir, *va., vr.* to seclude

reclutar, *va.* to recruit

recobrar, *va.* to recover

recoger, *va.* to take back; to gather, pick up; to shelter; **recogerse,** to take shelter or refuge; to retire, to rest

recomendación, *f.* recommendation

recomendar, *va.* to recommend

recompensa, *f.* recompense

reconciliación, *f.* reconciliation

reconciliar, *va., vr.* to reconcile

reconocer, *va.* to examine closely; to acknowledge favors received; to admit; to recognize; (mil.) to reconnoiter

reconocimiento, *m.* recogni-

tion; gratitude; reconnaissance; **reconocimiento médico,** medical examination

reconstituyente, *m.* (med.) tonic

reconstruir, *va.* to reconstruct

recopilar, *va.* to compile; to abridge

recordar, *va., vr.* to remind; to remember; *vn.* to call to mind

recorrer, *va.* to run over, peruse; to travel over

recorrido, *m.* run, line; expedition

recortar, *va.* to cut away, trim

recorte, *m.* cutting; **recorte de periódico,** newspaper clipping

recostar, *va.* to lean against; **recostarse,** to recline, rest

recrear, *va., vr.* to amuse, delight, recreate

recreo, *m.* recreation, pleasure; recess

rectamente, *adv.* justly, rightly

rectángulo, *m.* rectangle

rectificar, *va.* to rectify

recto, *adj.* straight, direct, right; just

recuerdo, *m.* remembrance, memory; souvenir; **recuerdos,** *pl.* regards

recuperar, *va.* to recover; **recuperarse,** to recover from sickness

recurso, *m.* recourse; resource; **recursos,** *pl.* means

rechazar, *va.* to repel, reject

red, *f.* net; web; network

redacción, *f.* editing; editor's office; editorial staff

redactar, *va.* to edit (a publication); to draw up, draft

redactor, *m.* editor

redimir, *va.* to redeem

redondo, *adj.* around; **a la redonda,** all around

reducción, *f.* reduction

reducir, *va.* to reduce

redundante, *adj.* redundant

reelección, *f.* re-election

reelegir, *va.* to re-elect

ref., referencia, ref., reference

refacción, *f.* repair; **piezas de**

refacción, spare parts
referencia, *f.* reference
referer, *va.* to refer, relate; **refererse,** to refer to, relate to
refinamiento, *m.* refinement
refinar, *va.* to refine
reflector, *m.* reflector, search light
reflejar, *va., vr.* to reflect
reflejo, *m.* reflex; reflection, light, glare
reflexionar, *vn.* to reflect, meditate
reforma, *f.* reform
reformar, *va., vr.* to reform, correct
reforzar, *va., vr.* to strengthen, fortify
refrán, *m.* proverb, saying
refrenar, *va.* to refrain, restrain
refrescante, *adj.* refreshing
refrescar, *va.* to refresh; *vn.* to cool; to take the air
refresco, *m.* refreshment; cold drink
refrigerador, *m.* refrigerator
refrigerar, *va.* to refrigerate
refuerzo, *m.* reinforcement
refugiado, refugiada, *n.* refugee
refugiar, *va.* to shelter; **refugiarse,** to take refuge
refuñufuñar, *vn.* to grumble
regadera, *f.* watering pot, sprinkler; (Sp. Am.) **baño de regadera,** shower bath
regalar, *va.* to make a present of
regalo, *m.* present, gift
regañar, *va.* to scold
regar, *va.* to water, irrigate; to spread
regateo, *m.* bargaining, act of haggling
regenerar, *va., vr.* to regenerate
regidor, *m.* governor, prefect
régimen, *m.* regime
regimiento, *m.* regiment
regio, *adj.* royal, kindly
región, *f.* region
regir, *va.* to rule, govern, direct; *vn.* to be in force
registrar, *va.* to register; in-

spect; to search; to record
registro, *m.* register, registration; record; inspection
regla, *f.* rule, statute, ruler
reglamento, *m.* by-law; regulations
regresar, *vn.* to return, go back
regreso, *m.* return, regression
regular, *va.* to regulate, adjust; *adj.* regular; ordinary
regularidad, *f.* regularity
rehabilitar, *va., vr.* to rehabilitate
rehusar, *va.* to refuse, decline
reina, *f.* queen
reinado, *m.* reign
reinar, *va.* to reign
reino, *m.* kingdom, reign
reintegrar, *va., vr.* to reintegrate, to restore
reir, *vn.* to laugh; **reirse de,** to laugh at
reiterar, *va.* to reiterate, repeat
reja, *f.* lattice; grating; railing
rejuvenecer, *vn.* to be rejuvenated
relación, *f.* relation; report; account; **relaciones,** connections
relacionar, *va.* to relate; to connect; to make acquainted
relámpago, *m.* flash of lightning
relatar, *va.* to relate
relatividad, *f.* relativity
relativo, *adj.* relative, pertaining
relato, *m.* account, narrative
relegar, *va.* to relegate, banish
relevar, *va.* to relieve, substitute
relevo, *m.* (mil.) relief
relieve, *m.* relief (sculpture); **bajo relieve,** bas-relief; **dar relieve,** to emphasize, highlight
religión, *f.* religion
religioso, *adj.* religious
reloj, *m.* clock, watch; **de reloj pulsera,** wrist watch
relojero, *m.* watchmaker
relucir, *vn.* to shine, glitter
rellenar, *va.* to refill; to stuff

remachar, *va.* to rivet

remangar, *va.* to tuck up (sleeves, dress, etc.)

remar, *vn.* to row

remetado, *adj.* utterly ruined; **loco remetado,** stark mad

rematar, *va.* to sell at auction; to finish

remate, *m.* end, conclusion; auction sale; **de remate,** absolutely, hopelessly

remediar, *va.* to remedy; to prevent

remedio, *m.* remedy, reparation; **sin remedio,** inevitable

remendar, *va.* to patch, mend

remesa, *f.* sending of goods; remittance of money

remiendo, *m.* patch, repair

reminiscencia, *f.* reminiscence

remitente, *m., f.* remitter, shipper, sender

remitir, *va.* to send, transmit

remojar, *va.* to soak

remolacha, *f.* beet

remolino, *m.* whirlwind; whirlpool

rémora, *f.* hindrance, cause of delay

remordimiento, *m.* remorse

remoto, *adj.* remote, distant

remunerar, *va.* to remunerate

Renacimiento, *m.* Renaissance

rencor, *m.* rancor, grudge

rendija, *f.* crevice, crack

rendir, *va.* to produce, yield; **rendirse,** to be fatigued; to surrender

renegar, *va.* to deny, disown; *vn.* to curse

renglón, *m.* written or printed line; (com.) part of one's income; items

reno, *m.* reindeer

renombre, *m.* renown

renovar, *va.* to renew, renovate, reform

renta, *f.* rent, income

renuncia, *f.* resignation

reñir, *va., vn.* to wrangle; to quarrel

reo, *m.* offender, criminal

Rep., República, Rep. Repub-lic

reparar, *va.* to repair; to consider, serve

repartir, *va.* to distribute

reparto, *m.* distribution; (theat.) cast of characters

repasar, *va., vn.* to revise, review

repaso, *m.* revision, review

repente, de repente, *adv.* suddenly

repentino, *adj.* sudden

repercusión, *f.* reverberation, repercussion

repetición, *f.* repetition

repetir, *va.* to repeat

repicar, *va.* to chime

repleto, *adj.* replete

réplica, *f.* reply, answer

replicar, *vn.* to reply, answer; to argue

repollo, *m.* cabbage head

reponer, *va.* to replace; to restore; **reponerse,** to recover lost health

reposo, *m.* rest, repose

representación, *f.* representation; performance

representante, *m., f.* representative

representar, *va.* to represent; to play on the stage

represión, *f.* repression

reprimir, *va.* to repress

reprochar, *va.* to reproach

reproducir, *va.* to reproduce

reptil, *m.* reptile

república, *f.* republic

repuesto, *m.* replacement; **piezas de repuesto,** spare parts

repugnante, *adj.* repugnant

reputación, *f.* reputation

requerir, *va.* to request, demand; to summon; to require

requisito *m.* requisite, requirement

res, *f.* head of cattle; beast; **carne de res,** beef

resaca, *f.* undertow

resaltar, *vn.* to rebound; to stand out; to be evident

resbalar, *va., vr.* to slip, slide

rescate, *m.* ransom

resentimiento, *m.* resentment

resentirse, *vr.* to resent

reseña, *f.* brief description

reserva, *f.* reserve; reservation; **con** or **bajo la mayor reserva,** in strictest confidence

reservado, *adj.* reserved, cautious

reserver, *va.* to reserve

resfriado, *m.* cold (disease)

resfriarse, *vr.* to catch cold

residencia, *f.* residence

residente, *m., f.* resident

residuo, *m.* residue

resignarse, *vr.* to be resigned

resistencia, *f.* resistance

resistir, *vn., va.* to resist, bear; to oppose

resolución, *f.* resolution

resolver, *va., vr.* to resolve, decide

resollar, *vn.* to breathe

resorte, *m.* spring (elastic body)

respaldar, *va.* to indorse; *m.* back (of seats)

respaldo, *m.* indorsement; back of a seat

respecto, *m.* relation, respect; **a** or **con respecto a,** in regard to

respetable, *adj.* respect

respetar, *va.* to respect

respetuoso, *adj.* respectful

respirar, *vn.* to breathe

resplandor, *m.* splendor, brilliance; light

responder, *va.* to answer

resbonsabilidad, *f.* responsibility

responsable, *adj.* responsible

respuesta, *f.* answer, reply

restante, *m.* rest, remainder

restar, *va.* to subtract; *vn.* to be left, remain

restaurante, *m.* restaurant

restaurar, *va.* to restore

restregar, *va.* to scrub, rub

restricción, *f.* restriction

restringir, *va.* to restrain

resucitar, *va., vn.* to revive

resuello, *m.* breath, breathing

resultado, *m.* result

resultar, *vn.* to result

resumen, *m.* summary

resumir, *va.* to resume

retar, *va.* to challenge

retardar, *va.* to retard, delay

retazo, *m.* remnant

retener, *va.* to retain

retina, *f.* retina

retirar, *va.* to withdraw, retire; **retirarse,** to retire, reretreat

reto, *m.* challenge

retocar, *va.* to retouch (a painting or a photograph)

retoño, *m.* sprout, shoot

retoque, *m.* finishing stroke; retouching

retórica, *f.* rhetoric

retornar, *va. vn.* to return, give back

retorno, *m.* return

retrasar, *va.* to defer, put off; **retrasarse,** to be late; to be backward

retraso, *m.* lateness; delay

retratar, *va.* to draw a portrait of; to photograph

retrato, *m.* portrait, photograph; effigy

retrete, *m.* water closet

retribución, *f.* retribution

reuma, *f.* rheumatism

reunión, *n. f.* meeting

reunir, *va., vr.* to reunite

reventar, *vn.* to burst

reverencia, *f.* reverence, respect; bow, curtsy

reverendo, *adj.* reverend

reverso, *m.* reverse

revés, *m.* reverse, wrong side; misfortune; **al revés,** backwards; inside out

revisar, *va.* to revise, review

revista, *f.* revision, review; magazine

revivir, *vn.* to revive

revolcarse, *vr.* to wallow

revolución, *f.* revolution

revolucionario, *adj., m.* revolutionary

revolver, *va.* to stir

revólver, *m.* revolver

rey, *m.* king

rezagado, *adj.* left behind; **cartas rezagadas,** unclaimed letters

rezar, *va.* to pray

riboflavina, *f.* riboflavin

rico, *adj.* rich, wealthy; delicious

ridiculizar, *va.* to ridicule
ridículo, *adj.* ridiculous
riego, *m.* irrigation, watering
riel, *m.* rail
rienda, *f.* rein of a bridle; **a rienda suelta**, without restraint
riesgo, *m.* risk, jeopardy
rifa, *f.* raffle, lottery
riguroso, *adj.* strict
rimar, *va., vn.* to rhyme
rinoceronte, *m.* rhinoceros,
riñón, *m.* kidney
río, *m.* river, stream
R. I. P., Requiescat In Pace, may (he, she) rest in peace
riqueza, *f.* riches, wealth
risa, *f.* laugh, laughter
risueño, *adj.* smiling, pleasant
ritmo *m.* rhythm; tempo
rito, *m.* rite, ceremony
rival, *m.*rival, competitor
rizo, *m.* curl, frizzle
róbalo or **robalo**, *m.* (zool.) bass
roble, *m.* oak tree
robo, *m.* robbery, theft
roca, *f.* rock, cliff
rociar, *va.* to sprinkle
rocío, *m.* dew
rodar, *vn.* to roll
rodear, *vn.* to encompass
rodilla, *f.* knee
rodillo, *m.* roller, cylinder
rogar, *va.* to entreat, beg; to pray
rojo, *adj.* red; ruddy; **Rojo**, *m.* Red (communist)
rol, *m.* list; roll; catalogue
rollo, *m.* roll; spiral
Roma, *f.* Rome
romance, *adj.* romance; *m.* Romance language; ballad; novel of chivalry
romano, romana, *adj., n.* Roman
romanticismo, *m.* romanticism
romántico, *adj.* romantic; *m.* romanticist
rompecabezas, *m.* riddle, puzzle
ron, *m.* rum
roncar, *vn.* to snore
ronquera, *f.* hoarseness

ropa, *f.* clothing
ropero, *m.* clothes closet
rosa, *f.* rose
rosado, *adj.* flushed; rosy, pink
rosario, *m.* rosary
rosbif, *m.* roast beef
rosca, *f.* screw and nut; rusk, twisted roll
roto, *adj.* broken; ragged; torn
rótula, *f.* kneecap
rotular, *va.* to self-address
rótulo, *m.* inscription, label; sign
rotura, *f.* fracture; breakage
r.p.m., revoluciones por minuto, r.p.m., revolutions per minute
rubí, *m.* ruby; **rubíes**, *pl.* jewels of a watch
rubia, *f.* blonde girl
rubio, *adj.* blond, fair
ruborizarse, *vr.* to blush, flush
rueda, *f.* wheel, circle
ruego, *m.* prayer; plea
ruido, *m.* noise
ruina, *f.* ruin,,downfall
ruiseñor, *m.* nightingale
rumba, *f.* rumba
rumbo, *m.* course, direction; pomp, ostentation
rumboso, *adj.* magnificent, pompous; liberal
rumor, *m.* rumor, report
ruptura, *f.* rupture, break
rural, *adj.* rural
Rusia, *f.* Russia
ruso, rusa, *n., adj.* Russian
rústico, *adj.* rustic, rural; unbound or in a paper cover (of books)
ruta, *f.* route, road
rutina, *f.* routine, habit

S

S., San or **Santo**, St. Saint; **segundo**, second; **sur**, So. or so., south
s., sustantivo, *n.* noun
S.ª, Señora, Mrs. Mistress.
S. A., Sociedad Anónima, Inc. Incorporated; **Su Alteza**, His or Her Highness

sábado, *m.* Saturday

sábana, *f.* bed sheet

sábelotodo, *m.* know-it-all

saber, *va.* to know; to be able to; *vn.* to be very sagacious; **saber a**, to taste of; *m.* learning, knowledge; **a saber**, to wit

sabiduría, *f.* knowledge, wisdom

sabiendas, a sabiendas, *adv.* knowingly, with awareness

sabio, *adj.* sage, wise; *m.* sage, scholar

sabor, *m.* taste, flavor

saborear, *va.* to enjoy, relish

sabroso, *adj.* delicious

sacar, *va.* to draw out; to pull out

sacarina, *f.* saccharine

sacerdote, *m.* priest, clergyman

saciar, *va.* to satiate, quench

saco, *m.* sack; bag; man's coat; jacket

sacramento, *m.* sacrament

sacrificar, *va., vr.* to sacrifice

sacrificio, *m.* sacrifice

sacudir, *va.* to shake, jerk

sagrado, *adj.* sacred

sal, *f.* salt; wit, grace

sala, *f.* hall, parlor

salado, *adj.* salted, salty

salar, *va.* to salt

salario, *m.* salary

salchicha, *f.* sausage

saldar, *va.* to settle, pay

saldo, *m.* balance; **saldo acreedor**, credit balance; **saldo deudor**, debit balance

salero, *m.* saltcellar; (coll.) gracefulness

saleroso, *adj.* graceful

salir *vn.* to go out, leave; to appear; to be issued or published

saliva, *f.* saliva

salón, *m.* parlor, hall, salon; **salón de belleza**, beauty parlor

salsa, *f.* sauce, dressing

saltar, *vn.* to leap, jump

salto, *m.* jump; leap, dive; **salto con pértiga**, pole vault; **salto de altura**, high jump;

salto de longitud, broad jump

salud, *f.* health

saludable, *adj.* healthful

saludar, *va.* to greet

saludo, *m.* salute; greeting.

Salvador, *m.* Saviour

salvadoreño, salvadoreña, *n., adj.* Salvadorian

salvar, *va.* to save, rescue

salvavidas, *m.* life preserver

salvo, *adj.* saved, safe; **sano y salvo**, safe and sound; *adv.* excepting

san, *adj.* saint (before masculine proper names)

sanar, *va., vn.* to heal, recover (health)

sanatoria, *m.* sanitarium, sanatorium

sanción, *f.* sanction

sancionar, *va.* to sanction

sandalia, *f.* sandal

sandía, *f.* watermelon

sangrar, *va., vn.* to bleed

sangre, *f.* blood

sangriento, *adj.* bloody

sanitario, *adj.* sanitary

sano, *adj.* sane; healthy.

Santiago, James

santiguar, *va., vr.* to make the sign of the cross

santo, santa, *adj., m.* saint; holy; sacred

sapo, *m.* toad

S. A. R., Su Alteza Real, His or Her Royal Highness

sarampión, *m.* measles

serape, *m.* serape, shawl

sarcasmo, *m.* sarcasm

sarcástico, *adj.* sarcastic

sardina, *f.* sardine

sargento, *m.* sergeant

sartén, *f.* frying pan

sastre, *m.* tailor

Satanás, *m.* Satan

sátira, *f.* satire

satisfacción, *f.* satisfaction; amends, apology

satisfacer, *va.* to atone; **satisfacerse**, to satisfy oneself

satisfactorio, *adj.* satisfactory

satisfecho, *adj.* satisfied

sauce, *m.* (bot.) willow

saxofón, *m.* saxophone

sazonar, *va.* to season; to mature

Sbre., **septiembre**, Sept., September.

S. C., **su casa**, your house, (expresssion of kind hospitality)

s. c. or **s/c.**, **su cargo** or **su cuenta**, (com.) your account; **su casa**, your house (expression of kind hospitality)

s/cta. or **s/c.**, **su cuenta**, (com.) your account

SE, **sudeste**, SE or S.E., southeast

sé, second person imperative singular of **ser**, to be; first person indicative singular of **saber**, to know

se, the reflexive pronoun, possessive to the person or thing that governs the verb. It frequently introduces the passive form of a verb, as **Se dice**, it is said

sebo, *m.* suet; tallow

secante, *m.* blotter

sección, *f.* section

seco, *adj.* dry; arid

secretaría, *f.* secretariat; secretary's office

secretario, **secretaria**, *n.* secretary

secreto, *adj.* secret; hidden; *m.* secret

secuestrar, *va.* to abduct

secundario, *adj.* secondary; **escuela secundaria**, high school

sed, *f.* thirst; **tener sed**, to be thirsty

seda, *f.* silk

sede, *f.* see, seat of episcopal power

sediento, *adj.* thirsty

sedimento, *m.* sediment

seducir, *va.* to seduce; to attract, charm

seductor, *adj.* attractive, fascinating; *m.* seducer

segregar, *va.* to segregate

seguida, *f.* following; succession; **en seguida**, immediately

seguir, *va.* to follow, pursue

según, *prep.* according to; **según aviso**, as per advice

segundo, *adj.* second; *m.* second (of time)

seguridad, *f.* security; certainty, safety, assurance

seguro, *adj.* secure, safe, sure; firm, constant; *m.* insurance

seis, *adj.* six, sixth (of the month); *m.* six

seiscientos, *adj.* six hundred

selección, *f.* selection

selecto, *adj.* select, choice

selva, *f.* forest

sellar, *va.* to seal, stamp

sello, *m.* seal; stamp; **sello de correo**, postage stamp

semana, *f.* week

semanal, *adj.* weekly

semanario, *adj.* weekly; *m.* weekly publication

sembrar, *va.* to sow, plant

semejante, *adj.* similar, like; *m.* fellow creature

semejanza, *f.* resemblance

semestral, *adj.* semiyearly

semestre, *m.* semester

semi, prefix denoting half

semianual, *adj.* semiannual

semifinal, *adj.* semifinal

senado, *m.* senate

senador, *m.* senator

sencillez, *f.* simplicity; naturalness, candor

sencillo, *adj.* simple; plain

senda, *f.* path, footpath

sendos, *adj. pl.* having one apiece

seno, *m.* breast, bosom; lap; sinus; asylum, refuge

sensación, *f.* sensation, feeling

sensato, *adj.* sensible, wise

sensible, *adj.* sensitive; regrettable; soft-hearted

sentado, *adj.* seated; **dar por sentado**, to take for granted

sentar, *va.* to sit; to seat; **sentarse**, to sit down

sentencia, *f.* sentence, opinion; verdict

sentenciar, *va.* to sentence, pass judgment

sentido, *m.* sense; reason; meaning

sentimental, *adj.* sentimental

sentimiento, *m.* sentiment; grief; feeling; sensation

sentir, *va.* to feel; to regret; to mourn; to think; to foresee; **sentirse**, to be hurt or offended

seña, *f.* sign, mark; password; **señas**, *pl.* address

señal, *f.* sign, signal

señalar, *va.* to mark; to point out

señor, *m.* lord; sir; master; **muy señor mio** or **nuestro**, dear sir; el **Señor**, the Lord

señora, *f.* lady; mistress\

señoría, *f.* lordship

señorita, *f.* young lady,miss

separación, *f.* separation

separado, *adj.* separate, apart; **por separado**, under separate cover

separar, *va.* to separate; **separarse**, to separate, to withdraw

sepelio, *m.* burial

septentrional, *adj.* northern

septiembre, *m.* September

séptimo, *adj.* seventh

sepulcro, *m.* sepulcher, grave, tomb

sequía, *f.* dryness; drought

ser, *vn.* to be; to exist; *m.* being, life

serenata, *f.* serenade

serenidad, *f.* serenity, quiet

sereno, *m.* night dampness; night watchman; *adj.* serene, calm; quiet

serie, *f.* series

seriedad, *f.* seriousness

serigrafía, *f.* silkscreen

serio, *adj.* serious, grave

serrucho, *m.* handsaw

servicial, *adj.* diligent

servicio, *m.* service

servidor, *m.* servant, waiter; **su servidor**, at your service; yours truly

servidora, *f.* maidservant; **su servidora**, at your service; yours truly

servil, *adj.* servile, cringing

servilleta, *f.* napkin

servir, *va.* to serve

sesenta, *m.*, *adj.* sixty

sesgo, *m.* bias

sesión, *f.* session, meeting

seso, *m.* brain

setenta, *m.*, *adj.* seventy

severo, *adj.* rigorous

sexagésimo, *adj.* sixtieth

sexismo, *m.* sexism

sexo, *m.* sex

sexto, *adj.* sixth

s/f., **su favor**, your favor

s/g: **su giro**, (com.) your draft

si, *conj.* if, whether; *m.* (mus.) si, seventh note of the scale

sí, *adv.* yes; indeed; *pron.* himself; herself; itself; themselves; **volver en sí**, to come to, to recover one's senses

sicoanalizar, *va.* to psychoanalyze

sicología, *f.* psychology

sideral, *adj.* sidereal, astral, space; **viajes siderales**, space travel

siderúrgico, siderúrgica, *adj.* pertaining to iron and steel

siempre, *adv.* always, ever

sien, *f.* temple (of the head)

sierra, *f.* saw; range of mountains

siete, *m.*, *adj.* seven

sífilis, *f.* syphilis

siglo, *m.* century

significado, *m.* meaning

signo, *m.* sign, mark

siguiente, *adj.* following, successive

sílaba, *f.* syllable

silbido, *m.* hiss; whistling

sima, *f.* abyss, gulf

símbolo, *m.* symbol; device

símil, *m.* (rhet.) simile

similar, *adj.* similar

simpatía, *f.* sympathy; charm; **tener simpatía por**, to like someone, to find (someone) pleasant and congenial

simpático *adj.* sympathetic; likable, charming

simpatizar, *vn.* to sympathize; to be congenial

simple, *adj.* simple, silly; insipid

simplificar, *va.* to simplify

simultáneo, *adj.* simultaneous

sin, *prep.* without; **sin embargo,** notwithstanding, nevertheless

sinceridad, *f.* sincerity

sincero, *adj.* sincere, honest

sindicato, *m.* syndicate

sinfonía, *f.* symphony

singular, *adj.* singular; unique

siniestro, *adj.* left (side); sinister; unhappy

sinnúmero, *m.* no end; numberless quantity

sino, *conj.* (after a negative), but; except; besides; only; *m.* destiny, fate.

sinónimo, *m.* synonym; *adj.* synonymous

sintético, *adj.* synthetic

síntoma, *m.* symptom

sinvergüenza, *m.* cad, bounder

siquiatra, *m.* psychiatrist

siquiera, *conj.* at least; though, although; **ni siquiera,** not even

sirena, *f.* foghorn, siren; mermaid

sirviente, sirvienta, *n.* servant

sistema, *m.* system, plan

sistemático, *adj.* systematic

situación, *f.* situation, state, condition

ski, *m.* ski

s/l or **s/L, su letra** (com.) your letter or draft

S. M., Su Majestad, His or Her Majesty

smoking, *m.* Tuxedo coat.

SO, sudoeste, SW or S.W. Southwest

s/o, su orden, (com.) your order

so, *prep.* under; below; **so pena de multa** or **muerte,** under penalty of fine or death

sobaco, *m.* armpit

sobar, *va.* to massage

soberanía, *f.* sovereignty

soberano, soberana, *adj., n.* sovereign

soberbio, *adj.* proud, haughty

soborno, *m.* bribe

sobra, *f.* surplus, excess; remainder; **de sobra,** over and above

sobrante, *m.* residue, surplus

sobrar, *vn.* to have more than is necessary; to be more than enough; to remain

sobre, *prep.* above, over; on, about; *m.* envelope

sobrecama, *f.* bedspread

sobrehumano, *adj.* superhuman

sobrellevar, *va.* to suffer, tolerate

sobremanera, *adv.* exceedingly

sobremesa, *f.* table cover; dessert; **de sobremesa,** immediately after dinner

sobrenombre, *m.* nickname

sobreponerse, *vr.* to master; to show oneself superior to

sobresaliente, *adj.* outstanding, excellent

sobretodo, *m.* overcoat

sobreviviente, *m., f.* survivor

sobrevivir, *vn.* to survive

sobrina, *f.* niece

sobrino, *m.* nephew

sobrio, *adj.* sober, frugal.

Soc., Sociedad, Soc., Society; Co., Company

sociable, *adj.* sociable

social, *adj.* social; **razón social,** firm name

socialista, *m., f.* socialist; *adj.* socialistic

sociedad, *f.* society, company, partnership; **sociedad anónima,** corporation

socio, socia, *n.* associate, partner, member

sociológico, *adj.* sociological

socorrer, *va.* to succor, help, rescue

socorro, *m.* help, aid

sofá, *m.* sofa, couch; **sofá cama,** studio couch

sofocar, *va.* to suffocate; to harass

soga, *f.* rope

sol, *m.* sun; a silver coin of Peru; (mus.) sol

solapa, *f.* lapel

solar, *m.* plot of ground; lot; *adj.* solar; **luz solar,** sun-

shine
solaz, *m.* solace, consolation
soldado, *m.* soldier
soleded, *f.* solitude; lonely place; desert
solicitar, *va.* to solicit; to apply for
solícito, *adj.* solicitous
solicitud, *f.* solicitude, application, petition; **a solicitud,** on request
sólido, *adj.* solid
solitario, a *i.* solitary, lonely
solo, *m.* (mus.) solo; **sola,** *adj.* alone, single
sólo, *adv.* only
soltar, *va.* to untie, loosen, to set at liberty; **soltarse,** to get loose
soltero, *adj.* unmarried; *m.* bachelor; **soltera,** bachelor girl
sollozo, *m.* sob
sombra, *f.* shade, shadow
sombrerera, *f.* hatbox
sombrerería, *f.* hat shop
sombrero, *m.* hat
sombrilla, *f.* parasol
someter, *va.* to submit; to subject
son, *m.* sound, report; Cuban musical rhythm
sonar, *vn.* to sound; to ring; **sonarse,** to blow one's nose
soneto, *m.* sonnet
sonido, *m.* sound
sonoro, *adj.* sonorous
sonreír, *vn., vr.* to smile
sonrisa, *f.* smile
sonrojarse, *vr.* to blush
soñar, *va., vn.* to dream
sopa, *f.* soup
soplar, *va.* to blow; to prompt; **soplarse,** to swell up
sopor, *m.* drowsiness
soporte, *m.* support; brassière
soportar, *va.* to suffer, bear
sorber, *va.* to sip
sordera, *f.* deafness
sordo, *adj.* deaf
sordomudo, sordomuda, *n., adj.* deaf and dumb; mute
sorprendente, *adj.* surprising
sorprender, *va.* to surprise
sorpresa, *f.* surprise

sorteo, *m.* raffle
sortija, *f.* ring; hoop
soso, *adj.* insipid, tasteless
sospecha, *f.* suspicion
sospechar, *va., vn.* to suspect
sospechoso, *adj.* suspicious
sostén, *m.* support
sostenido, *m.* (mus.) sharp (#)
sostenimiento, *m.* sustenance; support
sótano, *m.* cellar, basement
soviet, *m.* soviet
soya, *f.* soybean
s/p, su pagaré, (com.) your promissory note
Sr. or **S.ʳ, Señor,** Mr., Mister
s/r, su remesa, (com.) your remittance or shipment
Sra. or **S.ʳᵃ, Señora,** Mrs., Mistress
Sres. or **S.ʳᵉˢ, Señores,** Messrs., Messieurs
Sría., Secretaría, secretary's office
srio, or **S.ʳⁱᵒ, secretario,** sec., secretary
Srta, or **S.ʳᵗᵃ, Señorita,** Miss
S. S or **s. s., seguro servidor,** devoted servant
S. S., Su Santidad, His Holiness
SS.ᵐᵒ P., Santísimo Padre, Most Holy Father
S.S.S. or **s.s.s., su seguro servidor,** your devoted servant, yours truly
SS. SS. SS. or **ss. ss. ss., sus seguros servidores,** your devoted servants, yours truly
Sto., Santo, St., Saint (masculine)
su, *pron.* his, her, its, one's; **sus,** their
suave, *adj.* smooth, soft
suavizar, *va., vr.* to soften
subasta, *f.* auction
subconsciente, *adj.* subconscious
súbdito, súbdita, *n., adj.* subject (of a king, etc.)
subgerente, *m.* assistant manager
subir, *vn.* to mount, climb; to increase
súbitamente, *adv.* suddenly

subjuntivo, *m.* (gram.) subjunctive

sublime, *adj.* sublime, exalted

submarino, *m.* submarine

subnormal, *adj.* subnormal

subordinar, *va.* to subordinate

subrayar, *va.* to underline

subsecuente, *adj.* subsequent

subsidio, *m.* subsidy, aid

subsiguiente, *adj.* subsequent

subsistir, *vn.* to subsist, last

subteniente, *m.* second lieutenant

subterfugio, *m.* subterfuge

subterráneo, *adj.* underground; *m.* subway; cave

suburbano, *adj.* suburban

suburbio, *m.* suburb

subvención, *f.* subsidy

subyugar, *va.* to subdue

suceder, *vn.* to succeed, inherit; to happen

sucesión, *f.* succession; issue, offspring; hereditary succession

sucesivo, *adj.* successive; **en lo sucesivo**, from now on

suceso, *m.* outcome, event

sucesor, sucesora, *n.* successor

sucio, *adj.* dirty filthy

sucre, *m.* sucre, monetary unit of Ecuador

Suc.ʳᵉˢ, Sucesores, successors

suculento, *adj.* succulent

sucumbir, *vn.* to succumb, perish

sucursal, *adj.* subsidiary; *f.* branch, annex

sud, *m.* south; south wind (used instead of **sur**, when joined to another word)

sudamericano, sudamericana, *adj., n.* South American

sudar, *va., vn.* to sweat, perspire

sudeste, *m.* southeast

sudoeste, *m.* southwest

sudor, *m.* sweat, perspiration

Suecia, *f.* Sweden

sueco, sueca, *n., adj.* Swedish

suegra, *f.* mother-in-law

suegro, *m.* father-in-law

suela, *f.* sole of the shoe

sueldo, *m.* salary, pay

suelo, *m.* floor; ground

suelto, *adj.* loose; *m.* change (money); newspaper item

sueño, *m.* sleep; vision, dream; **tener sueño**, to be sleepy

suero, *m.* whey; serum (of blood)

suerte, *f.* chance, lot, fate; **tener suerte**, to be lucky

suficiente, *adj.* sufficient

sufijo, *m.* suffix

sufragio, *m.* vote, suffrage

sufrido, *adj.* long suffering

sufrimiento, *m.* sufferance, patience

sufrir, *va.* to suffer, bear with patience; to undergo

suicidarse, *vr.* to commit suicide

suicidio, *m.* suicide

Suiza, *f.* Switzerland

suizo, suiza, *n., adj.* Swiss

sujetar, *va.* to subdue; to subject; to hold; to fasten

sujeto, *adj.* subject, liable, exposed; *m.* subject, topic

sultán, *m.* sultan

suma, *f.* sum; substance

sumar, *va.* to add, sum up

sumario, *m.* summary

suministrar, *va.* to supply, furnish

suntuoso, *adj.* sumptuous

superar, *va.* to surpass, excel

supercarretera, *f.* superhighway

superhombre, *m.* superman

superintendente, *m.* superintendent

superior, *adj.* superior; upper (in geography); **parte superior**, topside; *m.* superior

superioridad, *f.* superiority

superlativo, *adj.*, *m.* superlative

supermercado, *m.* supermarket

superstición, *f.* superstition

super.ᵗᵉ, superintendente, supt., superintendent

suplente, *adj.* alternate

súplica, *f.* petition, request

suplicar, *va.* to entreat; to

pray, plead

suplir, *va.* to supply; to supplant

supl.^{te}, **suplente,** sub., substitute

suponer, *va.* to suppose, surmise

suposición, *f.* supposition, conjecture, basis

supremo, *adj.* supreme:

supresión, *f.* suppression

suprimir, *va.* to suppress; to abolish

supuesto, *m.* supposition; *adj.* supposed, false, assumed; **por supuesto,** of course

sur, *m.* south; south wind

suroeste, *m.* southwest

surtir, *va.* to supply, provide

susceptible, *adj.* susceptible

suscitar, *va.* to excite, stir up

suscribir, *va., vr.* to subscribe; to sign

suscripción, *f.* subscription

suscriptor, suscriptora, *n.* subscriber

susodicho, *adj.* above-mentioned, aforesaid

suspender, *va.* to suspend, stop, cease; to raise up

suspenso, *adj.* suspended, unfinished

suspicaz, *adj.* suspicious, distrustful

suspirar, *vn.* to sigh

suspiro, *m.* sigh

sustancia, *f.* substance

sustancioso, *adj.* substantial, nutritious

sustantivo, *adj., m.* noun

sustento, *m.* sustenance, support

sustitución, *f.* substitution

sustituir, *va.* to substitute

sustituto, sustituta, *adj., n.* substitute

susto, *m.* fright, terror

sustracción, *f.* subtraction

sustraer, *va.* to subtract; **sustraerse,** to retire, withdraw

sutil, *adj.* subtle

sutileza, *f.* subtlety, cunning; finesse; delicacy

suyo, suya, *adj.* his, hers, theirs, one's; his, her, its

own, one's own or their own; **los suyos,** *m. pl.* their own, close friends, relations

T

tabaco, *m.* tobacco

tabla, *f.* board; table; **las tablas,** the stage

tablero, *m.* chessboard; checkerboard; blackboard

tableta, *f.* tablet

tablilla, *f.* tablet, slab; bulletin board

taburete, *m.* stool

tacaño, *adj.* miserly, stingy

taco, *m.* stopper, stopple; wad; billiard cue; (Mex.) sandwich made with a **tortilla**

tacón, *m.* shoe heel

tacto, *m.* touch; tact

tacha, *f.* fault, defect

tachar, *va.* to find fault with; to blot, efface

tafetán, *m.* taffeta

tajada, *f.* slice

tajar, *va.* to cut, chop

tal, *adj.* such; **con tal que,** provided that; **¿qué tal?** how goes it? **tal vez,** perhaps

taladro, *m.* drill

talco, *m.* talc, talcum

talego, *m.* sack

talento, *m.* talent

talón, *m.* heel; (com.) receipt, check; check stub

talonario, *m.* check stubs; **libro talonario,** checkbook; receipt book

talla, *f.* stature, size

tallado, *adj.* cut, carved, engraved

tallar, *va.* to carve in wood

tallarín, *m.* noodle (for soup)

talle, *m.* shape, figure, size; waist

taller, *m.* workshop

tallo, *m.* shoot, sprout, stem

tamal, *m.* tamale

tamaño, *m.* size, shape

tambalear, *vn., vr.* to stagger, waver

también, *adv.* also, too, likewise; as well

tambor, *m.* drum; drummer;

iron cylinder

tamborito, *m.* national folk dance of Panama

tampoco, *adv.* neither, not either (used to enforce a foregoing negative)

tan, *adv.* so, so much, as well. as much; **tan pronto como,** as soon as

tanda, *f.* turn; rotation; shift

Tánger, Tangier

tangible, *adj.* tangible

tango, *m.* tango

tanque, *m.* tank; reservoir; pool

tanto, *m.* certain sum or quantity; *adj.* so much, as much; very great; *adv.* so, in such a manner; a long time; **mientras tanto,** meanwhile; **por lo tanto,** therefore; **tantos,** *pl.* score, points

tapa, *f.* lid, cover

tapacubos, *m.* hub cap

tapar, *va.* to cover; to close; to conceal, hide

tapete, *m.* rug; runner

tapizar, *va.* to upholster

tapón, *m.* cork, plug

taquigrafía, *f.* shorthand, stenography

taquígrafo, taquígrafa, *n.* stenographer

taquilla, *f.* box office

tararear, *va.* to hum (a tune)

tardanza, *f.* tardiness, delay

tardar, *vn., vr.* to delay, put off; **a más tardar,** at the latest

tarde, *f.* afternoon, early evening **buenas tardes,** good afternoon; *adv.* late

tardío, *adj.* slow, tardy

tarea, *f.* task

tarifa, *f.* tariff, charge, rate, fare; price list

tarima, *f.* platform

tarjeta, *f.* card; **tarjeta, postal,** post card

tarro, *m.* jar; mug

tartamudear, *vn.* to stutter, stammer

tasar, *va.* to appraise, value

taxi, *m.* taxicab

taza, *f.* cup; cupful; bowl

te, *pron.* objective and dative cases of **tú** (thou)

té, *m.* tea

teatral, *adj.* theatrical

testro, *m.* theater

tecla, *f.* key of an instrument; key of a typewriter

teclado, *m.* keyboard

técnico, *adj.* technical; **técnica,** *f.* technique; *m.* technician

tecnológico, *adj.* technological

techo, *m.* roof, ceiling; (coll.) dwelling house; **bajo techo,** indoors

tedio, *m.* disgust; boredom

teja, *f.* roof tile

tejer, *va.* to weave, knit

tejido, *m.* texture, web; textile, fabric; (anat.) tissue

telaraña, *f.* cobweb

telef., teléfono, tel., telephone

telefonear, *va., vn.* to telephone

telefonista, *m., f.* telephone operator

teléfono, *m.* telephone

teleg., telegrama, tel., telegram; **telégrafo,** tel. telegraph

telegrafiar, *va., vn.* to telegraph

telégrafo, *m.* telegraph

telegrama, *m.* telegram

telerreceptor, *m.* television set

telescopio, *m.* telescope

televisión, *f.* television

telón, *m.* curtain, backdrop in a theater

tema, *m.* theme; subject

temblor, *m.* trembling, tremor; earthquake

temer, *va., vn.* to fear; to doubt

temeroso, *adj.* timid

temible, *adj.* dreadful, inspiring awe or fear

temor, *m.* dread, fear

témpano, *m.* tympanum; block; iceberg

temperatura, *f.* temperature

tempestad, *f.* tempest; storm

templo, *m.* temple, church

temporada, f. period, season

temporal, adj. temporary; m. tempest, storm

temprano, adj. early, anticipated; adv. early, prematurely

tenacidad, f. tenacity

tenaz, adj. tenacious; stubborn

tender, va. to spread, expand, extend; to have a tendency

tendón, m. tendon, sinew

tenedor, tenedora, f. holder; payee (of bill of exchange); **tenedor de libros,** bookkeeper, accountant; m. fork

tener, va. to take, hold; to possess; to have; **tener cuidado,** to be careful

tenería, f. tanyard, tannery

teniente, m. lieutenant

tenis, m. tennis

tenor, m. kind; condition, nature; meaning; (mus.) tenor

tensión, f. tension, strain

tentación, f. temptation

tentar, va. to touch; to grope; to tempt

tentativa, f. attempt, trial

ten.te, teniente, Lt. or Lieut., Lieutenant

tentempié, m. snack, bite

teñir, va. to tinge, dye

teoría, f. theory

tequila, m. tequila (a Mexican liquor)

tercero, adj. third; m. third person; mediator

tercio, m., adj. third

terciopelo, m. velvet

terco, adj. stubborn

terminante, adj. decisive; absolute, strict

terminar, va. to finish

término, m. term; end; boundary; limit; **término medio,** average

termómetro, m. thermometer

termos, m. thermos bottle

ternero, ternera, n. calf; veal; heifer

terneza, f. tenderness

ternura, f. tenderness

terquedad, f. obstinacy

terraza, f. terrace, veranda

terremoto, m. earthquake

terreno, m. land, ground

terrestre, adj. earthly

terrible, adj. terrible, dreadful

territorial, adj. territorial

territorio, m. territory

terror, m. terror, dread

terruño, m. native land

terso, adj. smooth, terse

tertulia, f. informal gathering; conversation

tesorería, f. treasury

tesorero, tesorera, n. treasurer

tesoro, m. treasure

testamento, m. will, testament

testar, va., vn. to make one's will; to bequeath

testarudo, adj. obstinate

testículo, m. testicle

testigo, m. witness

testimonio, m. testimony

teta, f. dug, teat

tétano, m. tetanus, lockjaw

tetera, f. teapot, teakettle

textil, adj., m. textile

texto, m. text

tez, f. complexion of the face; hue

ti, pron. objective or dative case of **tu**

tía, f. aunt

tibio, adj. lukewarm

tiburón, m. shark

tictac, m. ticktock

tiempo, m. time, term; season; weather; tempo

tienda, f. shop; tent

tierno, adj. tender; young; delicate, soft

tierra, f. earth; soil; land, ground; native country

tieso, adj. stiff, hard, firm; taut

tifoideo, adj. typhoid; **tifoidea,** f. typhoid fever

tigre, m. tiger

tijeras, f. pl. scissors

tilde, f. tilde, diacritical sign of the letter **ñ**

timbrazo, n. sharp bell ring

timbre, m. postage stamp; call bell; timbre

timidez, f. timidity

tímpano, _m._ kettledrum; eardrum

tina, _f._ tub; **tina de baño**, bathtub

tinaja, _f._ large earthen jar for water

tiniebla, _f._ darkness, obscurity

tino, _m._ good aim; tact; good judgment

tinta, _f._ tint, hue; ink

tinte, _m._ tint, dye

tintero, _m._ inkwell

tintorería, _f._ dry cleaning shop

tío, _m._ uncle

típico, _adj._ typical

tipo, _m._ type, model, pattern; rate, standard; **tipo de cambio**, rate of exchange

tipográfico, _adj._ typographical

tira, _f._ strip

tirabtizón, _m._ corkscrew

tirada, _f._ cast, throw; stroke (golf); edition, issue; presswork

tirador, _m._ doorknob; door knocker

tiranía, _f._ tyranny

tirano, _adj._ tyrannical; **tirana**, _n._ tyrant

tirante, _adj._ taut; **tirantes**, _m. pl._ suspenders

tirar, _va._ to throw, toss, cast; to pull, draw; to shoot; _vn._ to tend, incline

tiritar, _vn._ to shiver

tiro, _m._ cast, throw; shot

tiroides, _adj._, _f._ (anat.) thyroid (gland)

tirón, _m._ pull, haul, tug; **de un tirón**, all at once, at one stroke

tiroteo, _m._ random shooting, skirmish

tísico, _adj._ tubercular

tisis, _f._ consumption, tuberculosis

titubeo, _m._ hesitation, wavering

tiza, _f._ chalk

tobillera, _f._ anklet; bobbysoxer

tobillo, _m._ ankle

tocador, _m._ dressing table, boudoir

tocar, _va._ to touch; (mus.) to play; to ring a bell; _vn._ to belong; to behoove, fall to one's share

tocayo, tocaya, _n._ namesake

tocino, _m._ bacon, salt pork

todavía, _adv._ yet, still

todopoderoso, _adj._ almighty

tolerante, _adj._ tolerant

tolerar, _vn._ to tolerate

tomar, _va._ to take, seize; to drink

tomate, _m._ tomato

tomo, _m._ tome; volume

tonada, _f._ tune, melody, air

tonelada, _f._ ton

tónico, _m._ tonic

tontería, _f._ nonsense

tonto, _adj._ stupid, foolish; **tonto, tonta**, _n._ fool, dunce

tope, _m._ butt, rub; scuffle; **topes**, _pl._ (rail.) buffers; _adj._ high; **precio tope**, ceiling price

tópico, _m._ topic, subject

toque, _m._ touch; bell ringing; (mil.) call

torbellino, _m._ whirlwind

torcer, _va._ to twist; distort; **torcerse**, to go crooked or astray

torcido, _adj._ twisted

toreo, _m._ bullfighting

torero, _m._ bullfighter

tormenta, _f._ storm, tempest

tormento, _m._ torment

torneo, _m._ tournament

tornillo, _m._ bolt; screw

torno, _m._ lathe; wheel; wheel and axle; dentist's drill

toro, _m._ bull

toronja, _f._ grapefruit

torpe, _adj._ dull, heavy; stupid, awkward

torpeza, _f._ heaviness, stupidity

torrente, _m._ torrent

torso, _m._ trunk, torso

torta, _f._ tart, cake

tortilla, _f._ omelet; (Mex.) kind of pancake

tortuga, _f._ tortoise; turtle

tos, _f._ cough

toser, _vn._ to cough

tostada, _f._ slice of toast; (Mex.)

open-faced meat tart

tostador, *m.* toaster

tostar, *va.* to toast

total, *m.* whole, totality; *adj.* total, entire

totalmente, *adv.* totally

tr., transitive, tr., transitive

traba, *f.* obstacle

trabajar, *va.*, *vn.* to work, labor

trabajo, *m.* work, labor; toil; workmanship; difficulty, trouble

trabajoso, *adj.* laborious

traducción, *f.* translation

traducir, *va.* to translate

traductor, traductora, *n.* translator

traer, *va.* to bring, carry, wear

tráfico, *m.* traffic, trade

tragaluz, *m.* skylight

tragar, *va.* to swallow, glut

trago, *m.* draft of liquor; drink

tragón, *adj.* gluttonous

traición, *f.* treason

traicionar, *va.* to betray

traidor, traidora, *n.* traitor; *adj.* treacherous

traje, *m.* dress, suit, costume; **traje espacial**, space suit

trajinar, *va.* to convey; to bustle about one's work

trama, *f.* plot, conspiracy; weft or woof (of cloth)

tramar, *va.* to weave; to plot

trámite, *m.* requirement; step, passage; (law) procedure

tramo, *m.* flight of stairs; span of a bridge; stretch, section

trampa, *f.* trap, snare; trap door; fraud; **hacer trampa**, to cheat

tramposo, *adj.* deceitful, swindling

trancar, *va.* to barricade

trance, *m.* danger; hypnotic condition; last stage of life; **a todo trance**, at all costs

tranquilidad, *f.* tranquility

tranquilizar, *va.*, *vr.* to soothe, quiet

tranquilo, *adj.* calm, quiet

transacción, *f.* transaction; adjustment

transición, *f.* transition

transigir, *va.* to compromise; *vn.* to give in

tránsito, *m.* passage; road, way; traffic

tranvía, *m.* streetcar

trapo, *m.* rag, tatter

tras, *prep.* after, behind

trasatlántico, *adj.*, *m.* transatlantic

trasbordar, *va.* to transfer, change cars

trascendencia, *f.* transcendency; importance

trascendental, *adj.* transcendental

trascribir, *va.* to transcribe, copy

trascurso, *m.* course (of time)

trasero, *adj.* hind, hinder; **asiento trasero**, back seat; *m.* buttock

trasferir, *va.* to transfer

trasformación, *f.* transformation

trasformar, *va.* to transform

trasfusión, *f.* transfusion

trasladar, *va.* to transport, transfer

trasmisión, *f.* transmission

trasmitir, *va.* to transmit, send

trasnochar, *vn.* to watch, sit up all night

trasparente, *adj.* transparent

traspasar, *va.* to pass over; to trespass; to transfer

trasplantar, *va.* to transplant

trasportar, *va.* to transport, convey; (mus.) to transpose

trasporte, *m.* transportation; transport

trastornado, *adj.* unbalanced, crazy

trastorno, *m.* confusion, upset, overthrow

tratable, *adj.* compliant, pliant; pleasant

tratado, *m.* treaty

tratar, *va.* to treat on a subject; to trade; to treat

trato, *m.* treatment; manner; deal; dealing

travesía, *f.* crossing, voyage; distance

trazar, *va.* to plan out; to project; to trace

trébol, m. (bot.) clover; **hoja de trébol**, cloverleaf

trece, m., adj. thirteen; thirteenth

trecientos, adj., m. three hundred

tregua, f. truce, recess; **sin tregua**, unceasingly

treinta, m., adj. thirty

tremendo, adj. tremendous

tren, m. train, retinue; (rail.) train

trepar, vn. to climb, crawl

tres, adj., m. three

trescientos, adj., m. three hundred

triangular, adj. triangular

triángulo, m. triangle

tribu, f. tribe

tribuna, f. tribune, rostrum

tribunal, m. tribunal, court of justice

tributar, va. to pay tribute

tributo, m. tribute; tax

tricolor, adj. tricolored

trigésimo, adj. thirtieth

trigueño, adj. swarthy, brunet

trimestre, m. quarter, space of three months

trinar, vn. to trill, quaver

trinchante, m. carver; carving knife

trinchera, f. trench

trineo, m. sleigh, sled

trío, m. (mus.) trio

tripa, f. gut, entrails, tripe, intestine

triple, adj. triple, treble

triplicar, va. to treble, triple

tripulación, f. crew of a ship

triste, adj. sad, mournful

tristeza, f. sadness

triunfal, adj. triumphal

triunfante, adj. triumphant

triunfar, vn. to triumph

triunfo, m. triumph; trump (in cards)

trivial, adj. trivial

triza, f. mite; bit, shred

trompa, f. trumpet; trunk (of elephants)

trompeta, f. trumpet, horn; m. trumpeter

trompo, m. spinning top

tronco, m. tree trunk; log of wood; origin

trono, m. throne

tropa, f. troop

tropezar, vn. to stumble

tropical, adj. tropical

trópico, m. tropics

tropiezo, m. stumble, trip

tropo, m. figu speech

trote, m. trot; **a trote**, in haste

trovador, trovadora, n. minstrel

trozo, m. piece, fragment

trucha, f. trout; crane

trueno, m. thunderclap

tu, pron. possessive sing. of pronoun **tú**

tú, pron. thou, you (sing. familiar form)

tuberculosis, f. tuberculosis

tubería, f. pipe line; tubing; piping

tubo, m. tube, pipe, duct

tuerca, f. nut (of a screw)

tuerto, adj. one-eyed; squint-eyed

tul, m. tulle (cloth)

tulipán, m. tulip

tullido, adj. crippled, maimed

tumba, f. tomb, grave

tumbar, va., vn. to tumble

tumor, m. tumor

túnel, m. tunnel

túnica, f. tunic

turbante, m. turban

turborreactor, m. turbojet

turbulento, adj. turbid, muddy; stormy, turbulent

turco, turca, n., adj. Turkish, Turk

turismo, m. touring, tourism

turista, m., f. tourist

turnar, vn. to alternate

turno, m. turn; shift

turquesa, f. turquoise

turquí, adj. turquoise blue

Turquía, f. Turkey

turrón, m. nougat, candy

tutora, f. tutoress

tuyo, tuya, adj. thine; **los tuyos**, pl. thy family, thy people, etc

U

u, *conj.* or (used instead of **o**, when the following word begins with **o** or **ho**)
ubicar, *vn., vr.* to be located
ubre, *f.* dug, teat, udder
Ud., usted, *pron.* you (sing.)
Uds., ustedes, *pron.* you
úlcera, *f.* ulcer
últimamente, *adv.* lately
útimo, *adj.* last, latest; late, latter; remote, final
últ.°, último, ult. last
ultrajar, *va.* to outrage; to abuse
ultramar, *adj., m.* overseas
umbral, *m.* threshold, doorstep; beginning
un, una, *adj.* a, an; one
unánime, *adj.* unanimous
unanimidad, *f.* unanimity
undécimo, *adj.* eleventh
ungüento, *m.* ointment
único, *adj.* unique, only
unidad, *f.* unity; unit
uniforme, *adj., m.* uniform
uniformidad, *f.* uniformity
union, *f.* unión
unir, *va.* to join, unite; **unirse,** to associate, get together
universal, *adj.* universal
universidad, *f.* university
universo, *m.* universe
uno, *m.* one; *adj.* one; sole, only
uña, *f.* nail; hoof; claw
urbanidad, *f.* good manners
urbe, *f.* metropolis
urgencia, *f.* urgency, need
urgente, *adj.* urgent
urinario, *adj.* urinary
urraca, *f.* magpie
uruguayo, uruguaya, *n., adj.* Uruguayan
usado, *adj.* used; worn
usar, *va.* to use, make use of; **usarse,** to be in use, be customary
uso, *m.* use, service; custom; mode
usted, *pron.* you (sing.); **ustedes,** you (plural); **usted mismo,** you yourself
útero, *m.* uterus, womb

útil, *adj.* useful, profitable; **útiles,** *m. pl.* utensils, tools
utilidad, *f.* utility; usefulness; profit
utilizar, *va.* to make use of
uva, *f.* grape

V

v., véase, vid., see, refer to; **verbo,** verb
v/, valor, val., value; amt., amount
V. A., Vuestra Alteza, Your Highness, **Versión Autorizada,** A. V., Authorized Version
vaca, *f.* cow
vacaciones, *f. pl.* holidays, vacations
vacante, *adj.* vacant; *f.* vacancy
vaciar, *va.* to empty, clear; to mold; *vn.* to fall, decrease (of waters)
vacilar, *vn.* to hesitate
vacío, *adj.* void, empty; unoccupied; *m.* vacuum; concavity
vacuna, *f.* vaccine
vacunar, *va.* to vaccinate
vacuno, *adj.* bovine
vagón, *m.* car, freight car, coach; **vagón cama,** sleeping car
vahído, *m.* dizziness
vainilla, *f.* vanilla
vaivén, *m.* fluctuation, motion
vajilla, *f.* table service, set of dishes
vale, *m.* promissory note, I.O.U
valenciano, valenciana, *adj., n.* Valencian, from Valencia
valentía, *f.* valor, courage
valer, *vn.* to be valuable, be deserving; to be valid; **valer la pena,** to be worthwhile; **valerse,** to employ; to have recourse to
vilidez, *f.* validity
válido, *adj.* valid; obligatory
valiente, *adj.* brave, courageous
vafija, *f.* valise; mail bag
valioso, *adj.* valuable

valor, *m.* value, price; courage, valor

valorar, *va.* to value

vals, *m.* waltz

valuación, *f.* valuation, appraisal

valle, *m.* valley

¡vamos! *interj.* well let's go! stop!

vanagloriarse, *vr.* to boast

vanidad, *f.* vanity

vanidoso, *adj.* vain, conceited

vano, *adj.* vain; useless; **en vano,** in vain

vapor, *m.* vapor, steam; steamer, steamship

vaquero, *m.* cowherd; herdsman, cowboy; *adj.* pertaining to cowboys

vara, *f.* rod; pole, staff; yard (measure); **vara alta,** sway, high hand

variación, *adj.* variation

variado, varied

variar, *va.* to vary, change; *vn.* to vary

variedad, *f.* variety; diversity

variedades, *f. pl.* variety show

varios, *adj. pl.* some, several

varón, *m.* man, male human being; man of respectability

varonil, *adj.* male, masculine; manful

vaselina, *f.* vaseline, petroleum jelly

vasija, *f.* pot

vaso, *m.* vessel; jar

vástago, *m.* bud, shoot; descendant

vasto, *adj.* vast, huge

¡vaya! *interj.* well, now!

Vd., usted, you (sing.)

vda., viuda, widow

Vds. or VV., ustedes, you (pl.)

V.E., Vuestra Excelencia, Your Excellency

véase, see, refer to

vecindad, *f.* neighborhood

vecindario, *m.* neighborhood

vecino, *adj.* neighboring; near; *m.* neighbor; inhabitant

vegetación, *f.* vegetation

vegetal, *adj., m.* vegetable

vegetar, *vn.* to vegetate

vegetariano, vegetariana, *adj., n.* vegetarian

vehículo, *m.* vehicle

veinte, *adj., m.* twenty

veintena, *f.* score, twenty

vejez, *f.* old age

vejiga, *f.* bladder; blister

vela, *f.* watch; watchfulness; candle

velada, *f.* evening entertainment, soiree

velar, *vn.* to watch

velo, *m.* veil; pretext

velocidad, *f.* speed

veloz, *adj.* swift

vello, *m.* down; gossamer; short downy hair

velludo, *adj.* hairy

vena, *f.* vein, blood vessel

venado, *m.* deer; venison

vencer, *va.* to conquer, vanquish; *vn.* to fall due

vencido, *adj.* conquered; due; **darse por vencido,** to give up, yield

venda, *f.* bandage

vendaje, *m.* bandage

vendar, *va.* to bandage

vendedor, vendedora, *n.* seller

vender, *va.* to sell

veneciano, veneciana, *adj., n.* Venetian

veneno, *m.* poison, venom

venenoso, *adj.* poisonous

veneración, *f.* veneration

venerar, *va.* to venerate

venéreo, *adj.* venereal

vengar, *va.* to revenge, avenge; **vengarse de,** to take revenge on

vengativo, *adj.* revengeful

venia, *f.* pardon; leave, permission; bow

venida, *f.* arrival; return

venidero, *adj.* future, coming, next; **próximo venidero,** the coming month

venir, *vn.* to come, arrive; to follow, succeed; to spring from

venta, *f.* sale; roadside inn

ventaja, *f.* advantage; handicap

ventajoso, *adj.* advantageous

ventana, *f.* window

ventarrón, *m.* violent wind

ventilación, *f.* ventilation

ventilador, *m.* ventilator; fan

ventilar, *va., vr.* to ventilate; to fan; to air; to discuss

ventura, *f.* luck, fortune; **por ventura,** by chance

venturoso, *adj.* lucky, fortunate; happy

ver, *va.* to see, look; to observe; **a ver,** let's see; **hacer ver,** to pretend; *m.* sense of sight, seeing; view; **a mi ver,** in my opinion

veracidad, *f.* veracity

veraneo, *m.* summering; **lugar de veraneo,** *m.* summer resort

verano, *m.* summer

veras, *f. pl.* truth, sincerity; de veras, in truth, really

veraz, *adj.* truthful

verbal, *adj.* verbal, oral

verbigracia, *adv.* for example, namely

verbo, *m.* (gram.) verb

verdad, *f.* truth, veracity

verdaderamente, *adv.* truly

verdadero, *adj.* true, real

verde, *m., adj.* green

verdor, *m.* verdure; green

verdulero, verdulera, *n.* vegetable seller

verdura, *f.* verdure; vegetables, garden stuff

vereda, *f.* path, trail

vergel, *m.* flower garden

vergonzoso, *adj.* bashful, shy; shameful

vergüenza, *f.* shame; bashfulness; confusion

verídico, *adj.* truthful

verificar, *va.* to verify, check; **verificarse,** to take place

verja, *f.* grate, lattice

verosímil, *adj.* plausible

verruga, *f.* wart, pimple

versión, *f.* version, interpretation

verso, *m.* verse, stanza

vértebra, *f.* vertebra

vertebrado, vertebrada, *m., adj.* vertebrate

verter, *va., vr.* to pour; *vn.* to flow

vespertino, *adj.* evening

vestíbulo, *m.* vestibule, lobby

vestigio, *m.* vestige, trace

vestir, *va.* to clothe, dress

veterano, *adj.* experienced, long practiced; *m.* veteran, old soldier

vez, *f.* turn, time; **una vez,** once; **a veces, algunas veces,** sometimes; **en vez de,** instead of; **otra vez,** again; **tal vez,** perhaps

vg., v.g., or **v.gr., verbigracia,** e.g., for example

vía, *f.* way, road, route; (rail.) railway, railway line; **vía aérea,** air mail

viaducto, *m.* viaduct; overpass

viajar, *vn.* to travel

viaje, *m.* journey, voyage; **viaje sencillo,** one-way trip; **viaje redondo** or **de ida y vuelta,** round trip

viajero, viajera, *n.* traveler

víbora, *f.* viper

vicecónsul, *m.* vice-consul

vicepresidente, *m.* vice-president vice-chairman

viceversa, *adj.* vice versa

vicio, *m.* vice, folly

víctima, *f.* victim; **víctimas,** *pl.* casualties

victoria, *f.* victory

victorioso, *adj.* victorious

vid, *f.* (bot.) vine

vida, *f.* life

vidriera, *f.* glass case; shop-window

vidrio, *m.* glass

viejo, *adj.* old; ancient

vienés, vienesa, *adj., n.* Viennese

viento, *m.* wind; air

vientre, *m.* belly

viernes, *m.* Friday; **Viernes Santo,** Good Friday

viga, *f.* beam (of timber)

vigente, *adj.* in force

vigésimo, *adj., m.* twentieth

vigilar, *va., vn.* to watch over

vigor, *m.* vigor, strength

vigoroso, *adj.* vigorous

villa, *f.* town

villano, *adj.* rustic, boorish; *m.* villain

vinagre, *m.* vinegar
vincular, *va.* to link
vínculo, *m.* link, bond
vindicar, *va.* to vindicate; to avenge
vino, *m.* wine
viña, *f.* vineyard; grapevine
violación, *f.* violation
violar, *va.* to violate; to ravish
violencia, *f.* violence
violentar, *va.* to enforce by violent means
violento, *adj.* violent
violeta, *f., adj.* violet
violín, *m.* violin, fiddle
violinista, *m., f.* violinist
violón, *m.* bass viol
violonchelo, *m.* violoncello
virar, *va.* (naut.) to tack; *vn.* to turn around
virgen, *adj., f.* virgin
viril, virile, manly
virología, *f.* virology
virtud, *f.* virtue
virtuoso, *adj.* virtuous
viruela, *f.* smallpox; **viruelas locas**, chicken pox
visa, *f.* visa
visita, *f.* visit; visitor
visitante, *m., f.* visitor
visitar, *va.* to visit
víspera, *f.* evening before; day before; **víspera de Año Nuevo**, New Year's Eve
vistazo, *m.* glance
visto, *adj.* obvious; **visto que**, considering that; **por lo visto**, apparently; **visto bueno**, O.K., all right, correct
vistoso, *adj.* beautiful, showy
vital, *adj.* vital, essential
vitalicio, *adj.* during life
vitalidad, *f.* vitality
vitamina, *f.* vitamin
vitrina, *f.* showcase
viuda, *f.* widow
viudo, *m.* widower
¡viva! *interj.* hurrah! hail!
vivacidad, *f.* vivacity
víveres, *m. pl.* provisions
viveza, *f.* liveliness, perspicacity
vividor, vividora, *n.* sponger
vivienda, *f.* dwelling house
viviente, *adj.* alive, living

vivir, *vn.* to live
vivo, *adj.* living; lively; ingenious, bright
V. M., Vuestra Majestad, Your Majesty
V.° B.°, visto bueno, O.K., all correct
vocablo, *m.* word, term
vocabulario, *m.* vocabulary
vocación, *f.* vocation, calling
vocal, *f.* vowel; *m.* member of a board of directors; *adj.* vocal, oral
vol., volumen, vol., volume; **voluntad**, will; (com.) good will
volante, *m.* steering wheel; flier, note, memorandum; ruffle
volcán, *m.* volcano
volcar, *va., vr.* to upset
voltear, *va.* to whirl, over set; *vn.* to tumble
volumen, *m.* volume; size
voluminoso, *adj.* voluminous
voluntario, *adj.* voluntary; *n.* volunteer
voluntarioso, *adj.* willful
volver, *va., vn.* to return; to turn; **volver en sí**, to recover one's senses
vómito, *m.* vomiting
voraz, *adj.* voracious, greedy
vos, *pron.* you ye
vosotros, vosotras, *pron. pl.* you
votación, *f.* voting
votante, *m., f.* voter
votar, *va., vn.* to vote
voto, *m.* vow; vote; wish; supplication to God; **hacer votos**, to wish well
voz, *f.* voice; word, term
V.P., Vicepresidente, Vice Pres., Vice-President
vuelo, *m.* flight
vuelta, *f.* turn; circuit; detour; return; **dar la vuelta**, to turn around; to go out for a short walk or ride
vuelto, *p. p.* of **volver**; *m.* (sp. Am.) change (money back from a payment)
vuestro, vuestra, *pron.* your, yours

vulgar, *adj.* vulgar, common, ordinary

vulgaridad, *f.* vulgarity

vulgarismo, *m.* slang

vulgo, *m.* populace, mob

VV or **V.V.**, **ustedes**, you (*pl.*)

W

wáter, *m.* lavatory

whiskey, *m.* whiskey

X

xenón, *m.* xenon

xilófono, *m.* (mus.) xylophone

xilografía, *f.* wood engraving

Y

y, *conj.* and

ya, *adv.* already; presently; immediately; **ya no**, no longer

yanqui, *adj.*, *n.* Yankee

yarda, *f.* yard (measure)

yate, *m.* yacht

yedra, *f.* ivy

yelmo, *m.* helmet

yema, *f.* yolk

yerba or **hierba**, *f.* herb; grass; **yerba buena**, mint; **yerba mate**, Paraguay tea; **yerbas** *pl.* greens, vegetables

yerno, *m.* son-in-law

yeso, *m.* gypsum; plaster, plaster cast

yo, *pron.* I; **yo mismo**, I myself

yodo, *m.* iodine

yuca, *f.* (bot.) yucca

yugo, *m.* yoke

yunque, *m.* anvil

yunta, *f.* couple, yoke

yute, *m.* jute (fiber)

Z

zacate, *m.* (Mex.) hay, grass

zafiro, *m.* sapphire

zafra, *f.* sugar crop

zalamero, **zalamera**, *n.*, *adj.* wheedler, flatterer

zambullirse, *vr.* to plunge into water, dive

zanahoria, *f.* carrot

zancada, *f.* long stride

zanco, *m.* stilt

zancudo, *adj.* long-shanked; wading (bird); *m.* (Sp. Am.) mosquito

zángano, *m.* drone; idler, sponger

zanja, *f.* ditch, trench

zapallo, *m.* (Sp. Am.) squash

zapatear, *va.*, *vn.* to strike with the shoe; to beat time with the sole of the shoe

zapatería, *f.* shoe store

zapatero, *m.* shoemaker; shoe seller

zapatilla, *f.* pump (shoe), slipper

zapato, *m.* shoe

zar, *m.* czar

zaraza, *f.* chintz; gingham

zarzamora, *f.* brambleberry; blackberry bush

zarzuela, *f.* variety of operetta, musical comedy

zeta, *f.* name of letter z

zigzag, *m.* zigzag

zona, *f.* zone, district

zoología, *f.* zoology

zoológico, *adj.* zoological

zoquete, *m.* block; (coll.) blockhead, numbskull

zorra, *f.* fox; (coll.) prostitute, strumpet

zorrillo, *m.* skunk

zorro, *m.* male fox; cunning fellow

zozobra, *f.* anxiety

zueco, *m.* wooden shoe

zumbar, *vn.* to resound, hum; to buzz; to ring (the ears)

zumbido, *m.* humming, buzzing sound

zumo, *m.* sap, juice

zurdo, *adj.* left; lefthanded

zurrapa, *f.* lees, dregs; trash

zurrar, *va.* to chastise with a whip; **zurrarse**, (coll.) to have an involuntary evacuation of the bowels

zutano, **zutana**, *n.* such a one; **zutano y fulano**, such and such a one, so and so

A

a, *art.* un, uno, una

A. B., Bachelor of Arts, Br. Bachiller

aback, *adv.* detrás, atrás; **to be taken aback,** quedar desconcertado

abandon, *vt.* abandonar

abate, *vt., vi.* minorar, disminuir

abbreviate, *vt.* abreviar

abbreviation, *n.* abreviación, abreviatura, *f.*

abdicate, *vt.* abdicar

abdomen, *n.* abdomen, vientre, *m.*

abduct, *vt.* secuestrar

abhor, *vt.* aborrecer

abide, *vi.* habitar, morar; **to abide by,** cumplir con; atenerse a

ability, *n.* habilidad, aptitud, *f.*

abnormal, *adj.* anormal

aboard, *adj.* abordo

abode, *n.* habitación,

abolish, *vt.* abolir

abominable, *adj.* abominable

abortion, *n.* aborto, *m.*

about, *prep.* cerca de; sobre; acerca; *adv.* aqui y allá; **to be about to,** estar a punto de

above, *prep.* encima, sobre; *adj.* arriba; **above all,** sobre todo, principalmente

aboveboard, *adj.* y *adv.* sincero, al descubierto

abreast, *adj.* de frente

abrupt, *adi.* repentino; rudo

abscess, *n.* absceso, *m.*

absence, *n.* ausencia, *f.*; **leave of absence,** licencia, *f.*

absent, *adj.* ausente

absent-minded, *adj.* distraido

abstain, *vi.* abstenerse

abstract, *vt.* abstraer; compendiar; *adj.* abstracto; *n.* extracto, *m.*

absurd, *adj.* absurdo

abundance, *n.* abundancia, *f.*

abundant, *adj.* abundante

abuse, *vt.* abusar; ultrajar; violar; *n.* abuso, engaño, *m.*

A.C., a.c., alternating cur-

rent, C.A., corriente alterna

academic, *adj.* académico

academy, *n.* academia, *f.*

accede, *vi.* acceder

accelerator, *n.* acelerador, *m.*

accent, *n.* acento, *m.*; tono, *m.*; *vt.* acentuar

accentuate, *vt.* acentuar

accept, *vt.* aceptar; admitir

acceptance, *n.* aceptación, *f.*

access, *n.* acceso, *m.*; entrada, *f.*

accessory, *adj.* accesorio; *n.* cómplice, *m.* y *f.*

accident, *n.* accidente, *m.*; casualidad, *f.*

accidental, *adj.* accidental, casual

acclaim, *vt.* aclamar, aplaudir

accommodate, *vt.* acomodar, ajustar

accommodating, *adj.* servicial

accompaniment, *n.* (mus.) acompañamiento, *m.*

accompany, *vt.* acompañar

accomplice, *n.* cómplice, *m.* y *f.*

accomplish, *vt.* efectuar, realizar

accord, *n.* acuerdo, convenio, *m.*

accordance, *n.* conformidad, *f.*, acuerdo, *m.*

according, *adj.* conforme; **according to,** según; **accordingly,** *adv.* de conformidad, por consiguiente

account, *n.* cuenta, *f.*; cálculo, *m.*; narración, *f.*; **on account of,** a causa de

accountant, *n.* contador, tenedor de libros, *m.*

accounting, *n.* contabilidad, *f.*

accredited, *adj.* autorizado

accumulate, *vt.* y *vi.* acumular

accurate, *adj.* exacto; atinado

accusation, *n.* acusación, *f.*; cargo, *m.*

accusative, *n.* acusativo, *m.*

accuse, *vt.* acusar; culpar

accustom, *vt.* acostumbrar

ace, *n.* as (de naipe), *m.*; as, aviador sobresaliente, *m.*; *adj.* extraordinario

ache, *n.* dolor, *m.*; *vi.* doler

achieve, *vt.* ejecutar; lograr

achievement, *n.* ejecución, *f.*; hazaña, *f.*

acid, *n.* ácido, *m.*; *adj.* ácido, agrio

acknowledge, *vt.* reconocer; confesar; **acknowledge receipt**, acusar recibo

acoustics, *n.* acústica, *f.*

acquaint, *vt.* enterar, familiarizar; **to be acquainted**, conocer

acquaintance, *n.* conocimiento, *m.*; conocido, *m.*

acquire, *vt.* adquirir

acre, *n.* acre, *m.* (medida)

across, *adv.* al otro lado; *prep.* a través de

acrylic, *adj.* acrílico

act, *vt.* representar; obrar; *vi.* hacer; *n.* acto, hecho, *m.*

ACTH, *n.* (med.) ACTH

acting, *adj.* interino, suplente

action, *n.* acción, operación, *f.*; batalla, *f.*; proceso, *m.*; actividad, *f.*

active, *adj.* activo; eficaz

activity, *n.* actividad, *f.*

actual, *adj.* real; efectivo

acute, *adj.* agudo; ingenioso

A.D.: (in the year of our Lord), D. de J. C. (después de J. C.)

ad, *n.* anuncio, aviso, *m.*

adamant, *adj.* inflexible

adapt, *vt.* adaptar

add, *vt.* sumar; agregar

adding, *n.* suma, *f.*; **adding machine**, calculadora, *f.*

addition, *n.* adición, *f.*

address, *vt.* hablar, dirigir la palabra; *n.* discurso, *m.*; dirección, *f.*

addressee, *n.* destinatario, *m.*

adhere, *vt.* adherir

adhesion, *n.* adherencia, *f.*

adhesive, *adj.* pegajoso, tenaz; **adhesive plaster, adhesive tape**, esparadrapo, *m.*

adjacent, *adj.* adyacente, contiguo

adjective, *n.* adjetivo, *m.*

adjourn, *vt.* y *vi.* clausurar (una reunión, etc.)

adjust, *vt.* ajustar, acomodar

adjustment, *n.* ajuste, arreglo, *m.*

Adm., Admiral, Almte., almirante

administer, *vt.* administrar

administration, *n.* administración

admirable, *adj.* admirable

admiral, *n.* almirante, *m.*

admiration, *n.* admiración, *f.*

admire, *vt.* admirar; contemplar

admirer, *n.* admirador, *m.*; pretendiente, *m.*

admission, *n.* admisión, entrada, *f.*

admit, *vt.* admitir, dar entrada; reconocer

adolescence, *n.* adolescencia, *f.*

adopt,, *vt.* adoptar

adoption, *n.* adopción, *f.*

adrift, *adj.* y *adv.* flotante, al garete

adult, *adj.* y *n.* adulto, adulta

advance, *vt.* avanzar; pagar adelantado; *vi.* progresar; *n.* adelanto, *m.*

advantage, *n.* ventaja, *f.*; provecho, *m.*; **to take advantage of**, aprovecharse de

advantageous, *adj.* ventajoso, útil

adventure, *n.* aventura, *f.*

adventurer, *n.* aventurero, *m.*

adverb, *n.* adverbio, *m.*

adversity, *n.* adversidid, *f.*

advertise, *vt.* avisar, anunciar

advertisement, *n.* aviso, anuncio, *m.*

advice, *n.* consejo, *m.*; parecer, *m.*

advisable, *adj.* prudente, conveniente

advise, *vt.* aconsejar; avisar

adviser, *n.* consejero, *m.*

advisory, *adj.* consultivo

aerial, *adj.* aéreo; *n.* antena, *f.*

aeronautics, *n.* aeronáutica, *f.*

aerosol bomb, *n.* bomba de aerosol, *f.*

aerospace, *n.* atmósfera y espacio exterior

affair, *n.* asunto, *m.*

affect, *vt.* conmover; afectar

affected, *adj.* afectado, fingido
affection, *n.* amor, afecto, *m.*
affectionate, *adj.* afectuoso
affiliation, *n.* afiliación, *f.*
affirmative, *adj.* afirmativo
affix, *vt.* anexar, fijar
afflict, *vt.* afligir
afford, *vt.* dar; proveer; tener los medios
afraid, *adj.* miedoso; **to be afraid,** tener miedo
Afro, *adj.* afro
after, *prep.* después de, detrás; *adv.* después
afternoon, *n.* tarde, *f.*
afterward, afterwards, *adv.* después
again, *adv.* otra vez
against, *prep.* contra
age, *n.* edad, *f.*; **of age,** mayor de edad; *vi.* envejecer
agent, *n.* agente, *m.*
aggravate, *vt.* agravar
aggression, *n.* agresión, *f.*
ago, *adv.* pasado, tiempo ha; **long ago,** hace mucho
agony, *n.* agonía, *f.*
agrarian, *adj.* agrario
agree, *vi.* convenir; consentir
agreeable, *adj.* agradable
agreement, *n.* acuerdo, *m.*; conformidad, *f.*
agricultural, *adj.* agrario, agrícola
agriculture, *n.* agricultura, *f.*
aid, *vt.* ayudar, socorrer; *n.* ayuda, *f.*; auxilio, *m.*
ailment, *n.* dolencia, *f.*
aim, *vt.* apuntar; aspirar a; *n.* designio, intento, *m.*; puntería, *f.*
air, *n.* aire, *m.*; tonada, *f.*; **air brush,** aerógrafo, *m.*; **air drill,** perforadora, *f.*; **air freight,** flete aéreo, *m.* **air-conditioned,** *adj.* con aire acondicionado
airlift, *n.* puente aéreo, *m.*
airplane, *n.* aeroplano, *m.*
airport, *n.* aeropuerto, *m.*
airtight, *adj.* herméticamente cerrado
aisle, *n.* pasillo, *m.*; pasadizo, *m.*
alarm, *n.* alarma, *f.*; **alarm**

clock, reloj despertador, *m.*; *vt.* alarmar
album, *n.* álbum, *m.*
alcoholic, *adj.* alcohólico
alderman, *n.* concejal, *m.*
ale, *n.* variedad de cerveza
alert, *adj.* alerto, vivo
algebra, *n.* álgebra, *f.*
alibi, *n.* (law) coartada, *f.*
alien, *n.* extranjero, extranjera
alike, *adj.* semejante, igual
alive, *adj.* vivo, viviente
all, *adj.* todo; *adv.* enteramente; **all right,** bueno, satisfactorio; *n.* todo, *m.*
allege, *vt.* alegar, declarar
allegiance, *n.* lealtad, *f.*
allegory, *n.* alegoría *f.*
allergen, *n.* alergeno, *m.*
allergic, *adj.* alérgico
alley, *n.* callejón, *m.*
allied, *adj.* aliado
alligator, *n.* lagarto, caimán, *m.*; **alligator pear,** aguacate, *m.*
allot, *vt.* asignar, repartir
allotment, *n.* asignación, *f.*; parte, porción, *f.*
allow, *vt.* conceder; permitir
allowance, *n.* ración, *f.*; mesada, *f.*
allude, *vt.* aludir
alluring, *adj.* seductor
ally, *n.* aliado, asociado, *m.*; *vt.* vincular
almanac, *n.* almanaque, *m.*
almighty, *adj.* omnipotente, todopoderoso
almond, *n.* almendra, *f.*
almost, *adv.* casi, cerca de
alms, *n.* limosna, *f.*
alone, *adj.* solo; *adv.* a solas
along, *adv.* a lo largo; junto con
aloof, *adj.* reservado, apartado
aloud, *adv.* recio; en voz alta
alphabet, *n.* alfabeto, *m.*
Alps, Alpes, *m. pl.*
already, *adv.* ya
also, *adv.* también
alter, *vt.* alterar, modificar
alteration, *n.* alteración, *f.*
alternate, *vt.* alternar, variar; *n.* suplente, *m.* y *f.*
altimeter, *n.* altímetro, *m.*

altitude, *n.* altitud, *f.*

alto, *n.* contralto, *f.*

aluminum, *n.* aluminio, *m.*

always, *adv.* siempre

A.M., Master of Arts, Maestro o Licenciado en Artes

A.M., a.m., before noon, A.M. antemeridiano

am (1ª persona del singular de indicativo del verbo **to be**), soy; estoy

amateur, *n.* aficionado, aficionada

amaze, *vt.* asombrar

amazing, *adj.* asombroso

ambassador, *n.* embajador, *m.*

ambition, *n.* ambición, *f.*

ambitious, *adj.* ambicioso

ambulance, *n.* ambulancia, *f.*

amen, *interj.* amén

amend, *vt.*, *vi.* enmendar

amendment, *n.* enmienda, reforma, *f.*

American, *n.* y *adj.* americano, americana

amiable, *adj.* amable

amid, amidst, *prep.* entre, en medio de

amino acid, *n.* aminoácido, *m.*

ammonia, *n.* amoniaco, *m.*

ammunition, *n.* munición, *f.*

among, amongst, *prep.* entre, en medio de

amount, *n.* suma, *f.*; monto, *m.*; *vi.* importar

ample, *adj.* amplio, vasto

amplify, *vt.* ampliar, extender

amputate, *vt.* amputar

amt., amount, *v/* valor

amuse, *vt.* divertir

amusement, *n.* diversión, *f.*, pasatiempo, *m.*

amusing, *adj.* divertido

an, *art.* un, uno, una

analysis, *n.* análisis, *m.* y *f.*

analyze, *vt.* analizar

anatomy, *n.* anatomía, *f.*

ancestors, *n. pl.* antepasados, *m. pl.*

ancestry, *n.* linaje, *m.*

anchor, *n.* ancla, áncora, *f.*; *vi.* echar anclas

ancient, *adj.* antiguo

and, *conj.* y; e (antes de palabras que empiezan con *i* o *hi*,

con excepción de *hie*)

Andalusian, *n.* y *adj.* andaluz, andalza

anecdote, *n.* anécdota, *f.*

anesthetic, *adj.* y *n.* anestésico, *m.*

angel, *n.* ángel, *m.*

anger, *n.* ira, cólera, *f.*; *vt.* enojar, encolerizar

Anglo-Saxon, *n.* y *adj.* anglosajón, anglosajona

angry, *adj.* enojado

anguish, *n.* ansia, angustia, *f.*

animal, *n.* y *adj.* animal, *m.*

animation, *n.* animación, *f.*

ankle, *n.* tobillo, *m.*

anniversary, *n.* aniversario, *m.*

announce, *vt.* anunciar, publicar; notificar, avisar

announcement, *n.* aviso, anuncio, *m.*, notificación, *f.*

announcer, *n.* anunciador, anunciadora; locutor, locutora

annoy, *vt.* molestar; fastidiar

annoyance, *n.* molestia, *f.*; fastidio, *m.*; (coll.) lata,

annual, *adj.* anual

annuity, *n.* pension, anualidad *f.*

annul, *vt.* anular, aniquilar

annulment, *n.* anulación, *f.*

anonymous, *adj.* anónimo

another, *adj.* otro, diferente

answer, *vi.* responder, contestar; *vt.* refutar; contestar; *n.* respuesta, contestación, *f.*

ant, *n.* hormiga, f

antenna, *n.* antena, *f.*

antibiotic, *n.* y *adj.* antibiótico, *m.*

anticipate, *vt.* anticipar, prevenir

antihistamine, *n.* antihistamina, *f.*

antiknock, *n.* antidetonante, *m.*

antimatter, *n.* antimateria, *f.*

antique, *adj.* antiguo; *n.* antigüedad, *f.*

antiseptic, *adj.* antiséptico

antitank gun, *n.* cañón anticarro o antitanque, *m.*

anvil, *n.* yunque, *m.*

anxiety, *n.* ansiedad, *f.*

anxious, *adj.* ansioso

any, *adj.* cualquier, algún

anyhow, *adv.* de cualquier modo; de todos modos

anyone, *pron.* alguno, cualquiera

anything, *pron.* algo

anyway, *adv.* como quiera; de todos modos

apart, *adv.* aparte; separadamente

apartment, *n.* departamento, apartamento, apartamiento

ape, *n.* mono, *m.*; *vt.* imitar

apiece, *adv.* por cabeza, por persona

apologize, *vi.* disculparse

apology, *n.* disculpa, *f.*

apostle, *n.* apóstol, *m.*

apparatus, *n.* aparato, *m.*

apparel, *n.* vestido, *m.*; ropa, *f.*

apparent, *adj.* evidente, aparente

appeal, *vi.* apelar; recurrir; atraer; *n.* súplica, *f.*; (law) apelación, *f.*; simpatía, atracción, *f.*

appear, *vi.* aparecer; ser evidente; salir

appearance, *n.* apariencia, *f.*; aspecto, *m.*

appease, *vt.* apaciguar, aplacar

appendicitis, *n.* apendicitis, *f.*

appendix, *n.* apéndice, *m.*

appetite, *n.* apetito, *m.*

appetizer, *n.* aperitivo, *m.*; entremés, *m.*

applaud, *vt.* aplaudir; aclamar

applause, *n.* aplauso, *f.*

apple, *n.* manzana, *f.*

appliance, *n.* utensilio, aparato, *m.*, herramienta, *f.*

application, *n.* solicitud, *f.*; aplicación, *f.*

apply, *vt.* aplicar; **to apply for,** solicitar; *vi.* dirigirse a, recurrir a

appoint, *vt.* nombrar, designar

appointment, *n.* nombramiento, *m.*; cita, *f.*, compromiso, *m.*

appraise, *vt.* tasar; valuar

appreciate, *vt.* apreciar

apprentice, *n.* aprendiz, *m.*

approach, *vt.* y *vi.* abordar; aproximarse; *n.* acercamiento, *m.*

appropriate, *vt.* apropiar, asignar (una partida); *adj.* apropiado

appropriation, *n.* apropiación, partido, *f.*

approval, *n.* aprobación, *f.*

approve, *vt.* aprobar

approximate, *adj.* aproximado

apricot, *n.* albaricoque, *m.*; (Mex.) chabacano, *m.*

April, *n.* abril, *m.*

apron, *n.* delantal, *m.*

apt, *adj.* apto, idóneo

aptitude, *n.* aptitud, *f.*

aquarium, *n.* acuario, *m.*

aqueduct, *n.* acueducto, *m.*

Arab, Arabian, *n.* y *adj.* árabe, *m.* y *f.*, arábigo, arábiga

arbitrary, *adj.* arbitrario

arbitration, *n.* arbitraje, *f.*

arbor, *n.* enramada, *f.*

arc, *n.* arco, *m.*

arch, *n.* arco (de círculo, de puente, etc.), *m.*

archbishop, *n.* arzobispo, *m.*

archipelago, *n.* archipiélago, *m.*

architect, *n.* arquitecto, *m.*

architecture, *n.* arquitectura *f.*

arctic, *adj.* ártico

ardent, *adj.* ardiente, apasionado

ardor, *n.* ardor, *m.*; pasión, *f.*

are, plural y 2ª persona del singular de indicativo del verbo **to be**

area, *n.* área, *f.*; espacio, *m.*; superfide, *f.*

arena, *n.* pista, *f.*

argue, *vi.* disputar, argüir

argument, *n.* argumento, *m.*, controversia, *f.*

arid, *adj.* árido, seco

arise, *vi.* levantarse

aristocracy, *n.* aristocracia, *f.*

aristocrat, *n.* aristócrata, *m.* y *f.*

arithmetic, *n.* aritmética, *f.*

ark, *n.* arca, *f.*

arm, *n.* brazo, *m.*; arma, *f.*

armament, n. armamento, m.

armistice, n. armisticio, m.

armor, n. armadura, f.

armored, adj. blindado, acorazado

army, n. ejército, m.

around, prep. en, cerca; adv. al rededor

arrange, vt. arreglar

arrangement, n. arreglo, m.

arrest, n. arresto, m.; detención, f.; vt. arrestar, prender

arrival, n. arribo, m.; llegada, f.

arrive, vi. arribar; llegar

arrow, n. flecha, f.; dardo, m.

arsenic, n. arsénico, m.

art, n. arte, m. y f.; ciencia, f.; **the fine arts**, las bellas artes

artery, n. arteria, f.

arthritis, n. artritis, f.

article, n. artículo, m.

artillery, n. artillería, f.

artisan, n. artesano, m.

artist, n. artista, m. y f.; pintor, pintora

artistic, adj. artístico

as, conj. y adv. como; mientras; pues; visto que, pues que; **as much**, tanto; **as far as**, hasta; **as to**, en cuanto a

ascend, vi. ascender, subir

ascent, n. subida, f.

ash, n. (bot.) fresno, m.; **ashes**, pl. ceniza, f.; **ash tray**, cenicero, m.

ashamed, adj. avergonzado; **to be ashamed**, tener vergüenza

ashore, adv. en tierra, a tierra

Asiatic, n. y adj. asiático, asiática

aside, adv. al lado, aparte

ask, vt. y vi. pedir; interrogar

asleep, adj. dormido; **to fall asleep**, dormirse

asparagus, n. espárrago, m.

aspect, n. aspecto, m.

aspire, vi. aspirar, desear

aspirin, n. aspirina, f.

ass, n. borrico, asno, m.

assail, vt. asaltar, atacar

assassin, n. asesino, m.

assassinate, vt. asesinar

assault, n. asalto, m.; vt. acometer, asaltar

assemble, vt. congregar, convocar; esamblar, armar; vi. juntarse

assembly, n. asamblea, junta, f.; congreso, m.; montaje, m.; **assembly line**, línea de montaje

assert, vt. sostener, mantener; afirmar

assertion, n. aserción, f.

assessment, n. impuesto, m.; catastro, m.

assessor, n. asesor, m.

asset, n. algo de valor; ventaja, f.; **assets**, pl. (com.) haber, activo, capital, m.

assign, vt. asignar, destinar

assignment, n. asignación, f.; tarea escolar, f.

assimilate, vt. asimilar

assist, vt. asistir, ayudar

assistance, n. asistencia, f.; socorro, m.

assistant, n. asistente, ayudante, m.

associate, vt. asociar; acompañar; adj. asociado; n. socio, compañero, m.

association, n. asociación, agrupación, f.; club, m.

assume, vt. asumir

assumption, n. suposición, f.; **Assumption**, n. Asuncion, f.

assurance, n. seguridad, convicción, f.

assure, vt. asegurar, afirmar

asthma, n. asma, f.

astonishing, adj. asombroso

astounding, adj. asombroso

astray, adj. y adv. extraviado, descaminado; **to lead astray**, desviar, seducir

astringent, adi. astringente

astronomy, n. astronomía, f.

astute, adj. astuto; aleve

asylum, n. asilo, refugio, m.; **insane asylum**, manicomio, m.

at, prep. a, en; **at once**, al instante; **at last**, al fin, por último

ate, pretérito del verbo **eat**

athlete, n. atleta, m. y f.

athletics, n. pl. deportes, m.

pl.

Atlantic, *n.* y *adj.* Atlántico

atmosphere, *n.* atmósfera. *f.;* ambiente, *m.*

atom, *n.* átomo, *m.;* **atom bomb,** bomba atómica

atomic, *adj.* atómico

atomizer, *n.* pulverizador, *m.*

atone, *vt.* expiar, pagar

attach, *vt.* prender; juntar, adherir; embargar

attachment, *n.* anexo, *m.*

attack, *vt.* atacar; *n.* ataque, *m.*

attain, *vt.* obtener, alcanzar

attempt, *vt.* probar, experimentar; procurar; *n.* tentative, *f.;* prueba, *f.*

attend, *vt.* asistir; *vi.* prestar atención

attendance, *n.* asistencia, *f.*

attention, *n.* atención,

attest, *vt.* atestiguar; dar fe

attire, *n.* atavío, *m.; vt.* adornar, ataviar

attitude, *n.* actitud, *f.*

attorney, *n.* abogado, *m.*

attract, *vt.* atraer

attraction, *n.* atracción, *f.;* atractivo, *m.*

attractive, *adj.* atractivo, seductor

attribute, *vt.* atribuir, imputar; *n.* atributo, *m.*

auburn, *adj.* y *n.* castaño rojizo

auction, *n.* subasta, *f.,* remate, *m.*

audacious, *adj.* audaz, temerario

audience, *n.* audiencia, *f.;* auditorio, *m.;* concurrencia, *f.*

audition, *n.* audición, *f.; vt.* conceder audición; *vi.* presentar audición

auditor, *n.* contador, *m.*

audio-visual, *adj.* audio-visual

August, *n.* agosto (mes), *m.*

aunt, *n.* tía,

auspices *n. pl.* auspicio, *m.;* protección

austere, *adj.* austero

austerity, *n.* austeridad, crueldad, severidad, *f.*

authentic, *adj.* auténtico

author, *n.* autor, escritor, *m.*

authority, *n.* autoridad, *f.*

authorization, *n.* autorización, *f.*

authorize, *vt.* autorizar

autobiography, *n.* autobiografía, *f.*

auto, *n.* auto, *m.*

autograph, *n.* y *adj.* autógrafo, *m.*

automate, *vt.* automatizar

automatic, *adj.* automático

automobile, *n.* automóvil, *m.*

autumn, *n.* otoño, *m.*

auxiliary, *adj.* auxiliar, asistente

avail, *vt.* aprovechar; *vi.* servir, ser ventajoso; *n.* provecho, *m.*

ave., avenue, av. avenida

avenue, *n.* avenida, *f.*

average, *n.* término medio, promedio, *m.; adj.* medio, mediano, común y corriente

aviation, *n.* aviación, *f.*

aviator, *n.* aviador, *m.*

avocado, *n.* aguacate, *m.*

avocation, *n.* diversión, afición, *f.*

avoid, *vt.* evitar, escapar

await, *vt.* aguardar; **awaiting your reply,** en espera de sus noticias

awake, *vt.* y *vi.* despertar; *adj.* despierto

award, *vt.* otorgar, adjudicar; *n.* premio, *m.,* adjudicación, *f.*

aware, *adj.* enterado; consciente

away, *adv.* ausente, fuera

awe, *n.* miedo, pavor, *m.;* temor reverencial, *m.*

awhile, *adv.* por un rato

awkward, *adj.* tosco, torpe

awning, *n.* toldo, *m.*

ax, axe, *n.* segur, *f.;* hacha, *f.*

axis, *n.* eje, *m.;* alianza, *f.*

axle, *n.* eje de una rueda

aye, ay, *adv.* sí

B

B.A., Bachelor of Arts, Br.

Bachiller

babe, n. nene, bebé, m.

baby, n. nene, infante, m.

baby-sit, vi. servir de niñera

bachelor, n. soltero, m.; bachiller, m.

back, n. dorso, m.; espalda, f.; lomo, m.; adj. posterior; vt. sostener, apoyar; adv. atrás, detrás

backbone, n. espinazo, m., espina dorsal f.

background, n. fondo, m.; ambiente, m.; antecedentes, m. pl.; educación, f.

backlash, n. reacción, f.

backup, n. (mil.) apoyo, m.; (com.) acumulación, congestión, f.; adj. suplente

backward, adj. retrógrado; **backwards**, adv. hacia atrás

bacon, n. tocino, m.

bacteria, n. pl. bacterias, f. pl.

badge, n. divisa, f.

baffle, vt. eludir; confundir

bag, n. saco, m.; bolsa, f.

baggage, n. equipaje, m.

bail, n. fianza, f.; fiador, m.; **to go bail for**, salir fiador

bait, vt. cebar; atraer; n. carnada, f.

bake, vt. cocer en horno

baker, n. panadero, m.

bakery, n. panadería, f.

balance, n. equilibria m.; resto, m.; balance, m.; saldo, m.; vt. equilibrar; saldar; considerar

balcony, n. balcón, m.; galería, f.

bald, adj. calvo

bale, n. bala, f.; paca, f.; vt. embalar

balk, vi. rebelarse (un caballo, etc.)

ball, n. bola, f.; pelota, f.; baile, m.

ballad, n. balada, f.; romance, m.

ballet, n. ballet, m.

ballot, n. balota, papeleta, f.

ballroom, n. salón de baile, m.

balm, n. bálsamo, m.

bamboo, n. bambú, m.

ban, n. edicto, m.; prohibición,

f.; vt. prohibir; excomulgar

banana, n. plátano, m.

band, n. venda, faja, f.; cuadrilla, f.; banda, f.; orquesta, vt. unir, juntar

bandage, n. venda, f.; vendaje, m.; vt. vendar

bandit, n. bandido, bandida

bane, n. veneno, m.; calamidad, f.

banish, vt. desterrar

banister, n. pasamano, m.

bank, n. orilla (de rio), ribera, f.; montón de tierra; banco, m.; **savings bank**, banco de ahorros; vt. poner dinero en un banco

banker, n. banquero, m.

banking, n. banca, f.; adj. bancario

bankrupt, adj. quebrado, en bancarrota

banner, n. bandera, estandarte, m.

banquet, n. banquete, m.

baptism, n. bautismo, bautizo, m.

baptize, vt. bautizar

bar, n. barra, f.; foro, m.; obstáculo, m.; cantina, f.; vt. impedir; excluir; **bars**, rejas, f. pl.

barbaric, adj. bárbaro, cruel, fiero

barbecue, n. barbacoa, f.

barbell, n. haltera, f.

barber, n. barbero, peluquero, m.

barbershop, n. peluquería, barbería, f.

bare, adj. desnudo, descubierto; simple; vt. desnudar, descubrir

barefoot, adj. descalzo

barely, adv. apenas

bargain, n. ganga, f.; vt. regatear

barge, n. chalupa, f.

baritone, n. barítono, m.

bark, n. corteza, f.; ladrido, m.; vi. ladrar

barley, n. cebada, f.

barn, n. granero, establo, m.

barnyard, n. corral, m.

barometer, n. barómetro, m.

barrack, n. cuartel, m.; barraca, f.

barrel, n. barril, m.; cañón de escopeta, m.

barren, adj. estéril; seco

barrier, n. barrera, f.

bartender, n. cantinero, m.

barter, vt. cambiar, trocar

base, n. fondo, m.; base, f.; contrabajo, m.; vt. apoyar; basar; adj. bajo, vil

baseball, n. baseball, beisbol m.; pelota de baseball

basement, n. sótano, m.

bashful, adj. vergonzoso

basic, adj. fundamental

basis, n. base, f.

basket, n. cesta, canasta, f.

basketball, n. baloncesto, m.; juego de balón, m.

bass, n. (mus.) contrabajo, m.; bajo, m.; (zool.) lobina, f., róbalo or robalo, m.; adj. bajo; **bass viol,** violonchelo, m.

bassinet, n. cesta-cuna, f.

basso, n. (mus.) bajo, m.

bastard, n. y adj. bastardo, bastarda

baste, vt. pringar la carne; hilvanar

bat, n. (baseball) bate, m.; murciélago, m.

batch, n. hornada, f.; conjunto, m.

bath, n. baño, m.

bathe, vt. y vi. bañar, bañarse

bathrobe, n. bata de baño, f.

bathroom, n. cuarto de baño, m.

bathtub, n. bañera, f.; tina de baño, f.

baton, n. batuta, f.

battalion, n. batallón, m.

batter, n. pasta culinaria, f.; (baseball) bateador, m.

battery, n. acumulador, m.

battle, n. batalla, f.

bawl, vt. gritar, vocear; chillar

bay, n. bahía, f.

bazaar, n. bazar, m.

bbl., barrel, brl., barril

B. C., Before Christ, A. de J.C., antes de Jesucristo

beach, n. playa, f.

beacon, n. faro, m.

bead, n. cuenta, chaquira, f.

beak, n. rayo de luz, m.; vi. brillar

bean, n. (bot.) haba, habichuela, f.; frijol, m.

bear, n. oso, m.; vt. soportar; parir; **to bear in mind,** tener presente

bearer, n. portador, portadora

bearing, n. comportamiento, m.; relación, f.

beast, n. bestia, f.

beastly, adj. bestial, brutal

beat, vt. golpear; batir; ganar (en un juego); vi. pulsar; palpitar; n. pulsación, f.; (mus) compás, m.

beater, n. batidor, m.

beautiful, adj. hermoso, hello

beautify, vt. embellecer

beauty, n. hermosura, belleza, f.; beauty parlor, salón de belleza, m.

beck, n. seña, f.; **at one's beck and call,** a la mano, a la disposición

beckon, vi. llamar con señas

become, vt. sentar, quedar bien; vi. hacerse, convertirse; llegar a ser

becoming, adj. que sienta o cae bien; decoroso

bed, n. cama

bedclothes, n. pl. cobertores, m. pl.; mantas, colchas, f. pl.

bedding, n. ropa de cama, f.

bedridden, adj. postrado en cama

bedroom, n. dormitorio, m.

bedspread, n. sobrecama, f.

bee, n. abeja, f.

beech, n. (bot.) haya, f.

beef, n. carne de res, f.

beefsteak, n. biftec, bistec, m.

beehive, n. colmena, f.

been, p. p. del verbo be

beer, n. cerveza, f.

beet, n. remolacha, betarraga, f.; (Mex.) betabel, m.

beetle, n. escarabajo, m.

befall, vi. sobrevenir

before, adv. más adelante; prep. antes de, ante; conj. antes que

beforehand, adv. de antemano

beg, vt. mendigar, pedir

began, pretérito del verbo **begin**

beggar, n. mendigo, mendiga; limosnero, limosnera

begin, vt. y vi. comenzar, principiar

beginning, n. principio, comienzo, m.

begun, p. p. del verbo begin

behalf, n. favor, patrocinio, m.; **in behalf of,** en pro de

behave, vi. comportarse

behavior, n. comportamiento, m.

behind, prep. detrás; atrás; adv. atrás

behold, vt. ver, contemplar

beige, n. color arena, m.

being, n. ser, m.; existencia, f.

belated, adj. atrasado

belch, vi. eructar (or erutar

Belgium, Bélgica

believe, vt. y vi. creer; pensar

bell, n. campana, f.; timbre, m.

bellow, vi. bramar; rugir

bellows, n. fuelle, m.

belly, n. vientre, m.; panza, barriga, f.

belong, vi. pertenecer

belongings, n. pl. propiedad, f.; efectos, m. pl.

beloved, adj. querido, amado

below, adv. y prep. debajo, inferior; abajo

belt, n. cinturón, m.; correa, f.

bend, vt. doblar, plegar; vi. inclinarse

beneath, adv. y prep. debajo, abajo

benediction, n. bendición, f.

benefactor, n. bienhechor, bienhechora

beneficial, adj. beneficioso, útil

beneficiary, n. beneficiario, beneficiaria

benefit, n. beneficio, m.; utilidad, f.; provecho, m.; vt. y vi. beneficiar

benevolent, adj. benévolo

bequest, n. legado, m.

bereavement, n. luto, duelo, m.

beret, n. boina, f.

berry, n. baya, f.

berth, n. litera, f.; camarote, m.

beseech, vt. suplicar, rogar

beside, besides, prep. al lado de; fuera de; adv. además

best, adj. y adv. mejor; **best man,** padrino de boda

bestow, vt. otorgar

bet, n. apuesta, f.; apostar

betatron, n. betatrón

betray, vt. traicionar; divulgar (algún secreto)

betrothed, adj. comprometido, prometido; n. prometido, prometida

better, adj. y adv. mejor; vt. mejorar; **betters,** n. pl. superiores, m. pl.

beverage, n. bebida, f.

bewail, vt. y vi. lamentar, deplorar

beware, vi. tener cuidado

bewilder, vt., vi. turbar; confundirse

beyond, prep. más allá; fuera de

bias, n. parcialidad, f.; sesgo, m.; **on the bias,** al sesgo; vt. inclinar, influir

biased, adj. predispuesto

bib, n. babero, m.

Bible, n. Biblia, f.

bicker, vi. reñir, disputar

bicycle, n. bicicleta, f.

bid, vt. convidar; mandar, ordenar; ofrecer; n. licitación, oferta f.

bide, vi. esperar, aguardar

biennial, adj. bienal

big, adj. grande

bile, n. bilis, f.; cólera, f.

bilingual, adj. bilingüe

bill, n. pico de ave, m.; cuenta, f.; factura, f.; **bill of fare,** menú, m.; vt. facturar; vi. arrullar

billfold, n. billetera, f.

billiards, n. billar, m.

billion, n. billón, m., millón de millones (en España, Inglaterra, y Alemania); mil millones (en Francia y los Estados Unidos)

bimonthly, adj. bimestral

bind, *vt.* atar; unir; encuadernar; obligar; *vi.* ser obligatorio

binder, *n.* encuadernador, *m.*

binding, *n.* venda, fala, *f.*; encuademación, *f.*

binoculars, *n. pl.* gemelos, binóculos, *m. pl.*

bioastronautics, *n. pl.* bioastronáutica, *f.*

biochemical, *adj.* bioquímico

biodegradable, *adj.* biodegradable, hecho de compuestos que se descomponen por bacterias

biography, *n.* biografía, *f.*

biology, *n.* biología, *f.*

biopsy, *n.* biopsia, *f.*

biosphere, *n.* biosfera, *f.*

birch, *n.* (bot.) abedul, *m.*

bird, *n.* ave, *f.*; pájaro, *m.*

birth, *n.* nacimiento, *m.*; origen, *m.*; parto, *m.*; linaje, *m.*; **to give birth,** dar a luz, parir

birthday, *n.* cumpleaños, natalicio, *m.*; **to have a birthday,** cumplir años

birthmark, *n.* lunar, *m.*

birthplace, *n.* lugar de nacimiento, *m.*

biscuit, *n.* galleta

bishop, *n.* obispo, *m.*; alfil (en el ajedrez), *m.*

bit, *n.* pedacito, *m.*; **two bits** (coll. E.U.A.), 25¢ (moneda de E.U.A.); *pretérito* del verbo **bite**

bite, *vt.* morder; *n.* mordida, *f.*; tentempié, *m.*

bitten, *p.* del verbo bite **bite**

bitter, *adj.* amargo

bitterness, *n.* amargor, *m.*; amargura, *f.*

biweekly, *adj.* quincenal; *adv.* quincenalmente

B/L, b.l., bill of lading, conto., conocimiento de embarque

blab, *vt., vi.* charlar, divulgar; chismear

black, *adj.* negro; oscuro; *n.* negro, *m.*

blackberry, *n.* zarzamora, mora, *f.*

blackboard, *n.* pizarra, *f.*; encerado, pizarrón, tablero, *m.*

blacksmith, *n.* herrero, *m.*

bladder, *n.* vejiga, *f.*

blade, *n.* brizna, hoja, *f.*

blame, *vt.* culpar

blameless, *adj.* inocente, intachable

bland, *adj.* blando, suave

blank, *adj.* en blanco; **blank form,** blanco, esqueleto, *m.*; *n.* blanco, espacio en blanco, *m.*

blanket, *n.* frazada, manta, *f.*; *adj.* general

blasé, *adj.* abúlico

blast, *n.* explosión, *f.*; chorro, *m.*; **blast furnace,** alto horno, *m.*

blaze, *n.* fuerg *m.*; incendio, *m.*; hoguera, *f.*; *vt.* resplandecer

bleach, *vt., vi.* blanquear

bleat, *n.* balido, *m.*; *vi.* balar

bled, *pretérito* y *p. p.* del verbo **bleed**

bleed, *vt., vi.* sangrar

blemish, *vt.* manchar; infamar; *n.* tacha, *f.*; infamia, *f.*; lunar, *m.*

blend, *vt.* mezclar, combinar; *vi.* armonizar; *n.* mezcla, *f.*; ammonia, *f.*

bless, *vt.* bendecir, santiguar

blessing, *n.* bendición, *f.*

blind, *adj.* ciego; oculto; *vt.* cegar; deslumbrar; *n.* subterfugio, *m.*; **Venetian blinds,** persianas

blindfold, *vt.* vendar los ojos

bink, *vi.* guiñar, parpadear

bliss, *n.* felicidad, *f.*; embeleso, *m.*

blister, *n.* vejiga, ampolla, *f.*; *vi.* ampollarse

bloat, *vi.* abotagarse

bloc, *n.* bloque, *m.*

block, *n.* bloque, *m.*; obstáculo, *m.*; manzana (de una calle), *f.*; *vt.* bloquear

blond, blonde, *n.* y *adj.* rubio, bia; (Mex.) güero, güera

blood, *n.* sangre, *f.*

blood bank, *n.* banco de sangre, *m.*

bloody, *adj.* sangriento

bloom, n. flor, f.; florecimiento, m.; vi. florecer

blossom, n. flor, f.; capullo, botón, m.; vi. florecer

blot, vt. manchar (lo escrito); cancelar; n. mancha, f.

blotter, n. papel secante, m.

blouse n. blusa, f.

blow, n. golpe, m.; vi. soplar, sonar; vt. soplar; inflar

blowout, n. reventazón, f.; (auto.) ruptura de neumático o llanta

blue, adj. azul, celeste

bluebird, n. (orn.) azulejo, m.

blues, n. pl. (coll.) melancolia, f.; tipo de jazz melancólico

bluff. n. risco escarpado, morro, m.; fanfarronada, f.; vi. engañar, hacer alarde

bluing, blueing, n. añil, m.

blunder, n. desatino, disparate, m.; vt. y vi. desatinar, equivocarse

blur, n. mancha, f.; vt. manchar; infamar

blvd., boulevard, bulevar, m.

boar, n. verraco, m.; **wild boar,** jabalí, m.

board, n. tabla, f.; mesa, f.; (naut.) bordo, m.; **board of directors,** directorio, m., junta directiva, f.; vt.abordar; entablar; vi. residir en casa de huéspedes; recibir huéspedes

boardinghouse, n. casa de huéspedes, pensión, f.

boast, n. jactancia, ostentación, f.; vi. presumir; jactarse

boastful. adj. iactancioso

boat, n. barco, m., embarcación, f.; barca, f.

bob, vi. menearse

bobby pin, n. horquilla, f.

bode, vt. y vi. presagiar

bodily, adj. y adv. corpóreo; en peso

body, n. cuerpo, m.; individuo, m.; gremio, m.

bodyguard, n. (mil.) guardaespaldas, m.

boil, vi. hervir, bullir; vt. cocer; n. (med.) nacido, m.

boiler, n. caldera, f.

boisterous, adj. ruidoso

bold, adj. audaz

bolt, n. tornillo, m.; cerrojo, m.

bom n. bomba, f.

bond, n. vínculo, lazo, m.; (com.) bono, m.

bone, n. hueso, m.; vt. deshuesar

boneless, adj. sin huesos, deshuesado

bonfire, n. hoguera, fogata, f.

bonnet, n. gorra, f.; bonete, m.

bony, adj. huesudo

boob, booby, n. tonto, tonta

book, n. libro, m.; vt. asentar en un libro, inscribir

bookcase, n. librero, m.

bookkeeper, n. tenedor de libros, m.

booklet, n. folleto, m.

bookstore, n. librería, f.

boom, n. estampido, m.; auge industrial, m.

boon, n. favor, m.

boost, vt. levantar; vi. aprobar con entusiasmo; n. ayuda, f., empuje, m.

boot, n. bota, f.; **to boot,** además, por añadidura

bootblack, n. limpiabotas, m.

booth, n. puesto, m.; cabina, f.; reservado, m.

bootlegger, n. contrabandista (usualmente de licores), m.

booty, n. botín, m.; presa, f.; saqueo, m.

border, n. orilla, f.; borde, m.; frontera, f.; vi. confinar; bordear

borderline, n. límite, m., orilla, f.; adj. incierto

boric, adj. bórico; **boric acid,** ácido bórico

boring, adj. fastidioso, latoso

born, adj. nacido; destinado; **to be born,** nacer

borne, p. p. del verbo **bear**

borrow, vt. pedir prestado

bosom, n. seno, pecho, m.

botanical, adj. botátnico

botany, n. botánica, f.

both, pron. y adj. ambos, ambas

bother, vt. molestar; incomodar; n. estorbo, m.; molestia, f.

bottle, _n._ botella, _f.; vt._ embotellar

bottleneck, _n._ cuello de botella, _m.;_ cuello de estrangulación, _m._

bottom, _n._ fondo, _m._

bottomless, _adj._ insondable; sin fondo

boudoir, _n._ tocador, _m.,_ recámara, _f._

bough, _n._ rama (de un árbol), _f._

bought, _pretérito y p. p._ del verbo **buy**

bouillon, _n._ caldo, _m._

boulevard, _n._ paseo, bulevar, _m._

bounce, _vi._ arremeter, brincar

bouncing, _adj._ fuerte, robusto

bound, _n._ límite, _m.;_ salto, _m.;vt._ confinar, limitar; _vi._ brincar; _pretérito y p. p._ del verbo **bind**; _adj._ destinado; **bound for,** con rumbo

boundary, _n._ límite, _m.;_ frontera, _f._

boundless, _adj._ ilimitado, infinito

bouquet, _n._ ramillete de flores, ramo, _m._

bout, _n._ encuentro, combate, _m._

bow, _vi._ encorvarse; hacer reverencia; _n._ reverencia, inclinación, _f._

bow, _n._ arco, _m.;_ lazo (de cinta, etc.), _m.;_ (naut.) proa, _f._

bowels, _n. pl._ intestinos, _m. pl.;_ entrañas, _f. pl._

bowl, _n._ taza, _f.;_ **wash bowl,** lavamanos, _m.;_ _vi._ jugar boliche o bolos

bowlegged, _adj._ patizambo

box, _n._ caja, _f.;_ cofre, _m.;_ **box office,** taquilla, _f.;_ _vi._ boxear

boxer, _n._ boxeador, pugilista, _m._

boxing, _n._ boxeo, pugilato, _m._

boy, _n._ muchacho, _m.;_ niño, _m.;_ **boy scout,** muchacho explorador, _m._

boycott, _n._ boicot, boicoteo, _m._

boyhood, _n._ niñez (varones), _f._

boyish, _adj._ pueril, propio de un niño varón

bra, _n._ brassière, _m.,_ soporte (para senos), _m._

bracelet, _n._ brazalete, _m.,_ pulsera, _f._

bracket, _n._ ménsula, _f.;_ (fig.) categoría, _f.;_ **brackets,** _pl._ (print.) corchetes, _m. pl._

brag, _n._ jactancia, _f.;_ _vi._ jactarse

brain, _n._ cerebro, _m._

brake, _n._ freno, _m._

branch, _n._ rama (de árbol), _f._

brand, _n._ marca, _f.;_ nota de infamia, _f.;_ marca de fábrica, _f.;_ _vt._ herrar (ganado); infamar

brandy, _n._ aguardiente, _m.;_ coñac, _m._

brass, _n._ latón, bronce, _m._

brave, _adj._ valiente

brawl, _n._ pelotera, _f._

bray, _vi._ rebuznar; _n._ rebuzno (del asno), _m._

breach, _n._ rotura, brecha, _f.;_ violación, _f._

bread, _n._ pan, _m._

break, _vt._ y _vi._ quebrar; violar; _n._ rotura, _f.;_ intrrrupción, _f._

break-even point, _n._ punto en que un negocio empieza a cubrir los gastos que ocasiona

breakfast, _n._ almuerzo, desayuno, _m._

breast, _n._ pecho, seno, _m.;_ tetas, _f. pl._

breath, _n._ aliento, _m.,_ respiración, _f.;_ soplo (de aire), _m._

breathe, _vt._ y _vi._ respirar; resollar

breathing, _n._ respiración, _f._

breathless, _adj._ falto de aliento

bred, _pretérito y p. p._ del verbo **breed; well bred,** bien educado, de buenos modales

breech, _n._ trasero, _m._

breeches, _n. pl._ calzones, _m. pl._

breed, _n._ casta, raza, _f.;_ _vt._ procrear, engendrar; educar

breeder reactor, _n._ reactor reproductor, _m._

breeding, _n._ crianza, _f.;_ modales, *m. pl.*

breeze, *n.* brisa, *f.*

brewery, *n.* cervecería, *f.*

bribe, *n.* cohecho, soborno, *m.;* *vt.* sobornar

brick, *n.* ladrillo, *m.*

bricklayer, *n.* albañil, *m.*

bridal, *adj.* nupcial

bride, *n.* novia, desposada, *f.*

bridegroom, *n.* novio, desposado, *m.*

bridesmaid, *n.* madrina de boda, *f.*

bridge, *n.* puente, *m.*

bridgework, *n.* puente dental, *m.*

bridle, *n.* brida, *f.,* freno, *m.;* *vt.* embridar; reprimir, refrenar

brief, *adj.* breve, sucinto; *n.* compendio *m.;* (law) escrito, *m.;* **brief case,** portapapeles, *m.*

brig, *n.* bergantín, *m.*

bright, *adj.* claro, brillante; vivo

brighten, *vt.* pulir, dar lustre; *vi.* aclarar

brightness, *n.* esplendor, *m.,* brillantez, *f.*

brilliance, brilliancy, *n.* brillantez, *f.,* brillo, esplendor, *m.*

brilliant, *adj.* brillante; luminoso; resplandeciente; *n.* brillante, *m.*

brim, *n.* borde, extremo *m.;* orilla, *f.;* ala (de sombrero), *f.*

bring, *vt.* llevar, traer; **to bring about,** efectuar; **to bring up,** educar

brink, *n.* orilla, *f.;* margen, *m.* y *f.,* borde, *m.*

broad, *adj.* ancho; **broad jump,** salto de longitud, *m.*

broadcast, *n.* radiodifusión, *f.;* *vt.* radiofundir, perifonear

broaden, *vt.* ensanchar

broad-minded, *adj.* tolerante

broil, *vt.* asar (carne, etc.)

broiler, *n.* parrilla, *f.*

broke, *pretérito* del verbo **break;** *adj.* (coll.) en bancarrota; sin dinero

broken, *adj.* roto, quebrado

broker, *n.* corredor, agente, *m.*

bronchitis, *n.* bronquitis, *f.*

brooch, *n.* broche, *m.*

brood, *n.* cría, nidada, *f.*

brook, *n.* arroyo, *m.,* quebrada, *f.*

broom, *n.* escoba, *f.*

broth, *n.* caldo, *m.*

brother, *n.* hermano, *m.*

brotherhood, *n.* hermandad; fraternidad, *f.*

brother-in-law, *n.* cuñado, *m.*

brotherly, *adj.* fraternal

brought, *pretérito* y *p. p.* del verbo **bring**

brow, *n.* ceja , *f.;* frente, *f.*

brown, *adj.* castaño, pardo; *vt.* dorar, tostar

bruise, *vt.* magullar; *n.* magulladura, contusión, *f.*

brunet, brunette, *n., adj.* trigueño, trigueña, moreno, morena

brush, *n.* escobilla, *f.;* brocha, *f.;* cepillo, *m.;* *vt.* acepillar

brutal, *adj.* brutal, bruto

brute, *n.* bruto, *m.;* *adj.* feroz, bestial

B.S., Bachelor of Science, Br. en C., Bachiller en Ciencias

bu., bushel, medida de áridos (Ingl. 36.37 litros; E.U. 35.28 litros)

bubble, *n.* burbuja, *f.;* *vi.* bullir; **bubble over,** borbotar; hervir

buckle, *n.* hebilla, *f.;* *vt.* afianzar

bud, *n.* pimpollo, botón, *m.;* capullo, *m.*

buddy, *n.* hermano, compañero, muchachito, *m.*

budget, *n.* presupuesto, *m.*

buffalo, *n.* búfalo, *m.*

buffers, *n. pl.* (rail.) parachoques, *m. pl.*

buffet, *n.* aparador, *m.;* ambigú, *m.*

bug, *n.* insecto, *m.*

bugle, *n.* clarín, *m.;* corneta, *f.*

bugler, *n.* corneta, trompetero, *m.*

build, *vt.* edificar; construir

builder, *n.* arquitecto, constructor, *m.*

building, n. edificio, m.; construcción, f.

bulb, n. bulbo, m.; **electric light bulb,** foco o bombilla de luz eléctrica

bulge, vi. combarse

bulk, n. masa, f.; bulto, volumen, m.; **in bulk,** a granel

bull, n. toro, m.

bulldog, n. bulldog, m.

bulldoze, vt. intimidar

bullet, n. bala, f.

bulletin, n. boletín, m.; **bulletin board,** tablilla para noticias, f.

bulletproof, adj. a prueba de bala

bullfight, n. corrida de toros, f.

bullfighter, n. torero, toreador, m.

bully, n. valentón, m.; rufián, m.; vi. fanfarronear

bulwark, n. baluarte, m.; vt. fortificar

bum, n. hombre vago, m.

bumblebee, n. abejón, abejorro, zángano, m.

bump, n. hinchazón, f.; golpe, m.; vt. y vi. chocar contra

bumper, n. amortiguador de golpes, m.; (auto) defensa, f.

bunch, n. ramo, racimo, m.

bundle, n. haz (de leña, etc.), m.; bulto, m.; vt. atar, hacer un lío o un bulto; **bundle up,** envolver; abrigarse

bunion, n. juanete, m.

bunk, n. (coll.) cama, f.; patraña, f.

buoy, n. boya, f.

burden, n. carga, f., cargo, m.; vt. cargar; gravar

bureau, n. armario, m.; tocador, m., cómoda, f., oficina, f.; departamento, m.

burglar, n. ladrón, m.

burial, n. entierro, m.

burlap, n. arpillera, f.

burlesque, adj. burlesco; vt. y vi. burlarse; parodiar

burn, vt. quemar, incendiar; vi. arder; n. quemadura, f.

burst, vi. reventar; abrirse; n. reventón, m.

bury, vt. enterrar, sepultar

bus, n. ómnibus, camión, m.

bushel, n. medida de áridos (Ingl. 36.37 litros; E.U. 35.28 litros)

business, n. negocio, m., ocupación, f.

businessman, n. comerciante, m.

businesswoman, n. mujer de negocios

bust, n. busto, m.

bustle, n. confusión, f.; ruido, m.

busy, adj. ocupado; atareado

busybody, n. entremetido, entremetida

but, prep. excepto; conj. y adv. menos; pero; solamente

butcher, n. carnicero, m.; vt. matar atrozmente

butt, n. cabezada (golpe de la cabeza), f.; colilla (de cigarro), f.

butter, n. mantequilla, manteca, f.

butterfly, n. mariposa, f.

buttermilk, n. suero de mantequilla, m.; (Mex.) jocoqui, m.

butterscotch, n. especie de dulce de azúcar y mantequilla

buttock, n. nalga, f.; anca, f.

button, n. botón, m.; vt. abotonar

buttonhole, n. ojal, m.

buxom, adj. robusto y rollizo

buy, vt. comprar

buzz, n. susurro, soplo, m.; vi. zumbar, cuchichear

buzzer, n. zumbador, m.

by, prep. por; a, en; de, con; al lado de, cerca de; adv. cerca, al lado de

bygone, adj. pasado

bylaws, n. pl. estatutos, m. pl., reglamento, m.

by-pass, n. desviación, f.; vt. evadir, eludir

by-product, n. derivado, m.

C

C., centigrade, C., centigrado;

current, corrte., cte., corriente

C.A., Central America, C.A. Centro América

cab, *n.* coche de plaza, coche de alquiler, *m.*

cabdriver, *n.* cochero, *m.*; (auto.) taxista, *m.* y *f.*

cabana, *n.* cabaña, *f.*

cabaret, *n.* cabaret, *m.*

cabbage, *n.* repollo, *m.*; berza, col, *f.*

cabin, *n.* cabaña, cabina, barraca, *f.*; camarote, *m.*

cabinet, *n.* gabinete, *m.*; ministerio, *m.*

cabinetmaker, *n.* ebanista, *m.*

cable, *n.* cable, cablegrama, *m.*

cablegram, *n.* cablegrama, *m.*

cackle, *vi.* cacarear, graznar; *n.* cacareo, *m.*; charla, *f.*

cactus, *n.* (bot.) cacto, *m.*

cad, *n.* sinverguenza, *m.*

cadence, *n.* cadencia, *f.*

cadet, *n.* cadete, *m.*

café, *n.* café, restaurante, *m.*

cafetería, *n.* restaurante en donde se sirve uno mismo

cake, *n.* bollo, *m.*; torta, *f.*; bizcocho, pastel, *m.*; *vi.* endurecerse; coagularse

calamity, *n.* calamidad, miseria *f.*

calcimine, *n.* lechada, *f.*

calcium, *n.* calcio, *m.*

calculate, *vt.* calcular, contar

calendar, *n.* calendario, *m.*

calf, *n.* ternero, ternera; cuero de ternero; **calf of the leg**, pantorrilla, *f.*

calfskin, *n.* piel de ternera, *f.*; becerro, *m.*

caliber, *n.* calibre, *m.*

calisthentics, *n. pl.* calisténica, gimnasia

call, *vt.* llamar nombrar; convocar, citar; *n.* llamada, *f.*; vocación, profesión, *f.*

calling, *n.* profesión, vocación, *f.*

callous, *adj.* calloso, endurecido; insensible

calm, *n.* calma, tranquilidad, *f.*; *vt.* calmar; aplacar; **to calm down**, serenar, serenarse

camera, *n.* cámara, *f.*

camouflage, *n.* (mil.) camuflage, *m.*, simulación, *f.*, engaño, *m.*

camp, *n.* campamento, campo, *m.*; *vi.* acampar

campaign, *n.* campaña, *f.*

campfire, *n.* hoguera en el campo

camphor, *n.* alcanfor, *m.*

campus, *n.* patio o terrenos de una universidad, etc

can, *vi.* poder, saber; *vt.* envasar en latas; *n.* lata, *f.*, bote de lata; **can opener**, abrelatas, *m.*

Canada, Canadá, *m.*

Canadian, *n.* y *adj.* canadiense

canal, *n.* canal, *m.*

Canal Zone, Zona del Canal, *f.*

Canaries, Canary Islands, Las Canarias, Islas Canarias, *f. pl.*

canary, *n.* canario, *m.*

canasta, *n.* canasta, *f.* (juego de naipes)

cancel, *vt.* cancelar, borrar, anular

cancer, *n.* cáncer, *m.*

candid, *adj.* cándido, ingenuo

candidate, *n.* candidato, candidata, aspirante (a un puesto, cargo, etc.), *m.* y *f.*

candied, *adj.* garapiñado, en almíbar

candle, *n.* vela, bujía, *f.*

candlestick, *n.* candelero, *m.*

candy, *n.* confite, bombón, dulce, *m.*

cane, *n.* caña, *f.*; bastón, *m.*

cannibal, *n.* caníbal, *m.*, antropófago, antropófaga

cannon, *n.* cañón, *m.*

canoe, *n.* canoa, *f.*; bote, *m.*; (Mex.) chalupa, *f.*; piragua, *f.*

canonize, *vt.* canonizar

cantaloupe, *n.* melón de verano, *m.*

canteen, *n.* (mil.) cantina, *f.*, especie de tienda de provisiones para soldados; cantimplora, *f.*

canvas, *n.* lona

canvass, *vi.* solicitar votos, etc
canyon, *n.* desfiladero, cañon, *m.*
cap, *n.* goffa, *f.*, cachucha, *f.*; **cap and gown**, traje académico o toga y birrete
cap., **capital letter**, may., letra mayúscula
capable, *adj.* capaz
capacity, *n.* capacidad, *f.*; inteligencia, habilidad, *f.*; **seating capacity**, cabida, *f.*, cupo, *m.*
cape, *n.* cabo, *m.*; capa, *f.*; capota, *f.*; capote, *m.*
Cape Horn, Cabo de Hornos,*m.*
Cape of Good Hope, Cabo de Buena Esperanza, *m.*
caper, *n.* travesura, *f.*; alcaparra, *f.*
capital, *adj.* capital, excelente; principal; **capital punishment**, pena de muerte; *n.* (arch.) capitel, *m.*; capital (la ciudad principal), *f.*; capital, fondo, *m.*; mayuscula, *f.*
capitalist, *n.* capitalista, *m.* y *f.*
captain, *n.* capitán, *m.*
capricious, *adj.* caprichoso
capsize, *vt.*, *vr.* volcar, volcarse
capt., **Captain**, cap., capitán
captain, *n.* capitán, *m.*
captivate, *vt.* cautivar
captive, *n.* cautivo, va, esclavo, esclava
capture, *n.* captura, *f.*; toma, *f.*; *vt.* apresar; capturar
car, *n.* carreta, *f.*; carro, *m.*; coche, *m.*
caravan, *n.* caravana, *f.*
carbon, *n.* carbón, *m.*; **carbon paper**, papel carbón
carburetor, *n.* carburador, *m.*
carcass, *n.* animal muerto, *m.*; casco, *m.*; armazón, *m.*
card, *n.* naipe, *m.*, carta, *f.*; tarjeta, *f.*
cardinal, *adj.* cardinal, principal; rojo, purpurado; *n.* cardenal, *m.*; (orn.) cardenal, *m.*
care, *n.* cuidado, *m.*; cargo, *m.*; vigilancia, *f.*; *vi.* cuidar, tener cuidado

career, *n.* carrera, profesión, *f.*
carefree, *adj.* sin cuidados
careful, *adj.* cuidadoso, solicito
careless, *adj.* descuidado
caress, *n.* caricia, *f.*; *vt.* acariciar, halagar
caretaker, *n.* velador, *m.*
carfare, *n.* pasaje (de tranvia), *m.*
carnation, *n.* (bot.) clavel, *m.*
carnival, *n.* carnaval, *m.*
carol, *n.* villancico, *m.*
carpenter, *n.* carpintero, *m.*
carpet, *n.* tapiz, *m.*; **carpet sweeper**, barredor de alfombra, *m.*
carport, *n.* cobertizo para auto
carriage, *n.* porte, talante, *m.*; coche, carruaje, *m.*; cureña de cañón, *f.*
carrier, *n.* portador, carretero, *m.*; **aircraft carrier**, porta aviones, *m.*; **carrier pigeon**, paloma mensajera, *f.*
carrot, *n.* zanahoria,
carry, *vt.* llevar, conducir; portar; cargar; **to carry on**, continuar; **to carry out**, llevar a cabo, realizar
cart, *n.* carro, *m.*; carreta, *f.*; carretón, *m.*; *vt.* y *vi.* acarrear
cartload, *n.* carretada,
cartoon, *n.* caricatura, *f.*
cartridge, *n.* cartucho, *m.*; **cartridge shell**, cápsula, *f.*
carve, *vt.* cincelar; trinchar, tajar; grabar; *vi.* esculpir
case, *n.* estado, *m.*; situación, *f.*; caso, *m.*; estuche, *m.*, caja, *f.*; (gram.) caso, *m.*
cash, *n.* dinero contante o efectivo; *vt.* cobrar o hacer efectivo (un cheque, etc.)
cashier, *n.* cajero, cajera
cashmere, *n.* casimir (tela), *m.*
cask, *n.* barril, tonel, *m.*
casket, *n.* ataúd, *m.*
casserole, *n.* cacerola, *f.*
cast, *vt.* tirar, lanzar; echar; modelar; *n.* tiro, golpe, *m.*; (theat.) reparto, *m.*; *adj.* fundido, **cast iron**, hierro colado; **cast steel**, acero fundido

castanets, *n. pl.* castañuelas, *f. pl.*

Castile, Castilla, *f.*

Castilian, *n.* y *adj.* castellano, castellana

castle, *n.* castillo, *m.*

castor, *adj.* descartado

castor, *n.* castor, *m.*; sombrero castor; **castor oil,** aceite de ricino, *m.*

casual, *adj.* casual, fortuito

casualty, *n.* casualidad, *f.*; acaso, accidente, *m.*; caso, *m.*; **casualties,** *n. pl.* víctimas de accidentes o de guerra, etc

cat, *n.* gato, *m.*, gata, **to let the cat out of the bag,** revelar un secreto

cat., catalog, catálogo; **catechism,** catecismo

catalogue, *n.* catálogo, *m.*

Catatonia, Cataluña, *f.*

Catalonian, *n.* y *adj.* catalán, catalana

cataract, *n.* cascada, catarata, *f.*; (med.) catarata, *f.*

catarrh, *n.* catarro, *m.*

catastrophe, *n.* catástrofe, *f.*

catch, *vt.* coger, agarrar; atrapar; *vi.* pegarse, ser contagioso; **to catch cold,** resfriarse; *n.* botín, *m.*, presa, *f.*; captura, *f.*; trampa, *f.*

catcher, *n.* (baseball) parador de la pelota, *m.*

catching, *adj.* contagioso

catchy, *adj.* atrayente, pegajoso

catechism, *n.* catecismo, *m.*

category, *n.* categoría, *f.*

caterpillar, *n.* oruga, *f.*

cathartic, *adj.* (med.) catártico; *n.* purgante, laxante, *m.*

cathedral, *n.* catedral, *f.*

catholic, *n.* y *adj.* católico, católica

catholicism, catolicismo, *m.*

catsup, *n.* salsa de tomate, *f.*

cattle, *n.* ganado, *m.*

caught, *pretérito* y *p. p.* del verbo **catch**

cauliflower, *n.* coliflor, *f.*

cause, *n.* causa, *f.*; razón, *f.*; motivo, *m.*; *vt.* motivar, causar

caution, *n.* prudencia, precaución, *f.*; aviso, *m.*; *vt.* advertir

cautious, *adj.* prudente, cauto

cavalier, *n.* caballero, *m.*

cavalry, *n.* caballería, *f.*

cave, *n.* caverna, *f.*

cc., c.c., cubic centimeter, centímetro cúbico

C.E., Civil Engineer, Ing. Civil, Ingeniero Civil

cede, *vt.* ceder, trasferir

ceiling, *n.* techo o cielo raso, *m.*; (avi.) cielo máximo; *adj.* máximo

celebrate, *vt.* celebrar

celebration, *n.* celebración, *f.*

celebrity, *n.* celebridad, fama, *f.*; persona célebre

celestial, *adj.* celestial

cell, *n.* celda, *f.*; célula, *f.*

cellar, *n.* sótano, *m.*, bodega, *f.*

cello, *n.* violonchelo, *m.*

cement, *n.* cemento, *m.*; *vt.* cimentar

cemetery, *n.* cementerio, *m.*

cen., cent., central, cent. central

censor, *n.* censor, *m.*; crítico, *m.*

censorship, *n.* censura, *f.*

censure, *n.* censura, reprensión, *f.*; *vt.* censurar, criticar

census, *n.* censo, encabezamiento, *m.*

cent, *n.* centavo, *m.*; céntimo, *m.*; per por ciento

cent., centigrade, C. centigrado; **century,** siglo

centennial, *n.* y *adj.* centenario, *m.*

center, *n.* centro, *m.*; *vt.* centrar; reconcentrar; *vt.* colocarse en el centro, reconcentrarse

centigrade, *adj.* centígrado

centigram, *n.* centigramo, *m.*

centimeter, *n.* centímetro, *m.*

centipede, *n.* ciempiés, *m.*

central, *adj.* central; céntrico

Central America, América Central, *f.*

centralize, *vt.* centralizar

century, *n.* centuria, *f.*; siglo, *m.*

ceramics, n. cerámica, f.

cereal, n. cereal, m.

cerebral, adj. cerebral

ceremony, n. ceremonia,

certain, adj. cierto, evidente

certainty, n. certeza, seguridad, f.; certidumbre, f.

certificate, n. certificado, m.; (com.) bono, m.; certificación, f.

certified, adj. certificado

certify, vt. certificar, afirmar; dar fe

chagrin, n. mortificación, f.; disgusto, m.

chain, n. cadena, f.; serie, sucesión, f.; vt. encadenar

chair, n. silla

chairman, n. presidente (de una reunión o junta) m.

chalk, n. greda, f.; tiza, f.; yeso, m.

challenge, n. desafío, m.; vt. desafiar; retar

chamber, n. cámara, f.; aposento, m.

champagne, n. vino de Champaña, champaña, m.

champion, n. campeón, campeona

championship, n. campeonato, m.

chance, n. ventura, suerte, oportunidad, casualidad, f., acaso, m.; riesgo, m.; **by chance,** si acaso; vi. acaecer, acontecer; adj. fortuito, casual

change, vt. cambiar; variar; vi. variar, alterarse; n. cambio, m.

channel, n. canal, m.; conducto, m.

chaos, n. caos, m.

chapel, n. capilla, f.

chaperon, n. dueña, f.; acompañante de respeto

chaplain, n. capellán, m.

chapter, n. capítulo, m.

character, n. carácter, m.; letra, f.; calidad, f.; (theat.) papel, m.; personaje, m.

characteristic, adj. característico; típico; n. rasgo, m. peculiaridad, f.

charge, vt. encargar, comisionar; cobrar; cargar; acusar; imputar; n. cargo, cuidado, m.; acusación, f.; costo, m.; ataque, m.

charity, n. caridad, beneficencia, f.

charm, n. encanto, m.; atractivo, m.; vt. encantar; seducir

charming, adj. seductor; simpático; encantador

charter, n. carta constitucional, f.; vt. fletar (un barco, etc.); estatuir; **charter member,** miembro o socio fundador, m.

chase, vt. cazar; perseguir; n. caza, f.

chaste, adj. casto; puro

chastise, vt. castigar

chastity, n. castidad, f.

chat, vi. charlar, platicar; n. plática, charla, conversación, f.

chauffeur, n. chofer, m.

cheap, adj. barato

cheapen, vt. abaratar; denigrar

cheat, vt. engañar, hacer trampa; n. trampista, trápala, m. y f.

check, vt. reprimir, refrenar; verificar, comprobar; n. cheque, m.; restrición, f.; freno, m.

checkers, n. juego de damas, m.

checkroom, n. guardarropa, m.

cheek, n. cachete, carrillo, m., mejilla, f.

cheer, n. alegría, f.; vt. animar, alentar; vi. regocijarse

cheerful, adj. alegre, jovial

chef, n. cocinero, m.

chemical, adj. químico; n. sustancia química

chemist, n. químico, química

chemistry, n. química, f.

cherish, vt. estimar

cherry, n. cereza, f.; adj. bermejo, rojo cereza

chess, n. juego de ajedrez, m.

chest, n. pecho, m.; cofre, m.; **chest of drawers,** cómoda, f.

chestnut, *n.* castaña. *adj.* castaño

chewing gum, *n.* chicle. *m.*

chick, *n.* pollito, polluelo. *m.*

chicken, *n.* pollo. *m.*; (fig.) joven. *m.* y *f.*; **chicken pox,** viruelas locas, varicela. *f.*

chief, *adj.* principal, capital; *n.* jefe. *m.*

child, *n.* niño, niña

childbirth, *n.* parto, alumbramiento. *m.*

childhood, *n.* infancia, niñez. *f.*

childish, *adj.* frívolo, pueril

children, *n. pl.* niños. *m. pl.*; hijos. *m. pl.*

Chilean, *n.* y *adj.* chileno, chilena

chill, *adj.* frío; *n.* frío. *m.*; escalofrío. *m.*; *vt.* enfriar; helar

chimney, *n.* chimenea. *f.*

chin, *n.* barba. *f.*

china, chinaware, *n.* porcelana, loza. *f.*

chintz, *n.* zaraza.

chip, *vt.* astillarse; *n.* astilla. *f.*; raspadura. *f.*

chirp, *m.* chirriar, gorjear; *n.* gorjeo, chirrido. *m.*

chisel, *n.* cincel. *m.*; *vt.* cincelar, grabar; (coll.) estafar, engañar

chivalrous, chivalric, *adj.* caballeroso

chivalry, *n.* caballería. *f.*; hazaña. *f.*

chives, *n.* cebolleta. *f.*

chlorine, *n.* cloro. *m.*

chloroform, *n.* cloroformo. *m.*

chocolate, *n.* chocolate. *m.*

choice, *n.* selección. *f.*; preferencia. *f.*; *adj.* selecto, escogido

choir, *n.* coro. *m.*

choose, *vt.* escoger, elegir

chop, *vt.* tajar, cortar; picar; *n.* chuleta. *f.*

choral, *adj.* coral

chord, *n.* (mus.) acorde. *m.*; cuerda. *f.*

chore, *n.* quehacer. *m.*; **chores,** *n. pl.* quehaceres de la casa. *m. pl.*

chorus, *n.* coro. *m.*

chose, *pretérito* del verbo **choose**

Christ, *n.* Jesucristo, Cristo. *m.*

christening, *n.* bautismo, bautizo. *m.*

Christian, *n.* y *adj.* cristiano, cristiana; **Christian name,** nombre de pila. *m.*

Christianity, *m.* cristianismo. *m.*

Christmas, *n.* Navidad, Pascua. *f.*; **Christmas gift,** aguinaldo. *m.*; **Christmas Eve,** Nochebuena. *f.*

chromium, *n.* cromo. *m.*

chronic, *adj.* crónico

chronicle, *n.* crónica. *f.*, informe. *m.*

chubby, *adj.* gordo, rechoncho

chuckle, *vi.* reírse entre dientes

chum, *n.* camarada. *m.* y *f.* compañero, compañera

church, *n.* iglesia. *f.*; templo. *m.*

C.I.F., c.i.f., cost, insurance and freight, c.s.f., costo, seguro y flete

cigar, *n.* cigarro, puro. *m.*

cigarette, *n.* cigarrillo, cigarro. *m.*

cinema, *n.* cinematógrafo. *m.*

CIO, C.I.O., Congress of Industrial Organizations, C.I.O., Congreso de Organizaciones Industriales (de E.U.A.)

cipher, *n.* cifra. *f.*, número. *m.*; cero. *m.*

circle, *n.* círculo. *m.*; rueda. *f.*; *vt.* circundar; cercar

circuit, *n.* circuito. *m.*

circular, *adj.* circular, redondo; *n.* carta circular. *f.*

circulate, *vi.* circular

circulation, *n.* circulación. *f.*

circumference, *n.* circunferencia. *f.*

circumstance, *n.* circunstancia, condición. *f.*; incidente. *m.*

circus, *n.* circo. *m.*

cite, *vt.* citar (a juicio); citar, referirse a

citizen, *n.* ciudadano, ciudadana

citizenship, *n.* ciudadanía, *f.*; nacionalidad, *f.*

citric, *adj.* cítrico

city, *n.* ciudad, *f.*; **city hall**, ayuntamiento, palacio municipal, *m.*

civic, *adj.* cívico; civics, *n.* instrucción cívica, *f.*

civil, *adj.* civil, cortés

civilian, *n.* particular, *m.*

civilization, *n.* civilización, *f.*

civilize, *vt.* civilizar

clad, *adj.* vestido, cubierto

claim, *vt.* reclamar; *n.* pretensión, *f.*; derecho, *m.*; reclamo, *m.*

clam, *n.* almeja, *f.*

clamorous, *adj.* clamoroso, estrepitoso

clamp, *n.* grapa, laña, *f.*; sujetador, *m.*; *vt.* sujetar, afianzar

clan, *n.* familia, tribu, *f.*

clandestine, *adj.* clandestino

clap, *vt.* palmotear, aplaudir

clapping, *n.* aplauso, palmoteo, *m.*

clarify, *vt.* y *vi.* clarificar, aclarar

clarinet, *n.* clarinete, *m.*

clash, *vi.* encontrarse; chocar; *n.* estrépito, *m.*; disputa, *f.*; choque, *m.*

clasp, *n.* broche, *m.*; hebilla, *f.*; sujetador, *m.*; abrazo, *m.*; *vt.* abrochar; abrazar

class, *n.* clase, *f.*; género, *m.*; categoría, *f.*

classic, *adj.* clásico; *n.* autor clásico; obra clásica

classical, *adj.* clásico

classify, *vt.* clasificar, graduar

classmate, *n.* condiscípulo, la

classroom, *n.* sala de clase, *f.*

clean, *adj.* limpio; casto; *vt.* limpiar

cleaning, *n.* limpieza, *f.*

cleanliness, *n.* limpieza, *f.*; aseo *m.*

clear: *adj.* claro, lúcido; neto; *vt.* clarificar, aclarar; absolver; *vi.* aclararse

clef, *n.* (mús.) clave, *f.*

clemency, *n.* clemencia, *f.*

clergy, *n.* clero, *m.*

clergyman, *n.* eclesiástico, *m.*

clerical, *adj.* clerical, eclesiástico; **clerica work**, trabajo de oficina

clerk, *n.* escribiente, *m.*; dependiente, *m.*

clever, *adj.* hábil; inteligente

cliff, *n.* precipicio, *m.*, barranca, *f.*

climate, *n.* clima, *m.*,

climax, *n.* culminación, *f.*

climb, *vt.* escalar, trepar; *vi.* subir

cling, *vi.* adherirse, pegarse

clinic, *adj.* clínico; *n.* clínica, *f.*; consultorio, *m.*

clip, *vt.* cortar a raíz; *n.* tijeretada, *f.*; grapa, *f.*; gancho, *m.*

clipper, *n.* (avi.) clíper, *m.*; trasquilador, *m.*; **clippers**, *n. pl.* tijeras podadoras, *f. pl.*

clipping, *n.* recorte, *m.*

cloak, *n.* capa, *f.*; capote, *m.*

cloakroom, *n.* guardarropa, *m.*

clock, *n.* reloj, *m.*; **alarm clock**, despertador, *m.*

clog, *n.* obstáculo, *m.*; *vt.* obstruir; *vi.* coagularse

close, *vt.* cerrar, tapar; *vi.* cerrarse; *adj.* avaro; *adv.* cerca

closet, *n.* ropero, *m.*

close-up, *n.* fotografía de cerca, *f.*

clot, *n.* coagulación, *f.*; *vi.* cuajarse, coagularse

cloth, *n.* paño, *m.*; mantel, *m.*; lienzo, *m.*; material, *m.*

clothe, *vt.* vestir, cubrir.

clothes, *n. pl.* vestidura, *f.*; ropaje, *m.*; **clothes closet**, ropero, *m.*

clothespin, *n.* gancho para tender la ropa, *m.*

clothing, *n.* ropa, *f.*

clove, *n.* (bot.) clavo, *m.*

clover, *n.* trébol, *m.*

cloverleaf, *n.* hoja de trébol, *f.*; **cloverleaf (highway crossing)**, *n.* hoja de trébol, *f.*

clown, *n.* payaso, payasa

club, *n.* club, *m.*, agrupación, *f.*; garrote, *m.*

clue, *n.* seña, *f.*; indicio, *m.*

clutch, *n.* (auto.) embrague,

m.; vt. embragar; agarrar

clutter, *vt.* poner en desorden; *vi.* atroparse

Co., co., company, Cía., Comp., Compañia; **county,** condado

coach, *n.* coche, *m.;* carroza, *f.;* vagón, *m.;* entrenador (en un deporte), *m.; vt.* entrenar, preparar

coarse, *adj.* basto; ordinario; rústico

coast, *n.* costa, *f.*

coat, *n.* saco, *m.,* casaca, *f.;* abrigo, *m.*

cobbler, *n.* remendón, *m.*

cobweb, *n.* telaraña,

cock, *n.* gallo, *m.*

cockroach, *n.* cucaracha, *f.*

cocktail, *n.* cóctail, coctel, *m.*

cocoa, *n.* cacao, *m.;* chocolate

coconut, *n.* coco, *m.*

cocoon, *n.* capullo, *m.*

cod, *n.* bacalao, *m.*

C.O.D., c.o.d., cash on delivery, collect on delivery, C.A.E., cóbrese al entregar

code, *n.* código, *m.;* clave, *f.*

codfish, *n.* bacalao, *m.*

cod-liver oil, *n.* aceite de hígado de bacalao, *m.*

coeducational, *adj.* coeducativo

coffee, *n.* café, *m.*

coffeepot, *n.* cafetera,

cog, *n.* diente (de rueda), *m.*

cogwheel, *n.* rueda dentada, *f.*

coherence, *n.* coherencia, *f.*

cohesion, *n.* coherencia, cohesión, *f.*

coiffure, *n.* peinado, tocado, *m.*

coil, *vt.* recoger; enrollar; *n.* (elec.) carrete, *m.;* bobina, *f.*

coin, *n.* cuña, *f.;* moneda acuñada; dinero, *m.; vt.* inventar

coincide, *vi.* coincidir

coincidence, *n.* coincidencia, *f.;* casualidad, *f.*

Col., Colonel, Cnel. Coronel

colander, *n.* coladera, colador, *m.*

cold, *adj.* frío; **to be cold,** hacer frío; tener frío; *n.* frío, *m.;* frialdad, *f.;* (med.) res-

friado, *m.*

coleslaw, *n.* ensalada de col cruda y picada

collaborate, *vt.* colaborar

collapse, *vi.* desplomarse; desmayarse; *n.* colapso, *m.;* derrumbe, desplome, *m.*

collapsible, *adj.* plegadizo

collar, *n.* collar, *m.;* cuello, *m.*

collarbone, *n.* clavícula,

collect, *vt.* recoger; cobrar

collection, *n.* colección, *f.;* colecta, *f.;* cobro, *m.*

collective, *adj.* colectivo

collectivization, *n.* colectivización, *f.*

collectivize, *vt.* colectivizar

collector, *n.* colector, *m.;* agente de cobros, *m.*

college, *n.* colegio, *m.;* escuela superior, universidad, *f.*

collie, *n.* perro de pastor, *m.*

collision, *n.* colisión, choque, *m.*

colon, *n.* colon, *m.;* dos puntos (signo de puntuación)

colonel, *n.* coronel, *m.*

colonial, *adj.* colonial

colony, *n.* colonia, *f.*

color, *n.* color, *m.*

colored, *adj.* colorado, pintado, teñido; de raza negra; con prejuicio

colorful, *adj.* pintoresco

coloring, *n.* colorido, *m.;* colorante, *m.*

colorless, *adj.* descolorido

colossal, *adj.* colosal

Columbus, Colón

column, *n.* columna, *f.*

columnist, *n.* diarista, *m.* y *f.,* periodista encargado de una sección especial

Com., Commander, jefe

coma, *n.* (med.) coma, *f.;* letargo, *m.*

comb, *n.* peine, *m.; vt.* peinar; cardar (la lana)

combat, *n.* combate, *m.;* batalla, *f.; vt.* y *vi.* combatir; resistir

combine, *vt.* combinar; *vi.* unirse

combustible, *adj.* y *n.* combustible, *m.*

combustion, n. combustión, f.

Comdr., Commander, jefe

come, vi. venir, acontecer; originar

comedian, n. comediante, m. y f., cómico, cómca

comedy, n. comedia, f.

comfort, n. consuelo, m.; comodidad, f.; vt. confortar; consolar

comfortable, adj. cómodo

comforter, n. colcha, f.

comforting, adj. consolador

comical, adj. chistoso, gracioso, bufo

coming, n. venida, llegada, f.; adj. venidero, entrante

comma , n. (gram.) coma, f.

command, vt. ordenar; mandar; n. orden, f.

commander, n. jefe, m., comandante, m.

commandment, n. mandamiento, m.

commemorate, vt. conmemorar; celebrar

comment, n. comentario, m.; vt. comentar

commentator, n. comentador, comentadora; (rad.) locutor, m.

commerce, n. comercio, m.

commercial, adj. comercial; n. (rad.) anuncio comercial, m.

commission, n. comisión, f.; vt. comisionar; encargar

commissioner, n. comisionado, delegado, m.

commit, vt. cometer; encargar; **to commit to memory,** aprender de memoria

committee, n. comité, m., comisión, junta, f.

commodity, n. mercancías, f. pl.

common, adj. común, público, general; ordinario

Common Market, n. Mereado Común, m.

commonwealth, n. república, f.; estado, m.; nación, f.

communicate, vt. comunicar, participar; vi. comunicarse

communication, n. comunicación, f.; **communications**

satellite, satélite de radiodifusión;

communion, n. comunion, f.; **to take communion,** comulgar

communism, n. comunismo, m.

communist, n. comunista, m. y f.

community, n. comunidad, f.; colectividad, f.; adj. comunal

commute, vt. conmutar; vi. viajar diariamente de un lugar a otro

compact, adj. compacto; sólido; n. polvera, f.; (auto.) coche o carro compacto

companion, n. compañero, companera; acompañante, m. y f.

companionship, n. camaradería, f., compañerismo m.

company, n. compañía, f.; sociedad, f.

compare, vt. comparar; confrontar

compartment, n. compartimiento, compartimento, m.

compass, n. compás, m. piedad, f.

compel, vt. obligar

compensate, vt. y vi. compensar

compensation, n. compensación

competent, adj. competente, capaz

competition, n. competencia, f.

competitor, n. competidor, competidora; rival, m. y f.

compile, vt. compilar

complain, vi. quejarse, lamentarse

complaint, n. queja, f.

complement, n. complemento, m.

complete, adj. completo; vt. completar, acabar

complex, adj. complejo, compuesto; n. complejo m.

compliance, n. condescendencia, f.; consentimiento, m.; **in compliance with,** de acuerdo con, aocediendo (a sus deseos, etc.)

complicate, *vt.* complicar

compliment, *n.* lisonja, *f.*; piropo, requiebro, *m.*

comply, *vi.* cumplir; condescender

compose, *vt.* componer; sosegar; **to compose oneself**, serenarse

composed, *adj.* sosegado, moderado; **to be composed of**, componerse de

composer, *n.* autor, autora; compositor, compositora

composite, *n.* compuesto, *m.*; mezcla, *f.*

composure, *n.* calma, tranquilidad, *f.*

compound, *vt.* combinar; *adj.* compuesto; *n.* compuesto, *m.*

comprehend, *vt.* comprender; contener

comprehension, *n.* comprensión, *f.*

compress, *vt.* comprimir, estrechar; *n.* (med.) fomento, *m.*

comprise, *vt.* comprender, incluir

compromise, *n.* compromiso, convenio, *m.*; *vt.* transigir

compulsory, *adj.* obligatorio, compulsivo

compute, *vt.* computar, calcular

computer, (electronic) *n.* calculador electrónico, *m.*

comrade, *n.* camarada, *m.* y *f.*; compañero, compañera

con., against, contra; **conclusion**, conclusión

concede, *vt.* conceder, admitir

conceit, *n.* presunción, *f.*

conceive, *vt.* concebir

concentrate, *vt.* y *vi.* concentrar

concentration, *n.* concentración, *f.*

concept, *n.* concepto, *m.*

conception, *n.* concepción, *f.*; concepto, *m.*

concern, *vt.* concernir, importar; pertenecer; *n.* negocio, *m.*; interés, *m.*

concerned, *adj.* interesado; mortificado

concerning, *prep.* tocante a, respecto a

concession, *n.* concesión, cesión, *f.*

conciliation, *n.* conciliación, *f.*

concise, *adj.* conciso, sucinto

conclude, *vt.* concluir

concord, *n.* concordia, armonía, *f.*

concrete, *adj.* concreto; *n.* hormigón, cemento, *m.*; **concrete mixer**, hormigonera, *f.*

concussion, *n.* concusión, *f.*

condemn, *vt.* condenar

condense, *vt.* condensar; comprimir

condescend, *vi.* condescender; consentir

condescending, *adj.* complaciente, afable

condition, *n.* condición, *f.*; requisto, *m.*; estado, *m.*

condolence, *n.* pésame, *m.*, condolencia, *f.*

condominium, *n.* condominio, *m.*, propiedad horizontal

conduct, *n.* conducta, *f.*; conducción (de tropas), *f.*; **safe conduct**, salvoconducto, *m.*

conduct, *vt.* conducir, guiar

conductor, *n.* conductor, *m.*; guía, director, *m.*

confection, *n.* confitura, *f.*; confección, *f.*; confite, *m.*

confederate, *vi.* confederarse; *adj.* confederado; *n.* confederado, *m.*

confederation, *n.* federación, confederación, *f.*

confer, *vi.* conferenciar; consultarse; *vt.* otorgar

conference, *n.* conferencia, *f.*; sesión, junta, *f.*

confess, *vt.* y *vi.* confesar, confesarse

confession, *n.* confesión, *f.*

confide, *vt.* y *vi.* confiar; fiarse

confidence, *n.* confianza, seguridad, *f.*

confident, *adj.* cierto; seguro; confiado

confidential, *adj.* confidencial

confine, *vt.* limitar; aprisionar; *vi.* confinar

confinement, n. prisión, f.; encierro, m.; parto, m.

confirm, vt. confirmar; ratificar

confirmation, n. confirmación, f.; ratificación, f.

confiscate, vt. confiscar, decomisar

conflict, n. conflicto, m.; vt. estar en conflicto

conform, vt. y vi. conformar

conformity, n. conformidad, f.

confound, vt. confundir; **confound it!** interj. ¡caracoles!

confront, vt. confrontar, comparar

comfrontation, n. enfrentamiento, m.; careo, m.

confuse, vt. confundir; desordenar

confused, adj. confuso, desorientado

confusion, n. confusión, f.

congeal, vt. y vi. congelar

congenial, adj. congenial, compatible; **to be congenial**, simpatizar

congratulate, vt. felicitar

congregate, vt. congregar, reunir

congregation, n. congregación, reunión, f.

congress, n. congreso, m.

conjecture, n. conjetura, suposición, f.; vt. conjeturar; pronosticar

conjugate, vt. conjugar

conjunction, n. conjunción, f.

connect, vt. juntar, enlazar; relacionar

connection, n. conexión, f.; **connections**, n. pl. relaciones, f. pl.

connoisseur, n. perito, perita, conocedor, conocedora

conquer, vt. conquistar; vencer

conqueror n. vencedor, conquistador, m.

conquest, n. conquista, f.

conscience, n. conciencia, f.; escrúpulo, m.

conscientious, adj. concienzúdo

conscious, adj. consciente;

consciously, adv. a sabiendas

consciousness, n. conocimiento, sentido, m.

conscription, n. reclutamiento obligatorio, m.

consecrate, vt. consagrar; dedicar

consecutive, adj. consecutivo

consent, n. consentimiento, m.; aprobación, f.; vi. consentir; aprobar

consequence, n. consecuencia, f.; importancia, f.

consequent, adj. consecutivo; consiguiente

conservation, n. conservación, f.

conservative, adj. conservador

conservatory, n. conservatorio, m.; invernadero, m.

conserve, vt. conservar, cuidar; hacer conservas

consider, vt. considerar, examinar; vi. pensar, deliberar; reflexionar

considerable, adj. considerable; importante; bastante

considerate, adj. consideitado, prudente

consideration, n. consideración, f.; deliberación, f.

considering, prep. en vista de

consign, vt. consignar

consignee, n. consignatario, consignataria

consist, vi. consistir

consistent, adj. consistente; congruente

consolation, n. consuelo, m.

console, vt. consolar

consolidate, vt. y vi. consolidar, consolidarse

consort, n. consorte, m. y f.; esposo, esposa

conspicuous, adj. conspicuo, llamativo

conspiracy, n. conspiración, f.; trama, f.; complot, m.

conspire, vt. y vi. conspirar, maquinar

constant, adj. constante; fiel

consternation, n. consternación, f.

constipation, *n.* estreñimiento, *m.*

constitute, *vt.* constituir

constitution, *n.* constitución, *f.*

constitutional, *adj.* constitucional, legal

constrain, *vt.* constreñir; restringir

construct, *vt.* construir

construction, *n.* construcción, *f.*

construe, *vt.* interpretar

consul, *n.* cónsul, *m.*

consulate, *n.* consulado, *m.*

consult, *vt.* y *vi.* consultar

consultation, *n.* consulta, deliberación, *f.*

consume, *vt.* y *vi.* consumir

consumer, *n.* consumidor, consumidora

consumption, *n.* consumo, *m.*; consunción, tisis, *f.*

contact, *n.* contacto, *m.*; **contact lenses,** lentes de contacto; *vt.* y *vi.* tocar; poner en contacto

contagious, *adj.* contagioso

contain, *vt.* contener, comprender; caber; reprimir

container, *n.* envase, *m.*; recipiente, *m.*

contaminate, *vt.* contaminar

contemplate, *vt.* contemplar; *vi.* meditar, pensar

contempt, *n.* desprecio, desdén, *m.*

contend, *vi.* contender, disputar, afirmar

content, *adj.* contento, satisfecho; *vt.* contentar; *n.* contento, *m.*; satisfacción, *f.*

content, *n.* contento, *m.*; contenido, *m.*; **contents,** *pl.* contenido, *m.*

contention, *n.* contención, *f.*

contentment, *n.* contentamiento, placer, *m.*

contest, *vt.* disputar, litigar; *n.* concurso, *m.*; competencia, *f.*

contestant, *n.* contendiente, litigante, *m.* y *f.*; concursante, *m.* y *f.*

continent, *n.* continente, *m.*

continental, *adj.* continental

contingent, *n.* contingente, *m.*; cuota, *f.*

continuation, *n.* continuación, *f.*; serie, *f.*

continue, *vt.* continuar; *vi.* durar, perseverar, persistir

continuity, *n.* continuidad, *f.*

continuous, *adj.* continuo

contour, *n.* contorno, *m.*

contract, *vt.* contraer; abreviar; contratar; *vi.* contraerse; *n.* contrato, pacto, *m.*

contraction, *n.* contracción, *f.*; abreviatura, *f.*

contradict, *vt.* contradecir

contradiction, *n.* contradicción, oposición, *f.*

contrail, *n.* estela de vapor, *f.*

contralto, *n.* contralto (voz), *m.*; contralto (persona), *m.* y *f.*

contrary, *adj.* contrario, opuesto; **on the contrary,** al contrario

contrast, *n.* contraste, *m.*; oposición, *f.*; *vt.* contrastar, oponer

contribute, *vi.* contribuir, ayudar

contributor, *n.* contribudador, contribudadora, contribuyente, *m.* y *f.*

contrite, *adj.* contrito, arrepentido

contrive, *vt.* inventar, maquinar

control, *n.* inspección, *f.*; control, *m.*; gobierno, *m.*; *vt.* restringir; gobernar; **to control oneself,** contenerse

convalescence, *n.* convalecencia, *f.*

convalescent, *adj.* convaleciente

convene, *vt.* convocar; *vi.* juntarse

convenience, *n.* conveniencia, comodidad, *f.*

convenient, *adj.* conveniente, cómodo

convent, *n.* convento, monasterio, *m.*

convention, *n.* convención, *f.*

conventional, *adj.* convencional; tradicional

conversation, n. conversación, plática, f.

converse, vi. conversar, platicar

convert, vt. convertir, reducir; vi. convertirse; n. converso, convertido, m.

convey, vt. trasportar; trasmitir; conducir

convict, n. reo, convicto, presidiario, m.

conviction, n. convicción, f.

convince, vt. convencer

convincing, adj. convincente

convulsion, n. convulsión, f.

cook, n. cocinero, cocinera; vt., vi. cocinar, guisar, cocer

cookbook, n. libro de cocina, m.

cooking, n. cocina, f.; arte de cocinar, m.

cool, adj. fresco; indiferente; vt. enfriar, refrescar

coop, n. gallinero, m.; vt. enjaular, encarcelar

cooperate, vi. cooperar

cooperation, n. cooperación f.

co-ordinate, vt. coordinar

co-ordination, n. coordinación, f.

cop, n. (coll.) policía, gendarme, m.

copper, n. cobre, m.; cobre (color), m.

copy, n. copia, f.; original, m.; ejemplar de algún libro; vt. copiar; imitar

copyright, n. propiedad de una obra literaria; derechos de autor, m. pl.; patente, f.

coquette, n. coqueta, f.

coral, n. coral, m.; adj. de coral

cord, n. cuerda, f.; cordel, m.; cordón, pasamano, m.

cordial, adj. cordial, amistoso; n. cordial (licor), m.

core, n. cuesco, m.; interior, corazón, m.; núcleo, m.

cork, n. corcho, m.

corkscrew, n. tirabuzón, m.

corn, n. maíz, m.; callo, m.

corncob, n. mazorca, f.

corned beef, n. cecina, f., carne de vaca en salmuera

corner, n. ángulo, m.; rincón, m.; esquina, f.

cornstalk, n. tallo de maíz

cornstarch, n. almidón de maíz, m.

Corp., corp., corporal, cabo; **corporation,** S.A. sociedad anónima

corporal, n. (mil.) cabo, m.; adj. corpóreo, corporal; material, físico

corporate, adj. colectivo

corporation, n. corporación, f.; gremio, m.; sociedad anónima, f.

corps, n. regimiento, m.; cuerpo, m.; **air corps,** cuerpo de aviación, m.

correct, vt. corregir, castigar; rectificar; adj. correcto, cierto

correction, n. corrección, f.

correspond, vi. corresponder; sostener correspondencia

correspondence, n. correspondencia, f.; reciprocidad, f.

correspondent, n. corresponsal, m.

corrugated, adj. corrugado

corrupt, vt. y vi. corromper; sobornar; adj. corrompido

corruption, n. corrupción, f.

cosmetic, adj. y n. cosmético, m.

cosmopolitan, cosmopolite, n. y adj. cosmopolita, m. y f.

cost, n. coste, costo, precio, m.; expensas, f. pl.; vi. costar

costly, adj. costoso, caro

costume, n. traje, m.; ropa, f.; disfraz, m.

cottage, n. cabaña, choza, f.; **cottage cheese,** requesón, m.

cotton, n. algodón, m.

couch, n. canapé, sofá, m.

cough, n. tos, f.; vi. toser

council, n. concilio, concejo, m.

counsel, n. consejo, aviso, m.; abogado, m.

counselor, counsellor, n. consejero, abogado, m.

count, vt. contar, numerar;

calcular; **to count on,** confiar, depender de; *n.* cuenta, *f.*; cálculo, *m.*; conde (título), *m.*

countdown, *n.* conteo, *m.*

counter, *n.* mostrador, *m.*

counteract, *vt.* contrarrestar

counterfeit, *adj.* falsificado

countless, *adj.* innumerable

country, *n.* país, *m.*; campo, *m.*; patria, *f.*; *adj.* campestre, rural

countryman, *n.* paisano, paisana, compatriota, *m. y f.*

county, *n.* condado, *m.*

couple, *n.* par, *m.*; *vt.* unir, parear, casar; *vi.* juntarse

coupon, *n.* cupón, talón, *m.*

courage, *n.* valor, *m.*

courageous, *adj.* valiente

course, *n.* curso, *m.*; carrera, *f.*; ruta, *f.*; rumbo, *m.*; plato, *m.*; **of course,** por supuesto

court, *n.* corte, *f.*; juzgado, tribunal, *m.*; palacio, *m.*; patio, *m.*; cortejo, *m.*; *vt.* cortejar

courteous, *adj.* cortés

courtesy, *n.* cortesía, *f.*

courtship, *n.* cortejo, *m.*; galantería, *f.*

cousin, *n.* primo, ma; **first cousin,** primo hermano, prima hermana

cover, *n.* cubierta, *f.*; *vt.* cubrir; tapar; ocultar

cow, *n.* vaca, *f.*

coward, *n.* cobarde, *m. y f.*

cowardice, *n.* cobardía, *f.*

cowardly, *adj.* cobarde

cowboy, *n.* vaquero, *m.*

cowhide, *n.* cuero, *m.*

co-worker, *n.* colaborador, colaboradora, compañero o compañera de trabajo

cozy, *adj.* cómodo y agradable

C.P.A., Certified Public Accountant, C.P.T., Contador Público Titulado

crab, *n.* cangrejo, *m.*; (Sp. Am.) jaiba, *f.*; **crab apple,** manzana silvestre, *f.*

crack, *n.* crujido, *m.*; hendedura, raja, *f.*; *vt.* hender, rajar; romper; *vi.* agrietarse

cracked, *adj.* quebrado, raja-

do; (coll.) demente

cracker, *n.* galleta, *f.*

cradle, *n.* cuna, *f.*

craft, *n.* arte, *m.*; artificio, *m.*; astucia, *f.*

crafty, *adj.* astuto

cramp, *n.* calambre, *m.*

crane, *n.* (orn.) grulla, *f.*; (mech.) grúa, *f.*

cranium, *n.* craneo, *m.*

crank, *n.* manivela, *f.*; manija, *f.*; (coll.) maniático, maniática

crash, *vi.* estallar, rechinar; estrellar; *n.* estallido, choque, *m.*

crazy, *adj.* loco

cream, *n.* crema, *f.*; nata, *f.*

creamy, *adj.* cremoso

crease, *n.* pliegue, *m.*; *vt.* plegar

create, *vt.* crear; causar

creation, *n.* creación, *f.*

creative, *adj.* creador

creator, *n.* criador, criadora; **the Creator,** el Criador

credit, *n.* crédito, *m.*; **credit card,** tarjeta de crédito, *f.*; *vt.* creer, fiar, acreditar

creditor, *n.* acreedor, acreedora

creep, *vi.* arrastrar; gatear

cremate, *vt.* incinerar cadáveres

cretonne, *n.* cretona, *f.*

crevice, *n.* raja, hendidura, *f.*

crew, *n.* (naut.) tripulación, *f.*

crime, *n.* crimen, delito, *m.*

criminal, *adj.* criminal, reo; *n.* reo convicto, criminal, *m. y f.*

crimson, *adj.* carmesí, bermejo

crinoline, *n.* crinolina, *f.*

cripple, *n.* lisiado, lisiada; *vt.* tullir

crisis, *n.* crisis, *f.*

crisp, *adj.* crespo; fresco, terso (aplícase a la lechuga, el apio, etc.)

crisscross, *adj.* entrelazado

criterion, *n.* criterio, *m.*

critic, *n.* crítico, *m.*

critical, *adj.* crítico; delicado

criticism, *n.* crítica, *f.*; censura, *f.*

criticize, *vt.* criticar, censurar

crochet, *n.* labor con aguja de gancho; *vt.* tejer con aguja de gancho

crocodile, *n.* cocodrilo, *m.*

crony, *n.* amigo (o conocido) antiguo

crook, *n.* gancho, *m.*; curva, *f.*; ladrón, ladrona

crooked, *adj.* torcido; perverso; tortuoso

crop, *n.* cosecha, *f.*; cabello cortado corto

cross, *n.* cruz, *f.*; *adj.* enojado; mal humorado; *vt.* atravesar, cruzar

crossing, *n.* (rail.) cruce, *m.*

crossword puzzle, *n.* crucigrama, rompecabezas, *m.*

crow, *n.* (orn.) cuervo, *m.*; canto del gallo; *vi.* cantar el gallo; alardear

crowd, *n.* multitud, *f.*; *vt.* amontonar

crowded, *adj.* concurrido, lleno de gente

crown, *n.* corona, *f.*; *vt.* coronar; recompensar

crown prince, *n.* príncipe heredero, *m.*

crucifix, *n.* crucifijo, *m.*

crucify, *vt.* crucificar; atormentar

crude, *adj.* crudo; tosco; **crude (ore, oil, etc.)** (mineral, petróleo, etc.) bruto

cruel, *adj.* cruel, inhumano

cruelty, *n.* crueldad, *f.*

cruise, *n.* travesía marítima; excursión, *f.*; *vi.* navegar; cruzar (el mar o el país)

crumb *n.* miga, *f.*

crumble, *vt.* desmigajar, desmenuzar; *vi.* desmoronarse

crumple, *vt.* arrugar, ajar

crunch, *vt.* crujir

crusade, *n.* cruzada, *f.*

crush, *vt.* apretar, oprimir; machacar

crust, *n.* costra, *f.*; corteza, *f.*

crutch, *n.* muleta, *f.*

cry, *vt.* y *vi.* gritar; exclamar; llorar; *n.* grito, *m.*; llanto, *m.*

crystal, *n.* cristal, *m.*

C.S.T., **Central Standard Time**, hora normal del centro (de E.U.A.)

cub, *n.* cachorro, *m.*

Cuban, *n.* y *adj.* cubano, cubana

cubbyhole, *n.* casilla, *f.*

cube, *n.* cubo, *m.*

cubic, cubical, *adj.* cúbico

cucumber, *n.* pepino, *m.*

cuddle, *vt.* y *vi.* abrazar; acariciarse

cue, *n.* rabo, *m.*, coleta, *f.*; apunte de comedia, *m.*; taco (de billar), *m.*

cuff, *n.* puño de camisa o de vestido, *m.*; **cuff links**, gemelos, *m. pl.*; (Sp. Am.) mancuernillas, *f. pl.*

culinary, *adj.* culinario

culminate, *vi.* culminar

culprit, *n.* delincuente, criminal, *m.*

cult, *n.* culto, *m.*

cultivate, *vt.* cultivar

cultivation, *n.* cultivo, *m.*

cultural, *adj.* cultural

culture, *n.* cultura, civilización, *f.*

cumbersome, *adj.* engorroso

cunning, *adj.* astuto; intrigante; *n.* astucia, sutileza, *f.*

cup, *n.* taza, *f.*

cupboard, *n.* armario, aparador, *m.*, alacena, *f.*

cupful, *n.* taza (medida), *f.*

cupola, *n.* cúpula, *f.*

curb, *n.* freno, *m.*; restricción, *f.*; orilla de la acera, *f.*; *vt.* refrenar

curdle, *vt.* y *vi* cuajar, coagular

cure, *n.* remedio, *m.*; *vt.* curar, sanar

cure-all, *n.* panacea, *f.*

curiosity, *n.* curiosidad, *f.*; rareza, *f.*

curious, *adj.* curioso

curl, *n.* rizo, *m.*; *vt.* rizar (el cabello); *vi.* rizarse, encresparse

currency, circulación, *f.*; moneda corriente, *f.*, dinero *m.*

current, *adj.* corriente, del día; *n.* corriente, *f.*

curse, *vt.* maldecir; *n.* maldición, f.

curtain, n. cortina, f.; telón (en los teatros), m.

curve, vt. encorvar; n. curva, combadura, f.

cushion, n. cojín, m., almohada, f.

custody, n. custodia, f.; cuidado, m.

custom, n. costumbre, f.; uso, m.; customs, n. pl. aduana, f.

customary, adj. usual, acostumbrado

customer, n. cliente, m. y f.

customhouse, n. aduana, f.

cut, vt. cortar; herir; to cut short, interrumpir; n. cortadura, f.; herida, f.; (print.) grabado, m.

cute, adj. gracioso, chistoso

cutlery, n. cuchillería, f.

cutlet, n. costilla, chuleta, f.

cutting, adj. cortante; sarcástico

cwt., hundredweight, ql., quintal

cycle, n. ciclo, m.

cyclone, n. ciclón, m.

cyclotron, n. ciclotrón, m.

cylinder, n. cilindro, m.

cypher, cipher, n. cifra, cero, m.

cyst, n. quiste, m.; lobanillo, m.

C. Z., Canal Zone, Z. del C. Zona del Canal

czar, n. zar, m.

D

d., date, fha., fecha; daughter, hija; day, día; diameter, diámetro; died, murió

D.A., District Attorney, fiscal

d/a, days after acceptance, d/v, días vista

dad, daddy, n. papá, m.

daffodil, n. (bot.) narciso, m.

dagger, n. daga, f., puñal, m.

dahlia, n. (bot.) dalia, f.

daily, adj. diario, cotidiano; adv. diariamente

dainty, adj. delicado; meticuloso, refinado

dairy, n. lechería, f.

daisy, n, margarita, f.

dam, n. dique, m.; presa, f.; represa, f.; vt. represar; tapar

damage, n. daño, detrimento, m.; perjuicio, m.; damages, n. pl. daños y perjuicios, m. pl.; vt. dañar

damask, n. damasco, m.

dame, n. dama, señora, f.

damn, vt. condenar; maldecir; damn!, damn it! interj. ¡maldito sea!

damp, adj. húmedo

dampen, vt. humedecer; desanimar

dampness, n. humedad, f.

dance, n. danza, f.; baile, m.; vi. bailar

dancer, n. danzarín, danzarina, bailarín, bailarina

dandelion, n. diente de león, amargón, m.

dandy, n. petimetre, m.; adj. (coll.) excelente

danger, n. peligro, riesgo, m.

dangerous, adj. peligroso

Danish, adj. danés, danesa; dinamarqués, dinamarquesa

D.A.R., Daughters of the American Revolution, Organización "Hijas de la Revolución Norteamericana."

dare, vi. atreverse, arriesgarse; vt. desafiar, provocar; n. reto, m.

daredevil, n. temerario, temeraria; calavera, m.

daring, n. osadía, f.; adj. temerario; emprendedor

dark, adj. oscuro, opaco; moreno, trigueño; n. oscuridad, f.; ignorancia, f.

darken, vt. y vi. oscurecer

darkness, n. oscuridad, f.; tinieblas, f. pl.

darling, n. predilecto, predilecta, favorito, favorita; adj. querido, amado

dash, n. arranque, m.; acometida, f.; (gram.) raya, f.; vt. arrojar, tirar; chocar, estrellar

data, n. pl. datos, m. pl.; data

processing, proceso de datos, proceso de información por computadoras

date, n. fecha, f.; cita, f.; (bot.) dátil, m.

dated, adj. fechado

daughter, n. hija, f.; **daughter-in-law,** nuera, f.

daunt, vt. intimidar

dauntless, adj. intrépido, affojado

davenport, n. sofá, m.

dawn, n. alba, f.; madrugada f.; vi. amanecer

day, n. día, m.; **day after tomorrow,** pasado mañana

daylight, n. día, m., luz del día, luz natural, f.

daze, vt. atolondrar

dazzle, vt. deslumbrar

D.C., District of Columbia, D.C., Distrito de Columbia, E.U.A.

d.c., direct current, C.D. corriente directa; C.C. corriente continua

DDT, DDT (insecticida), m.

dead, adj. muerto; marchito; **dead letter,** carta no reclamada

deaden, vt. amortecer

deadlock, n. paro, m.; desacuerdo, m.

deadly, adj. mortal

deaf, adj. sordo

deaf-mute, n. sordomudo, sordomuda

deafness, n. sordera, f.

deal, n. negocio, convenio, m.; (com.) trato, m.; mano (en el juego de naipes), f.; vt. tratar; dar (las cartas)

dealer, n. comerciante, m.

dealing, n. trato, m.; comercio, m.; **dealings,** n. pl. transacciones, f. pl.; relaciones, f. pl.

dean, n. deán, decano, m.

dear, adj. querido; costoso, caro

death, n. muerte, f.

debate, n. debate, m.; vt. y vi. deliberar; disputar

debit, n. debe, cargo, m.; vt. adeudar

debris, n. despojos, escom-

bros, m. pl.

debt, n. deuda, f.; débito, m.

debtor, n. deudor, deudora

debut, n. estreno, debut, m.

debutante, n. debutante, f.

Dec., December, dic., diciembre

decade, n. década, f.

decay, vi. decaer, declinar; degenerar; n. decadencia, f.; (dent.) caries, f.

deceased, n. y adj. muerto, muerta, difunto, difunta

deceit, n. engaño, fraude, m.

deceitful, adj. fraudulento, engañoso

December, n. diciembre, m.

decency, n. decencia, f.; modestia, f.

decent, adj. decente, razonable

decimal, adj. decimal

decipher, vt. descifrar

decision, n. decisión, determinación, resolución, f.

decisive, adj. decisivo

deck, n. (naut.) bordo, m., cubierta, f.; baraja de naipes, f.; vt. adornar

declare, vt. declarar, manifestar

decline, vt. (gram.) declinar; rehusar; vi. decaer; n. declinación, f.; decadencia, f.; declive, m.

decorate, vt. decorar, adornar; condecorar

decoy, vt. atraer (algún pájaro); embaucar, engañar

decrease, vt. y vi. disminuir, reducir

decree, n. decreto, edicto, m.; vt. decretar, ordenar

dedicate, vt. dedicar; consagrar

dedication, n. dedicación, f.; dedicatoria, f.

deduct, vt. deducir, sustraer

deduction, n. deducción, rebaja, f.; descuento, m.

deed, n. hecho, m.; hazaña, f.; (com.) escritura, f.

deem, vi. juzgar, estimar

deep, adj. profundo; subido (aplícase al color); intenso

deepen, vt. profundizar

deepfreeze, n. congeladora, f.

deer, n. sing. y pl. ciervo, ciervos, venado, venados, m.

deface, vt. desfigurar

defame, vt. difamar; calumniar

default, n. defecto, m., falta, f.; vt. y vi. faltar, delinquir

defeat, n. derrota, f.; vt. derrotar; frustrar

defend, vt. defender; proteger

defendant, n. (law) demandado, demandada, acusado, acusada

defender, n. defensor, abogado, m.

defer, vt. diferir, posponer

deference, n. deferencia, f.; respeto, m.

defiance, n. desafío, m.

deficiency, n. deficiencia, f.

deficit, n. déficit, m.

define, vt. definir; determinar

definite, adj. definido; concreto

definition, n. definición, f.

deform, vt. deformar, desfigurar

deformity, n. deformidad, f.

defraud, vt. defraudar; frustrar

defray, vt. costear; sufragar

defrost, vt. descongelar, deshelar

defy vt. desafiar, retar

degrade, vt. degradar; deshonrar

degree, n. grado, m.; rango, m.; **by degrees,** gradualmente

deject, vt. abatir, desanimar

del., delegate, delegado; **delete,** suprímase

delay, vt. retardar; vi. demorar; n. demora, f.

delegate, vt. delegar, diputar; n. delegado, delegada, diputado, diputada

delegation, n. delegación, f.

delete, vt. suprimir

deliberate, vt. deliberar, considerar; adj. premeditado

deliberation, n. delibera ción, f.

delicacy, n. delicadeza, f.; manjar, m.

delicate, adj. delicado

delicious, adj. delicioso

delight, n. delicia, f.; deleite, m.; vt. y vi. deleitar

delightful, adj. delicioso; deleitable

delinquency, n. delincuencia, f.

delinquent, n. y adj. delincuente, m. y f.

deliver, vt. entregar; libertar; relatar; partear

delivery, n. entrega, f.; liberación, f.; parto, m.

deluxe, adj. de lujo

demand, n. demanda, f.; vt. pedir, exigir

demented, adj. demente, loco

demitasse, n. tacita (de café), f.

democracy, n. democracia, f.

democrat, n. demócrata, m. y f.

demolish, vt. demoler, arrasar

demon, n. demonio, diablo, m.

demonstrate, vt. demostrar

demonstration, n. demostración, f.

demonstrative, adj. demostrativo, expresivo

demotion, n. (mil.) degradación, f.; descenso de rango

den, n. caverna, f.; cuarto de lectura o de estudio, m.

denim, n. mezclilla, tela gruesa de algodón, f.

Denmark, Dinamarca

denomination, n. denominación, f.

denominational, adj. sectario

denominator, n. (math.) denominador, m.

denote, vt. denotar, indicar

denounce, vt. denunciar

dense, adj. denso, espeso; estúpido

dent, n. abolladura, f.; mella, f.; vt. abollar

dental, adj. dental

dentifrice, adj. y n. dentífrico, m.

dentist, n. dentista, m.

denture, n. dentadura postiza, f.

deodorant, adj., m. desodorante

depart, vi. partir; irse, salir; morir

department, n. departamento, m.

departure, n. partida, salida, f.; desviación, f.

depend, vi. depender

dependable, adj. digno de confianza

dependent, n. dependiente, m.

depict, vt. pintar, retratar; describir

deplete, vt. agotar, vaciar

deplorable, adj. deplorable

deplore, vt. deplorar, lamentar

deport, vt. deportar

deportment, n. conducta, f.

deposit, vt. depositar; n. depósito, m.

depot, n. (rail.) estación, f.

depressed, adj. deprimido

depression, n. depresión, f.

deprive, vt. privar, despojar

dept., department, dep., depto., departamento

depth, n. profundidad, f.; abismo, m.

deputy, n. diputado, delegado, m.

derail, vt. descarrilar

derivation, n. derivación, f.

derive, vt. y vi. derivar; proceder

descend, vi. descender

descendant, n. descendiente, m. y f.

describe, vt. describir

description, n. descripción, f.

desert, n. desierto, m.; merecimiento, m.; vt. abandonar; vi. (mil.) desertar

desertion, n. deserción, f.

design, vt. designar, proyectar; diseñar; n. diseño, plan, m.

designate, vt. designar, señalar

designer, n. dibujante, proyectista, m. y f.

desire, n. deseo, m.; vt. desear

desk, n. escritorio, pupitre, m.

desolation, n. desolación, destrucción, f.

despair, n. desesperación, f.; vi. desesperar

desperate, adj. desesperado; furioso

desperation, n. desesperación, f.

despise, vt. despreciar; desdeñar

despite, n. despecho, m.; prep. a despecho de

despondent, adj. abatido, desalentado

despot, n. déspota, m. y f.

dessert, n. postre, m.

destination, n. destino, m.

destine, vt. destinar, dedicar

destiny, n. destino, hado, m.; suerte, f.

destitute, adj. carente; necesitado

destroy, vt. destruir

destruction, n. destrucción, ruina, f.

detach, vt. separar, desprender

detail, n. detalle, m.; particularidad, f.; (mil.) destacamento, m.; **in detail,** al por menor; detalladamente; vt. detallar

detect, vt. descubrir; discernir

detective, n. detective, m.

détente, n. relajación en la tensión, distensión, f.

deter, vt. disuadir

deteriorate, vt. deteriorar

determination, n. determinación, f.

determine, vt. determinar, decidir; **to be determined,** proponerse

detest, vt. detestar, aborrecer

detract, vt. disminuir; vi. denigrar

detriment, n. detrimento, perjuicio m.

develop, vt. desarrollar; revelar (una fotografía)

development, n. desarrollo, m.

deviate, vi. desviarse

device, n. invento, m.; aparato, mecanismo, m.

devil, n. diablo, demonio, m.

devise, vt. inventar; idear

devoid, *adj.* vacío; carente

devote, *vt.* dedicar; consagrar

devotion, *n.* devoción, *f.*; dedicación, *f.*

devout, *adj.* devoto, piadoso

dew, *n.* rocío, *m.*

diabetes, *n.* diabetes, *f.*

diabolic, diabolical, *adj.* diabólico

diagnose, *vt.* diagnosticar

diagnosis, *n.* diagnosis, *f.*

diagonal, *n.* y *adj.* diagonal, *f.*

diagram, *n.* diagrama, *f.*

dial, *n.* esfera de reloj, *f.*; cuadrante, *m.*; **dial telephone,** teléfono automático, *m.*

dialect, *n.* dialecto, *m.*

diameter, *n.* diámetro, *m.*

diamond, *n.* diamante, *m.*; brillante, *m.*; oros (de baraja), *m. pl.*

diaper, *n.* pañal, *m.*

diarrhea, *n.* diarrea, *f.*

diary, *n.* diario, *m.*

dictate, *vt.* dietar

dictation, *n.* dictado, *m.*

dictator, *n.* dictador, *m.*

dictatorship, *n.* dictadura, *f.*

diction, *n.* dicción, *f.*

dictionary, *n.* diccionario, *m.*

did, *pretérito* del verbo **do**

die, *vi.* morir, expirar; marchitarse; *n.* dado, *m.*; molde, *m.*, matriz, *f.*

diet, *n.* dieta, *f.*; régimen, *m.*; *vi.* estar a dieta

differ, *vi.* diferenciarse; contradecir

difference, *n.* diferencia, *f.*

different, *adj.* diferente

difficult, *adj.* difícil

difficulty, *n.* dificultad, *f.*

digest, *vt.* digerir, clasificar; *vi.* digerir; *n.* extracto, compendio, *m.*

digestion, *n.* digestión, *f.*

dignified, *adj.* serio, grave

dignity, *n.* dignidad, *f.*

dike, *n.* dique, canal, *m.*

dilate, *vt.* y *vi.* dilatar, extender

diligent, *adj.* diligente, aplicado

dim, *adj.* turbio de vista; oscuro; *vt.* oscurecer

dime, *n.* moneda de plata de diez centavos en E. U. A.

dimension, *n.* dimensión, *f.*

diminish, *vt.* y *vi.* disminuir

diminutive, *adj.* y *n.* diminutivo, *m.*

dine, *vi.* comer, cenar

diner, *n.* coche comedor, *m.*

dining, *adj.* comedor; **dining car,** coche comedor; **dining room,** comedor, *m.*

dinner, *n.* comida, cena, *f.*

dip, *vt.* remojar, sumergir; *vi.* sumergirse; inclinarse; *n.* inmersión, *f.*

diphtheria, *n.* difteria, *f.*

diploma, *n.* diploma, *f.*

diplomacy, *n.* diplomacia, *f.*

diplomat, *n.* diplomático, *m.*

diplomatic, *adj.* diplomático

direct, *adj.* directo, derecho, recto; *vt.* dirigir

direction, *n.* dirección, manejo, *m.*; rumbo, *m.*

director, *n.* director, *m.*

directory, *n.* directorio, *m.*; guía,

dirt, *n.* suciedad, mugre, *f.*

dirty, *adj.* sucio; vil, bajo; *vt.* ensuciar

disadvantage, *n.* desventaja, *f.*

disagree, *vi.* discordar, estar en desacuerdo; hacer daño (el alimento)

disagreeable, *adj.* desagradable

disagreement, *n.* desacuerdo, *m.*

disappear, *vi.* desaparecer

disappearance, *n.* desaparición, *f.*

disappoint, *vt.* decepcionar

disappointment, *n.* decepción, *f.*

disapproval, *n.* desaprobación, censura, *f.*

disapprove, *vt.* desaprobar

disarmament, *n.* desarme, *m.*

disaster, *n.* desastre, *m.*

disastrous, *adj.* desastroso

disbursement, *n.* desembolso, *m.*

discard, *vt.* descartar; *n.* descarte (en el juego de naipes), *m.*

discharge, *vt.* descargar, pagar (una deuda, etc.); despedir; *n.* descarga, *f.*; descargo, *m.*

disciple, *n.* discípulo, *m.*

discipline, *n.* disciplina, *f.*; *vt.* disciplinar

disclose, *vt.* descubrir, revelar

discomfort, *n.* incomodidad, *f.*

disconnect, *vt.* desunir, separar

discontent, *n.* descontento, *m.*; *adj.* malcontento

discontinue, *vt.* descontinuar

discotheque, *n.* discoteca, *f.*

discount, *n.* descuento, *m.*; rebaja, *f.*; *vt.* descontar

discourage, *vt.* desalentar, desanimar

discouragement, *n.* desaliento, *m.*

discover, *vt.* descubrir

discovery, *n.* descubrimiento, *m.*

discretion, *n.* discreción, *f.*

discriminate, *vt.* distinguir

discrimination, *n.* discriminación, *f.*

discuss, *vt.* discutir

discussion, *n.* discusión, *f.*

disease, *n.* mal, *m.*; enfermedad, *f.*

diseased, *adj.* enfermo

disfigure, *vt.* desfigurar, afear

disgrace, *n.* deshonra, *f.*; desgracia, *f.*; *vt.* des honrar

disgraceful, *adj.* deshonroso, vergonzoso

disguise, *vt.* disfrazar; simular; *n.* disfraz, *m.*; máscara, *f.*

disgust, *n.* disgusto, *m.*; aversión, *f.*; *vt.* disgustar, repugnar

dish, *n.* fuente, *f.*, plato, *m.*

dishearten, *vt.* desalentar, descorazonar

disillusion, *n.* desengaño, *m.*, desilusión, *f.*; *vt.* desengañar

disinfect, *vt.* desinfectar

disinfectant, *n.* desinfectante, *m.*

disloyal, *adj.* desleal; infiel

disloyalty, *n.* deslealtad, *f.*

disobedient, *adj.* desobediente

disobey, *vt.* desobedecer

disorder, *n.* desorden, *m.*

disorderly, *adj.* desarreglado, confuso

dispatch, *n.* despacho, *m.*; embarque, *m.*; *vt.* despachar; embarcar; remitir

dispel, *vt.* disipar, dispersar

dispensary, *n.* dispensario, *f.*

dispensation, *n.* dispensa, *f.*

dispense, *vt.* dispensar; distribuir

displaced, *adj.* desplazado, dislocado

display, *vt.* desplegar; exponer; ostentar; *n.* exhibición, *f.*; ostentación, *f.*

displease, *vt.* disgustar; ofender; desagradar

dispose, *vt.* disponer; dar; *vt.* vender; trasferir

disposition, *n.* disposición, *f.*; indole, *f.*; carácter, *m.*

dispute, *n.* disputa, controversia, *f.*; *vt.* y *vi.* disputar

disqualify, *vt.* inhabilitar

disregard, *vt.* desatender, desdeñar; *n.* desatención, *f.*

disreputable, *adj.* despreciable

disrupt, *vt.* y *vi.* desbaratar, hacer pedazos; desorganizar

dissatisfaction, *n.* descontento, disgusto, *m.*

disseminate, *vt.* diseminar, propagar

dissension, *n.* disensión, discordia, *f.*

dissipation, *n.* disipación, *f.*; libertinaje, *m.*

dissolve, *vt.* y *vi.* disolver

dissuade, *vt.* disuadir

distance, *n.* distancia, *f.*

distant, *adj.* distante, lejano; esquivo

distasteful, *adj.* desagradable

distinct, *adj.* distinto, diferente; claro, sin confusión

distinction, *n.* distinción, diferencia, *f.*

distinguish, *vt.* distinguir; discernir; **distinguished,** *adj.* distinguido, eminente

distress, *n.* aflicción, *f.*; *vt.* angustiar, acongojar

distribute, vt. distribuir, repartir

distributor, n. distribuidor, distribuidora

district, n. distrito, m.

distrust, vt. desconfiar; n. desconfianza, f.

disturb, vt. perturbar, estorbar

ditch, n. zanja, f.

dive, vi. sumergirse, zambullirse; bucear; n. zambullidura, f.; (Mex.) clavado, m.

diver, n. buzo, m.

diversion, n. diversión, f.; pasatiempo, m.

diversity, n. diversidad, f.

divert, vt. desviar; divertir

divide, vt. dividir; repartir; desunir; vi. dividirse

dividend, n. dividendo, m.

divine, adj. divino; sublime

diving, n. buceo, m.; **diving suit,** escafandra, f.

divinity, n. divinidad, f.

division, n. división, f.

divorce, n. divorcio, m.; vt. y vi. divorciar, divorciarse

DNA, deoxyribonucleic acid, ácido ribonucleico

do, vt. hacer, ejecutar; vi. obrar

docile, adj. dócil, apacible

doctor, n. doctor, médico, m.

doctrine, n. doctrina, f.

document, n. documento, m.

dodge, vt. evadir, esquivar

does, tercera persona del singular del verbo **do**

dog, n. perro, m.

doghouse, n. perrera, f., casa de perro; (coll.) **to be in the doghouse,** estar castigado, estar en desgracia

dolly, n. pañito de adorno, m.

doings, n. pl. hechos, m. pl.

doll, n. muñeca, f.

dollar, n. dólar, peso (moneda de E.U.A.), m.

dome, n. cúpula, f.

domestic, adj. doméstico

domesticate, vt. domesticar

dominate, vt. y vi. dominar

domination, n. dominación, f.

domineering, adj. tiránico

Dominican Republic, República Dominicana, f.

domino, n. dominó, m.

donate, vt. donar, contribuir

donation, n. contribución, donación, f.

done, adj. hecho; cocido, asado; p. p. del verbo **do**

donkey, n. burro, asno, m.

doom, n. condena, f.; suerte, f.; vt. sentenciar, condenar

door, n. puerta, f.

doorbell, n. timbre de llamada, m.

doorknob, n. tirador, m. perilla, f.

doorman, n. portero, m.

doorstep, n. umbral, m.

doorway, n. puerta de entrada, f.

dope, n. narcótico, m., droga heroica, f.; (coll.) información, f.

dormitory, n. dormitorio, m.

dot, n. punto, m.

doubt, n. duda, sospecha, f.; vt. y vi. dudar

doubtful, adj. dudoso

doubtless, adj. indudable

dough, n. masa, pasta, f.

doughnut, n. rosquilla, f., especie de buñuelo

dove, n. paloma, f.

dowdy, adj. desaliñado

down, n. plumón, m.; bozo, vello, m.; **ups and downs,** vaivenes, m. pl.; adv. abajo

downcast, adj. cabizbajo

downfall, n. ruina, decadencia, f.

downpour, n. aguacero, m.

downstairs, adv. abajo; n. piso inferior, m.

downtown, n. centro, m., parte céntrica de una ciudad

doze, vi. dormitar

dozen, n. docena, f.

D.P., displaced person, persona desplazada

Dr., Doctor, Dr., Doctor

draft, n. dibujo, m.; (com.) giro, m; corriente de aire; (mil.) conscripción, f.; **rough draft,** borrador, m.; vt. dibujar; redactar

draftsman, n. dibujante, m.

drag, vt. arrastrar; vi. arrastrarse; *n.* rémora, *f.*; (coll.) influencia, *f.*

dragon, *n.* dragón, *m.*

dragonfly, *n.* libélula, *f.*

drain, *vt.* desaguar; colar; *n.* desaguadero, *m.*

drainage, *n.* desagüe, *m.*; saneamiento, *m.*

drake, *n.* ánade macho, *m.*

drama, *n.* drama, *m.*

dramatic, dramatical, *adj.* dramático

dramatics, *n.* arte dramático; declamación, *f.*

drank, *pretérito* del verbo **drink**

drape, *n.* cortina, *f.*; *vt.* vestir; colgar decorativamente

drapery, *n.* cortinaje, *m.*

draw, *vt.* tirar, traer; atraer; dibujar; girar, librar una letra de cambio

drawback, *n.* desventaja, *f.*

drawer, *n.* gaveta, *f.*; **drawers,** *n. pl.* calzones, *m. pl.*; calzoncillos, *m. pl.*

drawing, *n.* dibujo, *m.*; rifa, *f.*; **drawing room,** sala de recibo, *f.*

dread, *n.* miedo, terror, *m.*; *vt.* y *vi.* temer

dreadful, *adj.* terrible, espantoso

dream, *n.* suero, *m.*; fantasía, *f.*; *vi.* soñar; imaginarse

dreary, *adj.* espantoso, triste

dregs, *n. pl.* heces, *f. pl.*; escoria, *f.*

drench, *vt.* empapar, molar

dress, *n.* vestido, *m.*; traje, *m.*; *vt.* vestir, ataviar; curar (las heridas); *vi.* vestirse

dresser, *n.* tocador, *m.*

dressing, *n.* curación, *f.*; salsa, *f.*

dressy, *adj.* (coll.) vistoso; te, de vestir

drift, *n.* significado, *m.*; (naut.) deriva, *f.*

drill, *n.* taladro, *m.*, barrena *f.*; (mil.) instrucción de reclutas; *vt.* taladrar; (mil.) disciplinar reclutas

drink, *vt.* y *vi.* beber; embriagarse; *n.* bebida, *f.*

drip, *vt.* y *vi.* gotear, destilar; *n.* gotera, *f.*

drive, *n.* paseo, *m.*; pulso, *m.*; *vt.* y *vi.* impeler; guiar, manejar, conducir; (mech.) impulsar; andar en coche

drive-in, *n.* restaurante o cine para automovilistas

driven, *p. p.* del verbo **drive**

driver, *n.* cochero, *m.*; carretero, *m.*; conductor, *m.*; chofer, *m.*

driving, *adj.* motriz; conductor; impulsor; **driving school,** autoescuela, *f.*, escuela de manejo

drizzle, *vi.* lloviznar; *n.* llovizna, *f.*

drone, *n.* zángano de colmena *m.*; haragán, *m.*

droop, *vi.* inclinarse, colgar; desanimarse

drop, *n.* gota, *f.*; **letter drop,** buzón, *m.*; *vt.* soltar; cesar; dejar caer

dropsy, *n.* hidropesía,

drove, *n.* manada, *f.*; rebaño, *m.*; *pretérito* del verbo **drive**

drown, *vt.* y *vi.* sumergir; anegar

drudgery, *n.* trabajo arduo y monótono

drug, *n.* droga, *f.*, medicamento, *m.*; *vt.* narcotizar

druggist, *n.* farmacéutico, boticario, *m.*

drugstore, *n.* botica, *f.*

drum, *n.* tambor, *m.*; tímpano (del oído), *m.*

drumstick, *n.* palillo de tambor; pata (de ave cocida), *f.*

drunk, *adj.* borracho, ebrio, embriagado; *p. p.* del verbo **drink**

drunkard, *n.* borrachón, *m.*

dry, *adj.* árido, seco; aburrido; **dry cleaning,** lavado en seco; *vt.* y *vi.* secar; enjugar

D.S.T., Daylight Saving Time, hora oficial (aprovechamiento de luz del día)

duck, *n.* ánade, *m.* y *f.*, pato, pata; *vt.* zambullir; *vi.* zambullirse; agacharse

due, *adj.* debido, adecuado; **to**

become due, (com.) vencerse (una deuda, un plazo, etc.); **dues,** n. pl. cuota, f.

dumb, adj. mudo; (coll.) estúpido

dump, n. vaciadero, depósito, m.; **dumps,** n. pl. abatimiento, m., murria, f.

dumpling, n. empanada, f.

dunce, n. tonto, tonta

dungeon, n. calabozo, m.

dupe, n. bobo, boba; víctima, f.; vt. engañar, embaucar

duplicate, n. duplicado, m.; copia, f.; vt. duplicar

durable, adj. durable, duradero

duration, n. duración, f.

during, prep. durante

dusk, n. crepúsculo, m.

dusky, adj. oscuro

dust, n. polvo, m.

duster, n. plumero, m.; bata corta de mujer

dusty, adj. polvoriento; empolvado

Dutch, adj. holandés, holandesa

duly, n. deber, m., obligación, f.; **custom duties,** derechos de aduana

dwarf, n. enano, enana

dwell, vi. habitar, morar

dwelling, n. habitación, residencia, f.

dye, vt. teñir, colorar; n. tinte, colorante, m.

dying, adj. agonizante, moribundo

dynamic, adj. dinámico, enérgico

dynamite, n. dinamita, f.

dynasty, n. dinastía, f.

dysentery, n. disentería, f.

E

E., east, E., este, oriente

ea., each, c/u., cada uno

each, adj. cada; pron. cada uno, cada una, cada cual

eager, adj. deseoso, ansioso

eagle, n. águila, f.

ear, n. oreja, f.; oído, m.; (bot.) espiga f.

earache, n. dolor de oído, m.

eardrum, n. tímpano, m.

early, adj. y adv. temprano

earmuff, n. orejera, f.

earn, vt. ganar, obtener

earnest, adj. fervoroso; serio

earnings, n. pl. ingresos, m. pl., ganancias, f. pl.

earphone, n. audífono, auricular, m.

earth, n. tierra, f.

earthly, adj. terrestre, mundano

earthquake, n. terremoto, m.

ease, n. facilidad, f.; **at ease,** sosegado; vt. aliviar

easel, n. caballete, m.

easily, adv. fácilmente

east, n. oriente, este, m.

Easter, n. Pascua de Resurrección, f.

easterly, eastern, adj. oriental, del este

easy, adj. fácil

eat, vt. comer

ebony, n. ébano, m.

eccentric, adj. excéntrico

ecclesiastic, adj. y n. eclesiástico, m.

echo, n. eco, m.; vi. resonar, repercutir (la voz)

eclipse, n. eclipse, m.; vt. eclipsar

ecological, adj. ecológico

ecology, n. ecología, f.

economic, economical, adj. económico

economics, n. economía, f.

economize, vt. y vi. economizar

economy, n. economía, f.; frugalidad, f.

edit, vt. redactar; dirigir (una publicación); revisar o corregir (un artículo, etc.)

edition, n. edición, f.; publicación, f.; impresión, f.; tirada, f.

editor, n. director, redactor (de una publicación), m.

editorial, n. editorial, m.

educate, vt. educar; enseñar

educated, adj. educado, instruido

education, n. educación, f.;

crianza, *f.*

educational, *adj.* educativo

eel, *n.* anguila, *f.*

efface, *vt.* borrar, destruir

effect, *n.* efecto, *m.*; realidad, *f.*; **effects**, *n. pl.* efectos, bienes, *m. pl.*; *vt.* efectuar, ejecutar

effective, *adj.* eficaz; efectivo; real

effervescent, *adj.* efervescente,

efficiency, *n.* eficiencia, *f.*

efficient, *adj.* eficaz; eficiente

effort *n.* esfuerzo, empeño, *m.*

effusive, *adj.* efusivo, expansivo

e.g., for example, p.ej., por ejemplo, vg. verbigracia

egg, *n.* huevo, *m.*

eggplant, *n.* (bot.) berenjena, *f.*

eggshell, *n.* cáscara o cascarón de huevo

egg-yolk, *n.* yema de huevo, *f.*

ego, *n.* ego, yo, *m.*

egoism, egotism, *n.* egoísmo, *m.*

Egypt, Egipto

Egyptian, *n.* y *adj.* egipcio, egipcia

eight, *adj.* y *n.* ocho, *m.*

eighteen, *adj.* y *n.* dieciocho, *m.*

eighteenth, *adj.* y *n.* décimoctavo, *m.*

eighth, *adj.* y *n.* octavo, *m.*

eighty, *adj.* y *n.* ochenta, *m.*

either, *pron.* y *adj.* cualquiera, uno de dos; *conj.* o, sea, ya, ora

elaborate, *vt.* elaborar; *adj.* elaborado, trabajado, primoroso

elapse, *vi.* pasar, trascurrir (el tiempo)

elated, *adj.* exaltado, animoso

elder, *adj.* que tiene más edad, mayor; *n.* anciano, antepasado, *m.*; eclesiástico, *m.*; (bot.) saúco, *m.*

elderly, *adj.* de edad madura

eldest, *adj.* el mayor, el más anciano

elect, *vt.* elegir

election, *n.* elección, *f.*; **elections**, elecciones, *f. pl.*

electoral, *adj.* electoral

electric, electrical, *adj.* eléctrico

electrician, *n.* electricista, *m.*

electricity, *n.* electricidad, *f.*

electrocute, *vt.* electrocutar

electronics, *n.* electrónica, *f.*

elegance, *n.* elegancia, *f.*

elegant, *adj.* elegante

element, *n.* elemento, *m.*; principio, *m.*

elemental, *adj.* elemental

elementary, *adj.* simple

elephant, *n.* elefante, *m.*

elevate, *vt.* elevar, alzar

elevation, *n.* elevación, *f.*; altura, *f.*

elevator, *n.* ascensor, elevador, *m.*

eleven, *n.* y *adj.* once, *m.*

eleventh, *n.* y *adj.* onceno, undécimo, *m.*

eligible, *adj.* elegible; deseable

eliminate, *vt.* eliminar, descartar

elope, *vi.* fugarse con un amante

elopement, *n.* fuga, huida (con un amante), *f.*

eloquence, *n.* elocuencia,

eloquent, *adj.* elocuente

else, *adj.* otro; *adv.* en lugar distinto; en forma distinta; **nothing else**, nada más; *conj.* de otro modo; si no

elsewhere, *adv.* en otra parte

elude, *vt.* eludir, evadir

elusive, *adj.* evasivo

emanate, *vi.* emanar

emancipation, *n.* emancipación, *f.*

embankment, *n.* dique, *m.*, presa, *f.*; terraplén, *m.*

embargo, *n.* embargo, *m.*; *vt.* embargar

embark, *vt.* y *vi.* embarcar; embarcarse

embarrass, *vt.* avergonzar, desconcertar

embarrassing, *adj.* penoso

embarrassment, *n.* vergüenza, pena, *f.*

embassy, *n.* embajada, *f.*

embezzle, *vt.* desfalcar
emblem, *n.* emblema, *m.*
embrace, *vt.* abrazar; contener; *n.* abrazo, *m.*
embroider, *vt.* bordar
emerge, *vi.* salir, surgir
emergency, *n.* emergencia, *f.*
emigrate, *vi.* emigrar
eminence, *n.* eminencia, excelencia, *f.*
eminent, *adj.* eminente
emotion, *n.* emoción, *f.*
emperor, *n.* emperador, *m.*
emphasis, *n.* énfasis, *m.*
emphasize, *vt.* recalcar
emphatic, *adj.* enfático
empire, *n.* imperio, *m.*
employ, *vt.* emplear, ocupar; *n.* empleo, *m.*
employee, *n.* empleado, empleada
employer, *n.* amo, patrón, *m.*
employment, *n.* empleo, *m.*; ocupación, *f.*
empress, *n.* emperatriz, *f.*
empty, *adj.* vacío; vano; *vt.* vaciar, verter
enable, *vt.* habilitar; facilitar
enamel, *n.* esmalte, charol, *m.*
enchanting, *adj.* encantador
encircle, *vt.* circundar
enclose, *vt.* cercar, circundar; incluir
enclosure, *n.* cercado, *m.*; anexo (en una carta), *m.*
encounter, *n.* encuentro, *m.*; duelo, *m.*; pelea, *f.*; *vi.* encontrarse
encourage, *vt.* animar, alentar
encouragement, *n.* estímulo, aliento, *m.*
encouraging, *adj.* alentador
encyclopedia, *n.* enciclopedia, *f.*
end, *n.* fin, *m.*; término, *m.*; propósito, intento, *m.*; *vt.* matar, concluir; terminar; *vi.* acabarse
endeavor, *vi.* esforzarse; intentar; *n.* esfuerzo, *m.*
ending, *n.* conclusión, *f.*; muerte, *f.*
endless, *adj.* infinito, perpetuo, sin fin
endorse, *vt.* endosar (una letra

de cambio)
endorsement, *n.* endorso o endoso, *m.*
endurance, *n.* duración, *f.*; paciencia, resistencia, *f.*
endure, *vt.* sufrir, aguantar, soportar; *vi.* durar
ENE, E.N.E., east-north-east, ENE, estenordeste
energetic, *adj.* enérgico, vigoroso
enforce, *vt.* poner en vigor
enforcement, *n.* compulsión, *f.*; cumplimiento (de una ley), *m.*
engage, *vt.* empeñar, obligar; ocupar; *vt.* comprometerse
engaged, *adj.* comprometido
engagement, *n.* noviazgo, compromiso, *m.*; cita, *f.*
engine, *n.* máquina, *f.*; locomotora, *f.*
engineer, *n.* ingeniero, *m.*; maquinista, *m.*
engineering, *n.* ingeniería, *f.*
England, Inglaterra, *f.*
English, *n.* y *adj.* inglés, *m.*; **English Channel,** Canal de la Mancha
Englishman, *n.* inglés, *m.*
Englishwoman, *n.* inglesa, *f.*
enjoy, *vt.* gozar; disfrutar de
enjoyable, *adj.* agradable
enjoyment, *n.* goce, disfrute, *m.*; placer, *m.*
enlarge, *vt.* ampliar; *vi.* extenderse, dilatarse
enlargement, *n.* aumento, *m.*; ampliación, *f.*
enlist, *vt.* alistar, reclutar; *vi.* inscribirse como recluta, engancharse
enliven, *vt.* animar; avivar
enormous, *adj.* enorme
enough, *adj.* bastante, suficiente; *adv.* suficientemente
enroll, *vt.* registrar, inscribir
ensemble, *n.* conjunto, *m.*
entangle, *vt.* enmarañar, embrollar
enter, *vt.* entrar, admitir; *vi.* entrar
enterprise, *n.* empresa, *f.*
enterprising, *adj.* emprendedor

entertain, vt. entretener; agasajar; divertir

entertaining, adj. divertido, chistoso

entertainment, n. festejo, m.; diversión, f., entretenimiento, m.

enthusiasm, n. entusiasmo, m.

enthusiastic, adj. entusiasmado, entusiasta

entire, adj. entero

entrance, n. entrada, f.; admisión, f. ingreso, m.

entreat, vt. rogar, suplicar,

entrust, vt. confiar

entry, n. entrada, f.; (com.) partida, f.

envious, adj. envioso

environment, n. ambiente, m.

environmental, adj. ambiental

envy, n. envidia, f.; vt. envidiar

epic, adj. épico; n. epopeya, f.

epidemic, adj. epidémico; n. epidemia, f.

epileptic, adj. y n. epiléptico, m.

episode, n. episodio, m.

epoch, n. época, era, f.

equal, adj. igual; semejante; n. igual, m.; vt. igualar

equality, n. igualdad, f.

equator, n. ecuador, m.

equilibrium, n. equilibrio, m.

equipment, n. equipo, m.

equitable, adj. equitativo

equivalent, n. y adj. equivalente, m.

era, n. edad, época, era, f.

erase, vt. borrár

eraser, n. goma de borrar, f., borrador, m.

erect, vt. erigir; establecer; adj. derecho, erguido

erosion, n. erosión, f.

err, vi. errar; desviarse

errand, n. recado, mensaje, m.

erroneous, adj. erróneo; falso

error, n. error, yerro, m.

eruption, n. erupción, f.

escalate, vi. crecer

escalator, n. escalera mecánica, f.

escapade, n. travesura, f.

escape, vt. evitar; escapar; vi. evadirse, salvarse; n. escapada, huida, fuga, f.

escort, n. escolta, f.; acompañant m.; vt. escoltar, acompañar

especial, adj. especial, excepcional; **especially,** adv. particularmente; sobre todo

essay, n. ensayo literario, m.

essence, n. esencia, f.

essential, adj. esencial

E.S.T., Eastern Standard Time, hora normal de la región oriental de E.U.A

establish, vt. establecer

establishment, n. establecimiento, m.

estate, n. patrimonio, m.; bienes, m. pl.; predio, m.

esteem, vt. estimar; n. consideración, f.

esthetic, adj. estético; **esthetics,** n. estética, f.

estimate, vt. estimar, apreciar, tasar; n. cálculo, m.; presupuesto, m.

estrogen, n. estrógeno, m.

etching, n. aguafuerte, f.

eternal, adj. eterno

eternity, n. eternidad, f.

ether, n. éter, m.

etiquette, n. etiqueta, f.

Europe, Europa f.

European, n. y adj. europeo, europea

evacuate, vt. evacuar

evacuation, n. evacuación, f.

evaluate, vt. avaluar, evaluar

evaporate, vi. evaporarse; **evaporated milk,** leche evaporada

even, adj. llano, igual; adv. aun, aun cuando; vt. igualar, allanar

evening, adj. vespertino; n. tarde, noche, f.

event, n. evento, acontecimiento, m.

eventful, adj. memorable

eventual, adj. eventual, fortuito; **eventually,** adv. finalmente, con el tiempo

ever, adj. siempre; **ever since,**

desde que

everlasting, *adj.* eterno

every, *adj.* todo, cada; **every day,** todos los días

everybody, *pron.* cada uno, cada una; todo el mundo

everyday, *adj.* ordinario, rutinario

everything, *n.* todo, *m.*

everywhere, *adv.* en todas partes

evil, *adj.* malo; *n.* malidad, *f.*; daño, *m.*; mal, *m.*

evoke, *vt.* evocar

evolution, *n.* evolución. desarrollo, *m.*

exact, *adj.* exacto, puntual; *vt.* exigir

exacting, *adj.* exigente

exaggerate, *vt.* exagerar

exaggeration, *n.* exageración, *f.*

examination, *n.* examen, *m.*

examine, *vt.* examinar

exasperation, *n.* exasperación, irritación, *f.*

excavate, *vt.* excavar

excavation, *n.* excavación, *f.*; cavidad, *f.*

exceed, *vt.* exceder

exceedingly, *adv.* altamente

excel, *vt.* sobresalir, superar

excellent, *adj.* excelente; sobresaliente

except, *vt.* exceptuar, excluir

exception, *n.* excepción, exclusión, *f.*

exceptional, *adj.* excepcional

excerpt, *vt.* extraer; extractar; *n.* extracto, *m.*

excess, *n.* exceso, *m.*

exchange, *vt.* cambiar; *n.* cambio, *m.*; bolsa, lonja, *f.*

excite, *vt.* excitar; estimular

excitement, *n.* excitación, *f.*, comoción, *f.*

exclaim, *vi.* exclamar

exclamation, *n.* exclamación, *f.*; **exclamation mark, exclamation point,** punto de admiraión

exclude, *vt.* excluir

exclusion, *n.* exclusión, exclusiva, *f.*; excepción, *f.*

exclusive, *adj.* exclusivo

excrement, *n.* excremento, *m.*

excursion, *n.* excursión, expedición, *f.*

excuse, *vt.* excusar; perdonar; *n.* excusa, *f.*

execute, *vt.* ejecutar; llevar a cabo, cumplir

execution, *n.* ejecución, *f.*

executioner, *n.* verdugo, *m.*

executive, *adj.* y *n.* ejecutivo, *m.*

exemplify, *vt.* ejemplificar

exempt, *adj.* exento; *vt.* eximir, exentar

exemption, *n.* exención, franquicia, *f.*

exercise, *n.* ejercicio, *m.*; ensayo, *m.*; práctica, *f.*; *vt.* hacer ejercicio; *vt.* ejercer

exhaust, *n.* (auto., avi.) escape, *m.*; *vt.* agotar, consumir

exhausting, *adj.* agotador

exhibit, *vt.* exhibir; mostrar; *n.* exhibición, *f.*

exhibition, *n.* exhibición, presentación, *f.*; espectáculo, *m.*

exile, *n.* destierro, *m.*; desterrado, *m.*; *vt.* desterrar, deportar

exist, *vi.* existir

existence, *n.* existencia, *f.*

existing, *adj.* actual, presente

exit, *n.* salida, *f.*

exorbitant, *adj.* exorbitante, excesivo

exotic, *adj.* exótico, extranjero

expand, *vt.* extender, dilatar

expansion, *n.* expansión, *f.*

expect, *vt.* esperar

expectant, *adj.* que espera; encinta, embarazada

expedite, *vt.* acelerar; expedir

expel, *vt.* expeler, expulsar

expenditure, *n.* gasto, desembolso, *m.*

expense, *n.* gasto, *m.*

expensive, *adj.* caro, costoso

experience, *n.* experiencia, *f.*; práctica, *f.*; *vt.* experimentar; saber

experienced, *adj.* experimentado; versado, perito

experiment, *n.* experimento, *m.*; prueba, *f.*; *vt.* experimentar

expert, *adj.* experto, diestro; perito; *n.* maestro, maestra; conocedor, conocedora; perito, perita

expiration, *n.* expiración, *f.;* muerte, *f.;* vencimiento (de una letra o pagaré, etc.), *m.*

expire, *vi.* expirar, morir

explain, *vt.* explicar

explanation, *n.* explicación, aclaración, *f.*

explode, *vt.* y *vi.* volar, es tallar, hacer explosión

explore, *vt.* explorar

explorer, *n.* explorador, *m.*

explosion, *n.* explosión, *f.*

export, *vt.* exportar

export, exportation, *n.* exportación, *f.*

expose, *vt.* exponer; mostrar; descubrir

exposition, *n.* exposición, exhibición, *f.*

express, *vt.* expresar, exteriorizar; *adj.* expreso, claro, a propósito; *n.* expreso, correo expreso, *m.*

expression, *n.* expresión, *f.*

expressive, *adj.* expresivo

expressway, *n.* autopista, *f.*

expropriate, *vt.* expropiar, confiscar

exquisite, *adj.* exquisito

extemporaneous, *adj.* extemporáneo, improviso

extend, *vt.* extender; **to extend (time),** prorrogar (un plazo)

extension, *n.* extensión, *f.;* prórroga, *f.*

extensive, *adj.* extenso; amplio

extent, *n.* extensión, *f.;* grado, *m.*

exterior, *n.* y *adj.* exterior, *m.*

exterminate, *vt.* exterminar

external, *adj.* externo, exterior

extinguish, *vt.* extinguir; suprimir

extra, *adj.* extraordinario, adicional; *n.* suplemento extraordinario de un periódico

extract, *vt.* extraer; extractar; *n.* extracto, *m.;* compendio, *m.*

extraction, *n.* extracción, *f.*

extraordinary, *adj.* extraordinario

extrasensory, *adj.* extrasensorio, extrasensoria

extravagance, *n.* extravagancia, *f.;* derroche, *m.*

extravagant, *adj.* extravagante, singular, excesivo; derrochador

extreme, *adj.* extremo; último; *n.* extremo, *m.*

extremity, *n.* extremidad, *f.*

exuberance, *n.* exuberancia, *f.*

exult, *vi.* regocijarse

eye, *n.* ojo, *m.,* vista, *f.*

eyeball, *n.* niña del ojo, *f.*

eyebrow, *n.* ceja, *f.*

eyeglass, *n.* anteojo, *m.*

eyelash, *n.* pestaña, *f.*

eyelid, *n.* párpado, *m.*

eyesight, *n.* vista, *f.*

eyestrain, *n.* cansancio o tensión de los ojos

F

F., Fellow, miembro de una sociedad científica o académica; **Fahrenheit,** Fahrenheit; **Friday,** vier., viernes

f., following, sig.^te, siguiente; **feminine,** *f.,* femenino; **folio,** fol., folio

fabricate, *vt.* fabricar, edificar; inventar (una leyen da, una mentira, etc.)

face, *n.* cara, faz, *f.;* fachada, *f.;* frente, *f.;* **to lose face,** sufrir pérdida de prestigio; **face value,** valor nominal o aparente; *vt.* encararse; hacer frente

facilitate, *vt.* facilitar

fact, *n.* hecho, *m.;* realidad, *f.;* **in fact,** en efecto, verdaderamente

factor, *n.* factor, *m.;* agente, *m.*

factory, *n.* fábrica, *f.,* taller, *m.*

faculty, *n.* facultad, *f.;* profesorado, *m.*

fade, *vi.* marchitarse; desteñirse

fail, *vt.* abandonar; decepcionar; reprobar (a un estudiante); vt. fallar, fracasar; n. falta, f.

failure, n. fracaso, m.; quiebra, bancarrota.

faint, vt. desmayarse

fair, adj. hermoso, bello; blanco; rubio; justo; n. feria, exposición, f.

fairly, adv. claramente; bastante; **fairly well,** bastante bien

fairness, n. hermosura, f.; equidad, f.

fairy, n. hada, f., duende, m.; **fairy tale,** cuento de hadas, m.

faith, n. fe, f.

faithful, adj. fiel, leal

faithless, adj. infiel

fake, adj. (coll.) falso, fraudulento; vt. (coll.) engañar; imitar

faker, n. farsante, m. y f.

fall, vi. caer, caerse; n. caída, f.; otoño, m.

false, adj. falso, pérfido; postizo

falsehood, n. falsedad, f.; mentira, f.

familiar, adj. familiar, casero, conocido

familiarity, n. familiaridad, f.

family, n. familia, f.; linaje, m.; clase, especie, f.

famine, n. hambre, f.; carestía, f.

fan, n. abanico, m.; ventilador, m.; aficionado, aficionada; vt. abanicar

fancy, n. fantasía, imaginación, f.; capricho, m.; adj. de fantasía; vt. y vi. imaginar; gustar de; suponer

far, adv. lejos; adj. lejano, distante, remoto

faraway, adj. lejano

fare, n. alimento, m., comida, f.; pasaje, m., tarifa, f.

farewell, n. despedida, f.

farfetched, adj. forzado, traído de los cabellos

farm, n. hacienda, granja, f.

farmer, n. labrador, labradora; hacendado, hacendada; agricultor, agricultora

farming, n. agricultura, cultivo, m.

far-off, adj. remoto, distante

far-reaching, adj. de gran alcance, trascendental

farsighted, adj. présbita, présbite; (fig.) precavido

farther, adj. y adv. mas lejos; más adelante

farthest, adj. más distante, más remoto; adv. a la mayor distancia

fascinate, vt. fascinar, encantar

fascinating, adj. fascinador, seductor

fashion, n. moda, f.; uso, m., costumbre, f.; vt. formar, amoldar

fashionable, adj. en boga, de moda; elegante

fast, vi. ayunar; n. ayuno, m.; adj. firme, estable; veloz; adv. de prisa

fasten, vt. afirmar, fijar

fat, adj. gordo; **to get fat,** engordar; n. gordo, m., gordura, f.; grasa, manteca, f.; sebo, m.

fate, n. hado, destino, m.

fateful, adj. funesto

father, n. padre, m.

father-in-law, n. suegro, m.

fatherland, n. patria f.

fatherless, adj. huérfano de padre

fatherly, adj. paternal

fatigue, n. fatiga, f., cansancio, m.

fatten, vt. cebar, engordar

faucet, n. grifo m.; **water faucet,** toma, llave, f., caño de agua, m.

favor, n. favor, beneficio, m.; **your favor,** su grata (carta); vt. favorecer, proteger, apoyar

favorable, adj. favorable, propicio; provechoso

favorite, n. y adj. favorito, favorita

FBI, Federal Bureau of Investigation, Departamento Federal de Investigación

fear, vt. y vi. temer, tener miedo; n. miedo, terror, pavor, m.

fearful, *adj.* temeroso; tímido

fearless, *adj.* intrépido

feasible, *adj.* factible, práctico

feast, *n.* banquete, festín, *m.*; fiesta, *f.*; *vt.* festejar; *vi.* comer opíparamente

feat, *n.* hecho, *m.*; acción, hazaña, *f.*

feather, *n.* pluma (de ave) *f.*

featherweight, *n.* peso pluma, *m.*

feature, *n.* facción del rostro; rasgo, *m.*; atracción principal; **double feature,** función de dos películas, *f.*; **features,** *n. pl.* facciones, *f. pl.*, fisonomía, *f.*

February, febrero, *m.*

federal, *adj.* federal

federation, *n.* confedera,ción, federación, *f.*

fee, *n.* paga, gratificación, *f.*; honorarios, derechos, *m. pl.*

feeble, *adj.* flaco, débil

feeble-minded, *adj.* retardado mentalmente

feed, *vt.* pacer; nutrir; alimentar; *n.* alimento, *m.*; pasto, *m.*

feeding, *n.* nutrición, alimento, *m.*

feel, *vt.* sentir; palpar

feeling, *n.* tacto, *m.*; sensibilidad, *f.*; sentimiento, *m.*

feet, *n. pl.* de **foot,** pies, *m. pl.*

feign, *vt.* y *vi.* inventar, fingir; simular

felicitation, *n.* felicitación, *f.*

fellow, *n.* compañero, camarada, *m.*; sujeto, *m.*; becario, *m.*

fellowship, *n.* beca (en una universidad), *f.*; camaradería, *f.*

female, *n.* hembra, *f.*; *adj.* femenino

feminine, *adj.* femenino

fence, *n.* cerca, valla, *f.*; *vt.* cercar; *vi.* esgrimir

fencing, *n.* esgrima, *f.*

fender, *n.* guardafango, *m.*

fertile, *adj.* fértil, fecundo

fertilizer, *n.* abono, *m.*

fervent, *adj.* ferviente; fervoroso

fervor, *n.* fervor, ardor, *m.*

festival, *n.* fiesta, *f.*

festive, *adj.* festivo, alegre

festivity, *n.* festividad, *f.*

fever, *n.* fiebre, *f.*

fiancé, *n.* novio, *m.*

fiancée, *n.* novia, *f.*

fickle, *adj.* voluble, inconstante

fiction, *n.* ficción, *f.*; invención, *f.*

fictitious, *adj.* ficticio; fingido

fiddle, *n.* violín, *m.*

fiddler, *n.* violinista, *m.* y *f.*

field, *n.* campo, *m.*; *adj.* campal

fierce, *adj.* fiero, feroz

fiery, *adj.* fogoso

fifteen, *n.* y *adj.* quince, *m.*

fifteenth, *n.* y *adj.* décimoquinto, *m.*

fifth, *n.* y *adj.* quinto, *m.*; quinto de galón (medida de vinos y licores)

fiftieth, *n.* y *adj.* quincuagésimo, *m.*

fifty, *n.* y *adj.* cincuenta, *m.*

fifty-fifty, *adj.* y *adv.* mitad y mitad

fight, *vt.* pelear; reñir; luchar; *n.* pelea, *f.*

fighter, *n.* luchador, luchadora; **fighter plane,** caza, *m.*

figure, *n.* figura, *f.*; cifra, *f.*; *vt.* figurar

file, *n.* archivo, *m.*; (mil.) fila, hilera, *f.*; lima, *f.*; *vt.* archivar; limar

filial, *adj.* filial

fill, *vt.* y *vi.* llenar, henchir; hartar; **to fill out,** llenar (un cuestionario, etc.)

filling, *n.* relleno, *m.*; orificación (de un diente), *f.*; **filling station,** estación de gasolina, *f.*

filly, *n.* potranca, *f.*

film, *n.* película, *f.*; membrana, *f.*

filter, *n.* filtro, *m.*; **filter-tip,** *adj.* de boquilla-filtro; *vt.* filtrar

filthy, *adj.* sucio, puerco

final, *adj.* final, último; definitivo; **finally,** *adv.* finalmente, por útimo; **finals,** último examen, juego, etc.

finality, n. finalidad, f.

finance, n. finaizas, f. pl.

financial, adj. financiero

find, vt. hallar, descubrir; n. hallazgo, descubrimiento, m.

fine, adj. fino; bueno; **the fine arts,** las bellas artes; n. multa, f.; vt. multar

finesse, n. sutileza, f.

finger, n. dedo, m.

fingernail, n. uña, f.

fingerprints, n. pl. impresiones digitales, f. pl.

finish, vt. acabar, terminar; n. conclusión, f., final, m.

fire, n. fuego, m.; candela, f.; incendio, m.; vi. (mil.) tirar, hacer fuego

firearms, n. pl. armas de fuego, f. pl.

firefly, n. luciérnaga, f., cocuyo, cucuyo, m.

fireman, n. bombero, m.; (rail.) fogonero, m.

fireplace, n. hogar, m., chimenea, f.

fireplug, n. boca de incendios, toma de agua, f.

fireproof, adj. a prueba de fuego, refractario

fireside, n.sitio cerca a la chimenea u hogar; vida de hogar

fireworks, n. pl. fuegos artificiales, m. pl.

firm, adj. firme, estable; n. (com.) empresa, razón social, f.

firmament, n. firmamento, m.

first, adj. primero; primario; delantero; **first aid,** primeros auxilios; adv. primeramente

first-class, adj. de primera clase

firsthand, adj. directo, de primera mano

fiscal, adj. fiscal, del fisco

fish, n. pez, m.; pescado, m.; vt. y vi. pescar

fisherman, n. pescador, m.

fishing, n. pesca, f.

fist, n. puño, m.

fit, adj. apto, idóneo, capaz; n. convulsión, f.; ataque, m.; vt. ajustar, acomodar, adaptar;

sentar, quedar bien

five, n. y adj. cinco, m.

fix, vt. fijar, establecer; componer

fixtures, n. pl. enseres, m. pl.; instalación (eléctrica), f.

flag, n. bandera, f.; pabellón, m.

flagpole, n. asta de bandera, f.

flamingo, n. (orn.) flamenco, m.

flap, n. bragueta, f.; solapa, f.; aleta, f.; vt. y vi. aletear; sacudir

flash, n. relámpago, m.; llamarada, f.; destello, m.; vi. relampaguear; brillar

flashback, n. interrupción de la continuidad de un relato

flashlight, n. linterna, linterna eléctrica de bolsillo, f.

flat, adj. plano; insípido; **flat tire,** llanta desinflada, neumático desinflado; n. (mus.) bemol, m.; apartamiento, apartamento, m.

flatten, vt. allanar; aplastar

flatter, vt. adular

flavor, n. sabor, gusto, m.

flavoring, n. condimento, m.

flaw, n. falta, tacha,

flawless, adj. sin tacha

flax, n. lino, m.

flaxseed, n. semill de lino, f.

flea, n. pulga, f.

flee, vi. escapar; huir

fleecy, adj. lanudo

fleeting, adj. pasajero, fugitivo

flesh, n. carne, f.

flew, pretérito del verbo **fly**

flexible, adj. flexible

flicker, vi. aletear, fluctuar; n. aleteo, m.; **flicker of an eyelash,** pestañeo, m.

flier, n. aviador, aviadora; tren muy rápido

flight, n. buida, fuga, f.; vuelo, m.

fling, vt. lanzar, echar; vi. lanzarse con violencia; n. tiro, m.; tentativa, f.

flirt, vi. coquetear; n. coqueta, f.

flirtation, n. coquetería, f.

float, vi. flotar; n. carro alegórico, m.; flotador, m.

flock, n. manada, f.; rebaño, m.; gentío, m.; vi. congregarse

flood, n. diluvio, m.; inundación, f.; vt. inundar

floor, n. suelo, piso, m.

flounder, n. (pez) rodaballo, m.

flour, n. harina, f.

flourish, vi. prosperar; n. floreo de palabras; rasgo (de una pluma), m.; lozanía, f.

flow, vi. fluir, manar; n. flujo, m.; corriente, f.

flower, n. flor, f.

flowery, adj. florido

flu, n. (coll.) influenza, gripe, f., trancazo, m.

fluent, adj. fluido; fluente, fácil; **fluently,** adv. con fluidez

fluorescent, adj. fluorescente; **fluorescent lighting,** aluminado fluorescente, m.

fluoridate, vt. fluorizar

fluoridation, n. fluoruración, f.

flush, vt. limpiar con un chorro de agua (por ej., un inodoro); vi. sonrojarse, ruborizarse; n. rubor, m.

fluster, vt. confundir, atropellar; vi. confundirse

flutter, vt. turbar, desordenar; vi. revolotear; flamear

fly, vt. y vi. volar; huir; n. mosca, f.; volante, m.

flying, n. vuelo, m.; aviación, f.; adj. volante, volador; de pasada

F.M. or **f.m., frequency modulation,** (rad.) modulación de frecuencia

f.o.b. or **F.O.B., frèe on board,** L.A.B., libre a bordo o f.a.b. franco a bordo

focus, n. foco, m., punto céntrico; enfoque, m.; vt. enfocar

foe, n. adversario, adversaria, enemigo, enemiga

fog, n. niebla, f.

foil, vt. vencer; frustrar

fold, n. redil, m.; plegadura, f., doblez, m.; vt. plegar, doblar

folder, n. folleto, m.; papelera, f.

foliage, n. follaje, m.

folk, n. gente, f.; **folk music,** música tradicional, f.; **folk song,** romance, m., copla, f.

folklore, n. folklore, m., tradiciones populares, f. pl.

follow, vt. seguir; vi. seguirse, resultar, provenir

following, n. séquito, cortejo, m.; profesión, f.; adj. próximo, siguiente

follow-up, adj. que sigue

fond, adj. afectuoso; aficionado; **to be fond of,** aficionarse, tener simpatía por

fondle, vt. mimar, acariciar

fondness, n. debilidad, f.; afición, f.

food, n. alimento, m.; comida, f.

fool, n. loco, loca, tonto, tonta, bobo, boba; vt. engañar; vi. tontear

foolish, adj. bobo, tonto, majadero

foolproof, adj. muy evidente, fácil hasta para un tonto

foot, n. pie, m.

football, n. futbol americano, m.; pelota de futbol, f.

footlights, n. pl. luces del proscenio; (fig.) el teatro, las tablas

footmark, n. huella, f.

footnote, n. anotación, glosa, f.; nota, f.

footprint, n. huella, pisada, f.

footstep, n. paso, m.; pisada, f.

footwear, n. calzado, m.

for, prep. para; por; conj. porque, pues; **what for?** ¿para qué?

forbear, vt. y vi. cesar, detenerse; abstenerse

forbearance, n. paciencia, f.

forbid, vt. prohibir; **God forbid!** Dios no quiera!

forbidden, adj. prohibido

force, n. fuerza, f.; poder, vigor, m.; valor, m.; **forces,** tropas, f. pl.; vt. forzar, violentar; obligar

forceful, adj. fuerte, poderoso; dominante

forceps, n. pl. pinzas, f. pl.
forearm, n. antebrazo, m.
forebear, n. antepasado, m.
foreboding, n. corazonada, f.
forecast, vt. y vi. proyectar, prever; n. previsión, f.; profecía f.; **weather forecast**, pronóstico del tiempo, m.
foreclosure, n. juicio hipotecario, m.
forefather, n. abuelo, antepasado, m.
forefinger, n. índice, m.
foregoing, adj. anterior, precedente
foreground, n. delantera, f.; primer plano, m.
foreign, adj. extranjero
foreigner, n. extranjero, extranjera, forastero, forastera
foreman, n. capataz, m.
forenoon, n. la mañana, las horas antes del mediodía
forerunner, n. precursor, precursora; predecesor, predecesora
foresee, vt. prever
foresight, n. previsión, f.
forest, n. bosque, m.; selva, f.
foreword, n. prefacio, prólogo, preámbulo, m.
forfeit, n. multa, f.; prenda, f.; vt. decomisar; perder
forget, vt. olvidar; descuidar
forgetful, adj. olvidadizo
forget-me-not, n. (bot.) nomeolvides, f.
forgive, vt. perdonar
forgiveness, n. perdón, m.
forgot, pretérito del verbo **forget**
forlorn, adj. abandonado, perdido
form, n. forma, f.; esqueleto, modelo, m.; modo, m.; **form letter**, carta circular, f.; vt. formar; concebir; vi. formarse
formal, adj. formal, metódico ceremonioso
formality, n. formalidad, f.
formation, n. formación, f.
former, adj. precedente; previo; **formerly**, adv. antiguamente, en tiempos pasados
formidable, adj. formidable,

terrible
forsaken, adj. desamparado
fort, n. fortaleza, f., fuerte, m.
forth, adv. en adelante; afuera; **and so forth**, y así sucesivamente, et cétera
forthcoming, adj. próximo
fortieth, n. y adj. cuadragésimo, m.
fortify, vt. fortificar
fortnight, n. quincena, f., quince días; dos semanas
fortress, n. (mil.) fortaleza, f.
fortunate, adj. afortunado, dichoso; **fortunately**, adv. felizmente, por fortuna
fortune, n. fortune, f.; suerte, f.
forty, n. y adj. cuarenta, m.
forum, n. foro, tribunal, m.
forward, n. delantero; precoz; atrevido; adv. adelante, más allá; vt. expedir, trasmitir
forwards, adv. adelante
foul, adj. sucio, detestable; **foul ball**, pelota foul (que cae fuera del primer o tercer ángulo del rombal de baseball); **foul play**, conducta falsa y pérfida; jugada sucia, f.
found, vt. fundar, establecer; basar
foundation, n. fundación, f.; fundamento, m., pie, m.; fondo, m.
founder, n. fundador, fundadora
fountain, n. fuente, f.; manantial, m.; **fountain pen**, plumafuente, estilográfica, f.
four, n. y adj. cuatro, m.
fourteen, n. y adj. catorce, m.
fourteenth, n. y adj. décimocuarto, m.
fourth, n. y adj. cuarto, m.
fox, n. zorra, f.; zorro, m.
foxy, adj. astuto
fracture, n. fractura, f.; vt. fracturar, romper
fragment, n. fragmento, trozo, m.
fragrance, n. fragancia, f.
fragrant, adj. fragante, oloroso
frame, n. marco, m.; bastidor,

m.; armazón, f.

France, Francia

franchise, n. franquicia, inmunidad, f.

frank, adj. franco, sincero; **frankly,** adv. francamente

frankfurter, n. salchicha, f.

fraternal, adj. fraternal

fraternity, n. fraternidad, f.

freak, n. monstruosidad, f.

freakish, adj. estrambótico

freckle, n. peca, f.

free, adj. libre; liberal; gratuito, gratis; vt. libertar; librar; eximir

freedom, n. libertad, f.

freethinker, n. librepensador, librepensadora

freeze, vi. helar, helarse; vt. helar, congelar

freezer, n. congelador, m.; **deep freezer,** congeladora, f., congelador, m.

freezing, n. congelación, f.

freight, n. carga, f.; flete, m.; porte, m.

French, adj. francés, francesa

Frenchman, n. francés, m.

frenzy, n. frenesí, m.; locura, f.

frequency, n. frecuencia, f.

frequent, adj. frecuente; **frequently,** adv. con frecuencia

fresh, adj. fresco; nuevo; atrevido

freshen, vt. refrescar

freshman, n. estudiante de primer año; novicio, novicia

fretful, adj. enojadizo

Friday, n. viernes, m.; **Good Friday,** Viernes Santo

fried, adj. frito

friend, n. amigo, amiga

friendless, adj. sin amigos

friendly, adj. amigable, amistoso

friendship, n. amistad, f.

fright, n. susto, terror, m.

frighten, vt. espantar

frightful, adj. espantoso

frivolous, adj. frívolo, vano

frolic, n. alegría, f.; travesura, f.; vi. retozar, juguetear

from, prep. de; desde; **from now on,** en lo sucesivo

front, n. frente, m.

frontier, n. frontera, f.

frontispiece, n. frontispicio, m.; portada, f.

frost, n. helada, f.

frosting, n. confitura o betún (para pasteles)

froth, n. espuma (de algún líquido), f.

frown, vi. fruncir el entrecejo; n. ceño, m.; mala cara, f.

froze, pretérito del verbo **freeze**

frozen, adj. helado; congelado

fruit, n. fruto, fruta; producto, m.

fruitcake, n. torta o pastel de frutas

fruitful, adj. fructífero, fértil

fruitless, adj. estéril; inútil

frustration, n. contratiempo, chasco, m.

fry, vt. freír

frying pan, n. sartén, f.

fudge, n. variedad de dulce de chocolate

fulfil, vt. cumplir, realizar

full, adj. lleno, repleto

full-grown, adj. desarrollado, crecido, maduro

fumigate, vt. fumigar

fun, n. chanza, burla, f.; diversión, f.; **to make fun of,** burlarse de; **to have fun,** divertirse

fund, n. fondo, (dinero), m.

fundamental, adj. fundamental, básico

funnel, n. embudo, m.

funny, adj. cómico

furlough, n. (mil.) licencia, f.; permiso, m.

furnace, n. horno, m.; caldera, f.

furnish, vt. proveer; equipar

furnished, adj. amueblado

furniture, n. mobiliario, m., muebles, m. pl.

furor, n. rabia, f.; entusiasmo, m.

further, adj. ulterior, más distante; adv. más lejos, más allá; aun; vt. adelantar, promover

furthermore, adv. además

furthest, *adj.* y *adv.* más lejos, más remoto

fuss, *n.* (coll.) alboroto, *m.*; *vi.* preocuparse por pequeñeces

fussy, *adj.* melindroso; exigente

future, *adj.* futuro, venidero; *n.* lo futuro, porvenir, *m.*

G

gain, *n.* ganancia, *f.*; interés, beneficio, *m.*; *vt.* ganar; conseguir

gall, *n.* hiel, *f.*; rencor, odio, *m.*; **gall bladder,** vesícula biliar, *f.*

gallant, *adj.* galante; *n.* galán, *m.*

gallantry, *n.* galantería, *f.*

gallery, *n.* galería,

galley, *n.* (naut.) galera, *f.*; **galley roof,** (print.) galerada, *f.*, primera prueba

gallon, *n.* galón, *m.*

gallop, *n.* galope, *m.*; *vi.* galopar

gallstone, *n.* cálculo biliario, *m.*

galvanometer, *n.* galvanómetro, *m.*

gamble, *vi.* jugar por dinero; aventurar

gambling, *n.* juego por dinero, *m.*

game, *n.* juego, *m.*

gamma globulin, *n.* gama globulina, *f.*

gang, *n.* cuadrilla, banda, pandilla, *f.*

gangster, *n.* rufián, *m.*

gap, *n.* boquete, *m.*; brecha, *f.*; laguna, *f.*

gape, *vi.* bostezar, boquear

garage, *n.* garaje, garage, *m.* cochera, *f.*

garb, *n.* vestidura, *f.*

garbage, *n.* basura, *f.*

garden, *n.* huerto, *m.*; jardín, *m.*

gardener, *n.* jardinero, jardinera

gardenia, *n.* gardenia, *f.*

gargle, *vt.* y *vi.* hacer gárgaras; *n.* gárgara, *f.*

garlic, *n.* (bot.) ajo, *m.*

garment, *n.* vestidura, *f.*

garrison, *n.* (mil.) guarnición, *f.*; fortaleza, *f.*

gas, *n.* gas, *m.*; **gas station,** gasolinera, *f.*

gasoline, *n.* gasolina, *f.*

gas-storage tank, *n.* gasómetro, *m.*

gate, *n.* puerta, *f.*

gateway, *n.* entrada, *f.*

gather, *vt.* recoger, amontonar, reunir; inferir; *vi.* juntarse

gathering, *n.* reunión, *f.*

gaze, *vi.* contemplar

gear, *n.* engtanaje, *m.*; **to put in gear,** embragar

geese, *n. pl.* de **goose,** gansos, *m. pl.*

gelatine, *n.* gelatina, *f.*

gem, *n.* joya, *f.*

Gen., General, Gral., General

gender, *n.* género, *m.*

gene, *n.* gen, *m.*

general, *adj.* general, común, usual; *n.* general, *m.*; **in general,** por lo común

generation, *n.* generación, *f.*

generator, *n.* generador, *m.*

generosity, *n.* generosidad, *f.*

generous, *adj.* generoso

genetics, *n.* genética, *f.*

genius, *n.* genio, *m.*

genocide, *n.* genocidio, *m.*

genteel, *adj.* gentil, elegante

Gentile, *n.* gentil, *m.* y *f.*

gentle, *adj.* suave, dócil

gentleman, *n.* caballero, *m.*

gentleness, *n.* gentileza, *f.*

genuine, *adj.* genuino, puro

geographic, **geographical,** *adj.* geográfico

geography, *n.* geografía, *f.*

geology, *n.* geología, *f.*

geometric, geometrical, *adj.* geométrico

geometry, *n.* geometría, *f.*; **solid geometry,** geometría del espacio

German, *n.* y *adj.* alemán, alemana

Germany, Alemania, *f.*

gesture, *n.* gesto, movimiento, *m.*

get, *vt.* obtener, conseguir; *vi.* llegar; ponerse

ghastly, *adj.* pálido, cadavérico

ghost, *n.* espectro, *m.*; fantasma, *m.*

giant, *n.* gigante, *m.*

gift, *n.* don, *m.*; presente, obsequio, *m.*

gifted, *adj.* hábil, talentoso

gigantic, *adv.* gigantesco

gin, *n.* ginebra, *f.*

ginger, *n.* jengibre, *m.*

gingerly, *adv.* cautelosamente; *adj.* cauteloso

gingham, *n.* zaraza, *f.*

giraffe, *n.* jirafa, *f.*

girdle, *n.* faja, cinturón, *m.*

girl, *n.* muchacha, niña, *f.*

girlhood, *n.* niñez, *f.*, juventud femenina

give, *vt.* y *vi.* dar, conceder; **to give birth**, dar a luz; **to give up**, rendirse, darse por vencido

given, *p. p.* del verbo **give**

gladiolus, *n.* gladiolo, *m.*

gladness, *n.* alegría, *f.*, regocijo, placer, *m.*

glamor, **glamour**, *n.* encanto, hechizo, *m.*, elegancia, *f.*

glamorous, *adj.* fascinador, encantador

glance, *n.* vistazo, *m.*; ojeada, *f.*; **at first glance**, a primera vista; *vt.* verligeramente

glare, *n.* deslumbramiento, *m.*; reflejo, *m.*; mirada penetrante; *vi.* relumbrar, brillar; echar miradas de indignación

glaring, *adj.* deslumbrante; penetrante

glass, *n.* vidrio, *m.*; vaso para beber; espejo, *m.*; **glasses**, *n. pl.* anteojos, *m. pl.*; *adj.* de vidrio

glassful, *n.* vaso, *m.*, vaso lleno

glassware, *n.* cristalería, *f.*

glee, *n.* alegría, *f.*; gozo, *m.*; **glee club**, coro, *m.*

glide, *vi.* deslizarse; planear

glider, *n.* (avi.) planeador, *m.*

glint, *n.* lustre, brillo, *m.*

glisten, *vi.* centellear

glitter, *vi.* destellar; *n.* destello

globe, *n.* globo, *m.*; esfera, *f.*; orbe, *m.*

gloom, *n.* oscuridad, melancolía, tristeza, *f.*

gloomy, *adj.* sombrío oscuro; triste, melancólico

glorify, *vt.* glorificar, celebrar

glorious, *adj.* glorioso

glory, *n.* gloria, fama, *f.*

glossy, *adj.* lustroso, brillante

glove, *n.* guante, *m.*

glow, *vi.* arder; relucir

glowworm, *n.* luciérnaga, *f.*

glue, *n.* cola, *f.*, sustancia glutinosa; *vt.* encolar, pegar

glutton, *n.* glotón, glotona

gm., **gram**, *g.*, gramo

G-Man, *n.* (E. U. A.) miembro de la policía secreta

go, *vi.* ir, irse, andar, caminar; partir; huir; to awa marcharse, salir; **to go away**, marcharse, salir; **to go back**, regresar; *n.* (coll.) energía, *f.*; **on the go**, en plena actividad

goal, *n.* meta, *f.*; fin, *m.*

goat, *n.* cabra, chiva, *f.*

gobbler, *n.* pavo, *m.*; glotón, glotona

goblet, *n.* copa, *f.*; cáliz, *m.*

goblin, *n.* duende, *m.*

God, *n.*; Dios, *m.*; **God willing**, Dios mediante

god, *n.* dios *m.*

godchild, *n.* ahijado, ahijada

godess, *n.* diosa, *f.*

godfather, *n.* padrino, *m.*

godmother, *n.* madrina, *f.*

godsend, *n.* bendición, cosa llovida del cielo

Godspeed, *n.* bienandanza, *f.*

goes, 3ª persona del singular del verbo **go**

gold, *n.* oro, *m.*

golden, *adj.* de oro; excelente

goldenrod, (bot.) vara de San José, vara de oro, *f.*

goldfish, *n.* carpa dorada, *f.*

goldsmith, *n.* orfebre, *m.*

good, *adj.* bueno; bondadoso; apto; perito

good-bye, *n.* adiós, *m.*

good-looking, *adj.* bien parecido, guapo

goodness, n. bondad, f.

goose, n. ganso, m.

gorge, n. barranco, m.

gorgeous, adj. primoroso

gorilla, n. (zool.) gorila.

gospel, n. evangelio, m.

gout, n. (med.) gota, f.

govern, vt. y vi. gobernar

governess, n. institutriz, f.

government, n. gobierno, m.

governor, n. gobernador, m.;
gobernante, m.

grace, n. gracia, f.; favor, m.;
to say grace, bendecir la mesa; vt. agraciar

graceful, adj. agraciado

gracious, adj. gentil, afable

grade, n. grado, m.; pendiente,
f.; nivel, m.; calidad, f.; **grade
school,** escuela premaria, m.

gradual, adj. gradual

graduate, vt. y vi. graduar,
graduarse, recibirse; n. gra-
duado, graduada

graduation, n. graduación, f.

grain, n. grano, m.; semilla, f.

gram, n. gramo (peso), m.

grammar, n. gramática, f.,
grammar school, escuela
primaria o elemental, f.

grammatical, adj. gramatical

grand, adj. grande, ilustre; espléndido; **grand piano,** piano
de cola, m.

grandchild, n. nieto, nieta

granddaughter, n. nieta, f.

grandeur, n. pompa, f.

grandfather, n. abuelo, m.

grandmother, n. abuela, f.

grandparent, n. abuelo, abuela

grandson, n. nieto, m.

granite, n. granito, m.

grant, vt. conceder; conferir;
granting that, supuesto que;
to take for granted, dar por
sentado; n. subvención, f.

grape, n. uva, f.

grapefruit, n. toronja, f.

graph, n. diagrama, m.; gráfico, m.

graphic, adj. gráfico; pintoresco

grasp, vt. empuñar, agarrar;

comprender; n. puño, puñado, m.; dominio, m.

grasping, adj. codicioso

grass, n. hierba, f.; yerba, f.,
césped, m.

grasshopper, n. saltamontes,
m.

grate, n. reja, verja, rejilla, f.;
vt. rallar; irritar

grateful, adj. agradecido

gratify, vt. gratificar

gratis, adj. gratuito, gratis;
adv. gratis, de balde

gratitude, n. gratitud, f.

grave, n. sepultura, f.; tumba,
fosa, f.; adj. grave, serio

graveyard, n. cementerio, m.

gravity, n. graveded, f.; seriedad, f.

gravy, n. jugo de la carne, m.,
salsa, f.

graze, vt. pastorear; tocar ligeramente; vi. rozar; pacer

grease, n. grasa, f.; vt. engrasar, lubricar

greasy, adj. grasiento

great, adj. gran, grande; ilustre; **greatly,** adv. grandemen-
te, muy, mucho

Great Britain, Gran Bretaña,
f.

great-grandchild, n. biznieto,
biznieta

great-grandparent, n. bisabuelo, bisabuela

Grecian, n. y adj. griego, griega

Greece, Grecia, f.

greed, greediness, n. voraci-
dad, f.; codicia, f.

greedy, adj. voraz, goloso; codicioso

Greek, n. adj. griego, griega

green, adj. verde, fresco; no
maduro; n. verde, m., verdor,
m.; **greens,** n. pl. verduras,
hortalizas, f. pl.

Greenland, Groenlandia, f.

greet, vt. saludar

greeting, n. saludo, m.

grew, pretérito del verbo **grow**

greyhound, n. galgo, lebrel, m.

grief, n. dolor, m., aflicción, f.

grieve, vt. agraviar, afligir; vi.
afligirse, llorar

grill, *vt.* asar en parrillas; *n.* parrilla, *f.*

grim, *adj.* feo; austero

grimace, *n.* mueca, *f.*

grime, *n.* suciedad, *f.*

grimy, *adj.* sucio

grin, *n.* risa franca, *f.*; *vi.* reirse francamente

grind, *vt.* moler; afilar

grinder, *n.* molinillo, *m.*; amolador, *m.*

grip, *vt.* agarrar, empuñar; *n.* maleta, *f.*

grippe, *n.* gripe, *f.*; influenza, *f.*

gripping, *adj.* emocionante

gristle, *n.* cartílago, *m.*

gritty, *adj.* arenoso

groan, *vi.* gemir; *n.* gemido, quejido, *m.*

grocer, *n.* abacero, *m.*; (Sp. Am.) abarrotero, *m.*

grocery, *n.* abacería, *f.*; **grocery store,** tienda de comestibles, *f.*; (Sp. Am.) tienda de abarrotes, *f.*

groom, *n.* criado, *m.*; mozo de caballos; novio, *m.*

gross, *n.* gruesa, *f.*; todo, *m.*

ground, *n.* tierra, *f.*; país, *m.*; terreno, suelo, *m.*

groundless, *adj.* infundado

group, *n.* grupo, *m.*

grow, *vt.* cultivar; *vi.* crecer

grown, *p. p.* del verbo **grow**

grown-up, *adj.* mayor de edad, maduro; *n.* persona mayor de edad

growth, *n.* crecimiento, *m.*; nacencia, *f.*, tumor, *m.*

grudge, *n.* rencor, odio, *m.*; envidia

grudgingly, *adv.* con repugnancia, de mala gana

gruff, *adj.* ceñudo, brusco

grumble, *vi.* gruñir; murmurar

grumpy, *adj.* regañón, quejoso

guarantee, *vt.* garantizar

guaranty, *n.* garante, *m.*; garantía, *f.*

guard, *n.* guarda, guardia, *f.*, centinela, *f.*, m. y *f.*; vigilante, *m.*; *vt.* defender; custodiar; *vi.* guardarse; prevenirse; velar

guardian, *n.* tutor, *m.*; guardián, *m.*

guess, *vt.* y *vi.* conjeturar; adivinar; *n.* conjetura, *f.*

guest, *n.* huésped, huéspeda, invitado, invitada, convidado, convidada

guide, *vt.* guiar, dirigir; *n.* guía, m y *f.*

guilt, *n.* delito, *m.*; culpa, *f.*

guilty, *adj.* culpable

guitar, *n.* guitarra, *f.*

gulf, *n.* golfo, *m.*; abismo , *m.*

Gulf Stream, *n.* corriente del Golfo de México, *f.*

gum, *n.* goma, *f.*; encía, *f.*; **chewing gum,** chicle, *m.*, goma de mascar, *f.*

gumbo, *n.* (bot.) quimbombó, *m.*

gumption, *n.* (coll.) iniciativa, inventiva, *f.*

gun, *n.* arma de fuego; fusil, *m.*; escopeta, *f.*; pistola, *f.*, revólver, *m.*

gunpowder, *n.* pólvora, *f.*

gust, *n.* soplo de aire, *m.*; ráfaga, *f.*

gusto, *n.* gusto, placer, *m.*

gut, *n.* intestino, *m.*, cuerda de tripa, *f.*; **guts,** *n. pl.* (coll.) valor, *m.*, valentía, *f.*

gutter, *n.* zanja, *f.*; caño, *m.*

guy, *n.* tipo, sujeto, *m.*

gymnasium, *n.* gimnasio, *m.*

gypsy, *n.* y *adj.* gitano, gitana

H

habit, *n.* hábito, vestido, *m.*; costumbre, *f.*

habitation, *n.* habitación, *f.*; domicilio, *m.*

habitual, *adj.* habitual

had, pretérito y *p. p.* del verbo **have**

haddock, *n.* (pez) merluza, *f.*

Hades, *n. pl.* los infiernos, *m. pl.*

hag, *n.* bruja, hechicera, *f.*

haggard, *adj.* ojeroso, trasnochado

hail, *n.* granizo, *m.*; saludo, *m.*; *vt.* saludar; *vi.* granizar; **hail!** *interj.* ¡viva!

hair, n. cabello pelo, m.

hairbrush, n. cepillo para el cabello, m.

hair-do, n. (coll.) peinado, m.

hairdresser, n. peluquero, m.; peinador, peinadora

hairpin, n. horquilla, f.

hairy, adj. peludo

hale, adj. sano, vigoroso

half, n. mitad, f.; adj. medio

half-breed, n. y adj. mestizo, mestiza

halfhearted, adj. indiferente, sin entusiasmo

half-hour, n. media hora, f.

halfway, adv. a medio camino, a medias

hall, n. vestíbulo, m., sala, f.; salón, colegio, m.; sala, f.; cámara, f.

hallow, vt. consagrar, santificar

Halloween, n. víspera de Todos los Santos, f.

hallway, n. vestíbulo, atrio, m.

halo, n. halo, nimbo, m., corona, f.

halves, n. pl. de **half**, mitades, f. pl., **by halves**, a medias

ham, n. jamón, m.

hamburger, n. carne picada de res; emparedado de carne molida

hammer, n. martillo, m.; vt. martillar

hamper, n. cesto grande (para ropa, etc.); vt. estorbar, impedir

hand, n. mano, f.; obrero, m.; mano o manecilla (de un reloj), f.; **at hand**, a la mano, vt. alargar; entregar

handbag, n. bolsa, f.; maletilla, f.

handcuff, n. manilla, f.; esposas, f. pl.

handful, n. puñado, m.

handicap, n. obstáculo, m.; ventaja, f. (en juegos)

handiwork, n. obra manual, f.

handkerchief, n. pañuelo, m.

handle, n. mango, m., asa, manigueta, f.; vt. manejar; tratar

handmade, adj. hecho a mano

handshake, n. apretón de manos, m.

handsome, adj. hermoso, bello

handwork, n. trabajo a mano, m.

handwriting, n. escritura, f.; caligrafía, f.; letra, f.

handy, adj. manual; diestro, hábil

hang, vt. colgar, suspender; ahorcar; vi. colgar; ser ahorcado; pegarse

hangnail, n. uñero, padrastro, m.

haphazard, adj. casual, descuidado

happen, vi. acontecer, suceder

happening, n. suceso, acontecimiento, m.

happily, adv. felizmente

happiness, n. felicidad, dicha, f.

happy, adj. feliz

hard, adj. duro, firme; difícil; severo, rígido

hard-boiled, adj. cocido hasta endurecerse; **hard-boiled eggs**, huevos duros, m. pl.

harden, vt. y vi. endurecer, endurecerse

hardly, adv. apenas

hardship, n. injusticia, f.; trabajo, m.

hardtop, n. toldo rígido; adj. con toldo rígido

hardware, n. ferretería, f.

hardy, adj. fuerte, robusto

hare, n. liebre, f.

harem, n. harén, m.

harm, n. mal, daño, m.; perjuicio, m.; vt. dañar, injuriar

harmful, adj. perjudicial

harmless, adj. inofensivo

hormonize, vt. y vi. armonizar

harmony, n. armonía, f.

harp, n. arpa, f.

harsh, adj. áspero, austero

harvest, n. cosecha, f.

has, 3ª persona del singular del verbo **have**

hash, n. jigote, picadillo, m.

hassock, n. cojín para los pies, m.

haste, n. prisa, f.

hasten, *vt.* y *vi.* acelerar, apresurar

hastily, *adv.* precipitadamente

hasty, *adj.* apresurado

hat, *n.* sombrero, *m.*

hatch, *vt.* criar pollos; empollar

hate, *n.* odio, *m.*; *vt.* odiar, detestar

hateful, *adj.* odioso, detestable

haul, *vt.* tirar, halar; acarrear

haunt, *vt.* frecuentar, rondar; perseguir; *n.* guarida, *f.*

haunted, *adj.* encantado, frecuentado por espantos

Havana, Habana

haven, *n.* puerto, *m.*; abrigo, asilo, *m.*

Hawaiian Islands, Islas Hawaianas, *f. pl.*

hawk, *n.* (orn.) halcón, gavilán, *m.*

hay, *n.* heno, *m.*; **hay fever**, romadizo, *m.*, fiebre del heno, *f.*

hazard, *n.* acaso, accidente, *m.*; riesgo, *m.*; *vt.* arriesgar; aventurar

haze, *n.* niebla, bruma, *f.*

hazel, *n.* avellano, *m.*; *adj.* castaño

hazelnut, *n.* avellano, *f.*

hazy, *adj.* anieblado, oscuro

H-Bomb, *n.* bomba H, *m.*

he, *pron.* él

head, *n.* cabeza, *f.*; jefe, *m.*; *vt.* gobernar, dirigir

headache, *n.* dolor de cabeza, *m.*; jaqueca, *f.*

headfirst, *adv.* de cabeza

headgear, *n.* tocado, *m.*

heading, *n.* título, membrete, *m.*

headline, *n.* encabezamiento, título (de un periódico, etc.), *m.*

headquarters, *n.* (mil.) cuartel general, *m.*; jefatura, administración, *f.*

headstrong, *adj.* testarudo, cabezudo

heal, *vt.* y *vi.* curar, sanar, cicatrizar

health, *n.* salud, sanidad, *f.*

healthy, *adj.* sano; saludable

heap, *n.* montón, *m.*; *vt.* amontonar, acumular

hear, *vt.* y *vi.* oír; escuchar

hearing, *n.* oído, *m.*, oreja, *f.*; audiencia, *f.*

hearsay, *n.* rumor, *m.*

hearse, *n.* carroza fúnebre, *f.*

heart, *n.* corazón, *m.*; alma, *f.*; interior, centro, *m.*; ánimo, valor, *m.*; **by heart**, de memoria; **heart attack**, ataque al corazón; **heart transplant**, trasplante de corazón, trasplante cardíaco

heartbroken, *adj.* transido de dolor

heartburn, *n.* acedía, *f.*

heartfelt, *adj.* expresivo, sentido, sincero

hearth, *n.* hogar, fogón, *m.*, chimenea, *f.*

heartless, *adj.* inhumano, cruel

heart-to-heart, *adj.* sincero, abierto; confidencial

hearty, *adj.* cordial

heat, *n.* calor, *m.*; ardor, *m.*; *vt.* calentar

heater, *n.* calorífero, *m.*; **hot-air heater**, calorífero de aire caliente

heathen, *n.* gentil, *m.* y *f.*, pagano, pagana

heating, *n.* calefacción, *f.*

heave, *vt.* alzar; elevar; (naut.) virar para proa; *vi.* palpitar

heaven, *n.* cielo, *m.*

heavenly, *adj.* celeste, divino

heaviness, *n.* pesadez, *f.*

heavy, *adj.* pesado

heavyweight, *n.* boxeador de peso mayor, *m.*

hectic, *adj.* inquieto, agitado

heed, *vt.* atender, observar; *n.* cuidado, *m.*; atención, precaución, *f.*

heel, *n.* talón, carcañal, calcañar, *m.*; tacón, *m.*; (coll.) canalla, *m.*

height, *n.* altura, elevación, *f.*

heighten, *vt.* realzar

heir, *n.* heredero, *m.*

heiress, *n.* heredera, *f.*

heirloom, *n.* reliquia de familia, *f.*

helicopter, *n.* helicóptero, *m.*

hell, *n.* infierno, *m.*

hello, *interj.* ¡qué hay! ¡qué hubo! (expresión de saludo)

helmet, *n.* yelmo, casco, *m.*

help, *vt. y vi.* ayudar, socorrer; aliviar, remediar; evitar; *n.* ayuda, *f.*; socorro, remedio, *m.*

helpful, *adj.* util, provechoso

helpless, *adj.* irremediable

hem, *n.* bastilla, *f.*; *vt.* bastillar

hemisphere, *n.* hemisferio, *m.*

hemoglobin, *n.* (med.) hemoglobina, *f.*

hemorrhage, *n.* hemorragia, *f.*

hemorrhoids, *n.* *pl.* hemorroides, almorranas, *f. pl.*

hemp, *n.* ciñamo, *m.*

hemstitch, *n.* (costura) vainica, *f.*; *vt.* (costura) hacer una vainica

hen, *n.* gallina, *f.*

henceforth, *adv.* de aquí en adelante; en lo sucesivo

hencoop, *n.* gallinero, *m.*

her, *pron.* su, ella, de ella, a ella

herald, *n.* heraldo, *m.*

herb, *n.* yerba, hierba, *f.*

herd, *n.* hato, rebaño, *m.*; manada, *f.*

here, *adv.* aquí, acá

hereabouts, *adv.* aquí al rededor

hereafter, *adv.* en lo futuro; *n.* estado venidero, el futuro, *m.*

hereditary, *adj.* hereditario

heredity, *n.* derecho de su cesión, *m.*; herencia, *f.*

heretofore, *adv.* antes, en tiempos pasados; hasta ahora

heritage, *n.* herencia, *f.*

hermetic, *adj.* hermético

hermit, *n.* ermitaño, *m.*

hero, *n.* héroe, *m.*

heroic, *adj.* heroico; **heroics,** *n. pl.* expresión o acto extravagantes

heroine, *n.* heroína, *f.*

heroism, *n.* heroísmo, *m.*

heron, *n.* garza, *f.*

herring, *n.* arenque, *m.*

hers, *pron.* suyo, de ella

herself, *pron.* si, ella misma

hesitate, *vi.* vacilar, titubear

hesitation, *n.* duda, *f.*, titubeo, *m.*

hiccough, *n.* hipo, *m.*; *vi.* tener hipo

hid, *pretérito* del verbo **hide**

hidden, *adj.* escondido; secreto

hide, *vt.* esconder; *vi.* esconderse; *n.* cuero, *m.*; piel, *f.*

hide-and-seek, *n.* escondite, *m.*

hideous, *adj.* horripilante

high, *adj.* alto, elevado; **high jump,** salto de altura, *m.*

highball, *n.* highball, *m.*, bebida compuesta de aguardiente con soda

high-grade, *adj.* de alta calidad, excelente

highland, *n.* tierra montañosa

Highness, *n.* Alteza, *f.*

highness, *n.* altura, *f.*

high-strung, *adj.* nervioso, excitable

highway, *n.* carretera, *f.*

hike, *n.* paseo a pie, *m.*

hilarious, *adj.* alegre y bullicioso

him, *pron.* le, a él

himself, *pron.* si, él mismo

hinder, *vt.* impedir, estorbar

hindrance, *n.* impedimento, obstáculo, *m.*; rémora, *f.*

hint, *n.* seña, *f.*; sugestión, insinuación, *f.*; *vt.* insinuar; sugerir; hacer señas

hip, *n.* cadera, *f.*

hippopotamus, *n.* hipopótamo, *m.*,

hippie, hippy, *n.* hippie, *m.* y *f.*

hire, *vt.* alquilar; arrendar; *n.* alquiler, *m.*; salario, *m.*

his, *pron.* su, suyo, de él

historian, *n.* historiador, *m.*

historic, historical, *adj.* histórico

history, *n.* historia, *f.*

hit, *vt.* golpear; atinar; *n.* golpe, *m.*; (coll.) éxito, *m.*

hive, *n.* colmena, *f.*

hives, n. (med.) urticaria, f.; ronchas, f. pl.

hoard, n. montón, m.; tesoro escondido, m.; vt. atesorar, acumular

hoax, n. burla, f.; petardo, m.; vt. engañar, burlar

hobby, n. afición, f.

hockey, n. hockey, m. juego de patinadores sobre el hielo

hog, n. cerdo, puerco, m.

hoist, vt. alzar; (naut.) izar; n. grúa, f.; cabria, f.; montacargas, m.

hold, vt. tener, asir; detener; sostener; contener; sujetar; pl. mantenerse

holdup, n. asalto, robo, m.

hole, n. agujero, m.; hoyo, m.; hueco, m.

holiday, n. día de fiesta, día festivo, m.; **holidays**, n. pl. vacaciones, f. pl.

Holland, Holanda

holly, n. (bot.) acebo, m.

holster, n. funda de pistola

holy, adj. santo

homage, n. homenaje, culto, m.

home, n. casa, morada, f. hogar, m.; adj. doméstico

homeland, n. patria, f.

homeless, adj. sin hogar

homely, adj. feo

homemade, adj. hecho en casa; casero

homemaker, n. ama de casa, f.

homesick, adj. nostálgico

homesickness, n. nostalgia, f.

homework, n. tarea, f.

homicide, n. homicidio, m.; homicida, m. y f.

honest, adj. honesto, probo; honrado; justo

honesty, n. honestidad, justicia, probidad, f.; honradez, f.

honey, n. miel, f.; dulzura, f.

honeybee, n. abeja obrera

honeycomb, n. panal, m.

honeysuckle, n. (bot.) madreselva, f.

honor, n. honra, f., honor, lauro, m.; vt. honrar; **to honor (a draft)**, (com.) aceptar

(un giro o letra de cambio)

honorable, adj. honorable; ilustre; respatable

honorary, adj. honorario

hood, n. caperuza, f.; gorro, m.; (auto.) cubierta del motor

hoodlum, n. (coll.) pillo, tunante, m.

hook, n. gancho, m.; anzuelo, m.; vt. enganchar

hop, n. salto m.; **hops**, (bot.) lúpulo, m.; vt. saltar, brincar

hope, n. esperanza, f.; vt. esperar

hopeless, adj. desesperado; sin remedio

hormone, n. hormón, m., hormona, f.

horn, n. cuerno, m.; corneta, f.; trompeta, f.; bocina, f.; klaxon, m.

hornet, n. abejón, m.

horoscope, n. horóscopo m.

horrible, adj. horrible

horrid, adj. horroroso

horrify, va. horrorizar

horror, n. horror, terror, m.

hors d'oeuvre, n. pl. entremés, m.

horse, n. caballo, m.

horseback, n. espinazo del caballo; **on horseback**, a caballo

horseman, n. jinete, m.

horsepower, n. caballo de fuerza o potencia, m.

horseshoe, n. herradura de caballo, f.

horticulture, n. horticultura, jardinería, f.

hose, n. medias, f. pl.; manguera, f.; tubo flexible, m.

hosiery, n. medias, f. pl.; calcetines, m. pl.

hospitable, adj. hospitalario

hospital, n. hospital, m.

hospitality, n. hospitalidad, f.

hospitalization, n. hospitalización, f.

hospitalize, vt. hospitalizar

host, n. anfitrión, m.; huésped, m.; hostia, f.

hostel, n. posada, hostería, f., hotel, m.

hostess, n. anfitriona, f.

hot, *adj.* caliente, cálido; ardiente; picante; (coll.) excitante agitado, violento; **hot line**, línea de emergencia

hotel, *n.* posada, fonda. *f.*, hotel, *m.*

hot-tempered, *adj.* colérico

hound, *n.* sabueso, *m.*

hour, *n.* hora, *f.*

hourly, *adv.* a cada hora; frecuentemente; *adj.* por hora, frecuente

house, *n.* casa, *f.*; linaje, *m.*; cámara (del parlamento), *f.*; **House of Representatives**, Cámara de Representantes; **to keep house**, ser ama de casa; *vt.* y *vi.* albergar, residir

housecoat, *n.* bata de casa

household, *n.* familia, *f.*; casa, *f.*; establecimiento, *m.*; **household management**, manejo doméstico, *m.*

housekeeper, *n.* ama de casa, jefe de familia, *f.*; ama de llaves, *f.*

housewife, *n.* ama de casa, *f.*

housework, *n.* quehaceres doméstiooo, *m. pl.*

housing, *n.* alojamiento, *m.*

how, *adv.* cómo, cuán; cuánto

however, *adv.* como quiera, como quiera que sea; sin embargo, no obstante

hub, *n.* cubo, *m.*; centro, *m.*; **hub cap**, tapacubos, *m.*

hubbub, *n.* alboroto, tumulto, *m.*

hue, *n.* color, *m.*; tez del rostro, *f.*; matiz, *m.*

hug, *vt.* abrazar, acariciar; *n.* abrazo, *m.*

huge, *adj.* vasto, enorme

hull, *n.* cáscara, *f.*; (naut.) casco (de un buque), *m.*; *vt.* descortezar, pelar

hullabaloo, *n.* tumulto, al boroto, *m.*

hum, *vi.* zumbar, susurrar, murmurar; *vt.* tararear (una canción, etc.); *n.* zumbido, *m.*

human, *n.* y *adj.* humano, humana

humane, *adj.* humano

humanitarian, *n.* filántropo,

filántropa; *adj.* humanitario

humanity, *n.* humanidad *f.*

humankind, *n.* el género o linaje humano *m.*

humble, *adj.* humilde, modesto; *vt.* humillar; **to humble oneself**, humillarse

humid, *adj.* humedo

humidity, *n.* humedad, *f.*

humiliate, *vt.* humillar

humiliation, *n.* humillación, mortificación, *f.*

humility, *n.* humildad, *f.*

humor, *n.* humor, *m.*; *vt.* complacer, dar gusto

humorist, *n.* humorista, *m.* y *f.*

humorous, *adj.* chistoso, jocoso

hump, *n.* giba, joroba, *f.*

hunch, *n.* giba, *f.*; (coll.) idea, *f.*

hunchback, *n.* joroba, *f.*; jorobado, jorobada

hundred, *adj.* cien, ciento; *n.* centenar, *m.*

hundredth, *n.* y *adj.* centésimo, *m.*

hundredweight, *n.* quintal, *m.*

hung, *pretérito* y *p.p.* del verbo **hang**

Hungary, Hungría

hunger, *n.* hambre, *f.*

hungry, *adj.* hambriento; **to be hungry**, tener hambre

hunk, *n.* pedazo grande, *m.*

hunt, *vt.* cazar; perseguir; buscar; *n.* caza, *f.*

hunter, *n.* cazador, *m.*; perro de monte, perro de caza, *m.*

hunting, *n.* montería, caza, *f.*

hurdle, *n.* valla, *f.*; obstáculo; **hurdles**, *pl.* carrera de vallas, *f.*

hurrah! *interj.* ¡viva!

hurricane, *n.* huracán, *m.*

hurry, *vt.* acelerar, apresurar, precipitar; *vi.* atropellarse, apresurarse; *n.* precipitación, *f.*; urgencia, *f.*

hurt, *vt.* dañar, hacer daño, herir; ofender; *n.* mal, daño, perjuicio, *m.*; herida, *f.*; *adj.* sentido; lastimado; perjudicado

husband, *n.* marido, esposo, *m.*

husky, *adj.* fuerte; robusto

hustle, *vt.* y *vi.* bullir; apurar (un trabajo); apurarse, andar de prisa

hut, *n.* cabaña, choza, *f.*

hydraulic, *adj.* hidráulico

hydrofoil, *n.* aereodeslizador, hidrofoil, *m.*

hydrogen, *n.* (chem.) hidrógeno, *m.*; **hydrogen bomb,** bomba de hidrógeno

hydroplane, *n.* (naut.) hidroplano, *m.*; (avi.) hidroavión, *m.*

hygiene, *n.* higiene, *f.*

hygienic, *adj.* higiénico

hymn, *n.* himno, *m.*

hyphen, *n.* guión, *m.*

hypnotic, *adj.* hipnótico

hypnotize, *vt.* hipnotizar

hypocrite, *n.* hipócrita, *m.* y *f.*

hypocritical, *adj.* hipócrita, disimulado

hypodermic, *adj.* hipodérmico

hysteria, *n.* histeria, *f.*, histerismo, *m.*

hysteric, hysterical, *adj.* histérico

hysterics, *n. pl.* paroxismo histérico, *m.*

I

I, *pron.* yo

ICBM, I.C.B.M., intercontinental ballistic missile, cohete balístico intercontinental

ice, *n.* hielo, *m.*; **ice skate,** patín de hielo, *m.*; **ice water,** agua helada

iceberg, *n.* témpano de hielo, *m.*

icebox, *n.* refrigerador, *m.*, nevera, *f.*

ice cream, *n.* helado, mantecado, *m.*, nieve, *f.*

iceman, *n.* repartidor de hielo, *m.*

icicle, *n.* carámbano, *m.*

icing, *n.*, betún o confitura (para pasteles)

icy, *adj.* helado; frío; (fig.) indiferente

idea, *n.* idea, *f.*; concepto, *m.*

ideal, *adj.* ideal

idealism, *n.* idealismo, *m.*

idealistic, *adj.* idealista

identical, *adj.* idéntico

identification, *n.* identificación, *f.*

identify, *vt.* identificar

idiomatic, idiomatical, *adj.* idiomático

idiot, *n.* idiota, *m.* y *f.*

idiotic, *adj.* tonto, bobo

idle, *adj.* ocioso, perezoso

idleness, *n.* ociosidad, pereza, *f.*

idol, *n.* ídolo, *m.*; imagen, *f.*

idolize, *vt.* idolatrar

idyl, *n.* idilio, *m.*

i.e., that is, i.e., es decir, esto es

if, *conj.* si; aunque; supuesto que

ignorance, *n.* ignorancia, *f.*

ignorant, *adj.* ignorante, inculto

ignore, *vt.* pasar por alto, desconocer

ill, *adj.* malo, enfermo; *adv.* mal, malament

ill-bred, *adj.* malcriado, descortés

illegal, *adj.* ilegal

illegible, *adj.* ilegible

illegitimate, *adj.* ilegítimo

ill-gotten, *adj.* mal habido

ill-humored, *adj.* malhumorado

illiterate, *adj.* analfabeto

ill-mannered, *adj.* malcriado, descortés

illuminate, *vt.* iluminar

illumination, *n.* iluminación, *f.*; alumbrado, *m.*

illumine, *vt.* iluminar

illustrate, *vt.* ilustrar; explicar

illustrated, *adj.* ilustrado, de grabados

illustration, *n.* ilustración, *f.*; ejemplo, *m.*; grabado, *m.*

illustrious, *adj.* ilustre, célebre

image, *n.* imagen, estatua, *f.*

imaginary, *adj.* imaginario

imagination, *n.* imaginación, *f.*

imagine, vt. imaginar; idear, inventar

imbecile, n. y adj. imbécil, m. y f.

imitate, vt. imitar, copiar

imitation, n. imitación, copia, f.

imitator, n. imitador, imitadora

immaculate, adj. inmaculado, puro

immature, adj. inmaturo

immediate, adj. inmediato; **immediately**, adv. en seguida

immense, adj. inmenso

immensity, n. inmensidad, f.

immerse, vt. sumergir

immersion, n. inmersión,

immigrant, n. inmigrante, m. y f.

immigrate, vi. inmigrar

immigration, n. inmigración, f.

imminent, adj. inminente

immobile, adj. inmóvil

immoral, adj. immoral, depravado

immorality, n. inmoralidad f.

immortal, adj. immortal

immune, adj. inmune, exento

immunity, n. inmunidad, franquicia, f.

immunize, vt. inmunizar

impair, vt. deteriorar; disminuir

impart, vt. comunicar

impartial, adj. imparcial

impartiality, n. imparcialidad, f.

impassable, adj. intransitable

impassive, adj. impasible

impatience, n. impaciencia, f.

impatient, adj. impaciente

impediment, n. impedimento, obstáculo, m.

impel, vt. impeler, impulsar

imperative, adj. imperativo, imprescindible

imperfect, adj. imperfecto, defectuoso; n. (gram.) pretérito imperfecto

imperfection, n. imperfección, f., defecto, m.

impersonate, vt. personificar;

representar

impersonation, n. personificación, f.; (theat.) representación, f.

impertinence, n. impertinencia, f.; descaro, m.

impertinent, adj. impertinente

impetuous, adj. impetuoso

implement, n. herramienta, f.; utensilio, m.; vt. ejecutar, completar

implicate, vt. implicar, envolver

implicit, adj. implícito

implied, adj. implícito

implore, vt. implorar, suplicar

imply, vt. implicar

impolite, adj. descortés

import, vt. importar; significar; n. importancia, f.; importe, m.; sentido, m.; **import duties**, derechos de importación, m. pl.

importance, n. importancia, f.

important, adj. importante

importing, adj. importador; n. importación, f.

impose, vt. imponer

imposing, adj. imponente

imposition, n. imposición, carga, f.

impossibility, n. imposibilidad, f.

impossible, adj. imposible

impostor, n. impostor, impostora

impotent, adj. impotente; incapaz

impress, vt. imprimir, estampar

impression, n. impresión, f.

impressive, adj. imponente

imprint, vt. imprimir; estampar; n. impresión, f.; huella, f.

imprisonment, n. prisión, f., encierro, m.

improbable, adj. inverosímil

impromptu, adj. extemporáneo

improper, adj. impropio, indecente

improve, vt. y vi. mejorar, perfeccionar; vi. progresar

improvement, n. mejoramiento, perfeccionamiento, m.

improvise, vt. improvisar

impulse, n. impulso, m.; ímpetu, m.

in., inch, pulgada; pl. das **inches,** plgs., pulgadas

inability, n. incapacidad, f.

inaccurate, adj. inexacto

inactive, adj. inanimado

inaugurate, vt. inaugurar

inauguration, n. inauguración, f.

Inc., Incorporated, (Sp. Am.) S.A., Sociedad Anónima, Ltda., Sociedad Limitada

incapable, adj. incapaz

incense, n. incienso, m.; vt. exasperar, provocar

incentive, n. incentivo, estímulo, m.

inch, n. pulgada, f.

incident, n. incidente m.

incidental, adj. accidental, casual

incite, vt. incitar, estimular

inclination, n. inclinación, propensión, f.; declive, m.

incline, vt. inclinar; vi. inclinarse; n. pendiente, f.

include, vt. incluir

inclusion, n. inclusión, f.

inclusive, adj. inclusivo

incognito, adj. y adv. de incógnito

incoherent, adj. incoherente

income, n. renta, f., entradas, f. pl.; **income tax,** impuesto sobre rentas

incomparable, adj. incomparable

incompatible, adj. incompatible

incompetent, adj. incompetente

incomplete, adj. incompleto

inconceivable, adj. inconcebible

inconvenience, n. incomodidad, vt. incomodar

inconvenient, adj. inconveniente

incorporate, vt. y vi. incorporar

incorporation, n. incorporación, f.

incorrect, adj. incorrecto

incorrigible, adj. incorregible

increase, vt. aumentar; vi. crecer, aumentarse; n. aumento, m.

incredible, adj. increíble

incubator, n. incubadora, f.

incur, vt. incurrir; ocurrir

incurable, adj. incurable

indebted, adj. endeudado, obligado,

indebtedness, n. deuda, obligación, f.

indecent, adj. indecente

indecision, n. indecisión, f.

indeed, adv. verdaderamente, de veras; sí

indefinite, adj. indefinido

indelible, adj. indeleble

indentation, n. margen, m.

independence, n. independencia ,

independent, adj. independiente

indescribable, adj. indesriptible

indestructible, adj. indestructible

index, n. índice, elenco, m.

India, n. India, f.

Indian, n. y adj. indiano, indiana; indio, india

indicate, vt. indicar

indication, n. indicación, f.; indicio, m.; señal, f.

indicative, n. (gram.) indicativo, m.; adj. indicativo

indict, vt. procesar

indictment, n. denuncia, f.

indifference, n. indiferencia, apatía, f.

indigenous, adj. indígena

indigent, adj. indigente, pobre

indigestion, n. indigestión, f.

indignation, n. indignación, f.

indignity, n. indignidad, f.

indirect, adj. indirecto

indiscreet, adj. indiscreto

indiscretion, n. indiscreción, imprudencia, f.

indispensable, adj. indispensable

indisposed, adj. indispuesto, achacoso

indistinct, adj. confuse; borroso

individual, adj. individual; n. individuo, m.

induce, vt. inducir, persuadir

inducement, n. motivo, móvil, aliciente, m.

indulgence, n. indulgencia, f., mimo, m.

indulgent, adj. indulgente

industrial, adj. industrial

industrialization, n. industrialización, f.

industrialize, vt. industrializar

industrious, adj. hacendoso; trabajador

industry, n. industria, f.

inefficiency, n. ineficacia, f.

inefficient, adj. ineficaz

inept, adj. inepto

inescapable, adj. ineludible

inevitable, adj. inevitable

inexcusable, adj. inexcusable

inexhaustible, adj. inagotable

inexpensive, adj. barato

inexperienced, adj. inexperto, sin experiencia

infallible, adj. infalible

infamy, n. infamia, f.

infancy, n. infancia, f.

infant, n. infante, m; niño, niña

infantile, adj. pueril, infantil; **infantile paralysis,** parálisis infantil, f.

infantry, n. infantería,

infect, vt. infectar

infection, n. infección,

infer, vt. inferir, deducir

inferior, adj. inferior

inferiority, n. inferioridad, f.; **inferiority complex,** complejo de inferioridad, m.

infinite, adj. infinito; **infinitely,** adv. infinitamente

infinitive, n. infinitivo, n.

infinity, n. infinidad, eternidad, f.

infirmary, n. enfermería, f.

inflame, vt. y vt. inflamar

inflammable, adj. inflamable

inflation, n. inflación, f.

inflection, n. inflexión, modulación de la voz, f.

inflict, vt. castigar; infligir (penas corporales, etc.)

influence, n. influencia, f.; vt. influir

influential, adj. influyente

influenza, n. (med.) influenza, gripe, f., trancazo, m.

inform, vt. informar

informal, adj. íntimo, sin formulismos

information, n. información, instrucción, f.; informe, m.; aviso, m.

ingenious, adj. ingenioso

ingenuity, n. ingeniosidad, inventiva, f.

ingratitude, n. ingratitud, f.

ingredient, n. ingrediente, m.

ingrown, adj. crecido hacia dentro; **ingrown nail,** uñero, m.

inhabit, vt. habitar

inhabitant, n. habitante, residente, m. y f.

inherent, adj. inherente

inherit, vt. heredar

inheritance, n. herencia, f.; patrimonio, m.

inhibition, n. inhibición, f.

inhuman, adj. inhumano

initial, n. y adj. inicial, f.

initiation, n. iniciación, f.

initiative, n. iniciativa, f.

inject, vt. inyectar

injection, n. inyección, f.

injure, vt. injuriar, ofender; hacer daño

injurious, adj. perjudicial, nocivo

injury, n. perjuicio, m.; daño, m.

injustice, n. injusticia, f.

ink, n. tinta, f.

inkling, n. insinuación, noción vaga, f.

inkstand, n. tintero, m.

inmate, n. inquilino, inquilina; preso, presa

inn, n. posada, f.

inner, adj. interior

innocence, n. inocencia, f.

innocent, adj. inocente

innovation, n. innovación, f.

inoculate, vt. inocular; inyectar

inoffensive, *adj.* inofensivo

input, *n.* (elec.) entrada, *f.*; (fig.) gasto, *f.*

inquest, *n.* indagación, *f.*

inquire, *vt.* preguntar (alguna cosa); *vi.* inquirir, examinar

inquiry, *n.* pregunta, *f.*; investigación, *f.*

inquisition, *n.* inquisición *f.*

inquisitive, *adj.* curioso, preguntón

insane, *adj.* loco, demente

insanity, *n.* locura, *f.*

inscription, *n.* inscripción, letra, leyenda, *f.*; letrero, *m.*; dedicatoria, *f.*

insect, *n.* insecto, bicho, *m.*

insecurity, *n.* inseguridad, *f.*

inseparable, *adj.* inseparable

insert, *vt.* insertar, meter

insertion, *n.* inserción, *f.*

inside, *n.* y *adj.* interior, *m.*; **insides**, (coll.) entrañas, *f. pl.*; **on the inside**, por dentro; *adv.* adentro, dentro; **inside out**, al revés

insignia, *n. pl.* insignias, *f. pl.*; estandartes, *m. pl.*

insignificant, *adj.* insignificante; trivial

insincere, *adj.* insincero

insincerity, *n.* insinceridad, *f.*

insinuate, *vt.* insinuar; *vi.* congraciarse

insinuation, *n.* insinuación, *f.*

insist, *vi.* insistir, persistir

insistence, *n.* insistencia, *f.*

insistent, *adj.* insistente, persistente

insolent, *adj.* insolente

insomnia, *n.* insomnio, *m.*

inspect, *vt.* inspeccionar

inspection, *n.* inspección, *f.*

inspector, *n.* inspector, *m.*

inspiration, *n.* inspiración, *f.*

inspire, *vt.* inspirar

installation, *n.* instalación *f.*

installment, instalment, *n.*; plazo, *m.*; **monthly installment**, mensualidad, *f.*

instant, *adj.* instante, urgente; presents; **the 20th instant**, el 20 del presente; **instantly**, *adv.* un instante; *n.* instante, momento, *m.*

instead, *adv.* en lugar de, en vez de

instigate, *vt.* instigar

instinct, *n.* instinto, *m.*

instinctive, *adj.* instintivo

institute, *vt.* instituir, establecer; *n.* instituto, *m.*

institution, *n.* institución, *f.*

instruct, *vt.* instruir, enseñar

instruction, *n.* instrucción, enseñanza, *f.*

instructor, *n.* instructor, *m.*

instrument, *n.* instrumento, *m.*

insufferable, *adj.* insufrible, insoportable

insufficient, *adj.* insuficiente

insulating, *adj.* (elec.) aislante

insurance, *n.* seguro, *m.*; **life insurance**, seguro de vida, *m.*

integration, *n.* integración, *f.*

integrity, *n.* integridad, *f.*

intellect, *n.* intelecto, *m.*

intellectual, *n.* intelectual, *m.* y *f.*; *adj.* intelectual, mental

intelligence, *n.* inteligencia, *f.*

intelligent, *adj.* inteligente

intend, *vt.* intentar; *vi.* proponerse

intense, *adj.* intenso; vehemente

intensify, *vt.* intensificar

intensive, *adj.* completo, concentrado

intent, *adj.* atento, cuidadoso; *n.* intento, designio, *m.*

intention, *n.* intención, *f.*; designio, *m.*; (fig.) mira, *f.*

intentional, *adj.* intencional

intercede, *vi.* interceder, mediar

interest, *vt.* interesar; empeñar; *n.* interés, provecho, *m.*

interesting, *adj.* interesante, atractivo

interfere, *vi.* intervenir

interference, *n.* mediación, ingerencia, *f.*

interjection, *n.* (gram.) interjección, *f.*

interlining, *n.* entretela, *f.*

interlude, *n.* intermedio, *m.*

intermediary, *adj.* y *n.* intermediario, intermediaria

interment, n. entierro, m.; sepultura, f.

interminable, adj. interminable

intermission, n. intermedio, m.

intern, vt. internar; encerrar; n. (med.) practicante, m.; médico interno (en un hospital), m.

international, adj. internacional

interpret, vt. interpretar

interpretation, n. interpretación, f.; versión, f.

interpreter, n. intérprete, m. y f.

interrogate, vt. interrogar, examinar

interrogation, n. interrogación, pregunta, f.

interrupt, vt. interrumpir

interruption, n. interrupción, f.

intersection, n. intersección, f.; bocacalle, f.

interval, n. intervalo, m.

intervene, vi. intervenir

intervention, n. intervención, f.

interview, n. entrevista, f.; vt. entrevistar

intestinal, adj. intestinal

intestine, adj. intestino; **intestines,** n. pl. intestinos, m. pl.

intimacy, n. intimidad, confianza, f.; familiaridad, f.

intimate, adj. íntimo, familiar; vt. insinuar, dar a entender

intolerable, adj. intolerable

intolerance, n. intolerancia, f.

intolerant, adj. intolerante

intoxicant, n. bebida alcohólica, f.

intoxicated, adj. ebrio, borracho.

intoxicating, adj. embriagante

intoxication, n. embriaguez, f.; intoxicación, f.

intransitive, adj. (gram.) intransitivo

intrepid, adj. arrojado, intrépido

intricate, adj. complicado;

complejo

intrigue, n. intriga, f.

introduce, vt. introducir, meter; **to introduce (a person),** presentar (a una persona)

introduction, n. introducción, f.; presentación, f.; prólogo, preámbulo, m.

intrude, vi. entremeterse, introducirse

intuition, n. intuición,

inundate, vt. inundar

inundation, n. inundación, f.

invade, vt. invadir

invalid, adj. inválido; nulo; n. inválido, inválida

invaluable, adj. inapreciable

invariable, adj. invariable

invasion, n. invasión, f.

inveigle, vt. persuadir

invent, vt. inventar

invention, n. invención, f.; invento, m.

inventor, n. inventor, m.

inventory, n. inventario, m.

invert, vt. invertir

invest, vt. investir; invertir

investigate, vt. investigar

investigation, n. investigación,

investment n. inversión, f.

invisible, adj. invisible

invitation, n. invitación, f.

invite, vt. convidar, invitar

invoice, n. factura, f.; vt. facturar

invoke, vt. invocar

involuntary, adj. involuntario

involve, vt. envolver, implicar

iodine, n. yodo, m.

I.O.U., IOU, I owe you, pagaré, vale

Ireland, Irlanda, f.

iris, n. arco iris, m.; (anat.) iris, m.; (bot.) flor de lis, f.

Irish, n. y adj. irlandés, irlandesa

iron, n. hierro, m.; vt. planchar

ironical, adj. irónico

ironing, n. planchado, m.

irony, n. ironía, f.

irradiate, vt. y vi. irradiar, brillar

irregular, adj. irregular

irrelevant, *adj.* no aplicable

irreproachable, *adj.* irreprochable

irresistible, *adj.* irresistible

irresponsible, *adj.* irresponsable

irrigation, *n.* riego, *m.;* irrigación, *f.*

irritate, *vt.* irritar, exasperar

is, 3ª persona del singular del verbo **be**

island, *n.* isla, *f.*

isolate, *vt.* aislar, apartar

isolation, *n.* aislamiento, *m.*

isthmus, *n.* istmo, *m.*

it, *pron.* él, ella, ello, lo, la le

italic, *n.* bastardilla, *f.*

Italy, Italia, *f.*

itch, *n.* picazón, *f.; vi.* picar

item, *n.* artículo, suelto, *m.;* (com.) renglón, *m.*

itinerary, *n.* itinerario, *m.*

its, *pron.* su, suyo

itself, *pron.* el mismo, la misma, lo mismo; sí; **by itself**, de por sí

ivory, *n.* marfil, *m.*

ivy, *n.* hiedra, *f.*

J

jack, *n.* (mech.) gato, *m.;* sota, *f.;* **jack pot**, premio grande, *m.*

jackass, *n.* burro, asno, *m.*

jacket, *n.* chaqueta, *f.,* saco, *m.;* envoltura, *f.*

jail, *n.* cárcel , *f.*

jam, *n.* compota, conserva, *f.;* apretadura, *f.;* aprieto, *m.; vt.* apiñar, apretar

janitor, *n.* portero, conserje, *m.*

January, *n.* enero, *m.*

Japan, japón, *m.*

Japanese, *n.* y *adj.* japonés, japonesa, nipón, nipóna

jar, *vi.* chocar; discordar; *n.* jarro, *m.*

jct., junction emp. empalme, *m.;* confluencia, *f.*

jealous, celoso

jealousy, *n.* celos, *m. pl.*

jeans, *n. pl.* pantalones ajustados de dril, generalmente

azules

jelly, *n.* jalea, gelatina, *f.*

jest, *n.* chanza, burla, *f.; vi.* chancear

Jesuit, *n.* jesuita, *m.*

Jesus Christ, Jesucristo

jet, *n.* (min.) azabache, *m.;* (mech.) mechero, *m.;* boquilla, *f.;* **jet plane**, avión de retropropulsión, *m.;* **jet propulsion**, propulsión por reacción, *f.*

Jew, *n.* judío, judía

jewel, *n.* joya, alhaja, *f.;* rubí (de un reloj), *m.*

jeweler, *n.* joyero, *m.*

jewelry, *n.* joyería, *f.*

Jewish, *adj.* judío

jiffy, *n.* (coll.) tris, momentito, *m.*

jilt, *vt.* dar calabazas, plantar

jingle, *vi.* retiñir, resonar; *n.* retintín, *m.*

job, *n.* empleo, *m.;* (Mex. coll.) chamba, *f.*

jockey, *n.* jinete, *m.*

join, *vt.* y *vi.* juntar, unir

joint, *n.* coyuntura, articulación, *f.; adj.* unido; participante; **jointly**, *adv.* conjuntamente, en común

joke, *n.* chanza, chiste, *m.; vi.* chancear, bromear

jolly, *adj.* alegre, jovial

jolt, *vt.* y *vi.* sacudir; *n.* sacudida, *f.*

journal, *n.* diario, periódico, *m.*

journalism, *n.* periodismo, *m.*

journalist, *n.* periodista, *m.* y *f.*

journey, *n.* jornada, *f.;* viaje, *m.; vi.* viajar

jowl, *n.* quijada, *f.*

joy, *n.* alegría, *f.;* júbilo, *m.*

joyful, joyous, *adj.* alegre

judge, *n.* juez *m.; vi.* juzgar; inferir

judgment, judgement, *n.* juicio, *m.;* opinión, *f.*

judicial, *adj.* judicial

jug, *n.* jarro, *m.*

juice, *n.* zumo, jugo, *m.*

juicy, *adj.* jugoso

jukebox, *n.* sinfonola, *f.*

July, n. (mes) julio, m.

jumble, n. mezcla, confusión, f.

jump, vi. saltar, brincar; n. salto, m.

junction, n. empalme, m.; bifurcación, f.

June, n. (mes) junio, m.

jungle, n. matorral, m.

junior, adj. más joven; n. estudiante de tercer año

junk, n. chatarra, f., hierro viejo, m.; baratijas, f. pl.

jury, n. jurado, m.

just, adj. justo; adv. sólo

justice, n. justicia, f., derecho, m.; juez, m.

justify, vt. justificar

juvenile, adj. juvenil

K

karate, n. karate, m.

kc., kilocycle, kc., kilociclo

keen, adj. agudo; penetrante, sutil, vivo

keep, vt. mantener, retener; guardar; **to keep accounts**, llevar cuentas; n. manutención, f.

keepsake, n. recuerdo, m.

kettle, n. caldera, olla, f.

key, n. llave, f.; (mus.) clave, f.; tecla, f.

keyboard, n. teclado, m.

keyhole, n. agujero de la llave, m.

kg., kilogram, kg., kilogramo

kick, vt. patear, acocear; vi. patear; (coll .) reclamar, objetar; n. puntapié, m., patada, f.; (coll.) efecto estimulador, m.

kid, n. cabrito, m.; (coll.) muchacho, muchacha

kidnap, vt. secuestrar

kidney, n. riñón, m., **kidney bean**, variedad de frijol

kill, vt. matar, asesinar

kilocycle, n. kilociclo, m.

kilogram, n. kilogramo, m.

kilometer, n. kilómetro, m.

kiloton, n. kilotón, m.

kilowatt, n. kilovatio, m.

kin, n. parentesco, m.; afinidad, f.

kind, adj. benévolo, bondadoso; n. género, m.; clase, f.

kindergarten, n. escuela de párvulos, f., jardín de la infancia, m.

kindness, n. benevolencia, f.

king, n. rey, m.

kingdom, n. reino, m.

kinky, adj. grifo; ensortijado

kinsfolk, n. parientes, m. pl.

kiss, n. beso, m.; vt. besar

kitchen. n. cocina, f.

kite, n. cometa, birlocha, f.

kitten, n. gatito, gatita

km., kilometer, km., kilómetro

knack, n. maña, destreza, f.

knee, n. rodilla, f.

kneecap, n. rótula, f.

kneel, vi. arrodillarse

knew, pretérito del verbo **know**

knife, n. cuchillo, m.

knight, n. caballero, m.

knit, vt. y vi. enlazar; tejer

knitting, n. tejido con agujas, m.

knives, n. pl. de **knife**, cuchillos, m. pl.

knock, vt. y vi. tocar; pegar; n. golpe, m.; llamada, f.

knockout, n. golpe decisivo, (en el boxeo), m.

knot, n. nudo, m.; lazo, m.; vt. anudar

know, vt. y vi. conocer, saber

know-how, n. conocimiento práctico, m.

knowledge, n. conocimiento, saber, m.

knuckle, n. coyuntura, f.

L

£, pound, £, libra esterlina, f.

label, n. marbete, m., etiqueta, f.; rótulo, m.; vt. rotular

labor, n. trabajo, m.; labor, f.; **to be in labor**, estar de parto; vt. y vi. trabajar; afanarse

laboratory, n. laboratorio, m.

laborer, n. trabajador, obrero, m.

lace, n. lazo, cordón, m.; enca-

je, m.; vt. amarrar (los cordo-
nes de los zapatos, etc.)

lack, vt. y vi. carecer; faltar
algo; n. falta, carencia, f.

lacquer, n. laca, f.

lad, n. mozo, muchacho, m.

ladder, n. escalera portátil, f.

ladle, n. cucharón, cazo, m.

lady, n. señora, señorita, dama, f.

lagoon, n. laguna, f.

laid, pretérito y p.p. del verbo
lay

lain, p.p. del verbo **lie**

lake, n. lago, m.

lamb, n. cordero, m.

lament, vt. y vi. lamentar;
lamento, m.

land, n. país, m.; región, f.; territorio, m.; tierra, f.; vt. y vi.
desembarcar; saltar en tierra

landlady, n. affendadora, f.

landlord, n. propietario, casero, m.

landmark, n. señal, marca, f.;
hecho o acontecimiento importante, m.

landslide, n. derrumbe, m.;
(pol.) mayoría de votos abru-
madora, f.

language, n. lengua, f.; lenguaje, idioma, m.

lantern, n. linterna, f.; farol,
m.

lapel, n. solapa, f.

lapse, n. lapso, m.; vi. caducar
(un plazo, etc.)

large, adj. grande, amplio

lark, n. (orn.) alondra, f.

larynx, n. laringe, f.

laser, n. rayo laser

last, n. doncella, moza, f.

last, adj. último; **at last,** al fin,
por último; vi. durar; subsis-
tir; n. horma de zapato, f.

late, adj. tardo, lento; difunto;
adv. tarde; **lately,** adv. re-
cientemente

later, adj. posterior; adv. más
tarde

lateral, adj. lateral

latest, adj. último; más reciente; **at the latest,** a mis
tardar

Latin, n. latín (lenguaje), m.;

n. y adj. latino, latina

Latin American, n. latinoamericano, latinoamericana

latitude, n. latitud, f.

latter, adj. posterior, último

laugh, vi. reir; n. risa, risota-
da, f.

laughter, n. risa, f.

laundress, n. lavandera, f.

laundry, n. lavandería, f.

lavatory, n. lavabo, lavatorio,
m.

lavish, adj. pródigo; gastador;
vt. disipar, prodigar

law, n. ley, f.; derecho, m.

lawful, adj. legal; legítimo

lawn, n. prado, césped, m.

lawsuit, n. pleito, m., demanda, f.

lawyer, n. abogado, m.

laxative, n. y adj. purgante,
laxante, m.

lay, vt. poner, colocar; poner
(un huevo)

lay, adj. laico, secular, seglar;
pretérito del verbo **lie**

layer, n. capa, f., estrato, m.

lazy, adj. perezoso

lb., pound, lb. libra

lead, vt. conducir, guiar; vi.
mandar, tener el mando; sobresalir, ser el primero; n. delantera, f.

lead, n. plomo, m.; **lead pencil,** lápiz, m.

leader, n. líder, guía, m.

leadership, n. capacidad dirigente, f.

leading, adj. principal

leaf, n. hoja (de una planta), f.;
hoja (de un libro), f.

leafy, adj. frondoso

league, n. liga, alianza, f.; le-
gua, f.

leak, n. fuga, f., goteo, m.; vi.
gotear, salirse o escaparse (el
agua, gas, etc.)

lean, vt. y vi. inclinar, apoyarse

leap, vi. saltar, brincar; n. salto, m.; **leap year,** año bisiesto, m.

learn, vt. y vi. aprender, conocer; saber

learning, n. erudición, f.; saber, *m.*

lease, *n.* contrato, arrendamiento, *m.*; *vt.* arrendar

least, *adj.* mínimo; *adv.* en el grado mínimo

leave, *n.* licencia, *f.*, permiso, *m.*; despedida, *f.*; *vt. y vi.* dejar, abandonar; salir

leaves, *n. pl.* de **leaf,** hojas, *f. pl.*

left, *adj.* izquierdo; *n.* izquierda, *f.*

leg, *n.* pierna, *f.*

legacy, *n.* legado, *m.*

legal, *adj.* legal, legítimo

legation, *n.* legación, embajada, *f.*

legislation, *n.* legislación *f.*

legislature, *n.* legislatura, *f.*

legitimate, *adj.* legítimo

leisure, *n.* ocio, *m.*; comodidad, *f.*; **at leisure,** cómodamente, con sosiego; **leisure hours,** horas o ratos libres

lemon, *n.* limón, *m.*

lemonade, *n.* limonada, *f.*

length, *n.* longitud, *f.*; duración, *f.*; distancia, *f.*

lengthen, *vt. y vi.* alargar

lengthy, *adj.* largo

Lent, *n.* cuaresma, *f.*

leopard, *n.* leopardo, *m.*

leprosy, *n.* lepra, *f.*

lesbian, *adj.* lesbiano

lesion, *n.* lesión, *f.*

less, *adj.* inferior, menos; *adv.* menos

lessen, *vt. y vi.* disminuir

lesson, *n.* lección, *f.*

let, *vt.* dejar, permitir; arrendar

letter, *n.* letra, *f.*; carta, *f.*

letterhead, *n.* membrete, *m.*

lettering, *n.* inscripción, leyenda, *f.*

lettuce, *n.* lechuga, *f.*

level, *adj.* llano, plano; *vt.* allanar; nivelar

liability, *n.* responsabilidad, *f.*; **liabilities,** (com.) pasivo, *m.*, créditos pasivos

liable, *adj.* sujeto, expuesto a; responsable; capaz

liar, *n.* mentiroso, mentirosa

liberal, *adj.* liberal; generoso

liberate, *vt.* libertar

liberty, *n.* libertad, *f.*

librarian, *n.* bibliotecario, bibliotecaria

library, *n.* biblioteca,. *f.*

license, licence, *n.* licencia, *f.*; permiso, *m.*

lick, *vt.* lamer, chupar; (coll.) golpear; derrotar (en una pelea, etc.)

lid, *n.* tapa, *f.*, tapadera, *f.*

lie, *n.* mentira, *f.*; *vi.* mentir, acostarse; descansar

lieutenant, *n.* teniente, *m.*

life, *n.* vida, *f.*; ser, *m.*

lifeboat, *n.* bote de salvamento, *m.*

lifeguard, *n.* vigilante, *m.*

lifeless, *adj.* muerto, inanimado

lift, *vt.* alzar, elevar

lift-off, *n.* despegue, lanzamiento, *m.*

light, *n.* luz, *f.*; claridad, *f.*; *adj.* ligero, liviano; claro; blondo; *vt.* encender; alumbrar

lighten, *vt.* iluminar; aligerar; aclarar

lighthouse, *n.* faro, *m.*

lighting, *n.* iluminación, *f.*

lightning, *n.* relámpago, *m.*

likable, *adj.* simpático, agradable

like, *adj.* semejante; igual; *adv.* como; *vt. y vi.* querer; gustar, agradar alguna cosa

likely , *adj.* probable

likeness, *n.* semejanza,. *f.*

lily, *n.* lirio, *m.*

limb, *n.* miembro (del cuerpo) *m.*; pierna, *f.*; rama (de un árbol), *f.*

lime, *n.* cal, *f.*; limón mexicano, *m.*

limelight, *n.* centro de atención pública

limit, *n.* límite, término, *m.*; *vt.* restringir

limited, *adj.* limitado

limp, *vi.* cojear; *n.* cojera, *f.*; *adj.* flojo, blando

linen, *n.* lienzo, lino, *m.*; tela de hilo; ropa blanca

linger, *vi.* demorarse

lingerie, *n.* ropa íntima, *f.*

link, *n.* eslabón, *n.*; vínculo, *m.*; *vt.* y *vi.* unir, vincular

linkup, *n.* acoplamiento, enlace, *m.*, unión, *f.*

lion, *n.* león, *m.*

lip, *n.* labio borde, *m.*

lipstick, *n.* lápiz para los labios, lápiz labial, *m.*

liquid, *adj.* y *n.* liquido, *m.*

liquor, *n.* licor, *m.*

Lisbon, Lisboa

lisp, *vi.* cecear

list, *n.* lista, *f.*, elenco, *m.*; catálogo, *m.*; *vt.* poner en lista; registrar

listen, *vi.* escuchar

liter, *n.* litro, *m.*

literal, *adj.* literal

literary, *adj.* literario

literature, *n.* literatura, *f.*

little, *adj.* pequeño; poco; chico; *n.* poco, *m.*

live, *vi.* vivir

live, *adj.* vivo

lively, *adj.* vivo, alegre

liver, *n.* hígado, *m.*

lives, *n. pl.* de **life**, vidas, *f. pl.*

livestock, *n.* ganado, *m.*; ganadería, *f.*

living, *n.* subsistencia, *f.*

lid, *n.* lagarto, *m.*, lagartija, *f.*

llama, *n.* (zool.) llama, *f.*

L.L.D., Doctor of Laws, Doctor en Derecho

load, *vt.* cargar; *n.* carga, *f.*

loaf, *n.* pan, *m.*; *vi.* holgazanear

loan, *n.* préstamo, *m.*; *vt.* prestar

loathe, *vt.* aborrecer, detestar

loaves, *n. pl.* de **loaf**, panes, *m. pl.*

lobby, *n.* vestíbulo, *m.*

lobster, *n.* langosta, *f.*

local, *adj.* local

locality, *n.* localidad, *f.*

locate, *vt.* ubicar, colocar

location, *n.* ubicación, *f.*

lock, *n.* cerradura, cerraja, *f.*; compuerta, *f.*; *vt.* y *vi.* cerrar con llave

locker, *n.* armario, *m.*; gaveta, *f.*

locket, *n.* medallón, guardape-

lo, *m.*

lockjaw, *n.* tétano, *m.*

locksmith, *n.* cerrajero, *m.*

locomotive, *n.* locomotora, *f.*

lodge, *n.* casita en el bosque, *f.*; logia, *f.*; *vt.* alojar; fijar en la memoria; *vi.* residir

lodging, *n.* hospedaje, *m.*

lofty, *adj.* alto, sublime

logic, *n.* lógica, *f.*

logical, *adj.* lógico

loin, *n.* ijada, *f.*, ijar, *m.*; **loins**, *n. pl.* lomos, *m. pl.*

loiter, *vi.* holgazanear

London, Londres

lone, *adj.* solitario

loneliness, *n.* soledad, *f.*

lonely, *adj.* **lonesome**

lonesome, *adj.* solitario, triste

long, *adj.* largo, prolongado; *adv.* durante mucho tiempo

longing, *n.* anhelo, *m.*

long-playing (records), *adj.* (discos) de larga ejecución

look, *vt.* y *vi.* mirar; parecer; buscar; *n.* aspecto, *m.*; mirada, *f.*

loom, *n.* telar, *m.*

loose, *adj.* suelto, desatado

loosen, *vt.* aflojar, desatar

loot, *n.* pillaje, botín, *m.*

lord, *n.* señor *m.*; amo, dueño, *m.*; lord (título de nobleza inglés), *m.*

lose, *vt.* y *vi.* perder, perderse

loss, *n.* pérdida, *f.*; **to be at a loss**, estar perplejo

lot, *n.* suerte, *f.*; lote, *m.*

lotion, *n.* loción *f.*

lottery, *n.* lotería, rifa, *f.*

loud, *adj.* ruidoso; fuerte, recio, alto; chillón

loudspeaker, *n.* altoparlante, altavoz, *m.*

lounge, *n.* sofá, canapé, *m.*; salón social, *m.*

louse, *n.* (*pl.* **lice**) piojo, *m.*

lovable, *adj.* digno de ser querido

love, *n.* amor, cariño, *m.*; *vt.* amar; querer

lovely, *adj.* bello

lover, *n.* amante, galán, *m.*

low, *adj.* bajo, pequeño; abatido; vil; *adv.* a precio bajo; en posición baja

lower, *adj.* más bajo; *vt.* bajar; disminuir

lowly, *adj.* humilde

lox, (liquid oxygen) *n.* oxígeno líquido, *m.*

loyal, *adj.* leal, fiel

loyalty, *n.* lealtad, *f.*

L.P., long-playing, L.E., larga ejecución (discos)

lubricant, *n.* y *adj.* lubricante, *m.*

luck, *n.* suerte, *f.*

luckily, *adv.* afortunadamente

lucky, *adj.* afortunado

lukewarm, *adj.* tibio

lullaby, *n.* canción de cuna

lumber, *n.* madera de construcción, *f.*

lump, *n.* protuberancia, *f.*; **lump of sugar,** terrón de azúcar, *m.*; *vi.* aterronarse; agrumarse

lunatic, *adj.* y *n.* loco, loca

lunch, *n.* merienda, *f.*, almuerzo, *m.*; *vi.* almorzar, merendar

luncheon, *n.* almuerzo, *m.*

lung, *n.* pulmón, *m.*

lure, *n.* señuelo, cebo, *m.*; *vt.* atraer, seducir

lurk, *vi.* espiar

luscious, *adj.* delicioso, atractivo

luster, lustre, *n.* lustre, *m.*, brillantez, *f.*

luxuriant, *adj.* exuberante

luxurious, *adj.* lujoso

luxury, *n.* lujo, *m.*

lyric, lyrical, *adj.* lírico

M

macaroni, *n.* macarrones, *m. pl.*

machine, *n.* máquina, *f.*; **machine gun,** ametralladora, *f.*

machinery, *n.* maquinaria, *f.*

machinist, *n.* maquinista, mecánico, *m.*

mackerel, *n.* (pez) escombro, *m.*, caballa, *f.*

mad, *adj.* loco, furioso

madam, madame, *n.* madama, señora, *f.*

made, *adj.* hecho, fabricado

made-to-order, *adj.* hecho a la medida o a la orden

made-up, *adj.* ficticio; pintado

madness, *n.* locura, *f.*

magazine, *n.* revista, *f.*

magic, *n.* magia, *f.*; *adj.* mágico

magician, *n.* mago, nigromante, *m.*

magistrate, *n.* magistrado, *m.*

magnanimous, *adj.* magnánimo

magnesia, *n.* magnesia, *f.*

magnet, *n.* imán, *m.*

magnetism, *n.* magnetismo, *m.*

magnificent, *adj.* magnífico

magnify, *vt.* magnificar

magnitude, *n.* magnitud, *f.*

magnolia, *n.* magnolia, *f.*

magpie, *n.* urraca, *f.*

mahogany, *n.* caoba, *f.*

maid, maiden, *n.* doncella, joven, *f.*; moza, criada, *f.*

maiden, *adj.* virgen, virginal; **maiden name,** nombre de soltera; *n.* doncella, joven, *f.*

mail, *n.* correo, *m.*; correspondencia, *f.*

mailbox, *n.* buzón, *m.*

mailman, *n.* cartero, *m.*

main, *adj.* principal; esencial; **main office,** casa matriz; **mainly,** *adv.* principalmente

maintain, *vt.* y *vi.* mantener, sostener; conservar

maintenance, *n.* mantenimiento *m.*

maize, *n.* maíz, *m.*

majestic, majestical, *adj.* majestuoso

majesty, *n.* majestad, *f.*

major, *adj.* mayor; *n.* (mil.) mayor, *m.*

majority, *n.* mayoría, *f.*; pluralidad, *f.*

make, *vt.* hacer, fabricar; obligar, forzar; *n.* hechura, *f.*

make-up, *n.* maquillaje, *m.*

malaria, *n.* paludismo, *m.*

male, *adj.* masculino; *n.* macho, *m.*

malice, *n.* malicia, *f.*

malicious, *adj.* malicioso

malignant, adj. maligno
malt, n. malta, f.
maltreat, vt. maltratar
mamma, mama, n. mamá, f.
mammal, n. mamífero, m.
man, n. hombre, m.; marido, m.
manage, vt. y vi. manejar, administrar
management, n. manejo, m., administración, dirección, f.; gerencia, f.
manager, n. administrador, director, m.; gerente, m.
mandolin, n. mandolina, f.
maneuver, n. maniobra, f.; vt. y vi. maniobrar
manger, n. pesebre, m.
mangle, n. planchadora mecánica, f.; vt. mutilar
manhood, n. virilidad, f.; edad viril, hombría, f.
manicure, n. manicuro, manicura; arte de arreglar las uñas; vt. arreglar las uñas
manifest, adj. manifiesto, patente
manikin, n. maniquí, m.
mankind, n. género humano, m., humanidad, f.
manly, adj. varonil
manner, n. manera, f., modo, m.; forma, f.; método, m.; **manners**, n. pl., modales, m. pl.
mansion, n. mansión, residencia, f.
manual, n. manual, m.; adj. manual; **manual training,** instrucción en artes y oficios
manufacture, n. manufactura, fabricación, f.; vt. fabricar, manufacturar
manuscript, n. manuscrito, escrito, m.; original, m.
many, adj. muchos, muchas
Maoism, n. maoísmo, m.
map, n. mapa, m.
maple, n. arce, m.
marble, n. mármol, m.; canica, bola, f.
March, n. marzo, m.
march, n. marcha, f.; vi. marchar, caminar
margin, n. margen, m. y f.;

borde, m.
marimba, n. marimba, f.
marina, n. estación de gasolina para los botes
marine, n. marina, f.; soldado de marina, m.; adj. marino
mariner, n. marinero, m.
marionette, n. títere, m.
maritime, adj. marítimo
mark, n. marca, f.; señal, nota, f.; seña, f.; calificación, vt. marcar; advertir
market, n. mercado, m.
marquis, n. marqués, m.
marriage, n. matrimonio, casamiento, m.
marry, vt. y vi. casar, casarse
marshal, n. mariscal, m.
martial, adj. marcial, guerrero
marvel, n. maravilla, f., prodigio, m.; vi. maravillarse
marvelous, adj. maravilloso
mascot, n. mascota, f.
masculine, adj. masculino; varonil
mash, vt. majar
mask, n. máscara, f.; vt. enmascarar; disimular
mason, n. albañil, m.; masón, m.
masquerade, n. mascarada, f.
mass, n. misa, f.; masa, f., bulto, m.; **masses**, n. pl. las masas, f. pl
massage, n. masaje, m., soba, f.; vt. sobar
massive, adj. macizo, sólido
master, n. amo, dueño, m.; maestro, m.; señor, m.; señorito, m.; patrón, m.; vt. domar, dominar
mat, n. estera, esterilla, f.
match, n. fósforo, m.; cerilla, f., cerillo, m.; partido, m.; contrincante, m., casamiento, m.; vt. igualar; aparear
mate, n. consorte, m. o f.; compañero, compañera; piloto, m.; vt. desposar; igualar
material, adj. material, físico; n. material, m., tela, f.
maternal, adj. maternal, materno
maternity, n. maternidad, f.
mathematical, adj. matemáti-

co
mathematics, n. pl. matemáticas, f. pl.

matinee, n. matiné, f.

matriculate, vt. matricular

matrimony, n. matrimonio, m.

matter, n. materia, sustancia, f.; asunto, objeto, m.; **what is the matter?** ¿de qué se trata?; vi. importar, ser importante

maximum, adj. máximo

May, n. mayo, m.

may, vi. poder; ser posible

maybe, adv. quizás, tal vez

mayonnaise, n. mayonesa, f.

mayor, n. corregidor, alcalde, m.

maze, n. laberinto, m.

M.C., Master of Ceremonies, Maestro de Ceremonias

M.D., Doctor of Medicine, Doctor en Medicina

me, pron. mi; me

meadow, n. prado, m.

meal, n. comida, f.; harina, f.

mean, adj. bajo, vil, despreciable; **means,** n. pl. medios, recursos, m. pl.; **by all means,** sin falta; **by no means,** de ningún modo; vt. y vi. significar; querer decir

meaning, n. significado, m.

meantime, adv. mientras tanto

meanwhile, adv. entretanto, mientras tanto

measles, n. pl. sarampión, m.; rubeola, f.

measure, n. medida, f.; (mus.) compás, m.; vt. medir

measurement, n. medición, f.; medida, f.

meat, n. carne, f.

mechanic, n. mecánico, m.

mechanical, adj. mecánico; rutinario

mechanics, n. pl. mecánica, f.

mechanism, n. mecanismo, m.

medal, n. medalla, f.

mediate, vt. mediar

medical, adj. médico

medicare, n. asistencia médica estatal para personas ma-

yores de 65 años

medicine, n. medicina, f.

mediocre, adj. mediocre

meditation, n. meditación, f.

medium, n. medio, m.; adj. mediano

meet, vt. y vi. encontrar, convocar, reunir

meeting, n. sesión, reunión, f.

melancholy, n. melancolía, f.

melodious, adj. melodioso

melodrama, n. melodrama, m.

melody, n. melodía, f.

melon, n. melón, m.

member, n. miembro, socio, m.

membership, n. personal de socios, m.

memo., memorandum, memorándum, m.

memorable, adj. memorable

memorandum, n. memorándum, volante, m.

memorial, n. memoria, f.; memorial, m.; adj. conmemorativo

Memorial Day, n. Día de los soldados muertos en la guerra (30 de mayo)

memorize, vt. memorizar, aprender de memoria

memory, n. memoria, f.; recuerdo, m.; retentiva, f.

men, n. pl. de **man,** hombres, m. pl.

menstruation, n. menstruación, f.

mentality, n. mentalidad, f.

mention, n. mención, f.; vt. mencionar; **don't mention it,** no hay de qué

menu, n. menú, m.

merchandise, n. mercancía, f.

merchant, n. comerciante, m.

merciful, adj. misericordioso

merciless, adj. inhumano

mercury, n. mercurio, m.

mercy, n. misericordia, f.

merge, vt. unir, combinar; vi. absorberse, fundirse, converger

meridian, n. meridiano, m.

meringue, n. merengue, m.

merit, n. mérito, m.; merecimiento, m.; vt. merecer

merry, adj. alegre, jovial

merry-go-round, n. caballitos, m. pl., tiovivo, m.

mess, n. (mil.) comida, f.; confusión, f.; aprieto, lio, m.; suciedad, f.

message, n. mensaje, m.

messenger, n. mensajero, mensajera

metal, n. metal,. m.; **metal shears,** cizalla, f.

meter, n. medidor, contador, m.; metro, m.

method, n. método, m.

methodical, adj. metódico

meticulous, adj. metictiloso

metric, adj. métrico

metropolis, n. metrópoli, capital, f.

Mexico, Méjico

mezzanine, n. (theat.) entresuelo, m., mezanina, f.

mfg., manufacturing, manuf., manufactura

mfr., manufacturer, fab. fabricante

mg., milligram, mg. miligramo

mice, n. pl. de **mouse,** ratones, m. pl.

microbe, n. microbio, m.

microphone, n. micrófono, m.

microscope, n. microscopio, m.

midday, n. mediodía, m.

middle, n. medio, centro, m., mitad, f.

middle-aged, adj. entrado en años, de edad madura

middle class, n. clase media, f.

midnight, n. media noche, f.

midwife, n. partera, f.

might, n. poder, m., fuerza, f.; pretérito del verbo **may**

mighty, adj. fuerte, potente

migraine, n. jaqueca, f.

migrate, vi. emigrar

mild, adj. apacible, suave

mile, n. milla , f.

mileage, n. kilometraje, m.

military, adj. militar

milk, n. leche, f.; vt. ordeñar

milkman, n. lechero, m.

milky, adj. lácteo; lechoso; lechero

Milky Way, n. Vía Láctea, f.

mill, n. molino, m.

milligram, n. miligramo, m.

millimeter, n. milímetro, m.

millinery, n. confección de sombreros para señora

million, n. millón, m.

millionaire, n. y adj. millonario, millonaria

mind, n. mente, f.; intención, f.; opinión, f.; ánimo, m.; vt. importar; obedecer; vi. tener cuidado; preocuparse;

mine, pron. mío, mía, míos, mías; n. mina, f.

miner, n. minero, m.

mineral, adj. y n. mineral, m.

miniature, n. miniatura, f.

minimum, n. mínimum, mínimo, m.; adj. mínimo:

mining, n. minería, f.

minister, n. ministro, pastor, m.

ministry, n. ministerio, m.

minnow, n. variedad de pez pequeño

minor, adj. menor, pequeño; (mus.) menor; n. menor (de edad), m. y f.

minority, n. minoridad, f.; minoría, f.

mint, n. (bot.) menta, f.; casa de moneda, f.; vt. acuñar

minuet, n. minué, m.

minus, prep. menos; adj. negativo; n. (math.) el signo menos

minute, adj. menudo, pequeño

minute, n. minuto, m.

miracle, n. milagro, m.; maravilla, f.

miraculous, adj. milagroso

mirror, n. espejo, m.

misbehave, vi. portarse mal

miscarriage, n. aborto, malparto, m.

miscellaneous, adj. misceláneo, mezclado

mischief, n. travesura, f.

mischievous, adj. travieso, pícaro

misdeed, n. delito, m.

miser, n. avaro, avara

miserable, *adj.* miserable, infeliz

miserly, *adj.* tacaño

misery, *n.* miseria, *f.*; infortunio, *m.*

misfortune, *n.* infortunio, *m.*; calamidad, *f.*

misgiving, *n.* recelo, *m.*; presentimiento, *m.*

mishap, *n.* desventura, *f.*; contratiempo, *m.*

misleading, *adj.* engañoso, desorientador

miss, *n.* señorita, *f.*; pérdida, falta, *f.*; *vt.* errar; echar de menos

missile, *n.* proyectil, *m.*

missing, *adj.* que falta; perdido

mission, *n.* misión, comisión, *f.*; cometido, *m.*

missionary, *n.* misionero, *m.*

missive, *n.* carta, misiva, *f.*

misspell, *vt.* deletrear mal, escribir con mala ortografía

mistake, *n.* equivocación, *f.*, error, *m.*; *vt.* equivocar; *vi.* equivocarse, engañarse

Mister, *n.* Señor (título), *m.*

mistress, *n.* ama, *f.*; señora, *f.*; concubina, *f.*

misunderstand, *vt.* entender mal una cosa

misunderstanding, *n.* mal entendimiento, *m.*

mm., millimeter, mm., milímetro

moan, *n.* lamento, gemido, *m.*; *vi.* afligirse,quejarse

mob, *n.* populacho, *m.*

mobile, *adj.* movedizo, móvil

mobilize, *vt.* movilizar

mock, *vt.* mofar, burlar; *n.* mofa, burla, *f.*; *adj.* ficticio, falso

mockingbird, *n.* (orn.) sinsonte, arrendajo, *m.*

mode, *n.* modo, *m.*; forma, *f.*; manera, *f.*

moderate, *adj.* moderado; módico

moderation, *n.* moderación, *f.*

modern, *adj.* moderno

modernistic, *adj.* modernista

modest, *adj.* modesto

modesty, *n.* modestia, decencia, *f.*, pudor, *m.*

modify, *vt.* modificar

moist, *adj.* húmedo, mojado

moisten, *vt.* humedecer

moisture, *n.* humedad, *f.*; jugosidad, *f.*

molar, *adj.* molar; **molar teeth,** muelas, *f. pl.*

molasses, *n.* melaza, *f.*

mold, *n.* moho, *m.*; molde, *m.*; matriz, *f.*; *vt.* enmohecer; moldar; formar; *vi.* enmohecerse

molding, *n.* molduras, *f. pl*

moldy, *adj.* mohoso

mole, *n.* topo, *m.*; lunar, *m.*

molt, *vi.* mudar, estar de muda las aves

moment, *n.* momento, rato, *m.*

momentary, *adj.* momentáneo

momentous, *adj.* importante

monarch, *n.* monarca, *m.*

monarchy, *n.* monarquía, *f.*

monastery, *n.* monasterio, *m.*

Monday, *n.* lunes, *m.*

monetary, *adj.* monetario

money, *n.* moneda, *f.*; dinero, *m.*; plata, *f.*; **paper money,** papel moneda

monk, *n.* monje, *m.*

monkey, *n.* mono, mona; simio, mia; **monkey wrench,** llave inglesa, *f.*

monogram, *n.* monograma, *m.*

monologue, *n.* monólogo, *m.*

monopolize, *vt.* monopolizar, acaparar

monopoly, *n.* monopolio, *m.*

monster, *n.* monstruo, *m.*

month, *n.* mes, *m.*

monthly, *adj.* mensual

monument, *n.* monumento, *m.*

mood, *n.* humor, talante, *m.*

moody, *adj.* caprichoso, veleidoso

moon, *n.* luna, *f.*

moonlight, *n.* luz de la luna *f.*

moose, *n.* (zool.) alce, *m.*

mop, *n.*(Sp. Am.) trapeador, *m.*; *vt.* (Sp. Am.) trapear

moral, *adj.* moral, ético; *n.* moraleja, *f.*; **morals,** *n. pl.* moralidad, conducta, *f.*

morale, n. moralidad, f.; animación, f.

morality, n. ética, moralidad, f.

moratorium, n. moratoria, f.

more, adj. más, adicional; adv. más, en mayor grado

moreover, adv. además

morning, n. mañana, f.; **good morning**, buenos días; adj. matutino

morphine, n. morfina, f.

mortal, adj. mortal; humano; n. mortal, m.

mortgage, n. hipoteca, f.; vt. hipotecar

mosquito, n. mosquito, m.

most, adj. más; adv. sumamente, en sumo grado; n. los más; mayor número; mayo valor; **mostly**, adv. por lo común; principalmente

motel, n. hotel para automovilistas, m.

mother, n. madre, f.

motherhood, n. maternidad, f.

mother-in-law, n. suegra, f.

motherless, adj. huérfana de madre

motif, n. motivo, tema, m.

motion, n. movimiento, m., moción, f.; **motion picture**, cinema, cinematógrafo, m.; vt. proponer

motionless, adj. inmóvil

motor, n. motor, m.

motorcade, n. procesión o desfile de automóviles

motorcar, n. automóvil, m.

motorcycle, n. motocicleta, f.

motorist, n. automovilista, motorista, m. y f.

motorman, n. motorista, m.

mountain, n. montaña, sierra, f., monte, m.

mountainous, adj. montañoso

mourn, vt. deplorar; vi. lamentar; llevar luto

mourning, n. luto, m.

mouse, n. ratón, m.

mouth, n. boca, f.

mouthful, n. bocado, m.

mouthpiece, n. boquilla, f.

move, vt. mover; proponer; emocionar;vt. moverse, me-

nearse; n. movimiento

movement, n. movimiento, m.; moción, f.

movie, n. **movies**, n. pl. (coll.) cine, cinema, cinematógrafo, m.

moving, adj. conmovedor; **moving picture**, cine, cinema, cinematógrafo, m.

mow, vt. guadañar, segar

mph, m.p.h., miles per hour, m.p.h. millas por hora

much, adj. y adv. mucho

mucous, adj. mocoso, viscoso

mud, n. lodo, m.

muddle, vt. enturbiar; confundir

muffin, n. bizcochuelo, m.

muffler, n. (auto.) silenciador, m., sordina, f.; desconectador, m.

mule, n. mula, f.

multimillionaire, n. multimillonario, multimillonaria

multiplication, n. multiplicación, f.

multiply, vt. y vi multiplicar

mumble, vt. y vi. gruñir; murmurar

municipal, adj. municipal

munition, n. municiones, f. pl.

murder, n. asesinato, homicidio, m.; vt. asesinar

murderer, n. asesino, asesinar

murmur, n. murmullo, m.; cuchicheo, m.; vi. murmurar

muscle, n. músculo, m.

muscular, adj. muscular

museum, n. museo, m.

mushroom, n. hongo, m.

music, n. música, f.

musical, adj. musical

musician, n. músico, m.

mustard, n. mostaza, f.

mute, adj. mudo, silencioso

mutilate, vt. mutilar

mutiny, n. motín, tumulto, m.

mutter, vt. y vi. murmurar, hablar entre dientes

mutton, n. carnero, m.

mutual, adj. mutuo, recíproco

my, pron. mi, mis

myself, pron.yo mismo

mysterious, adj. misterioso

mystery, n. misterio, m.

myth, n. fábula, f.; mito, m.

mythology, n. mitología,

N

nab, vt. atrapar, prender

nag, n. jaca, f.; jaco, m.; vt. y vi. regañar, sermonear

nail, n. uña, f.; garra, f.; clavo, m.; vt. clavar

naked, adj. desnudo

name, n. nombre, m.; fama, reputación, f.

nameless, adj. sin nombre

namely, adv. a saber

namesake, n. tocayo, tocaya

nap, n. siesta, f.; pelo (de una tela), m.

napkin, n. servilleta, f.

narcotic, adj. narcótico

narrate, vt. narrar, relatar

narrative, n. relato, m.

narrow, adj. angosto, estrecho

narrowminded, adj. intolerante

NASA, National Aeronautics and Space Administration, Administración Nacional de Aeroná tica y del Espacio

nasal, adj. nasal

nasty, adj. sucio, puerco; desagradable

natal, adj. nativo; natal

nation, n. nación, f.

national, adj. nacional

nationality, n. nacionalidad, f.

native, adj. nativo; n. natural, m. y f.

NATO, North Atlantic Treaty Organization, OTAN, Organización del Tratado del Atlántico Norte

natural, adj. natural; sencillo; n. (mus.) becuadro, m.

nature, n. naturaleza, f.; indole, f.; **good nature,** buen humor, m.

naught, n. nada, f.; cero, m.

naughty, adj. travieso, pícaro

nausea, n. náusea, basca, f.

naval, adj. náutico, naval

navel, n. ombligo, m.

navigable, adj. navegable

navigate, vt. y vi. navegar

navigation, n. navegación, f.

navy, n. marina, f.

NE, N.E., n.e., northeast, N.E., nordeste

near, prep. cerca de, junto a; adv. casi; cerca, cerca de; adj. cercano

nearby, adj. cercano, próximo; adv. cerca, a la mano

neat, adj. pulido; ordenado

necessary, adj. necesario

necessity, n. necesidad, f.

neck, n. cuello, m.

necklace, n. collar, m.

necktie, n. corbata, f.

nectar, n. néctar, m.

negative, adj. negativo; n. negativa, f.

neglect, vt. descuidar, desatender; n. negligencia, f.

negligee, n. bata de casa, f.

negligence, n. negligencia, f.

negotiation, n. negociación, f.

negro, n. negro, negra

neighbor, n. vecino, vecina

neighborhood, n. vecindad, f.; vecindario, m.; inmediación, cercanía, f.

neither, conj. ni; adj. ninguno; pron. ninguno, ni uno ni otro

nephew, n. sobrino, m.

nerve, n. nervió, m.; (coll.) descaro, m.

nest, n. nido, m.

net, n. red, f.; malla, f.; adj. neto, líquido

Netherlands, Países Bajos, m. pl.

network, n. red radiodifusora o televisora, f.

neuralgia, n. neuralgia, f.

neutral, adj. neutral

neutrality, n. neutralidad, f.

neutron bomb, n. bomba de neutrón

never, adv. nunca, jamás; **never mind,** no importa

nevertheless, adv. no obstante

new, adj. nuevo

newcomer, n. recién llegado, recién llegada

newlywed, n. recién casado, recién casada

news, n. pl. novedad, f., nuevas, noticias, f. pl.

newsboy, *n.* vendedor de periódicos, *m.*

newspaper, *n.* gaceta, *f.*; periódico, *m.*; diario, *m.*

next, *adj.* próximo; entrante, venidero; *adv.* inmediatamente después

niacin, *n.* niacina, *f.*

nice, *adj.* fino; elegante

nickel, *n.* níquel, *m.*

nickel-plated, *adj.* niquelado

nickname, *n.* apodo, *m.*

niece, *n.* sobrina, *f.*

night, *n.* noche, *f.*; **good night**, buenas noches

nightgown, *n.* camisón, *m.*, camisa de dormir, *f.*

nightingale, *n.* ruiseñor, *m.*

nightmare, *n.* pesadilla, *f.*

nimble, *adj.* ligero, ágil

nine, *n.* y *adj.* nueve, *m.*

nineteen, *n.* y *adj.* diez y nueve, diecinueve, *m.*

nineteenth, *n.* y *adj.* décimonono, *m.*

ninety, *n.* y *adj.* noventa, *m.*

ninth, *n.* y *adj.* nono, noveno, *m.*

nitrogen, *n.* nitrógeno, *m.*

no, *adv.* no; *adj.* ningún, ninguno; **by no means**, **in no way**, de ningún modo

No., north, N., norte

nobility, *n.* nobleza, *f.*

noble, *n.* y *adj.* noble, *m.* y *f.*

nobody, *pron.* nadie, ninguno, ninguna; *n.* persona insignificante, *f.*

noise, *n.* ruido, *m.*

noiseless, *adj.* sin ruido

noisy, *adj.* ruidoso

nominate, *vt.* nombrar, proponer (a alguien para un pueso, cargo, etc.)

nominative, *n.* (gram.) nominativo, *m.*

none, *pron.* nadie, ninguno

nonsense, *n.* tontería, *f.*; disparate, absurdo, *m.*

nonsensical, *adj.* absurdo; tonto

nonstop, *adj.* directo, sin parar

noodle, *n.* tallarín, fideo, *m.*

noon, *n.* mediodía, *m.*

noonday, *n.* mediodía, *m.*

north, *n.* norte, *m.*; *adj.* septentrional

northeast, *n.* nordeste, *m.*

northerly, **northern**, *adj.* septentrional

North Pole, *n.* Polo Artico, Polo Norte, *m.*

northward, **northwards**, *adv.* hacia el norte

northwest, *n.* noroeste, *m.*

Norway, Noruega

nose, *n.* nariz, *f.*; olfato, *m.*

not, *adv.* no

notary, notario, *m.*

note, *n.* nota, *f.*; billete, *m.*; consecuencia, *f.*; comentario, *m.*; (mus.) nota, *f.*; *vt.* notar, observar

notebook, *n.* librito de apuntes, *m.*

noted, *adj.* afamado, célebre

noteworthy, *adj.* notable

nothing, *n.* nada, *f.*

notice, *n.* noticia, *f.*; aviso, *m.*; nota, *f.*; *vt.* observar

noticeable, *adj.* notable, reparable

notify, *vt.* notificar

notion, *n.* noción, *f.*; opinion, *f.*; idea, *f.*; **notions**, *n. pl.* mercería, *f.*

notorious, *adj.* notorio

notwithstanding, *conj.* no obstante, aunque

noun, *n.* sustantivo, *m.*

nourish, *vt.* nutrir, alimentar

nourishing, *adj.* nutritivo

novel, *n.* novela, *f.*; *adj.* novedoso, original

novelist, *n.* novelista, *m.* y *f.*

novice, *n.* novicio, novicia

nowadays, *adv.* hoy día

nowhere, *adv.* en ninguna parte

nucleus, *n.* núcleo, *m.*

nude, *adj.* desnudo

nuisance, *n.* estorbo, *m.*; (coll.) lata, *f.*

null, *adj.* nulo, inválido

numb, *adj.* entumecido; *vt.* entumecer

number, *n.* número, *m.*; cantidad, *f.*; cifra, *f.*; *vt.* numerar

numeral, *adj.* numeral; *n.* número, m. cifra, f.

numerator, n. (math.) numerador, m.

numerical, adj. numérico

nun, n. monja, f.

nuptial, adj. nupcial; **nuptials,** n. pl. nupcias, f. pl.

nurse, n. enfermera, f.; miñera, f.; **wet nurse,** nodriza, nutriz, f.; vt. criar, amamantar; cuidar (un enfermo)

nursery, n. cuarto de los niños, m.; criadero, m.

nursemaid, n. niñera, aya, f.; (Sp. Am.) nana, f.

nut, n. nuez, f.; tuerca, f.

nutmeg, n. nuez moscada, f.

nutrition, n. nutrición, f.

nutritious, nutritive, adj. nutritivo, alimenticio

NW, N.W., n.w., north-west, NO, noroeste

nylon, n. nylon, m.

nymph, n. ninfa, f.

O

oak, n. roble, m., encina, f.

oasis, n. oasis, m.

oath, n. juramento, m.; blasfemia, f.

obedience, n. obediencia, f.

obedient, adj. obediente

obey, vt. obedecer

object, n. objeto, m.; punto, m.; (gram.) complemento, m.; vt. objetar

objection, n. objeción, f.

objective, n. meta, f.; objetivo, m.

obligation, n. obligación, f.; compromiso, m.

oblige, vt. obligar; complacer, favorecer

obliging, adj. servicial; condescendiente

obscene, adj. obsceno

obscure, adj. oscuro

obscurity, n. oscuridad, f.

observation, n. observación, f.

observatory, n. observatorio, m.

observe, vt. observer, mirar; notar; guarder (una fiesta, etc.)

obsession, n. obsesión, f.

obsolete, adj. anticuado

obstacle, n. obstáculo, m.

obstetrician, n. partera, m.

obstinate, adj. terco, porfiado

obstruction, n. obstrucción, f.

occasion, n. ocasión, vt. ocasionar causar

occasional, adj. ocasional, casual

occident, n. occidente, m.

occupation, n. ocupación, f.; empleo, m.; quehacer, m.

occupy, vt. ocupar, emplear

ocean, n. océano, m.

o'clock, del reloj; por el reloj; **at two o'clock,** a las dos

October, n. octubre, m.

odds, n. pl. differencia, disparidad, f.; **odds and ends,** trozos o fragmentos sobrantes

odor, odour, n. olor, m.; fragancia, f.

off, adj. y adv. lejos, a distancia; **hands off,** no tocar

offend, vt. ofender, irritar

offense, n. ofensa, f.; crimen, delito, m.

offensive, adj. ofensivo; n. (mil.) ofensiva, f.

offer, vt. ofrecer; vi. ofrecerse; n. oferta, propuesta, f.

office, n. oficina, f.; cargo, m.

officer, n. oficial, m.; funcionario, m.; agente de policía, m.

official, adj. oficial; n. oficial, funcionario, m.; **officially,** adv. oficialmente

offset, vt. balancear, compensar

offspring, n. prole, f.; descendencia, f.

oft, often, oftentimes, adv. muchas veces, frecuentemente, a menudo

ogre, n. ogro, m.

oil, n. aceite, m.; petróleo, m.; vt. aceitar, engrasar

oilcloth, n. encerado, hule, m.

oily, adj. aceitoso

ointment, n. ungüento, m.

O. K., all correct, correcto, V.º B.º, visto bueno

okay, adj. y adv. bueno, está

bien; *vt.* aprobar; dar el visto bueno; *n.* aprobación, *f.*, visto bueno

okra, *n.* (bot.) quimbombó, *m.*

old, *adj.* viejo; antiguo

old-fashioned, *adj.* anticuado, fuera de moda

olive, *n.* olivo, *m.*; oliva, aceituna, *f.*; **olive oil**, aceite de oliva

omelet, omelette, *n.* tortilla de huevos, *f.*

omen, *n.* agüero, *m.*

omission, *n.* omisión, *f.*; descuido, *m.*

omit, *vt.* omitir

omnibus, *n.* ómnibus, *m.*

on, *prep.* sobre, encima, en; de; a; *adv.* adelante, sin cesar

once, *adv.* una vez; **at once**, en seguida

one, *adj.* un, uno

oneself, *pron.* sí mismo

one-sided, *adj.* unilateral, parcial

one-way, *adj.* en una sola dirección

onion, *n.* cebolla, *f.*

only, *adj.* único, solo; mero; *adv.*; solamente

opal, *n.* ópalo, *m.*

open, *adj.* abierto; sincero, franco; cándido; *vt.* abrir; descubrir; *vi.* abrirse

opening, *n.* abertura

open-minded, *adj.* liberal; imparcial

opera, ópera, *f.*

operate, *vi.* obrar; operar

operating room, *n.* quirófano, *m.*

operation, *n.* operación, *f.*; funcionamiento, *m.*

opponent, *n.* antagonista, *m.* y *f.*; contendiente, *m.* y *f.*

opportune, *adj.* oportuno

opposite, *adj.* opuesto; contrario; frente; *n.* antagonista, *m.* y *f.*, adversario, adversaria

opposition, *n.* oposición

optic, optical, *adj.* óptico

optimism, *n.* optimismo, *m.*

optimistic, *adj.* optimista

or, *conj.* o; ó (entre números); u (antes de o y ho)

oral, *adj.* oral, vocal; **orally**, *adv.* oralmente, de palabra

orange, *n.* naranja, *f.*

orangeade, *n.* naranjada, *f.*

oration, *n.* oración, *f.*, discurso, *m.*

orator, *n.* orador, oradora

orchestra, *n.* orquesta, *f.*

orchid, *n.* orquídea, *f.*

order, *n.* orden, *m.* y *f.*; mandato, *m.*; encargo, *m.*; (com.) pedido, *m.*; **out of order**, descompuesto; *vt.* ordenar, arreglar; hacer un pedido

ordinary, *adj.* ordinario

organ, *n.* órgano, *m.*

organdy, *n.* organdí, *m.*

organ-grinder, *n.* organillero, *m.*

organic, *adj.* orgánico

organism, *n.* organismo, *m.*

organist, *n.* organista, *m.* y *f.*

organization, *n.* organización,

organize, *vt.* organizar

orient, *n.* oriente, *m.*

oriental, *adj.* oriental

origin, *n.* origen, principio, *m.*

original, *adj.* original

originality, *n.* originalidad, *f.*

originate, *vt.* y *vi.* originar; provenir

ornament, *n.* adorno, *m.*

orphan, *n.* y *adj.* huérfano, huérfana

orphanage, *n.* orfanato, *m.*

ostrich, *n.* avestruz, *m.*

other, *pron.* y *adj.* otro

otherwise, *adv.* de otra manera, por otra parte

ounce, *n.* onza, *f.*

our, ours, *pron.* nuestro, nuestra, nuestros, nuestras

ourselves, *pron. pl.* nosotros mismos

out, *adv.* fuera, afuera; *adj.* de fuera; **out!** *interj.* ¡fuera!

outcome, *n.* consecuencia, *f.* resultado, *m.*

outdoor, *adj.* al aire libre, fuera de casa

outdoors, *adv.* al aire libre, a la intemperie

outer, *adj.* exterior

outfit, *n.* vestido, *m.*, vesti-

menta, *f.*; *vt.* equipar, ataviar
outgoing, *adj.* saliente, de salida
outgrow, *vt.* quedar chico (vestido, calzado, etc.)
outing, *n.* excursión campestre, *f.*
outlaw, *n.* bandido, *m.*
outlet, *n.* salida, *f.*; desagüe, *m.*; sangrador, tomadero, *m.*
outline, *n.* contorno, *m.*; bosquejo, *m.*; silueta, *f.*; *vt.* esbozar
outlook, *n.* perspectiva, *f.*
out-of-date, *adj.* anticuado
outrage, *n.* ultraje, *m.*
outrageous, *adj.* atroz
outside, *n.* superficie, *f.*; exterior, *m.*; *adv.* afuera
outskirts, *n. pl.* suburbios, *m. pl.*; afueras, *f. pl.*
outstanding, *adj.* sobresaliente, notable
oval, *n.* óvalo, *m.*; *adj.* oval, ovalado
ovary, *n.* ovario, *m.*
oven, *n.* horno, *m.*
over, *prep.* sobre, encima; **all over,** por todos lados; **over and over,** repetidas veces
overboard, *adv.* (naut.) al agua, al mar
overcoat, *n.* abrigo, *m.*
overcome, *vt.* vencer; superar; salvar (obstáculos)
overeat, *vi.* hartarse, comer demasiado
overflow, *vt.* rebosar; desbordar; *n.* superabundancia, *f.*
overkill, *n.* capacidad destructiva superior a la necesaria
overlook, *vt.* pasar por alto, tolerar; descuidar
overnight, *adv.* durante o toda la noche; *adj.* de una noche
overpass, *n.* paso superior, *m.*
overpower, *vt.* predominar
oversea, overseas, *adv.* ultramar; *adj.* de ultramar
oversight, *n.* equivocación, *f.*; olvido, *m.*
overthrow, *vt.* derribar, derrocar; *n.* derrocamiento, *m.*
overtime, *n.* trabajo en exceso

de las horas regulares
overture, *n.* (mus.) obertura, *f.*
overweight, *n.* exceso de peso
overwhelming, *adj.* abrumador
overwork, *vt.* hacer trabajar demasiado; *vi.* trabajar demasiado
owe, *vt.* deber, tener deudas; estar obligado
owl, owlet, *n.* lechuza, *f.*
own, *adj.* propio; **my own,** mío, mía; *vt.* poseer; **to own up,** confesar
owner, *n.* dueño, dueña, propietario, propietaria
ox, *n.* buey, *m.*
oxygen, *n.* oxígeno, *m.*
oyster, *n.* ostra, *f.*, ostión, *m.*
oz., ounce, ounces, onz., onza, onzas

P

pace, *n.* paso, *m.*, marcha, *f.*; *vi.* pasear
pacemaker, *n.* (med.) aparato cardiocinético, *m.*, marcador de paso, marcapasos, *m.*
Pacific, *n.* Pacífico, *m.*
package, *n.* bulto, *m.*; paquete, *m.*
packing, *n.* envase, *m.*; empaque, *m.*; relleno, *m.*
pad, *n.* cojincillo, *m.*, almohadilla, *f.*, relleno, *m.*; **pad (of paper),** bloc (de papel), *m.*; *vt.* rellenar
paddle, *vi.* remar; *n.* canalete (especie de remo), *m.*; pala (para remar), *f.*
page, *n.* página, *f.*; paje, *m.*
pageant, *n.* espectáculo público, *m.*, procesión, *f.*
pail, *n.* cubo, *m.*
pain, *n.* dolor, *m.*
painful, *adj.* doloroso; penoso
painstaking, *adj.* laborioso
paint, *vt. y vi.* pintar; *n.* pintura, *f.*
painter, *n.* pintor, pintora
painting, *n.* pintura, *f.*
pair, *n.* par, *m.*; *vt.* parear; *vi.* aparearse
pajamas, *n. pl.* pijamas, *m. pl.*

pal, *n.* compañero, compañera, gran amigo, gran amiga

palace, *n.* palacio, *m.*

palate, *n.* paladar, *m.*

pale, *adj.* pálido

paleness, *n.* palidez, *f.*

palm, *n.* (bot.) palma, *f.*; palma (de la mano), *f.*

Palm Sunday, *n.* domingo de Ramos, *m.*

pamper, *vt.* mimar

pamphlet, *n.* folleto, libreto, *m.*

Panama, Panama

Panamanian, *n.* y *adj.* panameño, panameña

pancake, *n.* especie de tortilla de masa que se cuece en una plancha metálica

pant, *vi.* palpitar; jadear; *n.* jadeo, *m.*; **pants**, *n. pl.* pantalones, *m. pl.*

panther, *n.* pantera, *f.*

panties, *n. pl.* pantalones (de mujer), *m. pl.*

pantry, *n.* despensa, *f.*

pants, *n. pl.* pantalones, *m. pl.*

paper, *n.* papel, *m.*; periódico, *m.*; *vt.* empapelar

paprika, *n.* pimentón, *m.*

par, *n.* equivalencia, *f.*; igualdad, *f.*; **at par**, a la par

parade, *n.* desfile, *m.*

paradise, *n.* paraíso, *m.*

paragraph, *n.* párrafo, *m.*

parallel, *n.* línea paralela, *f.*; *adj.* paralelo; *vt.* parangonar; ser paralelo a

paralysis, *n.* parálisis, *f.*

paralytic, paralytical, *adj.* paralítico

paralyze, *vt.* paralizar

paramount, *adj.* supremo, superior

parasite, *n.* parásito, *m.*

parcel, *n.* paquete, *m.*; bulto, *m.*; **parcel post**, paquete postal, *m.*

pardon, *n.* perdón, *m.*, gracia, *f.*; *vt.* perdonar

parent, *n.* padre, *m.*; madre, *f.*; **parents**, *n. pl.* padres, *m. pl.*

parental, *adj.* paternal; maternal

parish, *n.* parroquia, *f.*

park, *n.* parque, *m.*; *vt.* estacionar (vehículos)

parking, *n.* estacionamiento (de automóviles), *m.*

parlor, *n.* sala, *f.*

parochial, *adj.* parroquial

parole, *n.* libertad condicional que se da a un prisionero; *vt.* y *vi.* libertar bajo palabra

parrot, *n.* papagayo, loro, *m.*

parson, *n.* párroco, *m.*

part, *n.* parte, *f.*; papel (de un actor), *m.*; obligación, *f.*; **in part**, parcialmente; *vt.* partir, separar, desunir; *vi.* separarse

participate, *vt.* participar

participle, *n.* (gram.) participio, *m.*

particular, *adj.* particular, singular

parting, *n.* separación, partida, *f.*; raya (en el cabello), *f.*

partition, *n.* partición, separación, *f.*; tabique, *m.*

party, *n.* partido, *m.*; fiesta, tertulia, *f.*

pass, *vt.* pasar; traspasar; *vi.* pasar, ocurrir, trascurrir; *n.* paso, camino, *m.*; pase, *m.*

passage, *n.* pasaje, *m.*; travesía, *f.*; pasadizo, *m.*

passenger, *n.* pasajero, pasajera

passing, *adj.* pasajero, transitorio; *n.* paso, *m.*; **in passing**, al pasar

passion, *n.* pasión, *f.*

passive, *adj.* pasivo

passport, *n.* pasaporte, *m.*

password, *n.* contraseña, *f.*

past, *adj.* pasado; **past tense**, (gram.) pretérito, *m.*; *n.* pasado, *m.*; *prep.* más allá de

paste, *n.* pasta, *f.*; engrudo, *m.*; *vt.* pegar (con engrudo)

pasteurize, *vt.* pasterizar

pastime, *n.* pasatiempo, *m.*

pastry, *n.* pastelería, *f.*

pasture, *n.* pasto, *m.*; *vt.* y *vi.* pastar, pacer

patch, *n.* remiendo, parche, *m.*; *vt.* remendar

patent, *n.* patente, *f.*, *vt.* patentar

paternal, *adj.* paternal

path, *n.* senda, *f.*, sendero, *m.*

patient, *adj.* paciente, sufrido; *n.* enfermo, enferma; paciente, doliente, *m.* y *f.*

patriot, *n.* patriota, *m.*

patriotic, *adj.* patriótico

patriotism, *n.* patriotismo, *m.*

patrol, *n.* patrulla, *f.*

patron, *n.* patrón, protector, *m.*; **patron saint,** santo patrón, *m.*

patronize, *vt.* patrocinar

pattern, modelo, *m.*; patrón, *m.*; muestra, *f.*

pauper, *n.* pobre, *m.* y *f.*, limosnero, limosnera

pause, *n.* pausa, *f.*; *vi.* pausar; deliberar

paw, *n.* garra, *f.*

pawn, *n.* prenda, *f.*; peón (de ajedrez), *m.*; *vt.* empeñar

pawnshop, *n.* casa de empeño, *f.*

pay, *vt.* pagar; saldar; *n.* paga, *f.*, pago, *m.*

payable, *adj.* pagadero

payload, *n.* carga útil, *f.*

payment, *n.* pago, *m.*, paga, *f.*, recompensa, *f.*

payola, *n.* cohecho, soborno *m.*

pea, *n.* guisante, *m.*; (Mex.) chícharo, *m.*

peace, *n.* paz, *f.*; **Peace Corps,** Cuerpo de Paz

peaceful, *adj.* pacífico, apacible

peach, *n.* melocotón, durazno, *m.*

peacock, *n.* pavo real, *m.*

peanut, *n.* cacahuate, cacahuete, maní, *m.*

peasant, *n.* campesino, campesina

pebble, *n.* guijarro, *m.*, piedrecilla, *f.*

peculiar, *adj.* peculiar, singular

pedal, *n.* pedal, *m.*

peddler, *n.* buhonero, *m.*

pedestal, *n.* pedestal, *m.*

pedestrian, *n.* peatón, peatona

pediatrician, *n.* (med.) pedia-

tra, *m.* y *f.*

pedigreed, *adj.* de casta escogida

peel, *vt.* descortezar, pelar; *n.* corteza, *f.*

peerless, *adj.* sin par

pen, *n.* pluma, *f.*; corral, *m.*

penalty, *n.* pena, *f.*; castigo, *m.*; multa, *f.*

pencil, *n.* pince, *m.*; lápiz, *m.*

pending, *adj.* pendiente

penetrate, *vt.* y *vi.* penetrar

penicillin, *n.* penicilina, *f.*

peninsula, *n.* península, *f.*

penitence, *n.* penitencia,

penitentiary, *n.* penitenciaria, *f.*

penknife, *n.* cortaplumas, *m.*

penmanship, *n.* caligrafía, *f.*

penniless, *adj.* indigente

penny, *n.* centavo, *m.*

pension, *n.* pensión, *f.*; *vt.* pensionar

people, *n.* gente, *f.*; pueblo, *m.*; nación, *f.*

pep, *n.* (coll.) energía, *f.*, entusiasmo, *m.*

pepper, *n.* pimienta, *f.*

peppermint, *n.* menta, *f.*

per, *prep.* por; **per capita,** por persona, por cabeza; **per cent,** por ciento (%)

perceive, *vt.* percibir, comprender

percentage, *n.* porcentaje, *m.*

perception, *n.* percepción, *f.*

percussion, *n.* percussión *f.*; **percussion section,** (mus.) batería, *f.*

perfect, *adj.* perfecto; *vt.* perfeccionar

perfection, *n.* perfección, *f.*

perforate, *vt.* perforar

perforation, *n.* perforación, *f.*

perform, *vt.* ejecutar; efectuar; realizar; *vi.* (theat.) representar

performance, *n.* ejecución, *f.*; cumplimiento, *m.*; actuación, *f.*; representación teatral, función, *f.*

perfume, *n.* perfume, *m.*

perhaps, *adv.* quizá, tal vez

peril, *n.* peligro, riesgo, *m.*

period, *n.* periodo, *m.*; época,

f.; punto, *m.*
periodic, *adj.* periódico
periodical, *n.* periódico, *m.*; *adj.* periodico
perish, *vi.* perecer
permanent, *adj.* permanente; **permanent wave**, ondulado permanente, *m.*
permission, *n.* permiso, *m.*, licencia, *f.*
permit, *vt.* permitir; *n.* permiso, *m.*
peroxide, *n.* peróxido, *m.*
perpendicular, *adj.* perpendicular
perpetual, *adj.* perpetuo
persecute, *vt.* perseguir
persecution, *n.* persecución, *f.*
perseverance, *n.* perseverancia, *f.*
persist, *vi.* persistir
persistent, *adj.* persistente
person, *n.* persona, *f.*
personal, *adj.* personal
personality, *n.* personalidad, *f.*
personnel, *n.* personal, *m.*
perspective, *n.* perspectiva, *f.*
perspiration, *n.* traspiración, *f.*, sudor, *m.*
perspire, *vi.* traspirar, sudar
persuade, *vt.* persuadir
pertain, *vi.* relacionar, tocar
perturb, *vt.* perturbar
perverse, *adj.* perverso
perversion *n.* perversión, *f.*
perversity, *n.* perversidad, *f.*
pervert, *vt.* perverter, corromper
pessimist, *n.* pesimista, *m.* y *f.*
pessimistic, *adj.* pesimista
pest, *n.* reste, pestilencia, *f.*
pet, *n.* favorito, favorita; *vt.* mimar
petition, *n.* petición, súplica, *f.*; *vt.* suplicar, pedir
pew, *n.* banco de iglesia, *m.*
phantom, *n.* espectro, fantasma, *m.*
pharmacist, *n.* boticario, farmacéutico, *m.*
pharmacy, *n.* farmacia, botica, *f.*
phase, *n.* fase, *f.*, aspecto, *m.*
philanthropic, **philanthropi-**

cal, *adj.* filantrópico
philately, *n.* filatelia, *f.*
Philippines, Filipinas
philosopher, *n.* filósofo *m.*
philosophy, *n.* filosofía *f.*
phone, *n.* (coll.) teléfono, *m.*; *vt.* (coll.) telefonear
phonetics, *n. pl.* fonética, *f.*
photo, *n.* (coll.) **photograph**
photogenic, *adj.* fotogénico
photograph, *n.* fotografía, *f.*; retrato, *m.*; *vt.* fotografiar, retratar
photographer, *n.* fotógrafo, *m.*
physic, *n.* purgante, *m.*, purga, *f.*; **physics**, *n. pl.* física, *f.*; *vt.* purgar, dar un purgante
physical, *adj.* físico
physician, *n.* médico, *m.*
physics, *n.* física, *f.*
physiology, *n.* fisiología, *f.*
physique, *n.* físico, *m.*
pianist, *n.* pianista, *m.* y *f.*
piano, *n.* piano, *m.*
pickle, *n.* encurtido, *m.*
pickpocket, *n.* ratero, ratera, ladrón, ladrona
picnic, *n.* merienda campestre, *f.*; día de campo, *m.*
picture, *n.* retrato, *m.*; **motion picture**, película, *f.*
picturesque, *adj.* pintoresco
pie, *n.* pastel, *m.*
piece, *n.* pedazo, *m.*; pieza, obra, *f.*
pier, *n.* muelle, *m.*
pig, *n.* cerdo, *m.*, puerco, puerca
pigeon, *n.* palomo, *m.*, paloma, *f.*
pile, *n.* pila, *f.*; montón, *m.*; **piles**, *n. pl.* hemorroides, almorranas, *f. pl.*; *vt.* amontonar, apilar
pill, *n.* píldora, *f.*
pillar, *n.* pilar, poste, *m.*, columna, *f.*
pillow, *n.* almohada, *f.*, cojín, *m.*
pillowcase, **pillowslip**, *n.* funda, *f.*
pilot, *n.* piloto, *m.*
pimento, *n.* pimiento, *m.*
pimple, *n.* grano, barro, *m.*

pin, n. alfiler, m.; prendedor, m.; **safety pin,** imperdible, alfiler de gancho; vt. asegurar con alfileres; fijar con clavija

pinafore, n. delantal de niña, m.

pinch, vt. pellizcar; vi. escatimar gastos; n. pellizco, m.; aprieto, m.

pineapple, n. piña, f.; ananá, ananás, f.

pink, n. (bot.) clavel, m.; adj. rosado, sonrosado

pint, n. pinta (medida de líquidos), f.

pious, adj. piadoso

pipe, n. tubo, conducto, caño, m.; pipa para fumar, f.

pirate, n. pirata, m.

pit, n. hoyo, m.

pitcher, n. cántaro, m.; (baseball) lanzador de pelota

pitiful, adj. lastimoso

pity, n. piedad, compasión, f.; vt. compadecer

pkg., package, bto., bulto, paquete

place, n. lugar, sitio, m.; local, m.; **to take place,** verificarse; vt. colocar; poner

plague, n. peste, plaga, f.; vt. atormentar

plain, adj. sencillo; simple; evidente; n. llano, m.

plan, n. plan, m.; vt. planear, proyectar

plane, n. (avi.) avión, m.; plano, m.; cepillo, m.

planet, n. planeta, m.

plant, n. planta, f.

plasma, n. plasma, m.

plastic, adj. plástico

plate, n. placa, f.; clisé, m.; plato, m.

platform, n. plataforma, tarima, f.

platter, n. fuente, f., plato grande, m.

play, n. juego, m.; recreo, m.; comedia, f.; vt. y vi. jugar; (mus.) tocar

playback, n. reproducción en magnetófono

playboy, n. muchacho travieso, hombre de mundo, cala-

vera, m.

playful, adj. juguetón, travieso

playground, n. campo de deportes o de juegos, m.

playmate, n. compañero o compañera de juego

plaything, n. juguete, m.

plea, n. ruego, m.; súplica, f.; petición, f.

plead, vt. alegar; suplicar

please, vt. agradar, complacer

pleasing, adj. agradable, grato

pleasure, n. placer, m.

plot, n. pedazo pequeño de terreno, trama, f.; complot, m.; vt. y vi. conspirar, tramar

plug, n; tapón, m.; (elec.) clavija, f.; vt. tapar; (elec.) conectar

plumber, n. plomero, m.

plunge, vt. y vi. sumergir, precipitarse

plus, prep. más

p.m., afternoon, p.m., pasado meridiano, tarde

pneumonia, n. neumonía, pulmonía, f.

pocket, n. bolsillo, m.

pockctbook, n. portamonedas, m., cartera, f.; (fig.) dinero, m.

pocketknife, n. cortaplumas, m.

poem, n. poema, m.

poet, n. poeta, m.

poetic, poetical, adj. poético

poetry, n. poesía, f.

point, n. punta, f.; punto, m.; **point of view,** punto de vista; vt. apuntar; **to point out,** señalar

poison, n. veneno, m.; vt. envenenar

poker, n. hurgón, m.; póker (juego de naipes), m.

Poland, Polonia

polar, adj. polar; **polar bear,** oso blanco, m.

Pole, n. polaco, polaca

pole, n. polo, m.; palo, m.; **pole vault,** salto con pértiga, m.

police, n. policía, f.

policeman, n. policía, m.

policewoman, n. mujer policía, f.

policy, n. póliza, f.; política, f.: sistema, m.

polite, adj. cortés

politeness, n. cortesía, f.

political, adj. político

politician, n. político, m.

politics, n. pl. política, f.

pond, n. charca, f.

ponder, vt. y vt. ponderar

pontoon, n. (avi.) flotador de hidroavión, m.

pony, n. caballito, m.

pool, n. charco. m.

poor, adj. pobre; deficiente

popcorn, n. palomitas de maíz, f. pl.

Pope, n. papa, m.

poplar, n. álamo temblón, m.

poppy, n. amapola, f.

popular, adj. popular

popularity, n. popularidad, f.

population, n. población, f.: número de habitantes, m.

populous, adj. populoso

porcelain, n. porcelana, f.

porch, n. pórtico, vestíbulo, m.

pork, n. carne de puerco, f.

port, n. puerto, m.; vino de Oporto, m.

portable, adj. portátil

porter, n. portero, m.; mozo, m.

portion, n. porción, ración, f.

portrait, n. retrato, m.

Portuguese, n. y adj. portugués, portuguesa

pose, n. postura, actitud

position, n. posición, situación, f.

positive, adj. positive, real

possess, vt. poseer

possession, n. posesión, f.

possessive, adj. posesivo

possibility, n. posibilidad, f.

possible, adj. posible

post, n. correo, m.; puesto, m.; empleo, m.; poste, m.; vt. fijar; **post no bills,** se prohíbe fijar carteles

postage, n. franqueo, m.

postal, adj. postal; **postal card,** tarjeta postal, f.

poster, n. cartel, cartelón, m.

posterity, n. posteridad, f.

postman, n. cartero, m.

postmark, n. sello o marca de la oficina de correos

post office, n. correo, m., oficina postal, f.

postpaid, adj. franco; con porte pagado

postpone, vt. posponer

postscript, n. posdata, f.

postwar, n. postguerra, f.

pot, n. olla, f.

potato, n. patata, papa, f.

potent, adj. potente

pouch, n. buche, m.; bolsa, f.

poultry, n. aves de corral, f. pl.

pound, n. libra, f.; **pound sterling,** libra esterlina, f.; vt. machacar

pour, vt. verter; vi. fluir con rapidez; llover a cántaros

poverty, n. pobreza, f.

POW, (prisoner of war), n. prisionero de guerra, m.

powder, n. polvo, m.; pólvora, f.; **powder puff,** borla o mota de empolvarse; vt. pulverizar; empolvar

power, n. poder, m.; potencia, f.

powerful, adj. poderoso

powerless, adj. impotente

pp., pages, págs., páginas; **past participle,** p. pdo., participio pasado

practice, n. práctica, f.; costumbre, f.; vt. y vi. practicar; ejercer; ensayar

praise, n. alabanza, f.; vt. alabar, ensalzar

pray, vt. y vi. rezar, rogar

prayer, n. oración, súplica, f.; **the Lord's Prayer,** el Padre Nuestro, m.

preach, vt. y vi. predicar

preacher, n. predicador, m.

preamble, n. preámbulo, m.

precaution, n. precaución, f.

precede, vt. preceder

precedent, adj. y n. precedente, m.

preceding, adj. precursor

precious, adj. precioso; valioso

precipitation, n. precipitación, f.

precise, adj. preciso, exacto

predecessor, n. predecesor, predecesora, antecesor, antecesora

predict, vt. predecir

predominate, vt. predominar

preface, n. prefacio, m.

prefer, vt. preferir

preferable, adj. preferible

preference, n. preferencia, f.

pregnant, adj. encinta

prejudice, n. prejuicio, m.

preliminary, adj. preliminar

premature, adj. prematuro

premier, n. primer ministro, m.

premiere, n. estreno, m.

premium, n. premio, m.; prima, f.

premonition, n. presentimiento, m.

preparation, n. preparación, f.; preparativo, m.

prepare, vt. preparar; vi. prepararse

preposition, n. preposición, f.

prescribe, vt. y vi. prescribir; recetar

prescription, n. receta medicinal, f.

presence, n. presencia, f.; **presence of mind,** serenidad de ánimo, f.

present, n. presente, regalo, m.; adj. presente; vt. presentar, regalar

presentable, adj. presentable, decente

preserve, vt. preservar, conservar; n. conserva, confitura, f.

preside, vi. presidir

presidency, n. presidencia, f.

president, n. presidente, m.

press, vt. planchar; oprimir, compeler; n. prensa, f.; imprenta, f.

pressing, urgente

pressure, n. presión, f.; **pressure gauge,** manómetro, m.

pretend, vt. simular, fingir

pretense, pretence, n. pretexto, m.; pretensión, f.

pretext, n. pretexto, m.

pretty, adj. bonito

prevent, vt. prevenir

prevention, n. prevención, f.

preventive, adj. y n. preventivo, m.

preview, n. exhibición preliminar, f.

previous, adj. previo

price, n. precio, valor, m.

priceless, adj. inapreciable

priest, n. sacerdote, cura, m.

primary, adj. primario

primitive, adj. primitivo

princess, n. princesa, f.

principal, adj. principal; n. principal, jefe, m.; rector, director (de un colegio), m.; capital (dinero empleado), m.

principle, n. principio, fundamento, m.

print, vt. estampar, imprimir; n. impresión, estampa, f.

printed, adj. impreso; **printed matter,** impresos, m. pl.

printer, n. impresor, m.

prison, n. prisión, cárcel, f.

prisoner, n. prisionero, prisionera

private, adj. privado; secreto; particular; **private enterprise,** empresa particular, f.; n. soldado raso, m.

prize, n. premio, m.

prizefighter, n. pugilista, boxeador, m.

pro, prep. para, pro; adj. en el lado afirmativo (de un debate, etc.); **the pros and cons,** el pro y el contra

probability, n. probabilidad, f.

probable, adj. probable

probation, n. prueba, f.; libertad condicional, f.

problem, n. problema, m.

proceed, vi. proceder; **proceeds,** n. pl. producto, rédito, m.

process, n. proceso, m.

procession, n. procesión, f.

produce, vt. producir; rendir

product, n. producto, m.

production, n. producción, f.

Prof., prof., professor, Prof., profesor

profit, n. ganancia, f.; provecho, m.; vt. y vi. aprovechar

profitable, adj. provechoso,

productivo

program, *n.* programa, *m.*; *vt.* programar

progress, *vt.* progreso, *m.*; adelanto, *m.*; *vi.* progresar

prohibit, *vt.* prohibir

prohibition, *n.* prohibición, *f.*

project, *vt.* proyectar, trazar; *n.* proyecto, *m.*

prominent, *adj.* prominente

promise, *n.* promesa, *f.*; *vt.* prometer

promising, *adj.* prometedor

promote, *vt.* promover

promotion, *n.* promoción, *f.*

prompt, *adj.* pronto, listo; **promptly,** *adv.* pronto; *vt.* apuntar (en el teatro)

pronoun, *n.* pronombre, *m.*

pronounce, *vt.* pronunciar

pronunciation, *n.* pronunciación, *f.*

proof, *n.* prueba, *f.*

proofread, *vt.* corregir pruebas

propaganda, *n.* propaganda, *f.*

propagandist, *adj.* y *n.* propagandista, propagador, *m.*

proper, *adj.* propio; debido

property, *n.* propiedad, *f.*

prophecy, *n.* profecía, *f.*

prophet, *n.* profeta, *m.*

proportion, *n.* proporción, *f.*

proposal, *n.* propuesta, proposición, *f.*; oferta, *f.*

propose, *vt.* proponer

proposition, *n.* proposición, propuesta, *f.*

proprietor, *n.* propietario, propietaria, dueño, dueña

prose, *n.* prosa, *f.*

prosecutor, *n.* acusador, *m.*

prospect, *n.* perspectiva, *f.*

prosper, *vt.* y *vi.* prosperar

prosperity, *n.* prosperidad, *f.*

prosperous, *adj.* próspero

prostitution, *n.* prostitución, *f.*

prostrate, *adj.* decaído, postrado

protect, *vt.* proteger, amparar

protection, *n.* protección, *f.*

protector, *n.* protector, protectora

protein, *n.* proteína, *f.*

protest, *vt.* y *vi.* protestar; *n.*

protesta, *f.*

Protestant, *n.* y *adj.* protestante, *m.* y *f.*

prove, *vt.* probar

proverb, *n.* proverbio, *m.*

provide, *vt.* proveer, surtir

provided, *adj.* provisto; **provided that,** con tal que

providence, *n.* providencia, *f.* ; economía, *f.*

province, *n.* provincia, *f.*; jurisdicción, *f.*

provision, *n.* provisión, *f.*; **provisions,** *n. pl.* comestibles, *m. pl.*

provisional, *adj.* provisional

proxy, *n.* apoderado, apoderada; **by proxy,** por poder

P.S., postscript, P.D., posdata

psalm, *n.* salmo, *m.*

psychiatry, *n.* siquiatría, *f.*

psychoanalyze, *vt.* sicoanalizar

psychology, *n.* sicología, *f.*

P. T. A.: Parent-Teacher Association, Asociación de Padres y Maestros

public, *adj.* y *n.* público, *m.*

publication, *n.* publicación, *f.*

publicity, *n.* publicidad, *f.*

publish, *vt.* publicar

puff, *n.* bufido, soplo, *m.*; bocanada, *f.*; **powder puff,** mota o borla para polvos, *f.*; *vt.* y *vi.* hinchar; soplar

puffy, *adj.* hinchado

pull, *vt.* tirar, halar.; *n.* tirón, *m.*. influencia, *f.*

pulpit, *n.* púlpito, *m.*

pump, *n.* bomba, *f.*; zapatilla, *f.*; *vt.* sondear; sonsacar

pumpkin, *n.* calabaza, *f.*

pun, *n.* equívoco, chiste, *m.*; juego de palabras, *m.*

punch, *n.* puñetazo, *m.*; ponche, *m.*

punctual, *adj.* puntual

punctuation, *n.* puntuación, *f.*

puncture, *n.* pinchazo, *m.*

punish, *vt.* castigar

punishment, *n.* castigo, *m.*

pupil, *n.* (anat.) pupila, *f.*; pupilo, *m.*; discípulo, discípula; **pupil of the eye,** niña del ojo, *f.*

puppy, *n.* perrillo, cachorro, *m.*

purgatory, *n.* purgatorio, *m.*

purple, *adj.* morado

purpose, *n.* intención, *f.;* **on purpose,** de propósito

purse, *n.* bolsa, *f.,* portamonedas, *m.*

pursue, *vt.* y *vi.* perseguir; seguir

pursuit, *n.* persecución, *f.*

puss, pussy, *n.* micho, gato, *m.*

put, *vt.* poner, colocar

puzzle, *n.* rompecabezas, *m.;* *vt.* y *vi.* confundir

pyramid, *n.* pirámide,

Q

qt., quantity, cantidad; **quart,** cuarto de galón.

quail, *n.* codorniz, *f.*

quake, *vi.* temblar, tiritar; *n.* temblor, *m.*

Quaker, *n.* y *adj.* cuáquero, cuáquera

qualification, *n.* aptitud, *f.;* requisito, *m.*

quantity, *n.* cantidad, *f.*

quarantine, *n.* cuarentena, *f.*

quarrel, *n.* riña, pelea, *f.;* *vt.* reñir, disputar

quart, *n.* un cuarto de galón, *m.*

quarter, *n.* cuarto, *m.;* cuarta parte; cuartel, *m.;* moneda de E.U.A. de 25 centavos de dólar

quarterly, *adj.* trimestral

quartet, *n.* cuarteto, *m.*

queen, *n.* reina, *f.;* dama (en el juego de aiedrez), *f.*

queenly, *adj.* majestuoso, como una reina

question, *n.* cuestión, *f.;* asunto, *m.;* duda, *f.;* pregunta, *f.;* *vi.* preguntar; *vt.* desconfiar, poner en duda

questionable, *adj.* dudoso

questionnaire, *n.* cuestionario, *m.*

quick, *adj.* veloz; ligero, pronto; **quickly,** *adv.* rápidamente

quiet, *adj.* quieto, tranquilo, callado; *n.* calma, serenidad, *f.;* *vt.* tranquilizar

quinine, *n.* quinina, *f.*

quiz, *vt.* examinar; *n.* examen *m.*

quorum, *n.* quórum, *m.*

quota, *n.* cuota, *f.*

quotation, *n.* cotización, cita, *f.;* **quotation marks,** comillas, *f. pl.*

quote, *vt.* citar; **to quote (a price),** cotizar (precio)

quotient, *n.* cuociente o cociente, *m.*

R

rabbit, *n.* conejo, *m.*

race, *n.* raza, *f.;* carrera, corrida, *f.;* *vi.* correr

rack, *n.* (mech.) cremallera, *f.*

racket, *n.* raqueta, *f.*

radar, *n.* radar, *m.*

radiance, *n.* esplendor, *m.*

radiator, *n.* calentador, *m.;* (auto.) radiador, *m.*

radio, *n.* radio, *m.* y *f.*

radio telescope, *n.* radiotelescopio *m.*

radius, *n.* (math., anat.) radio, *m.*

rage, *n.* rabia, *f.;* furor, *m.,* cólera, *f.;* *vi.* rabiar, encolerizarse

rail, *n.* balaustrada, *f.;* (rail.) carril, riel, *m.;* **by rail,** por ferrocarril

railing, *n.* baranda, *f.,* barandal *m.;* carril, *m.*

railroad, *n.* ferrocarril, *m.*

railway, *n.* ferrocarril, *m.*

rain, *n.* lluvia, *f.;* *vi.* llover

rainbow, *n.* arco iris, *m.*

raincoat, *n.* impermeable, *m.*

raindrop, *n.* gota de lluvia, *f.*

rainy, *adj.* lluvioso

raise, *vt.* levantar, alzar

raisin, *n.* pasa, *f.*

ran, *pretérito* del verbo **run**

ranch, *n.* hacienda, *f.;* rancho, *m.*

random, *n.* ventura, casualidad, *f.;* **at random,** al azar

rang, *pretérito* del verbo **ring**

range, *vt.* clasificar; *vi.* fluctuar; alcance, *m.*; cocina económica, estufa, *f.*

rank, *n.* fila, hilera, *f.*; clase, *f.*; grado, rango, *m.*

ransom, *vt.* rescatar; *n.* rescate, *m.*

rape, *n.* fuerza, *f.*; estupro, *m.*; *vt.* estuprar

rash, *adj.* precipitado, temerario; *n.* roncha, *f.*; erupción, *f.*; sarpullido, *m.*

raspberry, *n.* frambuesa, *f.*

rat, *n.* rata, *f.*

rate, *n.* tipo, *m.*, tasa, *f.*; precio, valor, *m.*; **at the rate of,** a razón de; *vt.* tasar, apreciar; calcular, calificar

rather, *adv.* más bien; bastante; mejor dicho

ratify, *vt.* ratificar

rattle, *vt.* y *vt.* hacer ruido; **to become rattled,** confundirse; *n.* sonajero, *m.*; matraca, *f.*

rattlesnake, *n.* culebra de cascabel, *f.*

raw, *adj.* crudo; en bruto; **raw materials,** primeras materias, *f. pl.*

ray, *n.* rayo (de luz), *m.*

rayon, *n.* rayón, *m.*

razor, *n.* navaja de afeitar, *f.*

rd., road, camino; **rod,** pértica

reach, *vt.* alcanzar; *vi.* extenderse, llegar

read, *vt.* leer; interpretar

reader, *n.* lector, lectora

readily, *adv.* prontamente; de buena gana

reading, *n.* lectura, *f.*

real, *adj.* real, verdado, efectivo; **real estate,** bienes raíces o inmuebles, *m. pl.*

realistic, *adj.* realista; natural

reality, *n.* realidad, *f.*

realize, *vt.* realizar; darse cuenta de

really, *adv.* realmente

reap, *vt.* segar

rear, *n.* retaguardia, *f.*; parte posterior, *f.*; *adj.* posterior; *vt.* criar, educar

reason, *n.* razón, *f.*; motivo, *m.*; *vt.* razonar, raciocinar

reasonable, *adj.* razonable

reassure, *vt.* volver a asegurar

rebate, *n.* rebaja, *f.*

rebel, *n.* rebelde, *m.* y *f.*; *adj.* insurrecto; *vi.* rebelarse; insubordinarse

rebirth, *n.* renacimiento, *m.*

rebuild, *vt.* reconstruir

receipt, *n.* recibo, *m.*; receta, *f.*

receive, *vt.* recibir; admitir

receiver, *n.* receptor, *m.*; recipiente, *m.*; audífono, *m.*

reception, *n.* recepción, *f.*

receptionist, *n.* recepcionista, *m.* y *f.*; recibidor, m

recess, *n.* receso, recreo, *m.*

recipe, *n.* receta de cocina, *f.*

recipient, *n.* receptor, receptora

reciprocal, *adj.* recíproco

reciprocate, *vi.* corresponder

recital, *n.* recitación, *f.*; concierto, *m.*

recitation, *n.* recitación.

recite, *vt.* recitar; declamar

recognition, *n.* reconocimiento, *m.*; agradecimiento, *m.*

recognize, *vt.* reconocer

recommend, *vt.* recomendar

recommendation, *n.* recomendación, *f.*

recompense, *n.* recompensa, *f.*; *vt.* recompensar

reconciliation, *n.* reconciliación, *f.*

record, *vt.* registrar; grabar; *n.* registro, archivo, *m.*; disco, *m.*; *adj.* sin precedente; **off-the-record,** confidencial, extraoficial

recover, *vt.* recobrar; *vi.* restablecerse

recovery, *n.* restablecimiento, *m.*

recruit, *vt.* reclutar; *n.* (mil.) recluta, *m.*

rectangle, *n.* rectángulo, *m.*

rectangular, *adj.* rectangular

rectify, *vt.* rectificar

recuperate, *vi.* restablecerse; *vt.* recobrar, recuperar

red, *adj.* rojo; colorado; **Red, (communist),** *n.*, *adj.* rojo (communista)

redbreast, n. petirrojo, pechirrojo, m.

redden, vi. enrojecer

redeem, vt. redimir

redeemer, n. redentor, redentora, salvador, salvadora; the **Redeemer,** el Redentor

red-haired, adj. pelirrojo

reduce, vt. reducir

reduction, n. reducción, rebaja, f.

refer, vt. y vi. referir, dirigir

referee, n. árbitro, m.

reference, n. referencia, f.

refill, vt. rellenar; n. relleno, m.

refine, vt. y vi. refinar, purificar

refinement, n. refinamiento, m.

reflect, vt. y vi. reflejar; reflexionar

reflection, n. reflexión, meditación, f.; reflejo, m.

reflex, adj. reflejo

reform, vt. y vi. reformar; n. reforma, f.

reformatory, n. reformatorio m.

refrain, vi. abstenerse; n. estribillo, m.

refresh, vt. refrescar

refreshment, n. refresco, refrigerio, m.

refrigerate, vt. refrigerar

refrigeration, n. refrigeración, f.

refrigerator, n. refrigerador, m.

refuge, n. refugio, asilo, m.

refugee, n. refugiado, refugiada

refuse, vt. rehusar, repulsar; n. desecho, m., sobra, f.

regard, vt. estimar; considerar; n. consideración, f.; respeto, m.; **regards,** m. pl. , recuerdos, m. pl., memorias, f. pl.; **in regard to,** en cuanto a, respecto a, con respecto a; **in this regard,** a este respecto

regime, n. régimen, m.

regiment, n. regimiento, m.

region, n. región, f.

regional, adj. regional

register, n. registro, m.; **cash register,** caja registradora, f.; vt. registrar; certificar (una carta); vi. matricularse, registrarse

regret, n. arrepentimiento, m.; pesar, m.; vt. lamentar, deplorar

regrettable, adj. lamentable, deplorable

regular, adj. regular; ordinario

regularity, n. regularidad, f.

rehabilitation, n. rehabilitación, f.

rehearsal, n. (theat.) ensayo, m.

rehearse, vt. (theat.) ensayar

reign, n. reinado, reino, m.; vi. reinar, prevalecer, imperar

reimburse, vt. rembolsar

rein, n. rienda, f.

reindeer, n. sing. y pl., reno(s), rangífero(s), m.

reinforced, adj. reforzado

relate, vt. referir

related, adj. emparentado

relation, n. relación, f.; parentesco, m.

relative, adj. relativo; n. pariente, m. y f.

relax, vt. aflojar; vi. descansar, reposar

relaxation, n. reposo, descanso, m.

relay, n. trasmisión, f.; **relay race,** carrera de relevos, f.

release, vt. soltar, libertar; dar al público

relentless, adj. inflexible

relevant, adj. pertinente; concerniente

reliable, adj. digno de confianza, responsable

relief, n. alivio, consuelo, m.

relieve, vt. aliviar; relevar

religion, n. religión, f. ; culto, m.

religious, adj. religioso

relish, n. sabor, m.; gusto, deleite, m.; condimento, m.

relocate, vt. establecer de nuevo

remain, vi. quedar, restar, permanecer

remark, n. observación, nota,

f., comentario, *m.*

remarkable, *adj.* notable, interesante

remedy, *n.* remedio, medicamento, *m.*; *vt.* remediar

remember, *vt.* recordar, tener presente; dar memorias; *vi.* acordarse

remit, *vt.* y *vi.* remitir

remittance, *n.* remesa, *f.*; remisión, *f.*

remorse, *n.* remordimiento, *m.*

remote, *adj.* remoto, lejano

remove, *vt.* remover, alejar; quitar

render, *vt.* rendir

rendezvous, *n.* cita (particularmente amorosa), *f.*

renew, *vt.* renovar

renewal, *n.* prórroga,

rent, *n.* renta, *f.*, alquiler, *m.*; *vt.* arrendar, alquilar

repair, *vt.* reparar; *n.* remiendo, *m.*, reparación, compostura, *f.*

repeal, *vt.* abrogar, revocar; *n.* revocación, *f.*

repeat, *vt.* repetir

repent, *vi.* arrepentirse

repentance, *n.* arrepentimiento, *m.*

repertoire, *n.* repertorio, *m.*

repetition, *n.* repetición, *f.*

reply, *vt.* replicar, contestar, responder; *n.* respuesta, contestación, *f.*

report, *vt.* informar; dar cuenta; *n.* rumor, *m.*; informe, *m.*

reporter, *n.* reportero, *m.*; periodista, *m.* y *f.*

represent, *vt.* representar

representation, *n.* representación, *f.*

representative, *adj.* representativo; *n.* representante, *m.* y *f.*; **House of Representatives,** Cámara de Representantes

reprint, *n.* reimpresión, *f.*

reproduce, *vt.* reproducir

reptile, *n.* reptil, *m.*

republic, *n.* república,

reputation, *n.* reputación, *f.*

request, *n.* solicitud, súplica, *f.*; *vt.* suplicar; pedir, solicitar

require, *vt.* requerir, demandar

requirement, *n.* requisito, *m.*

rescue, *n.* rescate, *m.*; *vt.* socorrer; salvar

research, *n.* investigación, *f.*

resemblance, *n.* semejanza, *f.*

resemble, *vi.* parecerse a

resent, *vt.* resentir

resentment, *n.* resentimiento, *m.*

reservation, *n.* reservación, *f.*

reserve, *vt.* reservar; *n.* reserva, *f.*

residence, *n.* residencia, *f.*

resident, *n.* y *adj.* residente, *m.* y *f.*

residential, *adj.* residencial

resign, *vt.* y *vi.* resignar, renunciar, ceder; conformarse

resignation, *n.* resignación, *f.*; renuncia, *f.*

resist, *vt.* y *vi.* resistir; oponerse

resistance, *n.* resistencia, *f.*

resolution, *n.* resolución, *f.*

resolve, *vt.* resolver; decretar; *vi.* resolverse

resort, *vi.* recurrir; *n.* recurso; **summer resort,** lugar de veraneo, *m.*

resource, *n.* recurso, *m.*

resourceful, *adj.* ingenioso, hábil

respect, *n.* respecto, *m.*; respeto, *m.*; *vt.* apreciar; respetar

respectable, *adj.* respetable; decente

respectful, *adj.* respetuoso;

respectfully, *adv.* respetuosamente

respond, *vt.* responder

response, *n.* respuesta, réplica, *f.*

responsibility, *n.* responsabilidad, *f.*

responsible, *adj.* responsable

rest, *n.* reposo, *m.*; resto, restante, *m.*; **rest room,** sala de descanso, *f.*; *vt.* poner a descansar; apoyar; *vi.* resposar, recostar

restaurant, *n.* restaurante, *m.* fonda, *f.*

restless, *adj.* inquieto
restore, *vt.* restaurar, restituir
restrain, *vt*, restringir
restrict, *vt.* restringir, limitar
result, *n.* resultado, *m.*; consecuencia, *f.*; *vi.* resultar
resurrect, *vt.* resucitar
retail, *n.* venta al por menor *f.*, menudeo, *m.*
retain, *vt.* retener, guardar
retire, *vt.* retirar; *vi.* retirarse, sustraerse
return, *vt.* devolver; *n.* retorno, *m.*; vuelta, *f.*
reunion, *n.* reunión, *f.*
Rev., Reverend, R., Reverendo
revelation, *n.* revelación, *f.*
reverend, *adj.* reverendo; venerable; *n.* sacerdote, *m.*
reverse, *n.* reverso (de una moneda), *m.*; revés, *m.*; *adj.* inverso; contrario
review, *n.* revista, *f.*; reseña, *f.*; repaso, *m.*; *vt.* (mil.) revistar; repasar
revise, *vt.* revisar
revoke, *vt.* revocar, anular
revolt, *vt.* rebelarse; *n.* rebelión, *f.*
revolting, *adj.* repugnante
revolution, *n.* revolución, *f.*
revolutionary, *n.* y *adj.* revolucionario, revolucionaria
revolve, *vi.* girar
revolver, *n.* revólver, *m.*, pistola, *f.*
reward, *n.* recompensa, *f.*; *vt.* recompensar
RFD, r.f.d., rural free delivery, distribución gratuita del correo en regiones rurales
rhinoceros, *n.* rinoceronte, *m.*
rhyme, *n.* rima, *f.*; *vi.* rimar
rhythm, *n.* ritmo, *m.*
rib, *n.* costilla, *f.*
riboflavin, *n.* riboflavina, *f.*
rice, *n.* arroz, *m.*
rich, *adj.* rico; opulento
riches, *n.* riqueza, *f.*; bienes, *m. pl.*
rid, *vt.* librar, desembarazar
riddle, *n.* enigma, rompecabezas, *m.*
ride, *vi.* cabalgar; andar en coche; *n.* paseo a caballo o en coche

ridge, *n.* espinazo, lomo, *m.*; cordillera, *f.*
ridiculous, *adj.* ridículo
riding, *n.* paseo a caballo o en coche; *adj.* relativo a la equitación
rifle, *n.* fusil, *m.*
right, *adj.* derecho, recto; justo; *adv.* rectamente; **to be right**, tener razón; *n.* justicia, *f.*; derecho, *m.*; mano derecha, *f.*; (pol.) derecha, *f.*
ring, *n.* círculo, cerco, *m.*; anillo, *m.*; campaneo, *m.*; *vt.* sonar; **to ring the bell**, tocar la campanilla, tocar el timbre; *vi.* resonar
rinse, *vt.* enjuagar
riot, *n.* pelotera, *f.*; motín, *m.*
ripe, *adj.* maduro, sazonado
ripen, *vt.* y *vi.* madurar
rise, *vi.* levantarse; nacer, salir (los astros); rebelarse; ascender; *n.* levantamiento, *m.*; subida, *f.*; salida (del sol), *f.*
risen, *p. p.* del verbo **rise**
risk, *n.* riesgo, peligro, *m.*; *vt.* arriesgar
risky, *adj.* peligroso
rival, *n.* rival, *m.* y *f.*
river, *n.* río, *m.*
R.N., registered nurse, enfermera titulada, *f.*
RNA, ribonucleic acid, *n.* ácido ribonucleico
roach, *n.* cucaracha, *f.*
road, *n.* camino, *m.*
roar, *vi.* rugir; bramar; *n.* rugido, *m.*
roast, *vt.* asar
rob, *vt.* robar, hurtar
robber, *n.* ladrón, ladrona
robbery, *n.* robo, *m.*
robe, *n.* manto, *m.*; toga, *f.*
robin, *n.* (orn.) petirrojo, pechirrojo, pechicolorado, *m.*
rock, *n.* roca, *f.*; *vt.* mecer; arrullar; *vi.* balancearse
rock n' roll, rock-and-roll, *n.* música y baile popular, rock, *m.*
rocket, *n.* cohete, *m.*; **rocket launcher**, lanzacohetes, *m.*

rocky, adj. peñascoso, rocoso, roqueño

rode, pretérito del verbo **ride**

role, n. papel, m., parte, f.

roll, vt. rodar; arrollar, enrollar; vi. rodar; girar; n. rollo, m.; lista, f.; panecillo, m.

Roman, adj. romano; manesco; n. y adj. romano, romana

romance, n. romance, cuento, m.; idilio, m.; aventura romántica, f.

romantic, adj. romántico; sentimental

roof, n. tejado, techo, m.; azotea, f.; paladar, m.

room, n. cuarto, m., habitación, cámara, f.; lugar, espacio, m.

roommate, n. compañero o compañera de cuarto

roomy, adj. espacioso

rooster, n. gallo, m.

rope, n. cuerda, f.

rosary, n. rosario, m.

rose, n. (bot.) rosa, f.; color de rosa; pretérito del verbo **rise**

rotary engine, n. máquina rotativa, máquina alternativa

rotate, vt. y vi. girar, alternarse

rotten, adj. podrido, corrompido

rough, adj. áspero; brusco

round, adj. redondo

rout, vt. derrotar

route, n. ruta, vía, f.

routine, n. rutina, f.

row, n. riña, pelea, f.

row, n. hilera, fila, f.; vt. y vi. remar, bogar

rowboat, n. bote de remos m.

royal, adj. real; regio

royalty, n. realeza, f.; **royalties,** n. pl. regalías, f. pl.

R.R., railroad, f.c., ferrocarril; **Right Reverend,** Reverendísimo

R.S.V.P., please answer, sírvase enviar respuesta

rub, vt. frotar, restregar

rubber, n. goma, f., caucho, m.; **rubbers,** n. pl. chanclos, zapatos de goma, m. pl.; adj. de goma, de caucho

rubbish, n. basura, f.; desechos, m. pl.

ruby, n. rubí, m.

rude, adj. rudo, grosero

rug, n. alfombra, f.

ruin, n. ruina, f.; perdición, f.; vt. arruinar; echar a perder

rule, n. mando, m.; regla, f.; norma, f.; vt. y vi. gobernar; dirigir

ruler, n. gobernante, m.; regla, f.

Rumanian, n. y adj. rumano, rumana

rumba, n. rumba, f.

rumor, n. rumor, runrún, m.

run, vi. correr; fluir, manar

rural, adj. rural, rústico

rush, n. prisa, f.; vi. ir de prisa, apresurarse

Russia, Rusia

Russian, n. y adj. ruso, rusa

rusty, adj. mohoso; enmohecido

rut, n. rutina, f.; brama, f.

ruthless, adj. cruel

rye, n. centeno, m.

S

S.A., Salvation Army, Ejército de Salvación; **South America, S.A.,** Sud América; **South Africa,** Sud África

sabotage, n. sabotaje, m.

saccharine, n. sacarina, f.

sack, n. saco, talego, m.

sacrament, n. sacramento, m.

sacred, adj. sagrado

sacrifice, n. sacrificio, m.; vt. y vi. sacrificar

sad, adj. triste

sadness, n. tristeza, f.

safe, adj. seguro; salvo; n. caja fuerte, f.

safeguard, vt. proteger

safety, n. seguridad, f.; **safety pin,** alfiler de gancho, imperdible, m.

sage, n. y adj. sabio, m.

sail, n. vela, f.; vi. navegar

sailboat, n. buque de vela, m.

sailor, n. marinero, m.

saint, n. santo, santa

sake, n. causa, razón, f.; amor,

m., consideración, *f.*

salad, *n.* ensalada, *f.*

salary, *n.* salario, sueldo, *m.*

sale, *n.* venta, *f.*; barata, *f.*

salesman, *n.* vendedor, *m.*

saliva, *n.* saliva, *f.*

saloon, *n.* cantina, taberna, *f.*

salt, *n.* sal, *f.*

salty, *adj.* salado

salute, *vt.* saludar; *n.* saludo, *m.*

salvation, *n.* salvación, *f.*

salve, *n.* ungüento, *m.*, pomada *f.*

sanatorium, *n.* sanatorio, *m.*

sanction, *n.* sanción, *vt.* sancionar

sandal, *n.* sandalia, *f.*

sandwich, *n.* sandwich, emparedado, *m.*

sane, *adj.* sano, sensato

sanetarium, *n.* sanatorio, *m.*

sanitary, *adj.* sanitario

sanity, *n.* cordura, *f.*

sap, *n.* savia, *f.*

sapphire, *n.* zafiro, *m.*

sarcasm, *n.* sarcasmo, *m.*

sarcastic, *adj.* sarcástico

sardine, *n.* sardina, *f.*

sat, *pretérito* y *p. p.* del verbo **sit**

Sat., Saturday, sáb. sábado

Satan, *n.* Satanás, *m.*

satin, *n.* raso, *m.*

satisfaction, *n.* satisfacción, *f.*

satisfactory, *adj.* satisfactorio

satisfy, *vt.* satisfacer

Saturday, *n.* sábado, *m.*

sauce, *n.* salsa, *f.*

sausage, *n.* salchicha, *f.*

save, *vt.* salvar; economizar

saving, *adj.* económico; **savings**, *n. pl.* ahorros, *m. pl.*

Saviour, *n.* Redentor, *m.*

saw, *n.* sierra, *f.*; *vt.* serrar; *pretérito* del verbo **see**

scaffold, *n.* andamio, *m.*

scald, *vt.* escaldar

scale, *n.* balanza, *f.*; báscula, *f.*; escala, *f.*; escama, *f.*; *vt.* escalar

scalp, *n.* cuero cabelludo, *m.*

scandal, *n.* escándalo, *m.*

Scandinavia, Escandinavia

scant, scanty, *adj.* escaso,

parco

scarce, *adj.* raro; **scarcely**, *adv.* apenas, escasamente

scare, *n.* susto, *m.*; *vt.* espantar

scarf, *n.* bufanda, *f.*

scarlet, *n.* y *adj.* escarlata, *f.*; **scarlet fever**, escarlatina, *f.*

scatter, *vt.* y *vi.* esparcir, derramarse

scene, *n.* escena, *f.*

scenery, *n.* vista, *f.*; (theat.) decoración, *f.*

schedule, *n.* plan, programa, *m.*

scheme, *n.* proyecto, plan, *m.*

scholar, *n.* estudiante, *m.* y *f.*; erudito, erudita

scholarly, *adj.* erudito

scholarship, *n.* beca, *f.*

school, *n.* escuela, *f.*; **high school**, escuela secundaria, *f.*

schoolteacher, *n.* maestro o maestra de escuela

science, *n.* ciencia, *f.*

scientific, *adj.* científico

scissors, *n. pl.* tijeras, *f. pl.*

scoff, *vt.* mofarse

scold, *vt.* y *vi.* regañar

scooter, *n.* patineta, *f.*

scope, *n.* alcance, *m.*

scorched, *adj.* chamuscado

score, *n.* veintena, *f.*; (mus.) partitura, *f.*; tanteo, *m.*; *vt.* tantear; calificar; *vi.* hacer tantos

scorn, *vt.* y *vi.* despreciar; *n.* desdén, menosprecio, *m.*

Scotland, Escocia

scoundrel, *n.* infame, *m.* y *f.*

scout, *n.* (mil.) centinela avanzada; **boy scout**, niño explorador; **girl scout**, niña exploradora; *vt.* (mil.) explorar

scrap, *n.* migaja, *f.*

scrapbook, *n.* álbum de recortes, *m.*

scrape, *vt.* y *vi.* raspar; arañar; *n.* dificultad, *f.*, lío, *m.*

scratch, *vt.* rascar, raspar; borrar

scream, *vi.* chillar; *n.* chillido, grito, *m.*

screen, *n.* tamiz, *m.*; biombo,

m.; pantalla, f.; vt. tamizar

screw, n. tornillo, m.; clavo de
rosca, m.; **screw driver,** destornillador, m.; **to screw in,**
atornillar

Scripture, n. Escritura Sagra-
da, f.

scuba, n. escafandra autónoma, f.

sculptor, n. escultor, m.

sculptress, n. escultora, f.

sculpture, n. escultura, f.

sea, n. mar, m. y f.; **sea plane,**
hidroavión, m.

seal, n. sello, m.; (zool.) foca,
f.; vt. sellar

seam, n. costura, f.

seamstress, n. costurera, f.

search, vt. examinar, registrar;
escudriñar; busca, f.

seasick, adj. mareado

season, n. estación, f.; tiempo,
m.; vt. sazonar

seasoning, n. condimento, m.

seat, n. silla, f.; localidad, f.

seat belt, n. cinturón de seguridad, cinturón de asiento

second, adj. segundo; n. segundo, m.; vt. apoyar

secondary, adj. secundario

secondhand, adj. de ocasión;
de segunda mano

secrecy, n. secreto, m.

secret, n. secreto, m.; adj. privado

secretariat, n. secretaría, f.

secretary, n. secretario, secretaria

sect, n. secta, f.

section, n. sección, f.

secure, adj. seguro; salvo; vt.
asegurar; conseguir

security, n. seguridad, f.; defensa, f.; fianza, f.

sedative, n. y adj. sedante,
calmante, m.

seduce, vt. seducir

see, vt. y vi. ver, observar

seem, vi. parecer

seen, p. p. del verbo **see**

seep, vi. colarse, escurrirse

segregation, n. segregación, f.

seize, vt. agarrar, prender

seldom, adv. rara vez

select, vt. elegir, escoger; adj.

selecto, escogido

selection, n. selección, f.

self, adj. propio, mismo

self-controlled, adj. dueño de
sí mismo

self-defense, n. defensa pro-
pia, f.

self-denial, n. abnegación, f.

selfish, adj. egoísta

semester, n. semestre, m.

semicolon, n. punto y coma,
m.

semifinal, adj. semifinal

semimonthly, adj. quincenal

seminary, n. seminario, m.

Sen., sen., Senate, senado;
Senator, senador; **senior,**
padre; socio más antiguo o
más caracterizado

senate, n. senado, m.

senator, n. senador, m.

send, vt. enviar, mandar

senior, adj. mayor; n. estudiante de cuarto año, m.

seniority, n. antigüedad, f.

sense, n. sensatez, f.; **common sense,** sentido común,
m.

sensible, adj. juicioso

sensitive, adj. sensible; sensi-
tivo

sentence, n. sentencia, f.;
(gram.) oración, f.; vt. sentenciar, condenar

sentiment, n. sentimiento, m.;
opinión, f.

sentimental, adj. sentimental

separate, vt. y vi. separar; adj.
separado

separation, n. separación, f.

September, n. septiembre, m.

serenade, n. serenata, f.;
(Mex.) gallo, m.

serene, adj. sereno

serenity, n. serenidad, f.

series, n. serie, cadena, f.

serious, adj. serio, grave

sermon, n. sermón, m.

serpent, n. serpiente, f.

servant, n. criado, criada; sirviente, sirvienta

serve, vt. y vi. servir

service, n. servicio, m.; servi-
dumbre, f.

session, n. sesión, f.

set, *vt.* poner, colocar, fijar; *vi.* ponerse (el sol o los astros); cuajarse; *n.* juego, *m.*, colección, *f.*

settle, *vt.* arreglar; calmar; solventar (deudas); *vi.* establecerse, radicarse; sosegarse

settlement, *n.* establecimiento, *m.*; liquidación, *f.*

seven, *n.* y *adj.* siete, *m.*

seventeen, *adj.* y *n.* diez y siete, diecisiete, *m.*

seventeenth, *adj.* décimoséptimo

seventh, *adj.* séptimo

seventy, *n.* y *adj.* setenta, *m.*

several, *adj.* diversos, varios

severe, *adj.* severo

sew, *vt.* y *vi.* coser

sewage, *n.* inmundicias, *f. pl.*; **sewage system,** alcantarillado, *m.*

sewer, *n.* cloaca, alcantarilla, *f.*; caño, *m.*

sewing, *n.* costura, *f.*; **sewing machine,** máquina de coser, *f.*

sex, *n.* sexo, *m.*

sexual, *adj.* sexual

shabby, *adj.* destartalado

shack, *n.* choza, cabaña, *f.*

shade, *n.* sombra, *f.*; matiz, *m.*

shadow, *n.* sombra, *f.*

shady, *adj.* opaco; sospechoso

shake, *vt.* sacudir; agitar; *vi.* temblar; **to shake hands,** darse las manos; *n.* sacudida, *f.*

shape, *vt.* y *vi.* formar; *n.* forma, figura, *f.*

share, *n.* parte, cuota, *f.*; (com.) acción, *f.*; participación, *f.*; *vt.* y *vi.* compartir

shark, *n.* tiburón, *m.*

sharp, *adj.* agudo, astuto; afilado; *n.* (mus.) sostenido, *m.*; **two o'clock sharp,** las dos en punto

sharpener, *n.* afilador, amolador, *m.*; **pencil sharpener,** tajalápices, *m.*

shatter, *vt.* y *vi.* destrozar, estrellar

shawl, *n.* chal, mantón, *m.*

she, *pron.* ella

sheep, *n. sing.* y *pl.* oveja(s), *f.*; carnero, *m.*

sheepish, *adj.* timido, cortado

sheet, *n.* pliego (de papel), *m.*; **bed sheet,** sábana, *f.*

shell, *n.* cáscara, *f.*; concha, *f.*; *vt.* descascarar, descortezar

shelter, *n.* asilo, refugio, *m.*

shepherd, *n.* pastor, *m.*

sheriff, *n.* alguacil, *m.*, funcionario administrativo de un condado

sherry, *n.* jerez, *m.*

shield, *n.* escudo, *m.*; *vt.* defender; amparar;

shift, *vt.* y *vi.* cambiarse; ingeniarse; *n.* tanda, *f.*

shin, *n.* espinilla, *f.*

shine, *vi.* lucir, brillar; *vt.* dar lustre (a los zapatos , etc.); *n.* brillo, *m.*

shining, *adj.* reluciente

shiny, *adj.* brillante

ship, *n.* buque, barco, *m.*; *vt.* embarcar; expedir

shipment, *n.* embarque, *m.*, remesa, *f.*

shirk, *vt.* esquivar, evitar

shirt, *n.* camisa, *f.*

shock, *n.* choque, *m.*; conmoción, *f.*; *vt.* chocar; sacudir; conmover; **shock absorber,** amortiguador, *m.*

shocking, *adj.* ofensivo

shoe, *n.* zapato, *m.*

shoemaker, *n.* zapatero, *m.*

shone, *pretérito* y *p. p.* del verbo **shine**

shop, *n.* tienda, *f.*; *vt.* hacer compras

shopping, *n.* compras, *f. pl.*

short, *adj.* corto; conciso

shorten, *vt.* acortar; abreviar

shortening, *n.* acortamiento, *m.*; manteca o grasa vegetal, *f.*

shorthand, *n.* taquigrafia, *f.*

shorts, *n. pl.* calzoncillos, *m. pl.*; pantalones cortos, *m. pl.*

shortsighted, *adj.* miope

shot, *n.* tiro, *m.*

shotgun, *n.* escopeta, *f.*

should, *subj.* y *condicional* de **shall**; usase como auxiliar de otros verbos

shoulder, n. hombro, m.

shout, vi. aclamar; gritar

shovel, n. pala, f.

show, vt. mostrar, enseñar, probar; n. espectáculo, m. función, f.

shower, n. aguacero, m.; vi. llover; vt. derramar profusamente

shrank, pretérito del verbo **shrink**

shred, n. triza, f.; jirón, m.; vt. picar, rallar

shrimp, n. camarón, m.

shrink, vi. encogerse

shrunk, p. p. del verbo **shrink**

shudder, vi. estremecerse

shut, vt. cerrar, encerrar

shy, adj. tímido

sick adj. malo, enfermo

sickly, adj. enfermizo

sickness, n. enfermedad, f.

side, n. lado, m.; costado, m.; facción, f.; partido, m.; adj. lateral

sidewalk, n. banqueta, acera, f.

sideways, adv. de lado

sift, vt. cerner; cribar

sigh, vi. suspirar, gemir; n. suspiro, m.

sign, n. señal, f., indigo, m.; signo, m.; letrero, m.; vt. y vi. firmar

signal, n. señal, seña, f.

signature, n. firma, f.

significance, n. importancia, significación, f.

silence, n. silencio, m.

silent, adj. silencioso

silk, n. seda, f.

silkscreen, n. serigrafía, f.

silky, adj. sedoso

sill, n. alfeiza, f.

silly, adj. tonto, bobo

silver, n. plata, f.

silvery, adj. plateado

similar, adj. similar

simple, adj. simple

simplicity, n. simplicidad, f.

simplify, vt. simplificar

simply, adv. simplemente

simultaneous, adj. simultáneo

sin, n. pecado, m., culpa, f.; vi.

pecar, faltar

since, adv. desde entonces; conj. puesto que; prep. desde, después

sincere, adj. sincere, franco

sincerity, n. sinceridad, f.

sinew, n. tendón, m.

sinful, adj. pecaminoso

sing, vt. y vi. cantar

singe, vt. chamuscar

singer, n. cantante, m. y f.

singing, n. canto, m.

single, adj. solo; soltero, soltera

sink, vt. y vi. hundir; n. fregadero, m.

sinner, n. pecador, pecadora

sinus, n. seno (cavidad) m.

sip, vt. y vi. sorber; n. sorbo, m.

sir, n. señor, m.

siren, n. sirena, f.

sister, n. hermana, f.

sister-in-law, n. cuñada, f.

sit, vi. sentarse

situation, n. situación, f.

six, n. y adj. seis, m.

sixteen, n. y adj. diez y seis, dieciseis

sixteenth, adj. y n. décimosexto, m.

sixth, n. y adj. sexto, m.

sixty, n. y adj. sesenta, m.

size, n. tamaño, m., talla, f.

sizzle, vi. chamuscar

skate, n. patín, m.; **ice skate,** patin de hielo, m.; **roller skate,** patín de ruedas, m.; vi. patinar

skeleton, n. esqueleto, m.; **skeleton key,** llave maestra, f.

sketch, n. esbozo, m.; bosquejo, m.; vt. bosquejar, esbozar

skill, n. destreza, pericia, f.

skillet, n. cazuela, sartén, f.

skilful, skilful, adj. práctico, diestro

skin, n. cutis, m.; piel, f.

skinny, adj. flaco

skip, vi. saltar, brincar; vt. pasar, omitir; n. salto, brinco, m.

skunk, n. zorrillo, zorrino, m.

sky, n. cielo, m.

skylight, n. claraboya, f.

skyscraper, n. rascacielos, m.

slander, vt. calumniar, infamar; n. calumnia, f.

slang, n. vulgarismo, m.

slap, n. manotada, f.; **slap on the face,** bofetada, f.; vt. dar una bofetada

slave, n. esclavo, esclava

slavery, n. esclavitud, f.

slay, vt. matar

slayer, n. asesino, m.

sleep, vi. dormir; n. sueño, m.

sleepless, adj. desvelado

sleepy, adj. soñoliento

sleet, n. cellisca, aguanieve, f.

sleeve, n. manga, f.

sleeveless, adj. sin mangas

slender, adj. delgado

slice, n. rebanada, f.; vt. rebanar, tajar

slide, vt. correr; vi. deslizarse; n. diapositiva, f.; **slide projector,** linterna de proyección, f.

slight, adj. leve; n. desaire, m.; vt. desairar

slim, adj. delgado, sutil

sling, n. honda, f.

slip, n. resbalón, m.; enagua, f.; vi. resbalar

slipper, n. zapatilla, f.

sloppy, adj. desaliñado

slot, n. hendedura, f.

slow, adj. tardío, lento; adv. despacio

slums, n. pl. barrios bajos, m. pl.; viviendas escuálidas, f. pl.

slumber, vt. dormitar; n. sueño ligero

slush, n. lodo, cieno, m.

sly, adj. astuto; furtivo

small, adj. pequenño, chico

smallpox, n. viruelas, f. pl.

smart, adj. inteligente; elegante

smear, vt. manchar; calumniar,

smell, vt. y vi. oler; olfatear; n. olfato, m.; olor, m.; hediondez, f.

smile, vi. sonreir, sonreirse; n. sonrisa, f.

smoke, n. humo, m.; vt. y vi. ahumar; fumar (tabaco)

smooth, adj. liso, pulido

smother, vt. sofocar

smuggling, n. contrabando, m.

snake, n. culebra, f.

snap, vt. y vi. romper; chasquear

snappy, adj. vivaz, animado

snapshot, n. instantánea, fotografía, f.

snare, n. trampa, f.

snarl, vi. enredar

snatch, vt. arrebatar

sneeze, vi. estornudar; n. estornudo, m.

sniff, vt. olfatear

snoop, vi. espiar, acechar

snooze, vi. dormitar

snore, vi. roncar

snow, n. nieve, f.; vi. nevar

snowfall, n. nevada, f.

snowflake, n. copo de nieve, m.

snowmobile, n. vehículo automotor para marchar sobre la nieve

snowshoe, n. raqueta de nieve, f.

so, adv. así; tal

So., South, S., Sur

soak, vt. y vi. remojar

soap, n. jabón, m.

soar, vi. remontarse

sob, n. sollozo, m.; vi. sollozar

sober, adj. sobrio; serio

soccer, n. futbol, m.

sociable, adj. sociable

social, adj. social; sociable; **social worker,** asistente social

socialism, n. socialismo, m.

socialize, vt. socializar; **socialized medicine,** medicina estatal

society, n. sociedad, f.; compañía, f.

sociology, n. sociología, f.

sock, n. calcetín, m.

socket, n. enchufe, m.; cuenca (del ojo), f.

sod, n. césped, m.; tierra, f.

soda, n. sosa, soda, f.; **baking soda,** bicarbonato de sosa o de soda

sofa, n. sofá, m.

soft, *adj.* blando, suave

soft-boiled, *adj.* pasado por agua

soften, *vt.* ablandar

soggy, *adj.* empapado

soil, *vt.* ensuciar, emporcar; *n.* tierra, *f.*

solar, *adj.* solar; **solar battery,** batería solar; **solar energy,** energía solar

sold, *p. p.* vendido

soldier, *n.* soldado, *m.*

sole, *n.* planta, *f.*; suela, *f.*; *adj.* único, solo

solicit, *vt.* solicitar; pedir

solid, *adj.* sólido, compacto; entero; *n.* sólido, *m.*

solid-fuel space rocket, *n.* cohete especial de combustible sólido, *m.*

solitary, *adj.* solitario

solitude, *n.* soledad, *f.*

solo, *n.* y *adj.* solo, *m.*

solve, *vt.* resolver, solucionar

some, *adj.* algún; cierto; algo de

somebody, *pron.* alguno, alguna

somehow, *adv.* de algún modo

something, *n.* alguna cosa; algo, *m.*; **something else,** alguna otra cosa

sometimes, *adv.* a veces

somewhere, *adv.* en alguna parte

son, *n.* hijo, *m.*

sonic barrier, *n.* obstáculo sonic *m.*

sonic boom, *n.* trueno sónico, estrépito sónico, *m.*

son-in-law, *n.* yerno, *m.*

soothe, *vt.* calmar, sosegar

sophisticated, *adj.* refinado; complicado

soprano, *n.* soprano, tiple, *m.* y *f.*

sore, *n.* llaga, úlcera, *f.*; *adj.* doloroso penoso; (coll.) enojado, resentido

sorority, *n.* hermandad de mujeres, *f.*

sorry, *adj.* triste; afligido

soul, *n.* alma, *f.*; esencia, *f.*

sound, *adj.* sano; entero; *n.* sonido, *m.*; *vt.* sondar; *vi.* sonar, resonar

soup, *n.* sopa, *f.*

sour, *adj.* agrio, ácido; *vt.* y *vi.* agriar, agriarse

south, *n.* sur, sud, *m.*

southeast, *n.* sureste, sudeste, *m.*

southern, *adj.* meridional

southwest, *n.* sudoeste, *m.*

souvenir, *n.* recuerdo, *m.*

sovereign, *n.* y *adj.* soberano, soberana

soviet, *n.* soviet, *m.*

sow, *n.* puerca, marrana, *f.*

sow, *vt.* sembrar, sementar

soybean, *n.* soya, *f.*

space, *n.* espacio, *m.*; lugar, *m.*; **space capsule,** cabina espacial; **space travel,** viajes espaciales o siderales

spaceship, *n.* astronave, *f.*

spacious, *adj.* espacioso

spade, *n.* azadón, *m.*; espada (naipe),

Spain, España, *f.*

span, *n.* espacio, trecho, *m.*

Spaniard, *n.* y *adj.* español, española

Spanish, *adj.* español

spank, *vt.* pegar, dar nalgadas

spare, *vt.* y *vi.* ahorrar, evitar; *adj.* de reserva; **spare time,** tiempo desocupado; **spare tire,** neumático o llanta de repuesto

spark, *n.* chispa, *f.*

spat, *n.* riña, *f.*; *vi.* reñir

spats, *n. pl.* polainas, *f. pl.*

speak, *vt.* y *vi.* hablar

speaker, *n.* orador, oradora

spear, *n.* lanza, *f.*; pica, *f.*

spearmint, *n.* hierbabuena, *f.*

special, *adj.* especial

specialize, *vt.* y *vi.* especializar

specimen, *n.* muestra, *f.*

spectacle, *n.* espectáculo, *m.*; **spectacles,** *n. pl.* anteojos, espejuelos, *m. pl.*

spectacular, *adj.* espectacular

spectator, *n.* espectador, espectadora

speculate, *vi.* especular

speech, *n.* habla, *f.*; discurso, *m.*

speechless, *adj.* sin habla
speed, *n.* rapidez, *f.*; *vt.* apresurar; *vi.* darse prisa
speedy, *adj.* veloz
spell, *n.* hechizo, encanto, *m.*; *vt. y vi.* deletrear
spelling, *n.* ortografía, *f.*; deletreo, *m.*
spend, *vt.* gastar; consumir
spendthrift, *n.* botarate, *m. y f.*
sphere, *n.* esfera, *f.*
spider, *n.* araña, *f.*
spill, *vt.* derramar, verter
spin, *vt.* hilar; *vt. y vi.* girar; *n.* vuelta, *f.*; paseo, *m.*
spinach, *n.* espinaca, *f.*
spinal, *adj.* espinal; **spinal column,** columna vertebral, espina dorsal, *f.*
spine, *n.* espina, *f.*
spiral, *adj.* espiral
spirit, *n.* espíritu, *m.*; ánimo, valor, *m.*; fantasma, *m.*
spirited, *adj.* vivo, brioso
spiritual, *adj.* espiritual
spit, *vt. y vi.* escupir
spite, *n.* rencor, *m.*; **in spite of,** a pesar de
spiteful, *adj.* rencoroso
splash, *vt.* salpicar
splendid, *adj.* espléndido
splint, *n.* astilla, *f.*; **splints,** *n. pl.* tablillas para entablillar
splinter, *n.* astilla, *f.*
split, *vt. y vi.* hender, rajar; *n.* hendidura, raja, *f.*
spleen, *n.* bazo, *m.*; esplín, *m.*
spoil, *vt. y vi.* dañar; pudrir; mimar demasiado; **spoils,** *n. pl.* despojo, botín, *m.*
spoke, *n.* rayo de rueda, *m.*; *pretérito del verbo* **speak**
sponsor, *n.* fiador, *m.*; padrino, *m.*; garante, *m. y f.*; anunciante (de un programa de radio, etc.), *m.*
spontaneous, *adj.* espontáneo
spool, *n.* bobina, carrete, carretel, *m.*
spoon, *n.* cuchara, *f.*
spoonful, *n.* cucharada, *f.*
sport, *n.* recreo, pasatiempo, *m.*; deporte, *m.*
sportsman, *n.* deportista, *m.*

spot, *n.* mancha, *f.*; sitio, lugar, *m.*; *vt.* manchar
spotless, *adj.* sin mancha
spotlight, *n.* proyector, *m.*
spouse, *n.* esposo, esposa
sprain, *vt.* dislocar; *n.* torcedura, *f.*
sprang, *pretérito del verbo* **spring**
spray, *vt.* rociar, pulverizar
spread, *vt. y vi.* extender; *n.* sobrecama, colcha, *f.*
spring, *vi.* brotar; provenir; saltar, brincar; *n.* primavera, *f.*; elasticidad, *f.*; muelle, resorte, *m.*
sprinkle, *vt.* rociar; salpicar; *vi.* lloviznar
spur, *n.* espuela, *f.*; **on the spur of the moment,** en un impulso repentino; *vt.* estimular
sputnik, *n.* sputnik, *m.*, satélite artificial
spy, *n.* espía, *m. y f.*; *vt. y vi.* espiar
sq., square, cuadrado, *m.*; plaza, *f.*
squabble, *vi.* reñir; *n.* riña, *f.*
squander, *vt.* malgastar
square, *adj.* cuadrado; equitativo; *n.* cuadro, *m.*; plaza, *f.*; *vt.* cuadrar; ajustar
squaw, *n.* mujer india de E.U.A
squeal, *vi.* gritar; delatar
squeeze, *vt.* apretar, estrechar; *n.* abrazo, *m.*; apretón, *m.*
squirrel, *n.* ardilla, *f.*
S.S., steamship, v., vapor; **Sunday School,** escuela dominical
St., Saint, Sto., San, Santo; Sta., Santa; **Strait,** Estrecho; **Street,** Calle
stable, *n.* establo, *m.*; *adj.* estable
stadium, *n.* estadio, *m.*
staff, *n.* báculo, palo, *m.*; personal, *m.*
stag, *n.* ciervo, *m.*; **stag party,** tertulia para hombres, *f.*
stage, *n.* escenario, *m.*; teatro, *m.*, las tablas, *f. pl.*; *vt.* poner

en escena

stagecoach, n. diligencia, f.

stagger, vi. vacilar, titubear; vt. escalonar, alternar

stainless, adj. limpio, inmaculado; inoxidable

stair, n. escalón, m.; **stairs**, n. pl. escalera, f.

stairway, n. escalera, f.

stake, n. estaca, f.; vt. apostar; arriesgar

stale, adj. viejo, rancio

stamina, n. resistencia, f.

stamp, vt. patear, dar golpes (con los pies); estampar, imprimir, sellar; n. sello, m.; estampa, f.; timbre, m.; **postage stamp**, sello de correo, m.

stand, vi. estar en pie o derecho; sostenerse; resistir; pararse; n. puesto, sitio, m.; tarima, f.

standard, n. norma, f.; **standard of living**, nivel o norma de vida; adj. normal

starch, n. almidón, m.; vt. almidonar

stare, vt. clavar la vista; n. mirada fija, f.

start, vi. sobrecogerse, estremecerse; vt. comenzar; n. sobresalto, m.; principio, m.

starter, n. iniciador, iniciadora; (auto.) arranque, m.

starve, vi. perecer de hambre

state, n. estado, m.; condición, f.; vt. declarar

statement, n. estado de cuenta, m.; declaración, f.

stateroom, n. camarote, m.; compartimiento, m.

statesman, n. estadista, m.

station, n. estación, **station wagon**, camioneta, f.

stationary, adj. estacionario, fijo

stationery, n. papel de escribir, m.

statistics, n. pl. estadística, f.

statue, n. estatua, f.

staunch, adj. firme; fiel

stay, n. permanencia, f.; vi. quedarse, permanecer

steady, adj. firme, fijo

steak, n. bistec, m.

steam, n. vapor, m.; **steamroller**, apisonadora, f.

steamship, n. vapor, m.

steep, adj. empinado

steeple, n. campanario, m.

steer, n. novillo, m.; vt. guiar, dirigir

stenographer, n. taquígrafo, taquígrafa, estenógrafo, estenógrafa; mecanógrafo, mecanógrafa

stenography, n. taquigrafía, estenografía

step, n. paso, escalón, m.; trámite, m.; gestión, f.; vi. dar un paso; andar; vt. pisar

stepbrother, n. medio hermano, hermanastro, m.

stepdaughter, n. hijastra, f.

stepfather, n. padrastro, m.

stepladder, n. escalera de mano, f.

stepmother, n. madrastra, f.

stepson, n. hijastro, m.

stereophonic, adj. estereofónico, estereofónica

sterling, adj. genuino, verdadero; **sterling silver**, plata esterlina,

stern, adj. austero, severo; n. (naut.) popa, f.

stew, vt. guisar; n. guisado, guiso, m.

steward, n. mayordomo, m.

stewardess, n. (avi.) azafata, aeromoza, f.

stick, n. palo, bastón, m.; vi. pegarse

sticky, adj. pegajoso

stiff, adj. tieso; rígido

stifle, vt. sofocar

still, vt. aquietar, aplacar; destilar; adj. silencioso, tranquilo; adv. todavía; no obstante

stilt, n. zanco, m.

stimulate, vt. estimular

stimulation, n. estímulo, m.

sting, vt. picar o morder (un insecto); n. aguijón m.

stingy, adj. tacaño, avaro

stipulate, vt. y vi. estipular

stir, vt. agitar; revolver; incitar

stirring, adj. emocionante

stitch, vt. coser; n. puntada,

f.; punto, *m.*

stock, *n.* linaje, *m.*; (com.) capital, principal, *m.*; (com.) acción, *f.*; ganado, *m.*; proveer, abastecer

stockholder, *n.* accionista, *m.* y *f.*

stole, *n.* estola, *f.*; *pretérito* del verbo **steal**

stomach, *n.* estómago, *m.*

stone, *n.* piedra, *f.*; hueso de fruta, *m.*; *vt.* apedrear; deshuesar

stood, *pretérito* y *p. p.* del verbo **stand**

stool, *n.* banquillo, *m.*; evacuación, *f.*

stop, *vt.* cesar, suspender, *vi.* pararse, hacer alto; *n.* parada, *f.*

store, *n.* almacén, *m.*; *vt.* proveer, abastecer

storeroom, *n.* deposito, *m.*

stork, *n.* cigüeña, *f.*

storm, *n.* tempestad, *f.*; *vi.* haber tormenta

stormy, *adj.* tempestuoso

story, *n.* cuento, *m.*; piso de una casa, *m.*

straight, *adj.* derecho, recto; *adv.* directamente, en línea recta

straighten, *vt.* enderezar

strain, *vt.* colar, filtrar; *vi.* esforzarse; *n.* tensión, tirantez, *f.*

strainer, *n.* colador, *m.*

strange, *adj.* extraño; raro

stranger, *n.* extranjero, extranjera

strap, *n.* correa, *f.*

strategy, *n.* estrategia, *f.*

strawberry, *n.* fresa; (Sp. Am.) frutilla, *f.*

stray, *vi.* extraviarse

stream, *n.* arroyo, *m.*; corriente, *f.*

streamline, *vt.* simplificar

street, *n.* calle, *f.*

streetcar, *n.* tranvía, *m.*

strength, *n.* fuerza, *f.*

strengthen, *vt.* reforzar

strenuous, *adj.* estrenuo

stress, *n.* fuerza, *f.*; acento, *m.*; tensión *f.*; *vt.* acentuar, dar énfasis

stretch, *vt.* y *vi.* tirar; extenderse

stretcher, *n.* estirador, *m.*; camilla, *f.*

strict, *adj.* estricto, riguroso

stride, *n.* tranco, *m.*; adelanto, avance, *m.*; *vt.* cruzar, pasar por encima; *vi.* andar a pasos largos

strike, *vt.* y *vi.* golpear; declararse en huelga

striking, *adj.* llamativo

string, *n.* cordón, *m.*; cuerda, *f.*; hilera, *f.*; **string bean,** habichuela verde, judía, *f.*, (Mex.) ejote, *m.*

strip, *n.* tira, faja, *f.*; *vt.* desnudar, despojar

stripe, *n.* raya, lista, *f.*

striped, *adj.* rayado

stroboscope, *n.* estroboscopio, *m.*

stroke, *n.* golpe, *m.*; caricia, *f.*; *vt.* acariciar

stroll, *vi.* vagar, pasearse, *m.*

strong, *adj.* fuerte

structure, *n.* edificio, *m.*

struggle, *n.* lucha, *f.*; *vi.* luchar

stubborn, *adj.* testarudo

student, *n.* estudiante, estudianta, alumno, alumna

studio couch, *n.* sofá cama

study, *n.* estudio, *m.*; gabinete, *m.*; *vt.* estudiar

stuff, *n.* materia, *f.*; *vt.* llenar; rellenar; *vi.* abracarse; tragar

stuffing, *n.* relleno, *m.*

stumble, *vt.* tropezar

stupendous, *adj.* estupendo

stupid, *adj.* estúpido

stupidity, *n.* estupidez, *f.*

sturdy, *adj.* fuerte, robusto

style, *n.* estilo, *m.*; moda, *f.*

stylish, *adj.* elegante, de moda

subconscious, *adj.* subconsciente

subject, *n.* tema, tópico, *m.*; asignatura, *f.*; *adj.* sujeto, sometido a; *vt.* sujetar, someter

submarine, *n.* y *adj.* submarino, *m.*

submerge, *vt.* sumergir

submission, *n.* sumisión, *f.*

submit, *vt.* someter, rendir

subordinate, *n.* y *adj.* subalterno, *m.*; *vt.* subordinar

subscribe, *vt.* y *vi.* suscribir

subscriber, *n.* suscriptor, suscriptora, abonado, abonada

subscription, *n.* suscripción, *f.*, abono, *m.*

subsequent, *adj.* subsiguiente, subsecuente

subsist, *vi.* subsistir; existir

substance, *n.* sustancia, *f.*

substantive, *n.* sustantivo, *m.*

substitute, *vt.* sustituir; *n.* suplente, *m.*

substitution, *n.* sustitución, *f.*

subtle, *adj.* sutil

subtract, *vt.* sustraer; restar

subtraction, *n.* sustracción, *f.*; resta, *f.*

suburb, *n.* suburbio, *m.*

suburban, *adj.* suburbano

subway, *n.* túnel, *m.*; ferrocarril subterráneo, *m.*

sucaryl, *n.* nombre comercial de un compuesto ezucarado parecido a la sacarina

succeed, *vt.* y *vi.* lograr, tener éxito; seguir

success, *n.* buen éxito, *m.*

successful, *adj.* próspero, dichoso; **to be successful,** tener buen éxito

succession, *n.* sucesión, *f.*; herencia, *f.*

successor, *n.* sucesor, sucesora

such, *adj.* y *pron.* tal, semejante

sudden, *adj.* repentino; **suddenly,** *adv.* de repente

sue, *vt.* y *vi.* demandar, poner pleito

suffer, *vt.* y *vi.* sufrir

suffice, *vt.* y *vi.* bastar

sufficient, *adj.* suficiente

suffocate, *vt.* y *vi.* sofocar

sufrage, *n.* sufragio, voto, *m.*

sugar, *n.* azúcar, *m.* y *f.*

suicide, *n.* suicidio, *m.*; suicida, *m.* y *f.*

suit, *n.* vestido, *m.*; traje, *m.*; pleito, *m.*; *vt.* y *vi.* adaptar; ajustarse; *vt.* sentar, caer bien

suitable, *adj.* adecuado

suitcase, *n.* maleta, *f.*

sulky, *adj.* malhumorado

sulphur, *n.* azufre, *m.*

sum, *n.* suma, *f.*

summary, *n.* sumario, *m.*

summer, *n.* verano, *m.*

summertime, *n.* verano, *m.*

summit, *n.* cumbre, *f.*

summon, *vt.* citar, convocar

sun, *n.* sol, *m.*

sunbeam, *n.* rayo de sol, *m.*

Sunday, *n.* domingo, *m.*

sunflower, *n.* girasol, *m.*

sung, *p. p.* del verbo **sing**

sunken, *p. p.* del verbo **sink**

sunlight, *n.* luz del sol, *f.*

sunny, *adj.* asoleado; alegre

sunrise, *n.* salida del sol, *f.*

sunset, *n.* ocaso, *f.*

sunshine, *n.* luz del sol, *f.*

sunstroke, *n.* insolación, *f.*

superb, *adj.* excelente

superhighway, *n.* supercarretera, *f.*

superhuman, *adj.* sobrehumano

superintendent, *n.* superintendente, mayordomo, *m.*

superior, *n.* y *adj.* superior, *m.*

superiority, *n.* superioridad, *f.*

superlative, *adj.* y *n.* superlativo, *m.*

superman, *n.* superhombre, *m.*

supermarket, *n.* supermercado, *m.*

supernatural, *adj.* sobrenatural

superpower, *n.* superpotencia, *f.*

superstitious, *adj.* supersticioso

supervise, *vt.* inspeccionar

supervision, *n.* dirección, inspección, *f.*

supervisor, *n.* superintendente, *m.* y *f.*; inspector, inspectora

supper, *n.* cena, *f.*

supply, *vt.* suplir, proporcionar; *n.* surtido, *m.*; provisión, *f.*; **supply and demand,** oferta y demanda

support, *vt.* sostener; soportar; basar; *n.* sustento, *m.*; apoyo, *m.*

suppose, *vt.* suponer

supposition, *n.* suposición, *f.*, supuesto, *m.*

suppress, *vt.* suprimir; reprimir

supremacy, *n.* supremacia, *f.*

supreme, *adj.* supremo

Supt., supt., superintendent, super.**te**, superintendente

sure, *adj.* seguro, cierto; **surely,** *adv.* sin duda

surgeon, *n.* cirujano, *m.*

surgery, *n.* cirugía, *f.*

surgical, *adj.* quirúrgico

surname, *n.* apellido, *m.*

surplus, *n.* sobrante, *m.*

surprise, *vt.* sorprender; *n.* sorpresa, *f.*

surprising, *adj.* sorprendente

surrender, *vt.* y *vi.* rendir; renunciar; *n.* rendición, *f.*

surround, *vt.* circundar, rodear

surroundings, *n. pl.* cercanías, *f. pl.*; ambiente, *m.*

survey, *vt.* inspeccionar, examinar; *n.* inspección, *f.*; apeo (de tierras), *m.*

surveying, *n.* agrimensura, *f.*

survive, *vt.* sobrevivir

survivor, *n.* sobreviviente, *m.* y *f.*

susceptible, *adj.* susceptible

suspect, *vt.* y *vi.* sospechar

suspend, *vt.* suspender, colgar

suspenders, *n. pl.* tirantes, *m. pl.*

suspense, *n.* incertidumbre, *f.*

suspicion, *n.* sospecha, *f.*

suspicious, *adj.* sospechoso

sustain, *vt.* sostener, sustentar

sustenance, *n.* sostenimiento, sustento, *m.*

SW, S.W., s.w., southwest, SO., Sudoeste

swallow, *n.* golondrina, *f.*; bocado, *m.*; *vt.* tragar

swam, *pretérito* del verbo **swim**

swan, *n.* cisne, *m.*

swap, *vt.* y *vi.* (coll.) cambalachear, cambiar

swarm, *n.* enjambre, *m.*; gentío, *m.*

swear, *vt.* y *vi.* jurar; juramentar

sweat, *n.* sudor, *m.*; *vi.* sudar; trasudar

sweater, *n.* suéter, *m.*

Sweden, Suecia

sweet, *adj.* dulce; grato

sweeten, *vt.* endulzar

sweetheart, *n.* novio, novia

sweetness, *n.* dulzura, *f.*

swell, *vi.* hincharse; *adj.* (coll.) espléndido

swelling, *n.* hinchazón, *f.*

swelter, *vi.* ahogarse de calor

swim, *vi.* nadar

swimming, *n.* natación, *f.*

swindle, *vt.* estafar; *n.* estafa, *f.*, petardo, *m.*

swing, *vt.* balancear, oscilar; mecerse; columpio, *m.*

switch, *n.* (elec.) interruptor, conmutador, *m.*; *vt.* desviar

switchboard, *n.* conmutador telefónico, *m.*

Switzerland, Suiza

swivel, *vt.* y *vi.* girar

swollen, *adj.* hinchado, inflado

sword, *n.* espada, *f.*

swordfish, *n.* pez espada, *m.*

swore, *pretérito* del verbo **swear**

sworn, *p. p.* del verbo **swear**

syllable, *n.* sílaba, *f.*

symbol, *n.* símbolo, *m.*

symbolic, *adj.* simbólico

sympathize, *vi.* simpatizar

sympathy, *n.* compasión, condolencia, *f.*; simpatía, *f.*

symphony, *n.* sinfonía, *f.*

symptom, *n.* síntoma, *m.*

syndicate, *n.* sindicato, *f.*

synonym, *n.* sinónimo, *m.*

synopsis, *n.* sinopsis, *f.*

synthesis, *n.* síntesis, *m.*

synthetic, *adj.* sintético

syrup, *n.* jarabe, *m.*

system, *n.* sistema, *m.*

T

table, *n.* mesa, *f.*

tablecloth, *n.* mantel, *m.*

tablespoon, n. cuchara, f.

tablespoonful, n. cucharada, f.

tablet, n. tableta, f.; pastilla, f.; (med.) oblea, f.

taboo, tabu, n. tabú, m.; adj. prohibido

tact, n. tacto, m.

tactful, adj. prudente

tactics, n. pl. táctica, f.

tactless, adj. sin tacto

taffeta, n. tafetán, m.

tail, n. cola, f., rabo, m.

tailor, n. sastre, m.

take, vt. tomar, coger, asir

talcum, n. talco, m.

tale, n. cuento, m.

talent, n. talento, m.; ingenio, m.; capacidad, f.

talk, vi. hablar, conversar; n. plática, charla, f.

tall, adj. alto, elevado

tallow, n. sebo, m.

tambourine, n. pandereta, f.

tame, adj. domesticado; manso; vt. domesticar

tang, n. sabor, m.

tangerine, n. mandarina f.

tangle, vt. y vi. enredar, embrollar

tango, n. tango, m.

tank, n. (mil) tanque, m.

tantalizing, adj. atormentador

tap, vt. tocar o golpear ligeramente; n. palmada suave, f.; **tap dance**, baile zapateado (de E. U. A.)

tape, n. cinta, f.; vt. vendar; grabar; **tape recorder**, magnetófono, m.

tar, n. alquitrán, m.

tardiness, n. tardanza, f.

tardy, adj. tardío; lento

target, n. blanco, m.; meta, f.

tariff, n. tarifa, f.

taste, n. gusto, m.; sabor, m.; vt. y vi. probar; tener sabor

tasteful, adj. de buen gusto

tasteless, adj. insípido

tasty, adj. gustoso

tattered, adj. andrajoso

tattletale, n. chismoso, chismosa

tavern, n. taberna, f.

tax, n. impuesto, m., contribu-

ción, f.; **income tax**, impuesto de rentas; vt. imponer tributos

taxi, n. taxímetro, m.

taxicab, n. taxímetro, automóvil de alquiler, m.; (Mex.) libre, m.

tea, n. té, m.

teach, vt. enseñar, instruir

teacher, n. maestro, maestra, profesor, profesora

teaching, n. enseñanza, f.

teacup, n. taza para té, f.

teakettle, n. tetera, f.

team, n. tiro de caballos, m.; (deportes) equipo, m.

teapot, n. tetera, f.

tear, vt. despedazar; n. rasgón, jirón, n.

tear, n. lágrima, f.

tearoom, n. salón de té, m.

teaspoon, n. cucharita, f.

teat, n. ubre, f.; teta, f.

technical, adj. técnico

technician, n. técnico, m.

technique, n. técnica, f.

tedious, adj. fastidioso

teen-ager, n. adolescente, m. y f.

teens, n. pl. números y años desde 13 hasta 20; periodo de trece a diecinueve años de edad

teeth, n. pl. de **tooth**, dientes, m. pl.

telecast, vt. y vi. televisar; n. teledifusión, f.

telegram, n. telegrama, m.

telegraph, n. telégrafo, m.; vt. telegrafiar

telepathy, n. telepatía, f.

telephone, n. teléfono, m.; **dial telephone**, teléfono automático, m.; vt. y vi. telefonear

teleprompter, n. apuntador electrónico, m.

telescope, n. telescopio, m.

television, n. televisión f.; **television set**, telerreceptor, aparto de televisión

temper, n. temperamento, m.; humor, genio, m.

temperament, n. temperamento, m.; carácter, genio, m.

temperate, *adj.* templado, moderado, sobrio

temperature, *n.* temperatura, *f.*

tempest, *n.* tempestad, *f.*

temple, *n.* templo, *m.*; sien, *f.*

temporarily, *adj.* temporalmente

tempt, *vt.* tentar; provocar

temptation, *n.* tentación, *f.*

tempting, *adj.* tentador

ten, *n.* y *adj.* diez, *m.*

tenant, *n.* inquilino, inquilina

tendency, *n.* tendencia, *f.*

tender, *adj.* tierno, delicado

tenderloin, *n.* filete, solomillo, *m.*

tenderness, *n.* terneza, *f.*

tennis, *n.* tenis, *m.*

tenor, *n.* (mus.) tenor, *m.*

tense, *adj.* tieso; tenso; *n.* (gram.) tiempo, *m.*

tension, *n.* tensión, *f.*

tent, *n.* tienda de campaña, *f.*

tentative, *adj.* tentativo

tenth, *n.* y *adj.* décimo, *m.*

tepid, *adj.* tibio

term, *n.* plazo, *m.*; tiempo, período, *m.*; **terms of payment**, condiciones de pago, *f. pl.*

terminate, *vt.* y *vi.* terminar

terrace, *n.* terraza, *f.*

terrestrial, *adj.* terrestre

terrible, *adj.* terrible

terrify, *vt.* espantar, llenar de terror

territory, *n.* territorio, *m.*

terror, *n.* terror, *m.*

test, *n.* ensayo, *m.*, prueba, *f.*; examen, *m.*; *vt.* ensayar, probar; examinar

Testament, *n.* Testamento, *m.*

testament, *n.* testamento, *m.*

testify, *vt.* testificar, atestiguar

testimony, *n.* testimonio, *m.*

text, *n.* texto, *m.*; tema, *m.*

textbook, *n.* libro de texto, *m.*

texture, *n.* textura, *f.*

than, *conj.* que o de (en sentido comparativo)

thank, *vt.* dar gracias; **thanks**, *n. pl.* gracias, *f. pl.*

thankful, *adj.* agradecido

Thanksgiving, **Thanksgiving Day**, *n.* día de dar gracias (en Estados Unidos)

that, *dem. pron.* ése, ésa, eso; aquél, aquélla, aquello; *rel. pron.* que, quien, el cual, la cual, lo cual; *conj.* que, por que, para que; *adj.* ese, esa, aquel, aquella

the, *art.* el, la, lo; los, las

theater, *n.* teatro, *m.*

theatrical, *adj.* teatral

thee, *pron.* (acusativo de **thou**) ti, a ti

theft, *n.* hurto, robo, *m.*

their, *adj.* su, suyo, soya; sus, suyos, suyas; **theirs**, *pron.* el suyo, la suya, los suyos, las suyas

them, *pron.* (*acusativo y dativo* de they) los, las, les; ellos, ellas

theme, *n.* tema, asunto, *m.*; (mus.) motivo, *m.*

themselves, *pron. pl.* ellos mismos, ellas mismas; sí mismos

then, *adv.* entonces, después; **now and then**, de cuando en cuando

theology, *n.* teología, *f.*

there, *adv.* allí, allá

thereafter, *adv.* después; subsiguientemente

thereby, *adv.* por medio de eso

therefore, *adv.* por lo tanto

thermometer, *n.* termómetro, *m.*

these, *pron. pl.* éstos, éstas; *adj.* estos, estas

thick, *adj.* espeso, grueso

thicken, *vt.* y *vi.* espesar

thief, *n.* ladrón, ladrona

thin, *adj.* delgado, flaco

thing, *n.* cosa, *f.*

think, *vt.* y *vi.* pensar; creer

thinking, *n.* pensamiento, *m.*; opinión, *f.*

third, *n.* y *adj.* tercero, *m.*

thirst, *n.* sed, *f.*

thirsty, *adj.* sediento; **to be thirsty**, tener sed

thirteen, *n.* y *adj.* trece, *m.*

thirteenth, *n.* y *adj.* décimotercio, *m.*

thirtieth, _n._ y _adj._ treintavo, _m.; adj._ trigésimo

thirty, _n._ y _adj._ treinta. _m._

this, _adj._ este, esta; esto; _pron._ éste, ésta

thorn, _n._ espina, _f._

those, _adj. pl._ de **that**, aquellos, aquellas; esos, esas; _pron._ aquéllos, aquéllas; ésos, ésas

though, _conj._ aunque; _adv._ (coll.) sin embargo

thought, _n._ pensamiento, _m.;_ concepto, _m.; pretérito_ y _p. p._ del verbo **think**

thoughtful, _adj._ pensativo; considerado

thoughtless, _adj._ inconsiderado

thousand, _n._ mil, _m.;_ millar, _m._

thousandth, _n._ y _adj._ milésimo, _m._

threader, _n._ (mech.) terraja, _f._

threat, _n._ amenaza, _f._

threaten, _vt._ amenazar

three, _n._ y _adj._ tres, _m._

thresh, _vt._ trillar

threshold, _n._ umbral, _m._

threw, _pretérito_ del verbo **throw**

thrice, _adv._ tres veces

thrift, _n._ frugalidad, _f._

thrifty, _adj._ ahorrativo, frugal

thrill, _vt._ emocionar; _vt._ estremecerse; _n._ emoción, _f._

thrilling, _adj._ emocionante

thrive, _vi._ prosperar

throat, _n._ garganta, _f._

throb, _vi._ palpitar, vibrar

throne, _n._ trono, _m._

throng, _n._ gentío, _m._

throttle, _n._ válvula reguladora, _f.;_ acelerador, _m._

through, _prep._ a través, por medio de; _prep_

throw, _vt._ echar, arrojar; _n._ tiro, _m._, tirada _f._

thrown, _p. p._ del verbo **throw**

thumbtack, _n._ chinche, tachuela, _f._

thunder, _n._ trueno, _m.;_ estrépito, _m.; vt._ y _vi._ tronar

Thursday, _n._ jueves, _m._

thwart, _vt._ frustrar

ticket, _n._ billete, _m.;_ (Sp. Am.) boleto, _m._, boleta, _f._

tickle, _vt._ hacer cosquillas a alguno; _vt._ tener cosquillas

tide, _n._ marea, _f._

tidings, _n. pl._ noticias, _f. pl._

tidy, _adj._ pulcro

tie, _vt._ atar; enlazar; _n._ nudo, _m.;_ corbata, _f._

tiger, _n._ tigre, _m._

tight, _adj._ tieso; apretado; (coll.) tacaño

tighten, _vt._ estirar; apretar

tigress, _n._ tigre hembra

tile, _n._ teja, _f.;_ azulejo, _m._

till, _prep._ y _conj._ hasta que, hasta; _vt._ cultivar, labrar

time, _n._ tiempo, _m.;_ (mus.) compás, _m.;_ edad, época, _f.;_ hora, _f.;_ vez, _f._

timely, _adj._ oportuno

timetable, _n._ itinerario, _m._

timid, _adj._ tímido

tin, _n._ estaño, _m.;_ hojalata, _f.;_ **tin can**, lata, _f._

tingle, _vi._ latir, punzar

tint, _n._ tinte, _m.; vt._ teñir, colorar

tiny, _adj._ pequeño, chico

tip, _n._ punta, extremidad, _f.;_ gratificación, propina, _f.;_ información oportuna; _vt._ dar propina; ladear; volcar

tiptoe, _n._ punta del pie, _f.;_ **on tiptoe**, de puntillas

tire, _n._ llanta, goma, _f.;_ neumático, _m._ ; _vt._ cansar, fatigar; _vi._ cansarse

tired, _adj._ cansado

tissue, _n._ (anat.) tejido, _m.;_ **tissue paper**, papel de seda, _m._

title, _n._ título, _m._

to, _prep._ a, para; por; de; hasta; en; con; que; _adv._ hacia determinado objeto; **he came to**, volvió en sí

toad, _n._ sapo, _m._

toast, _vt._ tostar; brindar; _n._ tostada, _f._, pan tostado, _m.;_ brindis, _m._

toaster, _n._ tostador, _m._

toastmaster, _n._ maestro de ceremonias, _m._

tobacco, _n._ tabaco , _m._

today, n. y adv. hoy m.

toddle, vi. tambalearse

toe, n. dedo del pie, m.

toenail, n. uña del dedo del pie, f.

together, adv. juntamente

toil, vi. afanarse; n. fatiga, f.; afán, m.

toilet, n. tocado, m.; excusado, retrete, m.

token, n. símbolo, m.; recuerdo, m.

told, pretérito del verbo **tell**

tolerence, n. tolerancia, f.

tolerate, vt. tolerar

toll, n. peaje, portazgo, m.; tañido, m.; **toll call,** llamada telefónica de larga distancia; vi. sonar las campanas

tomato, n. tomate, m.

tomb, n. tumba, f.

tomorrow, n. y adv. mañana, f.

ton, n. tonelada, f.

tongue, n. lengua, f.

tonic, n. tónico, reconstituyente, m.; (mus.) tónica, f.

tonight, n. y adv. esta noche

tonsil, n. amígdala, f.

too, adv. demasiado; también

took, pretérito del verbo **take**

tool, n. herramienta, f.

toot, vt. y vi. sonar una bocina

tooth, n. diente, m.

toothache, n. dolor de muelas, m.

toothbrush, n. cepillo de dientes, m.

toothpaste, n. pasta dentífrica, f.

toothpick, n. escarbadientes, palillo de dientes, m.

top, n. cima, cumbre, f.; trompo, m.

topaz, n. topacio, m.

topcoat, n. sobretodo, abrigo, m.

topic, n. tópico, asunto, m.

topsy-turvy, adv. patas arriba, desordenadamente

torch, n. antorcha, f.

tore, pretérito del verbo **tear**

toreador, n. torero, m.

torment, n. tormento, m.; vt. atormentar

torn, adj. destrozado; descosido; p. p. del verbo **tear**

torpedo, n. torpedo, m.

tortoise-shell, adj. de carey

torture, n. tortura, f., martirio, m.; vt. atormentar, torturar

toss, vt. tirar, lanzar, arrojar; agitar, sacudir; vi. agitarse; menearse

tot, n. niñito, niñita

total, n. total, m.; adj. entero, completo

totter, vi. tambalear

touch, vt. tocar, palpar; emocionar, conmover; n. tacto, m.; toque, contacto, m.

touching, adj. conmovedor

tough, adj. tosco; correoso; fuerte, vigoroso

toughen, vi. endurecerse; vt. endurecer

touring, n. turismo, m.

tourist, n. turista, m. y f.; viajero, viajera; **tourist court,** posada para turistas, f.

tournament, n. torneo, concurso, m.

toward, towards, prep. hacia, con dirección a

town, n. pueblo, m., población, f.

trace, n. huella, pisada, f.; vestigio, m.; vt. delinear, trazar

track, n. vestigio, m.; huella, pista, f.; vía f.

trade, n. comercio, tráfico, m.; negocio, trato, m.; vt. comerciar, negociar

trade-mark, n. marca de fábrica, f.

traffic, n. tráfico, m.

trail, vt. y vi. rastrear; arrastrar; n. rastro, m.; pisada, f.; sendero, m.

trailer, n. carro de remolque, m.

train, vt. enseñar, adiestrar; entrenar; n. tren, m.; cola (de vestido), f.

training, n. educación, disciplina, f.; entrenamiento, m.

traitor, n. traidor, m.

transact, vt. negociar, transigir

transaction, *n.* transacción, *f.*

transatlantic, *adj.* trasatlántico

transfer, *vt.* trasferir; *n.* traspaso, *m.*; trastado, *m.*

transform, *vt.* y *vi.* trasformar

transfusion, *n.* trasfusión, *f.*

transient, *adj.* pasajero, transitorio

transit, *n.* transito, *m.*

transition, *n.* transición, *f.*

transitive, *adj.* transitivo

translate, *vt.* traducir

translation, *n.* traducción, *f.*

translator, *n.* traductor, traductora

transmission, *n.* (mech.) caja de cambios, *f.*

transmit, *vt.* trasmitir

transom, *n.* travesaño, *m.*

transparent, *adj.* trasparente

transport, *vt.* trasportar

transportation, *n.* trasportación, *f.*, trasporte, *m.*

trap, *n.* trampa, *f.*; *vt.* atrapar

trapeze, *n.* trapecio, *m.*

trash, *adj.* despreciable

travel, *vt.* y *vi.* viajar

traveler, *n.* viajero, viajera

tray, *n.* bandeja, *f.*; (Mex.) charola, *f.*

treacherous, *adj.* traidor

treachery, *n.* traición, *f.*

tread, *vt.* y *vi.* pisar, hollar; *n.* pisada, *f.*

treason, *n.* traición, *f.*

treasure, *n.* tesoro, *m.*; *vt.* atesorar; apreciar

treasurer, *n.* tesorero, tesorera

treasury, *n.* tesorería, *f.*

treat, *vt.* y *vi.* tratar; regalar; *n.* convite, *m.*

treatment, *n.* trato, *m.*; tratamiento, *m.*

treaty, *n.* tratado, *m.*

tree, *n.* árbol, *m.*

tremble, *vi.* temblar

tremendous, *adj.* tremendo; inmenso

trench, *n.* trinchera, *f.*

trespass, *vt.* traspasar, violar

trial, *n.* prueba, *f.*; ensayo, *m.*; (law) juicio, *m.*

triangle, *n.* triángulo, *m.*

triangular, *adj.* triangular

tribe, *n.* tribu, *f.*

tribulation, *n.* tribulación, *f.*

tribunal, *n.* tribunal, *m.*

tribute, *n.* tributo, *m.*

tricycle, *n.* triciclo, velocípedo, *m.*

trill, *n.* trino, *m.*

trillion, *n.* trillón, *m.*, la tercera potencia de un millón, o 1,000,000,000,000,000,000 (en la América Ibera, España Inglaterra, y Alemania); un millón de millones, o 1,000,000,000,000 (en Francia y los Estados Unidos)

trim, *adj.* bien ataviado; *n.* adorno, *m.*; *vt.* adornar, ornar; recortar

trinket, *n.* joya, alhaja, *f.*

trio, *n.* terceto, trío, *m.*

trip, *vt.* saltar, brincar; hacer tropezar; *vi.* tropezar; *n.* viaje, *m.*

triple, *adj.* triple

triplicate, *vt.* triplicar; *adj.* triplicado

trite, *adj.* trivial, banal

triumph, *n.* triunfo, *m.*; *vi.* triunfar; vencer

triumphant, *adj.* triunfante

trivial, *adj.* trivial, vulgar

trolley, *n.* tranvía, *m.*

trombone, *n.* trombón, *m.*

troop, *n.* tropa, *f.*

tropics, *n. pl.* trópico, *m.*

tropical, *adj.* tropical

troubadour, *n.* trovador, *m.*

trouble, *vt.* incomodar, molestar; *vi.* incomodarse; *n.* pena, *f.*; molestia, *f.*; trabajo, *m.*

troubled, *adj.* afligido

troublesome, *adj.* molesto, fastidioso

trousers, *n. pl.* calzones, pantalones, *m. pl.*

trousseau, *n.* ajuar de novia, *m.*

trout, *n.* trucha, *f.*

truce, *n.* tregua, *f.*

truck, *n.* camión, *m.*

true, *adj.* verdadero, cierto

truly, *adv.* en verdad

trumpet, *n.* trompeta, trompa, *f.*

trunk, n. tronco, m.; baúl, cofre, m.; **trunk (of an elephant),** trompa, f.

trunks, n. pl. calzones, m. pl.

trust, n. confianza, f.; crédito, m.; vt. y vi. confiar

trustee, n. fideicomisario, depositario, m.

trustworthy, adj. digno de confianza

truth, n. verdad, f.

truthful, adj. verídico, veraz

truthfulness, n. veracidad, f.

try, vt. y vi. probar; experimentar; intentar

trying, adj. cruel, penoso

tub, n. tina, f.

tube, n. tubo, caño, m.

tuberculosis, n. tuberculosis, tisis, f.

tug, vt. tirar con fuerza; arrancar

tugboat, n. remolcador, m.

tuition, n. instrucción, enseñanza, f.

tumble, vt. caer, voltear; n. caída, f.

tumor, n. tumor, m.

tuna, n. (bot.) tuna, f.; **tuna fish,** atún, m.

tune, n. tono, m.; tonada, f.; vt. afinar (un instrumento musical)

tunic, n. túnica, f.

tunnel, n. túnel, m.

turban, n. turbante, m.

turbojet, n. turborreactor, m.

turf, n. césped, m.

turkey, n. pavo, m.

Turkey, n. Turquía, f.

Turkish, adj. turco

turmoil, n. confusión, f.

turn, vt. volver, trocar; vi. volver, girar, voltear; n. vuelta, f.; giro, m.; turno, m.

turnip, n. (bot.) nabo, m.

turquoise, n. turquesa, f.

turtle, n. tortuga, f.

turtledove, n. tórtola, f

tuxedo, n. smoking, m.

tweezers, n. pl. pinzas, f. pl.; tenacillas, f. pl.

twelfth, n. y adj. duodécimo, m.

twelve, n. y adj. doce, m.

twentieth, n. y adj. vigésimo, m.

twenty, n. y adj. veinte, m.

twice, adv. dos veces

twig, n. varita, varilla, f.

twilight, n. crepúsculo, m.

twine, vt. torcer, enroscar; vi. entrelazarse

twinge, n. punzada, f.; vt. arder; sufrir dolor (de una punzada, etc.)

twinkle, vi. parpadear; n. pestañeo, m.

twinkling, n. pestañeo, m.; momento, m.

twirl, vt. voltear; hacer girar

twist, vt. y vi. torcer

two, n. y adj. dos , m.

type, n. tipo, m.; clase, f.; vt. y vi. escribir en máquina

typewrite, vt. escribir a máquina

typewriter, n. máquina de escribir, f.

typhoid, adj. tifoideo; **typhoid fever,** fiebre tifoidea, f.

typical, adj. típico

typing, n. mecanografía, f.

typist, n. mecanógrafo, mecanógrafa

typographical, adj. tipográfico

tyranny, n. tiranía, f.

tyrant, n. tirano, m.

U

U., University, Universidad

udder, n. ubre, f.

ugliness, n. fealdad, f.

ugly, adj. feo

ulcer, n. úlcera, f.

ultimatum, n. ultimátum, m.

ultra, adj. extremo, excesivo

ultrasonic, adj. ultrasónico

umbrella, n. paraguas, m.

umpire, n. árbitro, m.; vt. arbitrar

UN, United Nations, N.U., Naciones Unidas

unable, adj. incapaz

unanimity, n. unanimidad, f.

unanimous, adj. unánime

unarmed, adj. desarmado

unassuming, adj. sin pretensiones

unattached, *adj.* separado; disponible

unattainable, *adj.* inasequible

unavoidable, *adj.* inevitable

unawares, *adv.* inadvertidamente

unbalanced, *adj.* trastornado

unbearable, *adj.* intolerable

unbiased, *adj.* imparcial

unbutton, *vt.* desabotonar

uncertain, *adj.* inseguro

uncertainty, *n.* incertidumbre, *f.*

uncle, *n.* tío, *m.*

uncomfortable, *adj.* incómodo

unconcerned, *adj.* indiferente

unconditional, *adj.* incondicional

unconscious, *adj.* inconsciente

undecided, *adj.* indeciso

under, *prep.* debajo de, bajo; *adv.* abajo

underage, *adj.* menor de edad

underclothing, *n.* ropa interior, *f.*

undergo, *vt.* sufrir; sostener

underground, *adj.* subterráneo

underhanded, *adj.* clandestino

underline, *vt.* subrayar

underneath, *adv.* debajo

underprivileged, *adj.* desvalido, necesitado

underscore, *vt.* subrayar

undershirt, *n.* camiseta, *f.*

undersigned, *n.* y *adj.* suscrito, suscrita

underskirt, *n.* enagua, *f.*; fondo, *m.*

understand, *vt.* entender, comprender

understanding, *n.* entendimiento, *m.*; *adj.* comprensivo

undertake, *vt.* y *vi.* emprender

undertaker, *n.* empresario o director de pompas fúnebres

undertaking, *n.* empresa, obra, *f.*

undertow, *n.* resaca, *f.*

underwear, *n.* ropa interior, *f.*

underweight, *adj.* de bajo peso

undesirable, *adj.* nocivo

undivided, *adj.* entero

undress, *vt.* desvestir; desnudar

unearth, *vt.* desenterrar; revelar, divulgar

unemployed, *adj.* desocupado

unending, *adj.* sin fin

unequal, *adj.* desigual

uneven, *adj.* desigual

unexpected, *adj.* inesperado

unfailing, *adj.* infalible

unfair, *adj.* injusto

unfamiliar, *adj.* desconocido

unfavorable, *adj.* desfavorable

unfit, *adj.* inepto, incapaz; indigno

unfold, *vt.* desplegar

unforeseen, *adj.* imprevisto

unforgettable, *adj.* inolvidable

unfortunate, *adj.* desafortunado, infeliz

unfounded, *adj.* infundado

unfurl, *vt.* desplegar

ungrounded, *adj.* infundado

unhappy, *adj.* infeliz

unharmed, *adj.* ileso, incólume

unhealthy, *adj.* malsano

unheard (of), *adj.* inaudito

unhurt, *adj.* ileso

uniform, *n.* y *adj.* uniforme, *m.*

uniformity, *n.* uniformidad, *f.*

union, *n.* unión, *f.*

unique, *adj.* único; singular

unison, *n.* concordancia, *f.*; **in unison,** al unísono

unit, *n.* unidad, *f.*

unite, *vt.* y *vi.* unir, juntarse

united, *adj.* unido, junto

United States of America, Estados Unidos de América

unity, *n.* unidad, *f.*; unión, *f.*

universal, *adj.* universal; **universal joint,** cardán, *m.*

universe, *n.* universo, *m.*

university, *n.* universidad, *f.*

unkind, *adj.* cruel

unknowingly, *adv.* sin saberlo

unknown, *adj.* desconocido

unlike, *adj.* desemejante

unlikely, *adj.* improbable

unlimited, *adj.* ilimitado

unlock, *vt.* abrir alguna cerradura

unlucky, *adj.* desafortunado

unmarried, *adj.* soltero, soltera

unnatural, *adj.* artificial

unnecessary, *adj.* innecesario

unofficial, *adj.* extraoficial

unpack, *vt.* desempacar

unpaid, *adj.* sin pagar, pendiente de pago

unpopular, *adj.* impopular

unprincipled, *adj.* sin escrúpulos

unravel, *vt.* desenredar; resolver

unreal, *adj.* fantástico, ilusorio

unreserved, *adj.* franco, abierto

unscrew, *vt.* destornillar

unscrupulous, *adj.* sin escrúpulos

unseemly, *adj.* indecoroso

unseen, *adj.* no visto

unselfish, *adj.* desinteresado

unsettled, *adj.* incierto, indeciso; **unsettled accounts**, cuentas por pagar

unsightly, *adj.* feo

unskilled, *adj.* inexperto

unsound, *adj.* inestable; falso

unsuitable, *adj.* inadecuado

untangle, *vt.* desenredar

untie, *vt.* soltar, desamarrar

until, *prep.* y *conj.* hasta, hasta que

untimely, *adj.* intempestivo

untold, *adj.* no relatado

unusual, *adj.* inusitado, poco común

unveil, *vt.* y *vi.* descubrir; revelar; estrenar

unwilling, *adj.* sin deseos; **unwillingly**, *adv.* de mala gana

unwind, *vt.* desenrollar

unwise, *adj.* imprudente

unworthy, *adj.* indigno, vil

unwritten, *adj.* verbal, no escrito

up, *adv.* arriba, en lo alto; *prep.* hasta; **to make up**, hacer las paces; inventar; compensar; maquillarse; **to bring up**, criar, educar; **to call up**, telefonear

upbringing, *n.* educación,

crianza, *f.*

upholster, *vt.* entapizar

upkeep, *n.* mantenimiento, *m.*

upon, *prep.* sobre encima

upper, *adj.* superior; más elevado

upright, *adj.* derecho, recto

uproar, *n.* tumulto, alboroto, *m.*

upset, *vt.* y *vi.* volcar, trastornar; *adj.* mortificado

upside-down, *adj.* al revés; de arriba abajo

upstairs, *adv.* arriba

up-to-date, *adj.* moderno, de ultima moda, reciente

upward, *adv.* hacia arriba

uranium, *n.* uranio, *m.*

urban, *adj.* urbano

urge, *vt.* y *vi.* incitar, instar

urgent, *adj.* urgente

urinate, *vi.* orinar, mear

urine, *n.* orina, *f.*, orines, *m. pl.*

U.S.A., **United States of America**, E.U.A. Estados Unidos de América

usable, *adj.* utilizable

usage, *n.* uso, *m.*

use, *n.* uso, *m.*, servicio, *m.*; *vt.* y *vi.* usar, emplear; acostumbrar

used, *adj.* gastado, usado

useful, *adj.* útil

usefulness, *n.* utilidad, *f.*

useless, *adj.* inútil

usher, *n.* acomodador, *m.*

usual, *adj.* común, ordinario; **usually**, *adv.* de costumbre

utensil, *n.* utensilio, *m.*

utility, *n.* utilidad, *f.*; **public utilities**, servicios públicos *m. pl.*

V

vacancy, *n.* vacante, *f.*

vacant, *adj.* vacío, vacante

vacation, *n.* vacación, *f.*

vaccinate, *vt.* vacunar

vaccination, *n.* vacuna, *f.*; vacunación, *f.*

vaccine, *n.* vacuna, *f.*

vacuum, *n.* vacío, *m.*; **vacuum cleaner**, aspiradora, *f.*, barredor al vacío, m.

vain, adj. vano, inútil; vanidoso, presentuoso

valet, n. criado, camarero, m.

valid, adj. válido

valley, n. valle, m.

valuable, adj. valioso; **valuables**, n. pl. tesoros, m. pl., joyas, f. pl.

value, n. valor, precio, importe, m.; vt. valuar, apreciar

vanilla, n. vainilla, f.

vanish, vi. desaparecer

vanity, n. vanidad, f.; **vanity case**, polvera, f.

variety, n. variedad, f.

various, adj. diferentes

varnish, n. barniz, m.; vt. barnizer; charolar

vary, vt. y vi. variar

vase, n. jarrón, florero, m.

vast, adj. vasto; inmenso

vault, n. bóveda, f.

veal, n. ternera, f.; **veal cutlet**, chuleta de ternera, f.

vegetable, adj. vegetal; n. vegetal, m.; **vegetables**, n. pl. verduras, hortalizas, f. pl.

vegetation, n. vegetación, f.

vehicle, n. vehículo, m.

veil, n. velo, m.; vt. encubrir, ocultar

vein, n. vena, f.

velocity, n. velocidad, f.

velvet, n. terciopelo, m.

velveteen, n. pana, f.

venerate, vt. venerar, honrar

veneration, n. veneración, f.

Venetian, n. y adj. veneciano, veneciana

Venezuelan, n. y adj. venezolano, venezolana

vengeance, n. venganza, f.

Venice, Venecia

venison, n. carne de venado, f.

ventilate, vt. ventilar

ventilation, n. ventilación, f.

veracity, n. veracidad, f.

veranda, n. terraza, f.

verb, n. (gram.) verbo, m.

verbal, adj. verbal, literal; **verbally**, adv. oralmente, de palabra

verbatim, adv. palabra por palabra

verdict, n (law) veredicto, m.; sentencia, f., dictamen, m.

verify, vt. verificar

versatile, adj. hábil para muchas cosas

verse, n. verso, m.

version, n. versión, traducción, f.

vessel, n. vasija, f., vaso, m.; buque, m.

vest, n. chaleco, m.

vestibule, n. zaguán, m.

vestige, n. vestigio, m.

vest-pocket, adj. propio para el bolsillo del chaleco; pequeño; **vest-pocket edition**, edición en miniatura, f.

veteran, n. y adj. veterano, veterana

vex, vt. contrariar; **vexed**, adj. molesto, contrariado

via, prep. por la vía de; por; **via airmail**, por vía aérea

viaduct, n. viaducto, m.

vice, n. vicio, m.

vice-consul, n. vicecónsul, m.

vice-president, n. vice-presidente, m.

vicinity, n. vecindad, proximidad, f.

victim, n. víctima, f.

victorious, adj. victorioso

victory, n. victoria, f.

video, n. televisión, f.

Vienna, Viena, f.

Viennese, n. y adj. vienés, vienesa

view, n. vista, f.; paisaje, m.; vt. mirar, ver

viewpoint, n. punto de vista, m.

vigor, n. vigor, m.

vigorous, adj. vigoroso

villa, n. quinta, f.

village, n. aldea, f.

villain, n. malvado, m.

vim, n. energía, f., vigor, m.

vindicate, vt. vindicar, defender

vine, n. vid, f.

vinegar, n. vinagre, m.

vineyard, n. viña, f., viñedo, m.

viol, n. (mus.) violón, m.

viola, n. (mus.) viola, f.

violate, vt. violar
violation, n. violación, f.
violence, n. violencia, f.
violent, adj. violento
violet, n. (bot.) violeta, f.
violin, n. violín, m.
violinist, n. violinista, m. y f.
virgin, n. virgen, f.; adj. virginal; virgen
virology, n. virología, f.
virtue, n. virtud, f.
virtuous, adj. virtuoso
virus, n. (med.) virus, m.
visa, n. visa, f.
viscount, n. vizconde, m.
vision, n. visión, f.
visit, vt. y vi. visitar; n. visita, f.
visitor, n. visitante, m. y f.
visualize, vt. vislumbrar
vital, adj. vital; **vital statistics,** estadística demográfica, f.
vitality, n. vitalidad, f.
vitamin, n. vitamina, f.
vivacious, adj. vivaz
vivacity, n. vivacidad, f.
vivid, adj. vivo, vivaz; gráfico
viz., adv. a saber, esto es
vocabulary, n. vocabulario, m.
vocal, adj. vocal
vocalist, n. cantante, m. y f.
vocation, n. vocación, carrera, profesión, f.; oficio, m.
vocational, adj. práctico, profesional; **vocational school,** escuela de artes y oficios, escuela práctica, f.
vogue, n. moda, f.; boga, f.
voice, n. voz, f.
void, n. y adj. vacío, m.; vt. anular
volcano, n. volcán, m.
volleyball, n. balonvolea, m.
volume, n. volumen, m.
voluntarily, adv. voluntariamente
volunteer, n. voluntario, m.
vote, n. voto, sufragio, m.; vt. votar
voter, n. votante, m. y f.
voucher, n. comprobante, recibo, m.
vow, n. voto, m.; vt. y vi. dedicar, consagrar; hacer votos;

jurar
vowel, n. vocal, f.
voyage, n. viaje marítimo, m.
v.t., transitive verb, v.tr., verbo transitivo
vulgar, adj. vulgar, cursi
vulgarity, n. vulgaridad, f.

W

w., week, semana; **west,** O., oeste; **width,** ancho; **wife,** esposa
wafer, n. hostia, f.; oblea, f.; galletica, f.
wag, vt. mover ligeramente; **to wag the tail,** menear la cola; n. meneo, m.
wage, vt. apostar; emprender; **wages,** n. pl. sueldo, salario, m.
wager, n. apuesta, f.; vt. apostar
wagon, n. carreta, f.; vagón, m.
wail, vi. lamentarse
waist, n. cintura, f.
waistline, n. cintura, f.
wait, vi. esperar, aguardar
waiter, n. sirviente, mozo, m.
waitress, n. camarera, criada, mesera, f.
wake, vi. velar; despertarse; vt. despertar; n. vigilia, f.; velorio m.
walk, vt. y vi. pasear, andar, caminar; n. páseo, m., caminata, f.
wallet, n. cartera, f.
walnut, n. nogal, m.; nuez, f.
wand, n. vara, varita, f.; batuta, f.
wander, vi. vagar, rodar; extraviarse
wanderer, n. peregrino, m.
want, vt. y vi. desear, querer, anhelar; faltar; vt. estar necesitado; n. falta, carencia, f.
war, n. guerra, f.
warden, n. custodio, guardián, m. alcalde, m.
wardrobe, n. guardarropa, f., ropero, m.; vestuario, m.
warehouse, n. almacén, depósito, m., bodega, f.
warhead, n. punta de comba-

te, *f.*

warm, *adj.* caliente; abrigador; cordial, caluroso; **to be warm,** hacer calor; tener calor; *vt.* calentar

warmth, *n.* calor, *m.*; ardor, fervor, *m.*

warn, *vt.* avisar; advertir

warrant, *vt.* autorizar; garantizar; *n.* decreto de prisión, *m.*; autorización, *f.*

warship, *n.* barco de guerra, *m.*

wart, *n.* verruga, *f.*

wartime, *n.* época de guerra, *f.*

was, 1ª y 3ª persona del singular del pretérito del verbo **be**

wash, *vt.* y *vi.* lavar; *n.* loción, ablución, *f.*; lavado, *m.*

washable, *adj.* lavable

washer, *n.* máquina lavadora, *f.*; (mech.) arandela, *f.*

washing, *n.* lavado, *m.*; ropa para lavar; **washing machine,** máquina de lavar, lavadora, *f.*

wasp, *n.* avispa, *f.*

waste, *vt.* desperdiciar; malgastar; *vi.* gastarse; *n.* desperdicio, *m.*; despilfarro, *m.*

wastebasket, *n.* cesta para papeles

wasteful, *adj.* despilfarrador

wastepaper, *n.* papel de desecho, *m.*

watch, *n.* vigilia, vela, *f.*; centinela, *f.*; reloj de bolsillo, *m.*; **wrist watch,** reloj de pulsera, *m.*; *vt.* observar; *vi.* velar, custodiar

water, *n.* agua, *f.*; **running water,** agua corriente, *f.*; **water closet,** retrete, *m.*; **water color,** acuarela, *f.*; **water meter,** contador de agua, *m.*; **water polo,** polo acuático, *m.*; **water skiing,** esquí náutico o acuático, *m.*; *vt.* irrigar, regar

watermelon, *n.* sandía, *f.*

waterproof, *adj.* a prueba de agua; impermeable

watery, *adj.* aguado

watt, *n.* vatio, *m.*

wattmeter, *n.* vatímetro, *m.*

wave, *n.* ola, onda, *f.*; *vt.* agitar, menear; *vi.* ondear; saludar

wavy, *adj.* ondeado, ondulado

wax, *n.* cera, **wax paper,** papel encerado, *m.*; *vt.* encerar

way, *n.* camino, *m.*, senda, ruta, *f.*; modo, *m.*, forma, *f.*; medio, *m.*; **by the way,** a propósito

we, *pron.* nosotros, nosotras

weak, *adj.* débil

weaken, *vt.* y *vi.* debilitar

wealth, *n.* riqueza, *f.*; bienes, *m. pl.*

wealthy, *adj.* rico, adinerado

weapon, *n.* arma, *f.*

wear, *vt.* gastar, consumir; llevar puesto, traer; *vi.* gastarse; *n.* uso, *m.*

weariness, *n.* cansancio, *m.*

weather, *n.* tiempo, *m.*, temperatura, *f.*

weave, *vt.* tejer; trenzar

web, *n.* red, *f.*

wed, *vt.* y *vi.* casar, casarse

wedding, *n.* boda, *f.*, casamiento, matrimonio, *m.*

wedge, *n.* cuña, *f.*; *vt.* acuñar; apretar

Wednesday, *n.* miércoles, *m.*

wee, *adj.* pequeñito

weed, *n.* mala hierba, *f.*

week, *n.* semana, *f.*

weekday, *n.* día de trabajo, *m.*

week-end, *adj.* de fin de semana

weekly, *adj.* semanal, semanario; *adv.* semanalmente

weigh, *vt.* y *vi.* pesar; considerar

weight, *n.* peso, *m.*; pesadez, *f.*

weightlessness, *n.* imponderabilidad, *f.*

weird, *adj.* extraño, sobrenatural, misterioso

welcome, *adj.* bienvenido; *n.* bienvenida, *f.*; *vt.* dar la bienvenida

weld, *vt.* soldar

welfare *n.* bienestar, *m.*

well, *n.* pozo, *m.*; *adj.* bueno, sano; *adv.* bien

well-being, *n.* felicidad, prosperidad, *f.*

well-bred, *adj.* bien educado, de buenos modales

well-done, *adj.* bien hecho; bien cocido

well-timed, *adj.* oportuno

well-to-do, *adj.* acomodado, rico

wench, *n.* mozuela, *f.*

went, *pretérto* del verbo **go**

were, 2ª persona del singular y plural del *pretérto* del verbo **be**

west, *n.* poniente, occidente oeste, *m.*

westerly, western, *adj.* occidental

West Indies, Antillas, *f. pl.*

wet, *adj.* húmedo, mojado; *vt.* molar, humedecer

whale, *n.* ballena, *f.*

wharf, *n.* muelle, *m.*

what, *pron.* qué; lo que, aquello que; **what is the matter?** ¿qué pasa?

whatever, *pron.* y *adj.* cualquier cosa, lo que sea

wheat, *n.* trigo, *m.*

wheel, *n.* rueda, *f.*

wheelbarrow, *n.* carretilla, *f.*

when, *adv.* cuando; cuándo

whence, *adv.* de donde; de quien

whenever, *adv.* siempre que

where, *adv.* donde; dónde

whereabouts, *n.* paradero, *m.*; *adv.* por donde, hacia donde

whereas, *conj.* por cuanto, mientras que; considerando

whereby, *adv.* con lo cual

wherein, *adv.* en lo cual

whereof, *adv.* de lo cual

whereon, *adv.* sobre lo cual

whereupon, *adv.* entonces, en consecuencia de lo cual

wherever, *adv.* dondequiera que

whet, *vt.* afilar, amolar; exciter

whether, *conj.* que; si; ora

whey, *n.* suero, *m.*

which, *pron.* que, el cual, la cual, los cuales, las cuales; cuál

whichever, *pron.* y *adj.* cualquiera que

whiff, *n.* bocanada de humo,

fumada, *f.*

while, *n.* rato, *m.*; vez, *f.*; momento, *m.*; **to be worth while,** valer la pena; *conj.* mientras, durante

whim, *n.* antojo, capricho, *m.*

whimsical, *adj.* caprichoso, fantástico

whip, *n.* azote, látigo, *m.*; *vt.* azotar

whipped cream, *n.* crema batida, *f.*

whirl, *vt.* y *vi.* girar; hacer girar; moverse rápidamente; *n.* remolino, *m.*; vuelta, *f.*

whirlwind, *n.* torbellino, remolino, *m.*

whisker, *m.* patilla, *f.*

whiskey, whisky, *n.* whiskey, *m.*

whisper, *vi.* cuchichear; *n.* cuchicheo, secreto, *m.*

whistle, *vt.* y *vi.* silbar; chiflar; *n.* silbido, *m.*; pito, *m.*

white, *adj.* blanco, pálido; cano, canoso; puro; *n.* color blanco; clara (de huevo)

white-haired, *adj.* canoso

whiten, *vt.* y *vi.* blanquear; blanquearse

who, *pron.* quien, que; quién

whoever, *pron.* quienquiera

whole, *adj.* todo, total; entero; *n.* todo, total, *m.*; **the whole,** conjunto, *m.*

wholehearted, *adj.* sincero, cordial

wholesale, *n.* venta al por mayor, *f.*

wholesome, *adj.* sano, saludable

whole-wheat, *adj.* de trigo entero

wholly, *adv.* totalmente

whom, *pron.* acusativo de **who** (quien)

whooping cough, *n.* tosferina, *f.*

whore, *n.* puta, *f.*

whose, *pron.* (genitivo de **who** y **which**) cuyo, cuya, cuyos, cuyas, de quien o de quienes

why, *adv.* ¿por qué?

wicked, *adj.* malvado, perverso

wide, *adj.* ancho, extenso;
   widely, *adv.* ampliamente
wide-awake, *adj.* despierto,
   alerta
widen, *vt.* ensanchar, ampliar
widespread, *adj.* diseminado
widow, *n.* viuda, *f.*
widower, *n.* viudo, *m.*
width, *n.* anchura, *f.*
wield, *vt.* manejar, empuñar
wife, *n.* esposa, mujer, *f.*
wild, *adj.* silvestre; salvaje
wilderness, *n.* desierto, *m.*,
   selva, *f.*
wilful, *adj.* voluntarioso
will, *n.* voluntad, *f.*; capricho,
   m.; testamento, *m.*; *vt.* legar,
   dejar en testamento; verbo
   auxiliar que indica futuro
willing, *adj.* deseoso, listo;
   willingly, *adv.* de buena gana
willow, *n.* (bot.) sauce, *m.*
win, *vt.* y *vi.* ganar, obtener
wind, *n.* viento, *m.*; pedo, *m.*
wind, *vt.* enrollar; dar cuerda
   (a un reloj, etc.); torcer; envolver; *vi.* serpentear
winded, *adj.* sin fuerzas
window, *n.* ventana, *f.*
windpipe, *n.* (anat.) tráquea, *f.*
windshield, *n.* parabrisas, *m.*
wine, *n.* vino, *m.*
wing, *n.* ala, *f.*; lado, costado,
   m.; **wings,** *pl.* (theat.) bastidores, *m. pl.*
wink, *vt.* y *vi.* guiñar, pestañear
winner, *n.* vencedor, vencedo-
   ra
winning, *adj.* atractivo; **win-
   nings,** *n. pl.* ganancias, *f. pl.*
winsome, *adj.* simpático
winter, *n.* invierno, *m.*
winterize, *vt.* acondicionar
   para uso invernal
wipe, *vt.* secar, limpiar; borrar;
   to wipe out, obliterar; arruinar
wire, *n.* alambre, *m.*; *vt.* alam-
   brar; *vi.* (coll.) telegrafiar, cablegrafiar
wireless, *n.* telegrafía inalám-
   brica, *f.*
wisdom, *n.* sabiduría, *f.*; jui-

cio, *m.*
wisdom tooth, *n.* muela del
   juicio, muela cordal, *f.*
wise, *adj.* sabio, juicioso, prudente
wish, *vt.* desear, querer; *n.* anhelo, deseo, *m.*
wishful, *adj.* deseoso; **wishful
   thinking,** ilusiones, *f. pl.*
wisp, *n.* fragmento, *m.*; pizca,
   f.
wit, *n.* ingenio, *m.*, agudeza,
   sal, *f.*; **to wit,** a saber
witch, *n.* bruja, hechicera, *f.*
with, *prep.* con; por; de; a
withdraw, *vt.* quitar; retirar;
   vi. retirarse, apartarse
wither, *vi.* marchitarse
withhold, *vt.* detener, retener
within, *prep.* dentro, adentro
without, *prep.* sin; fuera,
   afuera; *adv.* exteriormente
withstand, *vt.* oponer, resistir
witness, *n.* testimonio, *m.*;
   testigo, *m.*; *vt.* atestiguar,
   testificar; *vi.* servir de testigo;
   presenciar
witty, *adj.* ingenioso
wives, *n. pl.* de **wife,** esposas,
   mujeres, *f. pl.*
wizard, *n.* hechicero, mago, *m.*
wobble, *vt.* bambolear
woe, *n.* dolor, *m.*, aflicción, *f.*
wolf, *n.* lobo, *m.*
wolves, *n. pl.* de **wolf,** lobos,
   m. pl.
woman, *n.* mujer, *f.*
womanhood, *n.* la mujer en
   general
womanly, *adj.* femenino
womb, *n.* útero, *m.*, matriz, *f.*
women, *n. pl.* de **woman,** mujeres, *f. pl.*
wonder, *n.* milagro, *m.*; prodigio, *m.*; maravilla, *f.*; *vi.* maravillarse (de)
wonderful, *adj.* maravilloso
won't, contracción de **will not**
woo, *vt.* cortejar
wood, *n.* madera, *f.*; leña, *f.*;
   woods, *pl.* bosque, *m.*
woodchuck, *n.* (zool.) marmo-
   ta, *f.*
woodcutter, *n.* leñador, *m.*
wooded, *adj.* arbolado

wooden, *adj.* de madera

woodland, *n.* bosque, *m.*; selva, *f.*

woodman, *n.* cazador, *m.*; guardabosque, *m.*

woodpecker, *n.* (orn.) picamaderos, *m.*

wool, *n.* lana, *f.*

woolen, *adj.* de lana

word, *n.* palabra, voz, *f.*; *vt.* expresar

wore, *pretérito* del verbo **wear**

work, *vi.* trabajar; funcionar; *vt.* trabajar; *n.* trabajo, *m.*

worker, *n.* trabajador, obrero, *m.*

workingman, *n.* obrero, *m.*

workroom, *n.* taller, *m.*

works, *n.* fábrica, *f.*, taller, *m.*

workshop, *n.* taller, *m.*

world, *n.* mundo, *m.*

worldly, *adj.* mundano

world-wide, *adj.* mundial

worm, *n.* gusano, *m.*

worn, *p. p.* del verbo **wear**

worn-out, *adj.* rendido, gastado

worry, *n.* cuidado, *m.*; preocupación, ansia, *f.*; *vt.* molestar, atormentar; *vi.* preocuparse

worse, *adj.* y *adv.* peor

worship, *n.* culto, *m.*; adoración, *f.*; *vt.* adorar, venerar

worst, *adj.* pésimo, malísimo; *n.* lo peor, lo más malo

worth, *n.* valor, precio, *m.*; mérito, *m.*, valía, *f.*; *adj.* meritorio, digno; **to be worth while,** merecer o valer la pensa

worthless, *adj.* inservible, sin valor

would, *pret.* y *subj.* de **will**, para expresar deseo, condición, acción

wound, *n.* herida, llaga, *f.*; *vt.* herir

wove, *pretérito* del verbo **weave**

woven, *p. p.* del verbo **weave**

wrangle, *vi.* reñir, discutir

wrap, *vt.* arrollar; envolver; *n.* abrigo, *m.*

wrapping, *n.* envoltura, *f.*

wrath, *n.* ira, cólera, *f.*

wreath, *n.* corona, guirnalda *f.*

wreck, *n.* naufragio, *m.*; destrucción, *f.*; colisión, *f.*, *vt.* arruinar; destruir

wren, *n.* (orn.) reyezuelo, *m.*

wrench, *vt.* arrancar; torcer; *n.* torcedura (del pie, etc.); destornillador, *m.*; **monkey wrench,** llave inglesa, *f.*

wrest, *vt.* arrancar, quitar a fuerza

wrestle, *vi.* luchar a brazo partido; *n.* lucha, *f.*

wrestling, *n.* lucha, *f.*

wretch, *n.* infeliz, *m.*; infame, *m.*

wretched, *adj.* infeliz, mísero

wriggle, *vi.* retorcerse; menearse

wring, *vt.* exprimir, torcer

wringer, *n.* torcedor, *m.*

wrinkle, *n.* arruga, *f.*; *vt.* arrugar

wrist, *n.* muñeca (de la mano), *f.*; **wrist watch,** reloj de pulsera, *m.*

write, *vt.* escribir

writer, *n.* escritor, escritora, autor, autora; novelista, *m.* y *f.*

writhe, *vt.* torcer; *vi.* contorcerse,

written, *p. p.* del verbo **write**

wrong, *n.* perjuicio, *m.*; injusticia, *f.*; error, *m.*; *adj.* incorrecto, erróneo; injusto; falso; *vt.* hacer un mal, injuriar; agraviar; **wrongly,** *adv.* mal, injustamente; al revés

wrote, *pretérito* del verbo **write**

wt., weight, P. peso

X

Xmas, Christmas, Navidad, Pascua de Navidad

X ray, *n.* rayo X o Roentgen; **X-ray picture,** radiografía, *f.*; *vt.* examinar con rayos X, radiografiar

Y

yacht, *n.* (naut.) yate, *m.*

yam, n. (bot.) batata, f.; (Sp. Am.) camote, m.

yank, vt. (coll.) sacudir, tirar de golpe; n. abreviatura de **yankee**

yankee, n. y adj. yanqui, m. y f.

yard, n. corral, m.; patio, m.; yarda (medida), f.

yardstick, n. yarda de medir, f.

yarn, n. estambre, m.; (coll.) cuento exagerado, m.

yawn, vi. bostezar; n. bostezo, m.

yd., yard, yd., yarda

year, n. año, m.

yearly, adj. anual; adv. anualmente

yearn, vi. anhelar

yearning, n. anhelo, m.

yeast, n. levadura, f.

yell, vi. aullar, gritar; n. grito, aullido, m.

yellow, adj., n. amarillo, m.

yelp, vt. latir, ladrar; n. aullido, latido, m.

yes, adv. sí

yesterday, adv. ayer; **day before yesterday,** anteayer

yet, adv. todavía, aún; conj. sin embargo

yield, vt. y vi. producir, rendir

yoke, n. yugo, m.; yunta, f.

yolk, n. yema (de huevo) f.

you, pron. tú, usted; vosotros, vosotras, ustedes

young, adj. joven; **young man,** joven, m.; **young woman,** joven, señorita, f.

youngster, n. jovencito, jovencita, chiquillo, chiquilla, muchacho , muchacha

your, yours, pron. tu, su, vuestro, de ustedes, de vosotros

yourself, pron. usted mismo; **yourselves,** ustedes mismos

youth, n. juventud, adolescencia, f.; joven, m.

youthful, adj. juvenil

Z

zeal, n. celo, ardor, ahinco , m.

zebra, n. cebra, f.

zero, n. cero, m.

zest, n. gusto, fervor, m.

zigzag, n. zigzag, m.

zinc, n. (chem.) cinc, zinc, m.; **zinc chloride,** cloruro de cinc, m.

zipper, n. cremallera, f.; cierre automático, m.

zone, n. zona, f.

zoo, n. jardín zoológico, m.

zoological, adj. zoológico

zoology, n. zoología, f.

A Taste of Spain

Spain offers a variety of food and that echoes throughout the western world. In the Americas, the Spanish style is reflected in the traditional dishes of Central and South America, as well as those of the Caribbean. We thought you might enjoy a sampling, some familiar and some not so familiar, but all guaranteed to be delicious.

Chili con Queso

---

2 tablespoons olive oil
½ cup onion, finely chopped
1 tablespoon flour
2 cups canned tomatoes, finely chopped, with liquid
½ cup green chilies, finely chopped
1 teaspoon chili powder
3 cups Monterey Jack cheese, shredded

---

1. Heat olive oil in a heavy skillet and sauté the onion until tender. Stir in flour and continue cooking for 2 minutes.
2. Stir in tomatoes, chilies, and chili powder. Simmer, stirring often, for 15 minutes or until the mixture has thickened somewhat.
3. Reduce the heat and add the cheese, stirring until melted. Serve warmed with fresh vegetables, tortilla chips, or bread for dipping.

Refried Beans

---

4 tablespoons bacon fat
2 tablespoons onions, finely chopped
2 cups kidney or pinto beans, cooked & drained
Salt

---

1. Heat the fat in a heavy skillet and sauté the onion just until soft.
2. Add beans to the pan and cook while mashing with a fork until all of the fat is absorbed and the beans are fairly dry.
3. Salt to taste.

NOTES: Flavor the beans with a bit of tomato paste, hot chili powder, or salsa.

—Spread refried beans over tortillas, or thin with a bit of broth to serve as a dip.

Party Quesadillas

This simplified version of the traditional Mexican preparation, sort of a cross between a quesadilla and a tostada, is a great way to add variety to a buffet or snack table.

½ cup mayonnaise
¼ cup salsa
2½ cups cheese, shredded
8 10-inch flour tortillas
Olive oil

1. Combine mayonnaise, salsa, and cheese.
2. Spread cheese mixture over 4 tortillas and cover with remaining 4 tortillas.
3. Brush tops with olive oil and brown under the broiler for about 1 minute. Turn, brush with olive oil, and brown the other side.
4. Cut into wedges and serve.

NOTES: Use any cheese that melts well such as Jack, Muenster, or cheddar.

For variety, garnish each serving with a thin avocado slice or spread with guacamole.

—Spread a thin layer of refried beans over the second tortilla before putting the sandwich together.

Easy Salsa

1 cup canned tomatoes, diced or crushed
¼ cup onions, finely chopped
1 small hot red or green pepper, minced
½ teaspoon coriander
1 clove garlic, minced
Pinch of cloves
Salt & pepper

Combine all measured ingredients well. Season with salt and pepper to taste. Refrigerate 1 to 2 hours to blend flavors. Serve with chips for dipping or over cold meat, poultry, or fish.

Chicken with Salsa

Serves 4

---

1 or 2 large chicken breasts, about 2 pounds
2 bay leaves
Pinch of thyme
¼ cup parsley, chopped

---

1. Place chicken breasts in a skillet with about ½ inch of water containing 1 bay leaf and a pinch of thyme. Bring water to a boil; reduce heat and simmer covered for 20 to 30 minutes or until cooked through. Set aside to cool.
2. While chicken cooks, prepare *Easy Salsa.*
3. Remove skin from chicken and carefully cut the flesh into ¼-inch-thick slices. Overlap slices on a serving platter or on individual plates and spread salsa over. Sprinkle with parsley. Serve cold.

For variety, green olives may be added to the sauce.

Spanish Chicken

Serves 4

---

2 tablespoons olive oil
2½ to 3 pound chicken, cut into serving pieces
1½ cups onions, sliced
¾ cup green peppers, cut into strips
½ cup lean smoked ham, finely chopped
1 teaspoon garlic, minced
4 cups tomatoes, fresh or canned, peeled, seeded, & finely chopped
Salt & pepper
12 each black & green olives, sliced

---

1. Heat 1 tablespoon olive oil in a heavy skillet and brown chicken lightly on all sides, adding more oil if needed. Remove chicken from the pan and set aside.
2. Add onion, pepper, ham, and garlic to the pan and sauté until the vegetables are barely soft.
3. Add tomatoes to the pan and bring to a boil.
4. Return chicken to the pan, turning to coat with sauce. Cook for 30 minutes, or until chicken is cooked through.
5. Remove chicken from the pan and boil until the sauce has thickened. Season to taste with salt and pepper. Stir in the olives, and serve.

Chicken with Green Chilies

Serves 4

¼ cup canned green chili peppers
1 cup onion, chopped
1 teaspoon garlic, crushed
¾ cup chicken broth
1 tablespoon vinegar
1 teaspoon sugar
½ teaspoon coriander seeds, finely ground
¼ teaspoon cinnamon, finely ground
¼ teaspoon cloves, finely ground
1 cup tomatoes, crushed or diced, drained
2 tablespoons olive oil
1 chicken, about 3 pounds, cut into serving pieces
Salt & pepper

1. In a blender, purée the chili peppers, onion, and garlic with the chicken broth or force the ingredients through a food mill and a strainer.
2. In a large bowl, combine purée with the vinegar, sugar, coriander, cinnamon, cloves and tomatoes; set aside.
3. Have ready a baking dish large enough to hold the chicken in one layer. In a heavy skillet, heat the olive oil and sauté the chicken a few pieces at a time, turning to brown well on all sides. As chicken pieces are ready, dip them in the bowl to coat with sauce and place them in the baking dish.
4. Pour remaining sauce over the chicken and bake at 350° for about 1 hour, or until chicken is cooked through. About 45 minutes into the baking, baste chicken parts with the sauce or turn them over.
5. When chicken is done, remove to a serving platter. Skim off fat and boil liquid in a sauce pan to reduce it. Serve over the chicken.

Skimming fat from pan juices is easier if the liquid is poured into a heatproof container and placed in the freezer. After a few minutes, fat will rise to the top. If time permits, chill for about 30 minutes and the fat will solidify.

Paella

A classic Spanish dish.

Serves 8

¼ cup olive oil
1 frying chicken, cut up, or about 3 pounds of chicken parts
½ cup onion, sliced or chopped
2 cloves garlic, minced
½ pound tomatoes, peeled, fresh or canned
2 cups rice, uncooked
1 teaspoon saffron dissolved in 4 cups water
Salt & pepper
1 cup peas, fresh or frozen
1 sweet red pepper, cut into strips
¼ pound medium shrimp, shelled
8 each clams and mussels in the shell

1. In a large skillet or kettle, heat the olive oil and brown the chicken on all sides.

2. Add the onion and continue to cook while stirring until the onion is transparent.

3. Add garlic, tomatoes, rice, saffron, and water. Stir to combine. Add salt and pepper to taste. Cover and cook for 15 minutes over low heat.

4. Stir the pot from top to bottom to prevent rice from browning. Arrange peas and red pepper strips over the top of the rice and cook for 10 more minutes.
   Note: If canned peas are used, add them with the seafood.

5. Arrange shrimp, clams, and mussels on top of the rice. Cover and cook for 5 to 10 minutes, or until the shellfish open. Serve in the skillet or kettle and enjoy!
   Note: Check the rice to be sure that it does not overcook. If the rice is already tender, steam the seafood in a separate pot with a small amount of water. If rice is very firm, cook for about 5 minutes longer before adding seafood.

NOTE: The traditional paella pan is a large covered skillet with metal handles on two sides, somewhat like a heavy wok with a flat bottom, although an iron kettle also serves very well.

Cocido (Spanish Stew)

Another classic, not so well known as paella, but one that qualifies as our all-time favorite. Don't let the long list of ingredients daunt you. Works great in a crock pot as well, using canned chick peas—merely combine all the ingredients and cook on low for several hours.

Serves 4

1 pound dried chick peas
1 pound lean beef, cut into 1-inch cubes
1 cup onion, chopped
1 cup fresh tomato, diced
¼ cup green pepper, chopped
1 clove garlic, minced
¼ pound Canadian bacon, diced
½ pound pumpkin, cut into 1-inch cubes
½ cup carrots, sliced thick
2 Spanish or Italian sausages, sliced thick
1 pound potatoes, peeled & cubed
½ pound green beans, cut in 1-inch pieces
½ teaspoon cumin
Salt & pepper

1. Soak chick peas overnight or boil for 2 minutes, then cover and allow to rest for 1 hour.

2. Add the beef, onion, tomatoes, green pepper, garlic, and Canadian bacon to the pot with the beans. Pour in sufficient water to cover and simmer with the pot covered, until the chick peas are tender, about 1 hour. If necessary, add more water as the beans cook.

3. Stir in the pumpkin, carrots, sausage, potatoes, green beans, and cumin. Cook for an additional 30 minutes, or until vegetables are tender.

4. Correct the seasoning and serve.

Tex-Mex Chili

3 thin strips bacon
1½ pounds lean beef, chuck or round, diced; or 1½
   pounds lean ground beef
1 cup onion, minced
2 cups tomatoes, canned, crushed or diced, with juice
1 bay leaf
½ teaspoon each cinnamon & salt
1 tablespoon cumin
3 tablespoons chili powder, or to taste

1. Over low heat in a large skillet, fry bacon until crisp and
   set aside.
2. In fat remaining in the pan, sauté beef, shaking the pan
   to brown on all sides. Add onion and continue cooking
   until lightly colored.
3. Crumble the bacon and return to the pan with tomato,
   bay leaf, cinnamon, salt, cumin, and chili powder. Cover
   and simmer for 1 hour.
4. Correct seasoning and serve with tortillas or crackers,
   chopped onion, and shredded cheese.

NOTES: If ground meat is used, brown in a small amount
of oil, then pour off the rendered fat before combining with
bacon fat and sautéed onions.

—**Serve** chili over beans, spaghetti, or rice.

—**Beans can be cooked with the chili**—add 3 to 4 cups of
cooked kidney, navy, or pinto beans for the final 30 minutes
of cooking.

—**For a spicier dish,** add chopped jalapeños or pepper
sauce.

—**If chili is too thick,** stir in a little water and cook for 5 to
10 minutes to blend flavors.

HEALTH NOTE: 2 tablespoons olive oil can be substituted
for the bacon and bacon fat.

For variety, use a mixture of beef and pork.

—Minced green peppers can be sautéed with the onions.

—A clove of garlic, minced, can be added to the pan with
the tomatoes and beans.

Arroz con Pollo (Chicken with Rice)

Serves 4

¼ cup olive oil
2½ to 3 pound chicken, cut into serving pieces
1 cup rice, uncooked
¼ cup onion, finely chopped
1 clove garlic, minced
2 cups canned tomatoes, diced, with liquid
½ teaspoon oregano
Dash of hot sauce
Salt & pepper
1 cup canned peas or frozen & cooked peas

1. Heat olive oil in a large, heavy skillet and brown chicken pieces on all sides. Remove chicken and set aside.
2. In the same pan, heat rice, onion, and garlic, stirring until onion is softened and the rice takes on a bit of color.
3. Return the chicken to the pan with tomatoes, oregano, hot sauce, and 1 cup water. Cover and simmer gently for 20 minutes or just until rice is soft, chicken is cooked through and most of the liquid has been absorbed.
4. Season with salt and pepper to taste and carefully mix in the peas. Continue cooking just to heat through.

Turkey Española

Serves 4

½ pound loose sausage, preferable Spanish
1 cup rice, uncooked
1 cup tomatoes, crushed or diced
¼ teaspoon saffron
2 cups chicken broth
1½ cups cooked turkey, diced
½ cup green peppers, cut into thin strips
¼ cup onion, finely chopped
½ teaspoon ground cumin
1 clove garlic, minced
2 tablespoons pimientos, chopped

more...

1. Brown the sausage in a large heavy skillet.
2. Add rice and cook until the rice takes on a bit of color.
3. Add tomatoes and cook for 5 minutes.
4. Dissolve saffron in the then add to the pan with turkey, peppers, onion, cumin, and garlic. Cook, covered, over low heat for 40 minutes or until rice is tender. Stir in pimientos and continue cooking just to heat through.

Pork Mexicaine

Serves 4

1 cup flat beer
2 tablespoons soy sauce
2 tablespoons brown sugar
1 tablespoon dry mustard
2 cloves garlic, minced
Hot pepper sauce or chili peppers
Salt & pepper
1½ pounds lean pork, sliced or cubed
1 fresh lime

1. Combine the beer, soy sauce, sugar, mustard, garlic, and hot sauce or peppers to taste in a saucepan. Heat briefly and stir just to combine flavors. Season with salt and pepper to taste. Set aside to cool.
2. Cover meat with the marinade and refrigerate overnight, stirring occasionally.
3. Thread meat on skewers or place loose in a broiler pan. Broil about 4 inches from the heat, basting often with the marinade, for 15 minutes or until the meat is cooked through.
4. Sprinkle with lime juice and serve.

NOTE: If wooden skewer are used, soak them in water for at least an hour ahead of time.

Chili Bake

1 pound lean ground beef
2 thin strips bacon
½ cup onion, minced
¼ cup green pepper, minced
¾ cup tomatoes, canned, crushed, with juice
¼ teaspoon each cinnamon, allspice, & salt
2 teaspoons chili powder, or to taste
Tortilla chips, about 5 ounces
½ cup cheddar cheese, shredded

1. In a large skillet, brown beef using a little oil if necessary. Drain off oil and set beef aside.

2. Over low heat in the same skillet, fry bacon until crisp and set aside.

3. Sauté onion and pepper in bacon grease, just until soft. Crumble bacon and return to pan with meat, tomato, cinnamon, allspice, salt, and chili powder. Simmer for about 1 hour covered.

4. In an oven dish, place alternating layers of chips and chili, beginning with chips and ending with chili. Cover with cheese and bake at 350° for 20 to 30 minutes.

Black Bean Soup

1 pound black beans
1 small onion, finely chopped
¼ cup celery, finely chopped
4 whole cloves
¼ pound pork or ham, finely chopped
2 tablespoons sherry
4 teaspoons lemon juice
1 teaspoon Worcestershire sauce
Pinch of sugar
Salt & pepper

1. Rinse beans in several changes of water until liquid runs clear. Cover with fresh water, boil for 2 minutes, and allow to stand, covered, for 2 hours. Add onion, celery, cloves, and meat. Cook for 2 hours, or until beans are soft, adding more water from time to time, if necessary.

more...